MARVEL MASTERWORKS

PRESENTS

THE AVENGERS

VOLUME 6

COLLECTING

THE AVENGERS NOS. 51-58,
ANNUAL NO. 2 & THE X-MEN NO. 45

ROY THOMAS • JOHN BUSCEMA

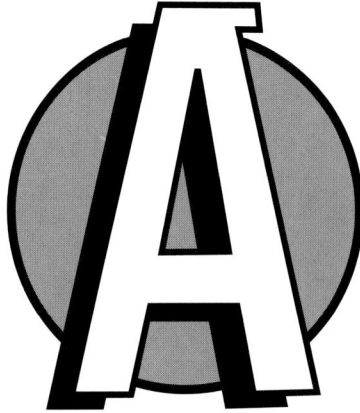

Collection Editor
Cory Sedlmeier

Book Design
Nickel DesignWorks

Senior Editor, Special Projects
Jeff Youngquist

Editor in Chief
Joe Quesada

Publisher
Dan Buckley

MARVEL MASTERWORKS: THE AVENGERS VOL. 6. Contains material originally published in magazine form as AVENGERS #51-58, ANNUAL #2 and X-MEN #45. First printing 2006. ISBN# 0-7851-2079-3. Published by MARVEL PUBLISHING, INC., a subsidiary of MARVEL ENTERTAINMENT, INC. OFFICE OF PUBLICATION: 417 5th Avenue, New York, NY 10016. Copyright © 1968 and 2006 Marvel Characters, Inc. All rights reserved. $49.99 per copy in the U.S. and $80.00 in Canada (GST #R127032852); Canadian Agreement #40668537. All characters featured in this issue and the distinctive names and likenesses thereof, and all related indicia are trademarks of Marvel Characters, Inc. No similarity between any of the names, characters, persons, and/or institutions in this magazine with those of any living or dead person or institution is intended, and any such similarity which may exist is purely coincidental. **Printed in the U.S.A.** ALAN FINE, President & CEO Of Marvel Toys and Marvel Publishing, Inc.; DAVID BOGART, VP Of Publishing Operations; DAN CARR, Executive Director of Publishing Technology; JUSTIN F. GABRIE, Managing Editor; STAN LEE, Chairman Emeritus. For information regarding advertising in Marvel Comics or on Marvel.com, please contact Joe Maimone, Advertising Director, at jmaimone@marvel.com or 212-576-8534.

10 9 8 7 6 5 4 3 2 1

MARVEL MASTERWORKS
CREDITS

THE
AVENGERS
NOS. 51-58, ANNUAL No. 2
& THE X-MEN No. 45

Writers: Roy Thomas
Gary Friedrich (*The X-Men No. 45*)

Pencilers: John Buscema (Nos. 51-58, Annual No. 2)
Don Heck (Annual No. 2; *The X-Men No. 45*)
Werner Roth (Annual No. 2; *The X-Men No. 45*)

Inkers: George Tuska (Nos. 51, 53, 54)
Vince Colletta (No. 52, Annual No. 2)
George Klein (Nos. 55-58)
Frank Giacoia (Annual No. 2)
John Tartaglione (*The X-Men No. 45*)

Letterers: Sam Rosen (Nos. 51, 52, 55-58; *The X-Men No. 45*)
Art Simek (Nos. 53, 54, Annual No. 2)
Joe Rosen (Annual No. 2)

Editor: Stan Lee

Color Reconstruction: Michael Kelleher (Nos. 51, 52, 54-58 & Annual No. 2)
Sno-Cone Digital (No. 53 & *The X-Men No. 45*)

Art Reconstruction: Michael Kelleher

Special Thanks: Kelly Borkert, Tom Brevoort, Ralph Macchio,
Michel Maillot, Roy Thomas & Scott Williams

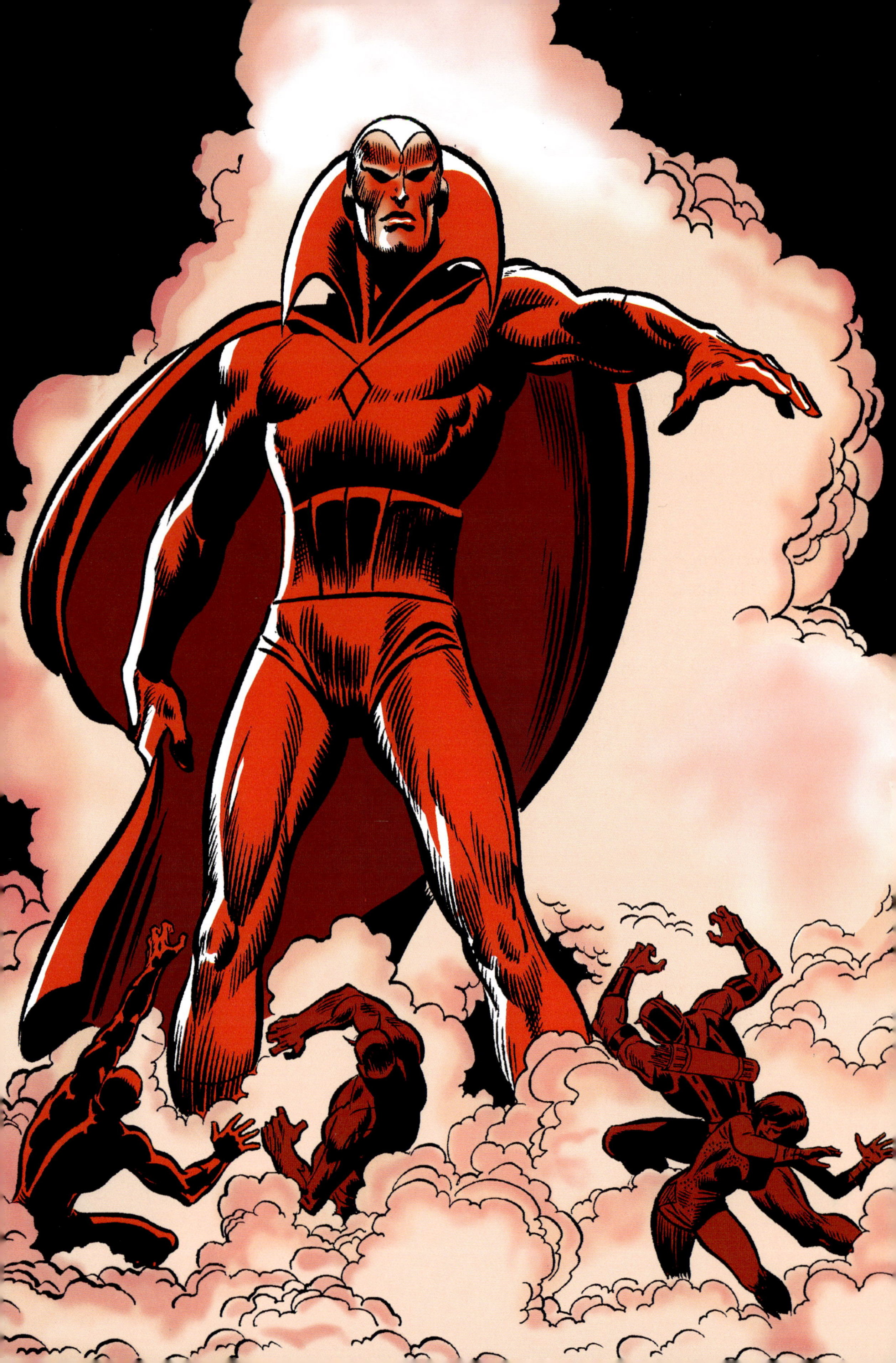

MARVEL MASTERWORKS
CONTENTS

INTRODUCTION
BY ROY THOMAS

John Buscema, that most talented of comic book artists, was always a mystery to me. He constantly claimed an utter disdain for the field ("I hate comics!" was one of his favorite lines); yet there was no one more dedicated to his craft in his own way. The hard-headed freelancer in him often seemed to be at battle with his more aesthetically inclined self. One day the former would hold sway, the next day the latter.

The first story in this volume, from *Avengers* #51, is a case in point. Two issues earlier, he had proclaimed he was tired of seeing other people "ruin" his pencils (but would he have *cared*, if he were really indifferent to the finished product as he always claimed, as long as his editors and public were happy with the finished product?), and he had inked #49-50 himself. The result had been a masterful romp through the hallowed halls of Olympus with a Hercules who looked as if he were drawn by Harold (*Prince Valiant*) Foster on steroids.

Then, just as suddenly, he announced he wanted to go back to only penciling the stories, because he could make more money that way. Inking took him too long, so that he didn't make as much money as when he penciled two pages in the same time, since inking rates were lower than penciling rates. Stan Lee, as Marvel's Editor-in-Chief, tried to indulge John as much as possible, to keep him happy.

And so George Tuska—himself a very popular penciler—was given the assignment of inking *The Avengers*. Myself, I never thought that a particularly happy combination, and George's cartoonier, simpler style seemed to me somewhat in conflict with John's more illustrative line.

In #51, it was time to get a bit more down-to-Earth...if that phrase really fits the Collector and the alien robot he sics on the ol' assemblers. This is one of those issues wherein I prevailed upon Stan to let me bring charter Avengers Thor and Iron Man back into the mag, even if only for a single issue. Besides wanting them to help sell the mag, I felt that those two and Cap (whom Stan had made me take out of the group some time before) *belonged* in the book. But, at least for a couple of years, Stan was adamant: the "big guns" could come back only for an occasional issue, and then had to depart—as do Goldilocks and Shellhead at the end of #51.

An oddity I cannot explain for the life of me: On the splash page of #51, there is a reference to the fact that Goliath is colored "the old way" (i.e., purple and gold) on the cover, while his outfit is the newer purple and red inside. This must've been a last-minute addition...and either Stan or I stuck that note on there at the last second, just to save readers from staying awake nights wondering if there was some subtle reason for the discrepancy. Actually, there was: namely, the right hand didn't always know what the left hand was doing.

#52 was inked by Vince Colletta. Once again, I have a clear vision of Buscema's pencils, and a lingering sadness that, so far as I know, there are no existing photocopies of the penciled pages. Although Vinnie was not primarily a penciler as Tuska was, I feel his inks were a bit better suited to John's style. Some would disagree. That's what makes horseracing...and comic books. If photocopies of those pencils still existed, they would show that John penciled the Black Panther sporting the full face mask he'd always worn previously. However, Stan wanted T'Challa to join the Avengers—probably agreeing with me at least to the extent that the mag needed one or two more popular heroes than a steady dose of second-stringers Goliath, Wasp, and Hawkeye—especially now that even Hercules had opted out.

The Panther, of course, was the first black super hero at Marvel—indeed, in all of American comic books—and Stan decreed that the mask should be altered so that part of his face showed. Besides, Stan often said he was never wild about a hero wearing a full face mask, because you couldn't see his expression. This always seemed to me an odd viewpoint coming from the co-creator of Spider-Man, but perhaps in the case of the son of T'Chaka it made sense. Oh, I'd have vetoed the change if I could've...but I couldn't, so I didn't worry about it. Besides, who was I to argue with the instincts of the guy who'd guided Marvel to such success over the past seven years?

Next, I came up with the Grim Reaper—the name of a minor 1940s hero at the Standard/Nedor comic group, which I felt would make an even better monicker for a villain. I asked John to give our Reaper a scythe, which the gent of legend had, and John went me one better, designing a scythe that was part of an armature worn by the baddie. And, just to give the Reaper one more "hook," I made him the brother of Simon Williams, the Wonder Man who'd made quite a splash in the Lee-Heck *Avengers* #9, but who'd been killed off therein.

X-Men #45 and *Avengers* #53 formed one story, with both halves reprinted here, just so you don't have to consult another recent Masterwork, *The X-Men, Vol. 5*. At that time I was in between my two stints on the original mutant series, but it was being scripted by my longtime friend (and drummer in our early-'60s rock'n'roll band) Gary Friedrich, who also had a staff job...so coordination was hardly a problem.

With this issue, genial George Tuska was back as inker, but this time it was *I* who tried an experiment with the Black Panther's outfit. I asked the colorist not to color the highlights on his costume dark blue, but to leave them white. (Here, I think I had in mind the effectiveness of another Standard/Nedor hero I'd liked in the late 1940s, the Black Terror, as drawn by the team of Mort Meskin and Jerry Robinson.) It didn't seem to work here, though, so with #54 I had the colorist go back to blue highlights.

In that issue, I launched a rather drastic sub-plot, which, in retrospect, I'll confess I view as a mistake: I had Jarvis, the Avengers' ever-faithful butler, suddenly turn traitor. Oh, I eventually justified his actions and even got him back in the heroes' good graces, but if I had it all to do over again—! But I don't, so I'll just have to hope the story entertains on its own, if only because #54 also introduced the New Masters of Evil (the old bunch had held forth in early Lee-Kirby issues)—and because the new grouping included the modern-day Black Knight who'd debuted in #48.

John drew a wonderful Black Knight and his winged stallion Aragorn. And if I don't begrudge the lack of extant photocopies of this issue's pencils quite as much as in other cases, it's because soon afterward John drew an exquisitely detailed and beautiful pencil illo of the Knight and his flying steed which has hung in my abode from that day to this.

I can't skim over this issue, though, without smiling to recall the source of one line of dialogue on p. 9. When the Crimson Cowl remarks to the Knight that he looks younger than he'd expected, the latter quips: "Should *my* mother had phoned *your* mother?" Michael Rennie had delivered that line a few years earlier in the movie version of Jean Kerr's play *Mary, Mary*. I've stolen just about every decent line in that film comedy, at one time or another!

Of course, in retrospect, it's the Crimson Cowl even more than the Black Knight who's important in #54, because he turns out to be—no, not Jarvis, but the gleaming metal robot who in this issue appears to be a mere automaton. By #55, it would turn out that the robot, not Jarvis, was actually behind the whole plot—and that he had a name: *Ultron-5*. Both with and without numerical suffixes, Ultron has become one of the longest-lived and most noteworthy villains in *Avengers* annals, and it's amusing that he had such an unpromising beginning.

Avengers #55 introduced a new inker: George Klein. George had been a mainstay of the 1940s Timely bullpen, then had inked Superman and other DC features for years. Serendipitously, he walked into the Marvel offices just as the other George's services were needed elsewhere as a penciler—and he had an ink style that reminded both Stan and me of that of joltin' Joe Sinnott. So he was assigned to *The Avengers* at once.

Oh, and in case you've wondered why the word "Mayhem" in our title, both on the cover and splash page, has quotation marks around it—you can chalk that up to a little run-in with the nice folks with the blue pencils over at the Comics Code Authority. Though there was nothing in the written Code against the use of the word "mayhem" in titles (as there was concerning "terror" and "horror"), its personnel were uneasy about a word that implied such violence. Somehow, either Stan or production manager Sol Brodsky convinced them that putting quotes around the word would take the edge off it—like we didn't really *mean* it—and, somehow, they accepted that reasoning. It was an odd little episode.

Ultron took a single issue off, so that in #56 John and I, by means of a bit of time travel, could add to the backstory of the death of Bucky related by Stan and Jack way back in #4. There were a few anomalies about that story I felt needed clearing up. Like, why were Cap and Bucky dressed in their Army uniforms rather than their costumes when they were strapped to that "drone plane"? Why was that prototype booby-trapped? And what was Baron Zemo's plan, barely hinted at in #4?

As a minor aside: the splash of this issue was the first time I managed to do something I'd wanted to do for a couple of years—namely, work a story's title into the artwork, rather than just have it floating above the action in a burst or ribbon. Artist/writer Bill Everett and I had both approached Stan about that earlier, but he preferred keeping the style as it was. Since then, though, a newcomer named Jim Steranko who both wrote and drew his S.H.I.E.L.D. stories hadn't bothered asking for permission to do what were termed "Eisneresque" things with titles; he just *did* them. I was aware that by roughly hand-lettering "Death Be Not Proud!" on the side of that splash-page bridge as I did, for Sam Rosen to ink, I'd be laying myself open to the charge of imitating Steranko—but I did it anyway. I knew the truth.

Actually, #55 was a lead-in to a more complex time travel story, in *Avengers Annual* #2, which was laid out in pencil by longtime *Avengers* artist Don Heck, with finished pencils by recent *X-Men* artist Werner Roth.

From the day I first laid eyes on (and purchased two copies of) *Fantastic Four* #1 in 1961, I was a fan of the Lee-Kirby approach to super heroes. But I remained likewise a fan of DC's Julius Schwartz and his creative teams, especially the parallel-world stories of what was called "Earth-Two," wherein alternate versions of current super-stars dwelt. This Annual was my first version of such a tale, with the new Avengers pitted against the old Avengers as they had been in issues #1-3.

As for the villain—well, actually, I'd wanted to call him simply "the Centurion." But, while I was holding onto that name for a character, jaunty Jim Steranko (yes, him again!) had used it in a S.H.I.E.L.D. story. Loath to abandon it entirely, I added an adjective ("Scarlet") to differentiate my Centurion from Jim's. Actually, both villains wound up being essentially one-shot wonders. I enjoyed coining the term "Herodotron" for the bad-guy's time-altering machine, christened of course after Herodotus, the ancient Greek "father of history." And, as the splash of "Part 2," I had dashin' Donnie draw an homage to a favorite 1940s DC cover of mine, Irwin Hasen's for *All-Star Comics* #35. I had no shame. Still don't.

The time travel angle of the story turned out all right, though reader Mark Gruenwald—himself a future Marvel writer and editor—took me to task for not following what he felt were the received rules of time travel stories. I was pretty unrepentant, though. The story either worked as a story or it didn't...and I always felt it basically did.

Besides the two-page pinup, John Buscema was on hand, too, drawing that weird little tale that follows the main saga. For, that year (1968), Stan decreed that each Annual's creative team would do a 5-page humor story about putting the issue together. John penciled ours in a style that reminded me of the work of Mort Drucker, then the chief movie parodist in *Mad*. But then, I shouldn't really have been surprised. John could draw anything you could get him to *want* to draw! But I'm embarrassed, in that little visual time capsule, to behold myself once again in the scraggly goatee and Nehru jacket I then wore. (Trust me—Nehru jackets were all the rage for about fifteen minutes there.) John, of course, skewered me perfectly, even if he didn't spare himself or his friend Don.

Actually, I gave up wearing my Nehru outfits around that time, after, one day, while I was wearing my orange one, a truck driver whistled at me on Second Avenue. And, a few weeks later, a bright and lovely blonde named Jean refused to marry me unless I shaved off my goatee. I happily complied; by then, I was just looking for an excuse.

After the ignominy of that little story, it's amazing that the next pair of issues are probably two of the best John and I did together of *The Avengers*.

Stan still wouldn't let me keep Cap (or Thor or Iron Man) in the book, but now he announced that he wanted me to add a new Avenger. I knew just who I wanted it to be: the Vision, that green-fleshed, other-dimensional entity from 1940s issues of *Marvel Mystery Comics*, originally done by Jack Kirby (and maybe his partner Joe Simon).

Stan, though, said no. He wanted a *new* character...and he wanted it to be an *android*. Why an android, he never said. But then, he didn't have to. He was The Man. He didn't give me any other instructions or explanation, but left everything up to me.

So, being the sly insubordinate that I was, I made up an android—called the Vision.

I sent John a picture of the '40s hero and asked him to add a diamond to his outfit—because I felt all good super heroes needed a chest symbol, and the Vision could make himself hard as diamond. I got the idea, as Golden Age comics fans recognized at once, from the Fawcett character called Spy Smasher.

Actually, I had another motive for adapting the Vision, instead of making up a totally new look and name. Much as I loved Marvel, I knew I wouldn't own any characters I created for it (any more than Stan and the artists did of the F.F., Spidey, or whomever), so I felt happier when, instead of making up something out of whole cloth, I could just adjust an old character, like the Vision—or the earlier Black Knight. That way, if the character one day became the hottest thing since sliced bread and a zillion-dollar movie was made about him, I wouldn't be quite as unhappy about not being paid anything for thinking up the character.

John did a marvelous job with the Vision. When he flew (the Vision, not John), John made him look as if he were not so much flying as floating, because he'd become lighter than air. Instinctively, John had him grasping the sides of his cape, something you didn't see other heroes do much.

Incidentally, on p. 3, panel 7, that drawing of the Vision walking through the wall of the Avengers Mansion doesn't look as much like John's work—because he didn't do it. Whatever John precisely drew (I don't recall), Stan was less than happy with it—so he pulled in staffer Marie Severin to redraw that single figure. In general, though, Stan loved those pencils as much as I did. I can still recall the day they arrived by mail—at my Brooklyn apartment, for some reason, instead of at the office—and I tore open the package to behold that wonderful artwork.

Stan and I did have one little set-to about the Vision. He was unhappy when the issue was printed and he saw I'd had the colorist make him red. He didn't think readers would like a red-faced character, but they didn't seem to mind. Why red? Well, we already had the green Hulk and blue Atlanteans. What was left?

Ultron-5 was back, as the evil genius behind the Vision. But the most noteworthy thing about the issue, besides the introduction of Vizh, is its final page. I'd asked John to draw a multi-panel scene of a kid finding Ultron's head and kicking it around a moment before he walks on, bored. When it came time to script that page, it occurred to me that Percy Shelley's sonnet "Ozymandias" would perfectly underscore the action, so I hand-wrote the lines of the poem, in upper and lower case, above the panels, exactly as I wanted Sam Rosen to letter them. I even ruled new top borders for the panels, so they'd all be of the same height, to better effect. It seems to have worked.

The next issue, I even thought up a story's title when I wrote the synopsis (a rarity for me or other Marvel writers at that time): "Even An Android Can Cry." And I asked John to letter it on the wall as the Panther crept along it. It's a gorgeous page, and I'm overjoyed that, because I took some of that art with me to my old stomping grounds of St. Louis, Missouri, at that time to a comics convention, there exists a photo of John's penciled splash, being ogled by someone—though whether it's by me or not, I neither know nor care.

I had fun doing an Oedipal trip in that issue, and relating the flashbacks in reverse chronological order, with each occurring earlier than the previous one, as the layers of the origin of Ultron-5 and of his and the Vision's relationship to the late Simon (Wonder Man) Williams were slowly peeled away. The story's final panel, of course, justified the title, as the Vision shed a tear upon realizing that the Avengers were treating him like a human being, rather than as an android. The Vision was, over the course of his earliest issues, learning to be human.

And, come to think of it—that was probably exactly what Stan Lee had in mind when he told me to bring an android into the group in the first place!

Roy

2006

Roy Thomas has been a writer and often editor in the comic book field since the mid-1960s, working exclusively for Marvel from 1965-80 and as a freelancer since the late 1980s. Whatever their derivation, he counts Marvel's second Vision and its third Black Knight among his favorite creations.

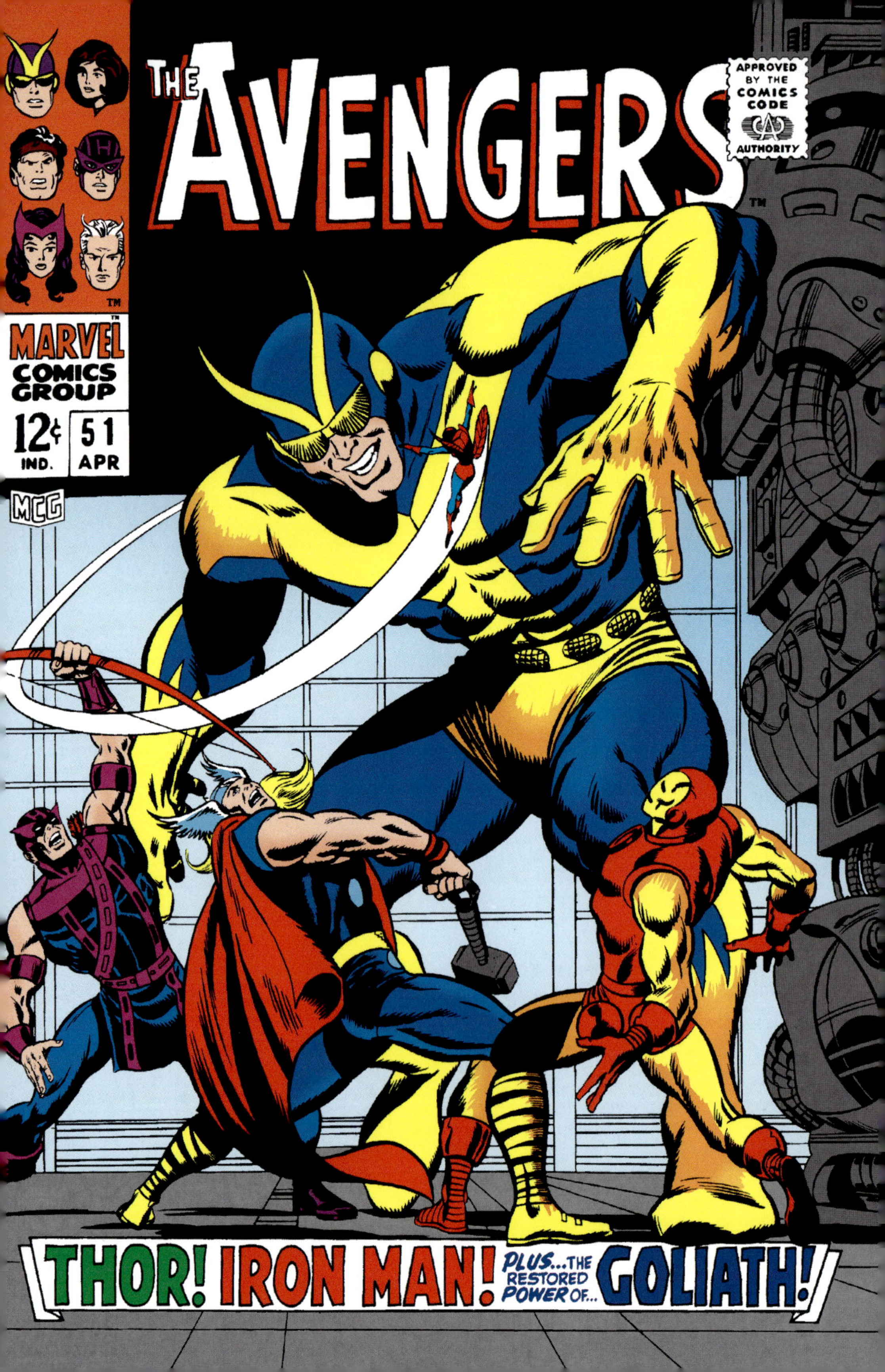

THE AVENGERS
APPROVED BY THE COMICS CODE AUTHORITY
MARVEL COMICS GROUP
12¢ IND.
51 APR
MCG
THOR! IRON MAN! PLUS...THE RESTORED POWER OF... GOLIATH!

THE MIGHTY AVENGERS!™
"IN THE CLUTCHES OF... THE COLLECTOR!"
HAVING RECENTLY LOST HIS ABILITY TO BECOME A GIANT-SIZED GOLIATH, HANDSOME HANK PYM WILL DO ANY-THING TO REGAIN HIS VANISHED POWER... OR, AT LEAST, SO HE THOUGHT--!
AAARRHH!
I'M TRYIN', MAN-MOUNTAIN--!
BUT, THE SWITCH IS STUCK! I CAN'T BUDGE IT!
HAWKEYE... TURN OFF THE VIBROTRON... FAST!!
MEANWHILE, HANK'S BEING BOMBARDED BY ZILLIONS OF ELECTRONS!
EVEN THAT NEW, SUPER-INSULATED SUIT OF HIS WON'T PROTECT HIM!
ZZZAK!
WE... WE'VE GOT TO DO SOMETHING... QUICKLY!
OTHERWISE... HANK WILL DIE WITHIN SECONDS!
FROM THE SANCTUM SANCTORUM OF SMILIN' STAN LEE COMES THIS ROY THOMAS-JOHN BUSCEMA TWO-MAN TOUR DE FORCE!
INKED AND EMBELLISHED BY: GEORGE TUSKA
LETTERED AND RELISHED BY: SAM ROSEN
BLUSHIN' BULLPEN NOTE: YES, WE KNOW WE ACCIDENTALLY COLORED HIGH-POCKETS THE OLD WAY ON OUR COVER! BUT, NOBODY'S PERFECT--LEAST OF ALL US!
FRANKLY, PILGRIM; WE KINDA ENVY YOU RIGHT NOW... 'CAUSE OF ALL THE GREAT GUEST STARS YOU'RE GONNA ENCOUNTER WITHIN THESE PULSE-POUNDING PAGES--!

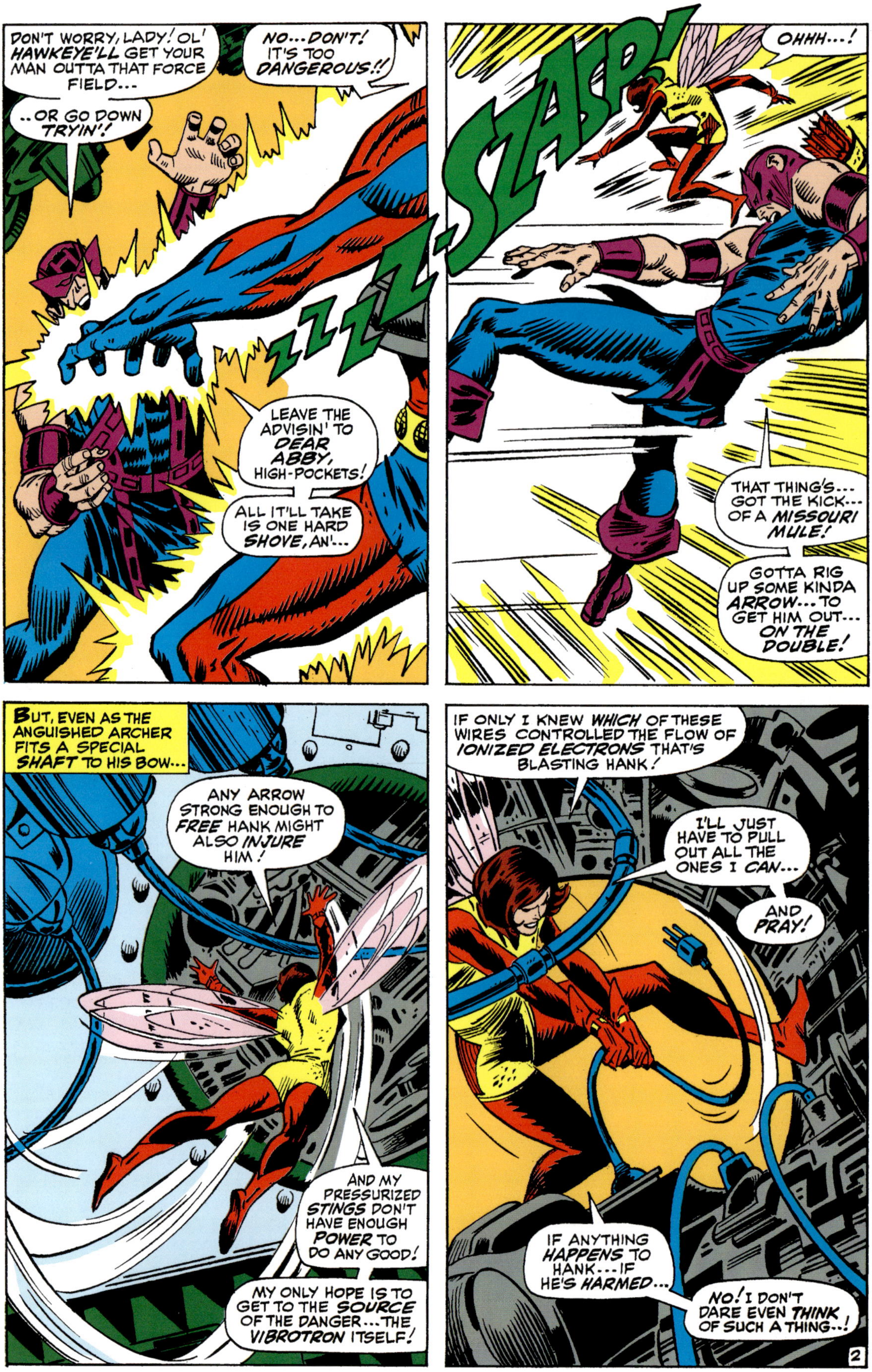
DON'T WORRY, LADY! OL' HAWKEYE'LL GET YOUR MAN OUTTA THAT FORCE FIELD...
..OR GO DOWN TRYIN'!
NO...DON'T! IT'S TOO DANGEROUS!!
LEAVE THE ADVISIN' TO DEAR ABBY, HIGH-POCKETS!
ALL IT'LL TAKE IS ONE HARD SHOVE, AN'...
ZZZZ-SZASP!
OHHH...!
THAT THING'S... GOT THE KICK... OF A MISSOURI MULE!
GOTTA RIG UP SOME KINDA ARROW... TO GET HIM OUT... ON THE DOUBLE!
BUT, EVEN AS THE ANGUISHED ARCHER FITS A SPECIAL SHAFT TO HIS BOW...
ANY ARROW STRONG ENOUGH TO FREE HANK MIGHT ALSO INJURE HIM!
AND MY PRESSURIZED STINGS DON'T HAVE ENOUGH POWER TO DO ANY GOOD!
MY ONLY HOPE IS TO GET TO THE SOURCE OF THE DANGER... THE VIBROTRON ITSELF!
IF ONLY I KNEW WHICH OF THESE WIRES CONTROLLED THE FLOW OF IONIZED ELECTRONS THAT'S BLASTING HANK!
I'LL JUST HAVE TO PULL OUT ALL THE ONES I CAN...
AND PRAY!
IF ANYTHING HAPPENS TO HANK... IF HE'S HARMED...
NO! I DON'T DARE EVEN THINK OF SUCH A THING..!
2

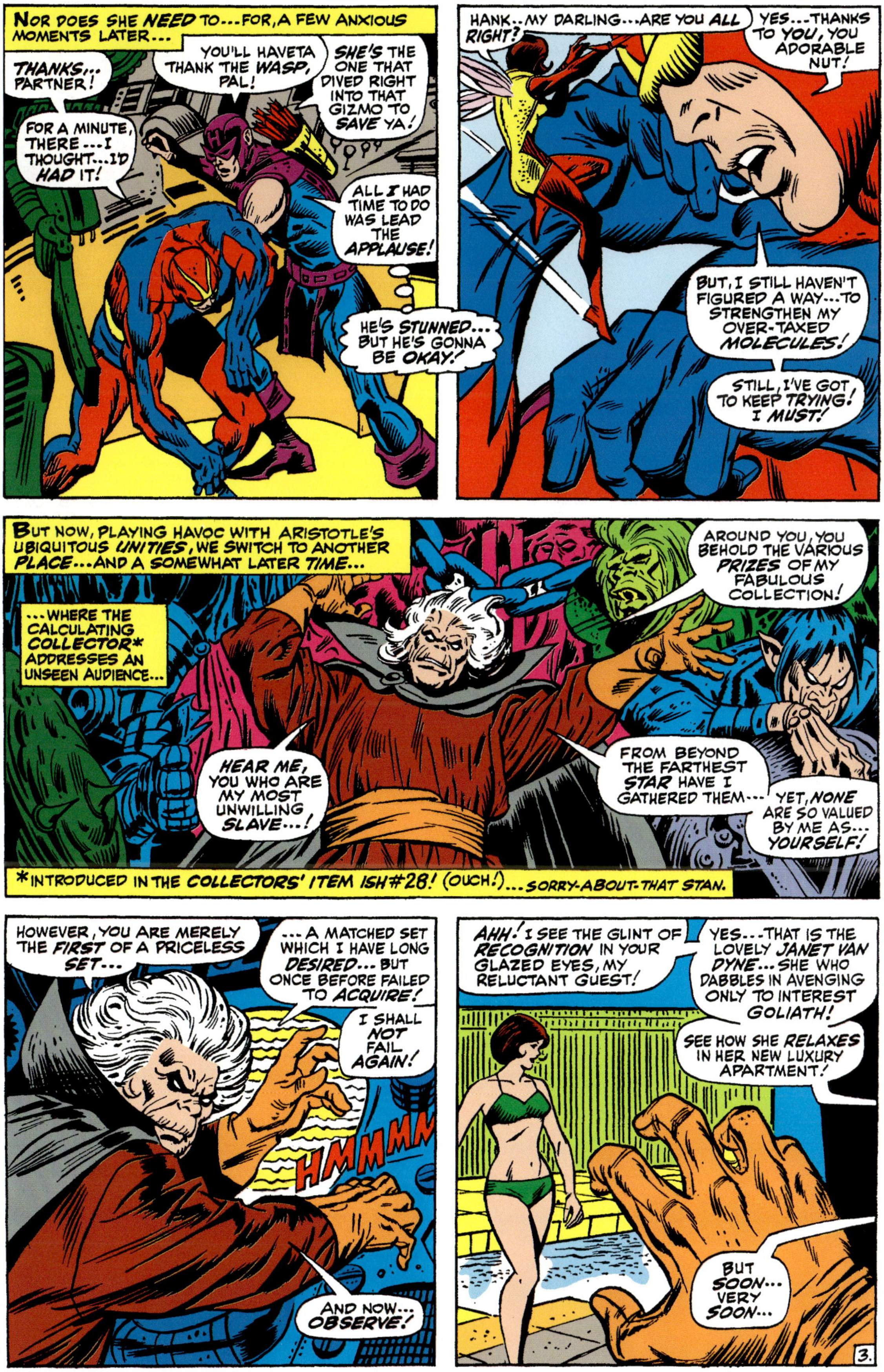
NOR DOES SHE NEED TO... FOR, A FEW ANXIOUS MOMENTS LATER...
THANKS... PARTNER!
YOU'LL HAVETA THANK THE WASP, PAL!
SHE'S THE ONE THAT DIVED RIGHT INTO THAT GIZMO TO SAVE YA!
FOR A MINUTE, THERE... I THOUGHT... I'D HAD IT!
ALL I HAD TIME TO DO WAS LEAD THE APPLAUSE!
HE'S STUNNED... BUT HE'S GONNA BE OKAY!
HANK.. MY DARLING... ARE YOU ALL RIGHT?
YES... THANKS TO YOU, YOU ADORABLE NUT!
BUT, I STILL HAVEN'T FIGURED A WAY... TO STRENGTHEN MY OVER-TAXED MOLECULES!
STILL, I'VE GOT TO KEEP TRYING! I MUST!
BUT NOW, PLAYING HAVOC WITH ARISTOTLE'S UBIQUITOUS UNITIES, WE SWITCH TO ANOTHER PLACE... AND A SOMEWHAT LATER TIME...
...WHERE THE CALCULATING COLLECTOR* ADDRESSES AN UNSEEN AUDIENCE...
AROUND YOU, YOU BEHOLD THE VARIOUS PRIZES OF MY FABULOUS COLLECTION!
HEAR ME, YOU WHO ARE MY MOST UNWILLING SLAVE...!
FROM BEYOND THE FARTHEST STAR HAVE I GATHERED THEM...
YET, NONE ARE SO VALUED BY ME AS... YOURSELF!
*INTRODUCED IN THE COLLECTORS' ITEM ISH #28! (OUCH!)... SORRY-ABOUT-THAT STAN.
HOWEVER, YOU ARE MERELY THE FIRST OF A PRICELESS SET...
...A MATCHED SET WHICH I HAVE LONG DESIRED... BUT ONCE BEFORE FAILED TO ACQUIRE!
I SHALL NOT FAIL AGAIN!
HMMMM
AND NOW... OBSERVE!
AHH! I SEE THE GLINT OF RECOGNITION IN YOUR GLAZED EYES, MY RELUCTANT GUEST!
YES... THAT IS THE LOVELY JANET VAN DYNE... SHE WHO DABBLES IN AVENGING ONLY TO INTEREST GOLIATH!
SEE HOW SHE RELAXES IN HER NEW LUXURY APARTMENT!
BUT SOON... VERY SOON...
3.

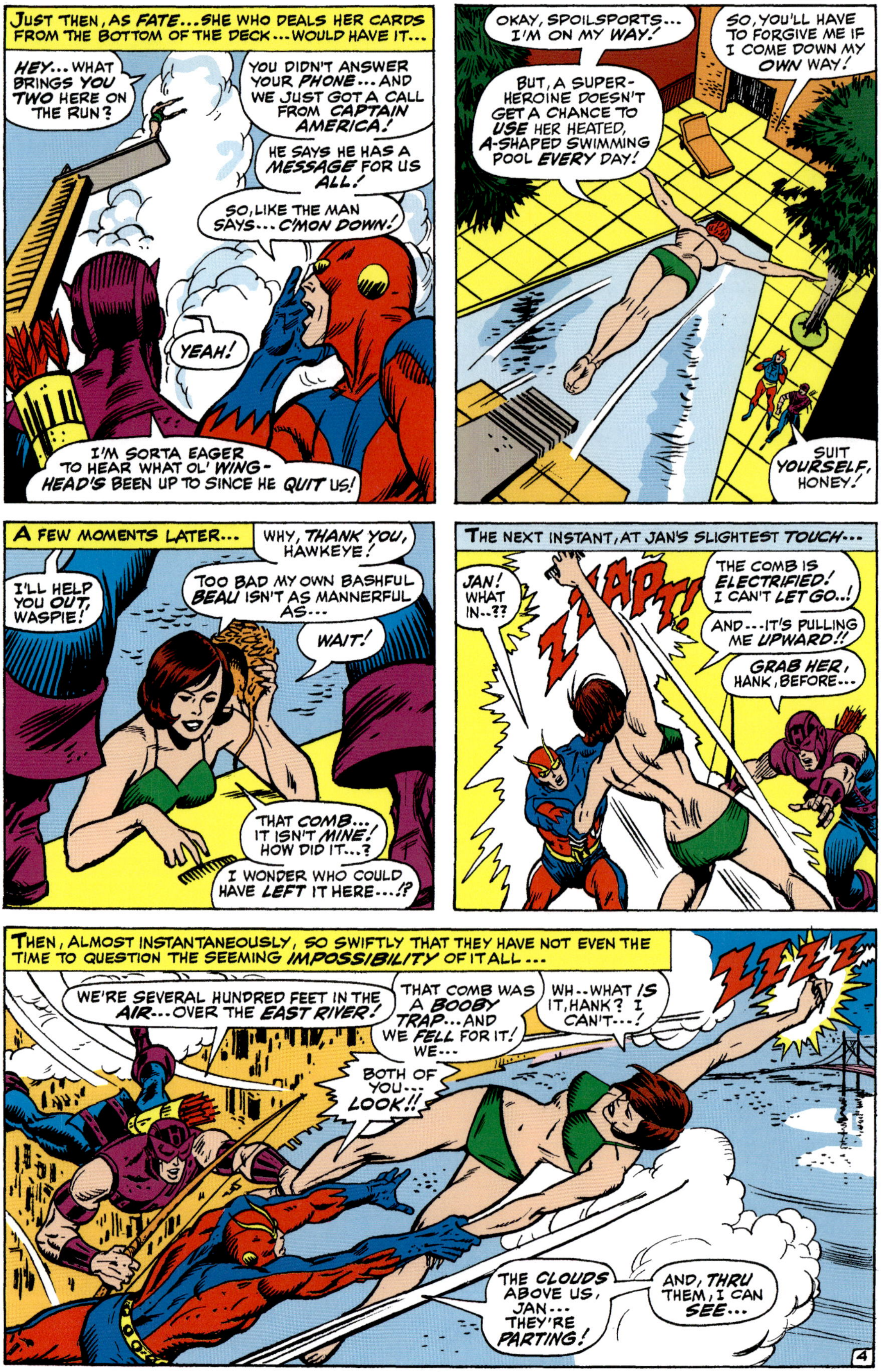
JUST THEN, AS FATE...SHE WHO DEALS HER CARDS FROM THE BOTTOM OF THE DECK...WOULD HAVE IT...
HEY...WHAT BRINGS YOU TWO HERE ON THE RUN?
YOU DIDN'T ANSWER YOUR PHONE...AND WE JUST GOT A CALL FROM CAPTAIN AMERICA!
HE SAYS HE HAS A MESSAGE FOR US ALL!
SO, LIKE THE MAN SAYS...C'MON DOWN!
YEAH!
I'M SORTA EAGER TO HEAR WHAT OL' WING-HEAD'S BEEN UP TO SINCE HE QUIT US!
OKAY, SPOILSPORTS... I'M ON MY WAY!
BUT, A SUPER-HEROINE DOESN'T GET A CHANCE TO USE HER HEATED, A-SHAPED SWIMMING POOL EVERY DAY!
SO, YOU'LL HAVE TO FORGIVE ME IF I COME DOWN MY OWN WAY!
SUIT YOURSELF, HONEY!
A FEW MOMENTS LATER...
I'LL HELP YOU OUT, WASPIE!
WHY, THANK YOU, HAWKEYE!
TOO BAD MY OWN BASHFUL BEAU ISN'T AS MANNERFUL AS---
WAIT!
THAT COMB... IT ISN'T MINE! HOW DID IT...?
I WONDER WHO COULD HAVE LEFT IT HERE...!?
THE NEXT INSTANT, AT JAN'S SLIGHTEST TOUCH...
JAN! WHAT IN..??
ZZAPT!
THE COMB IS ELECTRIFIED! I CAN'T LET GO..!
AND---IT'S PULLING ME UPWARD!!
GRAB HER, HANK, BEFORE---
THEN, ALMOST INSTANTANEOUSLY, SO SWIFTLY THAT THEY HAVE NOT EVEN THE TIME TO QUESTION THE SEEMING IMPOSSIBILITY OF IT ALL...
ZZZZ
WE'RE SEVERAL HUNDRED FEET IN THE AIR...OVER THE EAST RIVER!
THAT COMB WAS A BOOBY TRAP...AND WE FELL FOR IT! WE---
WH--WHAT IS IT, HANK? I CAN'T---!
BOTH OF YOU--- LOOK!!
THE CLOUDS ABOVE US, JAN... THEY'RE PARTING!
AND, THRU THEM, I CAN SEE...
4

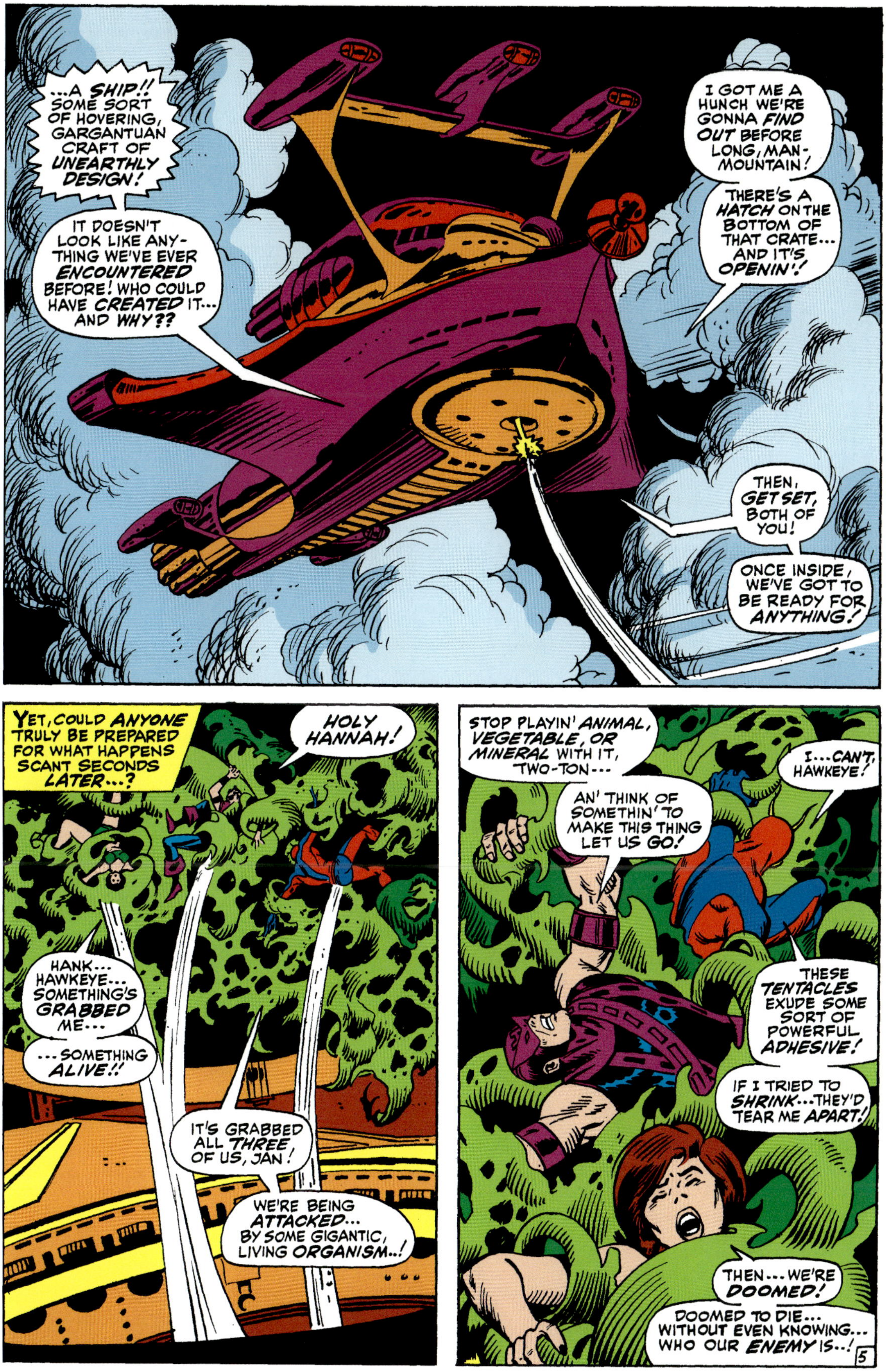
...A SHIP!! SOME SORT OF HOVERING, GARGANTUAN CRAFT OF UNEARTHLY DESIGN!
IT DOESN'T LOOK LIKE ANYTHING WE'VE EVER ENCOUNTERED BEFORE! WHO COULD HAVE CREATED IT... AND WHY??
I GOT ME A HUNCH WE'RE GONNA FIND OUT BEFORE LONG, MAN-MOUNTAIN!
THERE'S A HATCH ON THE BOTTOM OF THAT CRATE... AND IT'S OPENIN'!
THEN, GET SET, BOTH OF YOU!
ONCE INSIDE, WE'VE GOT TO BE READY FOR ANYTHING!
YET, COULD ANYONE TRULY BE PREPARED FOR WHAT HAPPENS SCANT SECONDS LATER...?
HOLY HANNAH!
HANK... HAWKEYE... SOMETHING'S GRABBED ME...
...SOMETHING ALIVE!!
IT'S GRABBED ALL THREE OF US, JAN!
WE'RE BEING ATTACKED... BY SOME GIGANTIC, LIVING ORGANISM..!
STOP PLAYIN' ANIMAL, VEGETABLE, OR MINERAL WITH IT, TWO-TON---
AN' THINK OF SOMETHIN' TO MAKE THIS THING LET US GO!
I...CAN'T, HAWKEYE!
THESE TENTACLES EXUDE SOME SORT OF POWERFUL ADHESIVE!
IF I TRIED TO SHRINK...THEY'D TEAR ME APART!
THEN...WE'RE DOOMED!
DOOMED TO DIE... WITHOUT EVEN KNOWING... WHO OUR ENEMY IS..!
5

Panel 1:

THEN, SUDDENLY, FROM THE CURVING CATWALK WHICH OVERLOOKS THE TRIO'S PLIGHT, A CACKLING *VOICE* IS HEARD... AND TWO SURPRISINGLY FAMILIAR *FIGURES* ARE SEEN...

YOU NEEDN'T BE SO *MELODRAMATIC*, MY DEAR MISS VAN DYNE! YOU'RE NOT GOING TO *PERISH*, YOU KNOW!

EVERYTHING IS STRICTLY UNDER *CONTROL!*

SHALL I *SAVE* THEM, COLLECTOR?

THE COLLECTOR! AND... *THOR!!*

Panel 2:

SAVE THEM, THUNDER GOD? FROM *WHAT?* THEY'RE REALLY IN *NO DANGER!*

MY VENUSIAN *RETRIEVER-ANEMONE* SIMPLY GETS A BIT *PLAYFUL* AT TIMES, THAT'S ALL!

A SIMPLE *STUN BEAM* FROM THIS DEVICE WILL PROVIDE WHAT LITTLE *RESCUING* THEY REQUIRE!

Panel 3:

BUT, TO THE AGONIZED AVENGERS, THE *CURE* SEEMS AS UNDESIRABLE AS THE *DISEASE*...

OHHHH...!

≡UNNHHH!≡

ZZZ ZASSS SKKK

Panel 4:

THEN, AFTER THE DISCIPLINED ALIEN ORGANISM HAS *DEPOSITED* HIS VICTIMS ON THE FLOOR...

THEY ARE UNCONSCIOUS! GOOD!

THOR...PUT THEM IN THE *CELL* WHICH I HAVE TEMPORARILY PROVIDED!

IN A... *CELL? NO--!!*

WHAT? YOU DARE REFUSE TO OBEY A COMMAND FROM YOUR *MASTER?*

6

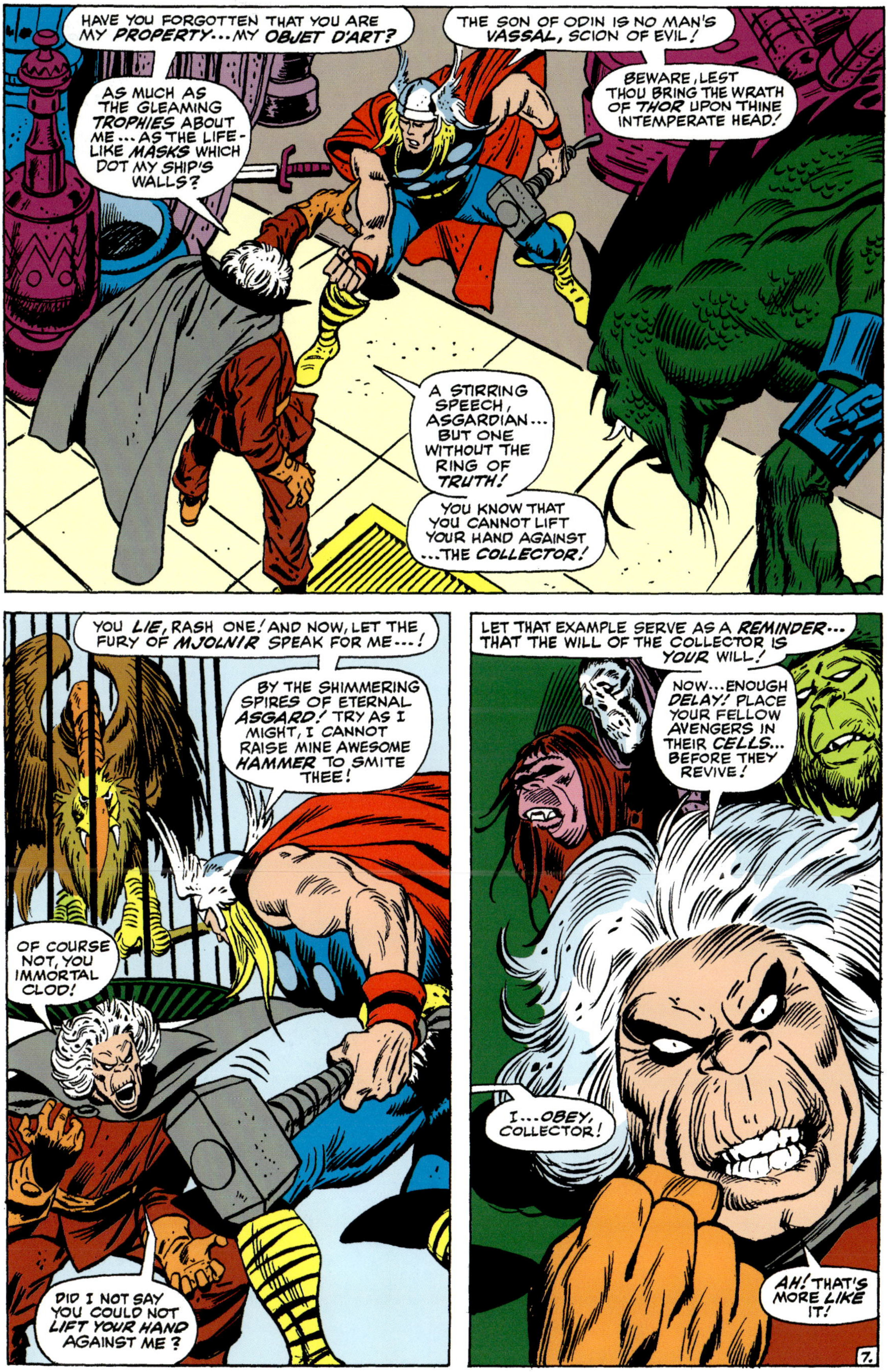
HAVE YOU FORGOTTEN THAT YOU ARE MY PROPERTY... MY OBJET D'ART?
AS MUCH AS THE GLEAMING TROPHIES ABOUT ME... AS THE LIFE-LIKE MASKS WHICH DOT MY SHIP'S WALLS?
THE SON OF ODIN IS NO MAN'S VASSAL, SCION OF EVIL!
BEWARE, LEST THOU BRING THE WRATH OF THOR UPON THINE INTEMPERATE HEAD!
A STIRRING SPEECH, ASGARDIAN... BUT ONE WITHOUT THE RING OF TRUTH!
YOU KNOW THAT YOU CANNOT LIFT YOUR HAND AGAINST ...THE COLLECTOR!
YOU LIE, RASH ONE! AND NOW, LET THE FURY OF MJOLNIR SPEAK FOR ME...!
BY THE SHIMMERING SPIRES OF ETERNAL ASGARD! TRY AS I MIGHT, I CANNOT RAISE MINE AWESOME HAMMER TO SMITE THEE!
OF COURSE NOT, YOU IMMORTAL CLOD!
DID I NOT SAY YOU COULD NOT LIFT YOUR HAND AGAINST ME?
LET THAT EXAMPLE SERVE AS A REMINDER... THAT THE WILL OF THE COLLECTOR IS YOUR WILL!
NOW... ENOUGH DELAY! PLACE YOUR FELLOW AVENGERS IN THEIR CELLS... BEFORE THEY REVIVE!
I... OBEY, COLLECTOR!
AH! THAT'S MORE LIKE IT!
7.

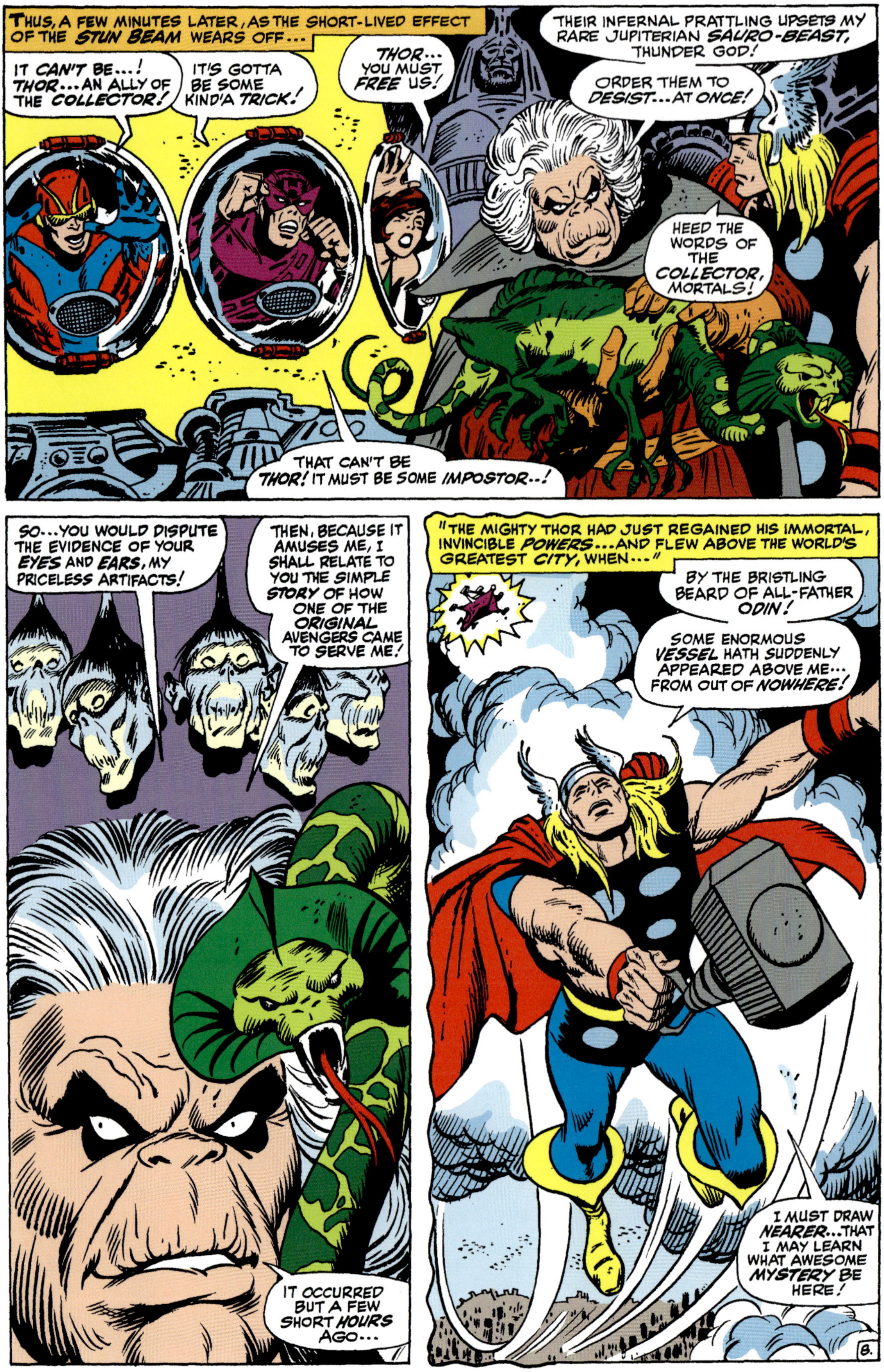
THUS, A FEW MINUTES LATER, AS THE SHORT-LIVED EFFECT OF THE STUN BEAM WEARS OFF...
IT CAN'T BE...! THOR...AN ALLY OF THE COLLECTOR!
IT'S GOTTA BE SOME KIND'A TRICK!
THOR...YOU MUST FREE US!
THEIR INFERNAL PRATTLING UPSETS MY RARE JUPITERIAN SAURO-BEAST, THUNDER GOD!
ORDER THEM TO DESIST...AT ONCE!
HEED THE WORDS OF THE COLLECTOR, MORTALS!
THAT CAN'T BE THOR! IT MUST BE SOME IMPOSTOR..!
SO...YOU WOULD DISPUTE THE EVIDENCE OF YOUR EYES AND EARS, MY PRICELESS ARTIFACTS!
THEN, BECAUSE IT AMUSES ME, I SHALL RELATE TO YOU THE SIMPLE STORY OF HOW ONE OF THE ORIGINAL AVENGERS CAME TO SERVE ME!
IT OCCURRED BUT A FEW SHORT HOURS AGO...
"THE MIGHTY THOR HAD JUST REGAINED HIS IMMORTAL, INVINCIBLE POWERS...AND FLEW ABOVE THE WORLD'S GREATEST CITY, WHEN..."
BY THE BRISTLING BEARD OF ALL-FATHER ODIN!
SOME ENORMOUS VESSEL HATH SUDDENLY APPEARED ABOVE ME...FROM OUT OF NOWHERE!
I MUST DRAW NEARER...THAT I MAY LEARN WHAT AWESOME MYSTERY BE HERE!
8.

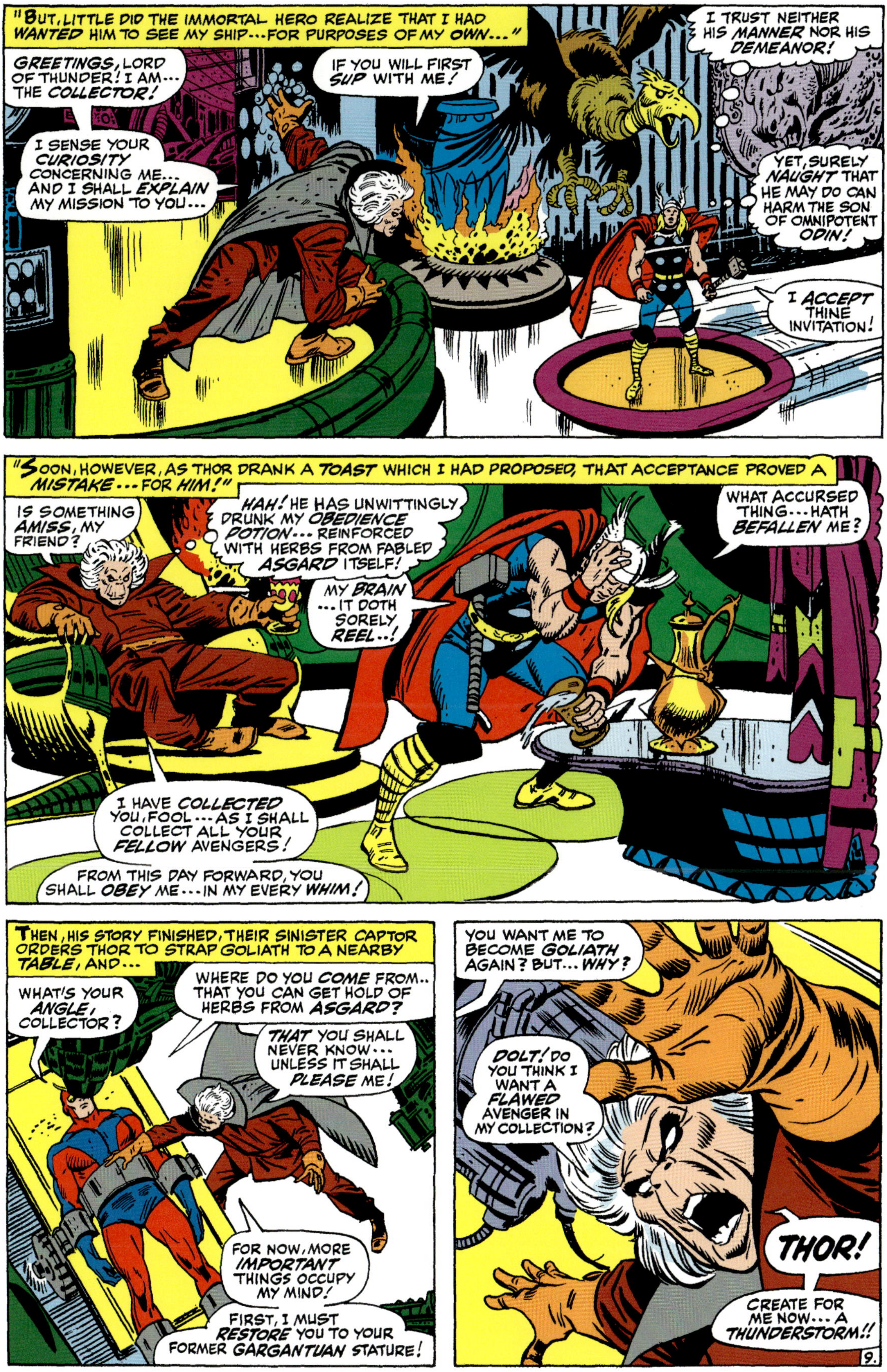
"BUT, LITTLE DID THE IMMORTAL HERO REALIZE THAT I HAD WANTED HIM TO SEE MY SHIP...FOR PURPOSES OF MY OWN..."
GREETINGS, LORD OF THUNDER! I AM... THE COLLECTOR!
I SENSE YOUR CURIOSITY CONCERNING ME... AND I SHALL EXPLAIN MY MISSION TO YOU...
IF YOU WILL FIRST SUP WITH ME!
I TRUST NEITHER HIS MANNER NOR HIS DEMEANOR!
YET, SURELY NAUGHT THAT HE MAY DO CAN HARM THE SON OF OMNIPOTENT ODIN!
I ACCEPT THINE INVITATION!
"SOON, HOWEVER, AS THOR DRANK A TOAST WHICH I HAD PROPOSED, THAT ACCEPTANCE PROVED A MISTAKE...FOR HIM!"
IS SOMETHING AMISS, MY FRIEND?
HAH! HE HAS UNWITTINGLY DRUNK MY OBEDIENCE POTION... REINFORCED WITH HERBS FROM FABLED ASGARD ITSELF!
MY BRAIN ...IT DOTH SORELY REEL..!
WHAT ACCURSED THING...HATH BEFALLEN ME?
I HAVE COLLECTED YOU, FOOL...AS I SHALL COLLECT ALL YOUR FELLOW AVENGERS!
FROM THIS DAY FORWARD, YOU SHALL OBEY ME...IN MY EVERY WHIM!
THEN, HIS STORY FINISHED, THEIR SINISTER CAPTOR ORDERS THOR TO STRAP GOLIATH TO A NEARBY TABLE, AND...
WHAT'S YOUR ANGLE, COLLECTOR?
WHERE DO YOU COME FROM.. THAT YOU CAN GET HOLD OF HERBS FROM ASGARD?
THAT YOU SHALL NEVER KNOW... UNLESS IT SHALL PLEASE ME!
FOR NOW, MORE IMPORTANT THINGS OCCUPY MY MIND!
FIRST, I MUST RESTORE YOU TO YOUR FORMER GARGANTUAN STATURE!
YOU WANT ME TO BECOME GOLIATH AGAIN? BUT... WHY?
DOLT! DO YOU THINK I WANT A FLAWED AVENGER IN MY COLLECTION?
THOR!
CREATE FOR ME NOW... A THUNDERSTORM!!
9.

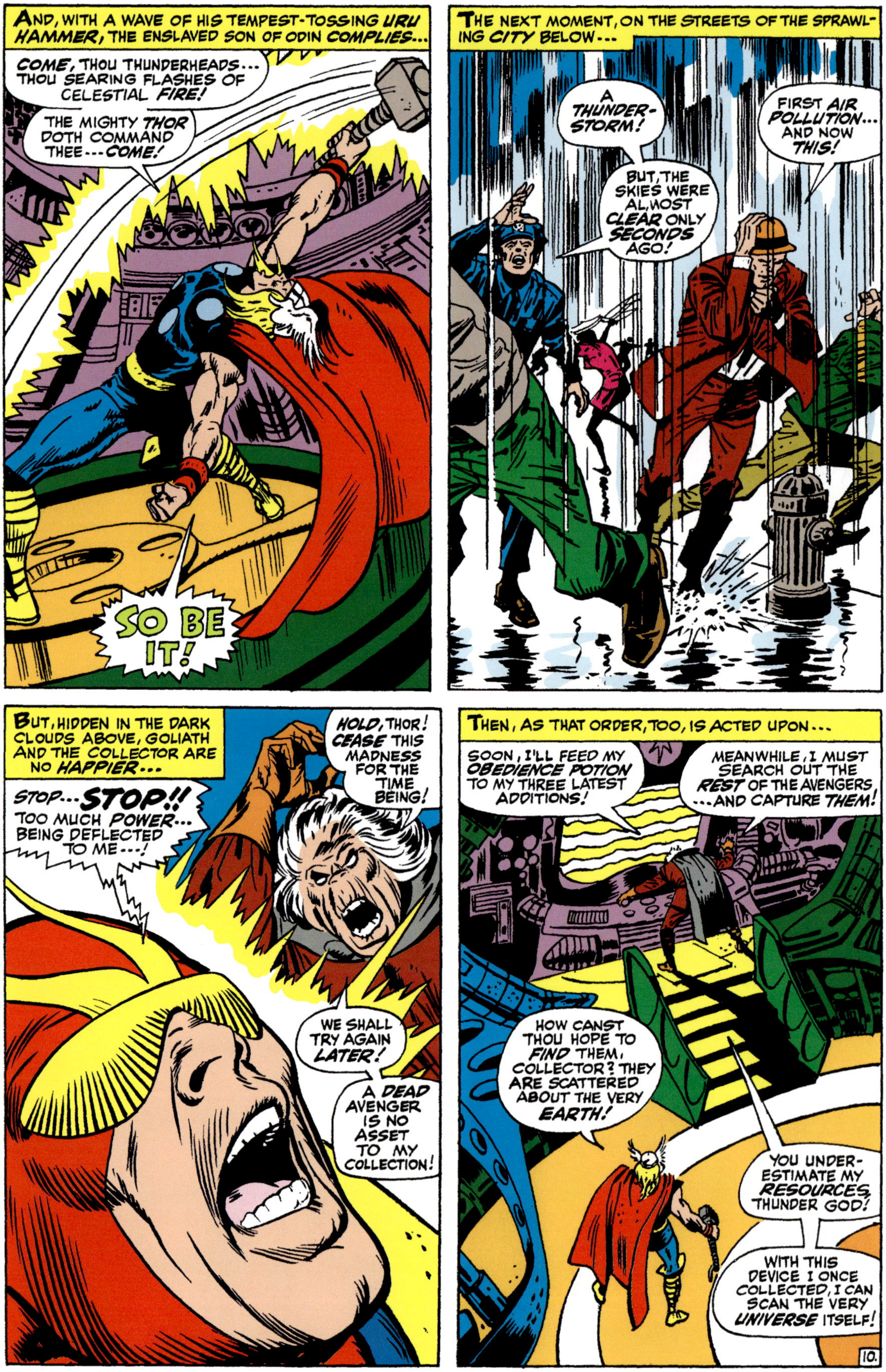
AND, WITH A WAVE OF HIS TEMPEST-TOSSING URU HAMMER, THE ENSLAVED SON OF ODIN COMPLIES...
COME, THOU THUNDERHEADS... THOU SEARING FLASHES OF CELESTIAL FIRE!
THE MIGHTY THOR DOTH COMMAND THEE---COME!
SO BE IT!
THE NEXT MOMENT, ON THE STREETS OF THE SPRAWLING CITY BELOW...
A THUNDER-STORM!
BUT, THE SKIES WERE ALMOST CLEAR ONLY SECONDS AGO!
FIRST AIR POLLUTION... AND NOW THIS!
BUT, HIDDEN IN THE DARK CLOUDS ABOVE, GOLIATH AND THE COLLECTOR ARE NO HAPPIER...
STOP...STOP!! TOO MUCH POWER... BEING DEFLECTED TO ME---!
HOLD, THOR! CEASE THIS MADNESS FOR THE TIME BEING!
WE SHALL TRY AGAIN LATER!
A DEAD AVENGER IS NO ASSET TO MY COLLECTION!
THEN, AS THAT ORDER, TOO, IS ACTED UPON...
SOON, I'LL FEED MY OBEDIENCE POTION TO MY THREE LATEST ADDITIONS!
MEANWHILE, I MUST SEARCH OUT THE REST OF THE AVENGERS ...AND CAPTURE THEM!
HOW CANST THOU HOPE TO FIND THEM, COLLECTOR? THEY ARE SCATTERED ABOUT THE VERY EARTH!
YOU UNDER-ESTIMATE MY RESOURCES, THUNDER GOD!
WITH THIS DEVICE I ONCE COLLECTED, I CAN SCAN THE VERY UNIVERSE ITSELF!
10.

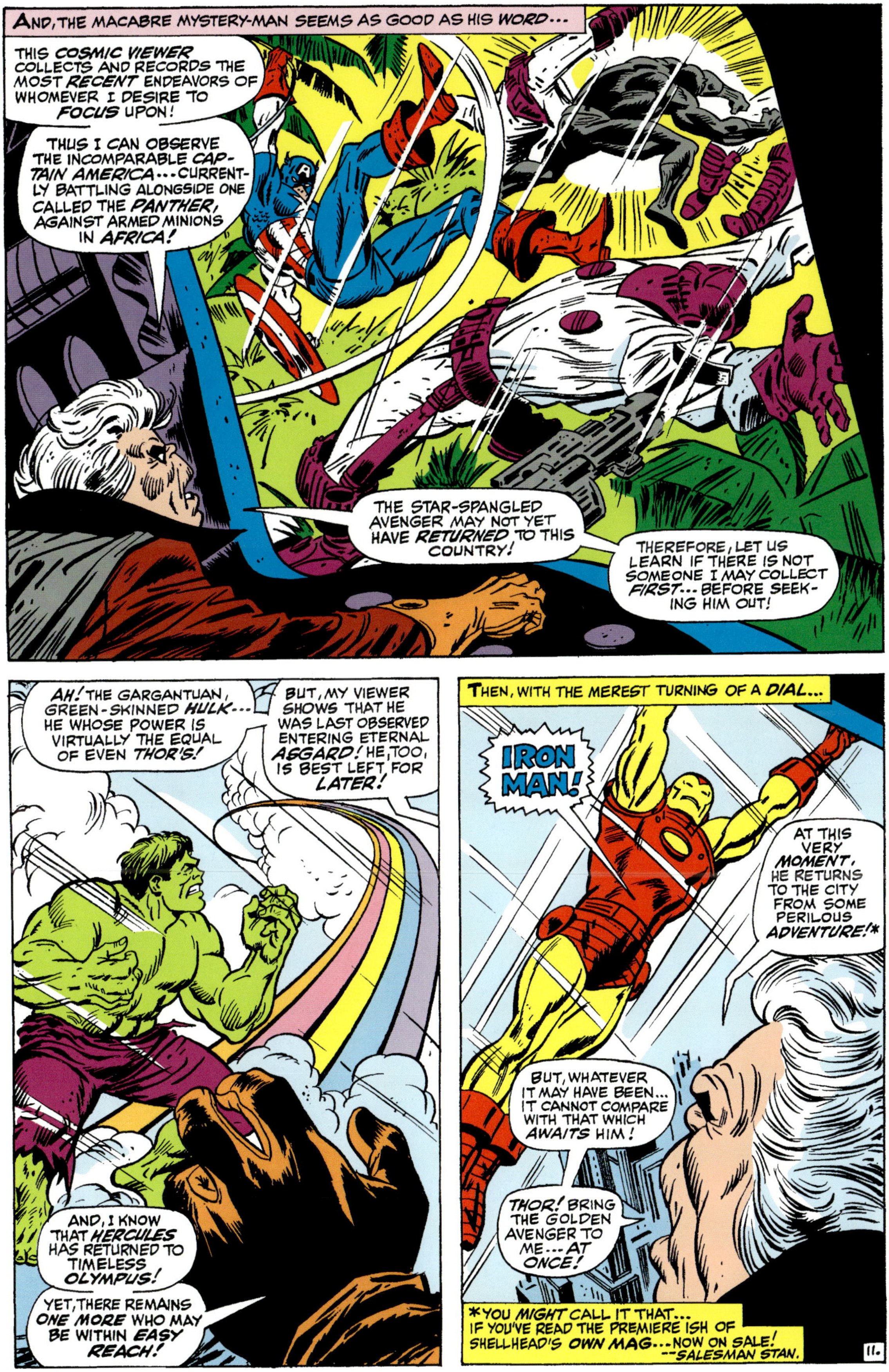
AND, THE MACABRE MYSTERY-MAN SEEMS AS GOOD AS HIS WORD...
THIS COSMIC VIEWER COLLECTS AND RECORDS THE MOST RECENT ENDEAVORS OF WHOMEVER I DESIRE TO FOCUS UPON!
THUS I CAN OBSERVE THE INCOMPARABLE CAPTAIN AMERICA... CURRENTLY BATTLING ALONGSIDE ONE CALLED THE PANTHER, AGAINST ARMED MINIONS IN AFRICA!
THE STAR-SPANGLED AVENGER MAY NOT YET HAVE RETURNED TO THIS COUNTRY!
THEREFORE, LET US LEARN IF THERE IS NOT SOMEONE I MAY COLLECT FIRST... BEFORE SEEKING HIM OUT!
AH! THE GARGANTUAN, GREEN-SKINNED HULK... HE WHOSE POWER IS VIRTUALLY THE EQUAL OF EVEN THOR'S!
BUT, MY VIEWER SHOWS THAT HE WAS LAST OBSERVED ENTERING ETERNAL ASGARD! HE, TOO, IS BEST LEFT FOR LATER!
AND, I KNOW THAT HERCULES HAS RETURNED TO TIMELESS OLYMPUS!
YET, THERE REMAINS ONE MORE WHO MAY BE WITHIN EASY REACH!
THEN, WITH THE MEREST TURNING OF A DIAL...
IRON MAN!
AT THIS VERY MOMENT, HE RETURNS TO THE CITY FROM SOME PERILOUS ADVENTURE!*
BUT, WHATEVER IT MAY HAVE BEEN... IT CANNOT COMPARE WITH THAT WHICH AWAITS HIM!
THOR! BRING THE GOLDEN AVENGER TO ME... AT ONCE!
*YOU MIGHT CALL IT THAT... IF YOU'VE READ THE PREMIERE ISH OF SHELLHEAD'S OWN MAG... NOW ON SALE! --SALESMAN STAN.
11.

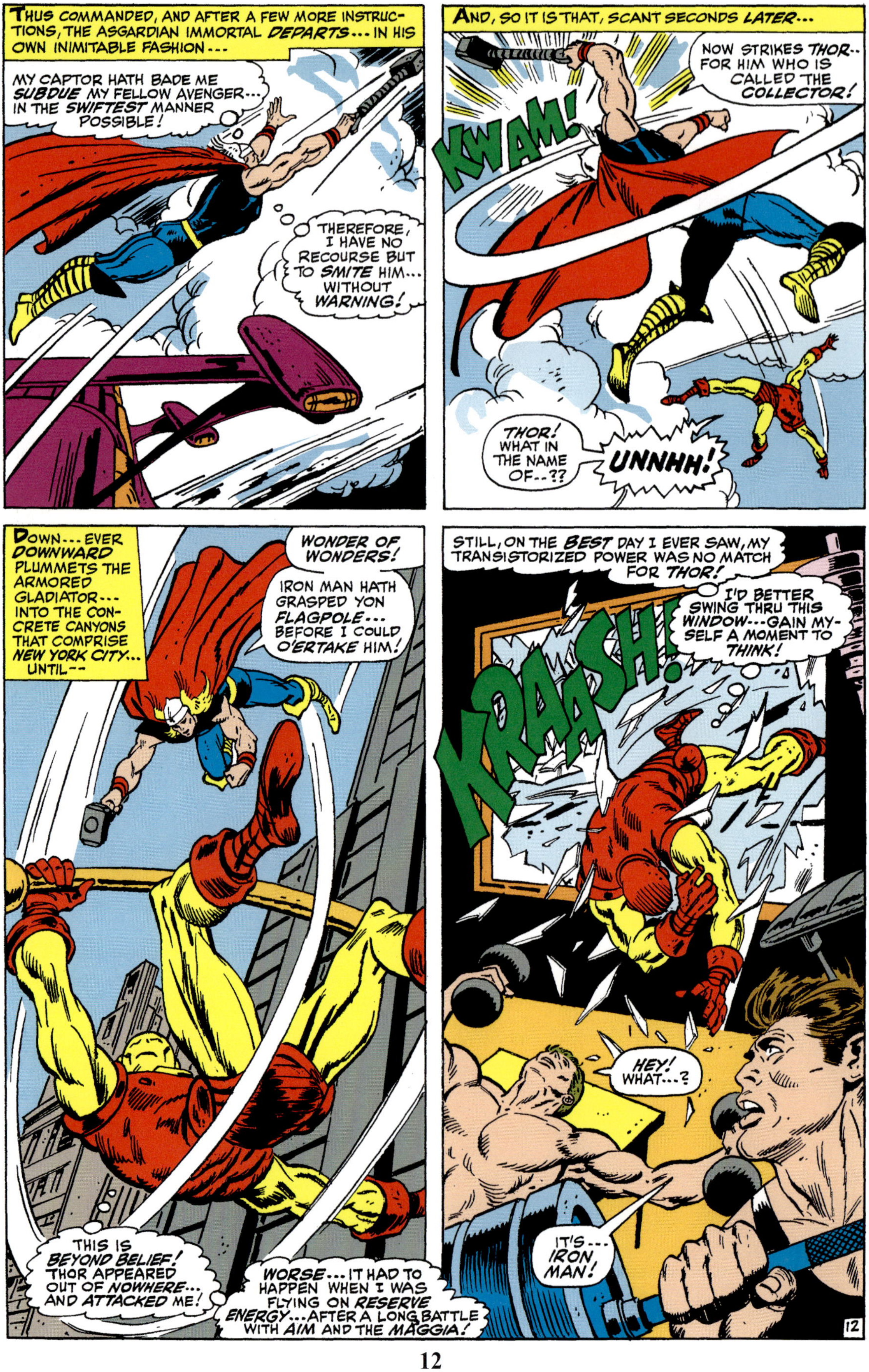
THUS COMMANDED, AND AFTER A FEW MORE INSTRUCTIONS, THE ASGARDIAN IMMORTAL DEPARTS... IN HIS OWN INIMITABLE FASHION...
MY CAPTOR HATH BADE ME SUBDUE MY FELLOW AVENGER... IN THE SWIFTEST MANNER POSSIBLE!
THEREFORE, I HAVE NO RECOURSE BUT TO SMITE HIM... WITHOUT WARNING!
AND, SO IT IS THAT, SCANT SECONDS LATER...
NOW STRIKES THOR.. FOR HIM WHO IS CALLED THE COLLECTOR!
KWAM!
THOR! WHAT IN THE NAME OF--??
UNNHH!
DOWN... EVER DOWNWARD PLUMMETS THE ARMORED GLADIATOR... INTO THE CONCRETE CANYONS THAT COMPRISE NEW YORK CITY... UNTIL--
WONDER OF WONDERS!
IRON MAN HATH GRASPED YON FLAGPOLE... BEFORE I COULD O'ERTAKE HIM!
THIS IS BEYOND BELIEF! THOR APPEARED OUT OF NOWHERE... AND ATTACKED ME!
WORSE... IT HAD TO HAPPEN WHEN I WAS FLYING ON RESERVE ENERGY... AFTER A LONG BATTLE WITH AIM AND THE MAGGIA!
STILL, ON THE BEST DAY I EVER SAW, MY TRANSISTORIZED POWER WAS NO MATCH FOR THOR!
I'D BETTER SWING THRU THIS WINDOW... GAIN MYSELF A MOMENT TO THINK!
KRAASH!
HEY! WHAT...?
IT'S... IRON MAN!
12

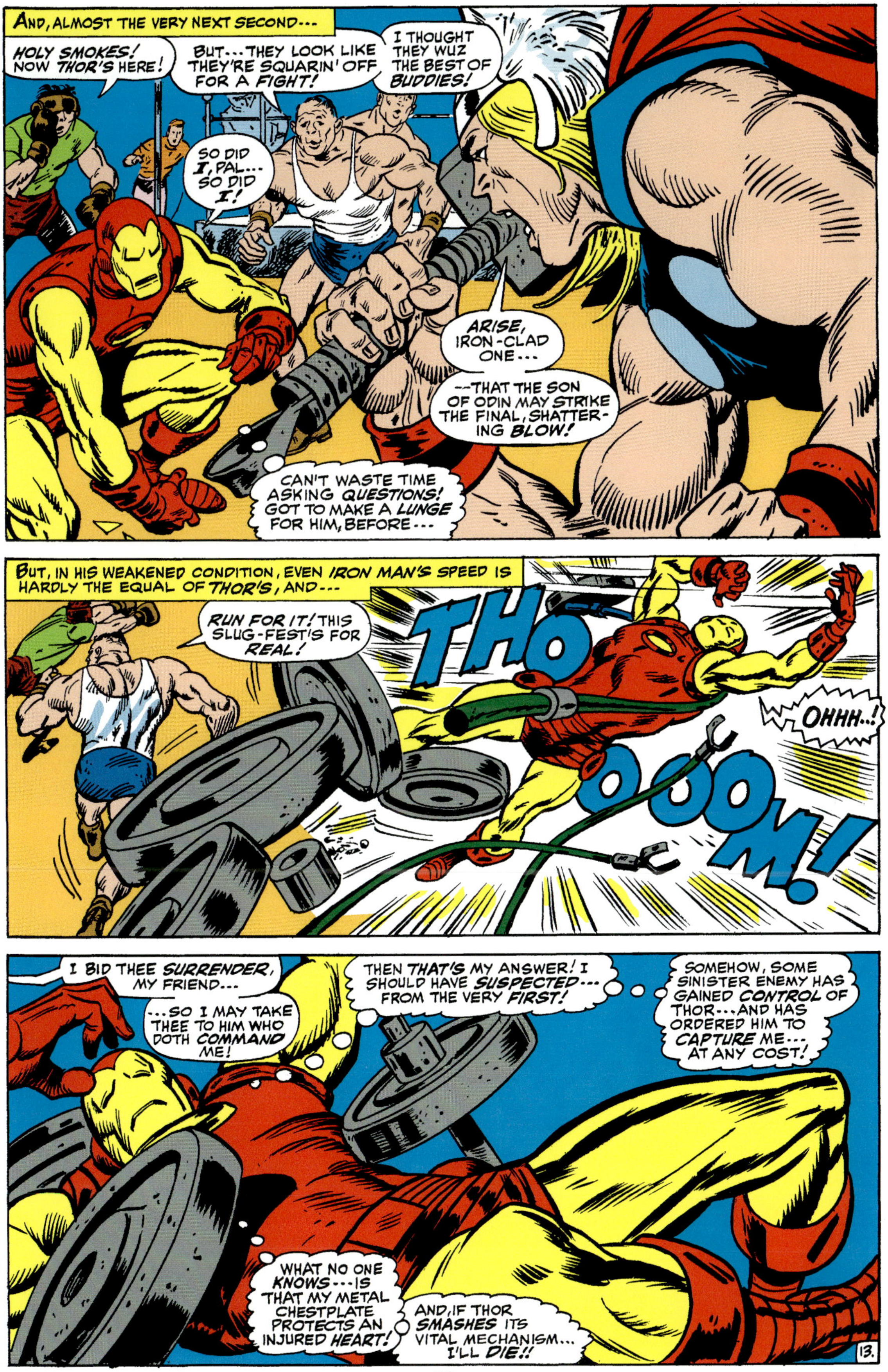
AND, ALMOST THE VERY NEXT SECOND---
HOLY SMOKES! NOW THOR'S HERE!
BUT--- THEY LOOK LIKE THEY'RE SQUARIN' OFF FOR A FIGHT!
I THOUGHT THEY WUZ THE BEST OF BUDDIES!
SO DID I, PAL... SO DID I!
ARISE, IRON-CLAD ONE---
--THAT THE SON OF ODIN MAY STRIKE THE FINAL, SHATTERING BLOW!
CAN'T WASTE TIME ASKING QUESTIONS! GOT TO MAKE A LUNGE FOR HIM, BEFORE---
BUT, IN HIS WEAKENED CONDITION, EVEN IRON MAN'S SPEED IS HARDLY THE EQUAL OF THOR'S, AND---
RUN FOR IT! THIS SLUG-FEST'S FOR REAL!
THOOOOM!
OHHH..!
I BID THEE SURRENDER, MY FRIEND---
...SO I MAY TAKE THEE TO HIM WHO DOTH COMMAND ME!
THEN THAT'S MY ANSWER! I SHOULD HAVE SUSPECTED--- FROM THE VERY FIRST!
SOMEHOW, SOME SINISTER ENEMY HAS GAINED CONTROL OF THOR---AND HAS ORDERED HIM TO CAPTURE ME--- AT ANY COST!
WHAT NO ONE KNOWS---IS THAT MY METAL CHESTPLATE PROTECTS AN INJURED HEART!
AND, IF THOR SMASHES ITS VITAL MECHANISM... I'LL DIE!!
13.

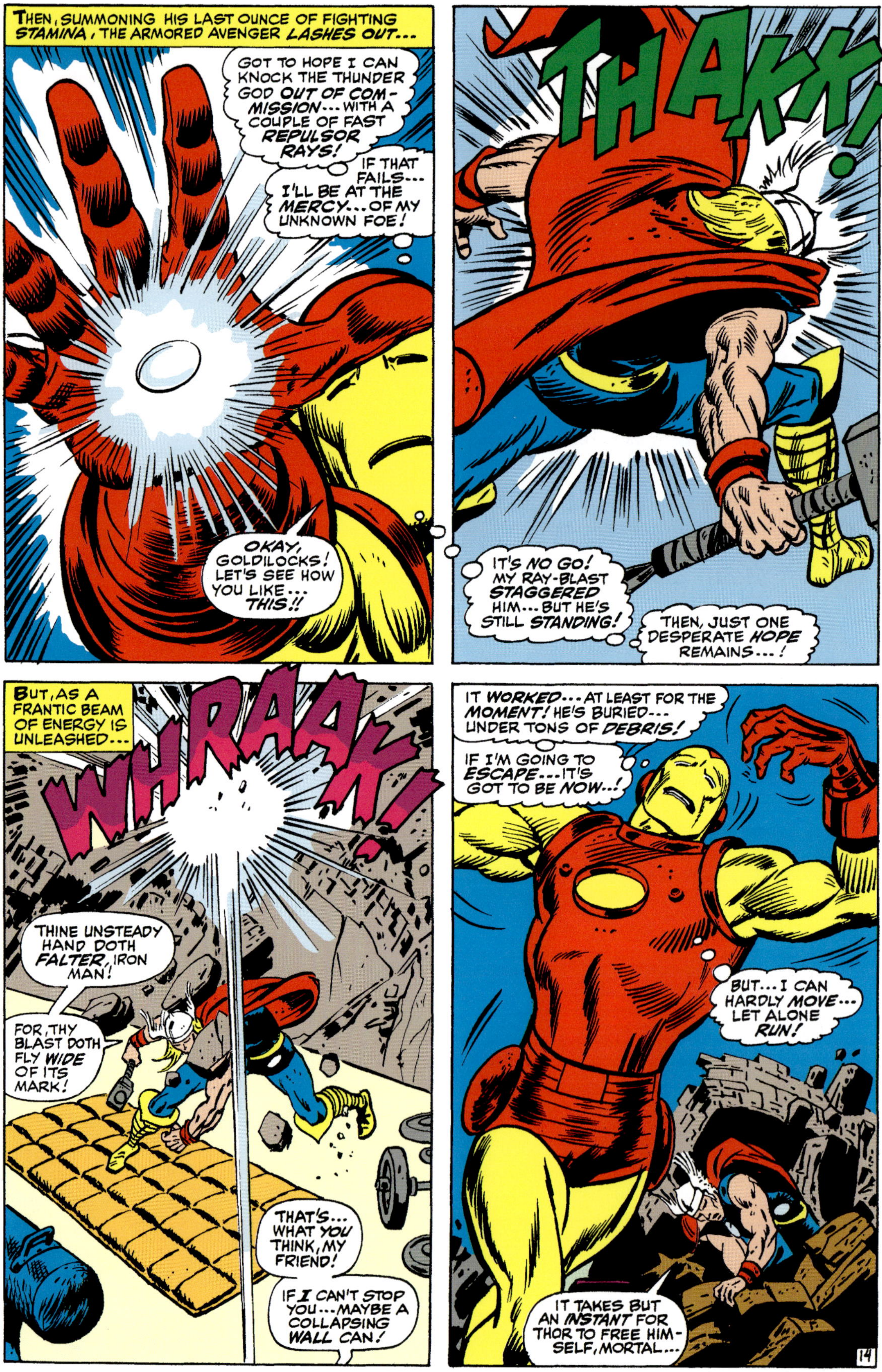
THEN, SUMMONING HIS LAST OUNCE OF FIGHTING STAMINA, THE ARMORED AVENGER LASHES OUT...
GOT TO HOPE I CAN KNOCK THE THUNDER GOD OUT OF COM-MISSION... WITH A COUPLE OF FAST REPULSOR RAYS!
IF THAT FAILS... I'LL BE AT THE MERCY... OF MY UNKNOWN FOE!
OKAY, GOLDILOCKS! LET'S SEE HOW YOU LIKE... THIS!!
THAKK!
IT'S NO GO! MY RAY-BLAST STAGGERED HIM... BUT HE'S STILL STANDING!
THEN, JUST ONE DESPERATE HOPE REMAINS...!
BUT, AS A FRANTIC BEAM OF ENERGY IS UNLEASHED...
WHRAAK!
THINE UNSTEADY HAND DOTH FALTER, IRON MAN!
FOR, THY BLAST DOTH FLY WIDE OF ITS MARK!
THAT'S... WHAT YOU THINK, MY FRIEND!
IF I CAN'T STOP YOU... MAYBE A COLLAPSING WALL CAN!
IT WORKED... AT LEAST FOR THE MOMENT! HE'S BURIED... UNDER TONS OF DEBRIS!
IF I'M GOING TO ESCAPE... IT'S GOT TO BE NOW...!
BUT... I CAN HARDLY MOVE... LET ALONE RUN!
IT TAKES BUT AN INSTANT FOR THOR TO FREE HIM-SELF, MORTAL...
14

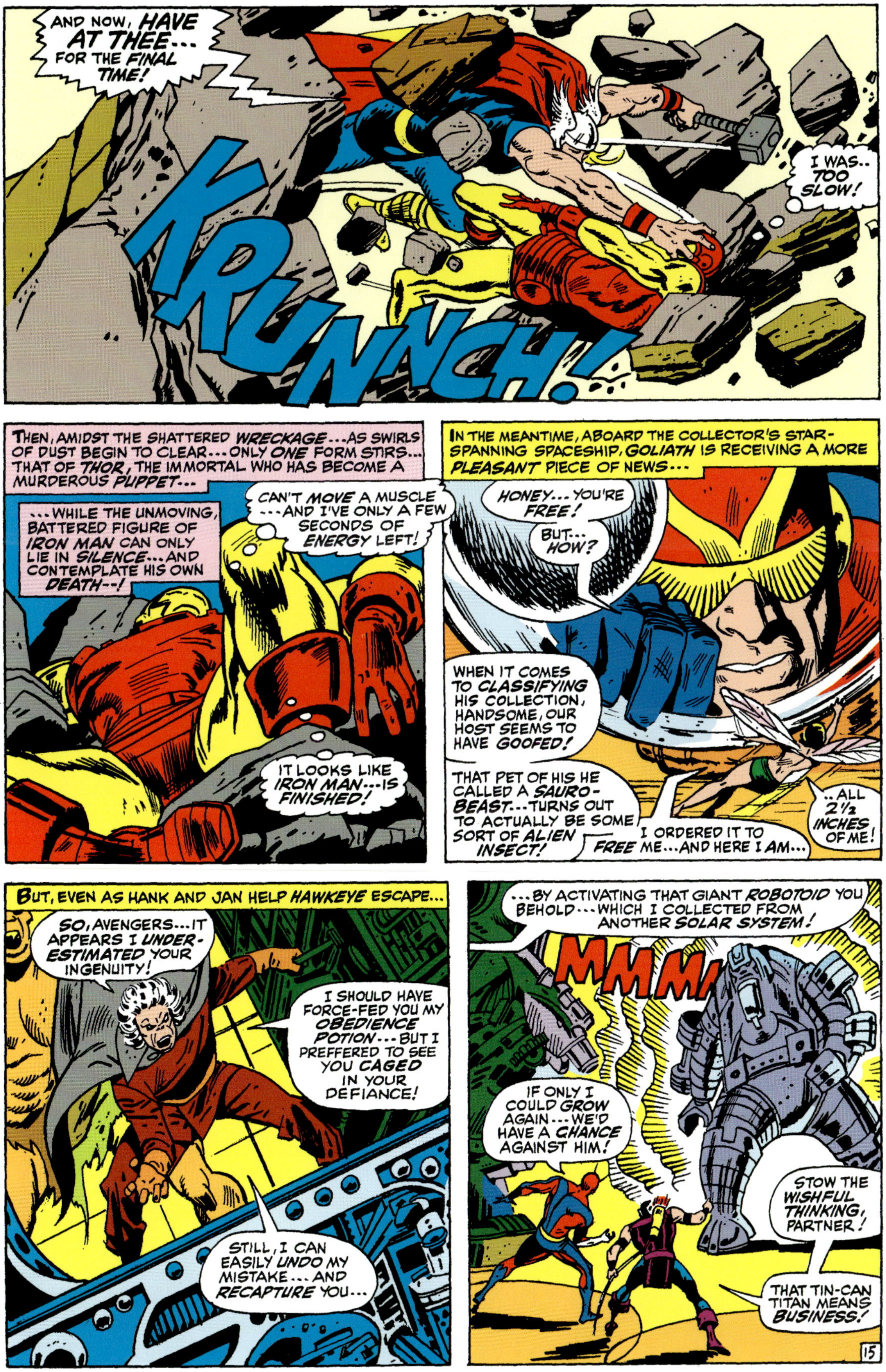
AND NOW, HAVE AT THEE... FOR THE FINAL TIME!
KRUNNCH!
I WAS.. TOO SLOW!
THEN, AMIDST THE SHATTERED WRECKAGE...AS SWIRLS OF DUST BEGIN TO CLEAR...ONLY ONE FORM STIRS... THAT OF THOR, THE IMMORTAL WHO HAS BECOME A MURDEROUS PUPPET...
...WHILE THE UNMOVING, BATTERED FIGURE OF IRON MAN CAN ONLY LIE IN SILENCE...AND CONTEMPLATE HIS OWN DEATH--!
CAN'T MOVE A MUSCLE ...AND I'VE ONLY A FEW SECONDS OF ENERGY LEFT!
IT LOOKS LIKE IRON MAN...IS FINISHED!
IN THE MEANTIME, ABOARD THE COLLECTOR'S STAR-SPANNING SPACESHIP, GOLIATH IS RECEIVING A MORE PLEASANT PIECE OF NEWS...
HONEY... YOU'RE FREE!
BUT... HOW?
WHEN IT COMES TO CLASSIFYING HIS COLLECTION, HANDSOME, OUR HOST SEEMS TO HAVE GOOFED!
THAT PET OF HIS HE CALLED A SAURO-BEAST...TURNS OUT TO ACTUALLY BE SOME SORT OF ALIEN INSECT!
I ORDERED IT TO FREE ME...AND HERE I AM...
..ALL 2½ INCHES OF ME!
BUT, EVEN AS HANK AND JAN HELP HAWKEYE ESCAPE...
SO, AVENGERS...IT APPEARS I UNDER-ESTIMATED YOUR INGENUITY!
I SHOULD HAVE FORCE-FED YOU MY OBEDIENCE POTION...BUT I PREFFERED TO SEE YOU CAGED IN YOUR DEFIANCE!
STILL, I CAN EASILY UNDO MY MISTAKE...AND RECAPTURE YOU...
...BY ACTIVATING THAT GIANT ROBOTOID YOU BEHOLD...WHICH I COLLECTED FROM ANOTHER SOLAR SYSTEM!
MMMM
IF ONLY I COULD GROW AGAIN...WE'D HAVE A CHANCE AGAINST HIM!
STOW THE WISHFUL THINKING, PARTNER!
THAT TIN-CAN TITAN MEANS BUSINESS!
15

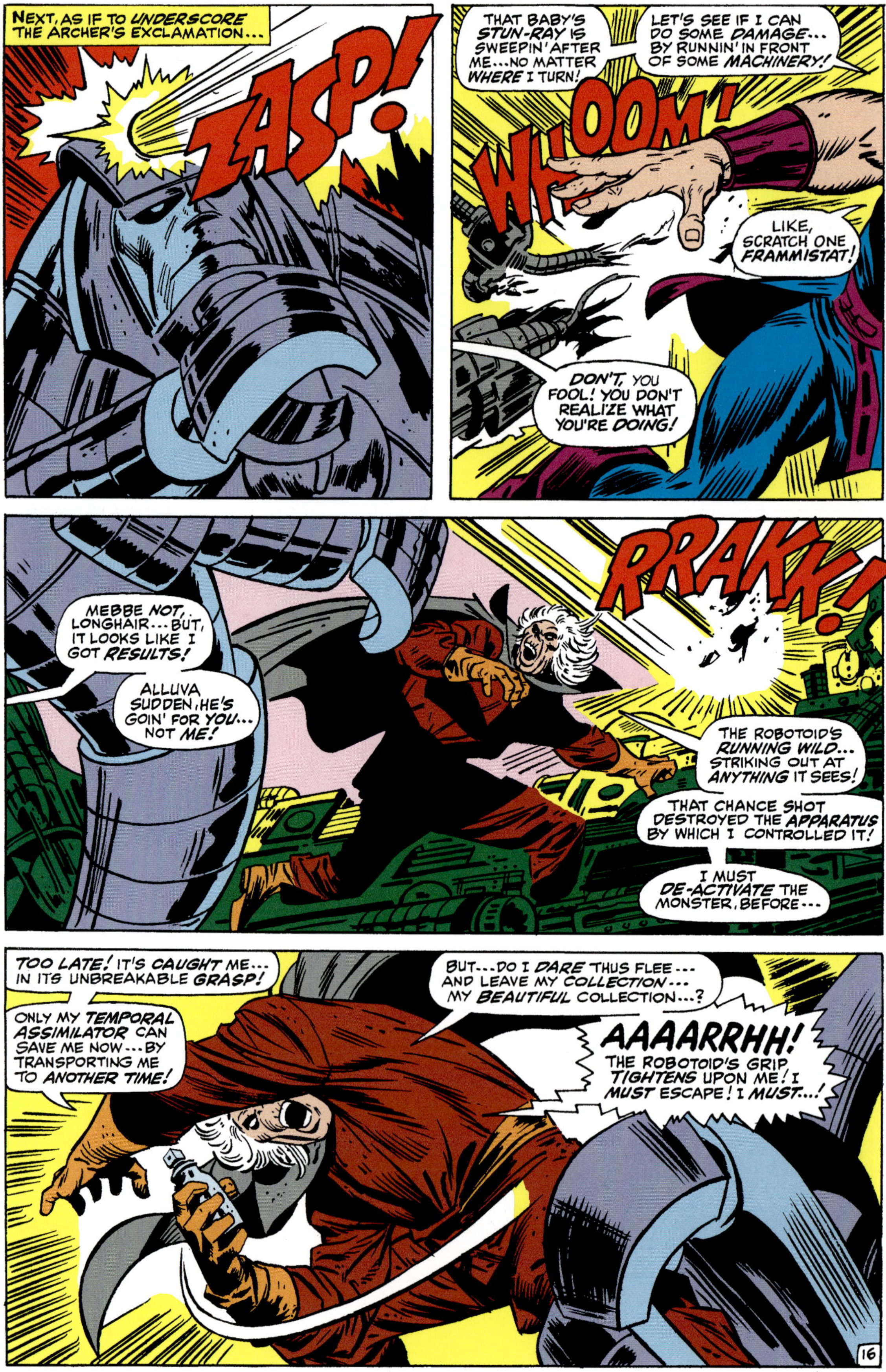
NEXT, AS IF TO UNDERSCORE THE ARCHER'S EXCLAMATION...
ZASP!
THAT BABY'S STUN-RAY IS SWEEPIN' AFTER ME...NO MATTER WHERE I TURN!
LET'S SEE IF I CAN DO SOME DAMAGE... BY RUNNIN' IN FRONT OF SOME MACHINERY!
WHOOM!
LIKE, SCRATCH ONE FRAMMISTAT!
DON'T, YOU FOOL! YOU DON'T REALIZE WHAT YOU'RE DOING!
RRAKK!
MEBBE NOT, LONGHAIR...BUT, IT LOOKS LIKE I GOT RESULTS!
ALLUVA SUDDEN, HE'S GOIN' FOR YOU... NOT ME!
THE ROBOTOID'S RUNNING WILD... STRIKING OUT AT ANYTHING IT SEES!
THAT CHANCE SHOT DESTROYED THE APPARATUS BY WHICH I CONTROLLED IT!
I MUST DE-ACTIVATE THE MONSTER, BEFORE---
TOO LATE! IT'S CAUGHT ME... IN ITS UNBREAKABLE GRASP!
ONLY MY TEMPORAL ASSIMILATOR CAN SAVE ME NOW...BY TRANSPORTING ME TO ANOTHER TIME!
BUT...DO I DARE THUS FLEE... AND LEAVE MY COLLECTION... MY BEAUTIFUL COLLECTION...?
AAAARRHH! THE ROBOTOID'S GRIP TIGHTENS UPON ME! I MUST ESCAPE! I MUST...!
16

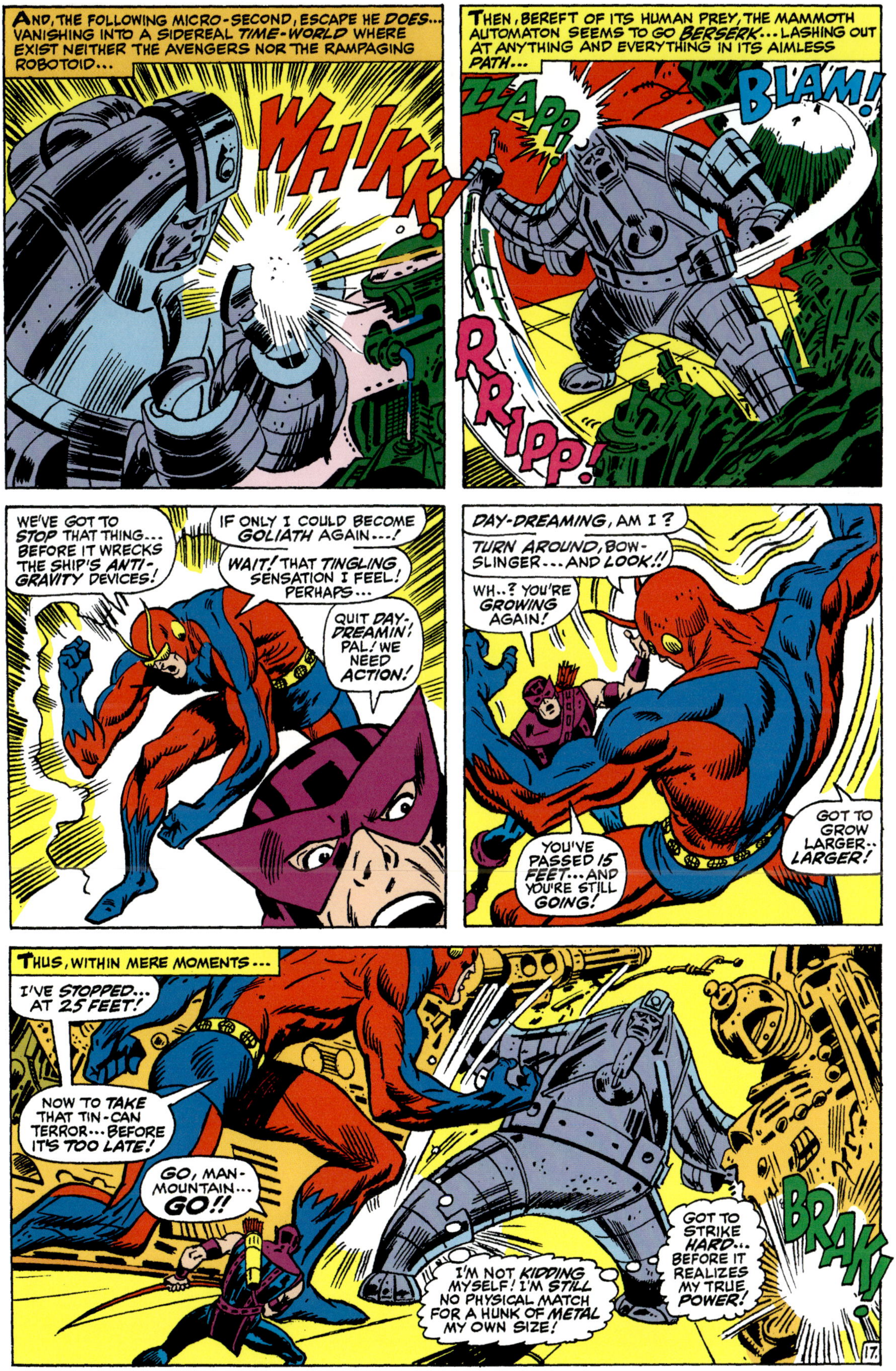

AND, THE FOLLOWING MICRO-SECOND, ESCAPE HE DOES... VANISHING INTO A SIDEREAL TIME-WORLD WHERE EXIST NEITHER THE AVENGERS NOR THE RAMPAGING ROBOTOID...
WHIKK!
THEN, BEREFT OF ITS HUMAN PREY, THE MAMMOTH AUTOMATON SEEMS TO GO BERSERK... LASHING OUT AT ANYTHING AND EVERYTHING IN ITS AIMLESS PATH...
ZZAPP!
BLAM!
RRIPP!
WE'VE GOT TO STOP THAT THING... BEFORE IT WRECKS THE SHIP'S ANTI-GRAVITY DEVICES!
IF ONLY I COULD BECOME GOLIATH AGAIN...!
WAIT! THAT TINGLING SENSATION I FEEL! PERHAPS...
QUIT DAY-DREAMIN', PAL! WE NEED ACTION!
DAY-DREAMING, AM I?
TURN AROUND, BOW-SLINGER... AND LOOK!!
WH..? YOU'RE GROWING AGAIN!
YOU'VE PASSED 15 FEET... AND YOU'RE STILL GOING!
GOT TO GROW LARGER.. LARGER!
THUS, WITHIN MERE MOMENTS...
I'VE STOPPED... AT 25 FEET!
NOW TO TAKE THAT TIN-CAN TERROR... BEFORE IT'S TOO LATE!
GO, MAN-MOUNTAIN... GO!!
I'M NOT KIDDING MYSELF! I'M STILL NO PHYSICAL MATCH FOR A HUNK OF METAL MY OWN SIZE!
GOT TO STRIKE HARD... BEFORE IT REALIZES MY TRUE POWER!
BRAK!
17

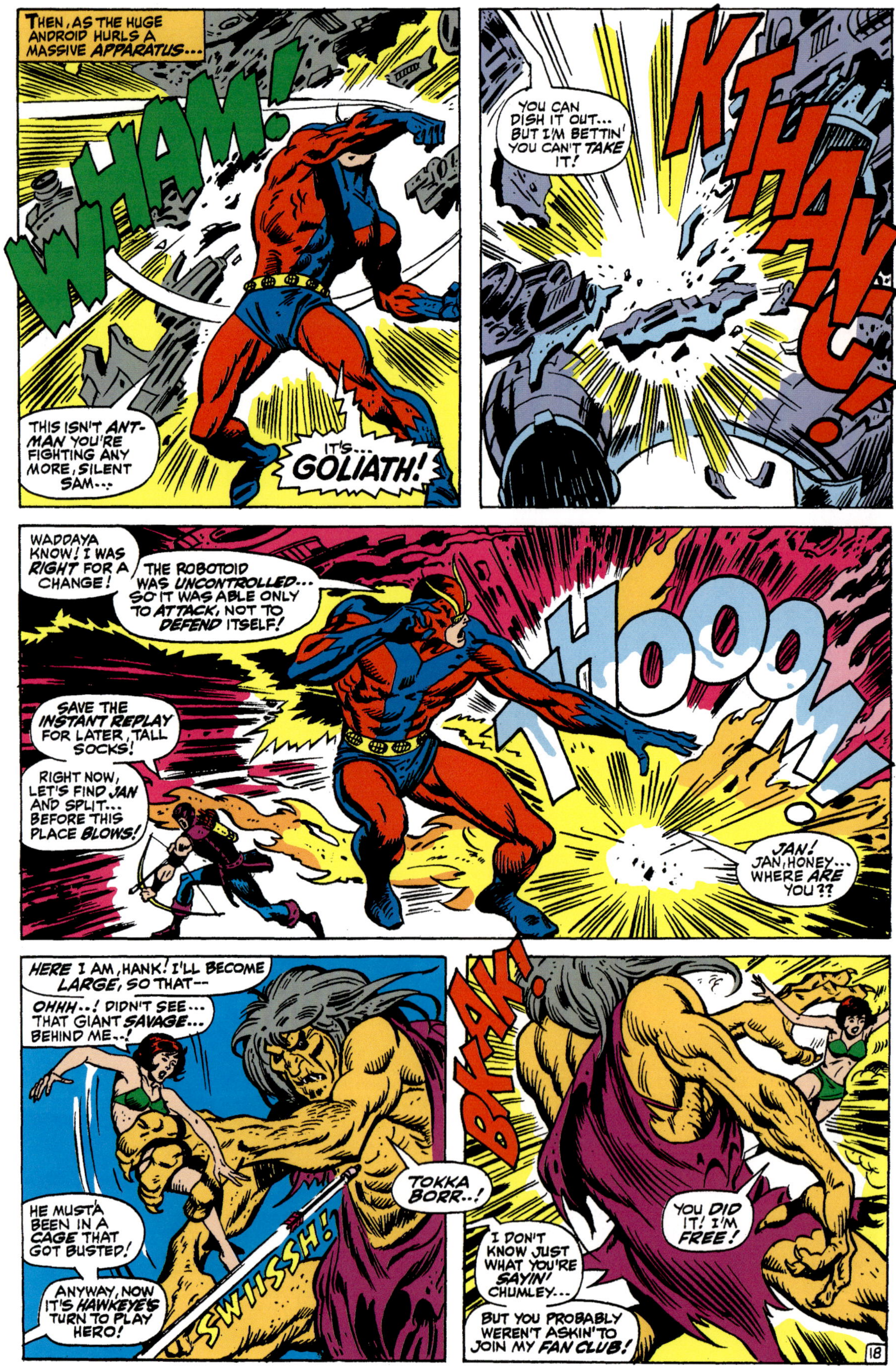
THEN, AS THE HUGE ANDROID HURLS A MASSIVE APPARATUS...
WHAM!
THIS ISN'T ANT-MAN YOU'RE FIGHTING ANY MORE, SILENT SAM...
IT'S... GOLIATH!
YOU CAN DISH IT OUT... BUT I'M BETTIN' YOU CAN'T TAKE IT!
KTHANG!
WADDAYA KNOW! I WAS RIGHT FOR A CHANGE!
THE ROBOTOID WAS UNCONTROLLED... SO IT WAS ABLE ONLY TO ATTACK, NOT TO DEFEND ITSELF!
SAVE THE INSTANT REPLAY FOR LATER, TALL SOCKS!
RIGHT NOW, LET'S FIND JAN AND SPLIT... BEFORE THIS PLACE BLOWS!
THOOOM!
JAN! JAN, HONEY... WHERE ARE YOU??
HERE I AM, HANK! I'LL BECOME LARGE, SO THAT--
OHHH..! DIDN'T SEE... THAT GIANT SAVAGE... BEHIND ME..!
HE MUSTA BEEN IN A CAGE THAT GOT BUSTED!
ANYWAY, NOW IT'S HAWKEYE'S TURN TO PLAY HERO!
SWIISSH!
TOKKA BORR..!
BKAK!
I DON'T KNOW JUST WHAT YOU'RE SAYIN' CHUMLEY...
BUT YOU PROBABLY WEREN'T ASKIN' TO JOIN MY FAN CLUB!
YOU DID IT! I'M FREE!
18

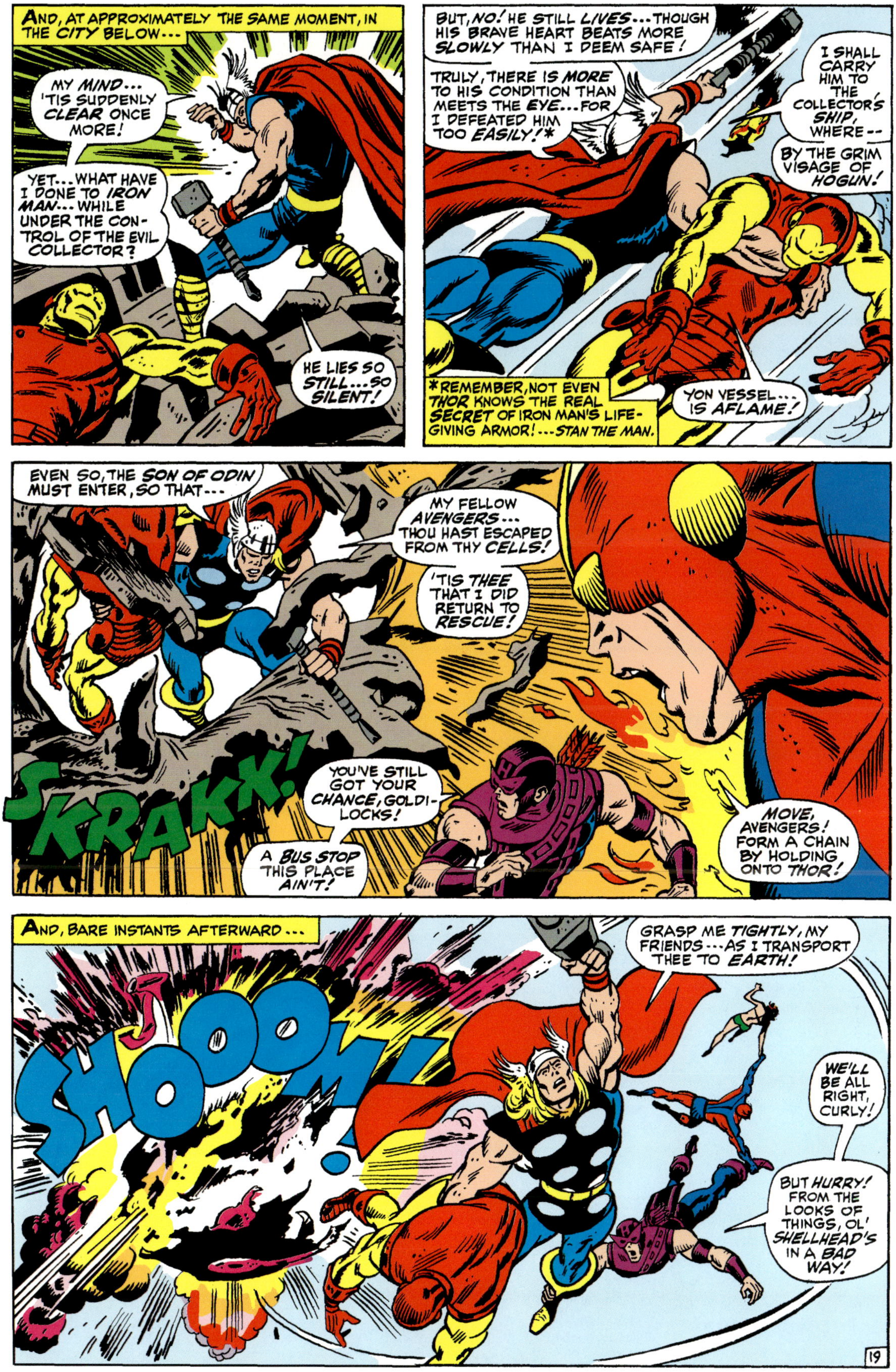

Panel 1:

AND, AT APPROXIMATELY THE SAME MOMENT, IN THE CITY BELOW...

MY MIND... 'TIS SUDDENLY CLEAR ONCE MORE!

YET... WHAT HAVE I DONE TO IRON MAN... WHILE UNDER THE CONTROL OF THE EVIL COLLECTOR?

HE LIES SO STILL... SO SILENT!

Panel 2:

BUT, NO! HE STILL LIVES... THOUGH HIS BRAVE HEART BEATS MORE SLOWLY THAN I DEEM SAFE!

TRULY, THERE IS MORE TO HIS CONDITION THAN MEETS THE EYE... FOR I DEFEATED HIM TOO EASILY!*

I SHALL CARRY HIM TO THE COLLECTOR'S SHIP, WHERE... BY THE GRIM VISAGE OF HOGUN!

YON VESSEL... IS AFLAME!

*REMEMBER, NOT EVEN THOR KNOWS THE REAL SECRET OF IRON MAN'S LIFE-GIVING ARMOR! --- STAN THE MAN.

Panel 3:

EVEN SO, THE SON OF ODIN MUST ENTER, SO THAT...

MY FELLOW AVENGERS... THOU HAST ESCAPED FROM THY CELLS!

'TIS THEE THAT I DID RETURN TO RESCUE!

SKRAKK!

YOU'VE STILL GOT YOUR CHANCE, GOLDI-LOCKS!

A BUS STOP THIS PLACE AIN'T!

MOVE, AVENGERS! FORM A CHAIN BY HOLDING ONTO THOR!

Panel 4:

AND, BARE INSTANTS AFTERWARD...

SHOOM!

GRASP ME TIGHTLY, MY FRIENDS... AS I TRANSPORT THEE TO EARTH!

WE'LL BE ALL RIGHT, CURLY!

BUT HURRY! FROM THE LOOKS OF THINGS, OL' SHELLHEAD'S IN A BAD WAY!

19

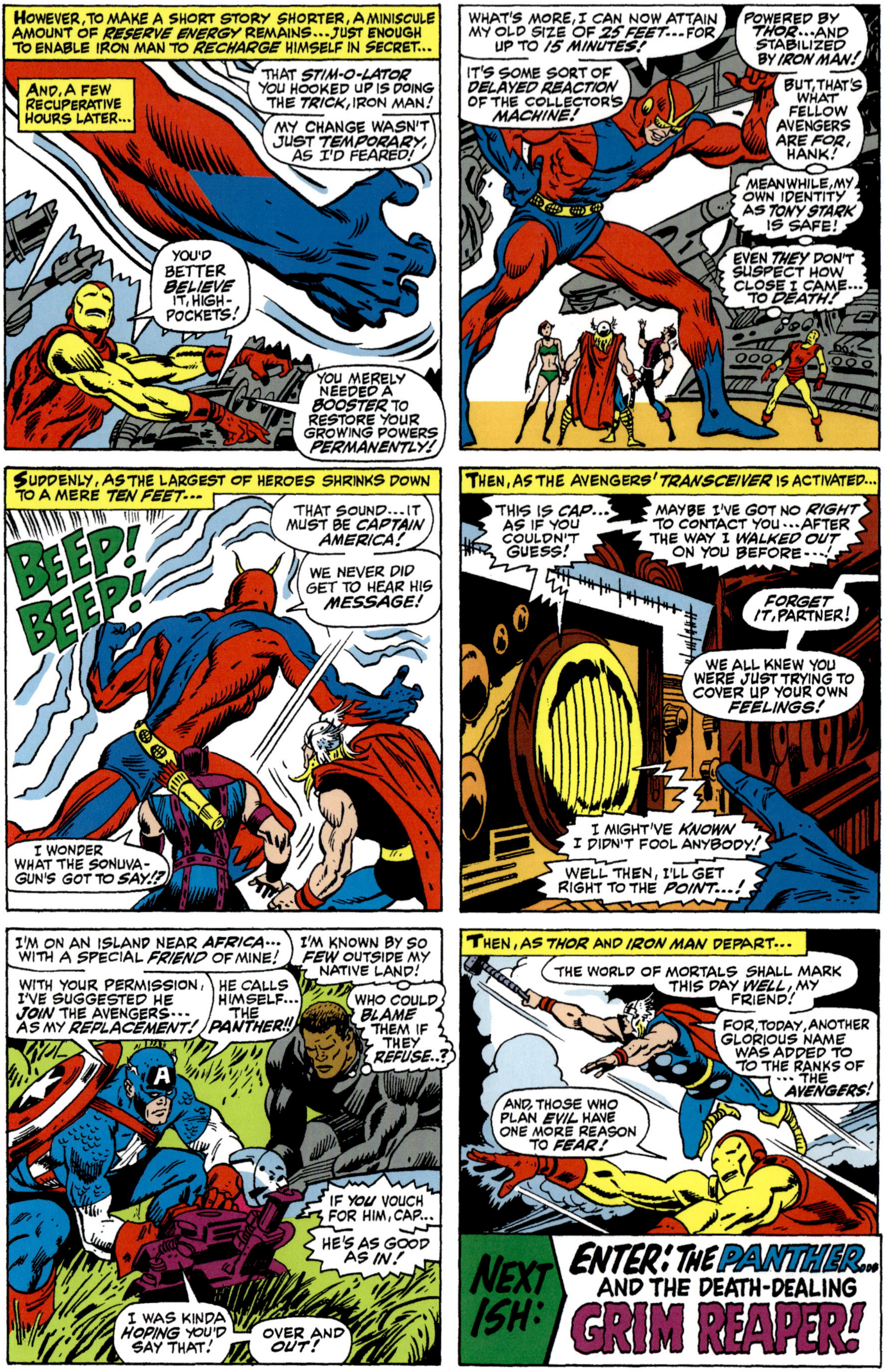

HOWEVER, TO MAKE A SHORT STORY SHORTER, A MINISCULE AMOUNT OF RESERVE ENERGY REMAINS... JUST ENOUGH TO ENABLE IRON MAN TO RECHARGE HIMSELF IN SECRET...
AND, A FEW RECUPERATIVE HOURS LATER...
THAT STIM-O-LATOR YOU HOOKED UP IS DOING THE TRICK, IRON MAN!
MY CHANGE WASN'T JUST TEMPORARY, AS I'D FEARED!
YOU'D BETTER BELIEVE IT, HIGH-POCKETS!
YOU MERELY NEEDED A BOOSTER TO RESTORE YOUR GROWING POWERS PERMANENTLY!
WHAT'S MORE, I CAN NOW ATTAIN MY OLD SIZE OF 25 FEET--FOR UP TO 15 MINUTES!
IT'S SOME SORT OF DELAYED REACTION OF THE COLLECTOR'S MACHINE!
POWERED BY THOR...AND STABILIZED BY IRON MAN!
BUT, THAT'S WHAT FELLOW AVENGERS ARE FOR, HANK!
MEANWHILE, MY OWN IDENTITY AS TONY STARK IS SAFE!
EVEN THEY DON'T SUSPECT HOW CLOSE I CAME... TO DEATH!
SUDDENLY, AS THE LARGEST OF HEROES SHRINKS DOWN TO A MERE TEN FEET---
BEEP! BEEP!
THAT SOUND---IT MUST BE CAPTAIN AMERICA!
WE NEVER DID GET TO HEAR HIS MESSAGE!
I WONDER WHAT THE SONUVA-GUN'S GOT TO SAY!?
THEN, AS THE AVENGERS' TRANSCEIVER IS ACTIVATED...
THIS IS CAP... AS IF YOU COULDN'T GUESS!
MAYBE I'VE GOT NO RIGHT TO CONTACT YOU...AFTER THE WAY I WALKED OUT ON YOU BEFORE---!
FORGET IT, PARTNER!
WE ALL KNEW YOU WERE JUST TRYING TO COVER UP YOUR OWN FEELINGS!
I MIGHT'VE KNOWN I DIDN'T FOOL ANYBODY!
WELL THEN, I'LL GET RIGHT TO THE POINT...!
I'M ON AN ISLAND NEAR AFRICA... WITH A SPECIAL FRIEND OF MINE!
I'M KNOWN BY SO FEW OUTSIDE MY NATIVE LAND!
WITH YOUR PERMISSION, I'VE SUGGESTED HE JOIN THE AVENGERS... AS MY REPLACEMENT!
HE CALLS HIMSELF... THE PANTHER!!
WHO COULD BLAME THEM IF THEY REFUSE..?
IF YOU VOUCH FOR HIM, CAP...
HE'S AS GOOD AS IN!
I WAS KINDA HOPING YOU'D SAY THAT!
OVER AND OUT!
THEN, AS THOR AND IRON MAN DEPART...
THE WORLD OF MORTALS SHALL MARK THIS DAY WELL, MY FRIEND!
FOR, TODAY, ANOTHER GLORIOUS NAME WAS ADDED TO TO THE RANKS OF ... THE AVENGERS!
AND, THOSE WHO PLAN EVIL HAVE ONE MORE REASON TO FEAR!
NEXT ISH: ENTER: THE PANTHER... AND THE DEATH-DEALING GRIM REAPER!

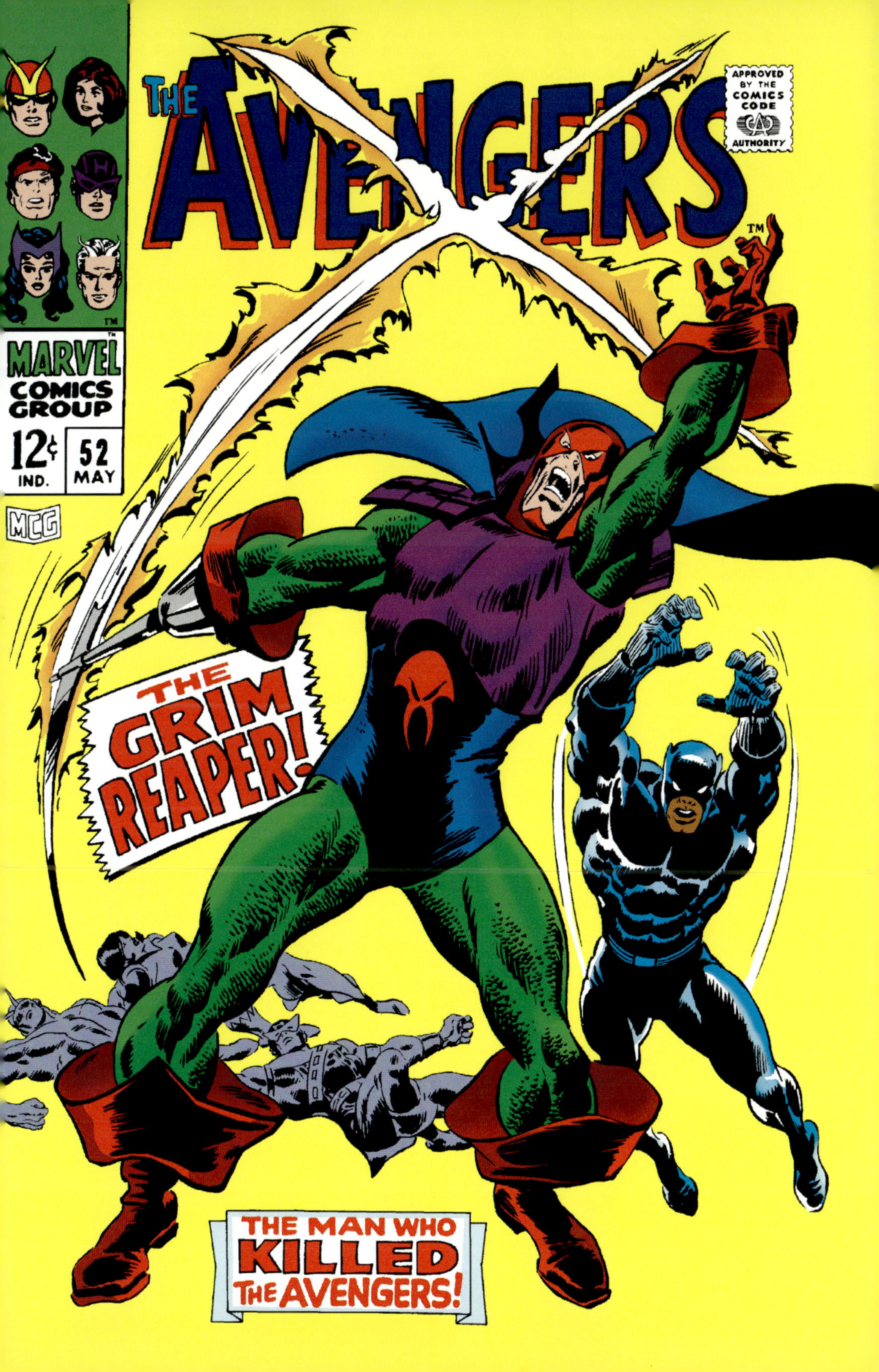
THE AVENGERS
APPROVED BY THE COMICS CODE AUTHORITY
MARVEL COMICS GROUP
12¢ IND.
52 MAY
MCG
THE GRIM REAPER!
THE MAN WHO KILLED THE AVENGERS!

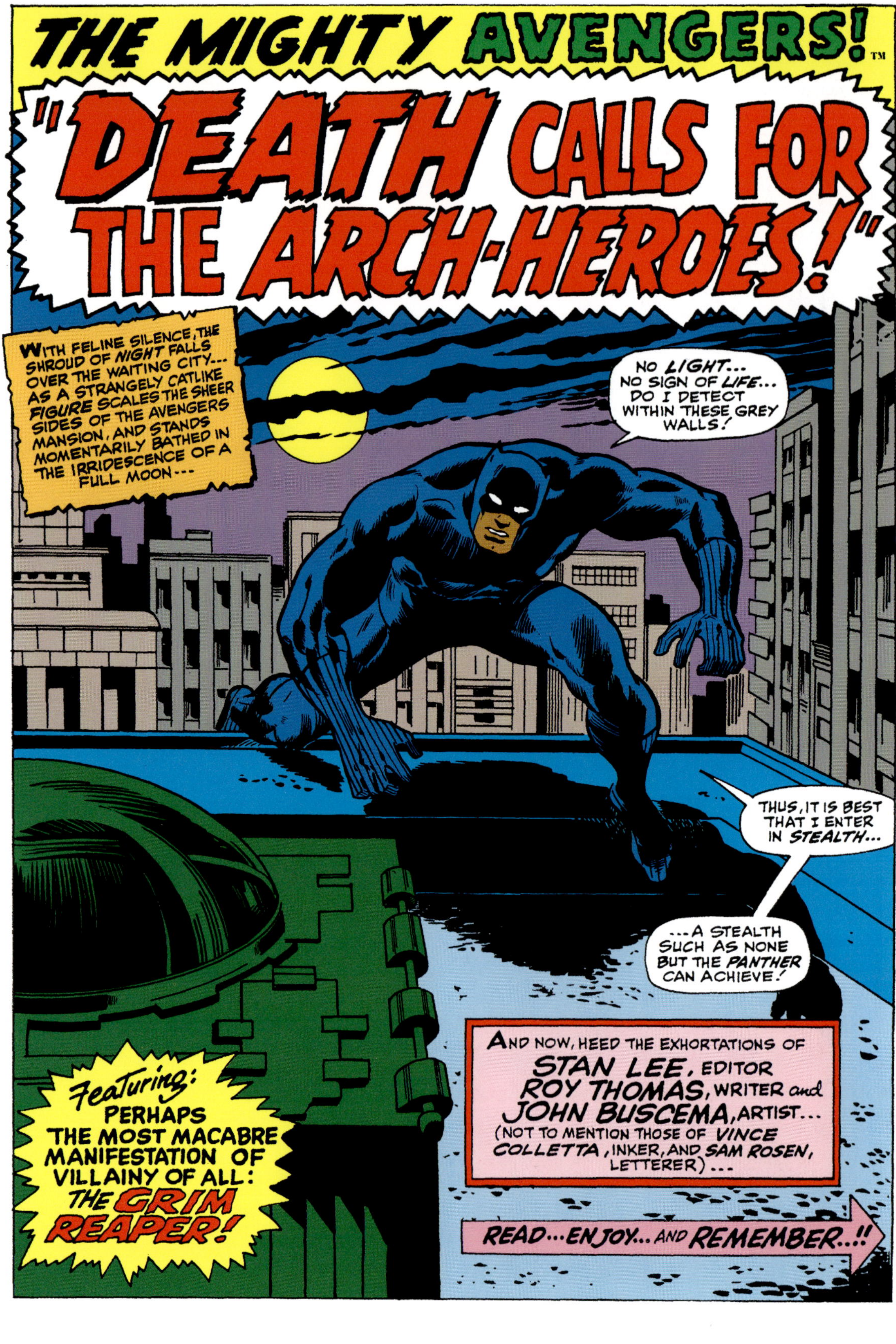
THE MIGHTY AVENGERS! ™
"DEATH CALLS FOR THE ARCH-HEROES!"
WITH FELINE SILENCE, THE SHROUD OF NIGHT FALLS OVER THE WAITING CITY... AS A STRANGELY CATLIKE FIGURE SCALES THE SHEER SIDES OF THE AVENGERS MANSION, AND STANDS MOMENTARILY BATHED IN THE IRRIDESCENCE OF A FULL MOON...
NO LIGHT... NO SIGN OF LIFE... DO I DETECT WITHIN THESE GREY WALLS!
THUS, IT IS BEST THAT I ENTER IN STEALTH...
...A STEALTH SUCH AS NONE BUT THE PANTHER CAN ACHIEVE!
AND NOW, HEED THE EXHORTATIONS OF STAN LEE, EDITOR ROY THOMAS, WRITER and JOHN BUSCEMA, ARTIST... (NOT TO MENTION THOSE OF VINCE COLLETTA, INKER, AND SAM ROSEN, LETTERER)...
Featuring: PERHAPS THE MOST MACABRE MANIFESTATION OF VILLAINY OF ALL: THE GRIM REAPER!
READ...ENJOY...AND REMEMBER..!!

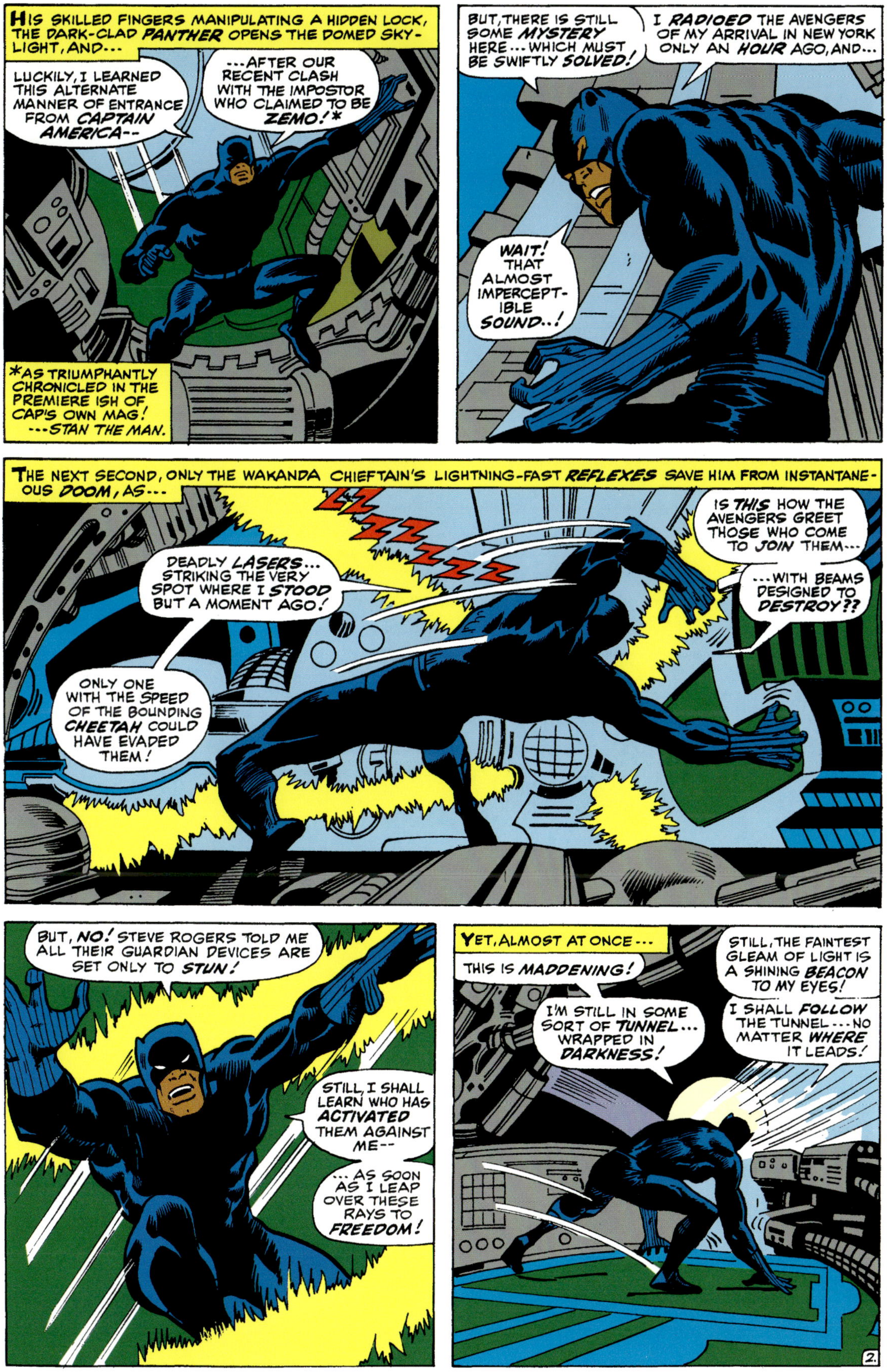

Panel 1: HIS SKILLED FINGERS MANIPULATING A HIDDEN LOCK, THE DARK-CLAD *PANTHER* OPENS THE DOMED SKYLIGHT, AND...

LUCKILY, I LEARNED THIS ALTERNATE MANNER OF ENTRANCE FROM *CAPTAIN AMERICA*--

...AFTER OUR RECENT CLASH WITH THE IMPOSTOR WHO CLAIMED TO BE *ZEMO!* *

*AS TRIUMPHANTLY CHRONICLED IN THE PREMIERE ISH OF CAP'S OWN MAG! --STAN THE MAN.

Panel 2: BUT, THERE IS STILL SOME *MYSTERY* HERE...WHICH MUST BE SWIFTLY *SOLVED!*

I *RADIOED* THE AVENGERS OF MY ARRIVAL IN NEW YORK ONLY AN *HOUR* AGO, AND...

WAIT! THAT ALMOST IMPERCEPTIBLE SOUND..!

Panel 3: THE NEXT SECOND, ONLY THE WAKANDA CHIEFTAIN'S LIGHTNING-FAST *REFLEXES* SAVE HIM FROM INSTANTANEOUS *DOOM*, AS...

DEADLY *LASERS*... STRIKING THE VERY SPOT WHERE I *STOOD* BUT A MOMENT AGO!

ONLY ONE WITH THE *SPEED* OF THE BOUNDING *CHEETAH* COULD HAVE EVADED THEM!

IS *THIS* HOW THE AVENGERS GREET THOSE WHO COME TO *JOIN* THEM...

...WITH BEAMS DESIGNED TO *DESTROY??*

Panel 4: BUT, *NO!* STEVE ROGERS TOLD ME ALL THEIR GUARDIAN DEVICES ARE SET ONLY TO *STUN!*

STILL, I SHALL LEARN WHO HAS *ACTIVATED* THEM AGAINST ME--

...AS SOON AS I LEAP OVER THESE RAYS TO *FREEDOM!*

Panel 5: YET, ALMOST AT ONCE...

THIS IS *MADDENING!*

I'M STILL IN SOME SORT OF *TUNNEL*... WRAPPED IN *DARKNESS!*

STILL, THE FAINTEST GLEAM OF LIGHT IS A SHINING *BEACON* TO MY EYES!

I SHALL *FOLLOW* THE TUNNEL...NO MATTER *WHERE* IT LEADS!

2.

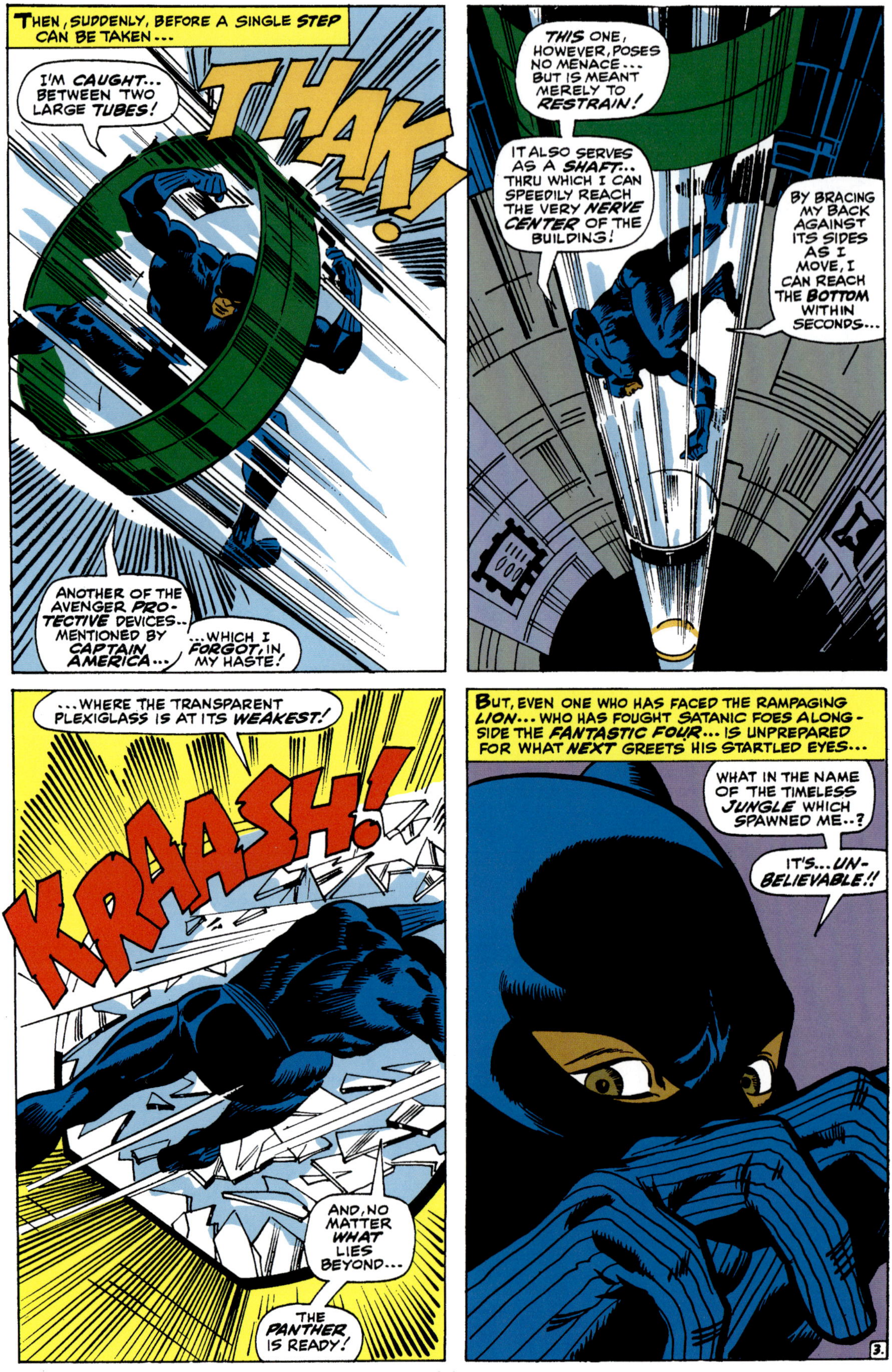
THEN, SUDDENLY, BEFORE A SINGLE STEP CAN BE TAKEN...
I'M CAUGHT... BETWEEN TWO LARGE TUBES!
THAK!
ANOTHER OF THE AVENGER PROTECTIVE DEVICES.. MENTIONED BY CAPTAIN AMERICA...
...WHICH I FORGOT, IN MY HASTE!
THIS ONE, HOWEVER, POSES NO MENACE... BUT IS MEANT MERELY TO RESTRAIN!
IT ALSO SERVES AS A SHAFT... THRU WHICH I CAN SPEEDILY REACH THE VERY NERVE CENTER OF THE BUILDING!
BY BRACING MY BACK AGAINST ITS SIDES AS I MOVE, I CAN REACH THE BOTTOM WITHIN SECONDS...
...WHERE THE TRANSPARENT PLEXIGLASS IS AT ITS WEAKEST!
KRAASH!
AND, NO MATTER WHAT LIES BEYOND...
THE PANTHER IS READY!
BUT, EVEN ONE WHO HAS FACED THE RAMPAGING LION... WHO HAS FOUGHT SATANIC FOES ALONG-SIDE THE FANTASTIC FOUR... IS UNPREPARED FOR WHAT NEXT GREETS HIS STARTLED EYES...
WHAT IN THE NAME OF THE TIMELESS JUNGLE WHICH SPAWNED ME..?
IT'S... UN-BELIEVABLE!!
3.

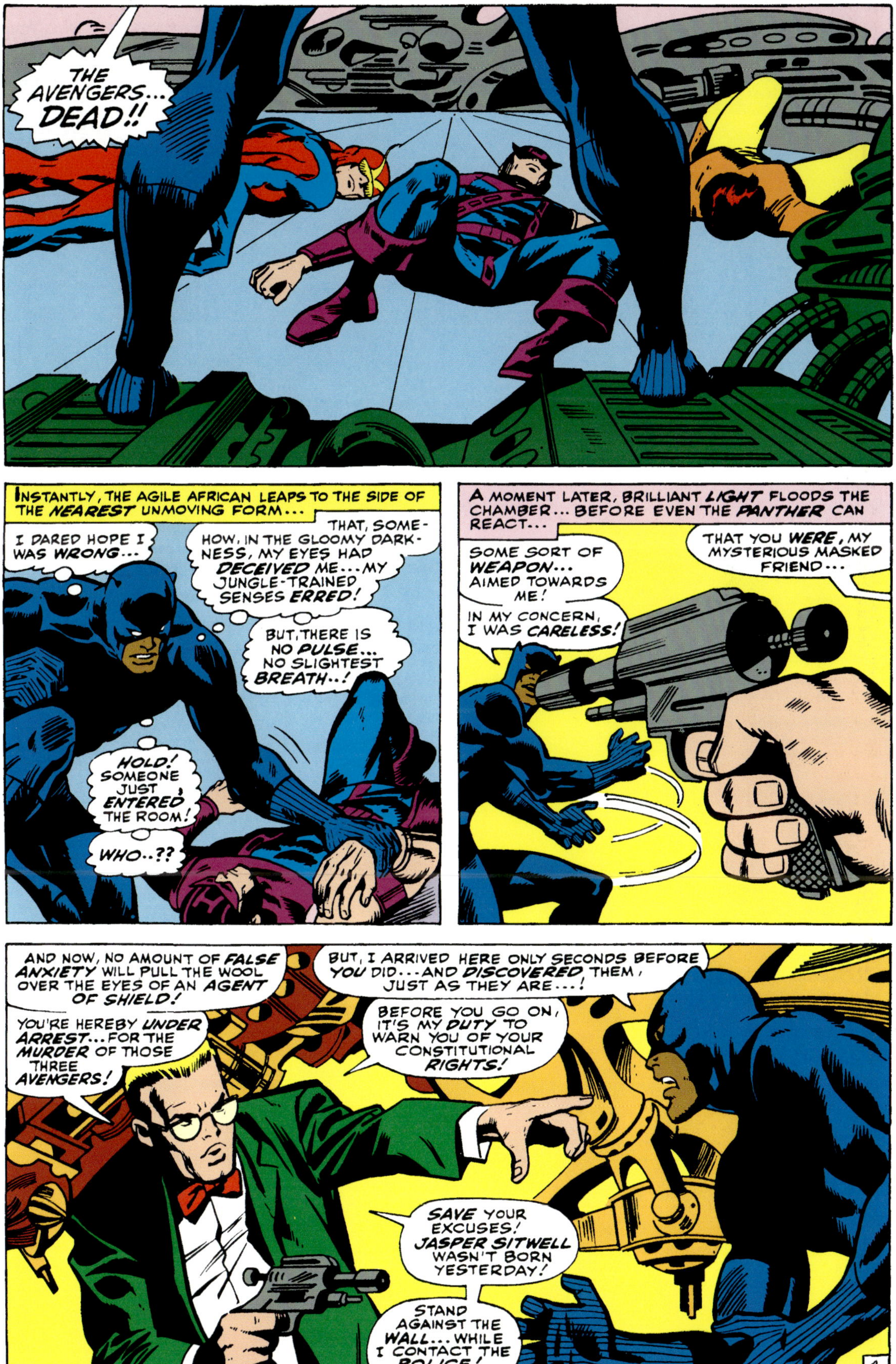
THE AVENGERS... DEAD!!
INSTANTLY, THE AGILE AFRICAN LEAPS TO THE SIDE OF THE NEAREST UNMOVING FORM...
I DARED HOPE I WAS WRONG...
THAT, SOMEHOW, IN THE GLOOMY DARKNESS, MY EYES HAD DECEIVED ME... MY JUNGLE-TRAINED SENSES ERRED!
BUT, THERE IS NO PULSE... NO SLIGHTEST BREATH..!
HOLD! SOMEONE JUST ENTERED THE ROOM!
WHO..??
A MOMENT LATER, BRILLIANT LIGHT FLOODS THE CHAMBER... BEFORE EVEN THE PANTHER CAN REACT...
SOME SORT OF WEAPON... AIMED TOWARDS ME!
IN MY CONCERN, I WAS CARELESS!
THAT YOU WERE, MY MYSTERIOUS MASKED FRIEND...
AND NOW, NO AMOUNT OF FALSE ANXIETY WILL PULL THE WOOL OVER THE EYES OF AN AGENT OF SHIELD!
YOU'RE HEREBY UNDER ARREST... FOR THE MURDER OF THOSE THREE AVENGERS!
BUT, I ARRIVED HERE ONLY SECONDS BEFORE YOU DID... AND DISCOVERED THEM, JUST AS THEY ARE...!
BEFORE YOU GO ON, IT'S MY DUTY TO WARN YOU OF YOUR CONSTITUTIONAL RIGHTS!
SAVE YOUR EXCUSES! JASPER SITWELL WASN'T BORN YESTERDAY!
STAND AGAINST THE WALL... WHILE I CONTACT THE POLICE!
4.

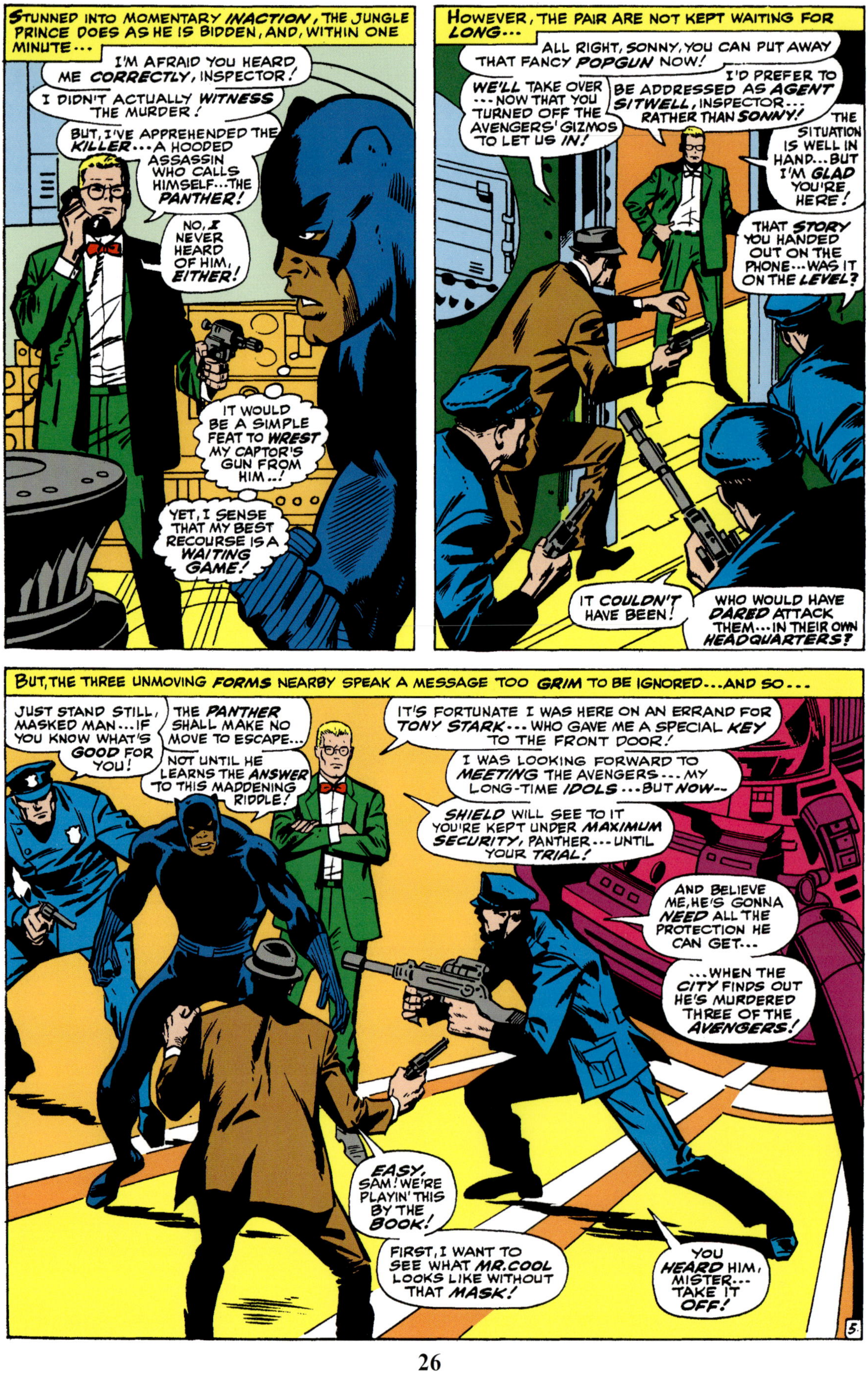
STUNNED INTO MOMENTARY INACTION, THE JUNGLE PRINCE DOES AS HE IS BIDDEN, AND, WITHIN ONE MINUTE...
I'M AFRAID YOU HEARD ME CORRECTLY, INSPECTOR!
I DIDN'T ACTUALLY WITNESS THE MURDER!
BUT, I'VE APPREHENDED THE KILLER... A HOODED ASSASSIN WHO CALLS HIMSELF... THE PANTHER!
NO, I NEVER HEARD OF HIM, EITHER!
IT WOULD BE A SIMPLE FEAT TO WREST MY CAPTOR'S GUN FROM HIM...!
YET, I SENSE THAT MY BEST RECOURSE IS A WAITING GAME!
HOWEVER, THE PAIR ARE NOT KEPT WAITING FOR LONG...
ALL RIGHT, SONNY, YOU CAN PUT AWAY THAT FANCY POPGUN NOW!
WE'LL TAKE OVER --- NOW THAT YOU TURNED OFF THE AVENGERS' GIZMOS TO LET US IN!
I'D PREFER TO BE ADDRESSED AS AGENT SITWELL, INSPECTOR... RATHER THAN SONNY!
THE SITUATION IS WELL IN HAND... BUT I'M GLAD YOU'RE HERE!
THAT STORY YOU HANDED OUT ON THE PHONE... WAS IT ON THE LEVEL?
IT COULDN'T HAVE BEEN!
WHO WOULD HAVE DARED ATTACK THEM... IN THEIR OWN HEADQUARTERS?
BUT, THE THREE UNMOVING FORMS NEARBY SPEAK A MESSAGE TOO GRIM TO BE IGNORED...AND SO...
JUST STAND STILL, MASKED MAN... IF YOU KNOW WHAT'S GOOD FOR YOU!
THE PANTHER SHALL MAKE NO MOVE TO ESCAPE...
NOT UNTIL HE LEARNS THE ANSWER TO THIS MADDENING RIDDLE!
IT'S FORTUNATE I WAS HERE ON AN ERRAND FOR TONY STARK... WHO GAVE ME A SPECIAL KEY TO THE FRONT DOOR!
I WAS LOOKING FORWARD TO MEETING THE AVENGERS... MY LONG-TIME IDOLS... BUT NOW--
SHIELD WILL SEE TO IT YOU'RE KEPT UNDER MAXIMUM SECURITY, PANTHER... UNTIL YOUR TRIAL!
AND BELIEVE ME, HE'S GONNA NEED ALL THE PROTECTION HE CAN GET...
...WHEN THE CITY FINDS OUT HE'S MURDERED THREE OF THE AVENGERS!
EASY, SAM! WE'RE PLAYIN' THIS BY THE BOOK!
FIRST, I WANT TO SEE WHAT MR. COOL LOOKS LIKE WITHOUT THAT MASK!
YOU HEARD HIM, MISTER... TAKE IT OFF!
5

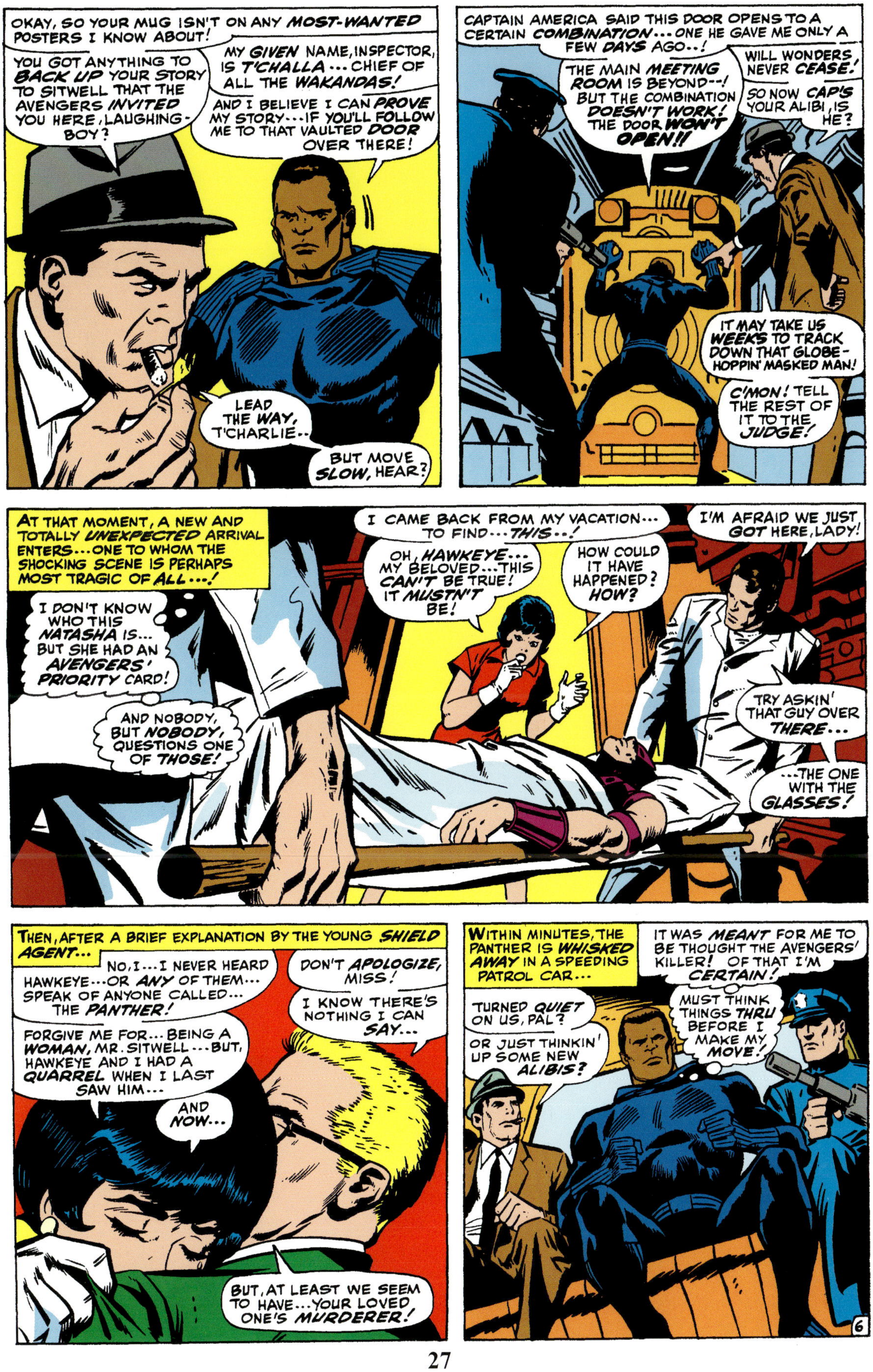
OKAY, SO YOUR MUG ISN'T ON ANY MOST-WANTED POSTERS I KNOW ABOUT!
YOU GOT ANYTHING TO BACK UP YOUR STORY TO SITWELL THAT THE AVENGERS INVITED YOU HERE, LAUGHING-BOY?
MY GIVEN NAME, INSPECTOR, IS T'CHALLA... CHIEF OF ALL THE WAKANDAS!
AND I BELIEVE I CAN PROVE MY STORY... IF YOU'LL FOLLOW ME TO THAT VAULTED DOOR OVER THERE!
LEAD THE WAY, T'CHARLIE..
BUT MOVE SLOW, HEAR?
CAPTAIN AMERICA SAID THIS DOOR OPENS TO A CERTAIN COMBINATION... ONE HE GAVE ME ONLY A FEW DAYS AGO..!
THE MAIN MEETING ROOM IS BEYOND--! BUT THE COMBINATION DOESN'T WORK! THE DOOR WON'T OPEN!!
WILL WONDERS NEVER CEASE!
SO NOW CAP'S YOUR ALIBI, IS HE?
IT MAY TAKE US WEEKS TO TRACK DOWN THAT GLOBE-HOPPIN' MASKED MAN!
C'MON! TELL THE REST OF IT TO THE JUDGE!
AT THAT MOMENT, A NEW AND TOTALLY UNEXPECTED ARRIVAL ENTERS... ONE TO WHOM THE SHOCKING SCENE IS PERHAPS MOST TRAGIC OF ALL...!
I DON'T KNOW WHO THIS NATASHA IS... BUT SHE HAD AN AVENGERS' PRIORITY CARD!
AND NOBODY, BUT NOBODY, QUESTIONS ONE OF THOSE!
I CAME BACK FROM MY VACATION... TO FIND... THIS..!
OH, HAWKEYE... MY BELOVED... THIS CAN'T BE TRUE! IT MUSTN'T BE!
HOW COULD IT HAVE HAPPENED? HOW?
I'M AFRAID WE JUST GOT HERE, LADY!
TRY ASKIN' THAT GUY OVER THERE...
...THE ONE WITH THE GLASSES!
THEN, AFTER A BRIEF EXPLANATION BY THE YOUNG SHIELD AGENT...
NO, I... I NEVER HEARD HAWKEYE... OR ANY OF THEM... SPEAK OF ANYONE CALLED... THE PANTHER!
FORGIVE ME FOR... BEING A WOMAN, MR. SITWELL... BUT, HAWKEYE AND I HAD A QUARREL WHEN I LAST SAW HIM...
AND NOW...
DON'T APOLOGIZE, MISS!
I KNOW THERE'S NOTHING I CAN SAY...
BUT, AT LEAST WE SEEM TO HAVE... YOUR LOVED ONE'S MURDERER!
WITHIN MINUTES, THE PANTHER IS WHISKED AWAY IN A SPEEDING PATROL CAR...
IT WAS MEANT FOR ME TO BE THOUGHT THE AVENGERS' KILLER! OF THAT I'M CERTAIN!
MUST THINK THINGS THRU BEFORE I MAKE MY MOVE!
TURNED QUIET ON US, PAL?
OR JUST THINKIN' UP SOME NEW ALIBIS?
6

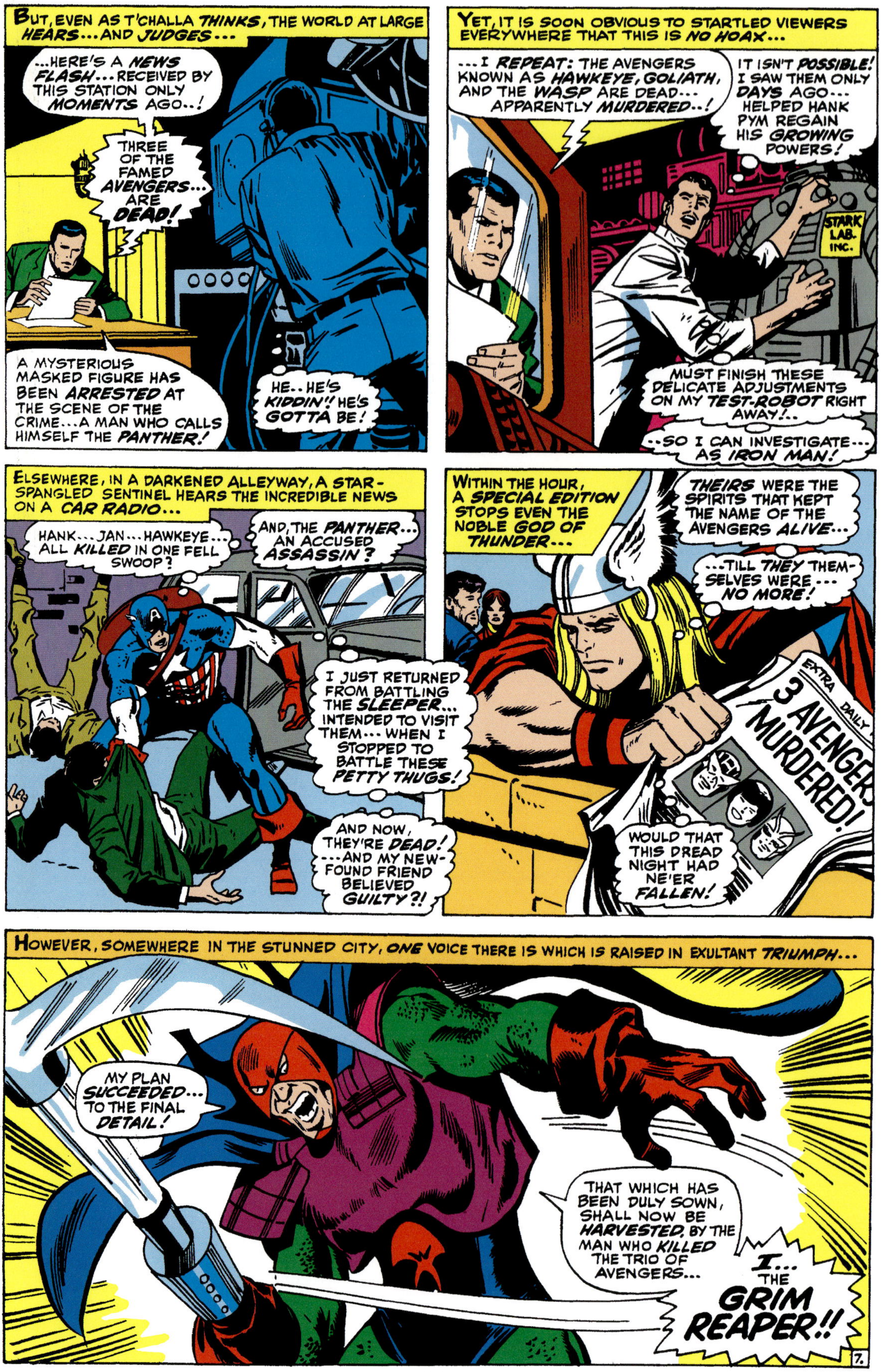
BUT, EVEN AS T'CHALLA THINKS, THE WORLD AT LARGE HEARS... AND JUDGES...
...HERE'S A NEWS FLASH... RECEIVED BY THIS STATION ONLY MOMENTS AGO..!
THREE OF THE FAMED AVENGERS... ARE DEAD!
A MYSTERIOUS MASKED FIGURE HAS BEEN ARRESTED AT THE SCENE OF THE CRIME... A MAN WHO CALLS HIMSELF THE PANTHER!
HE..HE'S KIDDIN'! HE'S GOTTA BE!
YET, IT IS SOON OBVIOUS TO STARTLED VIEWERS EVERYWHERE THAT THIS IS NO HOAX...
...I REPEAT: THE AVENGERS KNOWN AS HAWKEYE, GOLIATH, AND THE WASP ARE DEAD... APPARENTLY MURDERED..!
IT ISN'T POSSIBLE! I SAW THEM ONLY DAYS AGO... HELPED HANK PYM REGAIN HIS GROWING POWERS!
STARK LAB. INC.
MUST FINISH THESE DELICATE ADJUSTMENTS ON MY TEST-ROBOT RIGHT AWAY!..
..SO I CAN INVESTIGATE... AS IRON MAN!
ELSEWHERE, IN A DARKENED ALLEYWAY, A STAR-SPANGLED SENTINEL HEARS THE INCREDIBLE NEWS ON A CAR RADIO...
HANK... JAN... HAWKEYE... ALL KILLED IN ONE FELL SWOOP?
AND, THE PANTHER... AN ACCUSED ASSASSIN?
I JUST RETURNED FROM BATTLING THE SLEEPER... INTENDED TO VISIT THEM... WHEN I STOPPED TO BATTLE THESE PETTY THUGS!
AND NOW, THEY'RE DEAD! ...AND MY NEW-FOUND FRIEND BELIEVED GUILTY?!
WITHIN THE HOUR, A SPECIAL EDITION STOPS EVEN THE NOBLE GOD OF THUNDER...
THEIRS WERE THE SPIRITS THAT KEPT THE NAME OF THE AVENGERS ALIVE...
...TILL THEY THEMSELVES WERE... NO MORE!
EXTRA DAILY
3 AVENGERS MURDERED!
WOULD THAT THIS DREAD NIGHT HAD NE'ER FALLEN!
HOWEVER, SOMEWHERE IN THE STUNNED CITY, ONE VOICE THERE IS WHICH IS RAISED IN EXULTANT TRIUMPH...
MY PLAN SUCCEEDED... TO THE FINAL DETAIL!
THAT WHICH HAS BEEN DULY SOWN, SHALL NOW BE HARVESTED, BY THE MAN WHO KILLED THE TRIO OF AVENGERS...
I... THE GRIM REAPER!!
7.

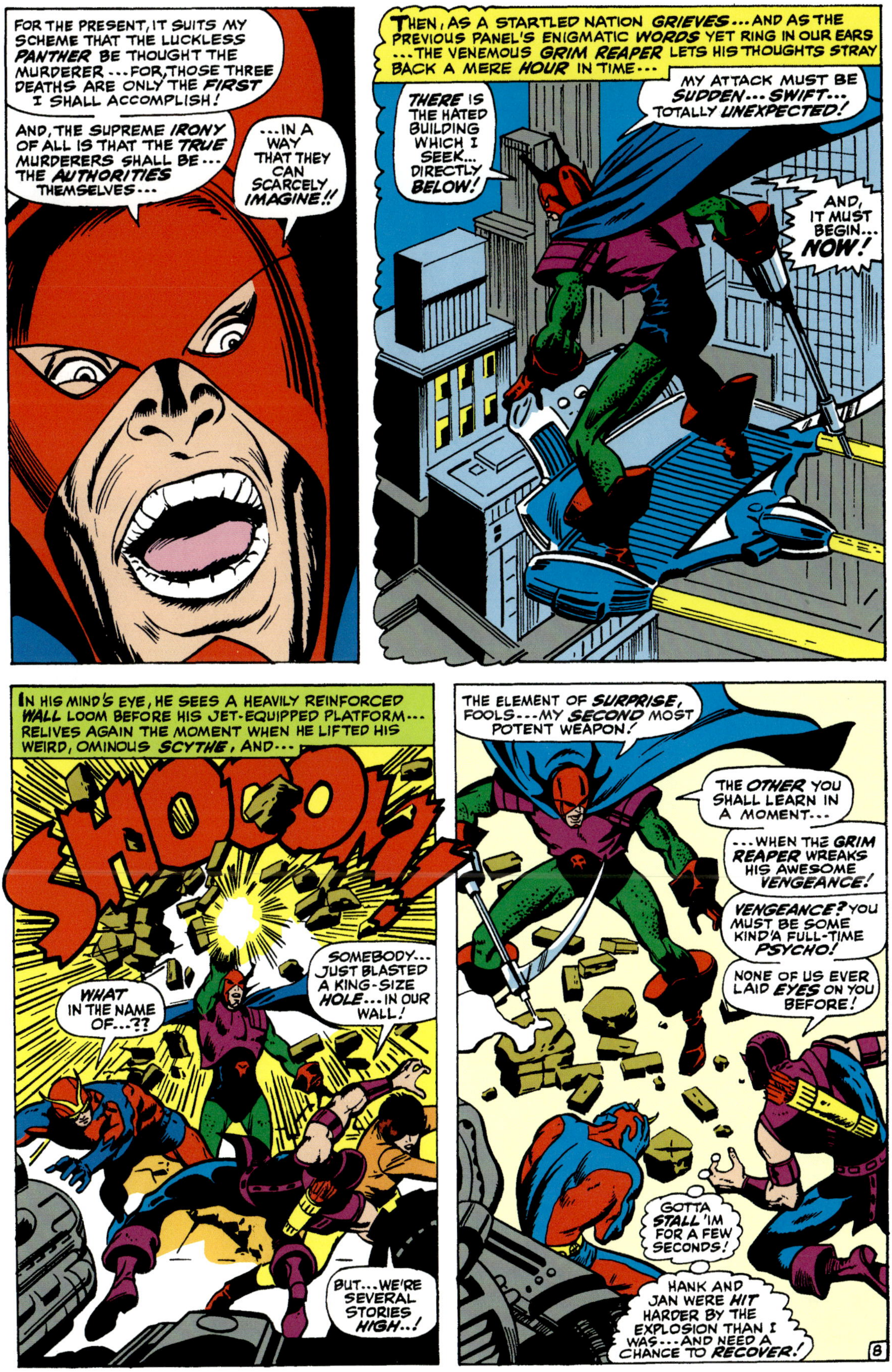

FOR THE PRESENT, IT SUITS MY SCHEME THAT THE LUCKLESS PANTHER BE THOUGHT THE MURDERER ... FOR, THOSE THREE DEATHS ARE ONLY THE FIRST I SHALL ACCOMPLISH!
AND, THE SUPREME IRONY OF ALL IS THAT THE TRUE MURDERERS SHALL BE ... THE AUTHORITIES THEMSELVES ...
... IN A WAY THAT THEY CAN SCARCELY IMAGINE!!
THEN, AS A STARTLED NATION GRIEVES ... AND AS THE PREVIOUS PANEL'S ENIGMATIC WORDS YET RING IN OUR EARS ... THE VENEMOUS GRIM REAPER LETS HIS THOUGHTS STRAY BACK A MERE HOUR IN TIME ...
THERE IS THE HATED BUILDING WHICH I SEEK... DIRECTLY BELOW!
MY ATTACK MUST BE SUDDEN ... SWIFT ... TOTALLY UNEXPECTED!
AND, IT MUST BEGIN... NOW!
IN HIS MIND'S EYE, HE SEES A HEAVILY REINFORCED WALL LOOM BEFORE HIS JET-EQUIPPED PLATFORM ... RELIVES AGAIN THE MOMENT WHEN HE LIFTED HIS WEIRD, OMINOUS SCYTHE, AND ...
SHOOOM!
WHAT IN THE NAME OF...??
SOMEBODY... JUST BLASTED A KING-SIZE HOLE... IN OUR WALL!
BUT... WE'RE SEVERAL STORIES HIGH..!
THE ELEMENT OF SURPRISE, FOOLS ... MY SECOND MOST POTENT WEAPON!
THE OTHER YOU SHALL LEARN IN A MOMENT ...
... WHEN THE GRIM REAPER WREAKS HIS AWESOME VENGEANCE!
VENGEANCE? YOU MUST BE SOME KIND'A FULL-TIME PSYCHO!
NONE OF US EVER LAID EYES ON YOU BEFORE!
GOTTA STALL 'IM FOR A FEW SECONDS!
HANK AND JAN WERE HIT HARDER BY THE EXPLOSION THAN I WAS ... AND NEED A CHANCE TO RECOVER!
8

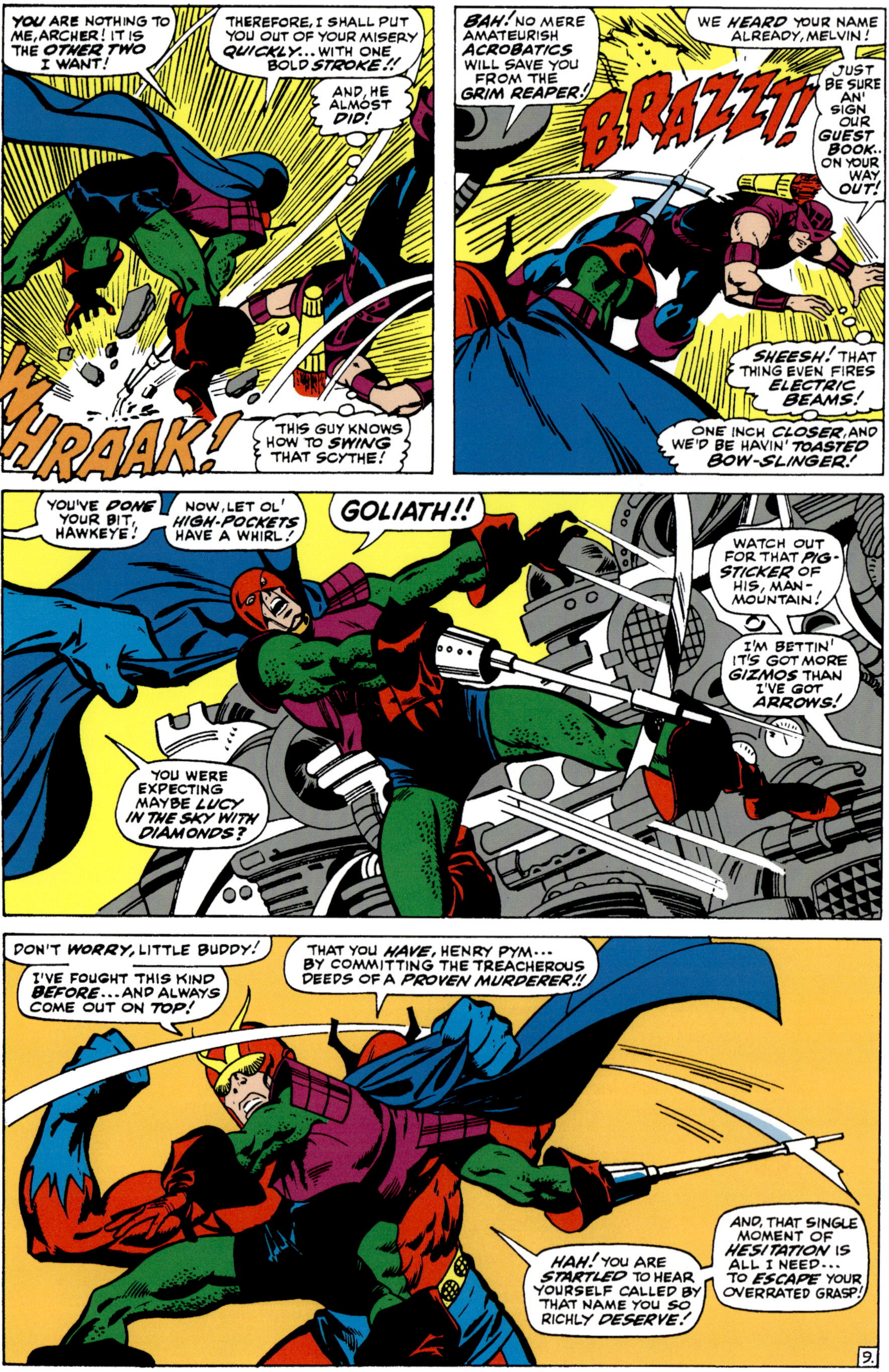

YOU ARE NOTHING TO ME, ARCHER! IT IS THE OTHER TWO I WANT!
THEREFORE, I SHALL PUT YOU OUT OF YOUR MISERY QUICKLY... WITH ONE BOLD STROKE!!
AND, HE ALMOST DID!
WHRAAK!
THIS GUY KNOWS HOW TO SWING THAT SCYTHE!
BAH! NO MERE AMATEURISH ACROBATICS WILL SAVE YOU FROM THE GRIM REAPER!
WE HEARD YOUR NAME ALREADY, MELVIN!
JUST BE SURE AN' SIGN OUR GUEST BOOK.. ON YOUR WAY OUT!
BRAZZT!
SHEESH! THAT THING EVEN FIRES ELECTRIC BEAMS!
ONE INCH CLOSER, AND WE'D BE HAVIN' TOASTED BOW-SLINGER!
YOU'VE DONE YOUR BIT, HAWKEYE!
NOW, LET OL' HIGH-POCKETS HAVE A WHIRL!
GOLIATH!!
WATCH OUT FOR THAT PIG-STICKER OF HIS, MAN-MOUNTAIN!
I'M BETTIN' IT'S GOT MORE GIZMOS THAN I'VE GOT ARROWS!
YOU WERE EXPECTING MAYBE LUCY IN THE SKY WITH DIAMONDS?
DON'T WORRY, LITTLE BUDDY!
I'VE FOUGHT THIS KIND BEFORE... AND ALWAYS COME OUT ON TOP!
THAT YOU HAVE, HENRY PYM... BY COMMITTING THE TREACHEROUS DEEDS OF A PROVEN MURDERER!!
HAH! YOU ARE STARTLED TO HEAR YOURSELF CALLED BY THAT NAME YOU SO RICHLY DESERVE!
AND, THAT SINGLE MOMENT OF HESITATION IS ALL I NEED... TO ESCAPE YOUR OVERRATED GRASP!
9.

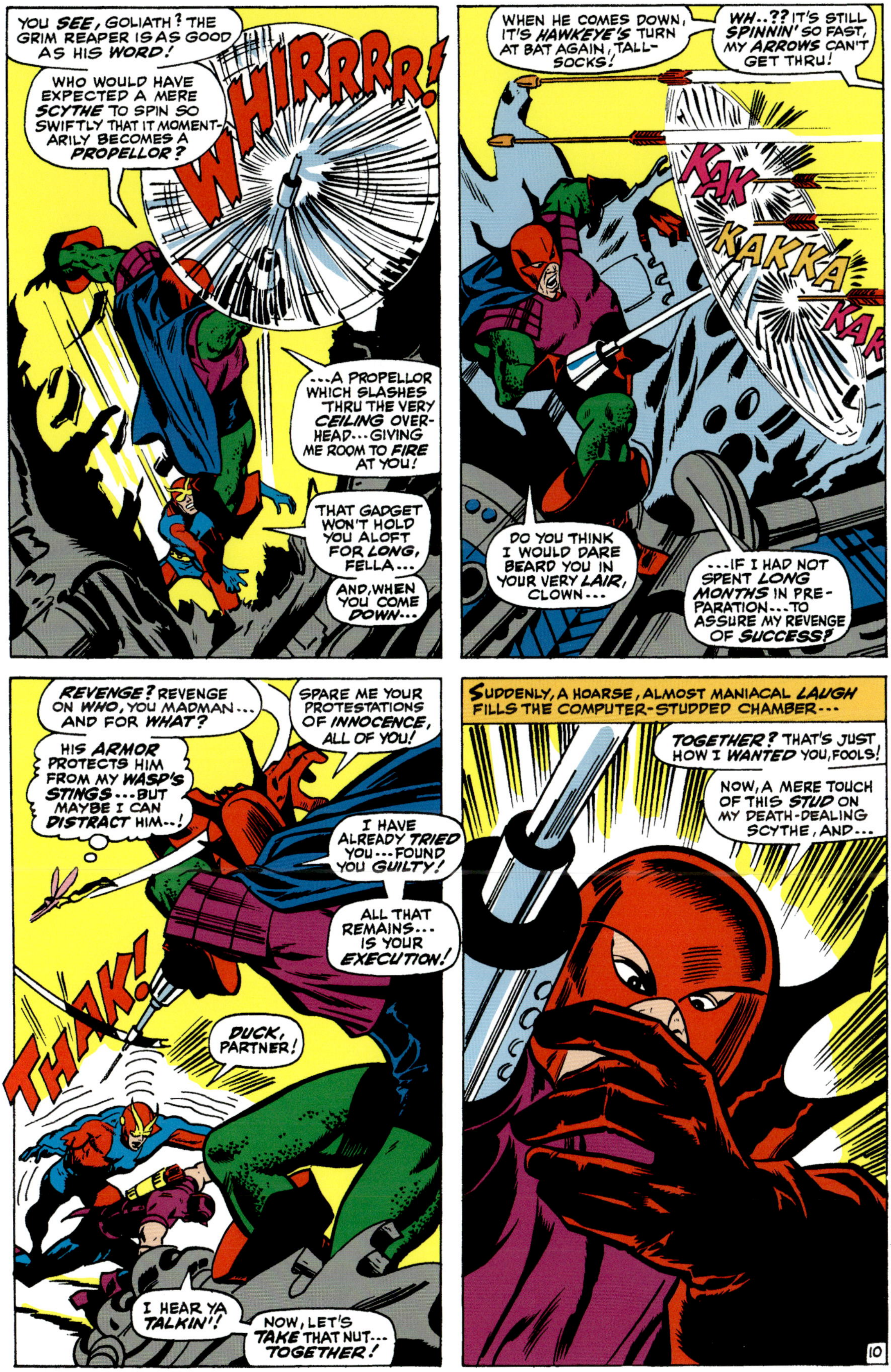
YOU SEE, GOLIATH? THE GRIM REAPER IS AS GOOD AS HIS WORD!
WHO WOULD HAVE EXPECTED A MERE SCYTHE TO SPIN SO SWIFTLY THAT IT MOMENTARILY BECOMES A PROPELLOR?
WHIRRRR!
...A PROPELLOR WHICH SLASHES THRU THE VERY CEILING OVERHEAD...GIVING ME ROOM TO FIRE AT YOU!
THAT GADGET WON'T HOLD YOU ALOFT FOR LONG, FELLA...
AND, WHEN YOU COME DOWN...
WHEN HE COMES DOWN, IT'S HAWKEYE'S TURN AT BAT AGAIN, TALL-SOCKS!
WH..?? IT'S STILL SPINNIN' SO FAST, MY ARROWS CAN'T GET THRU!
KAK
KAKKA
KAK
DO YOU THINK I WOULD DARE BEARD YOU IN YOUR VERY LAIR, CLOWN...
...IF I HAD NOT SPENT LONG MONTHS IN PREPARATION...TO ASSURE MY REVENGE OF SUCCESS?
REVENGE? REVENGE ON WHO, YOU MADMAN... AND FOR WHAT?
SPARE ME YOUR PROTESTATIONS OF INNOCENCE, ALL OF YOU!
HIS ARMOR PROTECTS HIM FROM MY WASP'S STINGS...BUT MAYBE I CAN DISTRACT HIM..!
I HAVE ALREADY TRIED YOU...FOUND YOU GUILTY!
ALL THAT REMAINS... IS YOUR EXECUTION!
THAK!
DUCK, PARTNER!
I HEAR YA TALKIN'!
NOW, LET'S TAKE THAT NUT... TOGETHER!
SUDDENLY, A HOARSE, ALMOST MANIACAL LAUGH FILLS THE COMPUTER-STUDDED CHAMBER...
TOGETHER? THAT'S JUST HOW I WANTED YOU, FOOLS!
NOW, A MERE TOUCH OF THIS STUD ON MY DEATH-DEALING SCYTHE, AND...
10

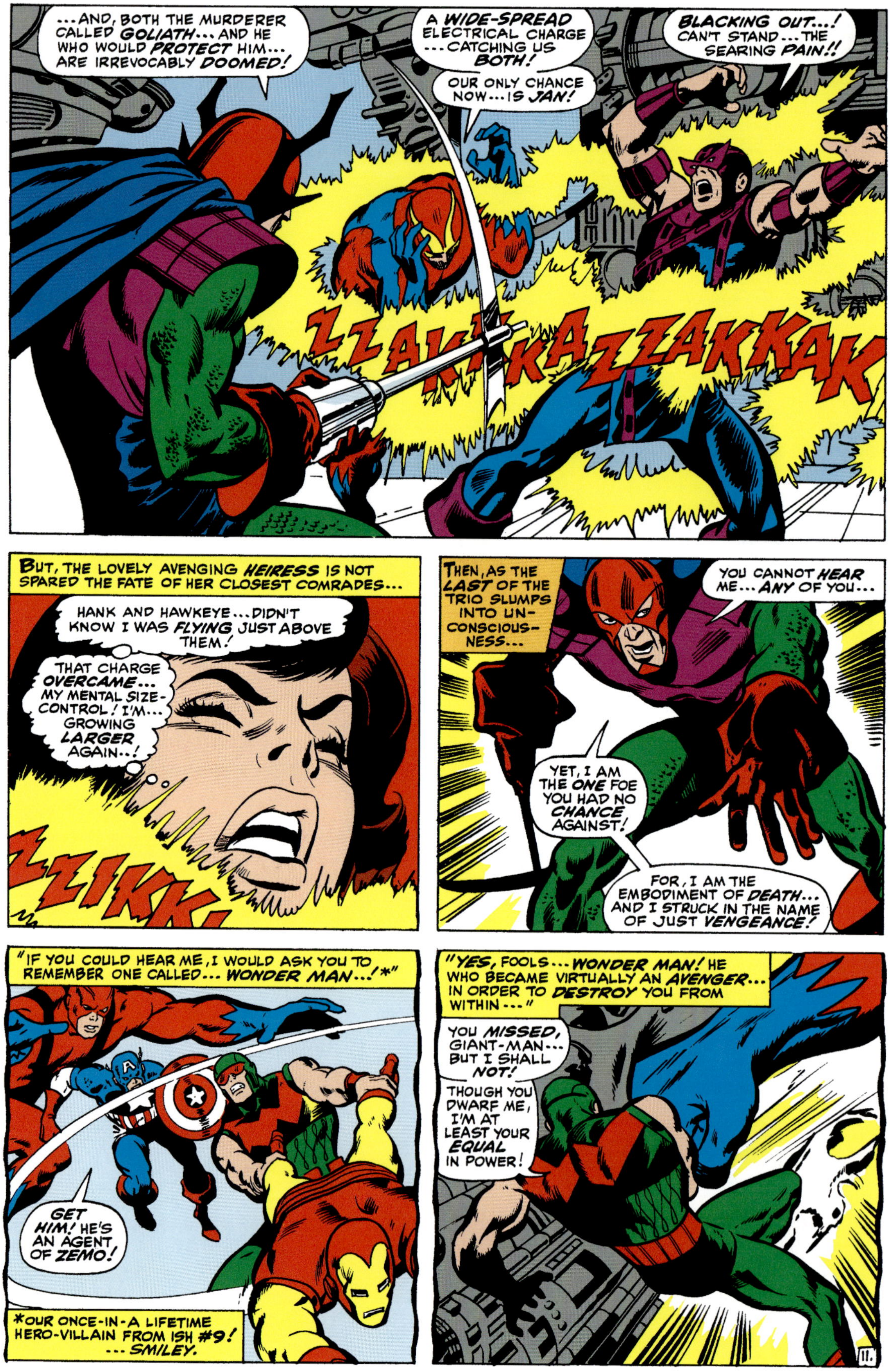
...AND, BOTH THE MURDERER CALLED GOLIATH... AND HE WHO WOULD PROTECT HIM... ARE IRREVOCABLY DOOMED!
A WIDE-SPREAD ELECTRICAL CHARGE ...CATCHING US BOTH!
OUR ONLY CHANCE NOW...IS JAN!
BLACKING OUT...! CAN'T STAND... THE SEARING PAIN!!
ZZAKKKAZZZAKKKAK
BUT, THE LOVELY AVENGING HEIRESS IS NOT SPARED THE FATE OF HER CLOSEST COMRADES...
HANK AND HAWKEYE...DIDN'T KNOW I WAS FLYING JUST ABOVE THEM.!
THAT CHARGE OVERCAME... MY MENTAL SIZE-CONTROL! I'M... GROWING LARGER AGAIN..!
ZZIKK!
THEN, AS THE LAST OF THE TRIO SLUMPS INTO UN-CONSCIOUS-NESS...
YOU CANNOT HEAR ME... ANY OF YOU...
YET, I AM THE ONE FOE YOU HAD NO CHANCE AGAINST!
FOR, I AM THE EMBODIMENT OF DEATH... AND I STRUCK IN THE NAME OF JUST VENGEANCE!
"IF YOU COULD HEAR ME, I WOULD ASK YOU TO REMEMBER ONE CALLED... WONDER MAN...!*"
GET HIM! HE'S AN AGENT OF ZEMO!
*OUR ONCE-IN-A LIFETIME HERO-VILLAIN FROM ISH #9! ...SMILEY.
"YES, FOOLS... WONDER MAN! HE WHO BECAME VIRTUALLY AN AVENGER... IN ORDER TO DESTROY YOU FROM WITHIN ..."
YOU MISSED, GIANT-MAN... BUT I SHALL NOT!
THOUGH YOU DWARF ME, I'M AT LEAST YOUR EQUAL IN POWER!
11.

Panel 1 (caption): "IN EVERY WAY, HE PROVED *MIGHTIER* THAN THE ONES WHO OPPOSED HIM! YET, BY SOME *TRICKERY,* HE WAS DEFEATED... *POISONED!*"

"AND THOSE WHO CALLED THEMSELVES *AVENGERS* STOOD BY AND WATCHED HIM *DIE...* AND DID *NOTHING* TO SAVE HIM..."

"THIS I *KNOW,* FOR SIMON WILLIAMS... WONDER MAN... WAS MY *BROTHER!*"

Panel 2 (caption): THE NEXT MOMENT, ALL THE VENEMOUS RANCOR IN HIS SOUL POURED OUT, THE *GRIM REAPER* GESTURES ONCE MORE WITH HIS MYSTERIOUS *SCYTHE,* AND...

THAT WHICH MY WEAPON HAS DONE, IT CAN *UNDO!*

ITS ELECTRICAL POWER SHALL NOW *RESTORE* THIS CHAMBER!

FOR, I HAVE *PLANS* IN MIND... PLANS THAT SHALL DESTROY THE *OTHERS* WHO LET MY BROTHER DIE...!

Panel 3 (caption): HOWEVER, WE'LL HAVE TO LET THE TANGLED SKEIN OF FATE *REMAIN* TWISTED A BIT LONGER... AS, RETURNING TO THE *PRESENT*--

IF HE'S REALLY AN *AFRICAN PRINCE* LIKE HE SAYS, WE CAN'T *BOOK* HIM!

THIS'D BE A JOB FOR THE *U.N.!*

SURE... BUT WE'VE GOT JUST *HIS* WORD ON THAT!

I CAN'T FIND THIS *WAKANDA* PLACE ON ANY *MAP!*

NOR *SHALL* HE... FOR ITS LOCATION IS *SECRET!*

BUT, I'VE ACCOMPLISHED MY *PURPOSE* IN ALLOWING MYSELF TO BE BROUGHT HERE...

Panel 4 (caption): AND NOW, IT IS TIME FOR THE *PANTHER* TO PROWL THE CITY ONCE MORE...

... TO LEARN IF THE GNAWING *SUSPICION* WHICH FILLS MY MIND... IS THE SENSES-STAGGERING *TRUTH!*

KRAASH!

HE'S MAKING A *BREAK* FOR IT!

AND HE MOVES LIKE *GREASED LIGHTNING!*

12

33

Panel 1 (caption): WITHIN MOMENTS, A GASPING, GAPING CROWD HAS FORMED ON THE STREETS OUTSIDE THE STATION...CREATING A SECOND HAZARD FOR THE POLICE...

THE GUY WE HEARD ABOUT ON TV--HE'S GETTING AWAY!

WHILE HE'S ON THE LOOSE, NOBODY'S SAFE!

IF ONLY THAT SHIELD AGENT HADN'T CUT OUT SO SOON...WAIT!!

THERE'S THE PANTHER...ON THAT LEDGE!

Panel 2: I HAD HOPED TO ELUDE THEM ...BY SCALING THIS ALMOST SHEER WALL!

BUT NOW...

YOU'RE TRAPPED, PANTHER...SO SURRENDER!

THIS IS THE ONLY WARNING BURST YOU'RE GETTING!

KTAHK

PTHIKK

BRAKKA

Panel 3: THE POLICE HAVE HIM CORNERED! HE'S GOTTA GIVE UP, OR...LOOK!!

HE...HE'S JUMPING...TOWARDS THE NEXT BUILDING!

HE LEAPS LIKE SOME JUNGLE BEAST...LIKE A REAL PANTHER!

BUT, IT'S TOO FAR! NOTHING THAT LIVES COULD JUMP THAT DISTANCE--!

Panel 4 (caption): FOR A FLEETING ETERNITY, THE HORRIFIED SPECTATORS AND POLICE BELOW HOLD THEIR BREATH...WHILE, HIGH ABOVE, TAUT MUSCLES STRAIN, ACHINGLY...

AND THEN...

HE MADE IT!!

THERE ARE A DOZEN EXITS FROM THAT BUILDING! WE'LL NEVER COVER THEM ALL IN TIME!

THE MAN WHO MURDERED THE AVENGERS...HAS ESCAPED!!

13

34

Panel 1:

BUT, MINUTES LATER, AS A JUNGLE *JUGGERNAUT* RACES THRU THE BACK ALLEYS OF NEW YORK...

THE CROWDS ARE *WRONG!* THE AVENGERS' KILLER *HASN'T* ESCAPED!

NOR *SHALL* HE.. WHILE THE *PANTHER* IS FREE TO STALK HIM!

AND, I BELIEVE I KNOW JUST WHERE HE *IS!*

--BEHIND THE VAULTED *DOOR* THAT WOULD NOT OPEN--

--IN *AVENGERS* HQ ITSELF!

Panel 2:

A SHORT TIME LATER, IN *ANOTHER* PART OF THE SPRAWLING CITY...

SOON... *VERY* SOON... THE OTHERS WHOM I SEEK WILL COME TO ME... AND I SHALL BE *WAITING*...

HERE, IN THE *AVENGERS'* OWN SECRET-STUDDED MANSION!

THOR.... IRON MAN.. CAPTAIN AMERICA....ALL MUST FALL BEFORE MY DEATH-DISPENSING *SCYTHE!*

ONLY THEN CAN THE SOUL OF MY BROTHER, *WONDER MAN,* REST IN PEACE!

Panel 3:

SO *THAT'S* YOUR MOTIVE... AN IN-SANE *REVENGE!*

AND, TO CARRY IT OUT, YOU'VE DEVISED A WEAPON WHICH CHILLS THE VERY *SOUL!*

BUT, I FOUND ANOTHER *ENTRANCE* HERE--ONE SUCH AS ONLY I COULD USE!

THE *PANTHER!!*

Panel 4:

YES, *ASSASSIN*... THE *PANTHER,* HE WHOM YOU WISHED TO *DIE* FOR YOUR UNSPEAKABLE CRIME!

BUT NOW, *WHO-EVER* YOU MAY BE, YOU'LL *PAY* FOR YOUR OWN DEEDS!

FLZT!

FOOL! KEEP *AWAY* FROM ME!

I AM THE *GRIM REAPER*... MINE IS THE SACRED *SCYTHE* OF *JUSTICE*..!

14

35

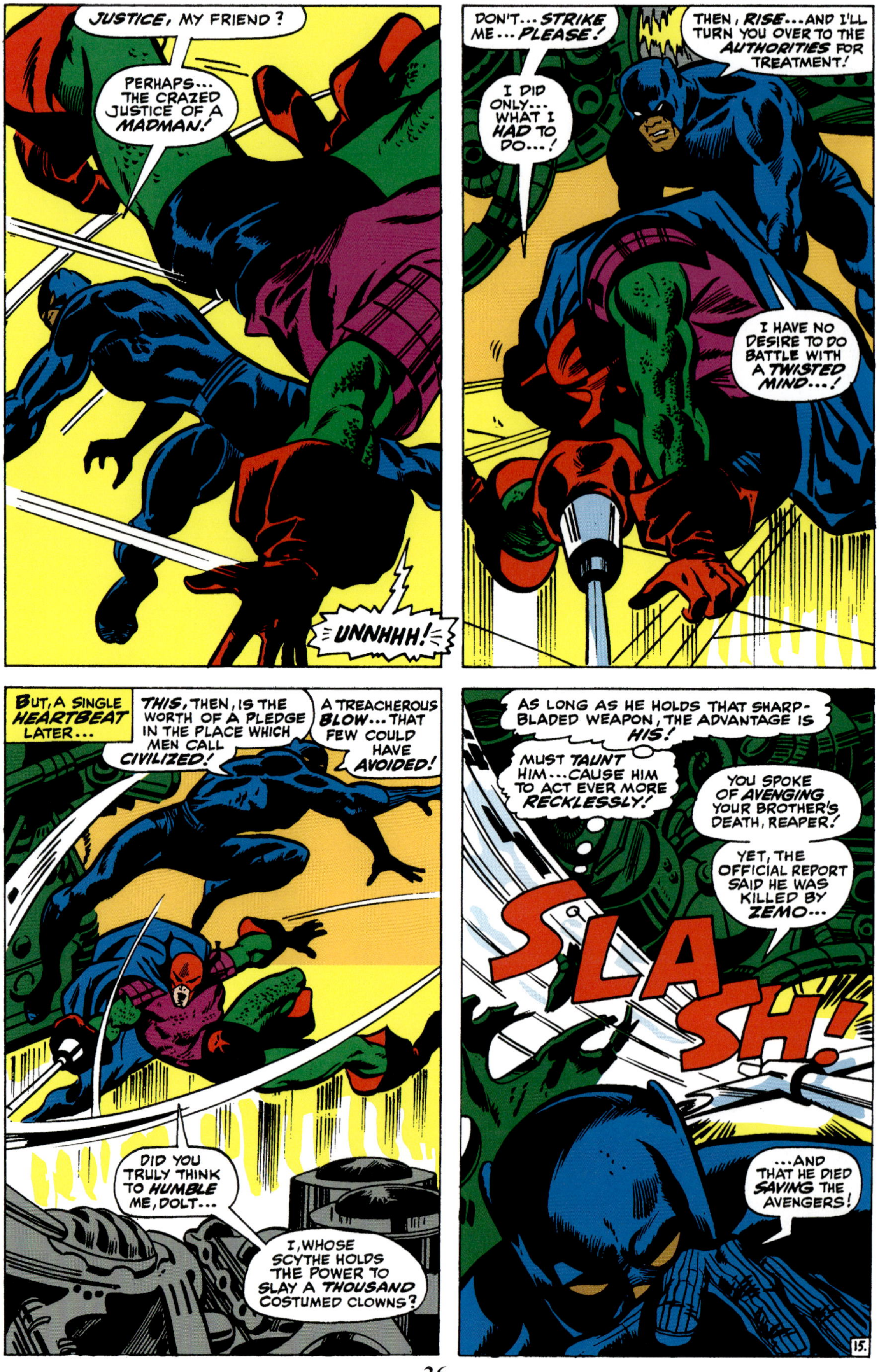
JUSTICE, MY FRIEND?
PERHAPS... THE CRAZED JUSTICE OF A MADMAN!
UNNHHH!
DON'T... STRIKE ME... PLEASE!
I DID ONLY... WHAT I HAD TO DO...!
THEN, RISE... AND I'LL TURN YOU OVER TO THE AUTHORITIES FOR TREATMENT!
I HAVE NO DESIRE TO DO BATTLE WITH A TWISTED MIND...!
BUT, A SINGLE HEARTBEAT LATER...
THIS, THEN, IS THE WORTH OF A PLEDGE IN THE PLACE WHICH MEN CALL CIVILIZED!
A TREACHEROUS BLOW... THAT FEW COULD HAVE AVOIDED!
DID YOU TRULY THINK TO HUMBLE ME, DOLT...
I, WHOSE SCYTHE HOLDS THE POWER TO SLAY A THOUSAND COSTUMED CLOWNS?
AS LONG AS HE HOLDS THAT SHARP-BLADED WEAPON, THE ADVANTAGE IS HIS!
MUST TAUNT HIM... CAUSE HIM TO ACT EVER MORE RECKLESSLY!
YOU SPOKE OF AVENGING YOUR BROTHER'S DEATH, REAPER!
YET, THE OFFICIAL REPORT SAID HE WAS KILLED BY ZEMO...
SLASH!
...AND THAT HE DIED SAVING THE AVENGERS!
15.

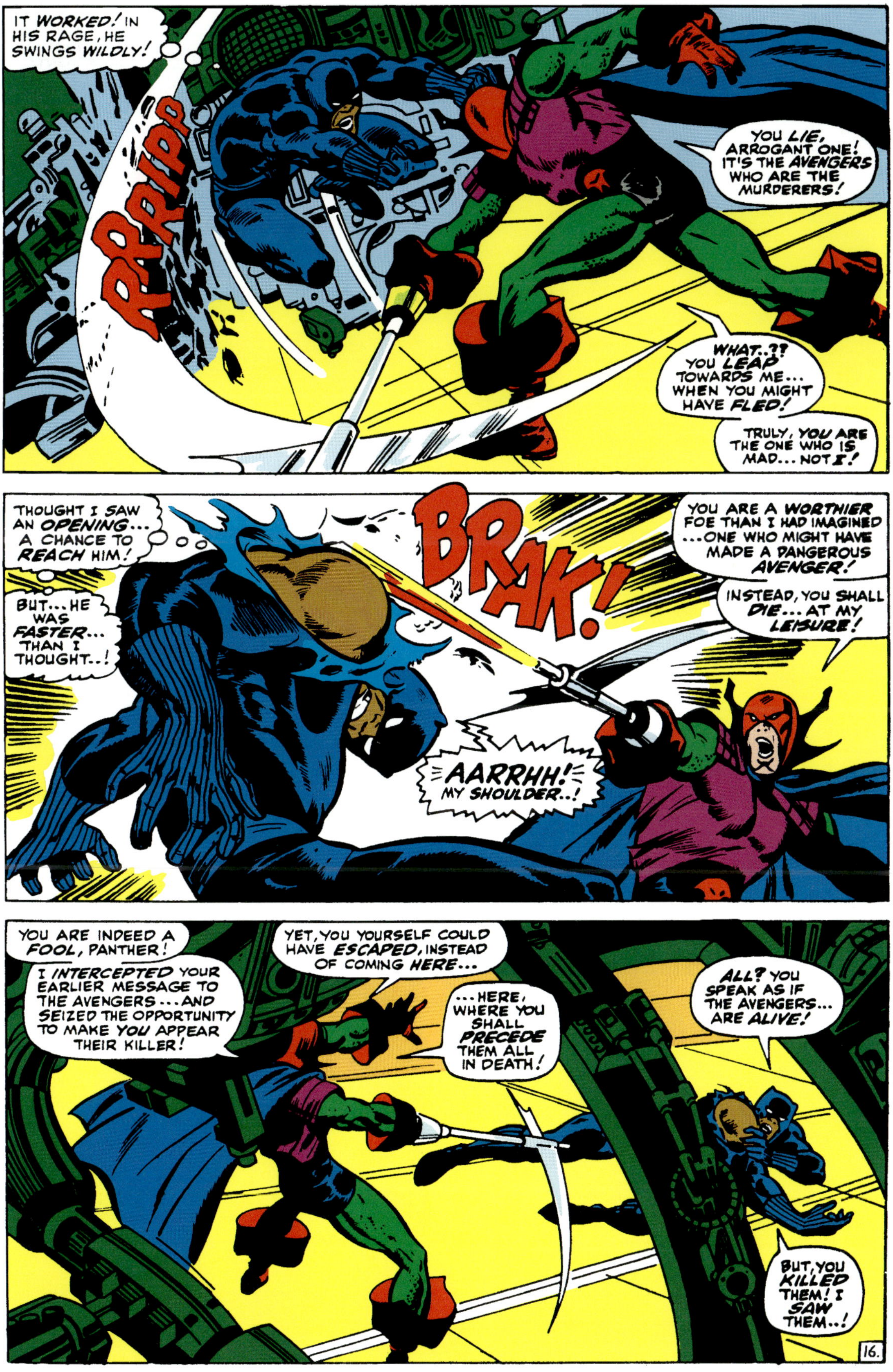
IT WORKED! IN HIS RAGE, HE SWINGS WILDLY!
RRRIPP
YOU LIE, ARROGANT ONE! IT'S THE AVENGERS WHO ARE THE MURDERERS!
WHAT..?? YOU LEAP TOWARDS ME... WHEN YOU MIGHT HAVE FLED!
TRULY, YOU ARE THE ONE WHO IS MAD... NOT I!
THOUGHT I SAW AN OPENING... A CHANCE TO REACH HIM!
BUT... HE WAS FASTER... THAN I THOUGHT..!
BRAK!
YOU ARE A WORTHIER FOE THAN I HAD IMAGINED ...ONE WHO MIGHT HAVE MADE A DANGEROUS AVENGER!
INSTEAD, YOU SHALL DIE... AT MY LEISURE!
AARRHH! MY SHOULDER..!
YOU ARE INDEED A FOOL, PANTHER!
I INTERCEPTED YOUR EARLIER MESSAGE TO THE AVENGERS... AND SEIZED THE OPPORTUNITY TO MAKE YOU APPEAR THEIR KILLER!
YET, YOU YOURSELF COULD HAVE ESCAPED, INSTEAD OF COMING HERE...
...HERE, WHERE YOU SHALL PRECEDE THEM ALL IN DEATH!
ALL? YOU SPEAK AS IF THE AVENGERS... ARE ALIVE!
BUT, YOU KILLED THEM! I SAW THEM..!
16.

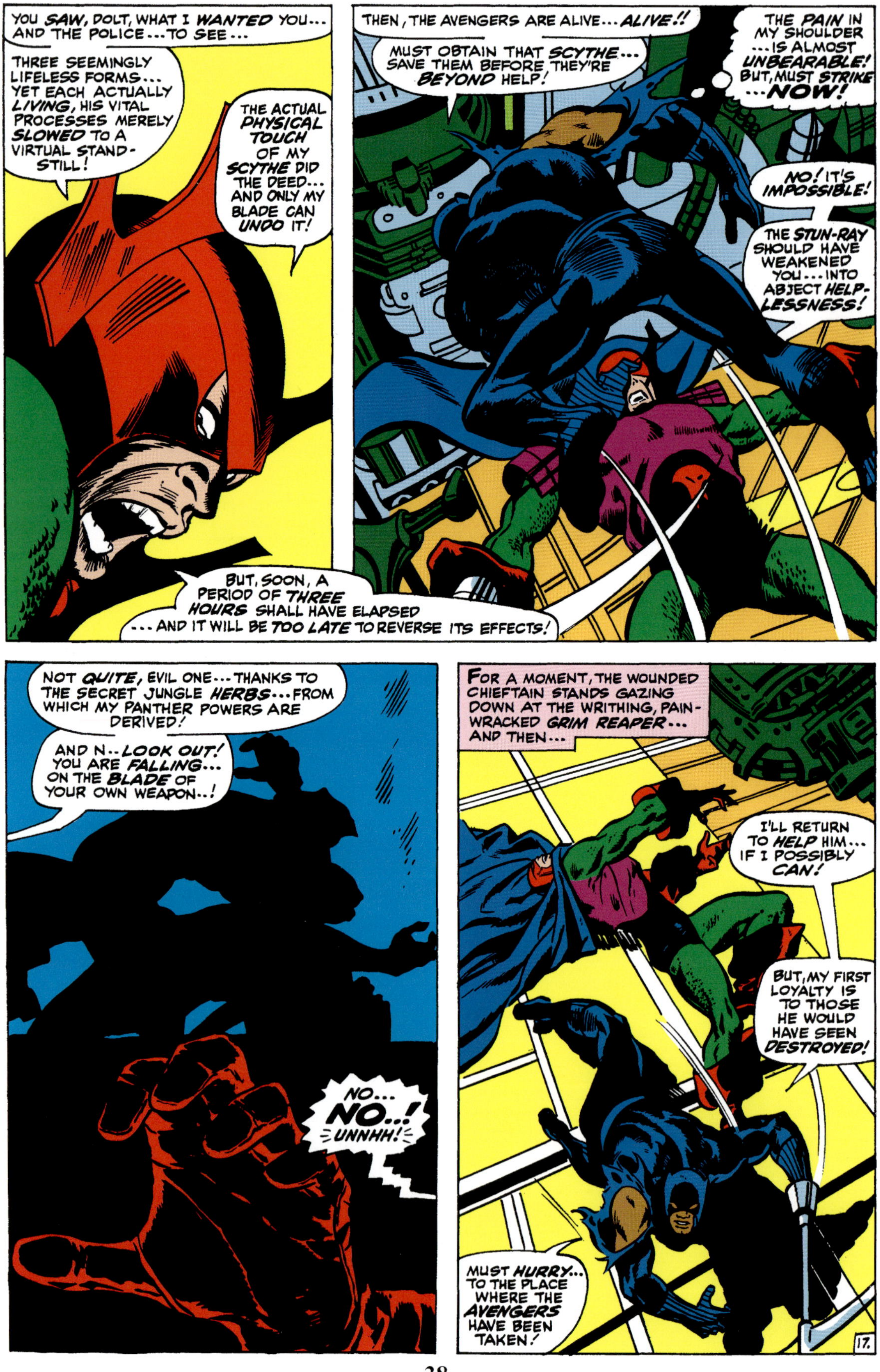
YOU SAW, DOLT, WHAT I WANTED YOU... AND THE POLICE... TO SEE...
THREE SEEMINGLY LIFELESS FORMS... YET EACH ACTUALLY LIVING, HIS VITAL PROCESSES MERELY SLOWED TO A VIRTUAL STAND-STILL!
THE ACTUAL PHYSICAL TOUCH OF MY SCYTHE DID THE DEED... AND ONLY MY BLADE CAN UNDO IT!
BUT, SOON, A PERIOD OF THREE HOURS SHALL HAVE ELAPSED ...AND IT WILL BE TOO LATE TO REVERSE ITS EFFECTS!
THEN, THE AVENGERS ARE ALIVE... ALIVE!!
MUST OBTAIN THAT SCYTHE... SAVE THEM BEFORE THEY'RE BEYOND HELP!
THE PAIN IN MY SHOULDER ...IS ALMOST UNBEARABLE! BUT, MUST STRIKE ...NOW!
NO! IT'S IMPOSSIBLE!
THE STUN-RAY SHOULD HAVE WEAKENED YOU... INTO ABJECT HELP-LESSNESS!
NOT QUITE, EVIL ONE... THANKS TO THE SECRET JUNGLE HERBS... FROM WHICH MY PANTHER POWERS ARE DERIVED!
AND N-- LOOK OUT! YOU ARE FALLING... ON THE BLADE OF YOUR OWN WEAPON..!
NO... NO..! UNNHH!
FOR A MOMENT, THE WOUNDED CHIEFTAIN STANDS GAZING DOWN AT THE WRITHING, PAIN-WRACKED GRIM REAPER... AND THEN...
I'LL RETURN TO HELP HIM... IF I POSSIBLY CAN!
BUT, MY FIRST LOYALTY IS TO THOSE HE WOULD HAVE SEEN DESTROYED!
MUST HURRY... TO THE PLACE WHERE THE AVENGERS HAVE BEEN TAKEN!
17.

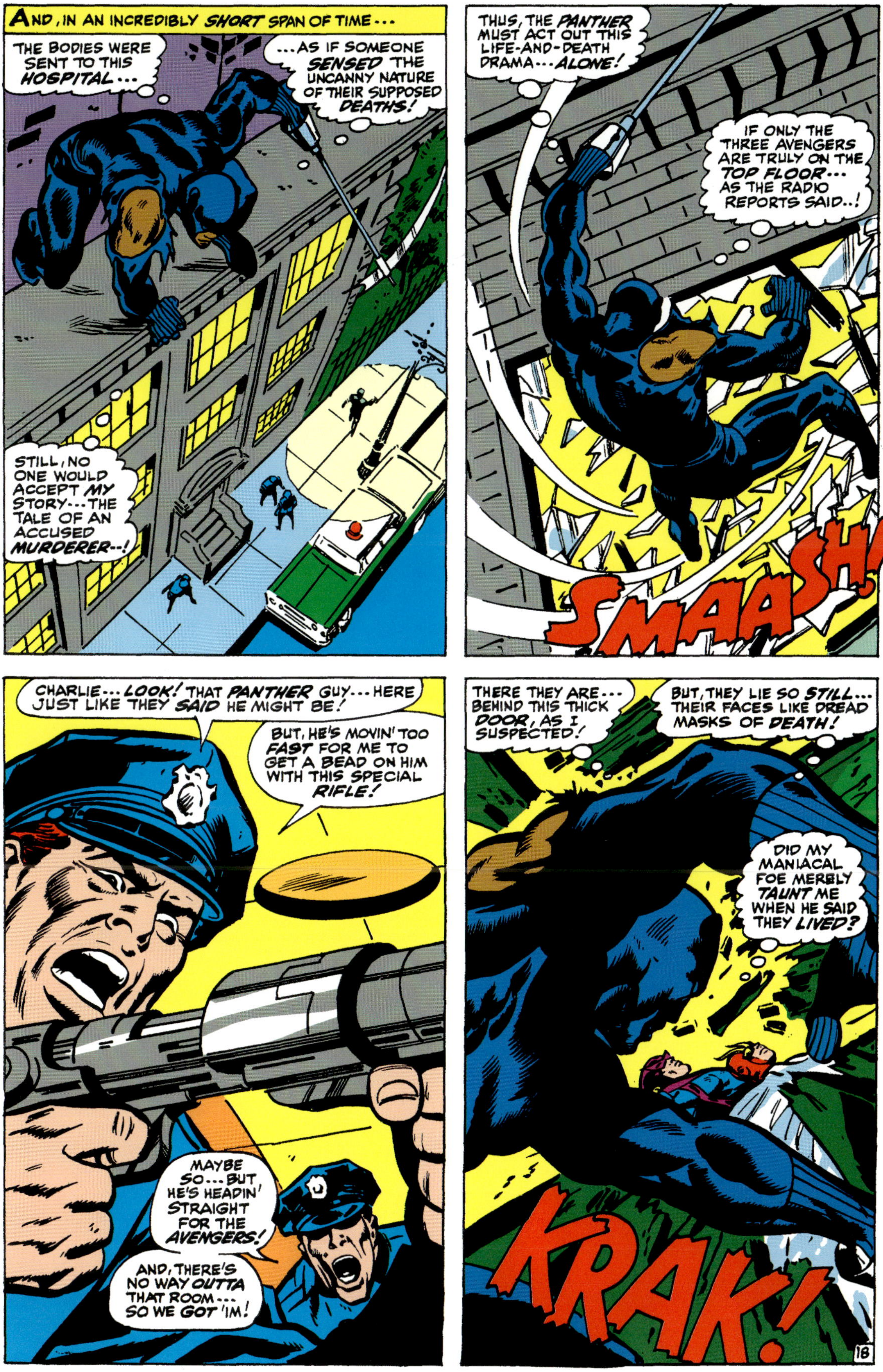
AND, IN AN INCREDIBLY SHORT SPAN OF TIME...
THE BODIES WERE SENT TO THIS HOSPITAL...
...AS IF SOMEONE SENSED THE UNCANNY NATURE OF THEIR SUPPOSED DEATHS!
STILL, NO ONE WOULD ACCEPT MY STORY...THE TALE OF AN ACCUSED MURDERER--!
THUS, THE PANTHER MUST ACT OUT THIS LIFE-AND-DEATH DRAMA...ALONE!
IF ONLY THE THREE AVENGERS ARE TRULY ON THE TOP FLOOR... AS THE RADIO REPORTS SAID..!
SMAASH!
CHARLIE...LOOK! THAT PANTHER GUY...HERE JUST LIKE THEY SAID HE MIGHT BE!
BUT, HE'S MOVIN' TOO FAST FOR ME TO GET A BEAD ON HIM WITH THIS SPECIAL RIFLE!
MAYBE SO...BUT HE'S HEADIN' STRAIGHT FOR THE AVENGERS!
AND, THERE'S NO WAY OUTTA THAT ROOM... SO WE GOT 'IM!
THERE THEY ARE... BEHIND THIS THICK DOOR, AS I SUSPECTED!
BUT, THEY LIE SO STILL... THEIR FACES LIKE DREAD MASKS OF DEATH!
DID MY MANIACAL FOE MERELY TAUNT ME WHEN HE SAID THEY LIVED?
KRAK!
18

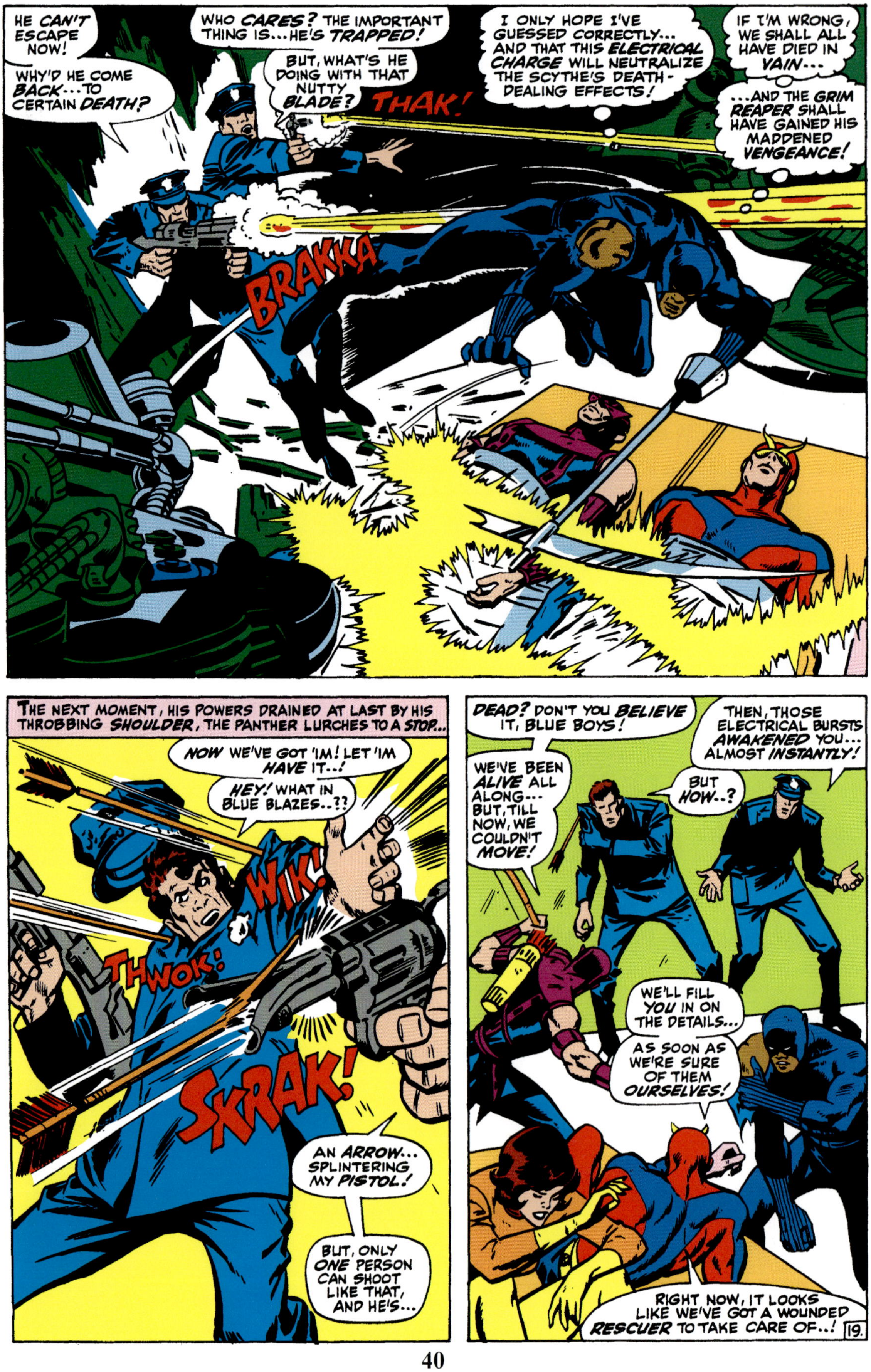
HE CAN'T ESCAPE NOW!
WHY'D HE COME BACK...TO CERTAIN DEATH?
WHO CARES? THE IMPORTANT THING IS...HE'S TRAPPED!
BUT, WHAT'S HE DOING WITH THAT NUTTY BLADE?
THAK!
I ONLY HOPE I'VE GUESSED CORRECTLY... AND THAT THIS ELECTRICAL CHARGE WILL NEUTRALIZE THE SCYTHE'S DEATH-DEALING EFFECTS!
IF I'M WRONG, WE SHALL ALL HAVE DIED IN VAIN...
...AND THE GRIM REAPER SHALL HAVE GAINED HIS MADDENED VENGEANCE!
BRAKKA
THE NEXT MOMENT, HIS POWERS DRAINED AT LAST BY HIS THROBBING SHOULDER, THE PANTHER LURCHES TO A STOP...
NOW WE'VE GOT 'IM! LET 'IM HAVE IT..!
HEY! WHAT IN BLUE BLAZES..??
WIK!
THWOK!
SKRAK!
AN ARROW... SPLINTERING MY PISTOL!
BUT, ONLY ONE PERSON CAN SHOOT LIKE THAT, AND HE'S...
DEAD? DON'T YOU BELIEVE IT, BLUE BOYS!
WE'VE BEEN ALIVE ALL ALONG... BUT, TILL NOW, WE COULDN'T MOVE!
BUT HOW..?
THEN, THOSE ELECTRICAL BURSTS AWAKENED YOU... ALMOST INSTANTLY!
WE'LL FILL YOU IN ON THE DETAILS...
AS SOON AS WE'RE SURE OF THEM OURSELVES!
RIGHT NOW, IT LOOKS LIKE WE'VE GOT A WOUNDED RESCUER TO TAKE CARE OF..!
19.

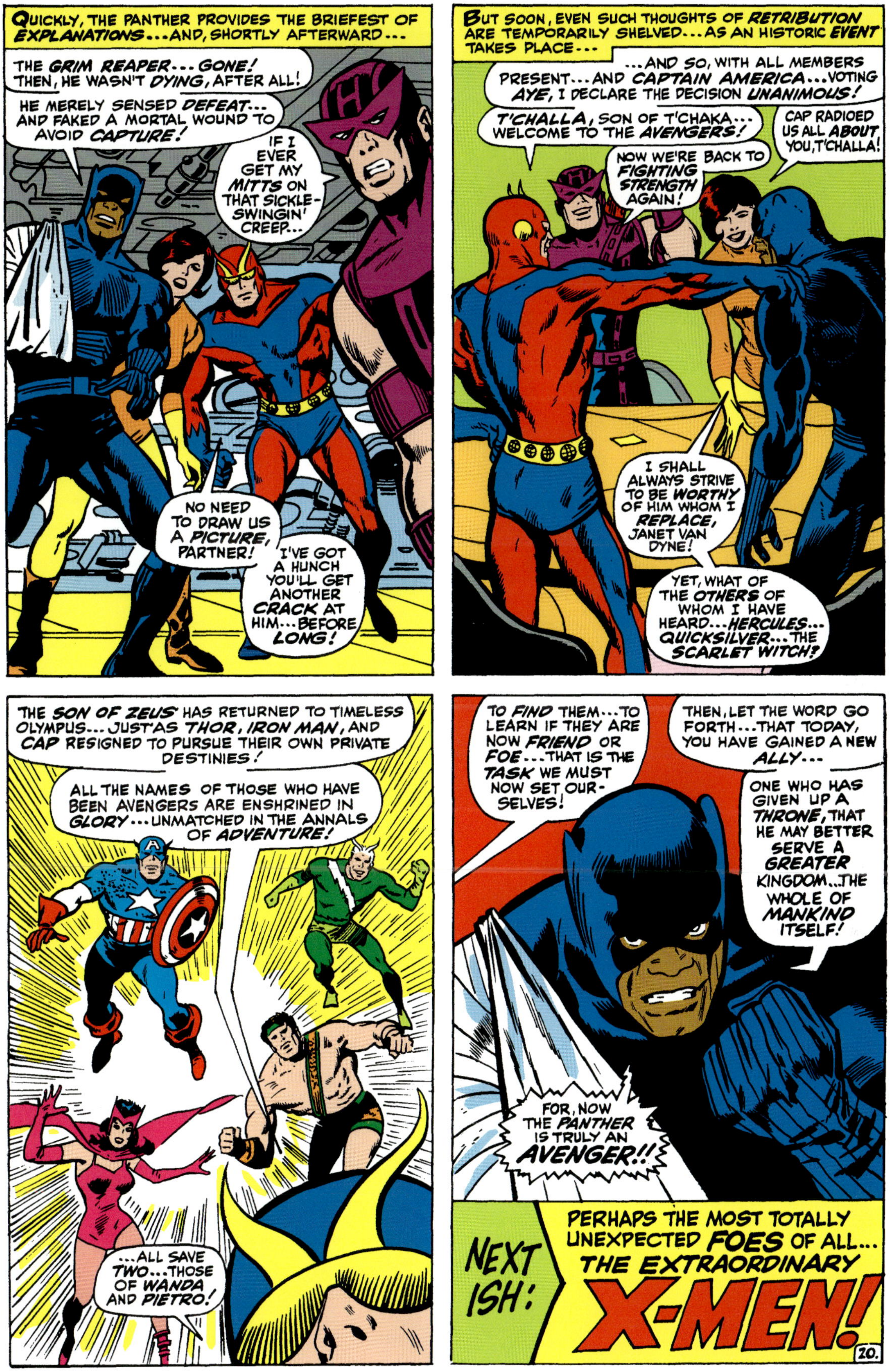
QUICKLY, THE PANTHER PROVIDES THE BRIEFEST OF EXPLANATIONS... AND, SHORTLY AFTERWARD...
THE GRIM REAPER... GONE! THEN, HE WASN'T DYING, AFTER ALL!
HE MERELY SENSED DEFEAT... AND FAKED A MORTAL WOUND TO AVOID CAPTURE!
IF I EVER GET MY MITTS ON THAT SICKLE-SWINGIN' CREEP...
NO NEED TO DRAW US A PICTURE, PARTNER!
I'VE GOT A HUNCH YOU'LL GET ANOTHER CRACK AT HIM... BEFORE LONG!
BUT SOON, EVEN SUCH THOUGHTS OF RETRIBUTION ARE TEMPORARILY SHELVED... AS AN HISTORIC EVENT TAKES PLACE...
...AND SO, WITH ALL MEMBERS PRESENT... AND CAPTAIN AMERICA... VOTING AYE, I DECLARE THE DECISION UNANIMOUS!
T'CHALLA, SON OF T'CHAKA... WELCOME TO THE AVENGERS!
NOW WE'RE BACK TO FIGHTING STRENGTH AGAIN!
CAP RADIOED US ALL ABOUT YOU, T'CHALLA!
I SHALL ALWAYS STRIVE TO BE WORTHY OF HIM WHOM I REPLACE, JANET VAN DYNE!
YET, WHAT OF THE OTHERS OF WHOM I HAVE HEARD... HERCULES... QUICKSILVER... THE SCARLET WITCH?
THE SON OF ZEUS HAS RETURNED TO TIMELESS OLYMPUS... JUST AS THOR, IRON MAN, AND CAP RESIGNED TO PURSUE THEIR OWN PRIVATE DESTINIES!
ALL THE NAMES OF THOSE WHO HAVE BEEN AVENGERS ARE ENSHRINED IN GLORY... UNMATCHED IN THE ANNALS OF ADVENTURE!
...ALL SAVE TWO... THOSE OF WANDA AND PIETRO!
TO FIND THEM... TO LEARN IF THEY ARE NOW FRIEND OR FOE... THAT IS THE TASK WE MUST NOW SET OUR-SELVES!
THEN, LET THE WORD GO FORTH... THAT TODAY, YOU HAVE GAINED A NEW ALLY...
ONE WHO HAS GIVEN UP A THRONE, THAT HE MAY BETTER SERVE A GREATER KINGDOM... THE WHOLE OF MANKIND ITSELF!
FOR, NOW THE PANTHER IS TRULY AN AVENGER!!
NEXT ISH:
PERHAPS THE MOST TOTALLY UNEXPECTED FOES OF ALL... THE EXTRAORDINARY X-MEN!
20.

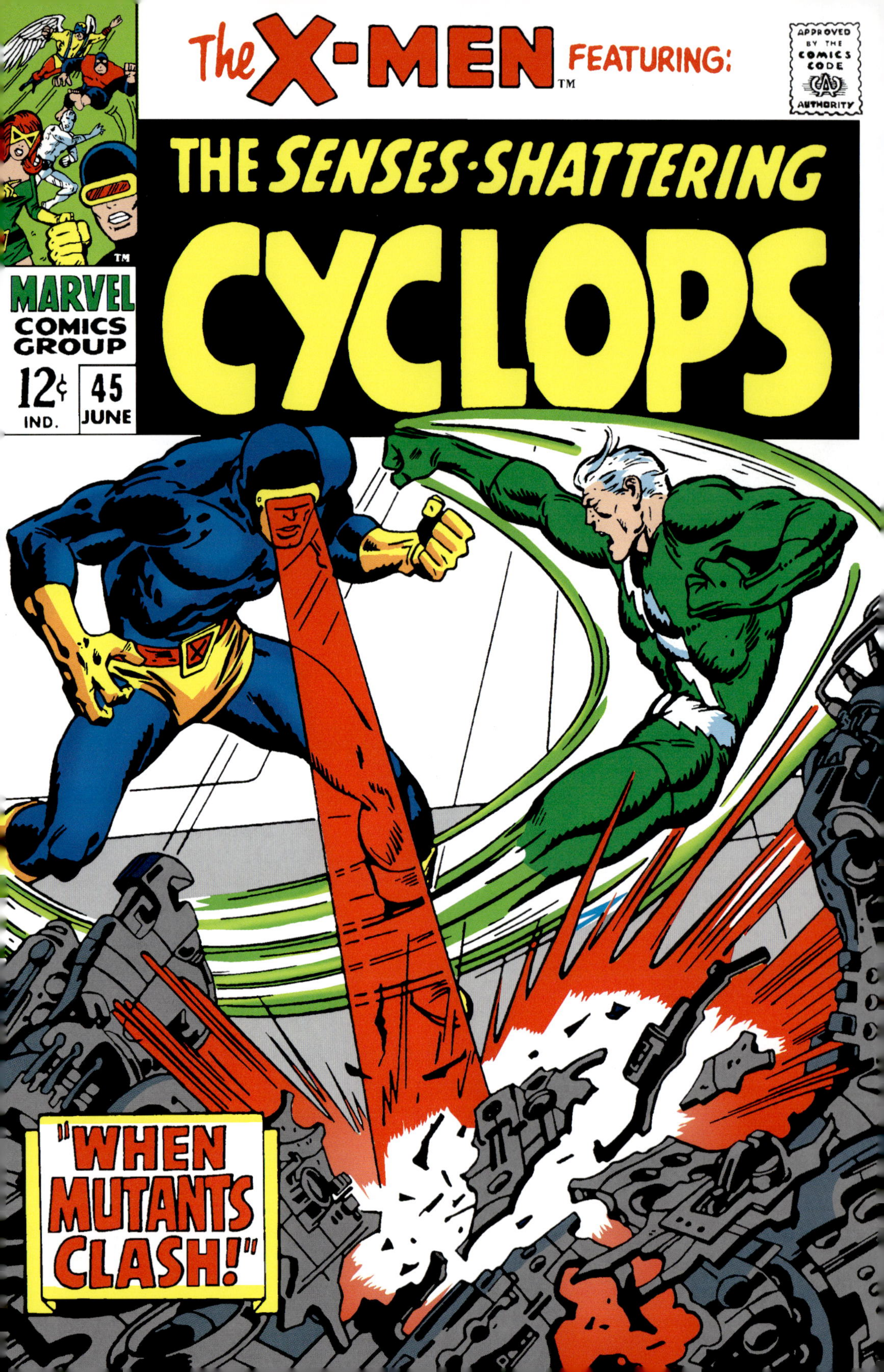
The X-MEN FEATURING:
APPROVED BY THE COMICS CODE AUTHORITY
MARVEL COMICS GROUP
12¢ IND.
45 JUNE
THE SENSES-SHATTERING
CYCLOPS
"WHEN MUTANTS CLASH!"

X-MEN! THE MOST UNUSUAL FIGHTING TEAM OF ALL TIME!™
"WHEN MUTANTS CLASH!"
WARREN'S BEEN GONE TOO LONG! HE SHOULD HAVE BEEN BACK WITH HELP BY NOW!*
MAGNETO MUST HAVE STOPPED HIM SOMEHOW... AND, IF HE DIDN'T REACH THE AVENGERS, THE X-MEN MAY WELL BE DOOMED!
UNLESS I CAN CONCENTRATE THE FULL FORCE OF MY OPTIC BLASTS ON A TINY PORTION OF THE LEAD SHIELD AROUND MY EYES... AND SOMEHOW BREAK FREE!
ROLL UP FOR THE MAGICAL MUTANTIA TOUR, MARVELITES! YOUR GALLANT GUIDES WILL BE... STAN LEE...EDITOR GARY FRIEDRICH..SCRIPTER DON HECK...LAY-OUT MAN WERNER ROTH...PENCILLER JOHN TARTAGLIONE...INKER SAM ROSEN...LETTERER
*BUT WE ALL KNOW THE HIGH-FLYING ANGEL WAS DELAYED BY A CRIMSON-CLAD SWINGER KNOWN AS THE RED RAVEN LAST ISH... DON'T WE? ...UNCERTAIN STAN.
AND, WITH THAT SENSES-SHATTERING SYNOPSIS FROM CYKE'S OWN LIPS... ALL WE CAN SAY IS TURN THE PAGE, MUTANT-WATCHER... 'CAUSE THAT'S WHERE THE ACTION IS--!

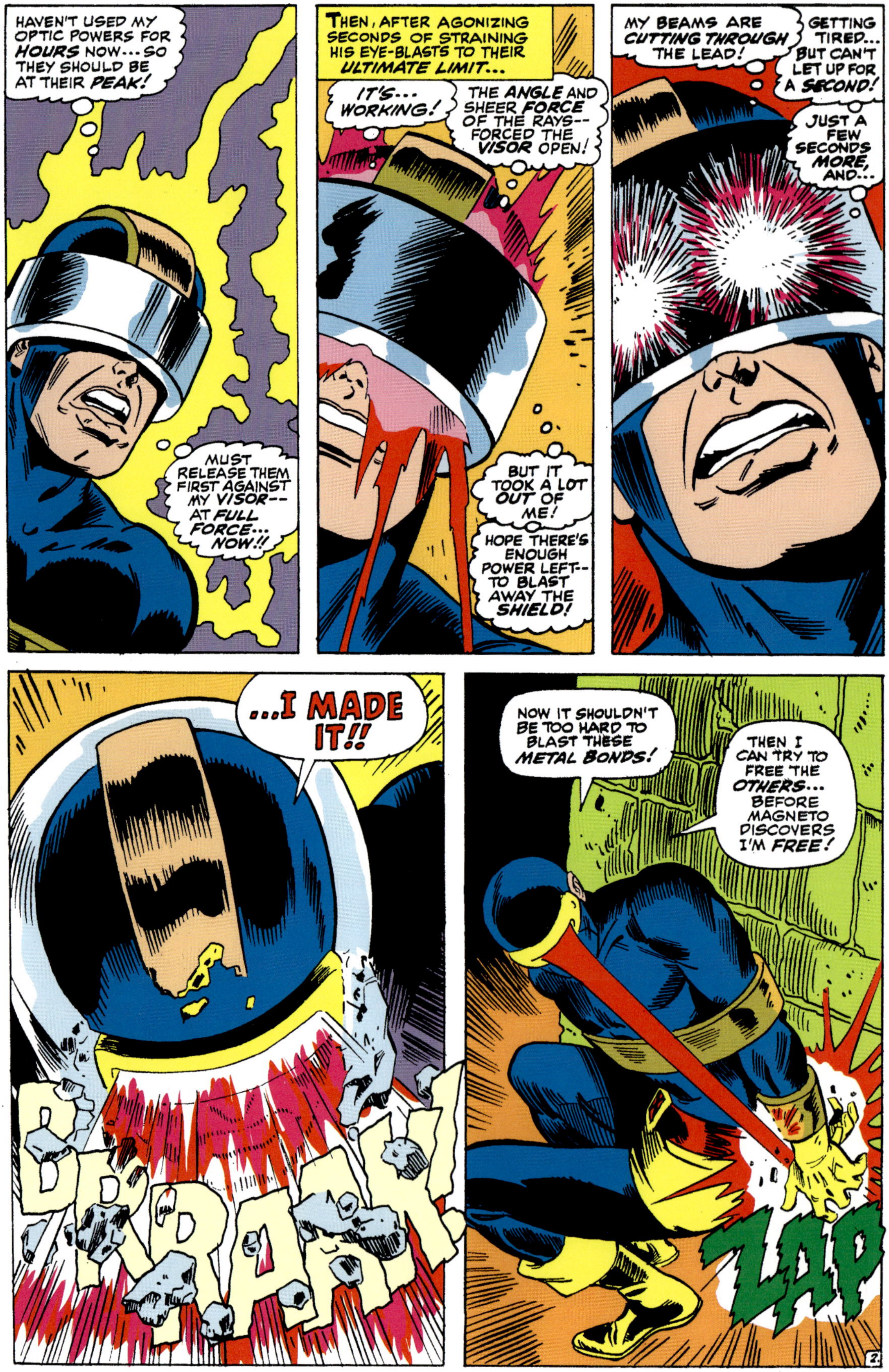
HAVEN'T USED MY OPTIC POWERS FOR HOURS NOW... SO THEY SHOULD BE AT THEIR PEAK!
MUST RELEASE THEM FIRST AGAINST MY VISOR-- AT FULL FORCE... NOW!!
THEN, AFTER AGONIZING SECONDS OF STRAINING HIS EYE-BLASTS TO THEIR ULTIMATE LIMIT...
IT'S... WORKING!
THE ANGLE AND SHEER FORCE OF THE RAYS-- FORCED THE VISOR OPEN!
BUT IT TOOK A LOT OUT OF ME!
HOPE THERE'S ENOUGH POWER LEFT-- TO BLAST AWAY THE SHIELD!
MY BEAMS ARE CUTTING THROUGH THE LEAD!
GETTING TIRED... BUT CAN'T LET UP FOR A SECOND!
JUST A FEW SECONDS MORE, AND...
...I MADE IT!!
NOW IT SHOULDN'T BE TOO HARD TO BLAST THESE METAL BONDS!
THEN I CAN TRY TO FREE THE OTHERS... BEFORE MAGNETO DISCOVERS I'M FREE!
ZAP
2

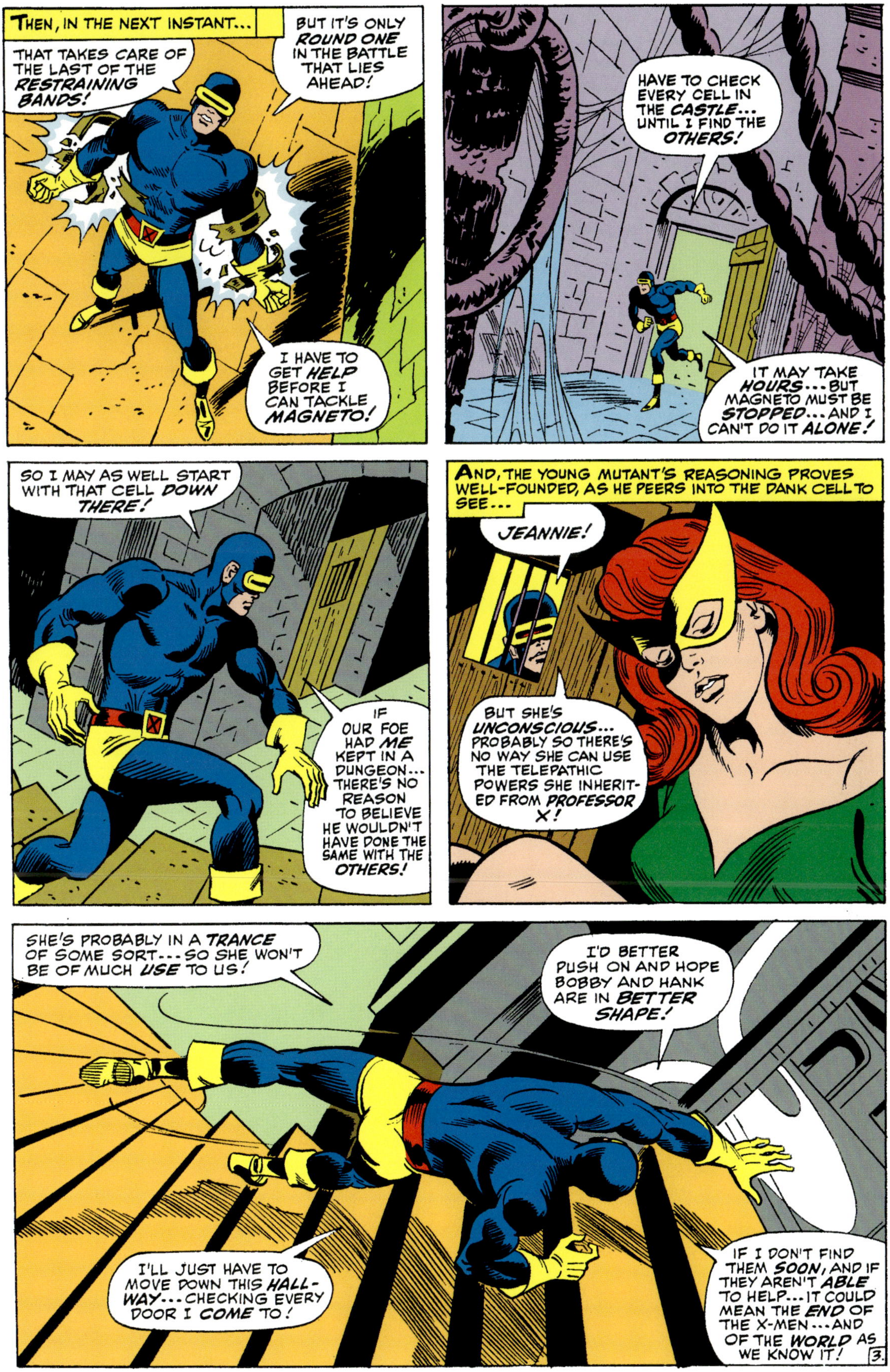
THEN, IN THE NEXT INSTANT...
THAT TAKES CARE OF THE LAST OF THE RESTRAINING BANDS!
BUT IT'S ONLY ROUND ONE IN THE BATTLE THAT LIES AHEAD!
I HAVE TO GET HELP BEFORE I CAN TACKLE MAGNETO!
HAVE TO CHECK EVERY CELL IN THE CASTLE... UNTIL I FIND THE OTHERS!
IT MAY TAKE HOURS... BUT MAGNETO MUST BE STOPPED... AND I CAN'T DO IT ALONE!
SO I MAY AS WELL START WITH THAT CELL DOWN THERE!
IF OUR FOE HAD ME KEPT IN A DUNGEON... THERE'S NO REASON TO BELIEVE HE WOULDN'T HAVE DONE THE SAME WITH THE OTHERS!
AND, THE YOUNG MUTANT'S REASONING PROVES WELL-FOUNDED, AS HE PEERS INTO THE DANK CELL TO SEE...
JEANNIE!
BUT SHE'S UNCONSCIOUS... PROBABLY SO THERE'S NO WAY SHE CAN USE THE TELEPATHIC POWERS SHE INHERIT-ED FROM PROFESSOR X!
SHE'S PROBABLY IN A TRANCE OF SOME SORT... SO SHE WON'T BE OF MUCH USE TO US!
I'D BETTER PUSH ON AND HOPE BOBBY AND HANK ARE IN BETTER SHAPE!
I'LL JUST HAVE TO MOVE DOWN THIS HALL-WAY... CHECKING EVERY DOOR I COME TO!
IF I DON'T FIND THEM SOON, AND IF THEY AREN'T ABLE TO HELP... IT COULD MEAN THE END OF THE X-MEN... AND OF THE WORLD AS WE KNOW IT!
3

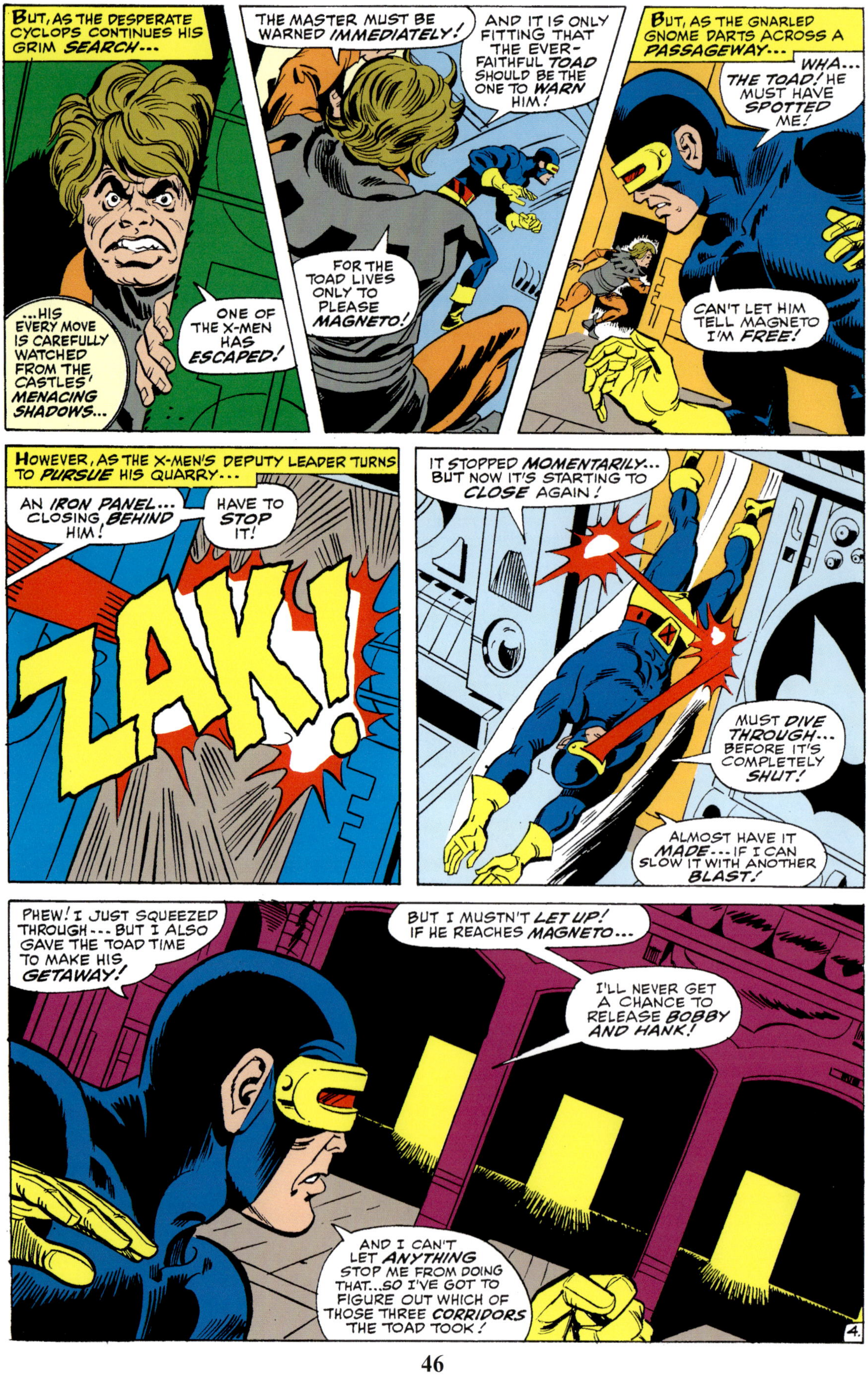
BUT, AS THE DESPERATE CYCLOPS CONTINUES HIS GRIM SEARCH...
...HIS EVERY MOVE IS CAREFULLY WATCHED FROM THE CASTLES' MENACING SHADOWS...
ONE OF THE X-MEN HAS ESCAPED!
THE MASTER MUST BE WARNED IMMEDIATELY!
AND IT IS ONLY FITTING THAT THE EVER-FAITHFUL TOAD SHOULD BE THE ONE TO WARN HIM!
FOR THE TOAD LIVES ONLY TO PLEASE MAGNETO!
BUT, AS THE GNARLED GNOME DARTS ACROSS A PASSAGEWAY...
WHA... THE TOAD! HE MUST HAVE SPOTTED ME!
CAN'T LET HIM TELL MAGNETO I'M FREE!
HOWEVER, AS THE X-MEN'S DEPUTY LEADER TURNS TO PURSUE HIS QUARRY...
AN IRON PANEL... CLOSING BEHIND HIM!
HAVE TO STOP IT!
ZAK!
IT STOPPED MOMENTARILY... BUT NOW IT'S STARTING TO CLOSE AGAIN!
MUST DIVE THROUGH... BEFORE IT'S COMPLETELY SHUT!
ALMOST HAVE IT MADE... IF I CAN SLOW IT WITH ANOTHER BLAST!
PHEW! I JUST SQUEEZED THROUGH... BUT I ALSO GAVE THE TOAD TIME TO MAKE HIS GETAWAY!
BUT I MUSTN'T LET UP! IF HE REACHES MAGNETO...
I'LL NEVER GET A CHANCE TO RELEASE BOBBY AND HANK!
AND I CAN'T LET ANYTHING STOP ME FROM DOING THAT...SO I'VE GOT TO FIGURE OUT WHICH OF THOSE THREE CORRIDORS THE TOAD TOOK!
4.

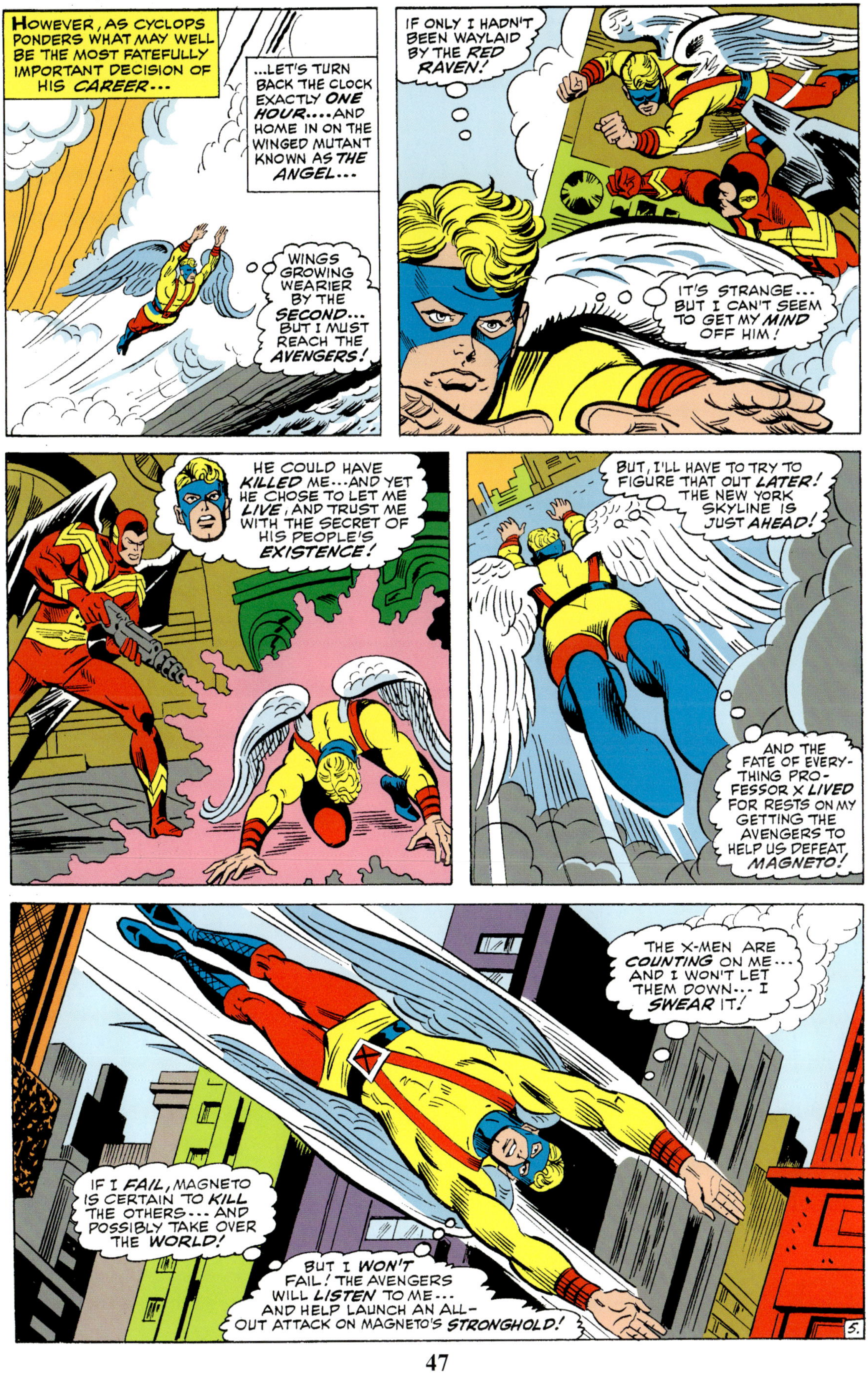
HOWEVER, AS CYCLOPS PONDERS WHAT MAY WELL BE THE MOST FATEFULLY IMPORTANT DECISION OF HIS CAREER...
...LET'S TURN BACK THE CLOCK EXACTLY ONE HOUR.... AND HOME IN ON THE WINGED MUTANT KNOWN AS THE ANGEL...
WINGS GROWING WEARIER BY THE SECOND... BUT I MUST REACH THE AVENGERS!
IF ONLY I HADN'T BEEN WAYLAID BY THE RED RAVEN!
IT'S STRANGE... BUT I CAN'T SEEM TO GET MY MIND OFF HIM!
HE COULD HAVE KILLED ME... AND YET HE CHOSE TO LET ME LIVE, AND TRUST ME WITH THE SECRET OF HIS PEOPLE'S EXISTENCE!
BUT, I'LL HAVE TO TRY TO FIGURE THAT OUT LATER! THE NEW YORK SKYLINE IS JUST AHEAD!
AND THE FATE OF EVERYTHING PROFESSOR X LIVED FOR RESTS ON MY GETTING THE AVENGERS TO HELP US DEFEAT MAGNETO!
THE X-MEN ARE COUNTING ON ME... AND I WON'T LET THEM DOWN... I SWEAR IT!
IF I FAIL, MAGNETO IS CERTAIN TO KILL THE OTHERS... AND POSSIBLY TAKE OVER THE WORLD!
BUT I WON'T FAIL! THE AVENGERS WILL LISTEN TO ME... AND HELP LAUNCH AN ALL-OUT ATTACK ON MAGNETO'S STRONGHOLD!
5.

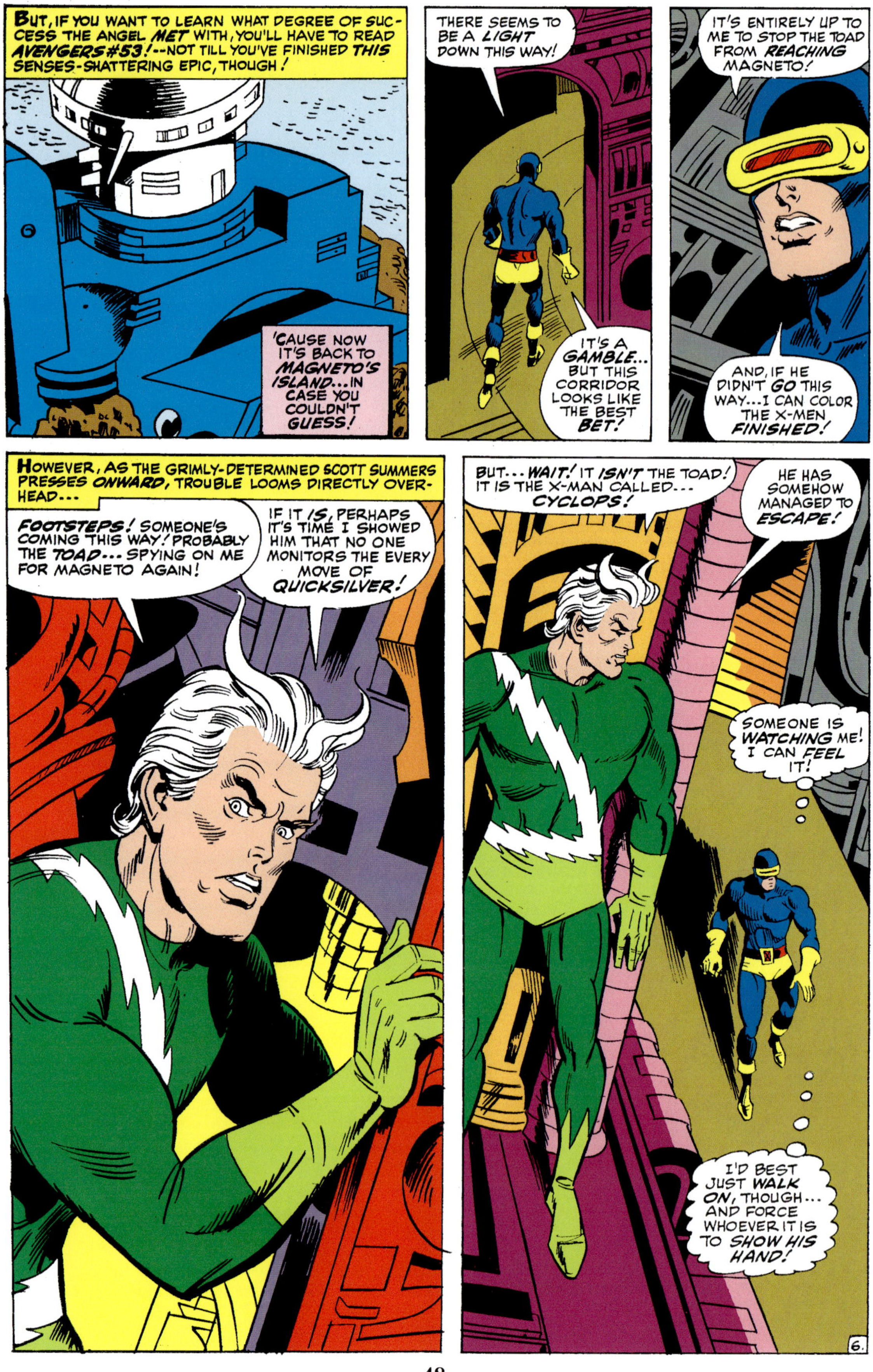

BUT, IF YOU WANT TO LEARN WHAT DEGREE OF SUCCESS THE ANGEL MET WITH, YOU'LL HAVE TO READ AVENGERS #53!--NOT TILL YOU'VE FINISHED THIS SENSES-SHATTERING EPIC, THOUGH!
'CAUSE NOW IT'S BACK TO MAGNETO'S ISLAND...IN CASE YOU COULDN'T GUESS!
THERE SEEMS TO BE A LIGHT DOWN THIS WAY!
IT'S A GAMBLE... BUT THIS CORRIDOR LOOKS LIKE THE BEST BET!
IT'S ENTIRELY UP TO ME TO STOP THE TOAD FROM REACHING MAGNETO!
AND, IF HE DIDN'T GO THIS WAY...I CAN COLOR THE X-MEN FINISHED!
HOWEVER, AS THE GRIMLY-DETERMINED SCOTT SUMMERS PRESSES ONWARD, TROUBLE LOOMS DIRECTLY OVERHEAD...
FOOTSTEPS! SOMEONE'S COMING THIS WAY! PROBABLY THE TOAD... SPYING ON ME FOR MAGNETO AGAIN!
IF IT IS, PERHAPS IT'S TIME I SHOWED HIM THAT NO ONE MONITORS THE EVERY MOVE OF QUICKSILVER!
BUT... WAIT! IT ISN'T THE TOAD! IT IS THE X-MAN CALLED... CYCLOPS!
HE HAS SOMEHOW MANAGED TO ESCAPE!
SOMEONE IS WATCHING ME! I CAN FEEL IT!
I'D BEST JUST WALK ON, THOUGH... AND FORCE WHOEVER IT IS TO SHOW HIS HAND!
6.

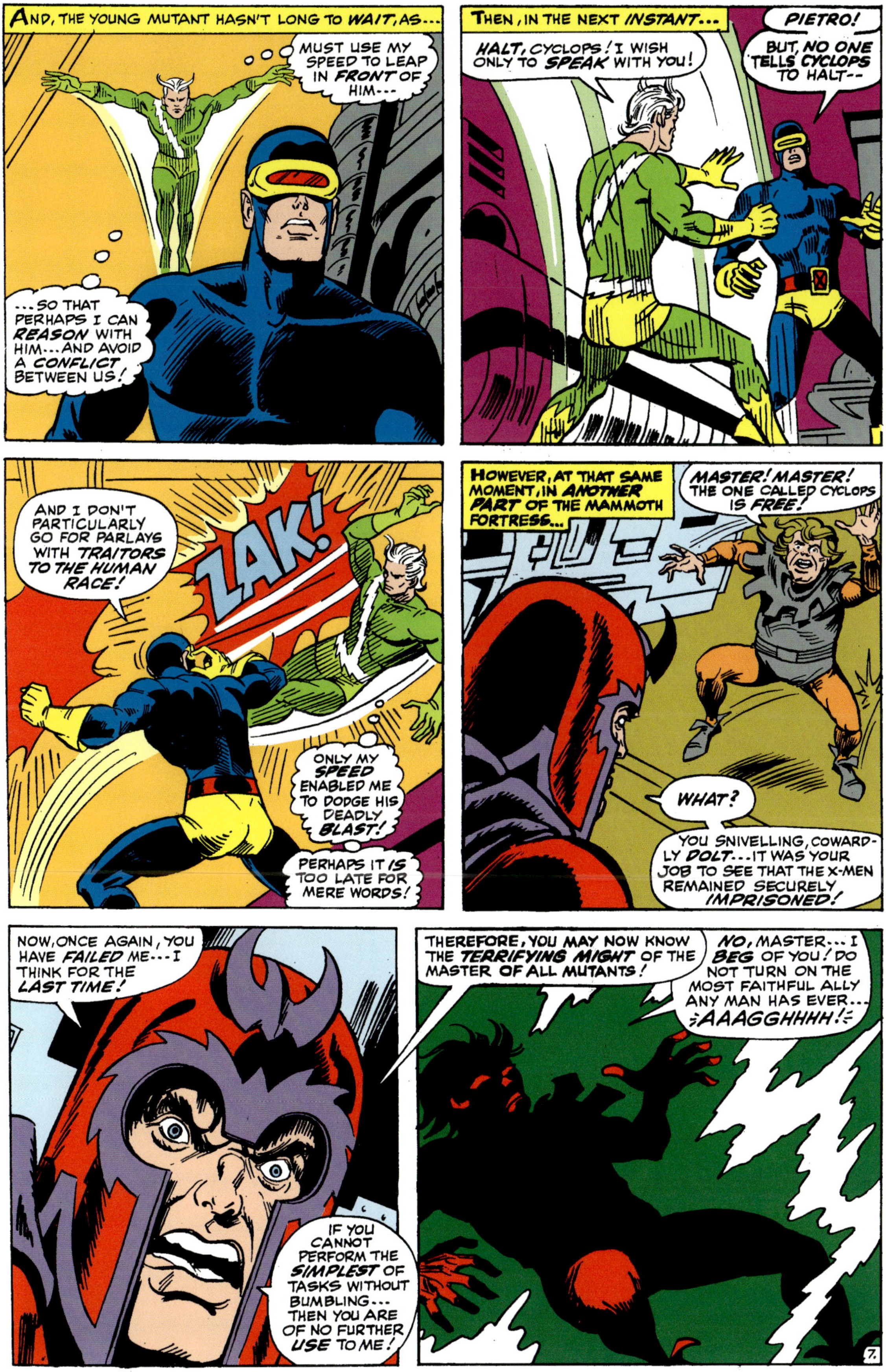
AND, THE YOUNG MUTANT HASN'T LONG TO WAIT, AS...
MUST USE MY SPEED TO LEAP IN FRONT OF HIM---
...SO THAT PERHAPS I CAN REASON WITH HIM...AND AVOID A CONFLICT BETWEEN US!
THEN, IN THE NEXT INSTANT...
HALT, CYCLOPS! I WISH ONLY TO SPEAK WITH YOU!
PIETRO!
BUT, NO ONE TELLS CYCLOPS TO HALT--
AND I DON'T PARTICULARLY GO FOR PARLAYS WITH TRAITORS TO THE HUMAN RACE!
ZAK!
ONLY MY SPEED ENABLED ME TO DODGE HIS DEADLY BLAST!
PERHAPS IT IS TOO LATE FOR MERE WORDS!
HOWEVER, AT THAT SAME MOMENT, IN ANOTHER PART OF THE MAMMOTH FORTRESS...
MASTER! MASTER! THE ONE CALLED CYCLOPS IS FREE!
WHAT?
YOU SNIVELLING, COWARDLY DOLT...IT WAS YOUR JOB TO SEE THAT THE X-MEN REMAINED SECURELY IMPRISONED!
NOW, ONCE AGAIN, YOU HAVE FAILED ME...I THINK FOR THE LAST TIME!
IF YOU CANNOT PERFORM THE SIMPLEST OF TASKS WITHOUT BUMBLING...THEN YOU ARE OF NO FURTHER USE TO ME!
THEREFORE, YOU MAY NOW KNOW THE TERRIFYING MIGHT OF THE MASTER OF ALL MUTANTS!
NO, MASTER...I BEG OF YOU! DO NOT TURN ON THE MOST FAITHFUL ALLY ANY MAN HAS EVER... AAAGGHHHH!
7.

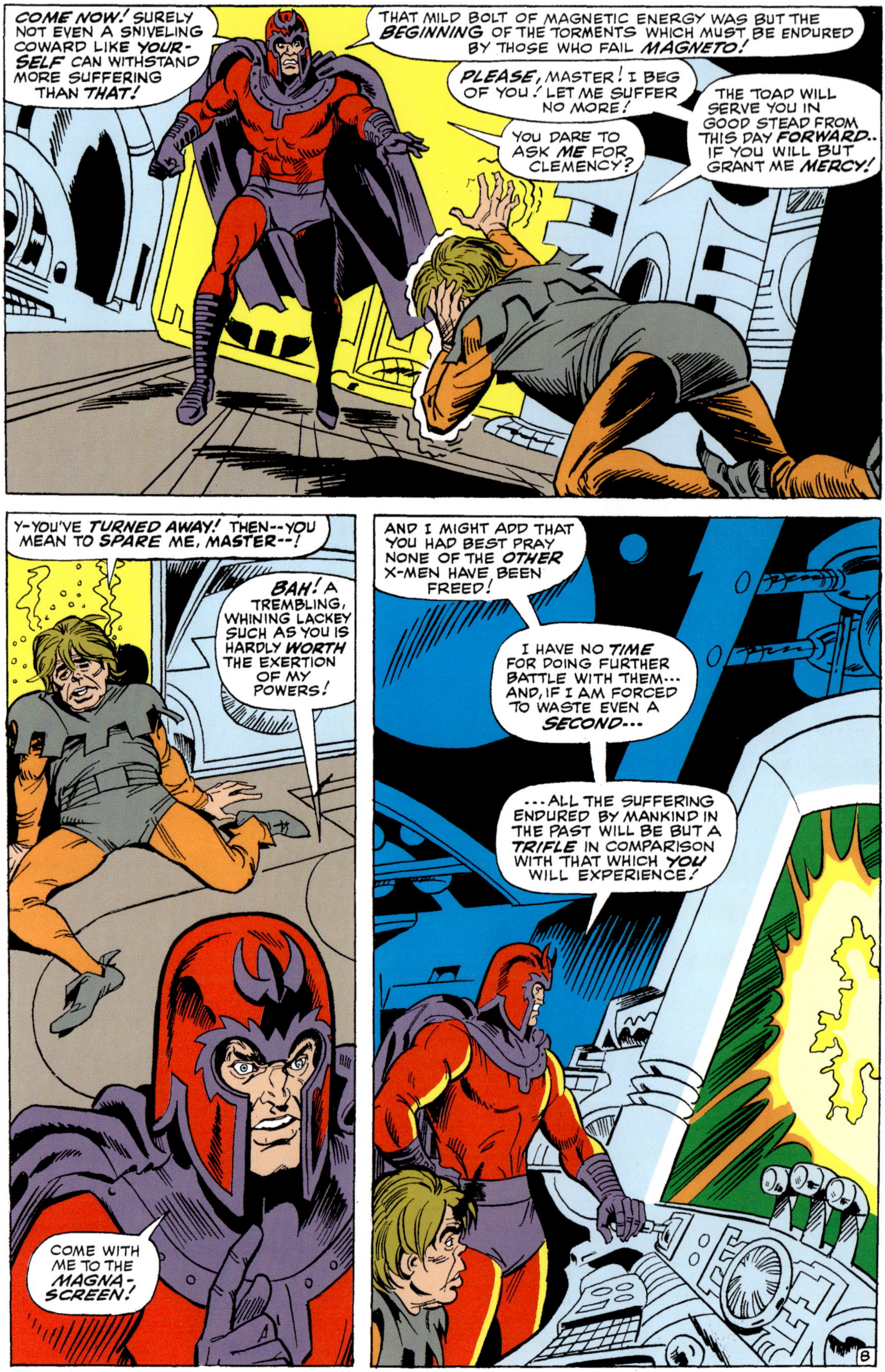
COME NOW! SURELY NOT EVEN A SNIVELING COWARD LIKE YOURSELF CAN WITHSTAND MORE SUFFERING THAN THAT!
THAT MILD BOLT OF MAGNETIC ENERGY WAS BUT THE BEGINNING OF THE TORMENTS WHICH MUST BE ENDURED BY THOSE WHO FAIL MAGNETO!
PLEASE, MASTER! I BEG OF YOU! LET ME SUFFER NO MORE!
THE TOAD WILL SERVE YOU IN GOOD STEAD FROM THIS DAY FORWARD.. IF YOU WILL BUT GRANT ME MERCY!
YOU DARE TO ASK ME FOR CLEMENCY?
Y-YOU'VE TURNED AWAY! THEN--YOU MEAN TO SPARE ME, MASTER--!
BAH! A TREMBLING, WHINING LACKEY SUCH AS YOU IS HARDLY WORTH THE EXERTION OF MY POWERS!
COME WITH ME TO THE MAGNA-SCREEN!
AND I MIGHT ADD THAT YOU HAD BEST PRAY NONE OF THE OTHER X-MEN HAVE BEEN FREED!
I HAVE NO TIME FOR DOING FURTHER BATTLE WITH THEM... AND, IF I AM FORCED TO WASTE EVEN A SECOND...
...ALL THE SUFFERING ENDURED BY MANKIND IN THE PAST WILL BE BUT A TRIFLE IN COMPARISON WITH THAT WHICH YOU WILL EXPERIENCE!
8

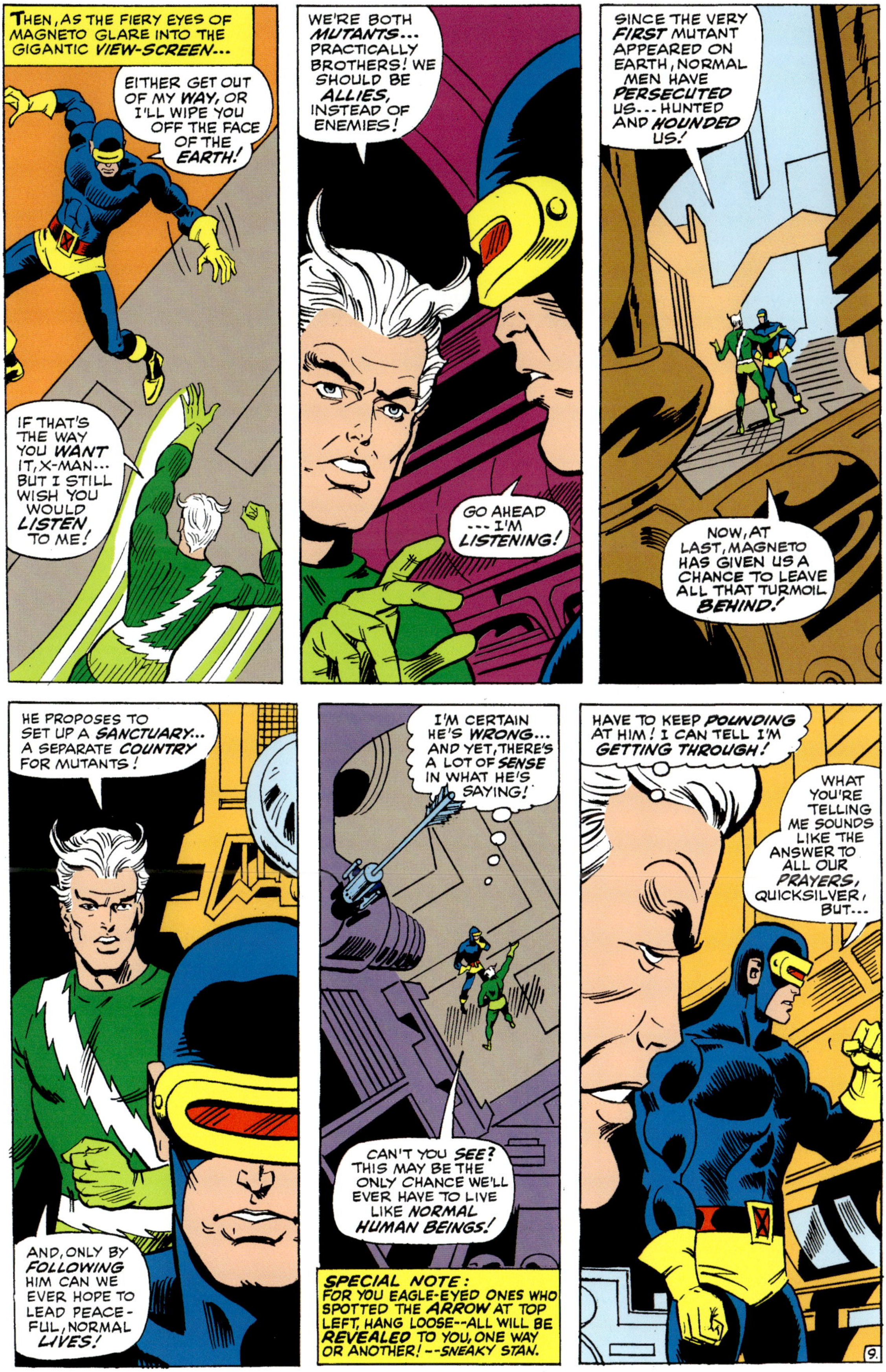
THEN, AS THE FIERY EYES OF MAGNETO GLARE INTO THE GIGANTIC VIEW-SCREEN...
EITHER GET OUT OF MY WAY, OR I'LL WIPE YOU OFF THE FACE OF THE EARTH!
IF THAT'S THE WAY YOU WANT IT, X-MAN... BUT I STILL WISH YOU WOULD LISTEN TO ME!
WE'RE BOTH MUTANTS... PRACTICALLY BROTHERS! WE SHOULD BE ALLIES, INSTEAD OF ENEMIES!
GO AHEAD --- I'M LISTENING!
SINCE THE VERY FIRST MUTANT APPEARED ON EARTH, NORMAL MEN HAVE PERSECUTED US... HUNTED AND HOUNDED US!
NOW, AT LAST, MAGNETO HAS GIVEN US A CHANCE TO LEAVE ALL THAT TURMOIL BEHIND!
HE PROPOSES TO SET UP A SANCTUARY... A SEPARATE COUNTRY FOR MUTANTS!
AND, ONLY BY FOLLOWING HIM CAN WE EVER HOPE TO LEAD PEACE-FUL, NORMAL LIVES!
I'M CERTAIN HE'S WRONG... AND YET, THERE'S A LOT OF SENSE IN WHAT HE'S SAYING!
CAN'T YOU SEE? THIS MAY BE THE ONLY CHANCE WE'LL EVER HAVE TO LIVE LIKE NORMAL HUMAN BEINGS!
SPECIAL NOTE: FOR YOU EAGLE-EYED ONES WHO SPOTTED THE ARROW AT TOP LEFT, HANG LOOSE--ALL WILL BE REVEALED TO YOU, ONE WAY OR ANOTHER! --SNEAKY STAN.
HAVE TO KEEP POUNDING AT HIM! I CAN TELL I'M GETTING THROUGH!
WHAT YOU'RE TELLING ME SOUNDS LIKE THE ANSWER TO ALL OUR PRAYERS, QUICKSILVER, BUT...
9.

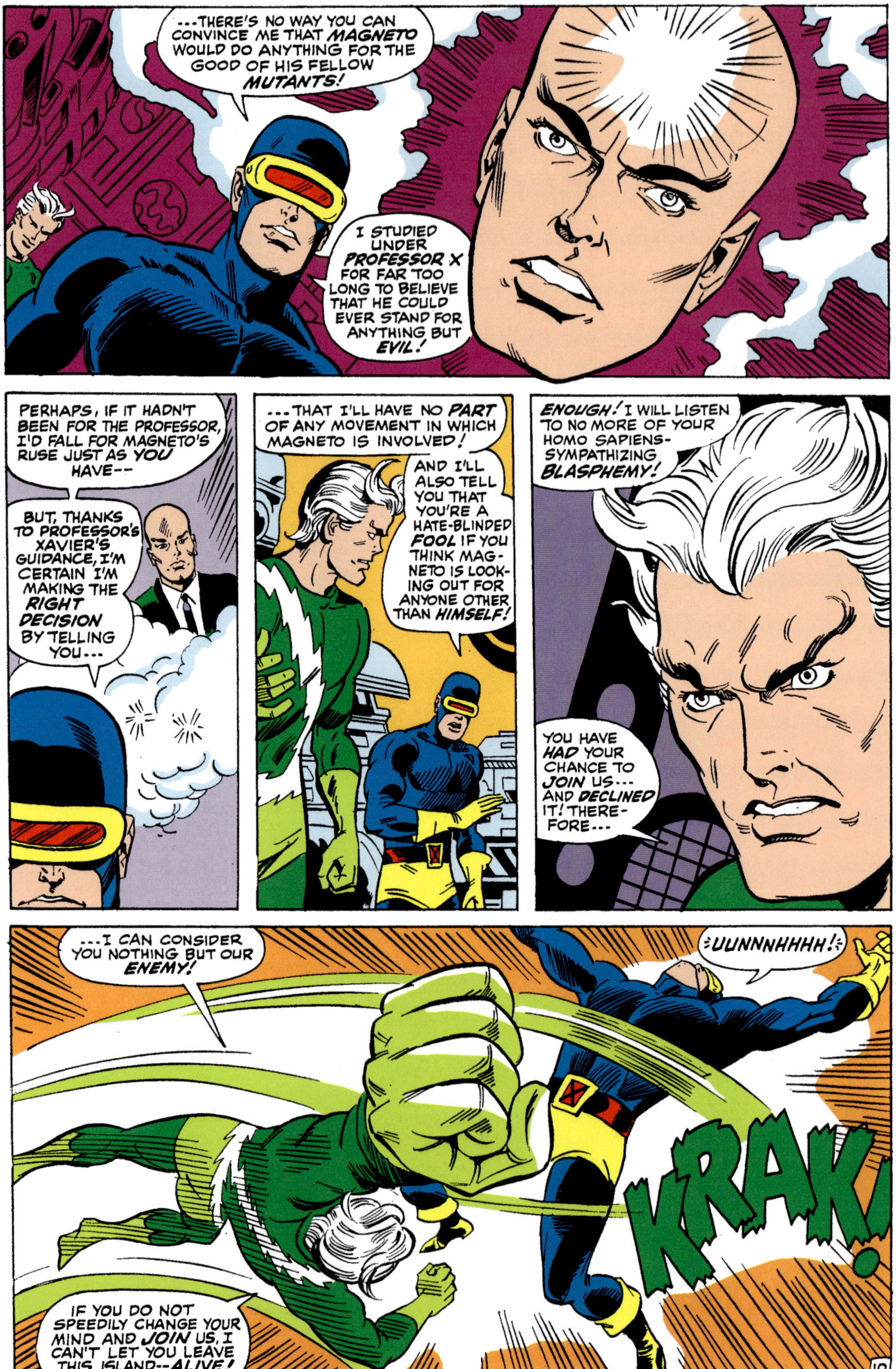
...THERE'S NO WAY YOU CAN CONVINCE ME THAT MAGNETO WOULD DO ANYTHING FOR THE GOOD OF HIS FELLOW MUTANTS!
I STUDIED UNDER PROFESSOR X FOR FAR TOO LONG TO BELIEVE THAT HE COULD EVER STAND FOR ANYTHING BUT EVIL!
PERHAPS, IF IT HADN'T BEEN FOR THE PROFESSOR, I'D FALL FOR MAGNETO'S RUSE JUST AS YOU HAVE--
BUT, THANKS TO PROFESSOR'S XAVIER'S GUIDANCE, I'M CERTAIN I'M MAKING THE RIGHT DECISION BY TELLING YOU...
...THAT I'LL HAVE NO PART OF ANY MOVEMENT IN WHICH MAGNETO IS INVOLVED!
AND I'LL ALSO TELL YOU THAT YOU'RE A HATE-BLINDED FOOL IF YOU THINK MAGNETO IS LOOKING OUT FOR ANYONE OTHER THAN HIMSELF!
ENOUGH! I WILL LISTEN TO NO MORE OF YOUR HOMO SAPIENS-SYMPATHIZING BLASPHEMY!
YOU HAVE HAD YOUR CHANCE TO JOIN US... AND DECLINED IT! THEREFORE...
...I CAN CONSIDER YOU NOTHING BUT OUR ENEMY!
UUNNNHHHH!
KRAK!
IF YOU DO NOT SPEEDILY CHANGE YOUR MIND AND JOIN US, I CAN'T LET YOU LEAVE THIS ISLAND--ALIVE!
10

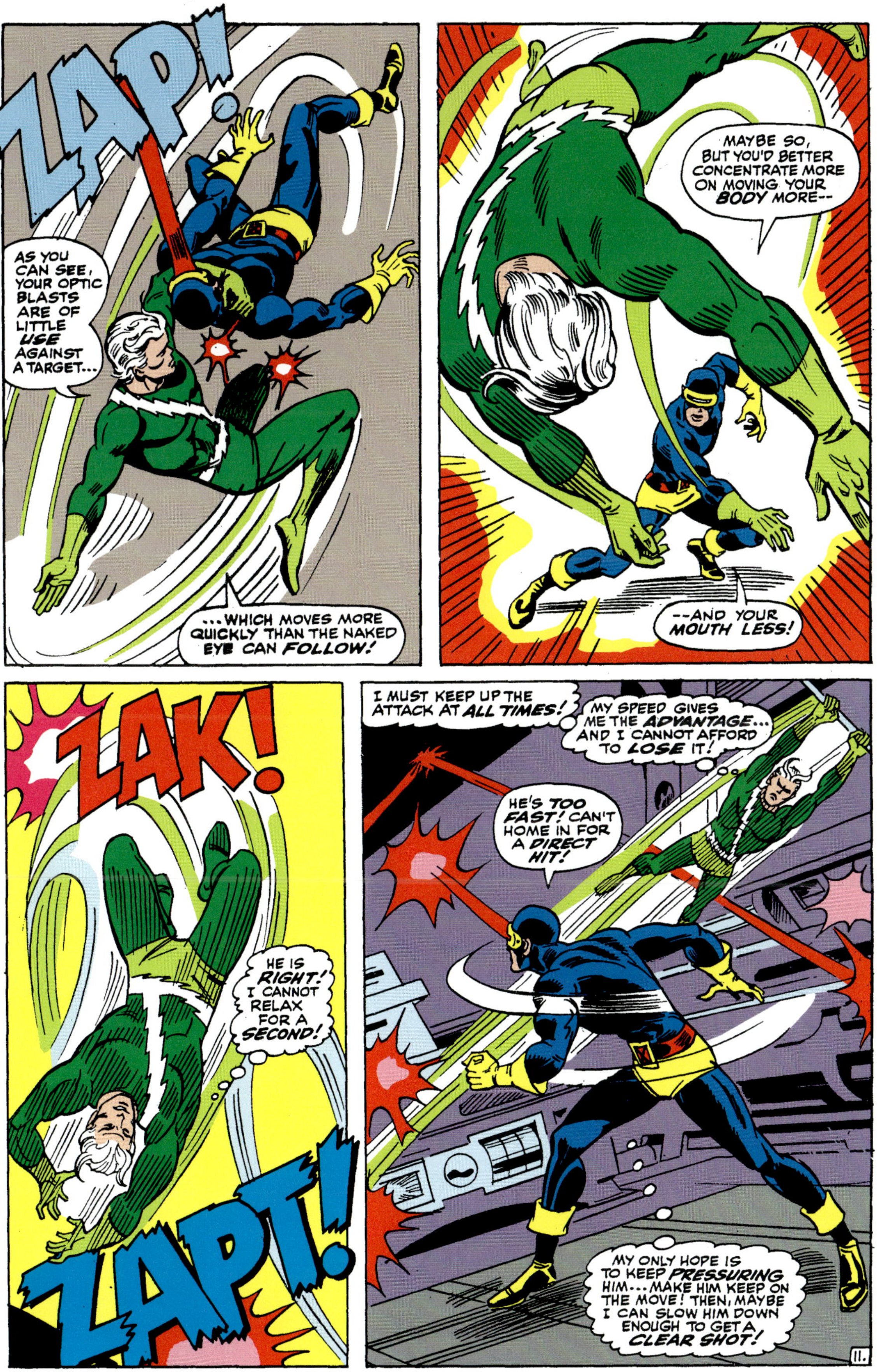
ZAP!
AS YOU CAN SEE, YOUR OPTIC BLASTS ARE OF LITTLE USE AGAINST A TARGET...
...WHICH MOVES MORE QUICKLY THAN THE NAKED EYE CAN FOLLOW!
MAYBE SO, BUT YOU'D BETTER CONCENTRATE MORE ON MOVING YOUR BODY MORE--
--AND YOUR MOUTH LESS!
ZAK!
HE IS RIGHT! I CANNOT RELAX FOR A SECOND!
ZAPT!
I MUST KEEP UP THE ATTACK AT ALL TIMES!
MY SPEED GIVES ME THE ADVANTAGE... AND I CANNOT AFFORD TO LOSE IT!
HE'S TOO FAST! CAN'T HOME IN FOR A DIRECT HIT!
MY ONLY HOPE IS TO KEEP PRESSURING HIM... MAKE HIM KEEP ON THE MOVE! THEN, MAYBE I CAN SLOW HIM DOWN ENOUGH TO GET A CLEAR SHOT!
11.

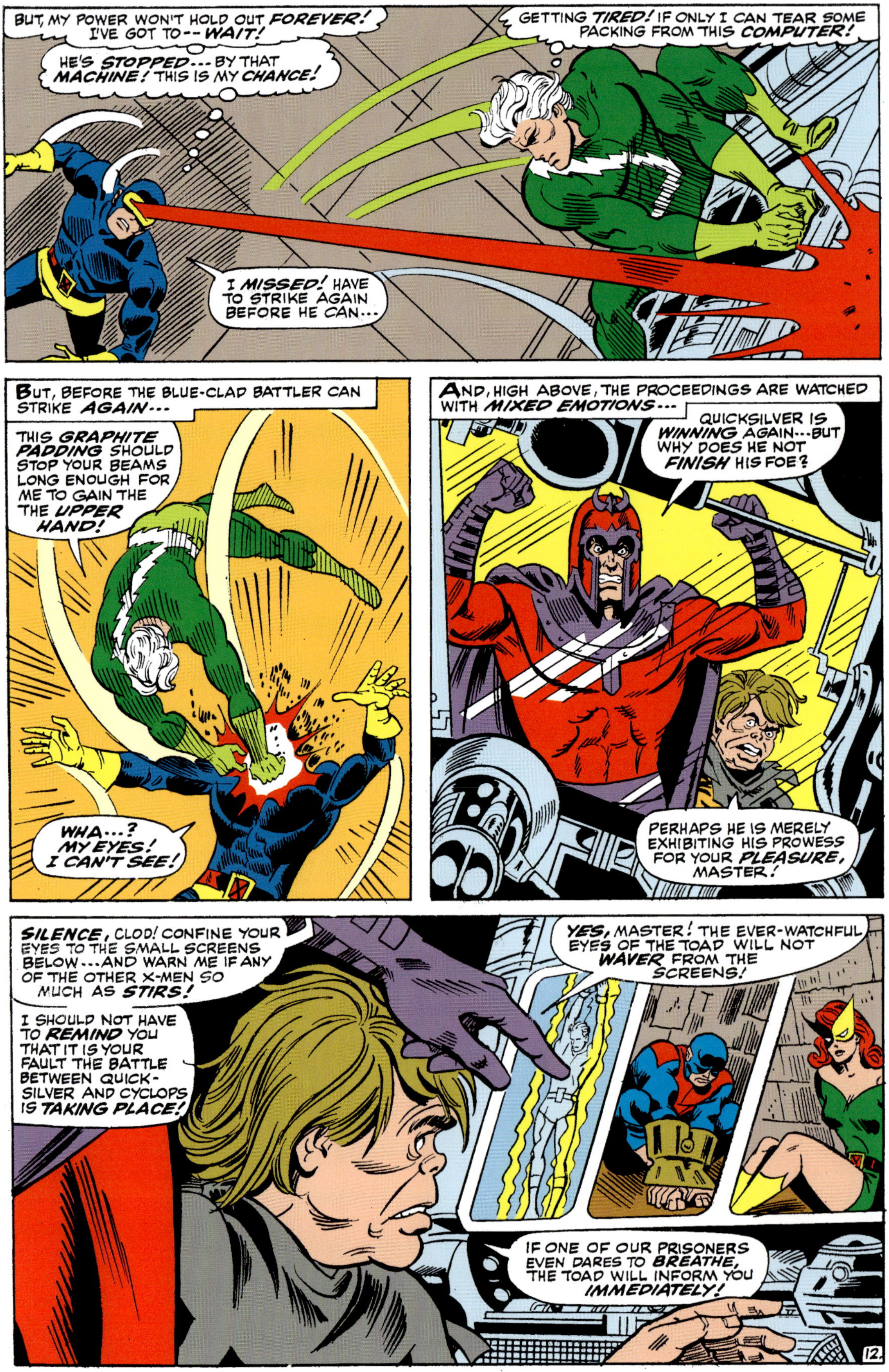
BUT, MY POWER WON'T HOLD OUT FOREVER! I'VE GOT TO -- WAIT!
HE'S STOPPED... BY THAT MACHINE! THIS IS MY CHANCE!
GETTING TIRED! IF ONLY I CAN TEAR SOME PACKING FROM THIS COMPUTER!
I MISSED! HAVE TO STRIKE AGAIN BEFORE HE CAN...
BUT, BEFORE THE BLUE-CLAD BATTLER CAN STRIKE AGAIN...
THIS GRAPHITE PADDING SHOULD STOP YOUR BEAMS LONG ENOUGH FOR ME TO GAIN THE THE UPPER HAND!
WHA...? MY EYES! I CAN'T SEE!
AND, HIGH ABOVE, THE PROCEEDINGS ARE WATCHED WITH MIXED EMOTIONS...
QUICKSILVER IS WINNING AGAIN...BUT WHY DOES HE NOT FINISH HIS FOE?
PERHAPS HE IS MERELY EXHIBITING HIS PROWESS FOR YOUR PLEASURE, MASTER!
SILENCE, CLOD! CONFINE YOUR EYES TO THE SMALL SCREENS BELOW...AND WARN ME IF ANY OF THE OTHER X-MEN SO MUCH AS STIRS!
I SHOULD NOT HAVE TO REMIND YOU THAT IT IS YOUR FAULT THE BATTLE BETWEEN QUICK-SILVER AND CYCLOPS IS TAKING PLACE!
YES, MASTER! THE EVER-WATCHFUL EYES OF THE TOAD WILL NOT WAVER FROM THE SCREENS!
IF ONE OF OUR PRISONERS EVEN DARES TO BREATHE, THE TOAD WILL INFORM YOU IMMEDIATELY!
12.

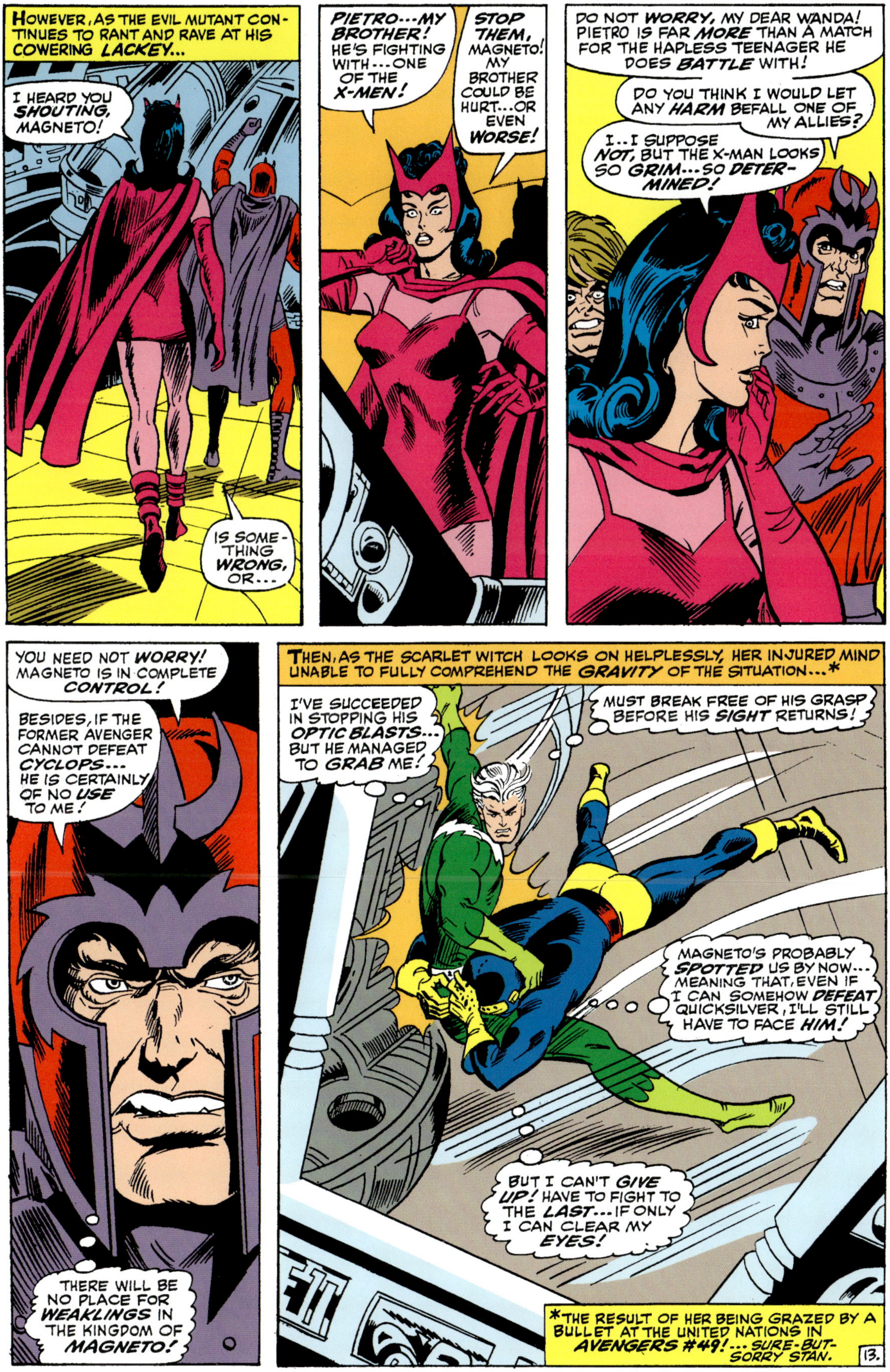

HOWEVER, AS THE EVIL MUTANT CONTINUES TO RANT AND RAVE AT HIS COWERING LACKEY...
I HEARD YOU SHOUTING, MAGNETO!
IS SOMETHING WRONG, OR...
PIETRO... MY BROTHER! HE'S FIGHTING WITH... ONE OF THE X-MEN!
STOP THEM, MAGNETO! MY BROTHER COULD BE HURT... OR EVEN WORSE!
DO NOT WORRY, MY DEAR WANDA! PIETRO IS FAR MORE THAN A MATCH FOR THE HAPLESS TEENAGER HE DOES BATTLE WITH!
DO YOU THINK I WOULD LET ANY HARM BEFALL ONE OF MY ALLIES?
I.. I SUPPOSE NOT, BUT THE X-MAN LOOKS SO GRIM... SO DETERMINED!
YOU NEED NOT WORRY! MAGNETO IS IN COMPLETE CONTROL!
BESIDES, IF THE FORMER AVENGER CANNOT DEFEAT CYCLOPS... HE IS CERTAINLY OF NO USE TO ME!
THERE WILL BE NO PLACE FOR WEAKLINGS IN THE KINGDOM OF MAGNETO!
THEN, AS THE SCARLET WITCH LOOKS ON HELPLESSLY, HER INJURED MIND UNABLE TO FULLY COMPREHEND THE GRAVITY OF THE SITUATION...*
I'VE SUCCEEDED IN STOPPING HIS OPTIC BLASTS... BUT HE MANAGED TO GRAB ME!
MUST BREAK FREE OF HIS GRASP BEFORE HIS SIGHT RETURNS!
MAGNETO'S PROBABLY SPOTTED US BY NOW... MEANING THAT, EVEN IF I CAN SOMEHOW DEFEAT QUICKSILVER, I'LL STILL HAVE TO FACE HIM!
BUT I CAN'T GIVE UP! HAVE TO FIGHT TO THE LAST... IF ONLY I CAN CLEAR MY EYES!
*THE RESULT OF HER BEING GRAZED BY A BULLET AT THE UNITED NATIONS IN AVENGERS #49! ... SURE-BUT-SORRY STAN.
13.

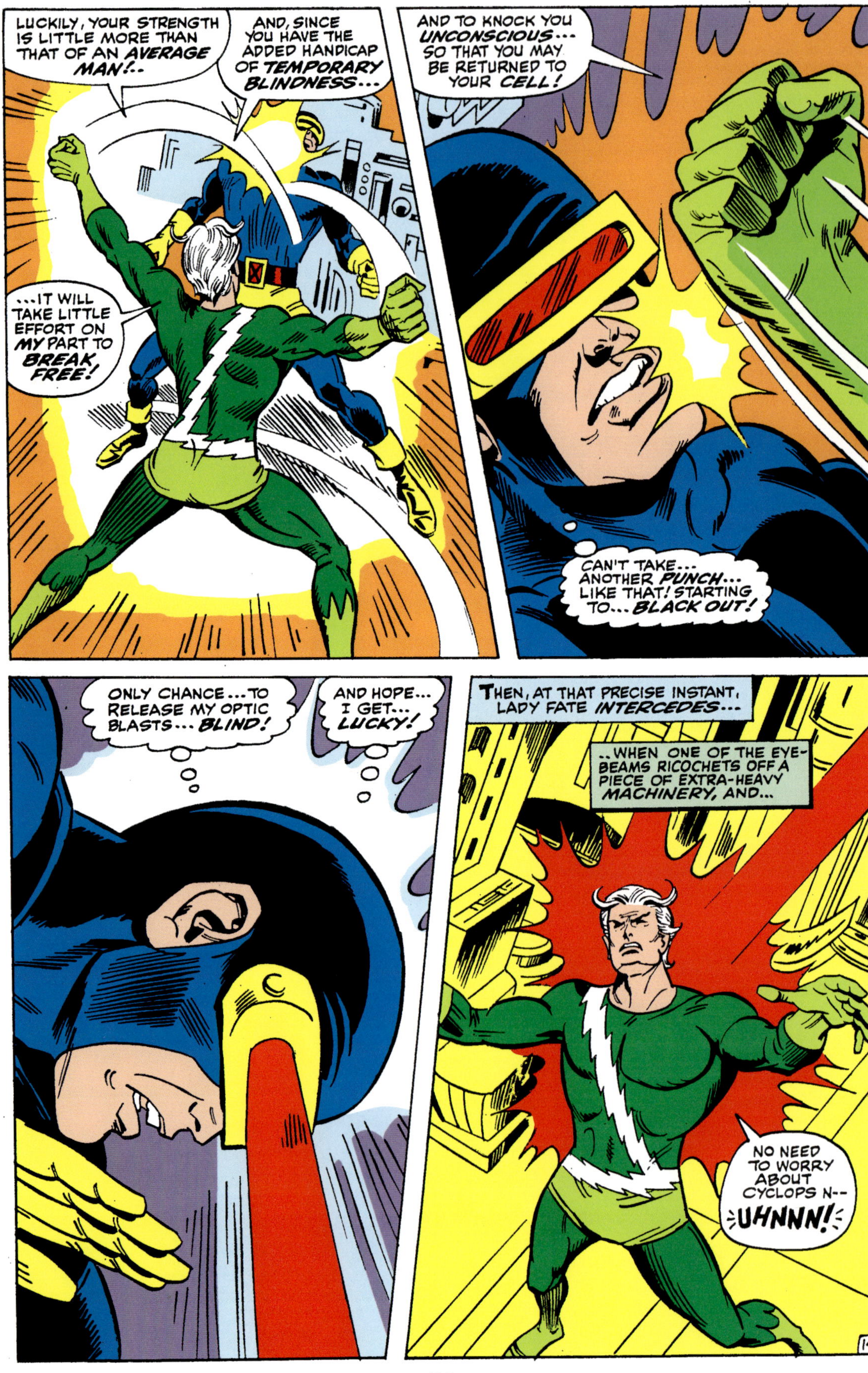
LUCKILY, YOUR STRENGTH IS LITTLE MORE THAN THAT OF AN AVERAGE MAN!..
AND, SINCE YOU HAVE THE ADDED HANDICAP OF TEMPORARY BLINDNESS...
...IT WILL TAKE LITTLE EFFORT ON MY PART TO BREAK FREE!
AND TO KNOCK YOU UNCONSCIOUS... SO THAT YOU MAY BE RETURNED TO YOUR CELL!
CAN'T TAKE... ANOTHER PUNCH... LIKE THAT! STARTING TO... BLACK OUT!
ONLY CHANCE...TO RELEASE MY OPTIC BLASTS... BLIND!
AND HOPE... I GET... LUCKY!
THEN, AT THAT PRECISE INSTANT, LADY FATE INTERCEDES...
..WHEN ONE OF THE EYE-BEAMS RICOCHETS OFF A PIECE OF EXTRA-HEAVY MACHINERY, AND...
NO NEED TO WORRY ABOUT CYCLOPS N--
UHNNN!
14

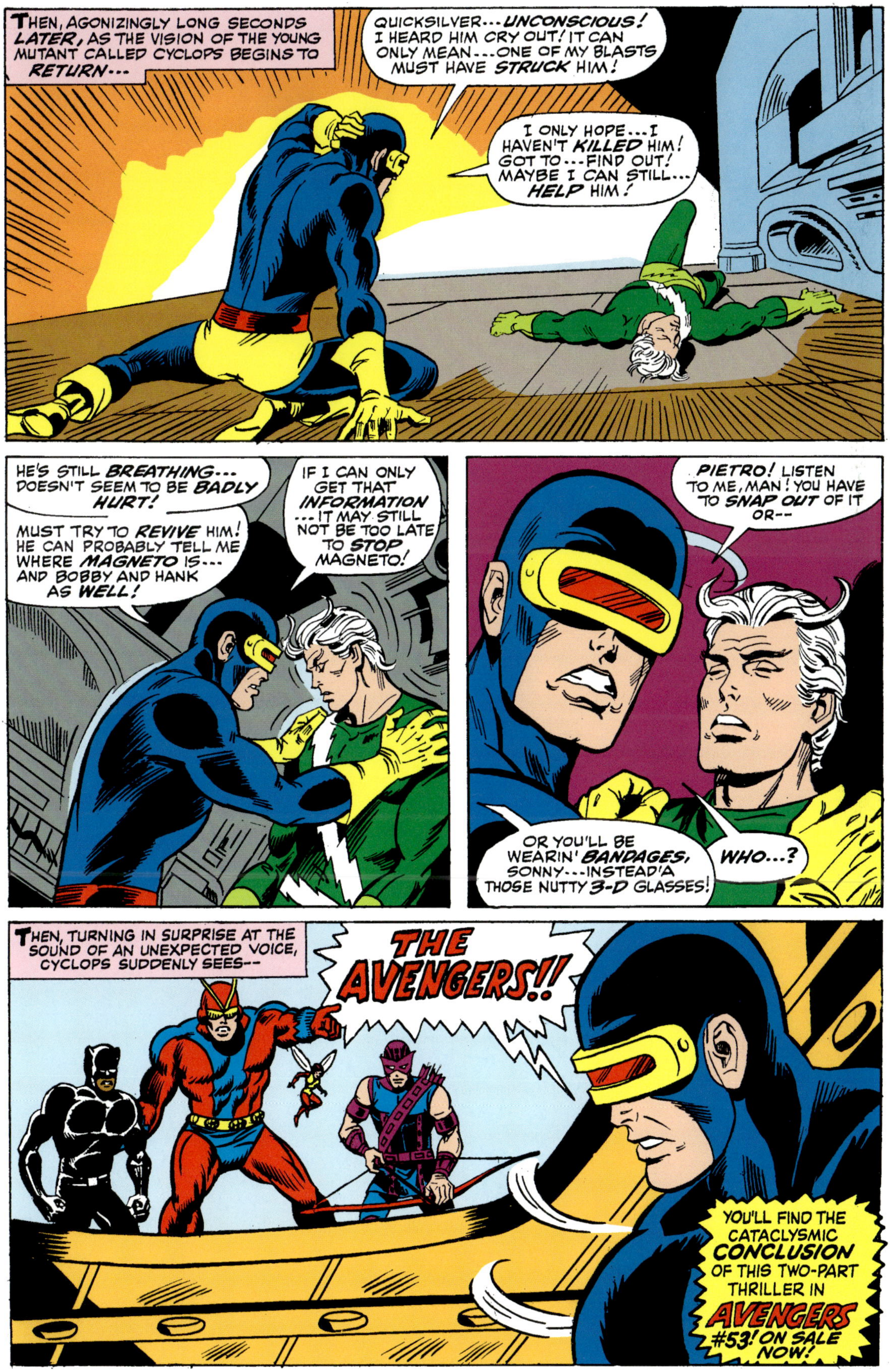
THEN, AGONIZINGLY LONG SECONDS LATER, AS THE VISION OF THE YOUNG MUTANT CALLED CYCLOPS BEGINS TO RETURN...
QUICKSILVER...UNCONSCIOUS! I HEARD HIM CRY OUT! IT CAN ONLY MEAN...ONE OF MY BLASTS MUST HAVE STRUCK HIM!
I ONLY HOPE...I HAVEN'T KILLED HIM! GOT TO...FIND OUT! MAYBE I CAN STILL...HELP HIM!
HE'S STILL BREATHING... DOESN'T SEEM TO BE BADLY HURT!
MUST TRY TO REVIVE HIM! HE CAN PROBABLY TELL ME WHERE MAGNETO IS... AND BOBBY AND HANK AS WELL!
IF I CAN ONLY GET THAT INFORMATION ...IT MAY STILL NOT BE TOO LATE TO STOP MAGNETO!
PIETRO! LISTEN TO ME, MAN! YOU HAVE TO SNAP OUT OF IT OR--
OR YOU'LL BE WEARIN' BANDAGES, SONNY...INSTEAD'A THOSE NUTTY 3-D GLASSES!
WHO...?
THEN, TURNING IN SURPRISE AT THE SOUND OF AN UNEXPECTED VOICE, CYCLOPS SUDDENLY SEES--
THE AVENGERS!!
YOU'LL FIND THE CATACLYSMIC CONCLUSION OF THIS TWO-PART THRILLER IN AVENGERS #53! ON SALE NOW!

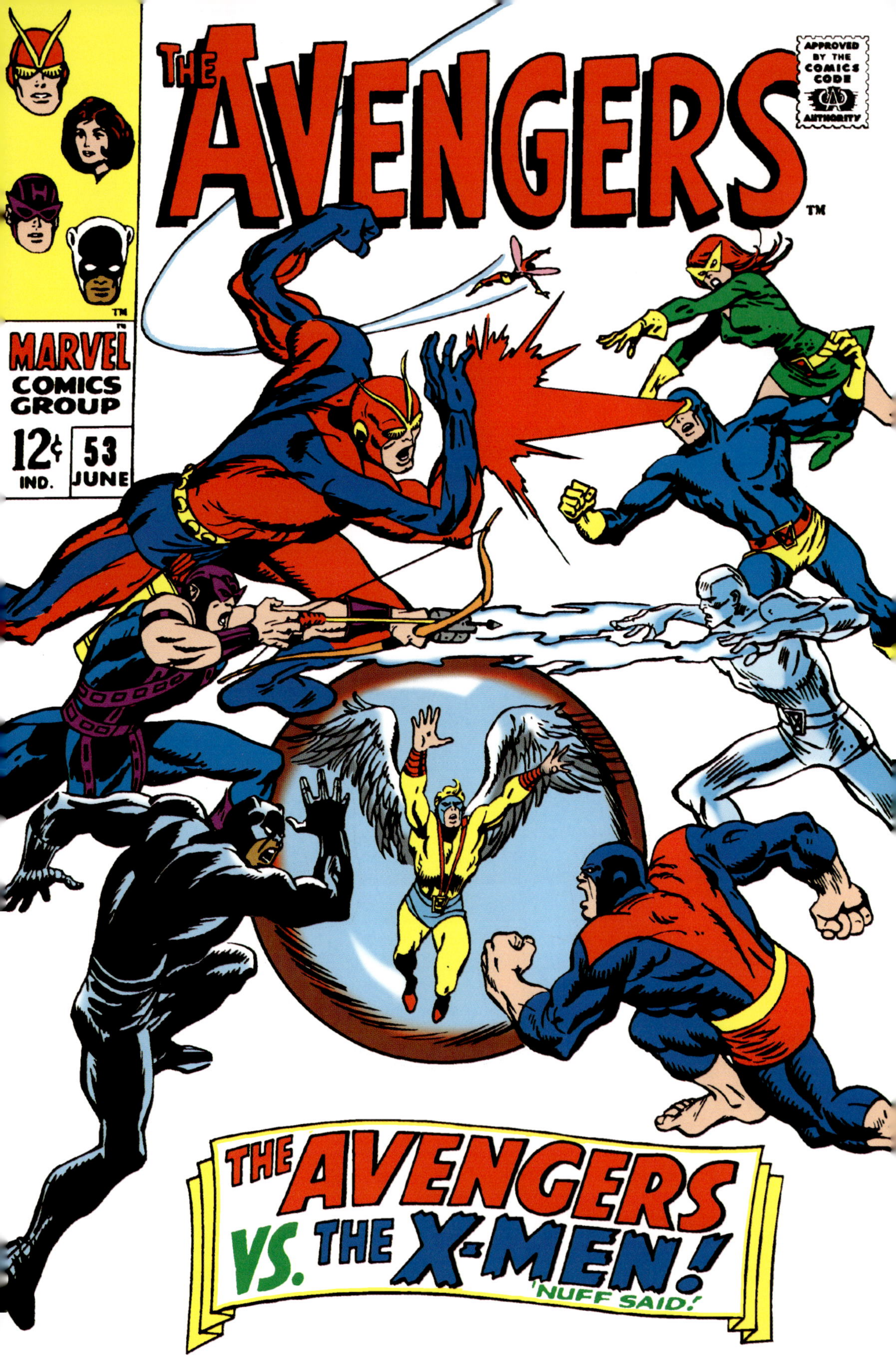
THE AVENGERS
APPROVED BY THE COMICS CODE AUTHORITY
MARVEL COMICS GROUP
12¢ IND.
53 JUNE
THE AVENGERS VS. THE X-MEN!
'NUFF SAID!

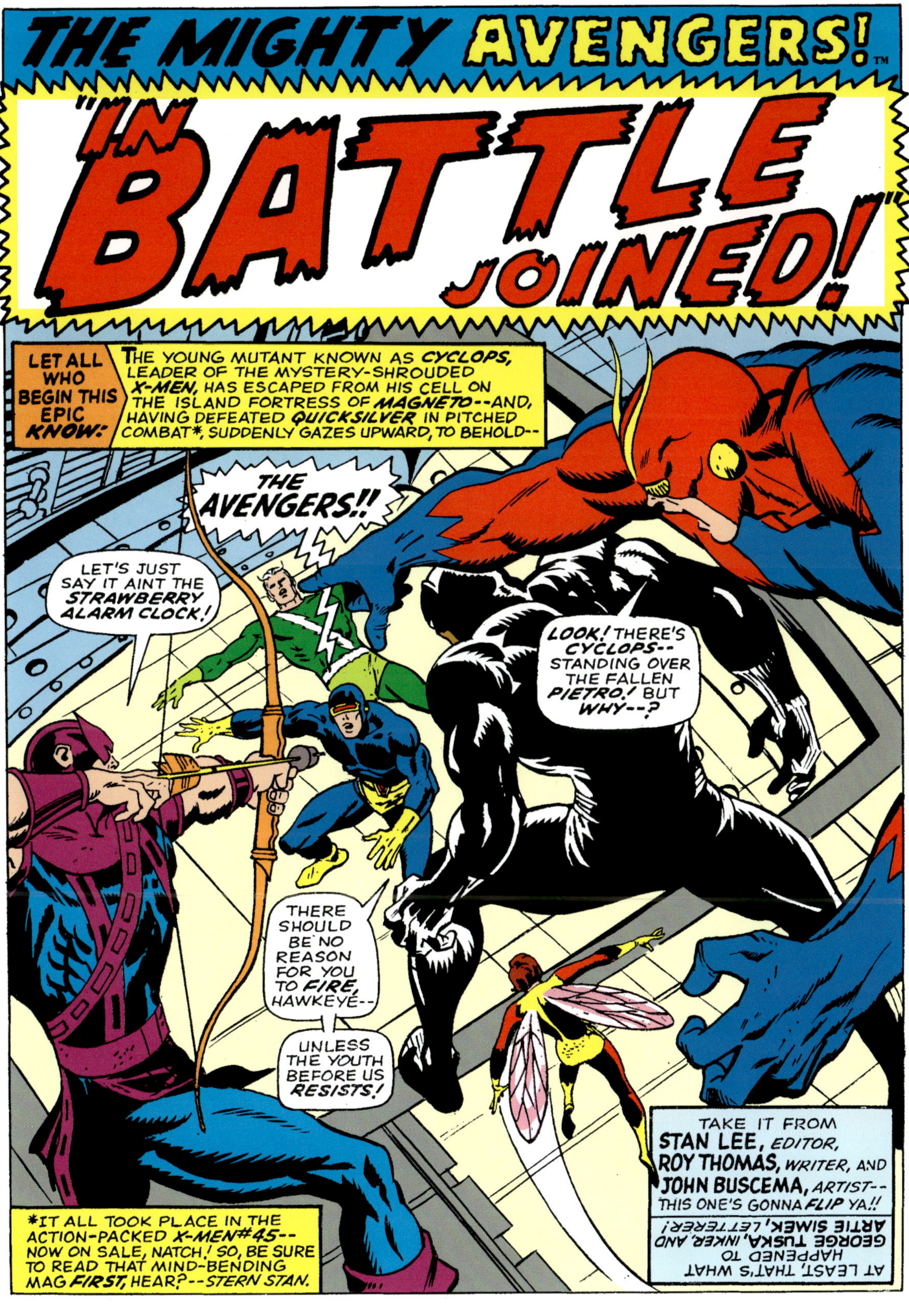
THE MIGHTY AVENGERS!™
"IN BATTLE JOINED!"
LET ALL WHO BEGIN THIS EPIC KNOW:
THE YOUNG MUTANT KNOWN AS CYCLOPS, LEADER OF THE MYSTERY-SHROUDED X-MEN, HAS ESCAPED FROM HIS CELL ON THE ISLAND FORTRESS OF MAGNETO--AND, HAVING DEFEATED QUICKSILVER IN PITCHED COMBAT*, SUDDENLY GAZES UPWARD, TO BEHOLD--
THE AVENGERS!!
LET'S JUST SAY IT AINT THE STRAWBERRY ALARM CLOCK!
LOOK! THERE'S CYCLOPS-- STANDING OVER THE FALLEN PIETRO! BUT WHY--?
THERE SHOULD BE NO REASON FOR YOU TO FIRE, HAWKEYE--
UNLESS THE YOUTH BEFORE US RESISTS!
TAKE IT FROM STAN LEE, EDITOR, ROY THOMAS, WRITER, AND JOHN BUSCEMA, ARTIST-- THIS ONE'S GONNA FLIP YA!!
AT LEAST, THAT'S WHAT HAPPENED TO GEORGE TUSKA, INKER, AND ARTIE SIMEK, LETTERER!
*IT ALL TOOK PLACE IN THE ACTION-PACKED X-MEN #45-- NOW ON SALE, NATCH! SO, BE SURE TO READ THAT MIND-BENDING MAG FIRST, HEAR?--STERN STAN.

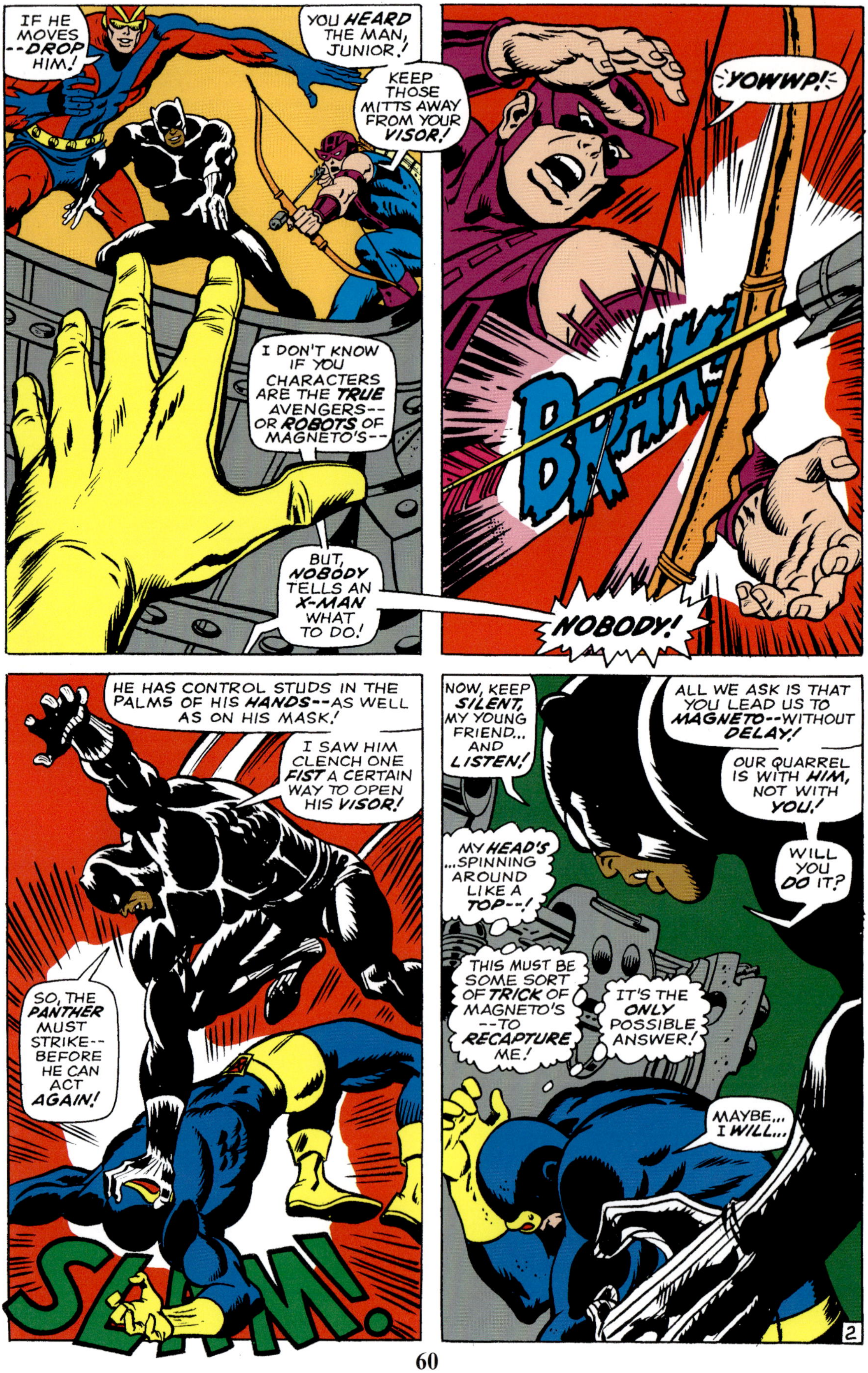
IF HE MOVES --DROP HIM!
YOU HEARD THE MAN, JUNIOR!
KEEP THOSE MITTS AWAY FROM YOUR VISOR!
I DON'T KNOW IF YOU CHARACTERS ARE THE TRUE AVENGERS-- OR ROBOTS OF MAGNETO'S--
BUT, NOBODY TELLS AN X-MAN WHAT TO DO!
YOWWP!
BRAK!
NOBODY!
HE HAS CONTROL STUDS IN THE PALMS OF HIS HANDS--AS WELL AS ON HIS MASK!
I SAW HIM CLENCH ONE FIST A CERTAIN WAY TO OPEN HIS VISOR!
SO, THE PANTHER MUST STRIKE-- BEFORE HE CAN ACT AGAIN!
SLAM!
NOW, KEEP SILENT, MY YOUNG FRIEND... AND LISTEN!
ALL WE ASK IS THAT YOU LEAD US TO MAGNETO--WITHOUT DELAY!
OUR QUARREL IS WITH HIM, NOT WITH YOU!
WILL YOU DO IT?
MY HEAD'S ...SPINNING AROUND LIKE A TOP--!
THIS MUST BE SOME SORT OF TRICK OF MAGNETO'S --TO RECAPTURE ME!
IT'S THE ONLY POSSIBLE ANSWER!
MAYBE... I WILL...
2

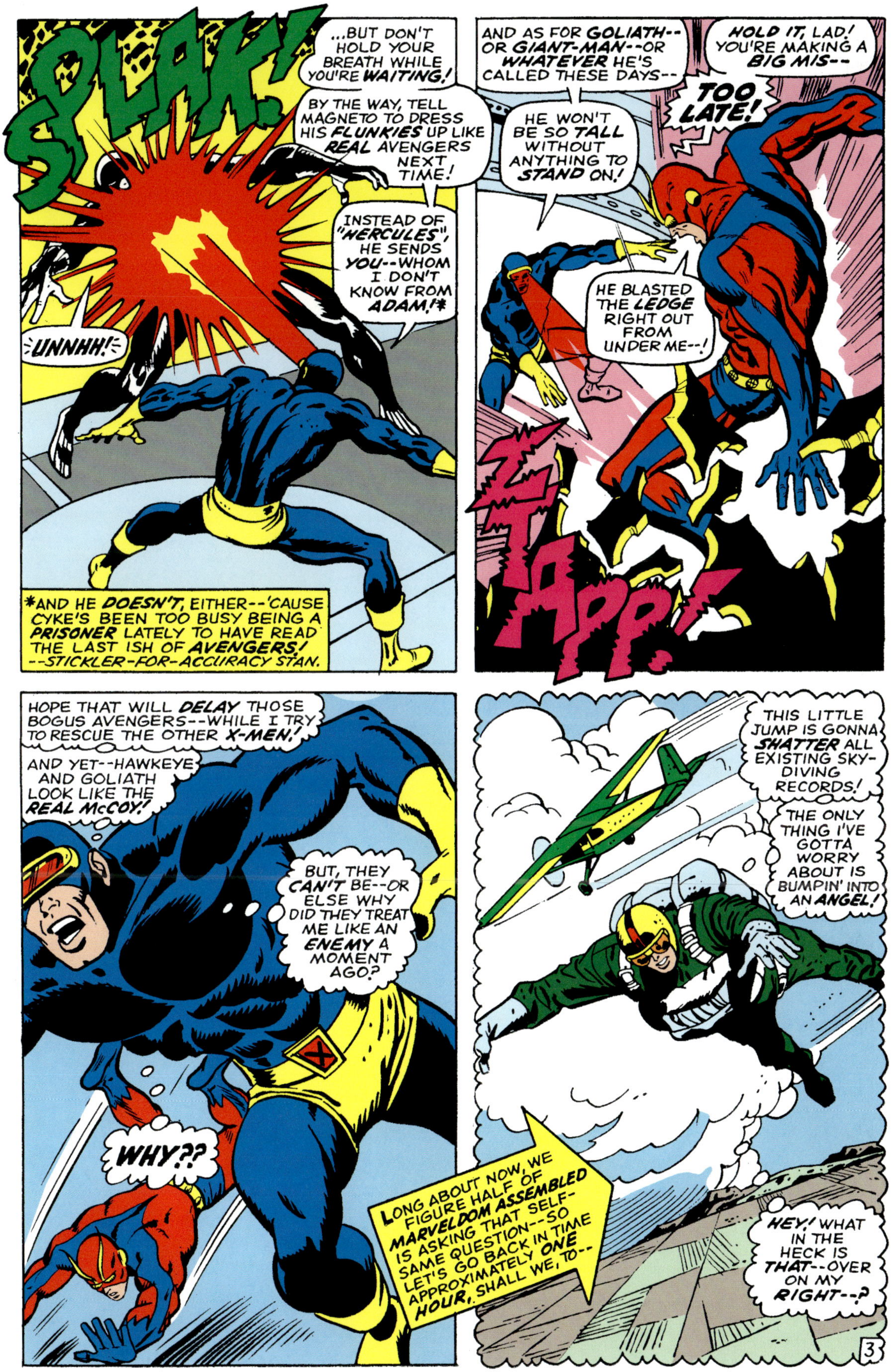
SPLAK!
...BUT DON'T HOLD YOUR BREATH WHILE YOU'RE WAITING!
BY THE WAY, TELL MAGNETO TO DRESS HIS FLUNKIES UP LIKE REAL AVENGERS NEXT TIME!
INSTEAD OF "HERCULES", HE SENDS YOU--WHOM I DON'T KNOW FROM ADAM!*
UNNHH!
*AND HE DOESN'T, EITHER--'CAUSE CYKE'S BEEN TOO BUSY BEING A PRISONER LATELY TO HAVE READ THE LAST ISH OF AVENGERS! --STICKLER-FOR-ACCURACY STAN.
AND AS FOR GOLIATH--OR GIANT-MAN--OR WHATEVER HE'S CALLED THESE DAYS--
HE WON'T BE SO TALL WITHOUT ANYTHING TO STAND ON!
HOLD IT, LAD! YOU'RE MAKING A BIG MIS--
TOO LATE!
HE BLASTED THE LEDGE RIGHT OUT FROM UNDER ME--!
ZTTAPP!
HOPE THAT WILL DELAY THOSE BOGUS AVENGERS--WHILE I TRY TO RESCUE THE OTHER X-MEN!
AND YET--HAWKEYE AND GOLIATH LOOK LIKE THE REAL McCOY!
BUT, THEY CAN'T BE--OR ELSE WHY DID THEY TREAT ME LIKE AN ENEMY A MOMENT AGO?
WHY??
LONG ABOUT NOW, WE FIGURE HALF OF MARVELDOM ASSEMBLED IS ASKING THAT SELF-SAME QUESTION--SO LET'S GO BACK IN TIME APPROXIMATELY ONE HOUR, SHALL WE, TO--
THIS LITTLE JUMP IS GONNA SHATTER ALL EXISTING SKY-DIVING RECORDS!
THE ONLY THING I'VE GOTTA WORRY ABOUT IS BUMPIN' INTO AN ANGEL!
HEY! WHAT IN THE HECK IS THAT--OVER ON MY RIGHT--?
3

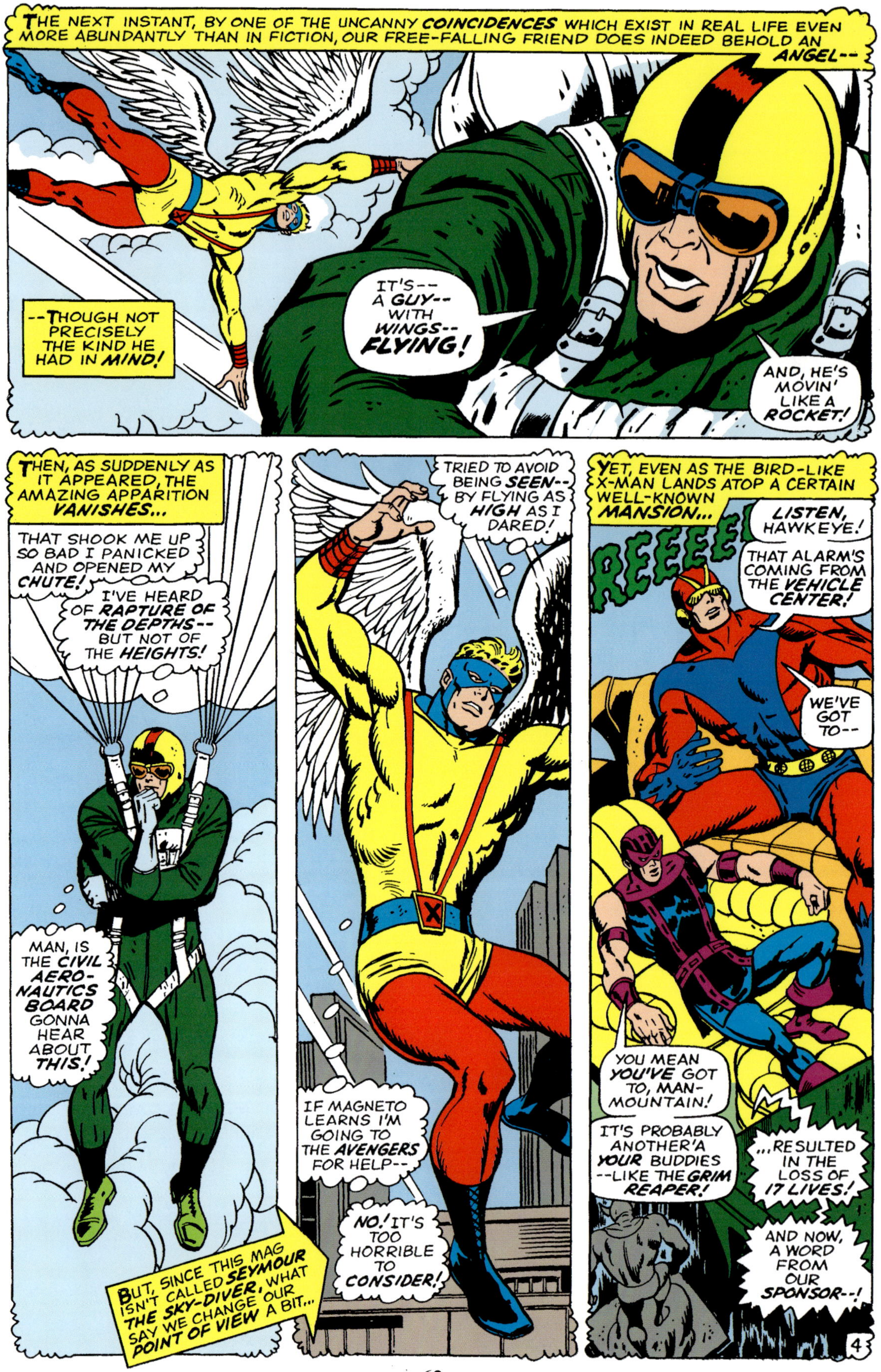

THE NEXT INSTANT, BY ONE OF THE UNCANNY COINCIDENCES WHICH EXIST IN REAL LIFE EVEN MORE ABUNDANTLY THAN IN FICTION, OUR FREE-FALLING FRIEND DOES INDEED BEHOLD AN ANGEL--
--THOUGH NOT PRECISELY THE KIND HE HAD IN MIND!
IT'S-- A GUY-- WITH WINGS-- FLYING!
AND, HE'S MOVIN' LIKE A ROCKET!
THEN, AS SUDDENLY AS IT APPEARED, THE AMAZING APPARITION VANISHES...
THAT SHOOK ME UP SO BAD I PANICKED AND OPENED MY CHUTE!
I'VE HEARD OF RAPTURE OF THE DEPTHS-- BUT NOT OF THE HEIGHTS!
MAN, IS THE CIVIL AERO-NAUTICS BOARD GONNA HEAR ABOUT THIS!
BUT, SINCE THIS MAG ISN'T CALLED SEYMOUR THE SKY-DIVER, WHAT SAY WE CHANGE OUR POINT OF VIEW A BIT...
TRIED TO AVOID BEING SEEN-- BY FLYING AS HIGH AS I DARED!
IF MAGNETO LEARNS I'M GOING TO THE AVENGERS FOR HELP--
NO! IT'S TOO HORRIBLE TO CONSIDER!
YET, EVEN AS THE BIRD-LIKE X-MAN LANDS ATOP A CERTAIN WELL-KNOWN MANSION...
REEEEE
LISTEN, HAWKEYE!
THAT ALARM'S COMING FROM THE VEHICLE CENTER!
WE'VE GOT TO--
YOU MEAN YOU'VE GOT TO, MAN-MOUNTAIN!
IT'S PROBABLY ANOTHER'A YOUR BUDDIES --LIKE THE GRIM REAPER!
...RESULTED IN THE LOSS OF 17 LIVES!
AND NOW, A WORD FROM OUR SPONSOR--!
4

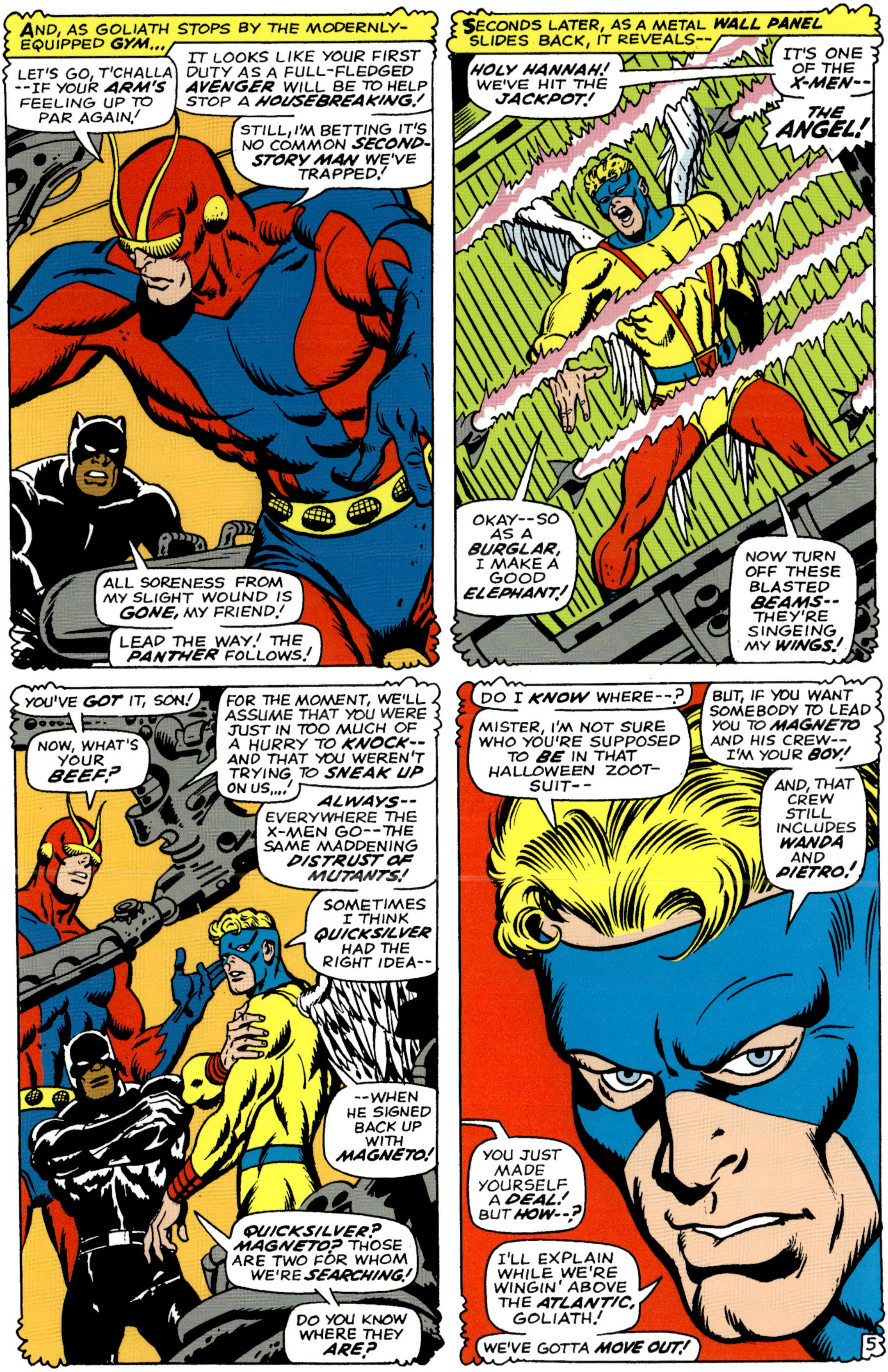
AND, AS GOLIATH STOPS BY THE MODERNLY-EQUIPPED GYM...
LET'S GO, T'CHALLA --IF YOUR ARM'S FEELING UP TO PAR AGAIN!
IT LOOKS LIKE YOUR FIRST DUTY AS A FULL-FLEDGED AVENGER WILL BE TO HELP STOP A HOUSEBREAKING!
STILL, I'M BETTING IT'S NO COMMON SECOND-STORY MAN WE'VE TRAPPED!
ALL SORENESS FROM MY SLIGHT WOUND IS GONE, MY FRIEND!
LEAD THE WAY! THE PANTHER FOLLOWS!
SECONDS LATER, AS A METAL WALL PANEL SLIDES BACK, IT REVEALS--
HOLY HANNAH! WE'VE HIT THE JACKPOT!
IT'S ONE OF THE X-MEN-- THE ANGEL!
OKAY--SO AS A BURGLAR, I MAKE A GOOD ELEPHANT!
NOW TURN OFF THESE BLASTED BEAMS-- THEY'RE SINGEING MY WINGS!
YOU'VE GOT IT, SON!
NOW, WHAT'S YOUR BEEF?
FOR THE MOMENT, WE'LL ASSUME THAT YOU WERE JUST IN TOO MUCH OF A HURRY TO KNOCK-- AND THAT YOU WEREN'T TRYING TO SNEAK UP ON US...!
ALWAYS-- EVERYWHERE THE X-MEN GO--THE SAME MADDENING DISTRUST OF MUTANTS!
SOMETIMES I THINK QUICKSILVER HAD THE RIGHT IDEA--
--WHEN HE SIGNED BACK UP WITH MAGNETO!
QUICKSILVER? MAGNETO? THOSE ARE TWO FOR WHOM WE'RE SEARCHING!
DO YOU KNOW WHERE THEY ARE?
DO I KNOW WHERE--?
MISTER, I'M NOT SURE WHO YOU'RE SUPPOSED TO BE IN THAT HALLOWEEN ZOOT-SUIT--
BUT, IF YOU WANT SOMEBODY TO LEAD YOU TO MAGNETO AND HIS CREW-- I'M YOUR BOY!
AND, THAT CREW STILL INCLUDES WANDA AND PIETRO!
YOU JUST MADE YOURSELF A DEAL! BUT HOW--?
I'LL EXPLAIN WHILE WE'RE WINGIN' ABOVE THE ATLANTIC, GOLIATH!
WE'VE GOTTA MOVE OUT!
5

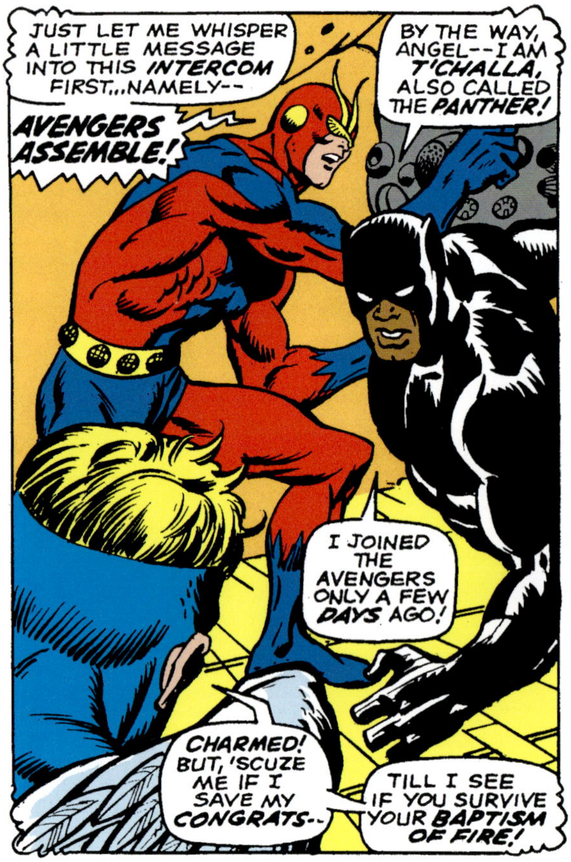
JUST LET ME WHISPER A LITTLE MESSAGE INTO THIS INTERCOM FIRST...NAMELY--
AVENGERS ASSEMBLE!
BY THE WAY, ANGEL--I AM T'CHALLA, ALSO CALLED THE PANTHER!
I JOINED THE AVENGERS ONLY A FEW DAYS AGO!
CHARMED! BUT, 'SCUZE ME IF I SAVE MY CONGRATS--
TILL I SEE IF YOU SURVIVE YOUR BAPTISM OF FIRE!

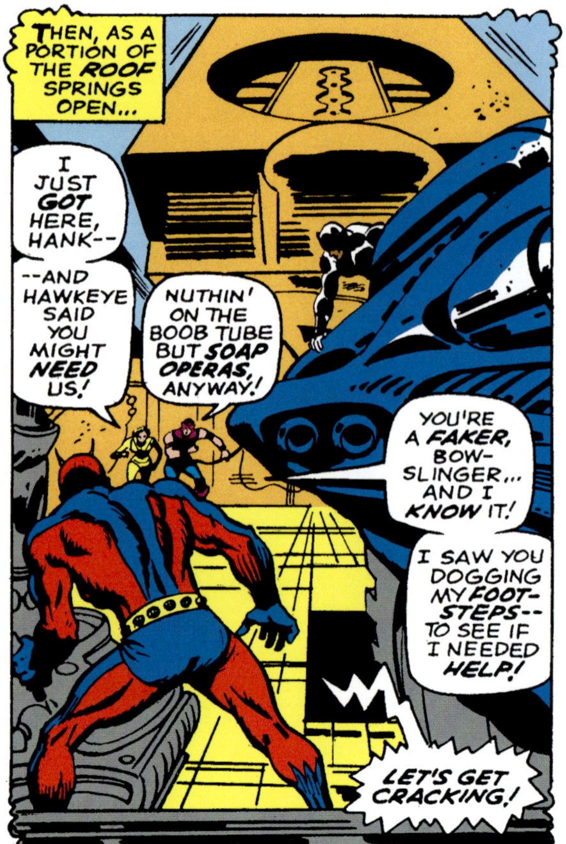
THEN, AS A PORTION OF THE ROOF SPRINGS OPEN...
I JUST GOT HERE, HANK--
--AND HAWKEYE SAID YOU MIGHT NEED US!
NUTHIN' ON THE BOOB TUBE BUT SOAP OPERAS, ANYWAY!
YOU'RE A FAKER, BOW-SLINGER... AND I KNOW IT!
I SAW YOU DOGGING MY FOOT-STEPS--TO SEE IF I NEEDED HELP!
LET'S GET CRACKING!

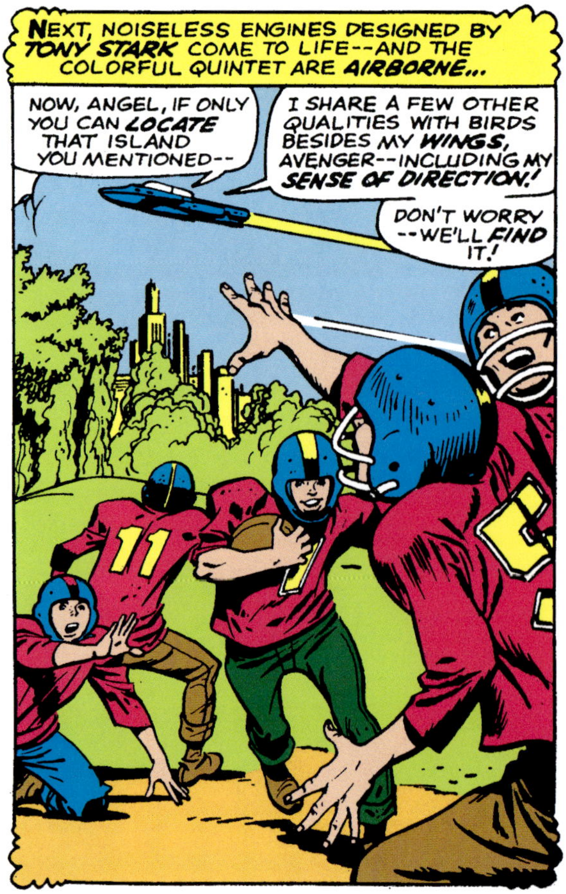
NEXT, NOISELESS ENGINES DESIGNED BY TONY STARK COME TO LIFE--AND THE COLORFUL QUINTET ARE AIRBORNE...
NOW, ANGEL, IF ONLY YOU CAN LOCATE THAT ISLAND YOU MENTIONED--
I SHARE A FEW OTHER QUALITIES WITH BIRDS BESIDES MY WINGS, AVENGER--INCLUDING MY SENSE OF DIRECTION!
DON'T WORRY--WE'LL FIND IT!
11

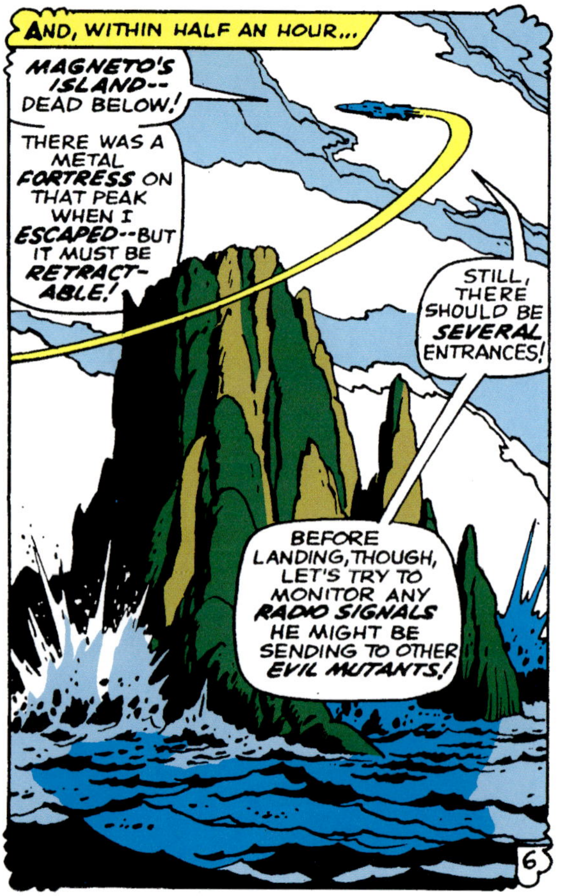
AND, WITHIN HALF AN HOUR...
MAGNETO'S ISLAND--DEAD BELOW!
THERE WAS A METAL FORTRESS ON THAT PEAK WHEN I ESCAPED--BUT IT MUST BE RETRACT-ABLE!
STILL, THERE SHOULD BE SEVERAL ENTRANCES!
BEFORE LANDING, THOUGH, LET'S TRY TO MONITOR ANY RADIO SIGNALS HE MIGHT BE SENDING TO OTHER EVIL MUTANTS!
6

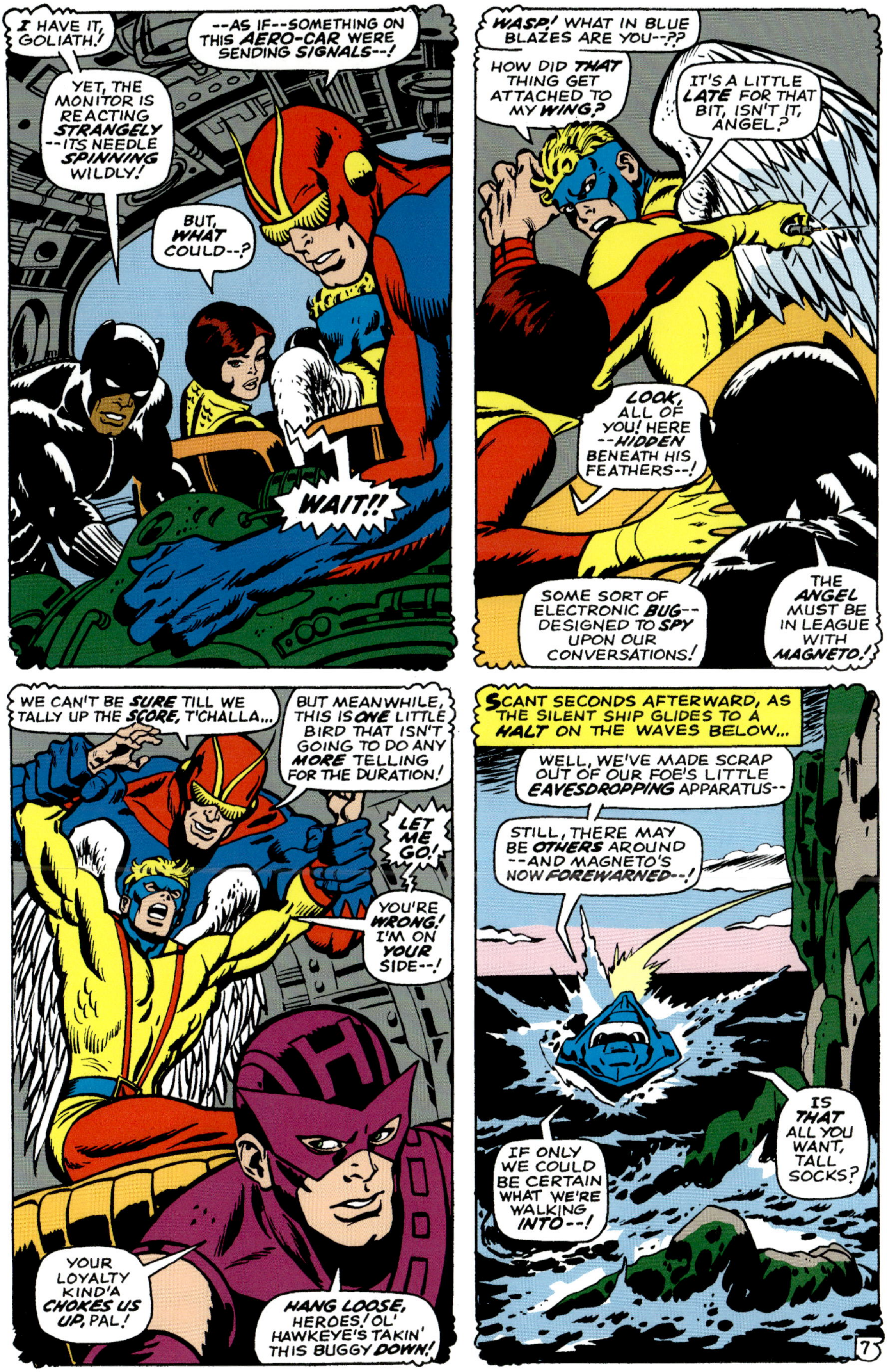
I HAVE IT, GOLIATH.!
--AS IF--SOMETHING ON THIS AERO-CAR WERE SENDING SIGNALS--!
YET, THE MONITOR IS REACTING STRANGELY --ITS NEEDLE SPINNING WILDLY!
BUT, WHAT COULD--?
WAIT!!
WASP! WHAT IN BLUE BLAZES ARE YOU--??
HOW DID THAT THING GET ATTACHED TO MY WING?
IT'S A LITTLE LATE FOR THAT BIT, ISN'T IT, ANGEL?
LOOK, ALL OF YOU! HERE --HIDDEN BENEATH HIS FEATHERS--!
SOME SORT OF ELECTRONIC BUG--DESIGNED TO SPY UPON OUR CONVERSATIONS!
THE ANGEL MUST BE IN LEAGUE WITH MAGNETO!
WE CAN'T BE SURE TILL WE TALLY UP THE SCORE, T'CHALLA...
BUT MEANWHILE, THIS IS ONE LITTLE BIRD THAT ISN'T GOING TO DO ANY MORE TELLING FOR THE DURATION!
LET ME GO!
YOU'RE WRONG! I'M ON YOUR SIDE--!
YOUR LOYALTY KIND'A CHOKES US UP, PAL!
HANG LOOSE, HEROES! OL' HAWKEYE'S TAKIN' THIS BUGGY DOWN!
SCANT SECONDS AFTERWARD, AS THE SILENT SHIP GLIDES TO A HALT ON THE WAVES BELOW...
WELL, WE'VE MADE SCRAP OUT OF OUR FOE'S LITTLE EAVESDROPPING APPARATUS--
STILL, THERE MAY BE OTHERS AROUND --AND MAGNETO'S NOW FOREWARNED--!
IF ONLY WE COULD BE CERTAIN WHAT WE'RE WALKING INTO--!
IS THAT ALL YOU WANT, TALL SOCKS?
7

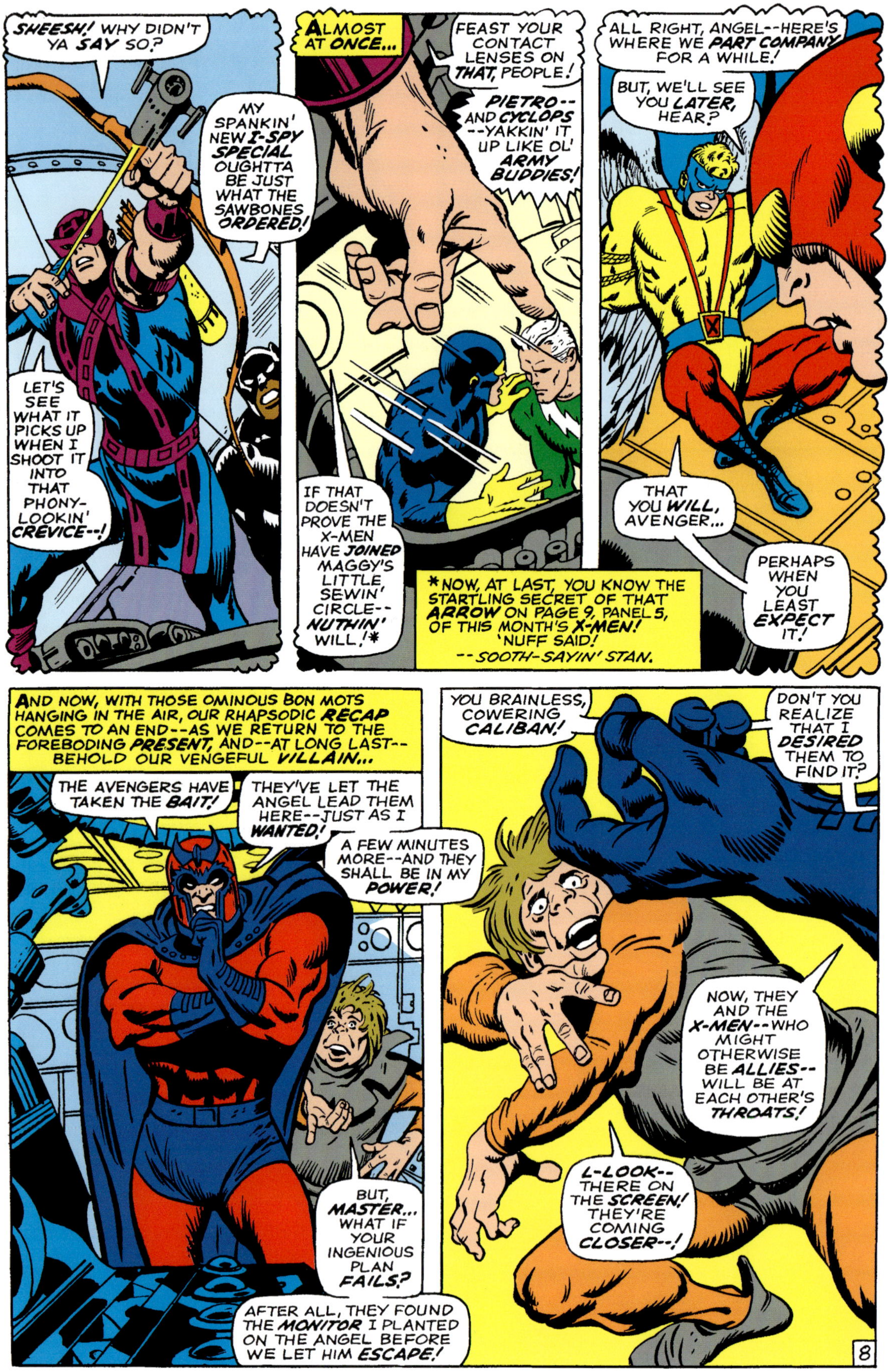
SHEESH! WHY DIDN'T YA SAY SO?
MY SPANKIN' NEW I-SPY SPECIAL OUGHTTA BE JUST WHAT THE SAWBONES ORDERED!
LET'S SEE WHAT IT PICKS UP WHEN I SHOOT IT INTO THAT PHONY-LOOKIN' CREVICE--!
ALMOST AT ONCE...
FEAST YOUR CONTACT LENSES ON THAT, PEOPLE!
PIETRO--AND CYCLOPS--YAKKIN' IT UP LIKE OL' ARMY BUDDIES!
IF THAT DOESN'T PROVE THE X-MEN HAVE JOINED MAGGY'S LITTLE SEWIN' CIRCLE--NUTHIN' WILL!*
*NOW, AT LAST, YOU KNOW THE STARTLING SECRET OF THAT ARROW ON PAGE 9, PANEL 5, OF THIS MONTH'S X-MEN! 'NUFF SAID! --SOOTH-SAYIN' STAN.
ALL RIGHT, ANGEL--HERE'S WHERE WE PART COMPANY FOR A WHILE!
BUT, WE'LL SEE YOU LATER, HEAR?
THAT YOU WILL, AVENGER...
PERHAPS WHEN YOU LEAST EXPECT IT!
AND NOW, WITH THOSE OMINOUS BON MOTS HANGING IN THE AIR, OUR RHAPSODIC RECAP COMES TO AN END--AS WE RETURN TO THE FOREBODING PRESENT, AND--AT LONG LAST--BEHOLD OUR VENGEFUL VILLAIN...
THE AVENGERS HAVE TAKEN THE BAIT!
THEY'VE LET THE ANGEL LEAD THEM HERE--JUST AS I WANTED!
A FEW MINUTES MORE--AND THEY SHALL BE IN MY POWER!
BUT, MASTER... WHAT IF YOUR INGENIOUS PLAN FAILS?
AFTER ALL, THEY FOUND THE MONITOR I PLANTED ON THE ANGEL BEFORE WE LET HIM ESCAPE!
YOU BRAINLESS, COWERING CALIBAN!
DON'T YOU REALIZE THAT I DESIRED THEM TO FIND IT?
NOW, THEY AND THE X-MEN--WHO MIGHT OTHERWISE BE ALLIES--WILL BE AT EACH OTHER'S THROATS!
L-LOOK--THERE ON THE SCREEN! THEY'RE COMING CLOSER--!
8

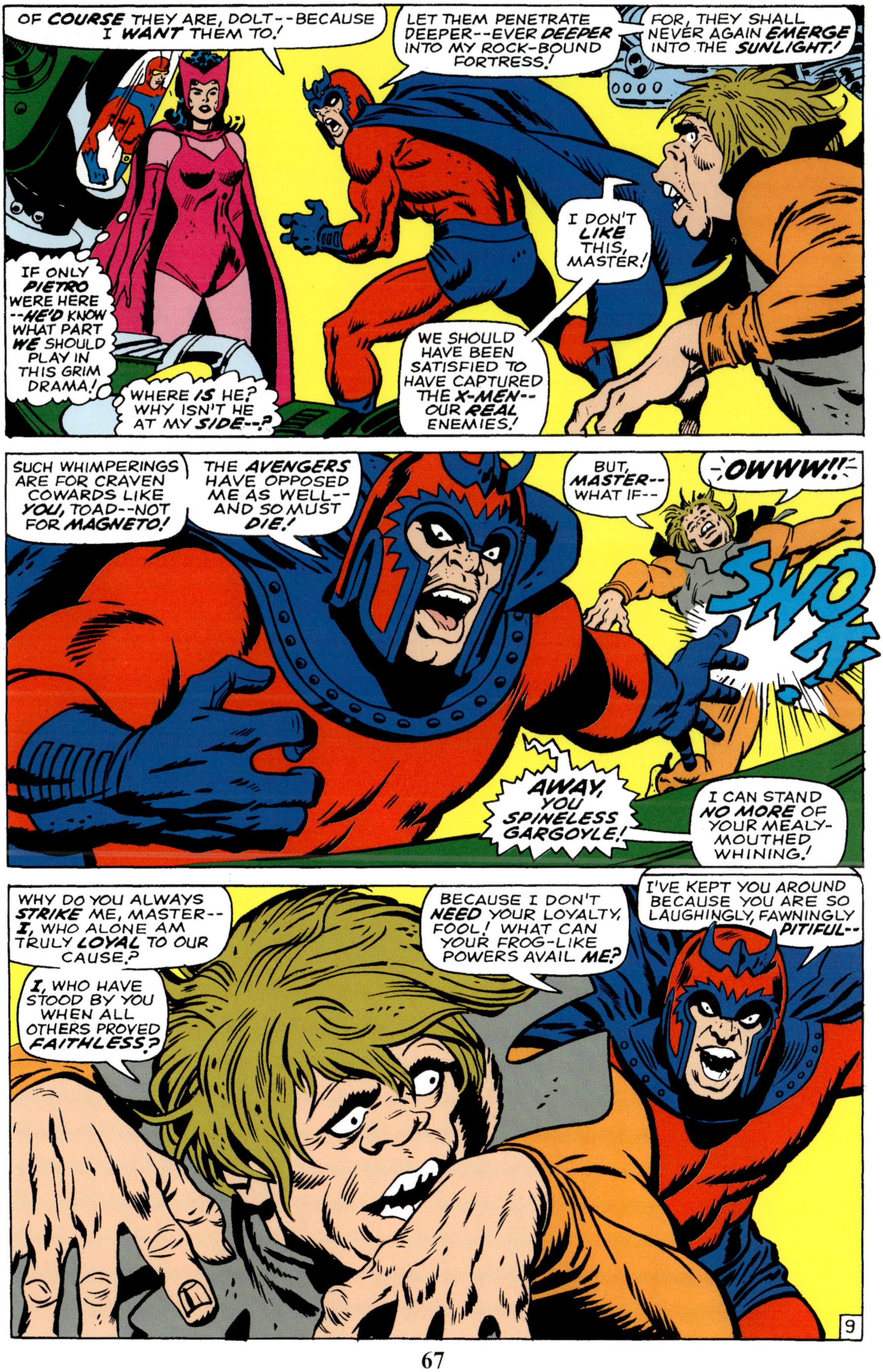
OF COURSE THEY ARE, DOLT--BECAUSE I WANT THEM TO!
LET THEM PENETRATE DEEPER--EVER DEEPER INTO MY ROCK-BOUND FORTRESS!
FOR, THEY SHALL NEVER AGAIN EMERGE INTO THE SUNLIGHT!
IF ONLY PIETRO WERE HERE --HE'D KNOW WHAT PART WE SHOULD PLAY IN THIS GRIM DRAMA!
WHERE IS HE? WHY ISN'T HE AT MY SIDE--?
I DON'T LIKE THIS, MASTER!
WE SHOULD HAVE BEEN SATISFIED TO HAVE CAPTURED THE X-MEN-- OUR REAL ENEMIES!
SUCH WHIMPERINGS ARE FOR CRAVEN COWARDS LIKE YOU, TOAD--NOT FOR MAGNETO!
THE AVENGERS HAVE OPPOSED ME AS WELL-- AND SO MUST DIE!
BUT, MASTER-- WHAT IF--
OWWW!!
SWOK!
AWAY, YOU SPINELESS GARGOYLE!
I CAN STAND NO MORE OF YOUR MEALY-MOUTHED WHINING!
WHY DO YOU ALWAYS STRIKE ME, MASTER-- I, WHO ALONE AM TRULY LOYAL TO OUR CAUSE?
I, WHO HAVE STOOD BY YOU WHEN ALL OTHERS PROVED FAITHLESS?
BECAUSE I DON'T NEED YOUR LOYALTY, FOOL! WHAT CAN YOUR FROG-LIKE POWERS AVAIL ME?
I'VE KEPT YOU AROUND BECAUSE YOU ARE SO LAUGHINGLY, FAWNINGLY PITIFUL--
9

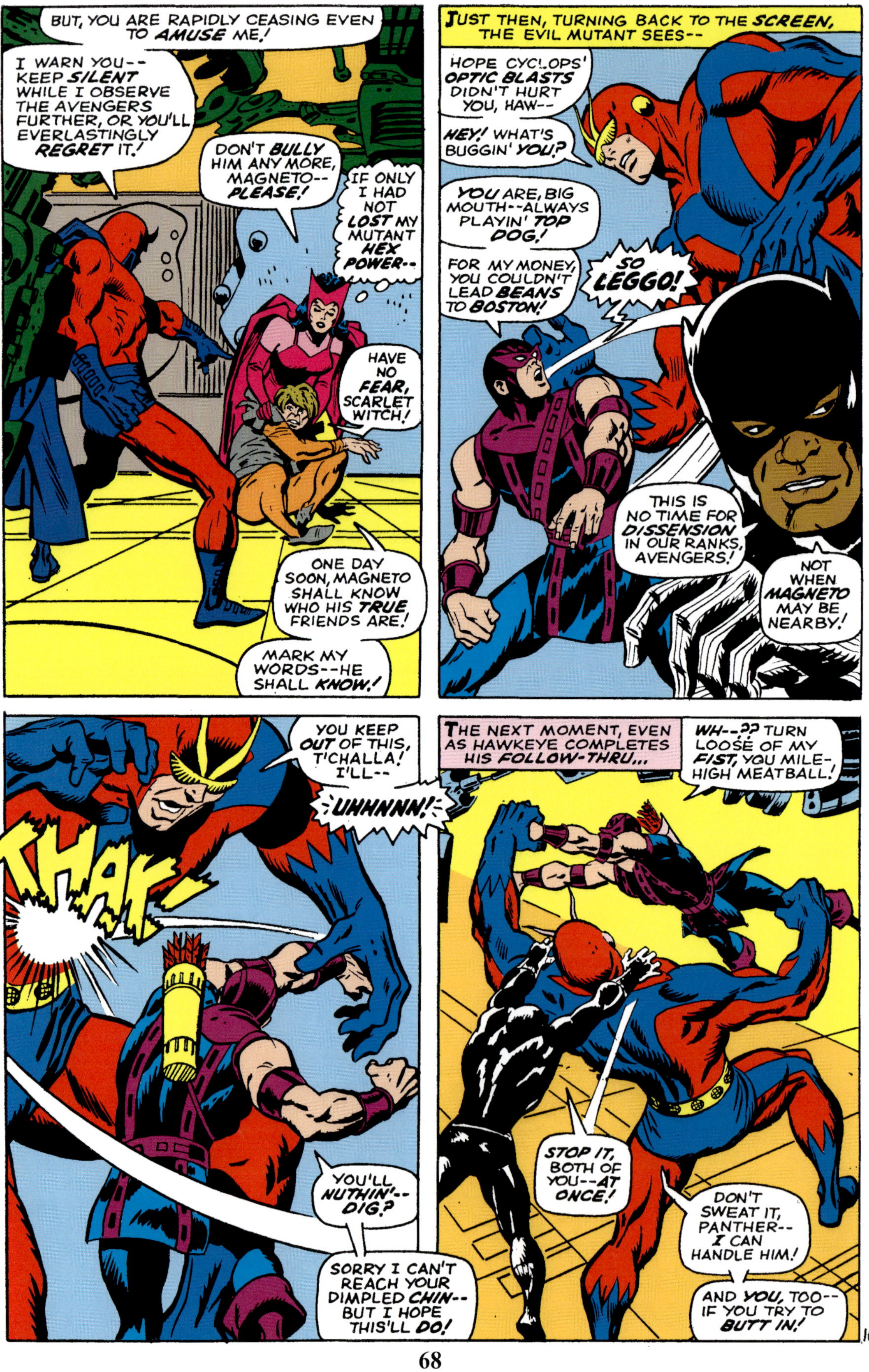

BUT, YOU ARE RAPIDLY CEASING EVEN TO AMUSE ME!
I WARN YOU-- KEEP SILENT WHILE I OBSERVE THE AVENGERS FURTHER, OR YOU'LL EVERLASTINGLY REGRET IT!
DON'T BULLY HIM ANY MORE, MAGNETO-- PLEASE!
IF ONLY I HAD NOT LOST MY MUTANT HEX POWER--
HAVE NO FEAR, SCARLET WITCH!
ONE DAY SOON, MAGNETO SHALL KNOW WHO HIS TRUE FRIENDS ARE!
MARK MY WORDS--HE SHALL KNOW!
JUST THEN, TURNING BACK TO THE SCREEN, THE EVIL MUTANT SEES--
HOPE CYCLOPS' OPTIC BLASTS DIDN'T HURT YOU, HAW--
HEY! WHAT'S BUGGIN' YOU?
YOU ARE, BIG MOUTH--ALWAYS PLAYIN' TOP DOG!
FOR MY MONEY, YOU COULDN'T LEAD BEANS TO BOSTON!
SO LEGGO!
THIS IS NO TIME FOR DISSENSION IN OUR RANKS, AVENGERS!
NOT WHEN MAGNETO MAY BE NEARBY!
YOU KEEP OUT OF THIS, T'CHALLA! I'LL--
UHHNNN!
THAK!
YOU'LL NUTHIN'-- DIG?
SORRY I CAN'T REACH YOUR DIMPLED CHIN-- BUT I HOPE THIS'LL DO!
THE NEXT MOMENT, EVEN AS HAWKEYE COMPLETES HIS FOLLOW-THRU...
WH--?? TURN LOOSE OF MY FIST, YOU MILE-HIGH MEATBALL!
STOP IT, BOTH OF YOU--AT ONCE!
DON'T SWEAT IT, PANTHER-- I CAN HANDLE HIM!
AND YOU, TOO-- IF YOU TRY TO BUTT IN!
10.

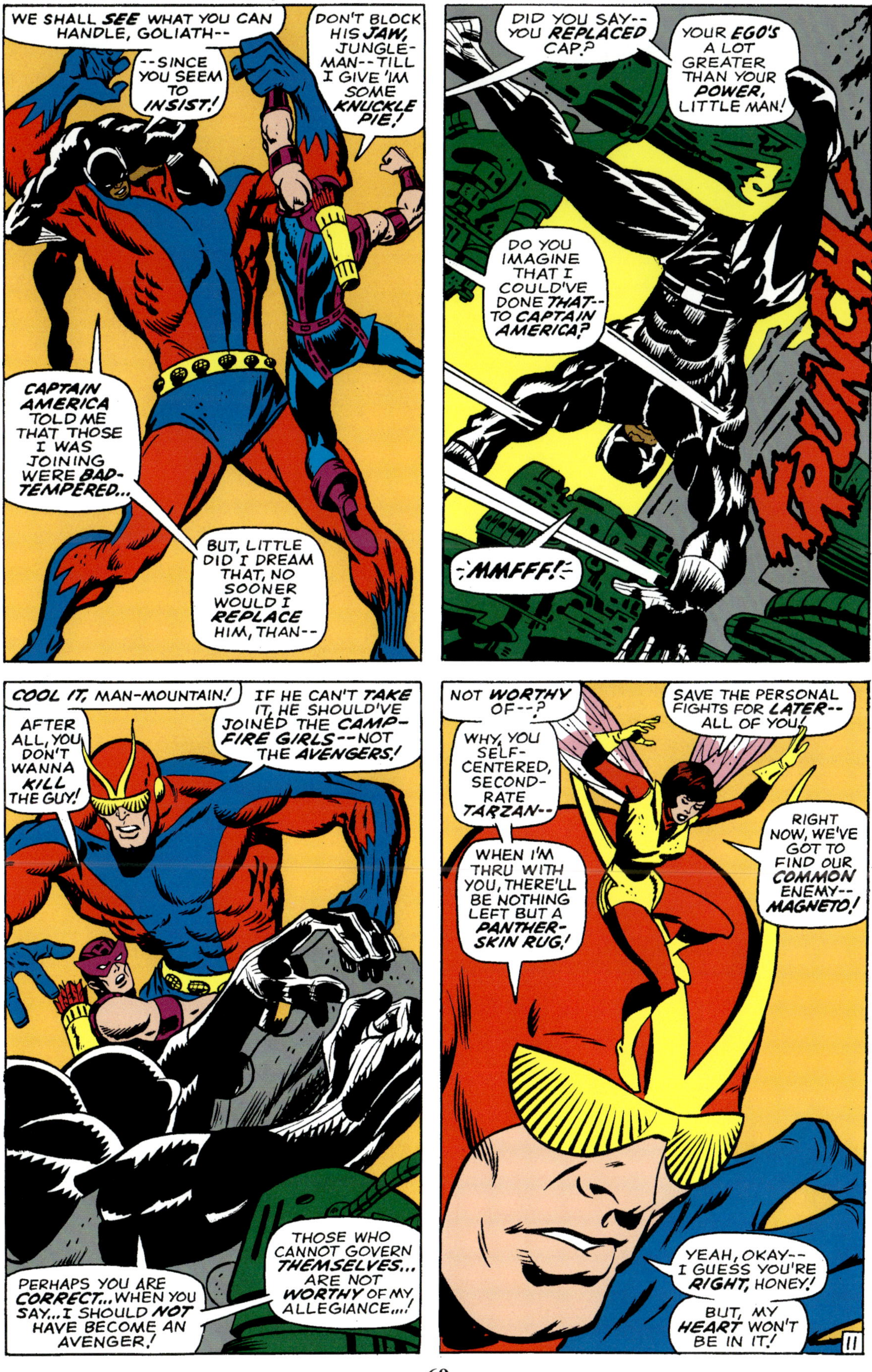

WE SHALL SEE WHAT YOU CAN HANDLE, GOLIATH--
--SINCE YOU SEEM TO INSIST!
DON'T BLOCK HIS JAW, JUNGLE-MAN--TILL I GIVE 'IM SOME KNUCKLE PIE!
CAPTAIN AMERICA TOLD ME THAT THOSE I WAS JOINING WERE BAD-TEMPERED...
BUT, LITTLE DID I DREAM THAT, NO SOONER WOULD I REPLACE HIM, THAN--
DID YOU SAY--YOU REPLACED CAP?
YOUR EGO'S A LOT GREATER THAN YOUR POWER, LITTLE MAN!
DO YOU IMAGINE THAT I COULD'VE DONE THAT--TO CAPTAIN AMERICA?
KRUNCH!
MMFFF!
COOL IT, MAN-MOUNTAIN!
AFTER ALL, YOU DON'T WANNA KILL THE GUY!
IF HE CAN'T TAKE IT, HE SHOULD'VE JOINED THE CAMP-FIRE GIRLS--NOT THE AVENGERS!
PERHAPS YOU ARE CORRECT...WHEN YOU SAY...I SHOULD NOT HAVE BECOME AN AVENGER!
THOSE WHO CANNOT GOVERN THEMSELVES... ARE NOT WORTHY OF MY ALLEGIANCE....!
NOT WORTHY OF--?
WHY, YOU SELF-CENTERED, SECOND-RATE TARZAN--
WHEN I'M THRU WITH YOU, THERE'LL BE NOTHING LEFT BUT A PANTHER-SKIN RUG!
SAVE THE PERSONAL FIGHTS FOR LATER--ALL OF YOU!
RIGHT NOW, WE'VE GOT TO FIND OUR COMMON ENEMY--MAGNETO!
YEAH, OKAY--I GUESS YOU'RE RIGHT, HONEY!
BUT, MY HEART WON'T BE IN IT!
11

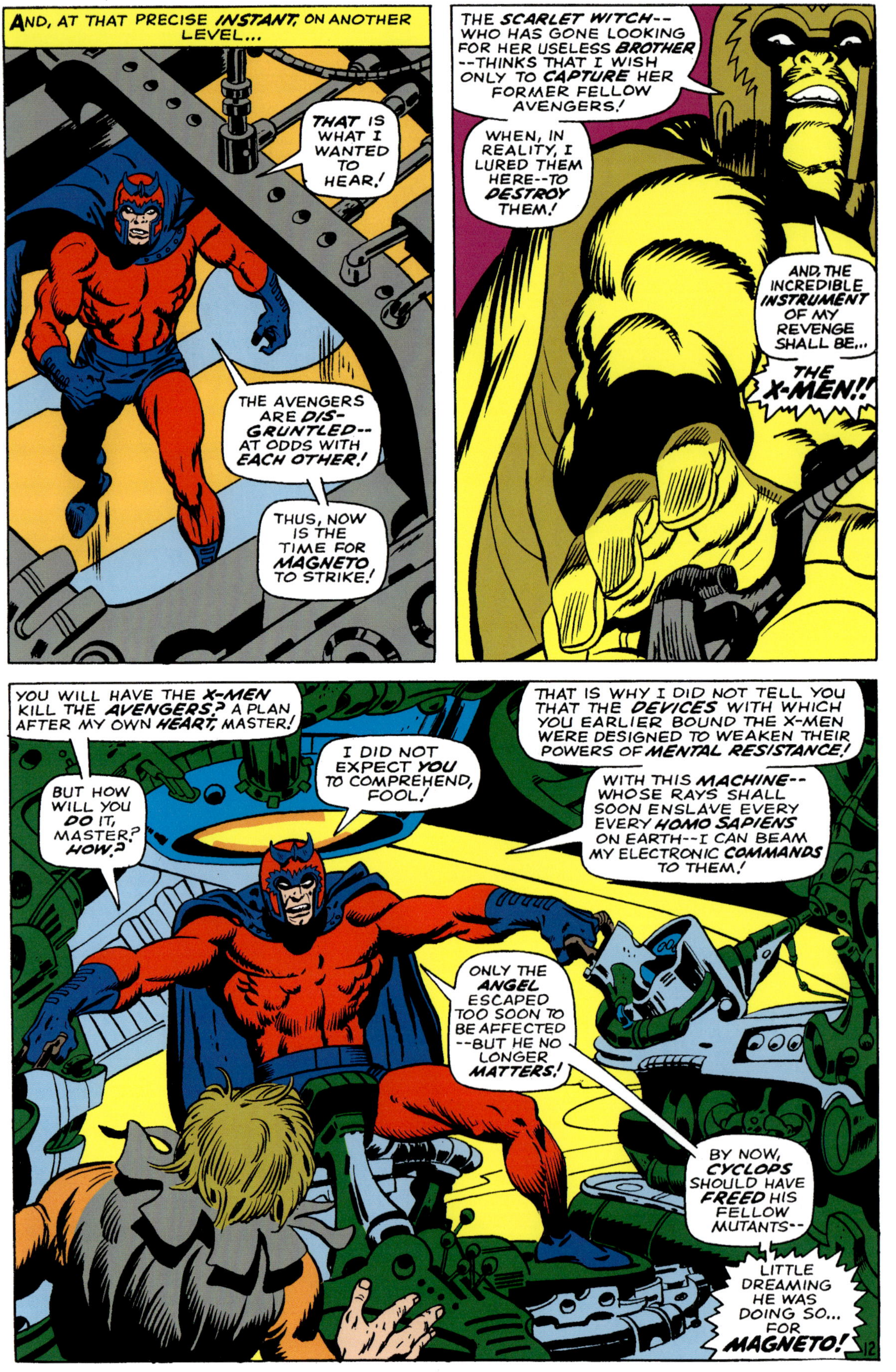
AND, AT THAT PRECISE INSTANT, ON ANOTHER LEVEL...
THAT IS WHAT I WANTED TO HEAR!
THE AVENGERS ARE DIS-GRUNTLED--AT ODDS WITH EACH OTHER!
THUS, NOW IS THE TIME FOR MAGNETO TO STRIKE!
THE SCARLET WITCH--WHO HAS GONE LOOKING FOR HER USELESS BROTHER--THINKS THAT I WISH ONLY TO CAPTURE HER FORMER FELLOW AVENGERS!
WHEN, IN REALITY, I LURED THEM HERE--TO DESTROY THEM!
AND, THE INCREDIBLE INSTRUMENT OF MY REVENGE SHALL BE...
THE X-MEN!!
YOU WILL HAVE THE X-MEN KILL THE AVENGERS? A PLAN AFTER MY OWN HEART, MASTER!
BUT HOW WILL YOU DO IT, MASTER? HOW?
I DID NOT EXPECT YOU TO COMPREHEND, FOOL!
THAT IS WHY I DID NOT TELL YOU THAT THE DEVICES WITH WHICH YOU EARLIER BOUND THE X-MEN WERE DESIGNED TO WEAKEN THEIR POWERS OF MENTAL RESISTANCE!
WITH THIS MACHINE--WHOSE RAYS SHALL SOON ENSLAVE EVERY EVERY HOMO SAPIENS ON EARTH--I CAN BEAM MY ELECTRONIC COMMANDS TO THEM!
ONLY THE ANGEL ESCAPED TOO SOON TO BE AFFECTED--BUT HE NO LONGER MATTERS!
BY NOW, CYCLOPS SHOULD HAVE FREED HIS FELLOW MUTANTS--
LITTLE DREAMING HE WAS DOING SO... FOR MAGNETO!
12

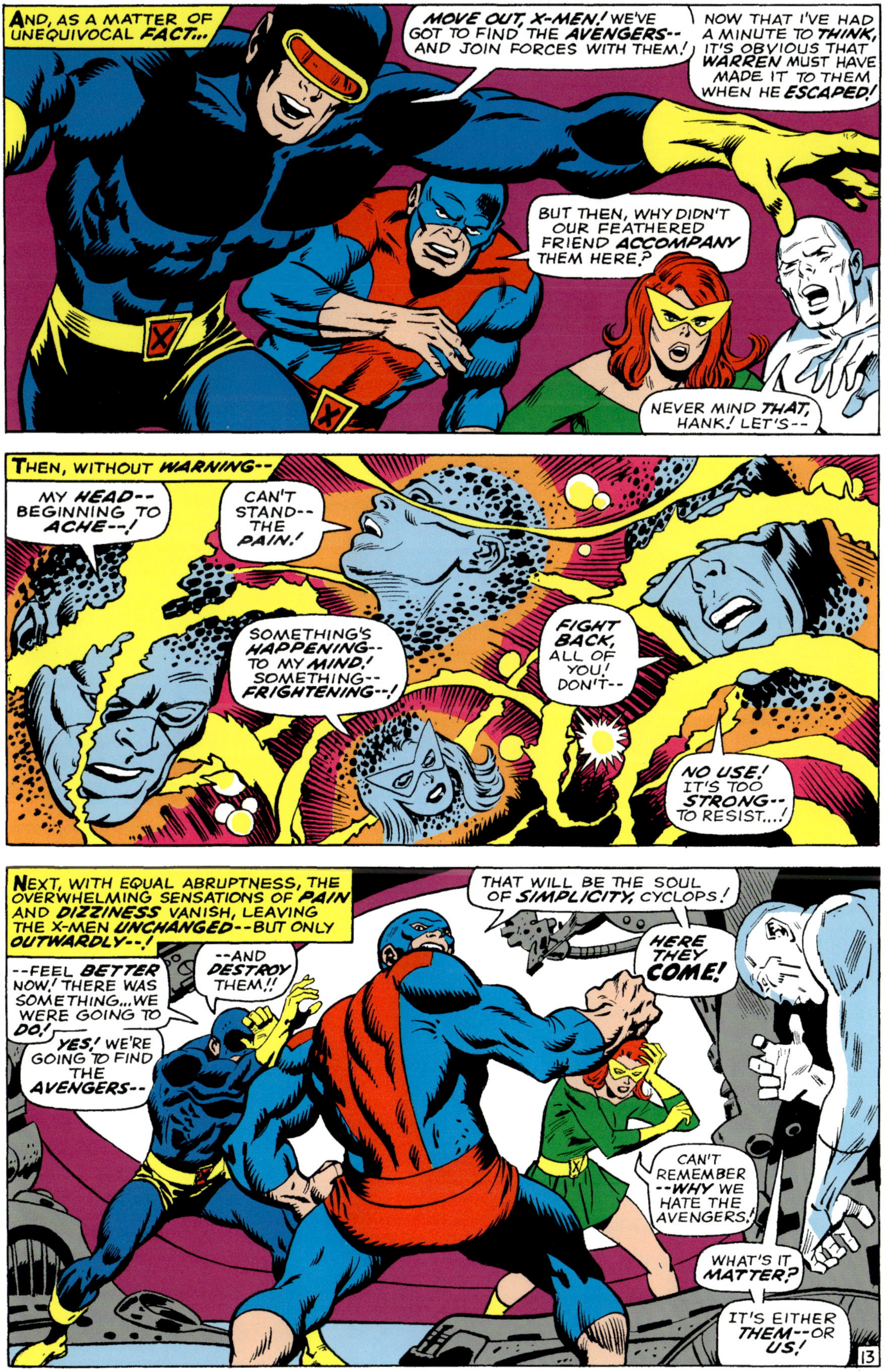

AND, AS A MATTER OF UNEQUIVOCAL FACT...
MOVE OUT, X-MEN! WE'VE GOT TO FIND THE AVENGERS-- AND JOIN FORCES WITH THEM!
NOW THAT I'VE HAD A MINUTE TO THINK, IT'S OBVIOUS THAT WARREN MUST HAVE MADE IT TO THEM WHEN HE ESCAPED!
BUT THEN, WHY DIDN'T OUR FEATHERED FRIEND ACCOMPANY THEM HERE?
NEVER MIND THAT, HANK! LET'S--
THEN, WITHOUT WARNING--
MY HEAD-- BEGINNING TO ACHE--!
CAN'T STAND-- THE PAIN!
SOMETHING'S HAPPENING-- TO MY MIND! SOMETHING-- FRIGHTENING--!
FIGHT BACK, ALL OF YOU! DON'T--
NO USE! IT'S TOO STRONG-- TO RESIST...!
NEXT, WITH EQUAL ABRUPTNESS, THE OVERWHELMING SENSATIONS OF PAIN AND DIZZINESS VANISH, LEAVING THE X-MEN UNCHANGED--BUT ONLY OUTWARDLY--!
--FEEL BETTER NOW! THERE WAS SOMETHING...WE WERE GOING TO DO!
--AND DESTROY THEM!!
YES! WE'RE GOING TO FIND THE AVENGERS--
THAT WILL BE THE SOUL OF SIMPLICITY, CYCLOPS!
HERE THEY COME!
CAN'T REMEMBER --WHY WE HATE THE AVENGERS!
WHAT'S IT MATTER?
IT'S EITHER THEM--OR US!
13

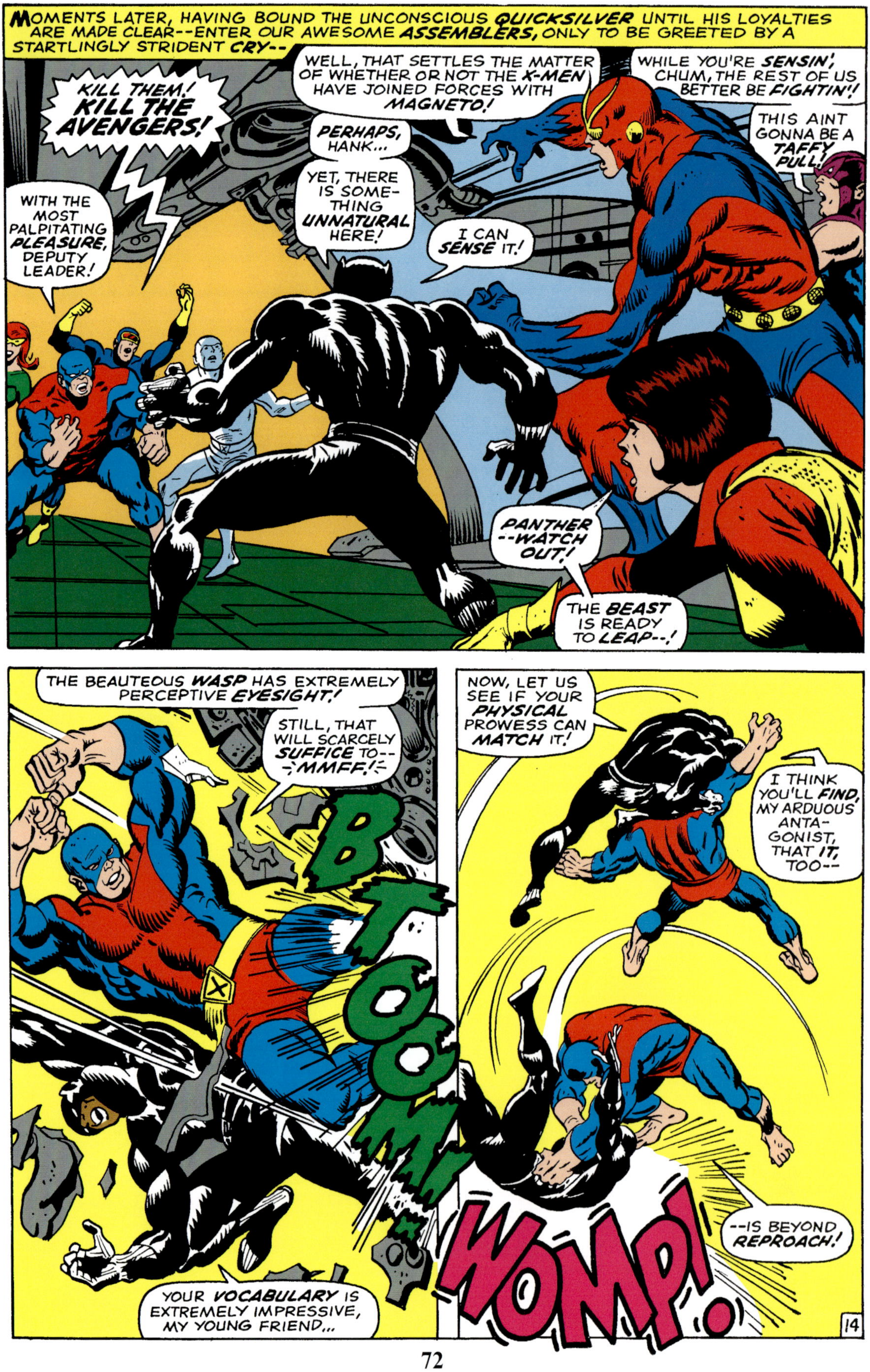
MOMENTS LATER, HAVING BOUND THE UNCONSCIOUS QUICKSILVER UNTIL HIS LOYALTIES ARE MADE CLEAR--ENTER OUR AWESOME ASSEMBLERS, ONLY TO BE GREETED BY A STARTLINGLY STRIDENT CRY--
KILL THEM! KILL THE AVENGERS!
WITH THE MOST PALPITATING PLEASURE, DEPUTY LEADER!
WELL, THAT SETTLES THE MATTER OF WHETHER OR NOT THE X-MEN HAVE JOINED FORCES WITH MAGNETO!
PERHAPS, HANK...
YET, THERE IS SOME-THING UNNATURAL HERE!
I CAN SENSE IT!
WHILE YOU'RE SENSIN', CHUM, THE REST OF US BETTER BE FIGHTIN'!
THIS AINT GONNA BE A TAFFY PULL!
PANTHER --WATCH OUT!
THE BEAST IS READY TO LEAP--!
THE BEAUTEOUS WASP HAS EXTREMELY PERCEPTIVE EYESIGHT!
STILL, THAT WILL SCARCELY SUFFICE TO-- -MMFF!-
BTOOM!
YOUR VOCABULARY IS EXTREMELY IMPRESSIVE, MY YOUNG FRIEND,..
NOW, LET US SEE IF YOUR PHYSICAL PROWESS CAN MATCH IT!
I THINK YOU'LL FIND, MY ARDUOUS ANTA-GONIST, THAT IT, TOO--
--IS BEYOND REPROACH!
WOMP!
14

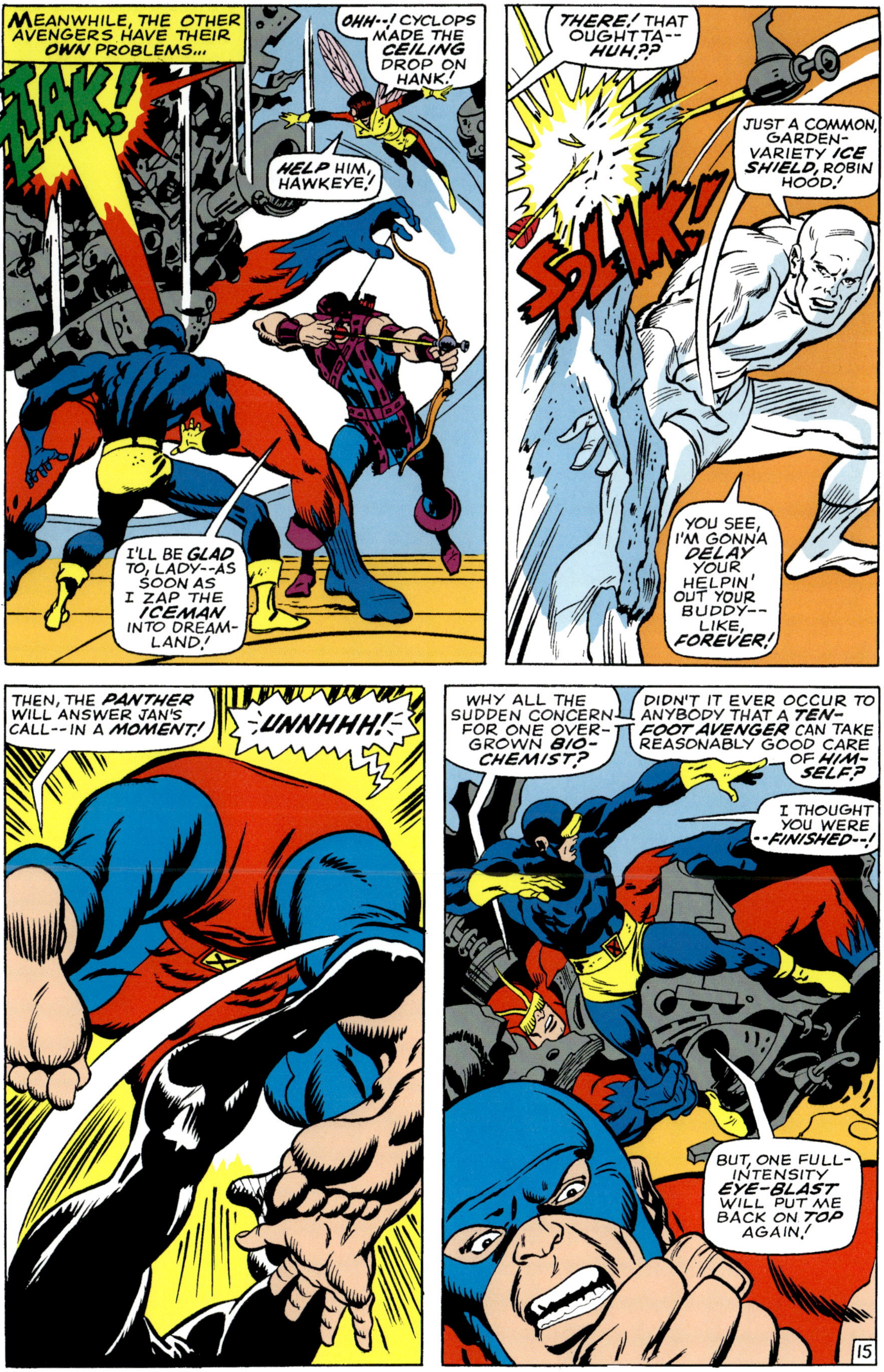
MEANWHILE, THE OTHER AVENGERS HAVE THEIR OWN PROBLEMS...
ZAK!
OHH--! CYCLOPS MADE THE CEILING DROP ON HANK!
HELP HIM, HAWKEYE!
I'LL BE GLAD TO, LADY--AS SOON AS I ZAP THE ICEMAN INTO DREAMLAND!
THERE! THAT OUGHTTA-- HUH??
SPLIK!
JUST A COMMON, GARDEN-VARIETY ICE SHIELD, ROBIN HOOD!
YOU SEE, I'M GONNA DELAY YOUR HELPIN' OUT YOUR BUDDY-- LIKE, FOREVER!
THEN, THE PANTHER WILL ANSWER JAN'S CALL--IN A MOMENT!
UNNHHH!
WHY ALL THE SUDDEN CONCERN FOR ONE OVERGROWN BIO-CHEMIST?
DIDN'T IT EVER OCCUR TO ANYBODY THAT A TEN-FOOT AVENGER CAN TAKE REASONABLY GOOD CARE OF HIMSELF?
I THOUGHT YOU WERE --FINISHED--!
BUT, ONE FULL-INTENSITY EYE-BLAST WILL PUT ME BACK ON TOP AGAIN!
15

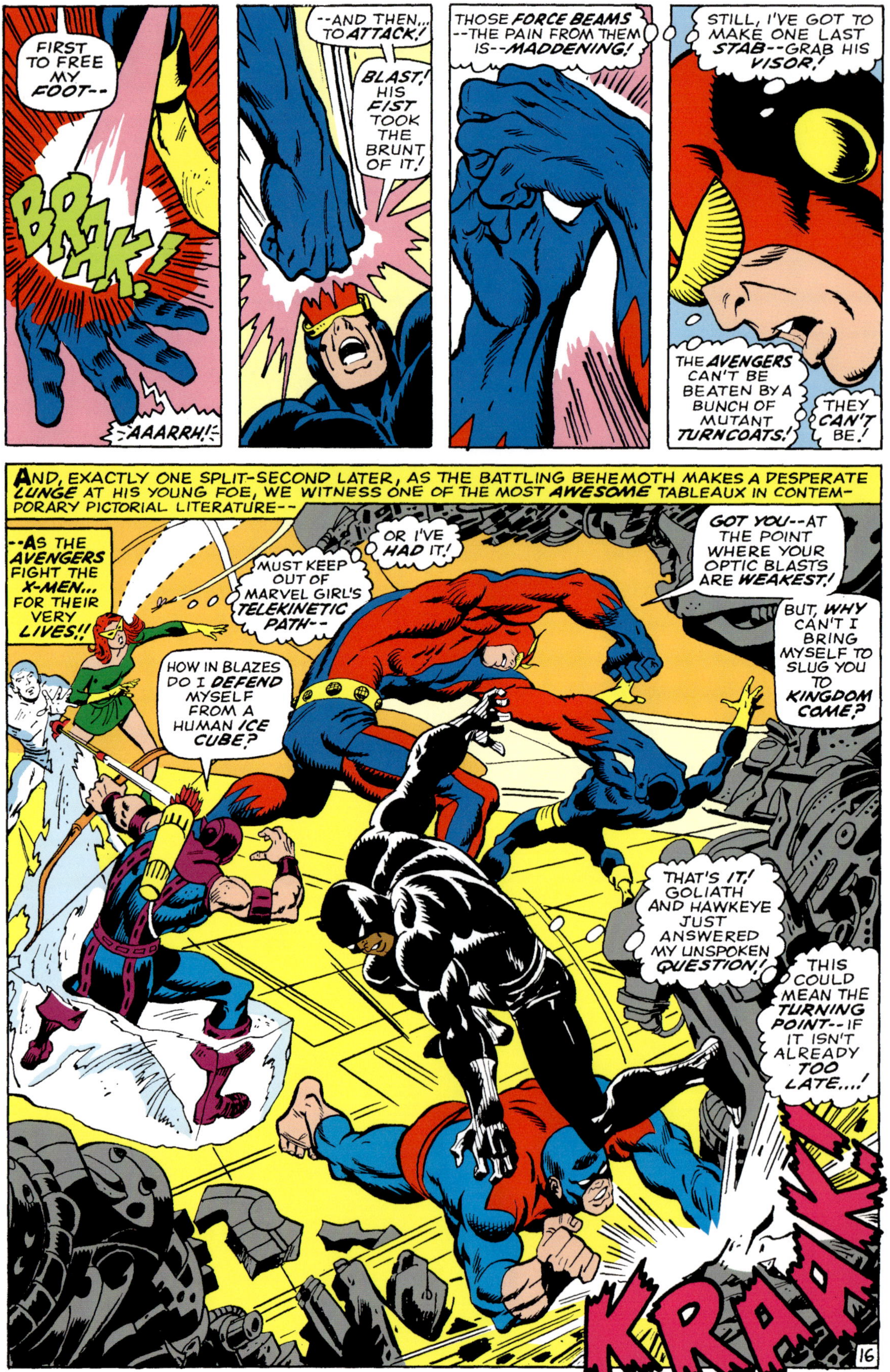
FIRST TO FREE MY FOOT--
BRAK!
AAARRH!
--AND THEN,... TO ATTACK!
BLAST! HIS FIST TOOK THE BRUNT OF IT!
THOSE FORCE BEAMS --THE PAIN FROM THEM IS--MADDENING!
STILL, I'VE GOT TO MAKE ONE LAST STAB--GRAB HIS VISOR!
THE AVENGERS CAN'T BE BEATEN BY A BUNCH OF MUTANT TURNCOATS!
THEY CAN'T BE!
AND, EXACTLY ONE SPLIT-SECOND LATER, AS THE BATTLING BEHEMOTH MAKES A DESPERATE LUNGE AT HIS YOUNG FOE, WE WITNESS ONE OF THE MOST AWESOME TABLEAUX IN CONTEMPORARY PICTORIAL LITERATURE--
--AS THE AVENGERS FIGHT THE X-MEN... FOR THEIR VERY LIVES!!
MUST KEEP OUT OF MARVEL GIRL'S TELEKINETIC PATH--
OR I'VE HAD IT!
GOT YOU--AT THE POINT WHERE YOUR OPTIC BLASTS ARE WEAKEST!
BUT, WHY CAN'T I BRING MYSELF TO SLUG YOU TO KINGDOM COME?
HOW IN BLAZES DO I DEFEND MYSELF FROM A HUMAN ICE CUBE?
THAT'S IT! GOLIATH AND HAWKEYE JUST ANSWERED MY UNSPOKEN QUESTION!
THIS COULD MEAN THE TURNING POINT--IF IT ISN'T ALREADY TOO LATE....!
KRAAK!
16

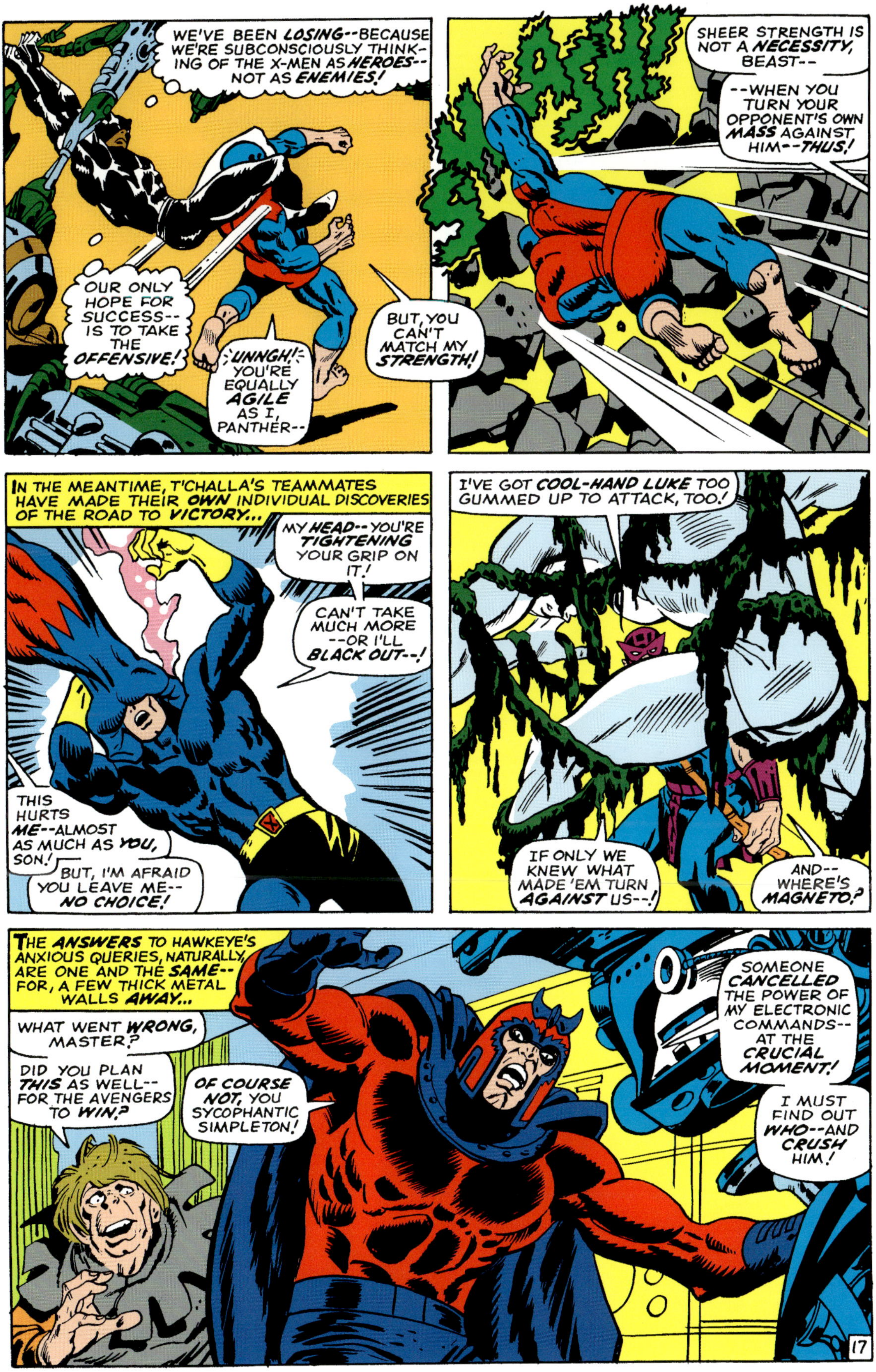
WE'VE BEEN LOSING--BECAUSE WE'RE SUBCONSCIOUSLY THINKING OF THE X-MEN AS HEROES--NOT AS ENEMIES!
OUR ONLY HOPE FOR SUCCESS--IS TO TAKE THE OFFENSIVE!
UNNGH! YOU'RE EQUALLY AGILE AS I, PANTHER--
BUT, YOU CAN'T MATCH MY STRENGTH!
YAAH!
SHEER STRENGTH IS NOT A NECESSITY, BEAST--
--WHEN YOU TURN YOUR OPPONENT'S OWN MASS AGAINST HIM--THUS!
IN THE MEANTIME, T'CHALLA'S TEAMMATES HAVE MADE THEIR OWN INDIVIDUAL DISCOVERIES OF THE ROAD TO VICTORY...
MY HEAD--YOU'RE TIGHTENING YOUR GRIP ON IT!
CAN'T TAKE MUCH MORE --OR I'LL BLACK OUT--!
THIS HURTS ME--ALMOST AS MUCH AS YOU, SON!
BUT, I'M AFRAID YOU LEAVE ME--NO CHOICE!
I'VE GOT COOL-HAND LUKE TOO GUMMED UP TO ATTACK, TOO!
IF ONLY WE KNEW WHAT MADE 'EM TURN AGAINST US--!
AND--WHERE'S MAGNETO?
THE ANSWERS TO HAWKEYE'S ANXIOUS QUERIES, NATURALLY, ARE ONE AND THE SAME--FOR, A FEW THICK METAL WALLS AWAY...
WHAT WENT WRONG, MASTER?
DID YOU PLAN THIS AS WELL--FOR THE AVENGERS TO WIN?
OF COURSE NOT, YOU SYCOPHANTIC SIMPLETON!
SOMEONE CANCELLED THE POWER OF MY ELECTRONIC COMMANDS--AT THE CRUCIAL MOMENT!
I MUST FIND OUT WHO--AND CRUSH HIM!
17

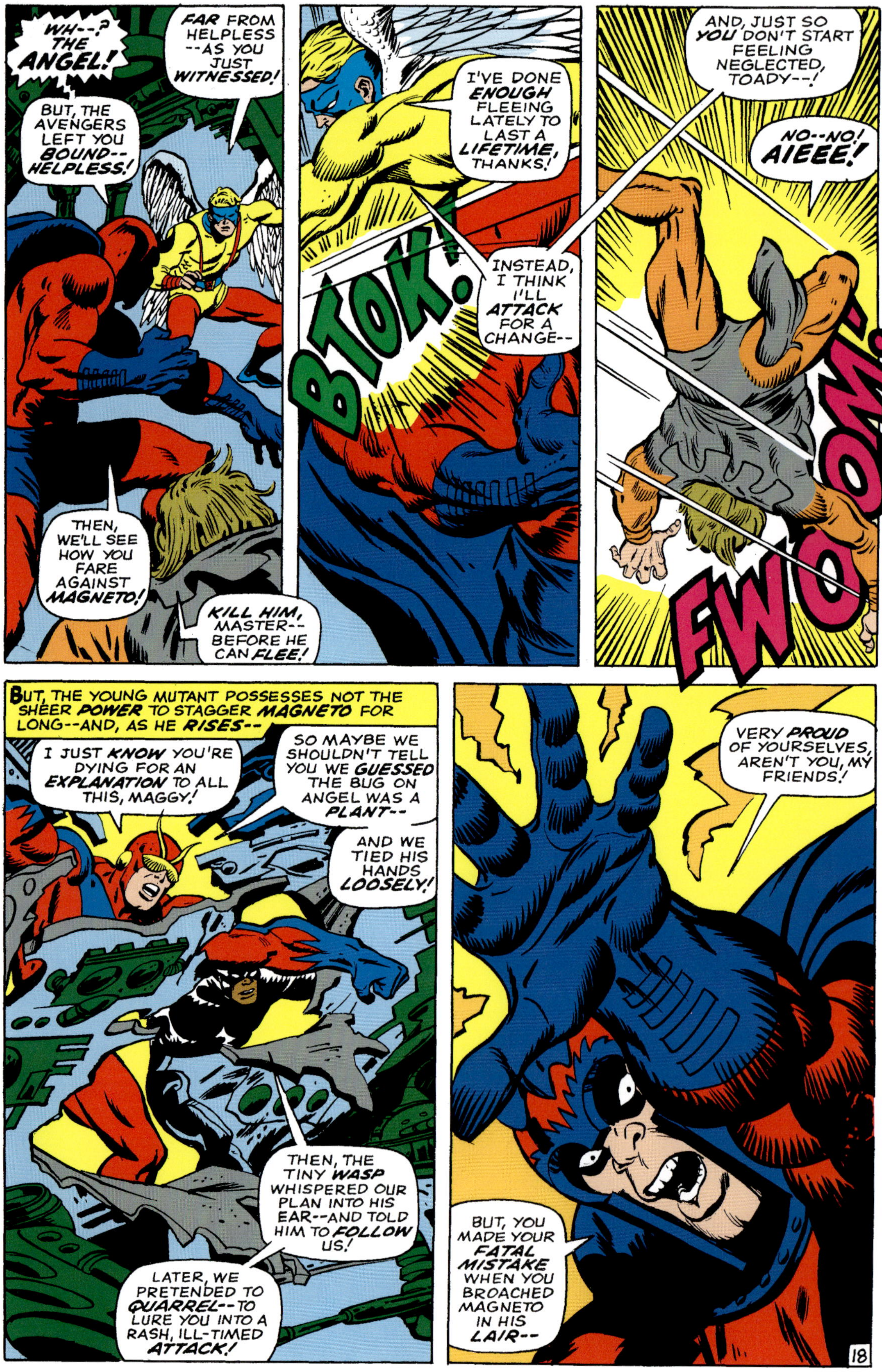
WH--? THE ANGEL!
BUT, THE AVENGERS LEFT YOU BOUND--HELPLESS!
FAR FROM HELPLESS --AS YOU JUST WITNESSED!
THEN, WE'LL SEE HOW YOU FARE AGAINST MAGNETO!
KILL HIM, MASTER-- BEFORE HE CAN FLEE!
I'VE DONE ENOUGH FLEEING LATELY TO LAST A LIFETIME, THANKS!
INSTEAD, I THINK I'LL ATTACK FOR A CHANGE--
BTOK!
AND, JUST SO YOU DON'T START FEELING NEGLECTED, TOADY--!
NO--NO! AIEEE!
FWOOM!
BUT, THE YOUNG MUTANT POSSESSES NOT THE SHEER POWER TO STAGGER MAGNETO FOR LONG--AND, AS HE RISES--
I JUST KNOW YOU'RE DYING FOR AN EXPLANATION TO ALL THIS, MAGGY!
SO MAYBE WE SHOULDN'T TELL YOU WE GUESSED THE BUG ON ANGEL WAS A PLANT--
AND WE TIED HIS HANDS LOOSELY!
THEN, THE TINY WASP WHISPERED OUR PLAN INTO HIS EAR--AND TOLD HIM TO FOLLOW US!
LATER, WE PRETENDED TO QUARREL--TO LURE YOU INTO A RASH, ILL-TIMED ATTACK!
VERY PROUD OF YOURSELVES, AREN'T YOU, MY FRIENDS!
BUT, YOU MADE YOUR FATAL MISTAKE WHEN YOU BROACHED MAGNETO IN HIS LAIR--
18

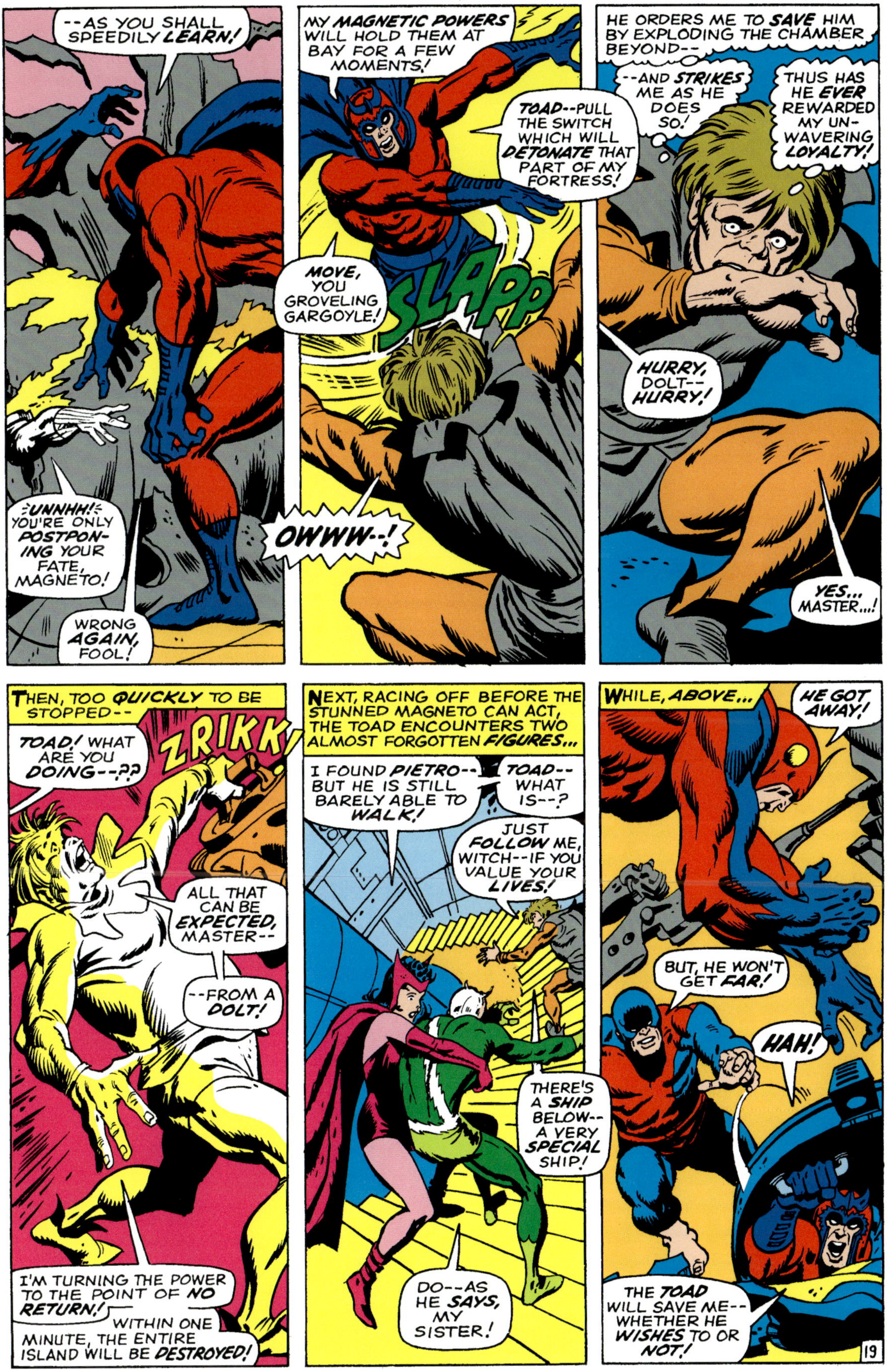
--AS YOU SHALL SPEEDILY LEARN!
UNNHH! YOU'RE ONLY POSTPONING YOUR FATE, MAGNETO!
WRONG AGAIN, FOOL!
MY MAGNETIC POWERS WILL HOLD THEM AT BAY FOR A FEW MOMENTS!
TOAD--PULL THE SWITCH WHICH WILL DETONATE THAT PART OF MY FORTRESS!
MOVE, YOU GROVELING GARGOYLE!
SLAPP
OWWW--!
HE ORDERS ME TO SAVE HIM BY EXPLODING THE CHAMBER BEYOND--
--AND STRIKES ME AS HE DOES SO!
THUS HAS HE EVER REWARDED MY UNWAVERING LOYALTY!
HURRY, DOLT-- HURRY!
YES... MASTER...!
THEN, TOO QUICKLY TO BE STOPPED--
TOAD! WHAT ARE YOU DOING--??
ZRIKK!
ALL THAT CAN BE EXPECTED, MASTER--
--FROM A DOLT!
I'M TURNING THE POWER TO THE POINT OF NO RETURN! WITHIN ONE MINUTE, THE ENTIRE ISLAND WILL BE DESTROYED!
NEXT, RACING OFF BEFORE THE STUNNED MAGNETO CAN ACT, THE TOAD ENCOUNTERS TWO ALMOST FORGOTTEN FIGURES...
I FOUND PIETRO-- BUT HE IS STILL BARELY ABLE TO WALK!
TOAD-- WHAT IS--?
JUST FOLLOW ME, WITCH--IF YOU VALUE YOUR LIVES!
THERE'S A SHIP BELOW-- A VERY SPECIAL SHIP!
DO--AS HE SAYS, MY SISTER!
WHILE, ABOVE...
HE GOT AWAY!
BUT, HE WON'T GET FAR!
HAH!
THE TOAD WILL SAVE ME-- WHETHER HE WISHES TO OR NOT!
19

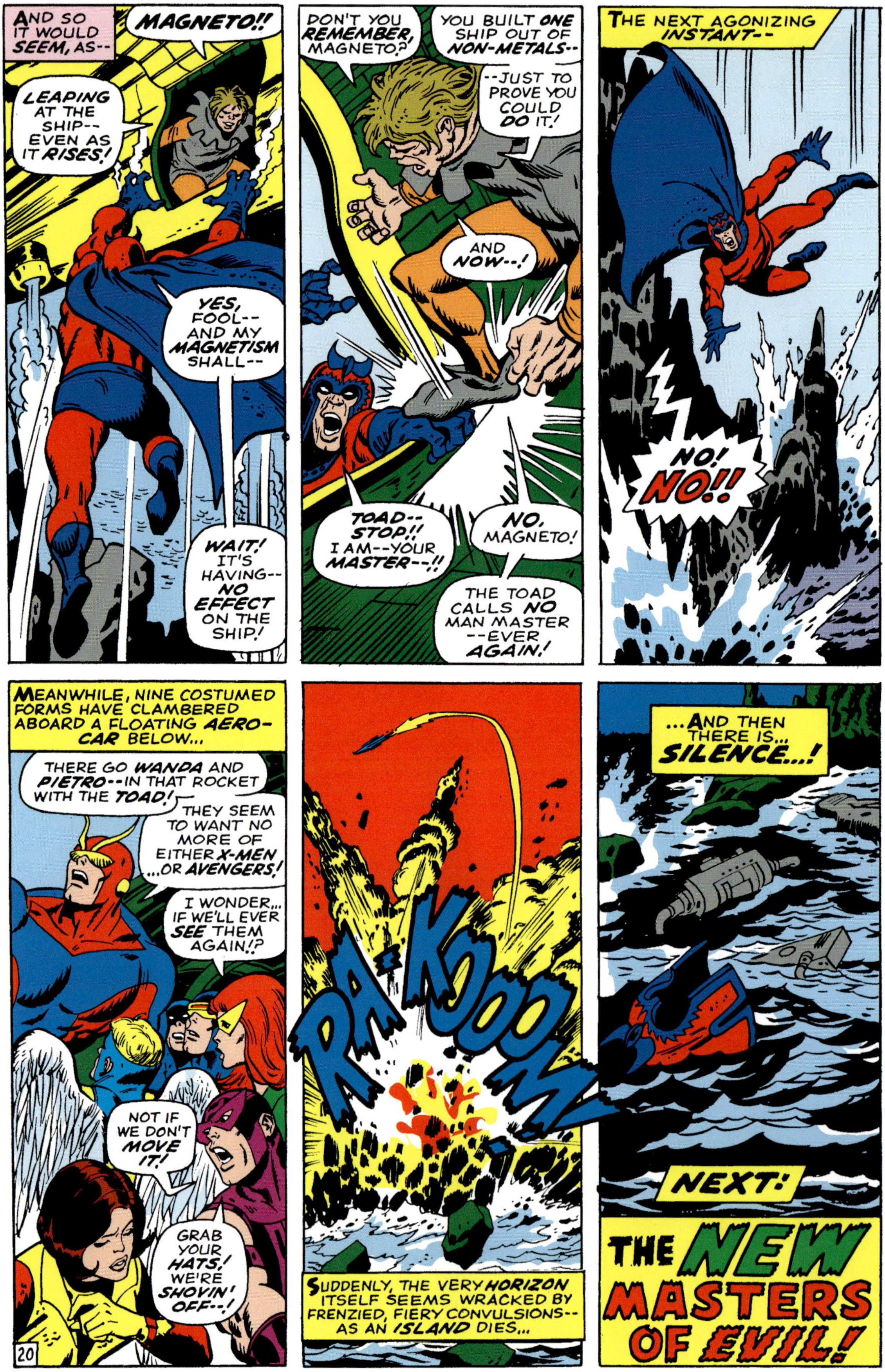
AND SO IT WOULD SEEM, AS--
MAGNETO!!
LEAPING AT THE SHIP--EVEN AS IT RISES!
YES, FOOL--AND MY MAGNETISM SHALL--
WAIT! IT'S HAVING--NO EFFECT ON THE SHIP!
DON'T YOU REMEMBER, MAGNETO?
YOU BUILT ONE SHIP OUT OF NON-METALS--
--JUST TO PROVE YOU COULD DO IT!
AND NOW--!
TOAD--STOP!! I AM--YOUR MASTER--!!
NO, MAGNETO!
THE TOAD CALLS NO MAN MASTER--EVER AGAIN!
THE NEXT AGONIZING INSTANT--
NO! NO!!
MEANWHILE, NINE COSTUMED FORMS HAVE CLAMBERED ABOARD A FLOATING AERO-CAR BELOW...
THERE GO WANDA AND PIETRO--IN THAT ROCKET WITH THE TOAD!
THEY SEEM TO WANT NO MORE OF EITHER X-MEN ...OR AVENGERS!
I WONDER... IF WE'LL EVER SEE THEM AGAIN!?
NOT IF WE DON'T MOVE IT!
GRAB YOUR HATS! WE'RE SHOVIN' OFF--!
20
RA-KOOOM!
SUDDENLY, THE VERY HORIZON ITSELF SEEMS WRACKED BY FRENZIED, FIERY CONVULSIONS--AS AN ISLAND DIES...
...AND THEN THERE IS... SILENCE...!
NEXT:
THE NEW MASTERS OF EVIL!

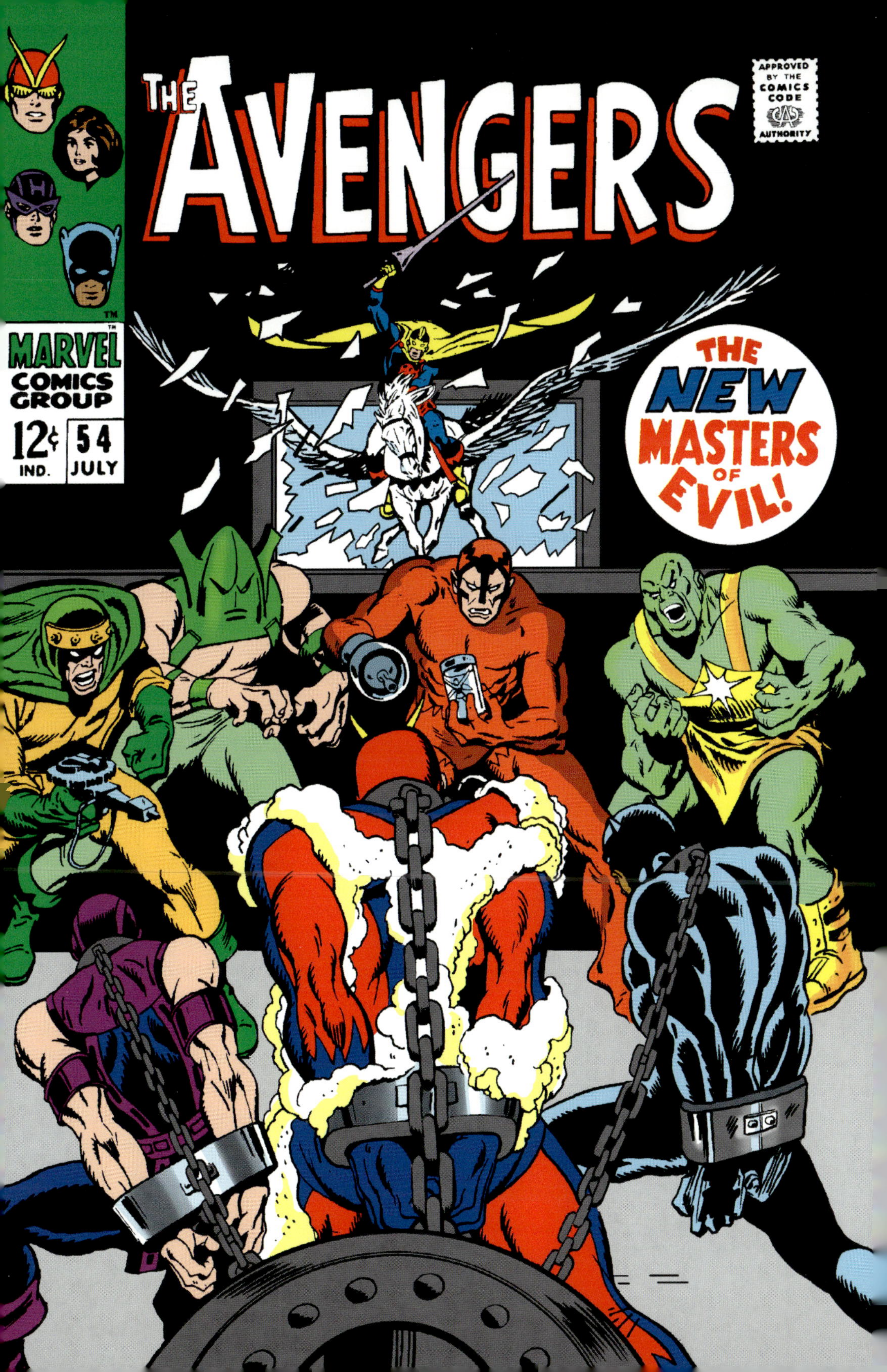
THE AVENGERS
APPROVED BY THE COMICS CODE AUTHORITY
MARVEL COMICS GROUP
12¢ IND.
54 JULY
THE NEW MASTERS OF EVIL!

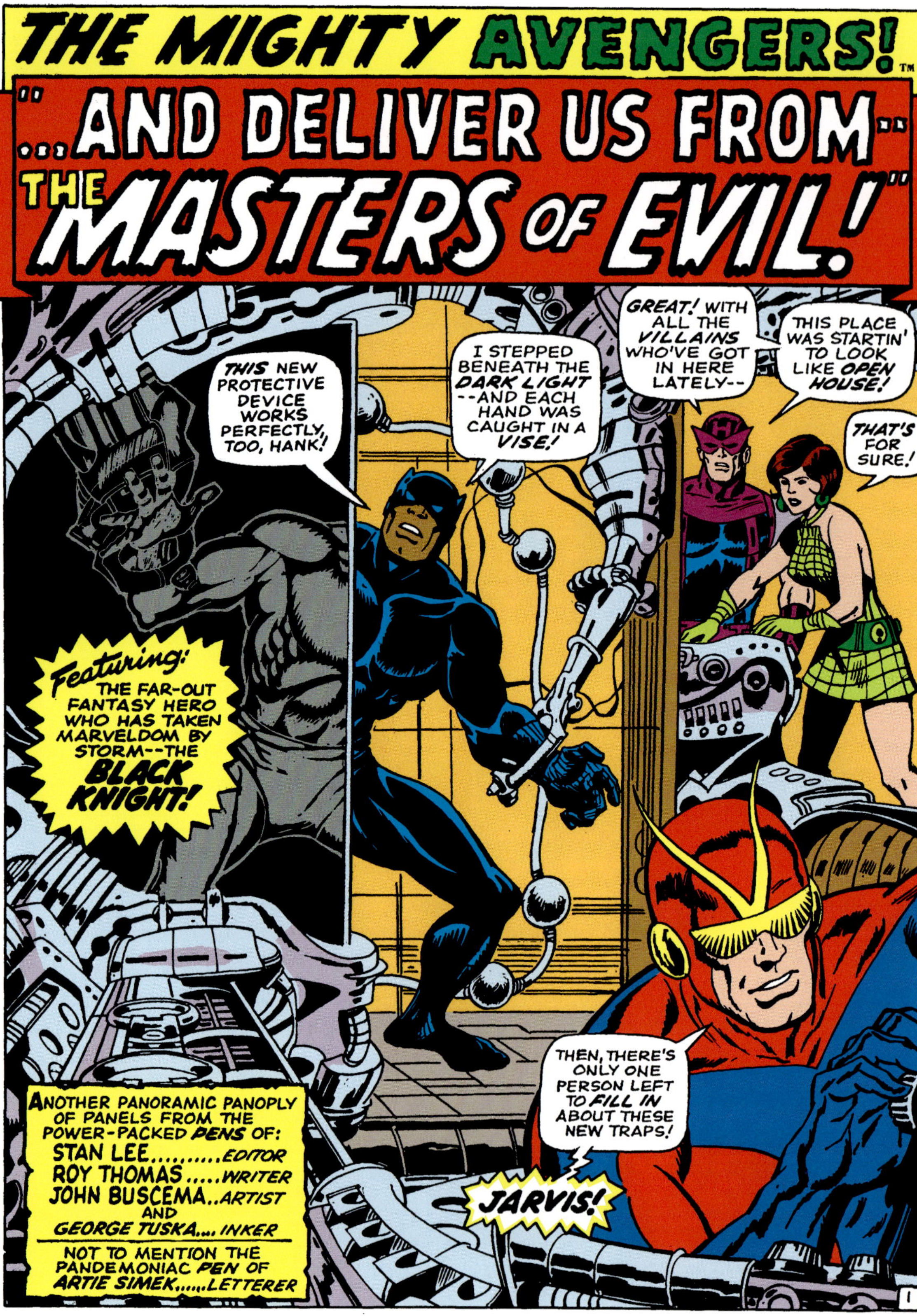
THE MIGHTY AVENGERS!
"...AND DELIVER US FROM--THE MASTERS OF EVIL!"
THIS NEW PROTECTIVE DEVICE WORKS PERFECTLY, TOO, HANK!
I STEPPED BENEATH THE DARK LIGHT --AND EACH HAND WAS CAUGHT IN A VISE!
GREAT! WITH ALL THE VILLAINS WHO'VE GOT IN HERE LATELY--
THIS PLACE WAS STARTIN' TO LOOK LIKE OPEN HOUSE!
THAT'S FOR SURE!
Featuring: THE FAR-OUT FANTASY HERO WHO HAS TAKEN MARVELDOM BY STORM--THE BLACK KNIGHT!
THEN, THERE'S ONLY ONE PERSON LEFT TO FILL IN ABOUT THESE NEW TRAPS!
JARVIS!
ANOTHER PANORAMIC PANOPLY OF PANELS FROM THE POWER-PACKED PENS OF: STAN LEE.........EDITOR ROY THOMAS.....WRITER JOHN BUSCEMA..ARTIST AND GEORGE TUSKA.... INKER
NOT TO MENTION THE PANDEMONIAC PEN OF ARTIE SIMEK......LETTERER
1

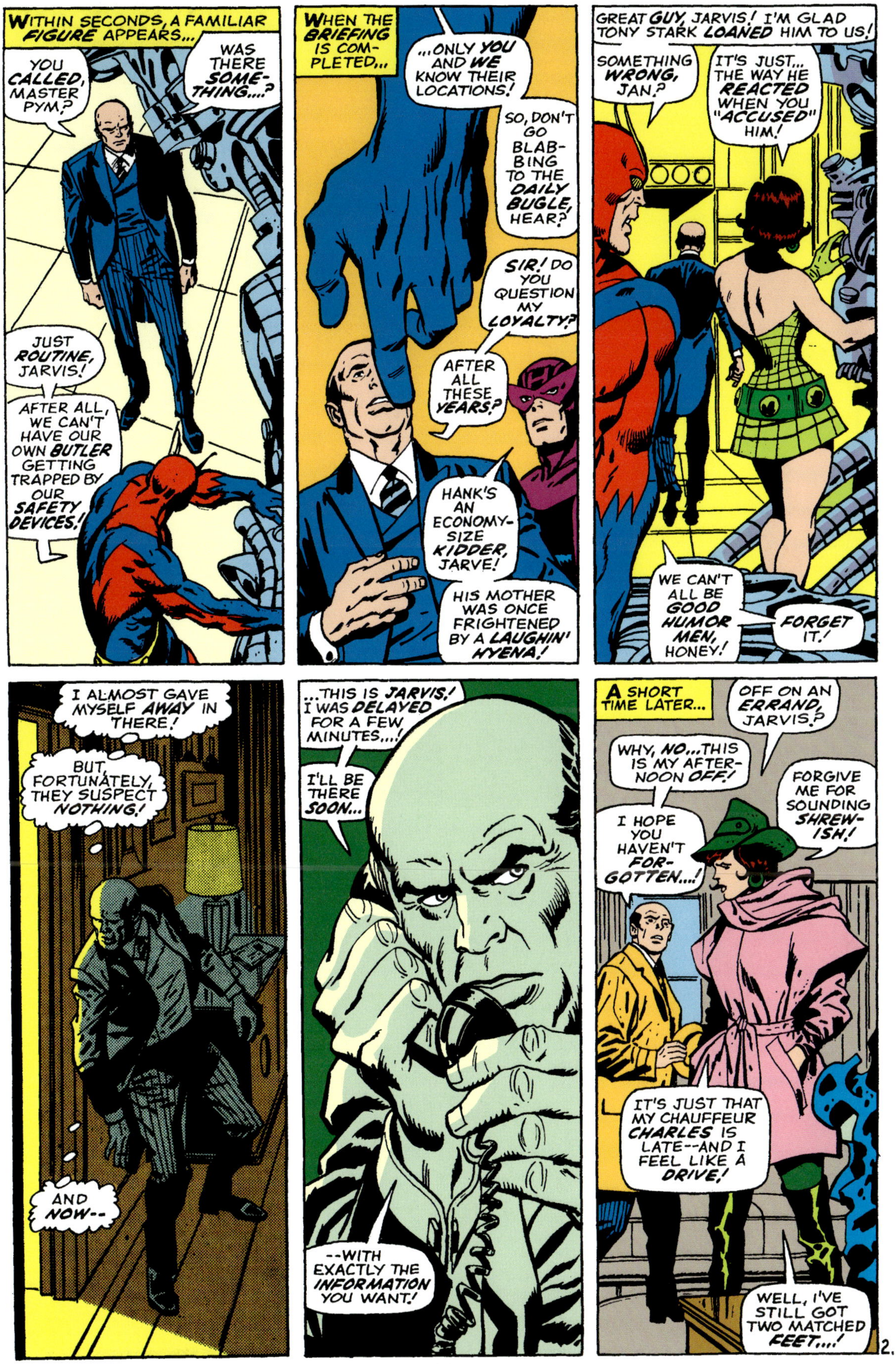
WITHIN SECONDS, A FAMILIAR FIGURE APPEARS...
YOU CALLED, MASTER PYM?
WAS THERE SOME-THING....?
JUST ROUTINE, JARVIS!
AFTER ALL, WE CAN'T HAVE OUR OWN BUTLER GETTING TRAPPED BY OUR SAFETY DEVICES!
WHEN THE BRIEFING IS COM-PLETED,...
...ONLY YOU AND WE KNOW THEIR LOCATIONS!
SO, DON'T GO BLAB-BING TO THE DAILY BUGLE, HEAR?
SIR! DO YOU QUESTION MY LOYALTY?
AFTER ALL THESE YEARS?
HANK'S AN ECONOMY-SIZE KIDDER, JARVE!
HIS MOTHER WAS ONCE FRIGHTENED BY A LAUGHIN' HYENA!
GREAT GUY, JARVIS! I'M GLAD TONY STARK LOANED HIM TO US!
SOMETHING WRONG, JAN?
IT'S JUST... THE WAY HE REACTED WHEN YOU "ACCUSED" HIM!
WE CAN'T ALL BE GOOD HUMOR MEN, HONEY!
FORGET IT!
I ALMOST GAVE MYSELF AWAY IN THERE!
BUT, FORTUNATELY, THEY SUSPECT NOTHING!
AND NOW--
...THIS IS JARVIS! I WAS DELAYED FOR A FEW MINUTES...!
I'LL BE THERE SOON...
--WITH EXACTLY THE INFORMATION YOU WANT!
A SHORT TIME LATER...
OFF ON AN ERRAND, JARVIS?
WHY, NO...THIS IS MY AFTER-NOON OFF!
FORGIVE ME FOR SOUNDING SHREW-ISH!
I HOPE YOU HAVEN'T FOR-GOTTEN...!
IT'S JUST THAT MY CHAUFFEUR CHARLES IS LATE--AND I FEEL LIKE A DRIVE!
WELL, I'VE STILL GOT TWO MATCHED FEET...!
2.

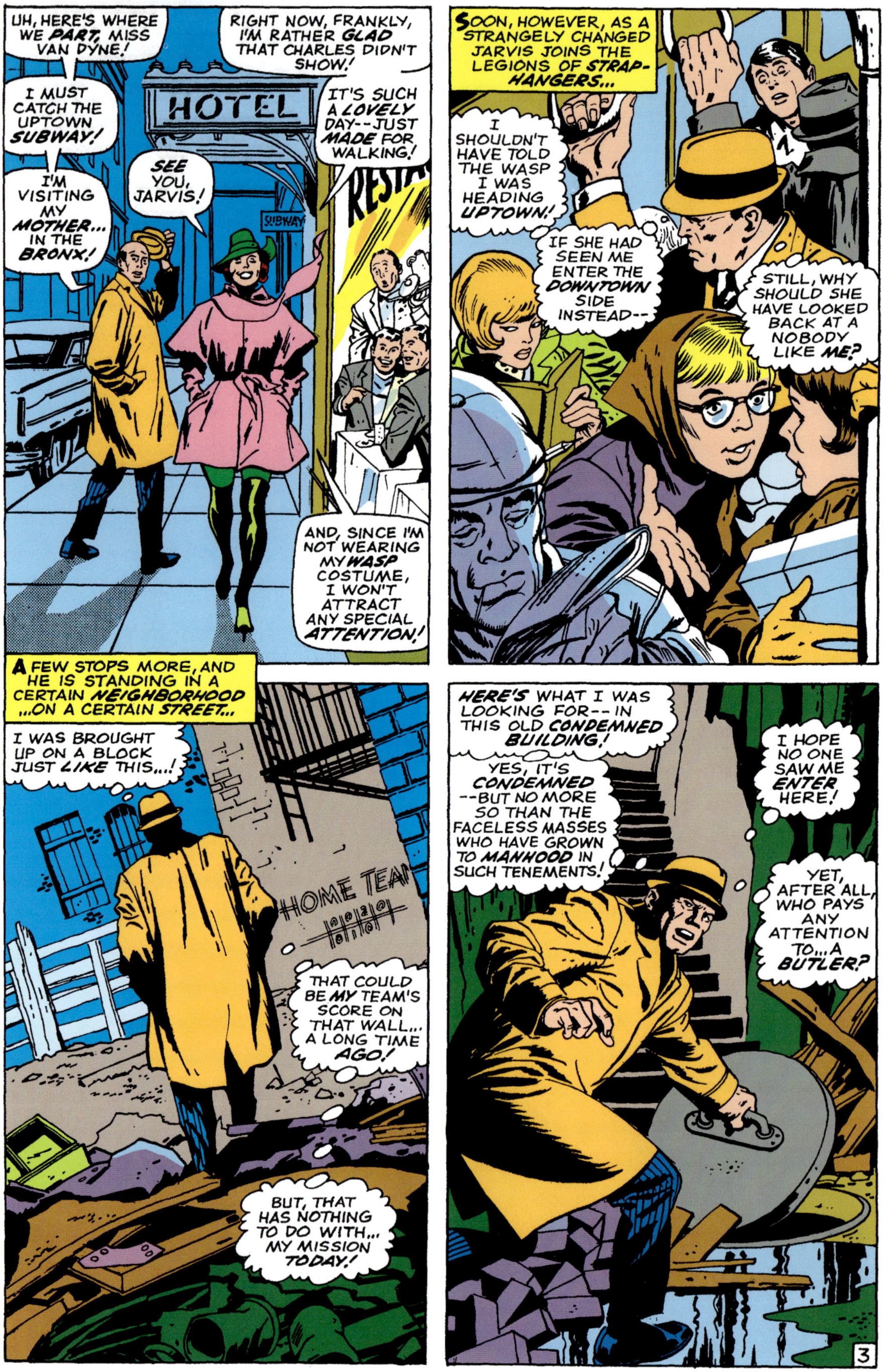

UH, HERE'S WHERE WE PART, MISS VAN DYNE!
I MUST CATCH THE UPTOWN SUBWAY!
I'M VISITING MY MOTHER... IN THE BRONX!
RIGHT NOW, FRANKLY, I'M RATHER GLAD THAT CHARLES DIDN'T SHOW!
IT'S SUCH A LOVELY DAY--JUST MADE FOR WALKING!
SEE YOU, JARVIS!
HOTEL
SUBWAY
AND, SINCE I'M NOT WEARING MY WASP COSTUME, I WON'T ATTRACT ANY SPECIAL ATTENTION!
SOON, HOWEVER, AS A STRANGELY CHANGED JARVIS JOINS THE LEGIONS OF STRAP-HANGERS...
I SHOULDN'T HAVE TOLD THE WASP I WAS HEADING UPTOWN!
IF SHE HAD SEEN ME ENTER THE DOWNTOWN SIDE INSTEAD--
STILL, WHY SHOULD SHE HAVE LOOKED BACK AT A NOBODY LIKE ME?
A FEW STOPS MORE, AND HE IS STANDING IN A CERTAIN NEIGHBORHOOD ...ON A CERTAIN STREET...
I WAS BROUGHT UP ON A BLOCK JUST LIKE THIS...!
HOME TEAM
THAT COULD BE MY TEAM'S SCORE ON THAT WALL... A LONG TIME AGO!
BUT, THAT HAS NOTHING TO DO WITH... MY MISSION TODAY!
HERE'S WHAT I WAS LOOKING FOR-- IN THIS OLD CONDEMNED BUILDING!
YES, IT'S CONDEMNED --BUT NO MORE SO THAN THE FACELESS MASSES WHO HAVE GROWN TO MANHOOD IN SUCH TENEMENTS!
I HOPE NO ONE SAW ME ENTER HERE!
YET, AFTER ALL, WHO PAYS ANY ATTENTION TO... A BUTLER?
3

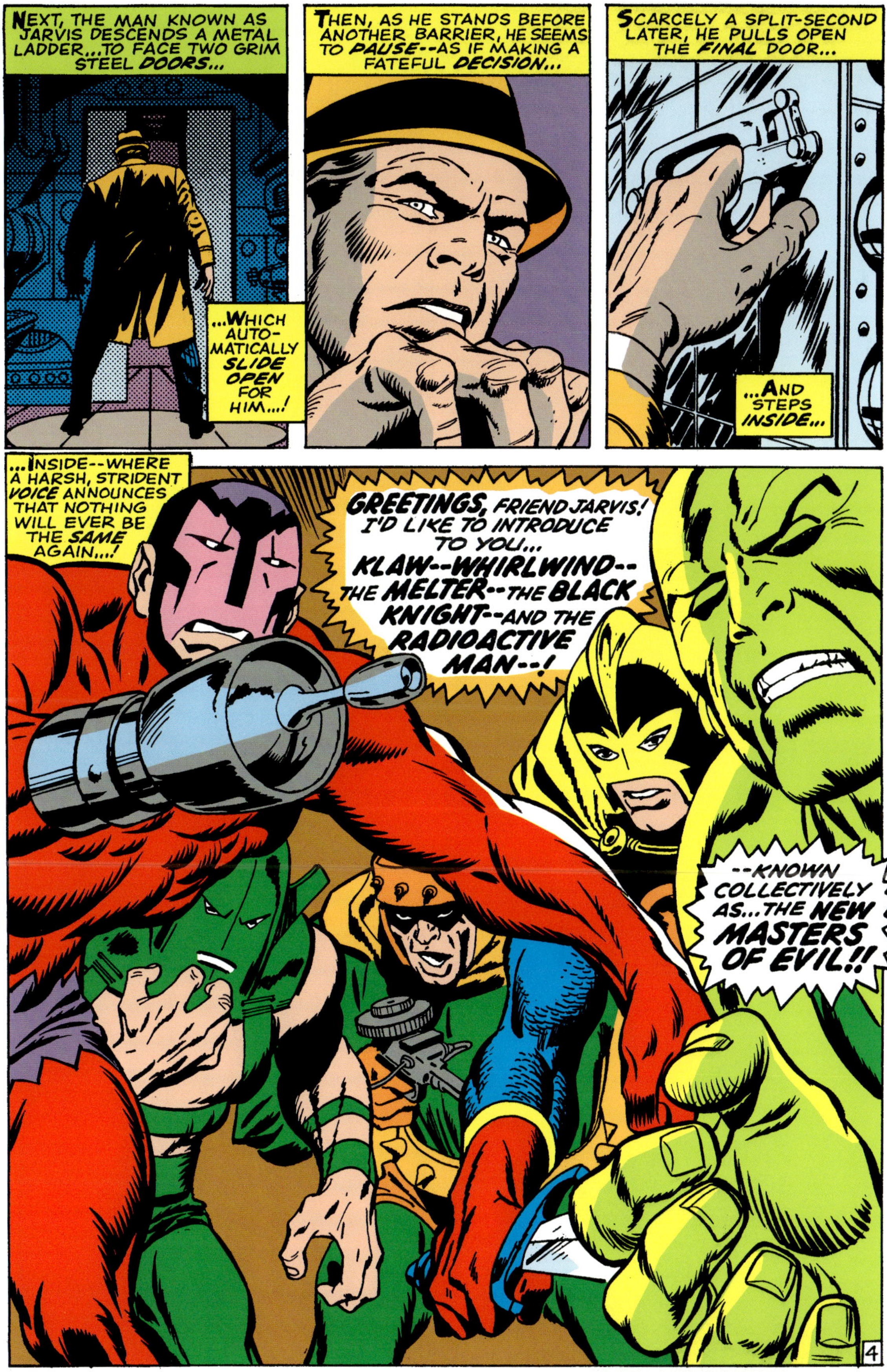

NEXT, THE MAN KNOWN AS JARVIS DESCENDS A METAL LADDER...TO FACE TWO GRIM STEEL DOORS...
...WHICH AUTO-MATICALLY SLIDE OPEN FOR HIM...!
THEN, AS HE STANDS BEFORE ANOTHER BARRIER, HE SEEMS TO PAUSE--AS IF MAKING A FATEFUL DECISION...
SCARCELY A SPLIT-SECOND LATER, HE PULLS OPEN THE FINAL DOOR...
...AND STEPS INSIDE...
...INSIDE--WHERE A HARSH, STRIDENT VOICE ANNOUNCES THAT NOTHING WILL EVER BE THE SAME AGAIN...!
GREETINGS, FRIEND JARVIS! I'D LIKE TO INTRODUCE TO YOU... KLAW--WHIRLWIND--THE MELTER--THE BLACK KNIGHT--AND THE RADIOACTIVE MAN--!
--KNOWN COLLECTIVELY AS...THE NEW MASTERS OF EVIL!!
4

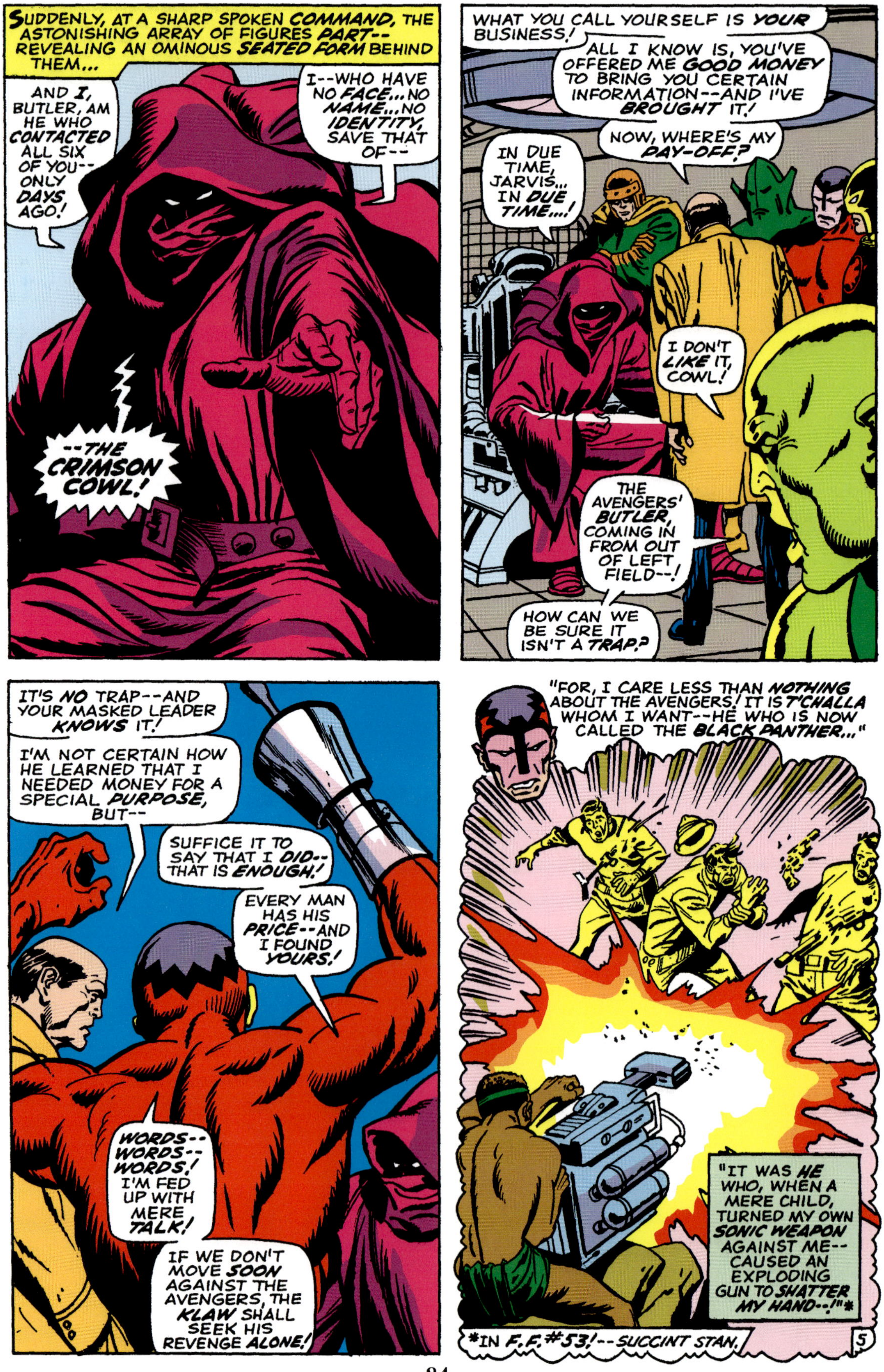
SUDDENLY, AT A SHARP SPOKEN COMMAND, THE ASTONISHING ARRAY OF FIGURES PART-- REVEALING AN OMINOUS SEATED FORM BEHIND THEM...
AND I, BUTLER, AM HE WHO CONTACTED ALL SIX OF YOU-- ONLY DAYS AGO!
I--WHO HAVE NO FACE... NO NAME... NO IDENTITY, SAVE THAT OF--
--THE CRIMSON COWL!
WHAT YOU CALL YOURSELF IS YOUR BUSINESS!
ALL I KNOW IS, YOU'VE OFFERED ME GOOD MONEY TO BRING YOU CERTAIN INFORMATION--AND I'VE BROUGHT IT!
NOW, WHERE'S MY PAY-OFF?
IN DUE TIME, JARVIS... IN DUE TIME...!
I DON'T LIKE IT, COWL!
THE AVENGERS' BUTLER, COMING IN FROM OUT OF LEFT FIELD--!
HOW CAN WE BE SURE IT ISN'T A TRAP?
IT'S NO TRAP--AND YOUR MASKED LEADER KNOWS IT!
I'M NOT CERTAIN HOW HE LEARNED THAT I NEEDED MONEY FOR A SPECIAL PURPOSE, BUT--
SUFFICE IT TO SAY THAT I DID-- THAT IS ENOUGH!
EVERY MAN HAS HIS PRICE--AND I FOUND YOURS!
WORDS-- WORDS-- WORDS! I'M FED UP WITH MERE TALK!
IF WE DON'T MOVE SOON AGAINST THE AVENGERS, THE KLAW SHALL SEEK HIS REVENGE ALONE!
"FOR, I CARE LESS THAN NOTHING ABOUT THE AVENGERS! IT IS T'CHALLA WHOM I WANT--HE WHO IS NOW CALLED THE BLACK PANTHER..."
"IT WAS HE WHO, WHEN A MERE CHILD, TURNED MY OWN SONIC WEAPON AGAINST ME-- CAUSED AN EXPLODING GUN TO SHATTER MY HAND--!"*
*IN F.F. #53!--SUCCINT STAN.
5

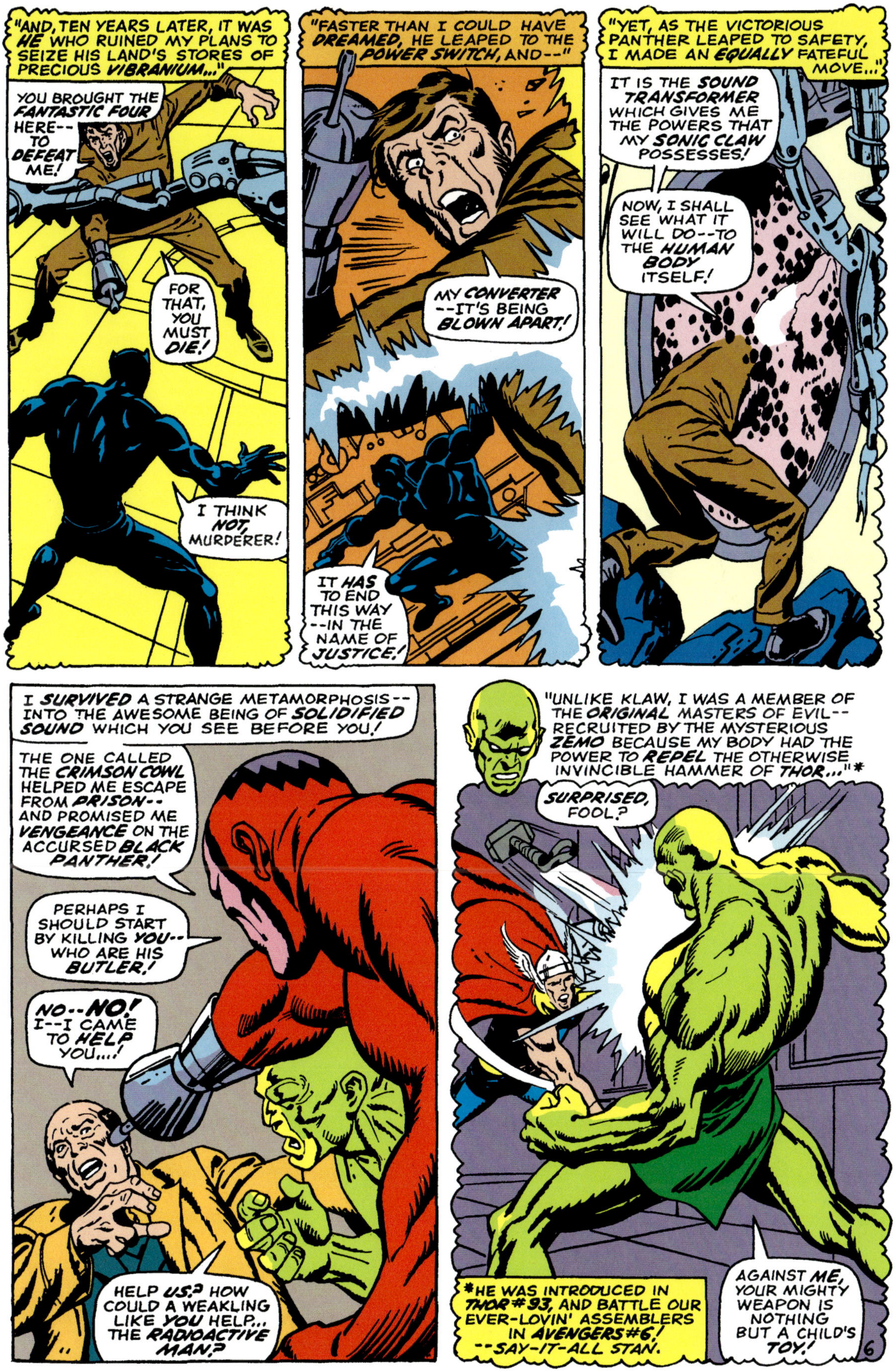
"AND, TEN YEARS LATER, IT WAS HE WHO RUINED MY PLANS TO SEIZE HIS LAND'S STORES OF PRECIOUS VIBRANIUM..."
YOU BROUGHT THE FANTASTIC FOUR HERE--TO DEFEAT ME!
FOR THAT, YOU MUST DIE!
I THINK NOT, MURDERER!
"FASTER THAN I COULD HAVE DREAMED, HE LEAPED TO THE POWER SWITCH, AND--"
MY CONVERTER--IT'S BEING BLOWN APART!
IT HAS TO END THIS WAY--IN THE NAME OF JUSTICE!
"YET, AS THE VICTORIOUS PANTHER LEAPED TO SAFETY, I MADE AN EQUALLY FATEFUL MOVE..."
IT IS THE SOUND TRANSFORMER WHICH GIVES ME THE POWERS THAT MY SONIC CLAW POSSESSES!
NOW, I SHALL SEE WHAT IT WILL DO--TO THE HUMAN BODY ITSELF!
I SURVIVED A STRANGE METAMORPHOSIS--INTO THE AWESOME BEING OF SOLIDIFIED SOUND WHICH YOU SEE BEFORE YOU!
THE ONE CALLED THE CRIMSON COWL HELPED ME ESCAPE FROM PRISON--AND PROMISED ME VENGEANCE ON THE ACCURSED BLACK PANTHER!
PERHAPS I SHOULD START BY KILLING YOU--WHO ARE HIS BUTLER!
NO--NO! I--I CAME TO HELP YOU...!
HELP US? HOW COULD A WEAKLING LIKE YOU HELP... THE RADIOACTIVE MAN?
"UNLIKE KLAW, I WAS A MEMBER OF THE ORIGINAL MASTERS OF EVIL--RECRUITED BY THE MYSTERIOUS ZEMO BECAUSE MY BODY HAD THE POWER TO REPEL THE OTHERWISE INVINCIBLE HAMMER OF THOR..."*
SURPRISED, FOOL?
*HE WAS INTRODUCED IN THOR #93, AND BATTLE OUR EVER-LOVIN' ASSEMBLERS IN AVENGERS #6! --SAY-IT-ALL STAN.
AGAINST ME, YOUR MIGHTY WEAPON IS NOTHING BUT A CHILD'S TOY!
6

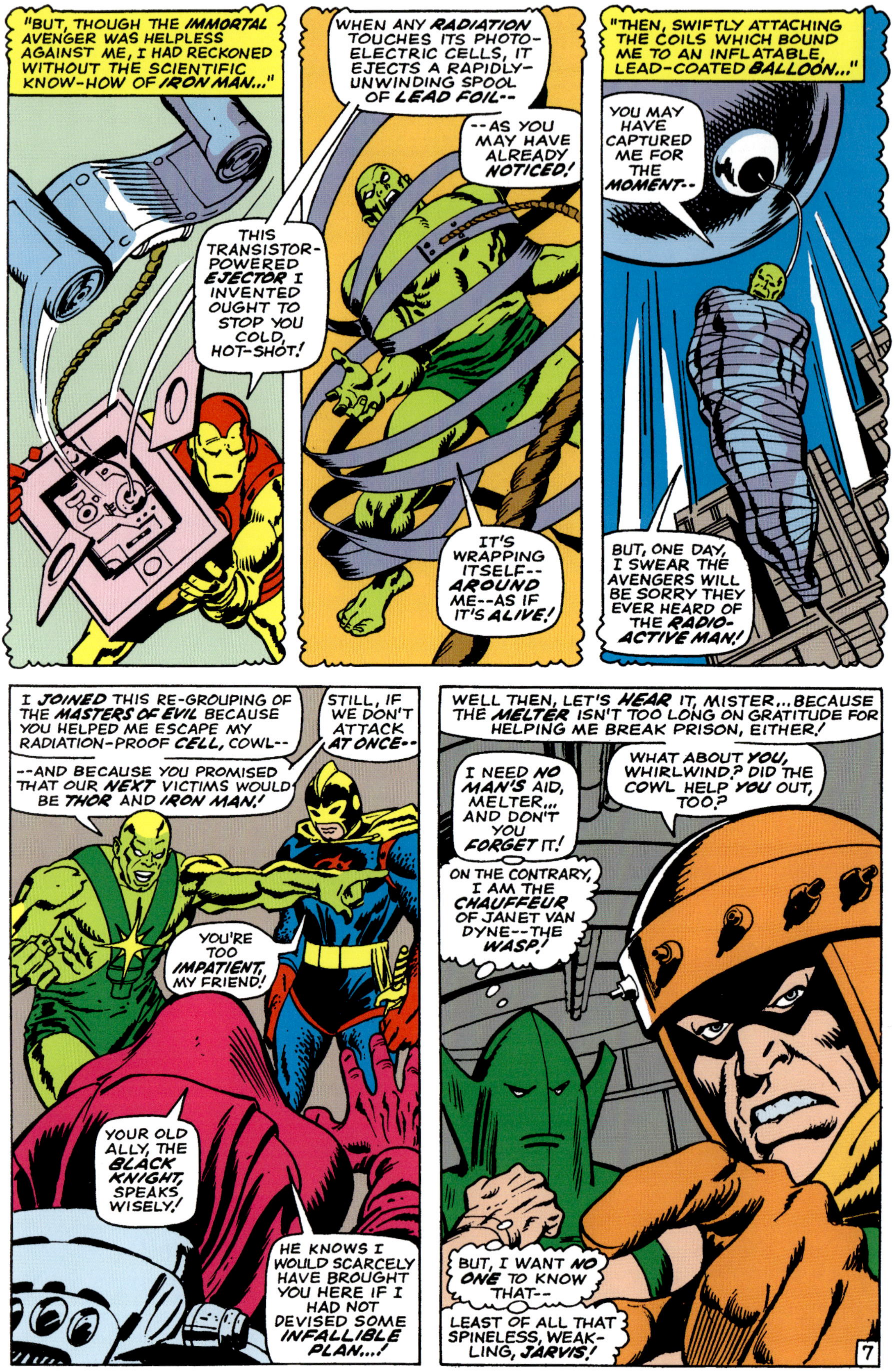
"BUT, THOUGH THE IMMORTAL AVENGER WAS HELPLESS AGAINST ME, I HAD RECKONED WITHOUT THE SCIENTIFIC KNOW-HOW OF IRON MAN..."
THIS TRANSISTOR-POWERED EJECTOR I INVENTED OUGHT TO STOP YOU COLD, HOT-SHOT!
WHEN ANY RADIATION TOUCHES ITS PHOTO-ELECTRIC CELLS, IT EJECTS A RAPIDLY-UNWINDING SPOOL OF LEAD FOIL--
--AS YOU MAY HAVE ALREADY NOTICED!
IT'S WRAPPING ITSELF--AROUND ME--AS IF IT'S ALIVE!
"THEN, SWIFTLY ATTACHING THE COILS WHICH BOUND ME TO AN INFLATABLE, LEAD-COATED BALLOON..."
YOU MAY HAVE CAPTURED ME FOR THE MOMENT--
BUT, ONE DAY, I SWEAR THE AVENGERS WILL BE SORRY THEY EVER HEARD OF THE RADIO-ACTIVE MAN!
I JOINED THIS RE-GROUPING OF THE MASTERS OF EVIL BECAUSE YOU HELPED ME ESCAPE MY RADIATION-PROOF CELL, COWL--
--AND BECAUSE YOU PROMISED THAT OUR NEXT VICTIMS WOULD BE THOR AND IRON MAN!
STILL, IF WE DON'T ATTACK AT ONCE--
YOU'RE TOO IMPATIENT, MY FRIEND!
YOUR OLD ALLY, THE BLACK KNIGHT, SPEAKS WISELY!
HE KNOWS I WOULD SCARCELY HAVE BROUGHT YOU HERE IF I HAD NOT DEVISED SOME INFALLIBLE PLAN...!
WELL THEN, LET'S HEAR IT, MISTER... BECAUSE THE MELTER ISN'T TOO LONG ON GRATITUDE FOR HELPING ME BREAK PRISON, EITHER!
WHAT ABOUT YOU, WHIRLWIND? DID THE COWL HELP YOU OUT, TOO?
I NEED NO MAN'S AID, MELTER... AND DON'T YOU FORGET IT!
ON THE CONTRARY, I AM THE CHAUFFEUR OF JANET VAN DYNE--THE WASP!
BUT, I WANT NO ONE TO KNOW THAT--
LEAST OF ALL THAT SPINELESS, WEAK-LING, JARVIS!
7

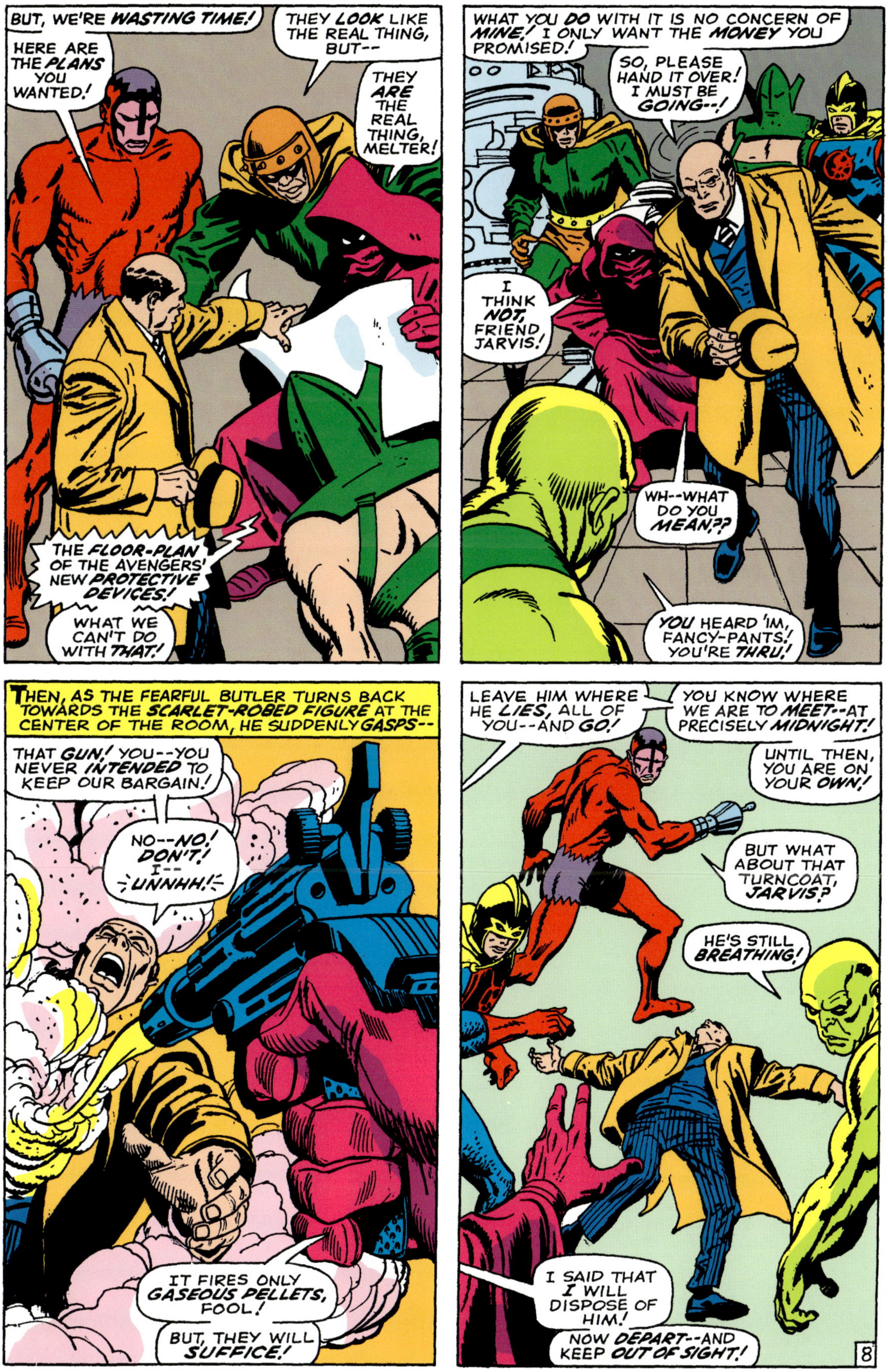

BUT, WE'RE WASTING TIME!
HERE ARE THE PLANS YOU WANTED!
THEY LOOK LIKE THE REAL THING, BUT--
THEY ARE THE REAL THING, MELTER!
THE FLOOR-PLAN OF THE AVENGERS' NEW PROTECTIVE DEVICES!
WHAT WE CAN'T DO WITH THAT!
WHAT YOU DO WITH IT IS NO CONCERN OF MINE! I ONLY WANT THE MONEY YOU PROMISED!
SO, PLEASE HAND IT OVER! I MUST BE GOING--!
I THINK NOT, FRIEND JARVIS!
WH--WHAT DO YOU MEAN??
YOU HEARD 'IM, FANCY-PANTS! YOU'RE THRU!
THEN, AS THE FEARFUL BUTLER TURNS BACK TOWARDS THE SCARLET-ROBED FIGURE AT THE CENTER OF THE ROOM, HE SUDDENLY GASPS--
THAT GUN! YOU--YOU NEVER INTENDED TO KEEP OUR BARGAIN!
NO--NO! DON'T! I-- UNNHH!
IT FIRES ONLY GASEOUS PELLETS, FOOL!
BUT, THEY WILL SUFFICE!
LEAVE HIM WHERE HE LIES, ALL OF YOU--AND GO!
YOU KNOW WHERE WE ARE TO MEET--AT PRECISELY MIDNIGHT!
UNTIL THEN, YOU ARE ON YOUR OWN!
BUT WHAT ABOUT THAT TURNCOAT, JARVIS?
HE'S STILL BREATHING!
I SAID THAT I WILL DISPOSE OF HIM!
NOW DEPART--AND KEEP OUT OF SIGHT!
8

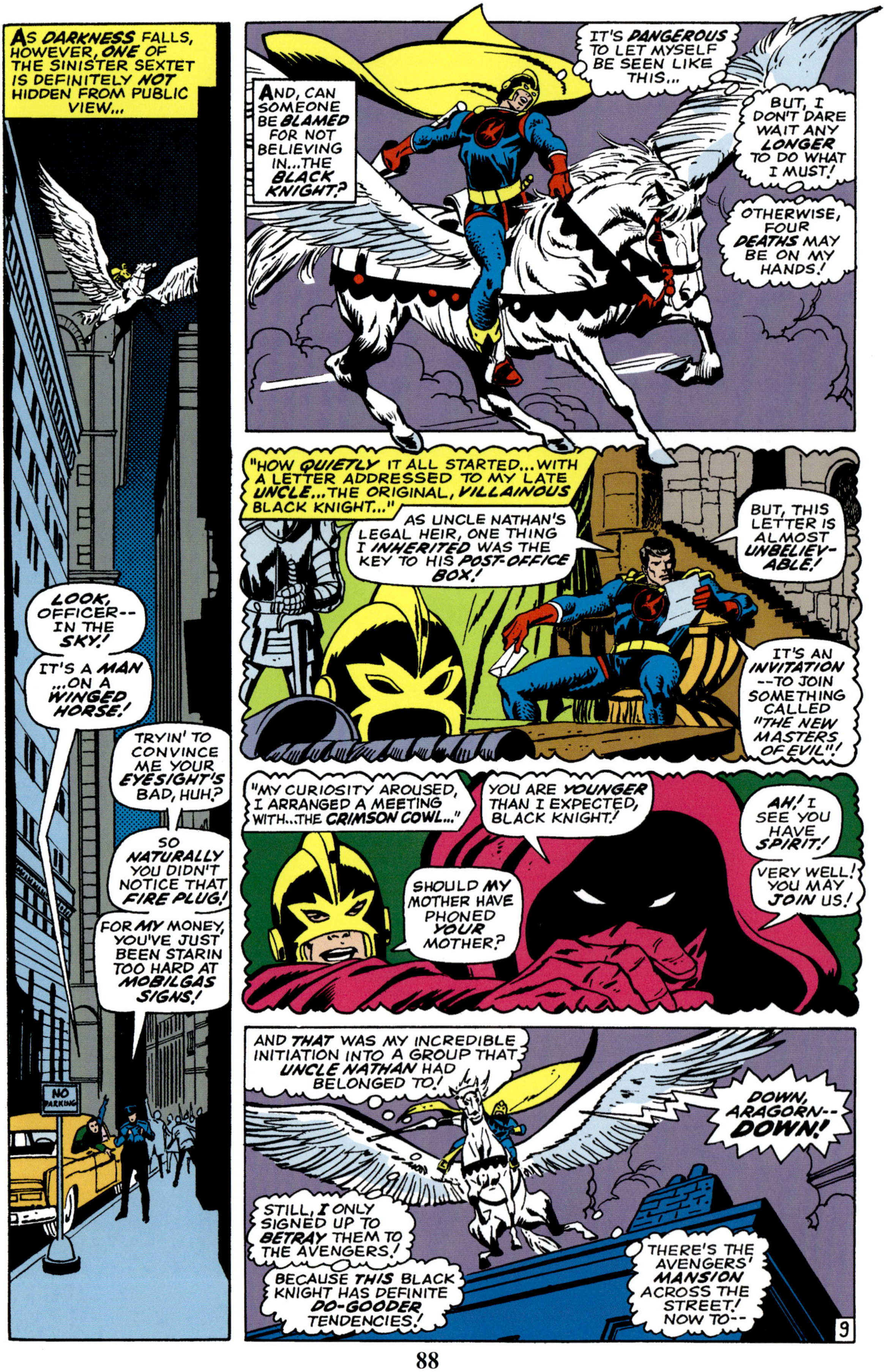
AS DARKNESS FALLS, HOWEVER, ONE OF THE SINISTER SEXTET IS DEFINITELY NOT HIDDEN FROM PUBLIC VIEW...
AND, CAN SOMEONE BE BLAMED FOR NOT BELIEVING IN...THE BLACK KNIGHT?
IT'S DANGEROUS TO LET MYSELF BE SEEN LIKE THIS...
BUT, I DON'T DARE WAIT ANY LONGER TO DO WHAT I MUST!
OTHERWISE, FOUR DEATHS MAY BE ON MY HANDS!
LOOK, OFFICER-- IN THE SKY!
IT'S A MAN ...ON A WINGED HORSE!
TRYIN' TO CONVINCE ME YOUR EYESIGHT'S BAD, HUH?
SO NATURALLY YOU DIDN'T NOTICE THAT FIRE PLUG!
FOR MY MONEY, YOU'VE JUST BEEN STARIN TOO HARD AT MOBILGAS SIGNS!
NO PARKING
"HOW QUIETLY IT ALL STARTED...WITH A LETTER ADDRESSED TO MY LATE UNCLE...THE ORIGINAL, VILLAINOUS BLACK KNIGHT..."
AS UNCLE NATHAN'S LEGAL HEIR, ONE THING I INHERITED WAS THE KEY TO HIS POST-OFFICE BOX!
BUT, THIS LETTER IS ALMOST UNBELIEV-ABLE!
IT'S AN INVITATION --TO JOIN SOMETHING CALLED "THE NEW MASTERS OF EVIL"!
"MY CURIOSITY AROUSED, I ARRANGED A MEETING WITH...THE CRIMSON COWL..."
YOU ARE YOUNGER THAN I EXPECTED, BLACK KNIGHT!
AH! I SEE YOU HAVE SPIRIT!
VERY WELL! YOU MAY JOIN US!
SHOULD MY MOTHER HAVE PHONED YOUR MOTHER?
AND THAT WAS MY INCREDIBLE INITIATION INTO A GROUP THAT UNCLE NATHAN HAD BELONGED TO!
DOWN, ARAGORN-- DOWN!
STILL, I ONLY SIGNED UP TO BETRAY THEM TO THE AVENGERS!
BECAUSE THIS BLACK KNIGHT HAS DEFINITE DO-GOODER TENDENCIES!
THERE'S THE AVENGERS' MANSION ACROSS THE STREET! NOW TO--
9

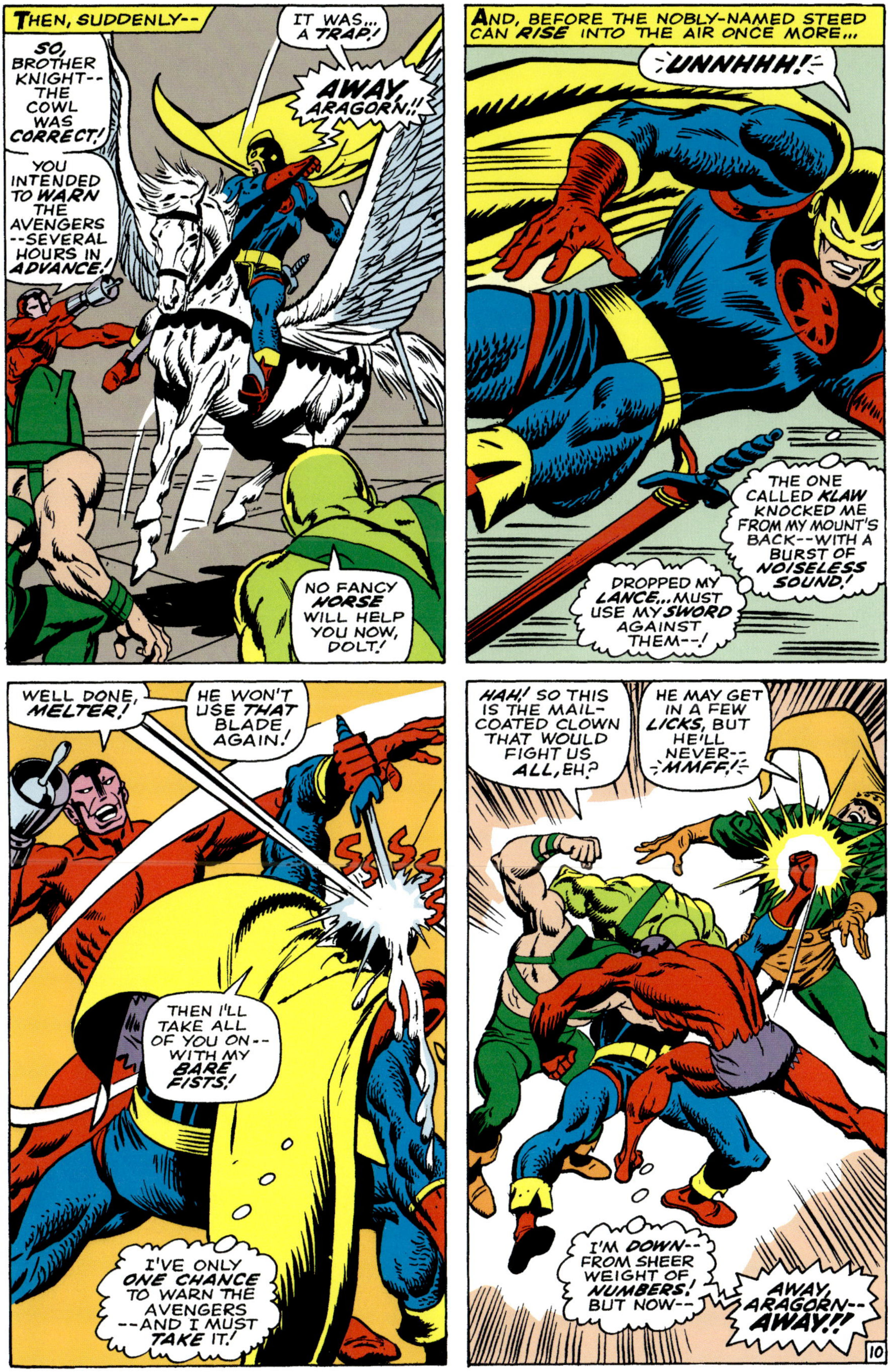
THEN, SUDDENLY--
SO, BROTHER KNIGHT-- THE COWL WAS CORRECT!
YOU INTENDED TO WARN THE AVENGERS --SEVERAL HOURS IN ADVANCE!
IT WAS... A TRAP!
AWAY, ARAGORN!!
NO FANCY HORSE WILL HELP YOU NOW, DOLT!
AND, BEFORE THE NOBLY-NAMED STEED CAN RISE INTO THE AIR ONCE MORE...
UNNHHH!
THE ONE CALLED KLAW KNOCKED ME FROM MY MOUNT'S BACK--WITH A BURST OF NOISELESS SOUND!
DROPPED MY LANCE... MUST USE MY SWORD AGAINST THEM--!
WELL DONE, MELTER!
HE WON'T USE THAT BLADE AGAIN!
THEN I'LL TAKE ALL OF YOU ON-- WITH MY BARE FISTS!
I'VE ONLY ONE CHANCE TO WARN THE AVENGERS --AND I MUST TAKE IT!
HAH! SO THIS IS THE MAIL-COATED CLOWN THAT WOULD FIGHT US ALL, EH?
HE MAY GET IN A FEW LICKS, BUT HE'LL NEVER-- MMFF!
I'M DOWN-- FROM SHEER WEIGHT OF NUMBERS! BUT NOW--
AWAY, ARAGORN-- AWAY!!
10

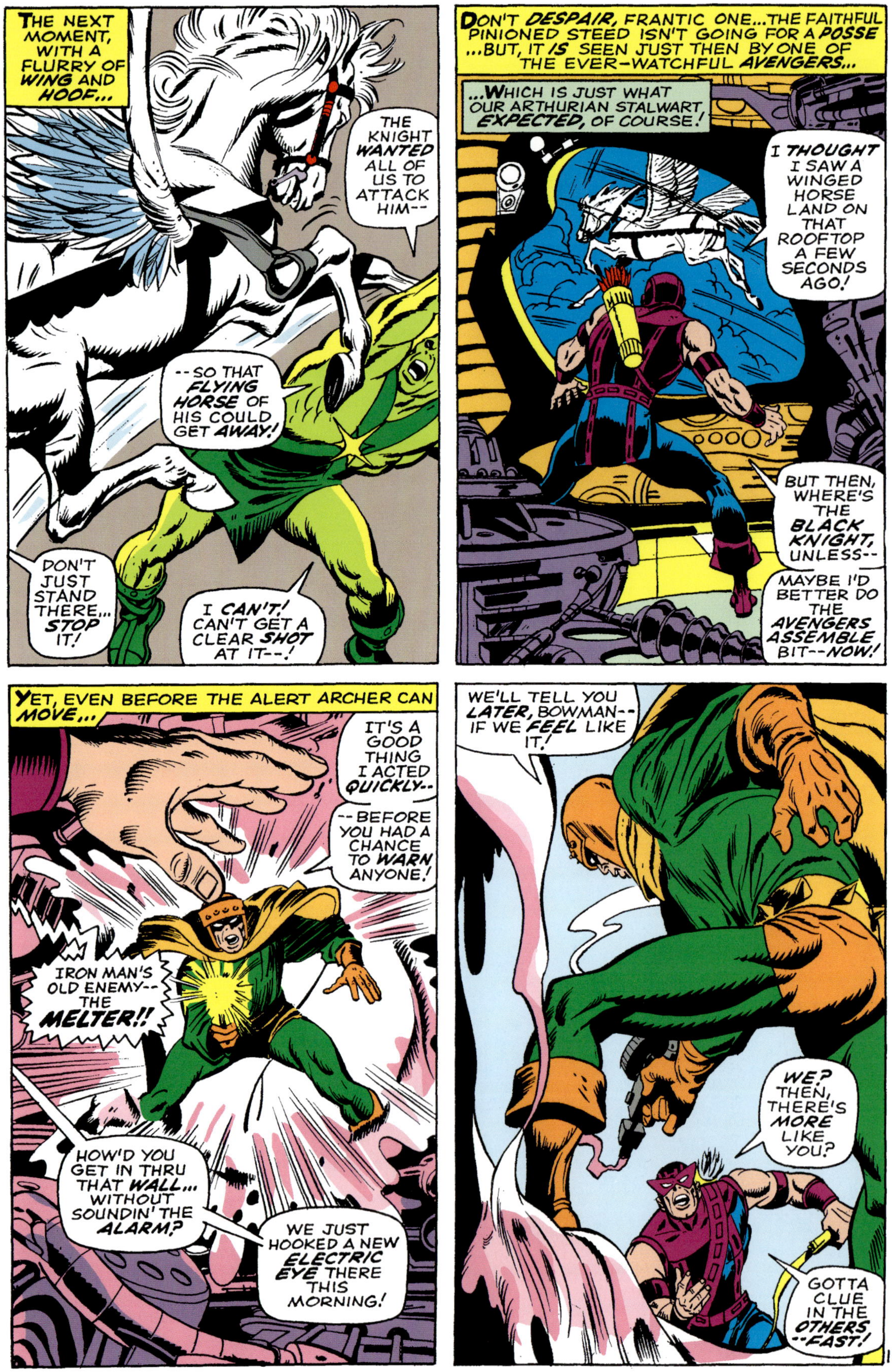
THE NEXT MOMENT, WITH A FLURRY OF WING AND HOOF...
THE KNIGHT WANTED ALL OF US TO ATTACK HIM--
--SO THAT FLYING HORSE OF HIS COULD GET AWAY!
DON'T JUST STAND THERE... STOP IT!
I CAN'T! CAN'T GET A CLEAR SHOT AT IT--!
DON'T DESPAIR, FRANTIC ONE...THE FAITHFUL PINIONED STEED ISN'T GOING FOR A POSSE ...BUT, IT IS SEEN JUST THEN BY ONE OF THE EVER-WATCHFUL AVENGERS...
...WHICH IS JUST WHAT OUR ARTHURIAN STALWART EXPECTED, OF COURSE!
I THOUGHT I SAW A WINGED HORSE LAND ON THAT ROOFTOP A FEW SECONDS AGO!
BUT THEN, WHERE'S THE BLACK KNIGHT, UNLESS--
MAYBE I'D BETTER DO THE AVENGERS ASSEMBLE BIT--NOW!
YET, EVEN BEFORE THE ALERT ARCHER CAN MOVE...
IT'S A GOOD THING I ACTED QUICKLY--
--BEFORE YOU HAD A CHANCE TO WARN ANYONE!
IRON MAN'S OLD ENEMY-- THE MELTER!!
HOW'D YOU GET IN THRU THAT WALL... WITHOUT SOUNDIN' THE ALARM?
WE JUST HOOKED A NEW ELECTRIC EYE THERE THIS MORNING!
WE'LL TELL YOU LATER, BOWMAN-- IF WE FEEL LIKE IT!
WE? THEN, THERE'S MORE LIKE YOU?
GOTTA CLUE IN THE OTHERS --FAST!
11.

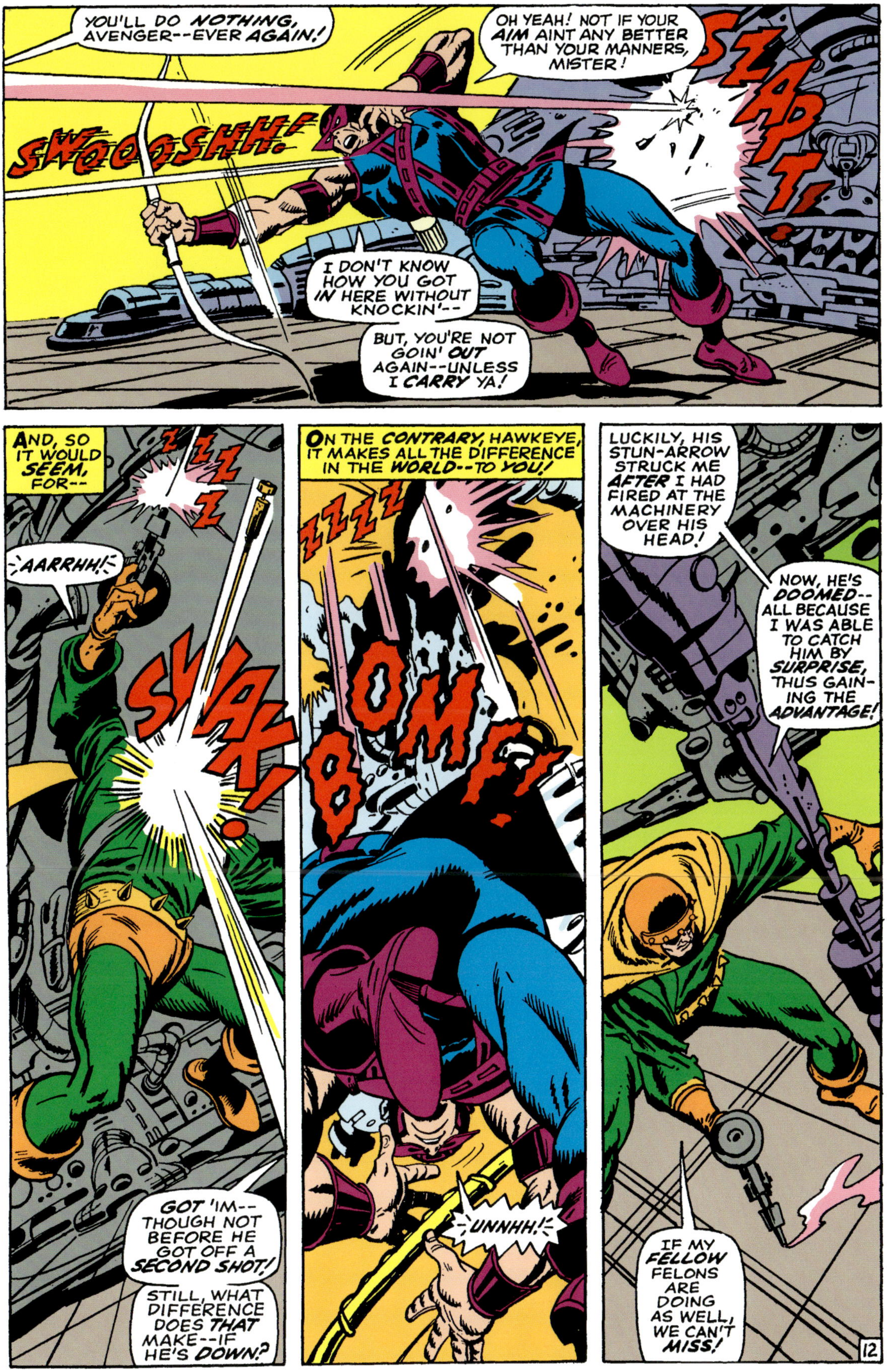
YOU'LL DO NOTHING, AVENGER--EVER AGAIN!
OH YEAH! NOT IF YOUR AIM AINT ANY BETTER THAN YOUR MANNERS, MISTER!
SZAPT!
SWOOOSHH!
I DON'T KNOW HOW YOU GOT IN HERE WITHOUT KNOCKIN'--
BUT, YOU'RE NOT GOIN' OUT AGAIN--UNLESS I CARRY YA!
AND, SO IT WOULD SEEM, FOR--
Z Z Z Z
AARRHH!
SWAK!
GOT 'IM--THOUGH NOT BEFORE HE GOT OFF A SECOND SHOT!
STILL, WHAT DIFFERENCE DOES THAT MAKE--IF HE'S DOWN?
ON THE CONTRARY, HAWKEYE, IT MAKES ALL THE DIFFERENCE IN THE WORLD--TO YOU!
ZZZZ
BOOM!
UNNHH!
LUCKILY, HIS STUN-ARROW STRUCK ME AFTER I HAD FIRED AT THE MACHINERY OVER HIS HEAD!
NOW, HE'S DOOMED--ALL BECAUSE I WAS ABLE TO CATCH HIM BY SURPRISE, THUS GAINING THE ADVANTAGE!
IF MY FELLOW FELONS ARE DOING AS WELL, WE CAN'T MISS!
12

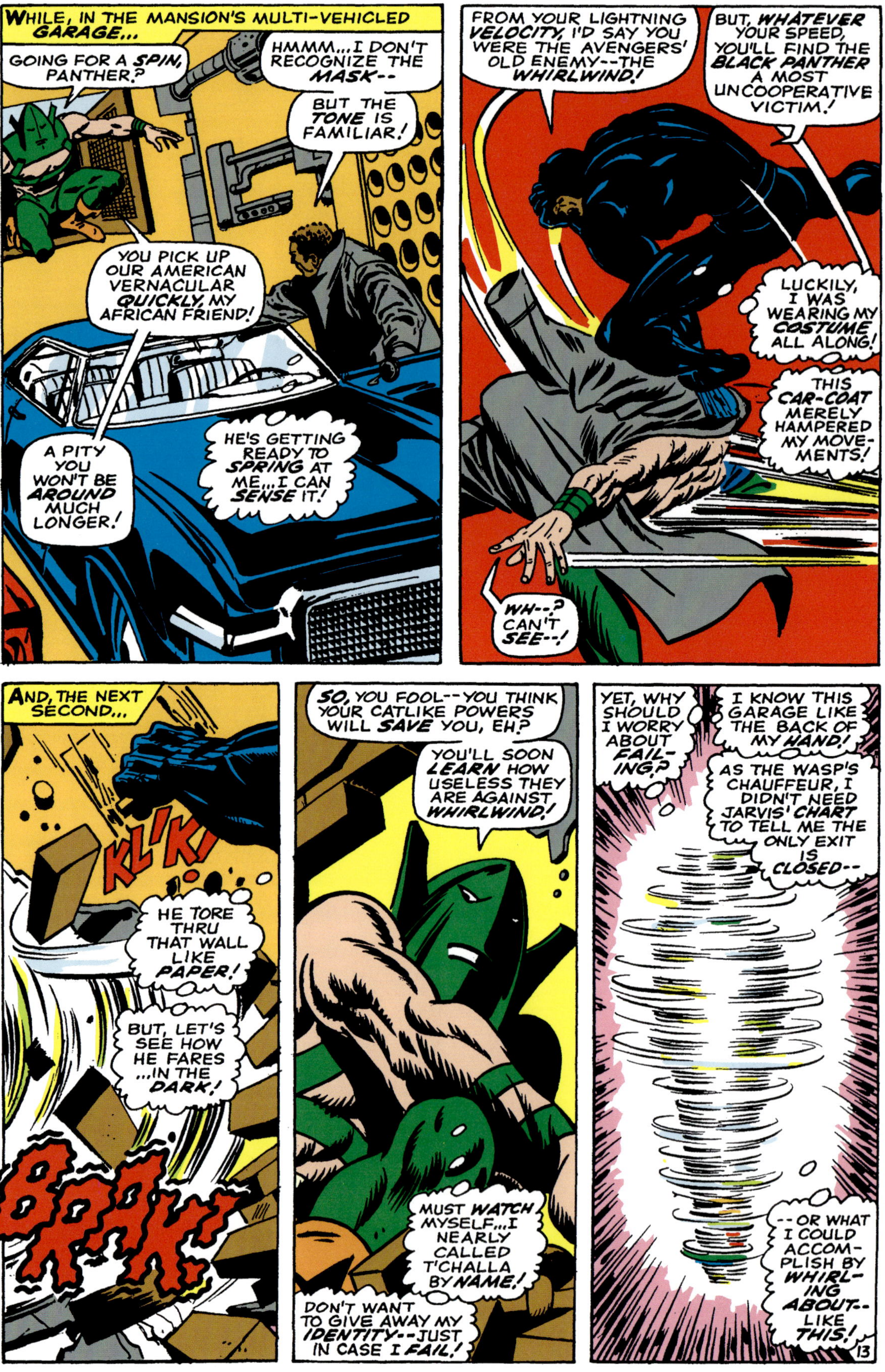
WHILE, IN THE MANSION'S MULTI-VEHICLED GARAGE...
GOING FOR A SPIN, PANTHER?
HMMM...I DON'T RECOGNIZE THE MASK--
BUT THE TONE IS FAMILIAR!
YOU PICK UP OUR AMERICAN VERNACULAR QUICKLY, MY AFRICAN FRIEND!
A PITY YOU WON'T BE AROUND MUCH LONGER!
HE'S GETTING READY TO SPRING AT ME...I CAN SENSE IT!
FROM YOUR LIGHTNING VELOCITY, I'D SAY YOU WERE THE AVENGERS' OLD ENEMY--THE WHIRLWIND!
BUT, WHATEVER YOUR SPEED, YOU'LL FIND THE BLACK PANTHER A MOST UNCOOPERATIVE VICTIM!
LUCKILY, I WAS WEARING MY COSTUME ALL ALONG!
THIS CAR-COAT MERELY HAMPERED MY MOVEMENTS!
WH--? CAN'T SEE--!
AND, THE NEXT SECOND...
KLIK!
HE TORE THRU THAT WALL LIKE PAPER!
BUT, LET'S SEE HOW HE FARES ...IN THE DARK!
BRAK!
SO, YOU FOOL--YOU THINK YOUR CATLIKE POWERS WILL SAVE YOU, EH?
YOU'LL SOON LEARN HOW USELESS THEY ARE AGAINST WHIRLWIND!
MUST WATCH MYSELF...I NEARLY CALLED T'CHALLA BY NAME!
DON'T WANT TO GIVE AWAY MY IDENTITY--JUST IN CASE I FAIL!
YET, WHY SHOULD I WORRY ABOUT FAILING?
I KNOW THIS GARAGE LIKE THE BACK OF MY HAND!
AS THE WASP'S CHAUFFEUR, I DIDN'T NEED JARVIS' CHART TO TELL ME THE ONLY EXIT IS CLOSED--
--OR WHAT I COULD ACCOMPLISH BY WHIRLING ABOUT--LIKE THIS!
13

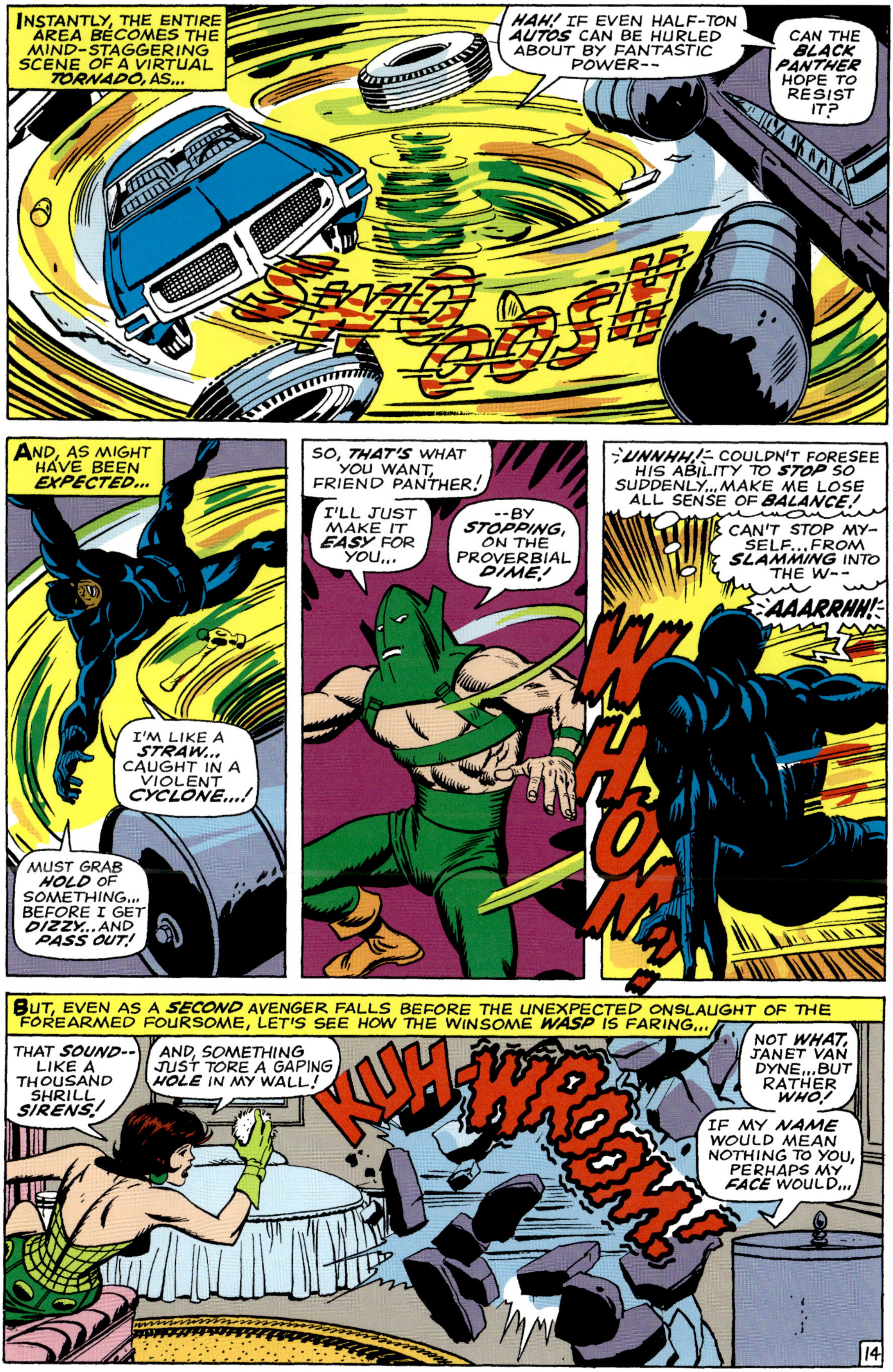
INSTANTLY, THE ENTIRE AREA BECOMES THE MIND-STAGGERING SCENE OF A VIRTUAL TORNADO, AS...
HAH! IF EVEN HALF-TON AUTOS CAN BE HURLED ABOUT BY FANTASTIC POWER--
CAN THE BLACK PANTHER HOPE TO RESIST IT?
SHOOOSH
AND, AS MIGHT HAVE BEEN EXPECTED...
I'M LIKE A STRAW... CAUGHT IN A VIOLENT CYCLONE...!
MUST GRAB HOLD OF SOMETHING... BEFORE I GET DIZZY...AND PASS OUT!
SO, THAT'S WHAT YOU WANT, FRIEND PANTHER!
I'LL JUST MAKE IT EASY FOR YOU...
--BY STOPPING, ON THE PROVERBIAL DIME!
UNNHH! COULDN'T FORESEE HIS ABILITY TO STOP SO SUDDENLY...MAKE ME LOSE ALL SENSE OF BALANCE!
CAN'T STOP MY-SELF...FROM SLAMMING INTO THE W--
AAARRHH!
WHOMM!
BUT, EVEN AS A SECOND AVENGER FALLS BEFORE THE UNEXPECTED ONSLAUGHT OF THE FOREARMED FOURSOME, LET'S SEE HOW THE WINSOME WASP IS FARING...
THAT SOUND-- LIKE A THOUSAND SHRILL SIRENS!
AND, SOMETHING JUST TORE A GAPING HOLE IN MY WALL!
KUH-WHOOM!
NOT WHAT, JANET VAN DYNE,...BUT RATHER WHO!
IF MY NAME WOULD MEAN NOTHING TO YOU, PERHAPS MY FACE WOULD...
14

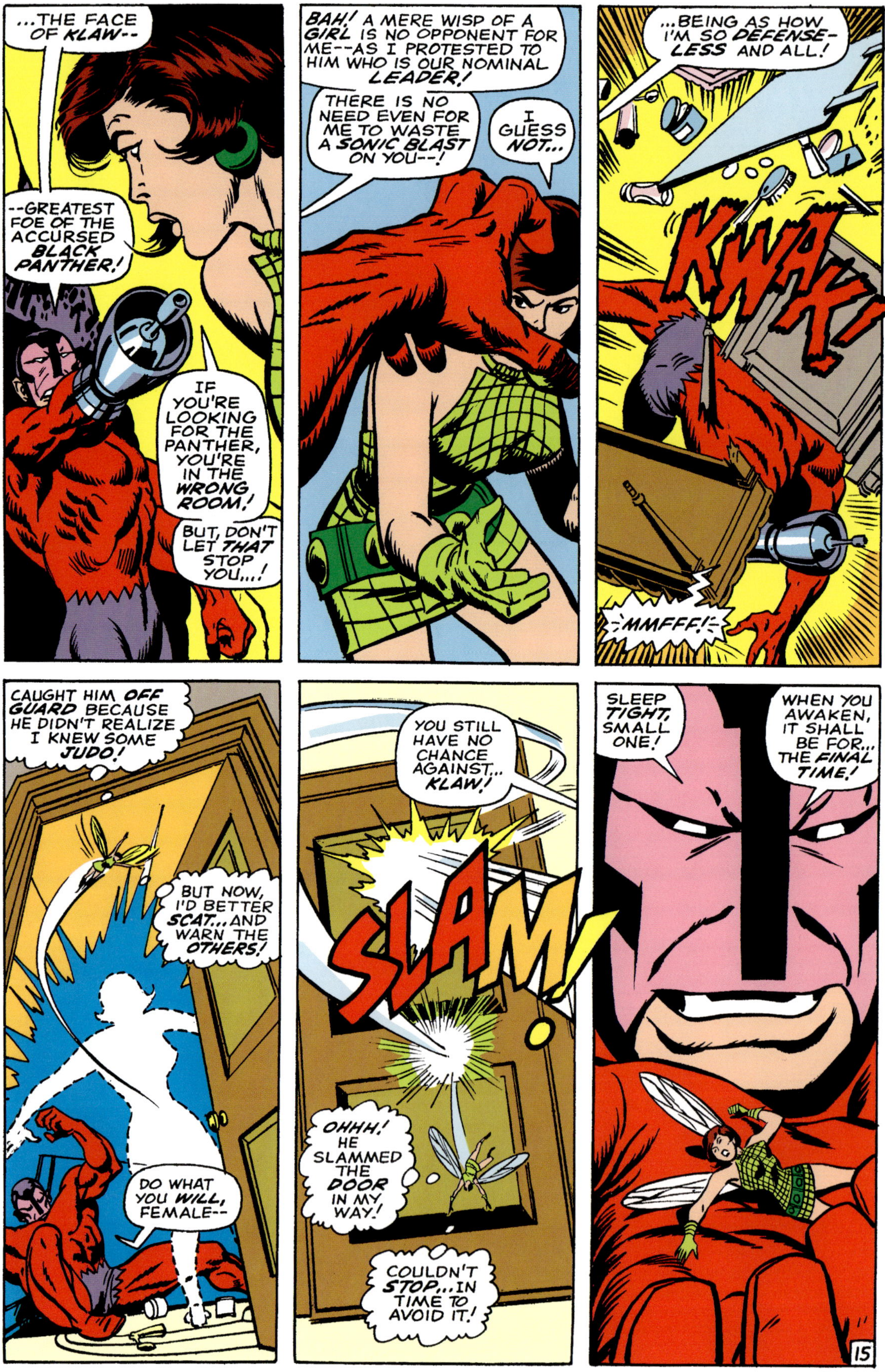
...THE FACE OF KLAW--
--GREATEST FOE OF THE ACCURSED BLACK PANTHER!
IF YOU'RE LOOKING FOR THE PANTHER, YOU'RE IN THE WRONG ROOM!
BUT, DON'T LET THAT STOP YOU...!
BAH! A MERE WISP OF A GIRL IS NO OPPONENT FOR ME--AS I PROTESTED TO HIM WHO IS OUR NOMINAL LEADER!
THERE IS NO NEED EVEN FOR ME TO WASTE A SONIC BLAST ON YOU--!
I GUESS NOT...
...BEING AS HOW I'M SO DEFENSELESS AND ALL!
KWAK!
MMFFF!
CAUGHT HIM OFF GUARD BECAUSE HE DIDN'T REALIZE I KNEW SOME JUDO!
BUT NOW, I'D BETTER SCAT... AND WARN THE OTHERS!
DO WHAT YOU WILL, FEMALE--
YOU STILL HAVE NO CHANCE AGAINST... KLAW!
SLAM!
OHHH! HE SLAMMED THE DOOR IN MY WAY!
COULDN'T STOP... IN TIME TO AVOID IT!
SLEEP TIGHT, SMALL ONE!
WHEN YOU AWAKEN, IT SHALL BE FOR... THE FINAL TIME!
15

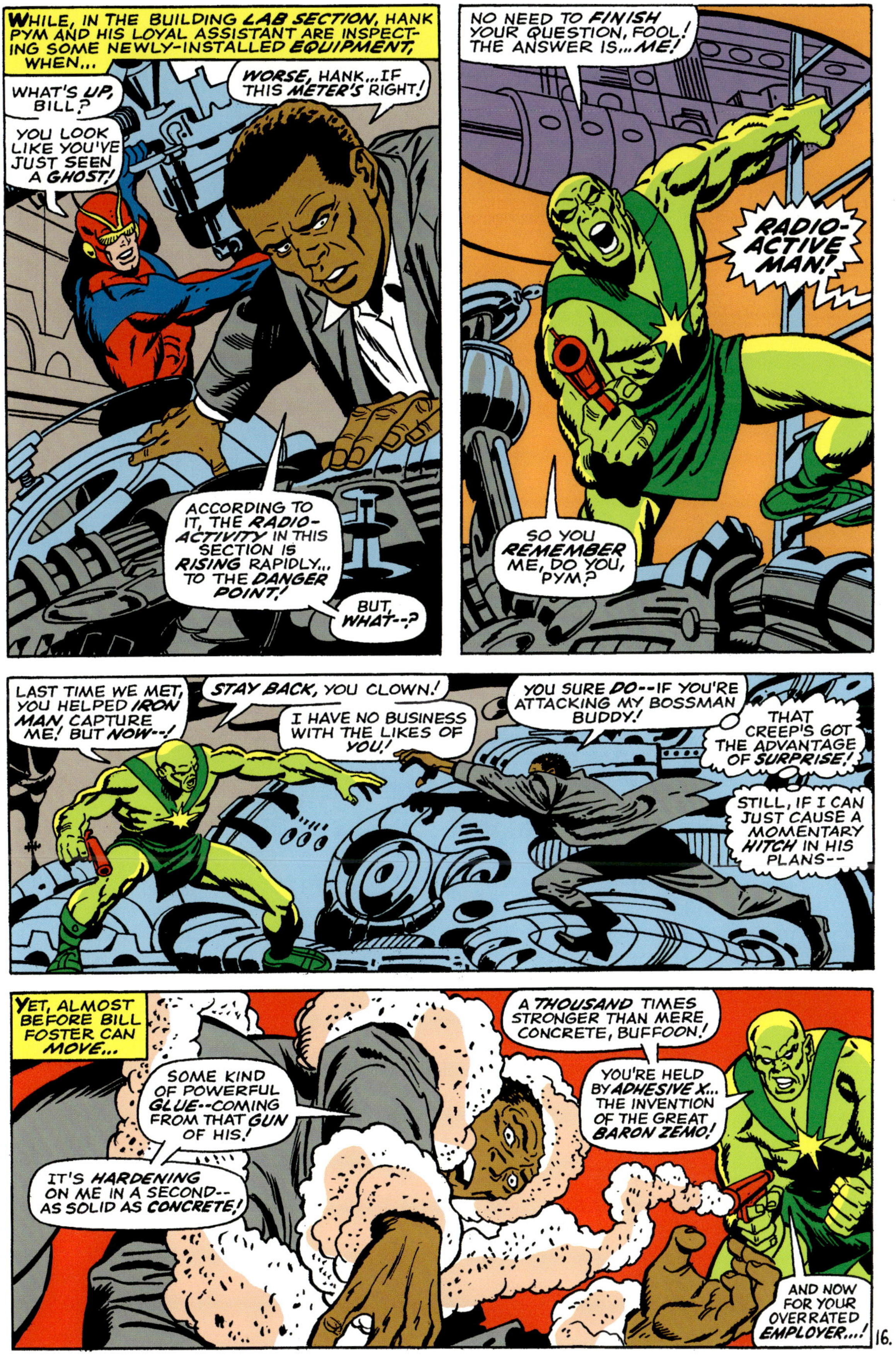
WHILE, IN THE BUILDING LAB SECTION, HANK PYM AND HIS LOYAL ASSISTANT ARE INSPECTING SOME NEWLY-INSTALLED EQUIPMENT, WHEN...
WHAT'S UP, BILL?
YOU LOOK LIKE YOU'VE JUST SEEN A GHOST!
WORSE, HANK...IF THIS METER'S RIGHT!
ACCORDING TO IT, THE RADIO-ACTIVITY IN THIS SECTION IS RISING RAPIDLY... TO THE DANGER POINT!
BUT, WHAT--?
NO NEED TO FINISH YOUR QUESTION, FOOL! THE ANSWER IS...ME!
RADIO-ACTIVE MAN!
SO YOU REMEMBER ME, DO YOU, PYM?
LAST TIME WE MET, YOU HELPED IRON MAN CAPTURE ME! BUT NOW--!
STAY BACK, YOU CLOWN!
I HAVE NO BUSINESS WITH THE LIKES OF YOU!
YOU SURE DO--IF YOU'RE ATTACKING MY BOSSMAN BUDDY!
THAT CREEP'S GOT THE ADVANTAGE OF SURPRISE!
STILL, IF I CAN JUST CAUSE A MOMENTARY HITCH IN HIS PLANS--
YET, ALMOST BEFORE BILL FOSTER CAN MOVE...
SOME KIND OF POWERFUL GLUE--COMING FROM THAT GUN OF HIS!
IT'S HARDENING ON ME IN A SECOND-- AS SOLID AS CONCRETE!
A THOUSAND TIMES STRONGER THAN MERE CONCRETE, BUFFOON!
YOU'RE HELD BY ADHESIVE X... THE INVENTION OF THE GREAT BARON ZEMO!
AND NOW FOR YOUR OVERRATED EMPLOYER...!
16.

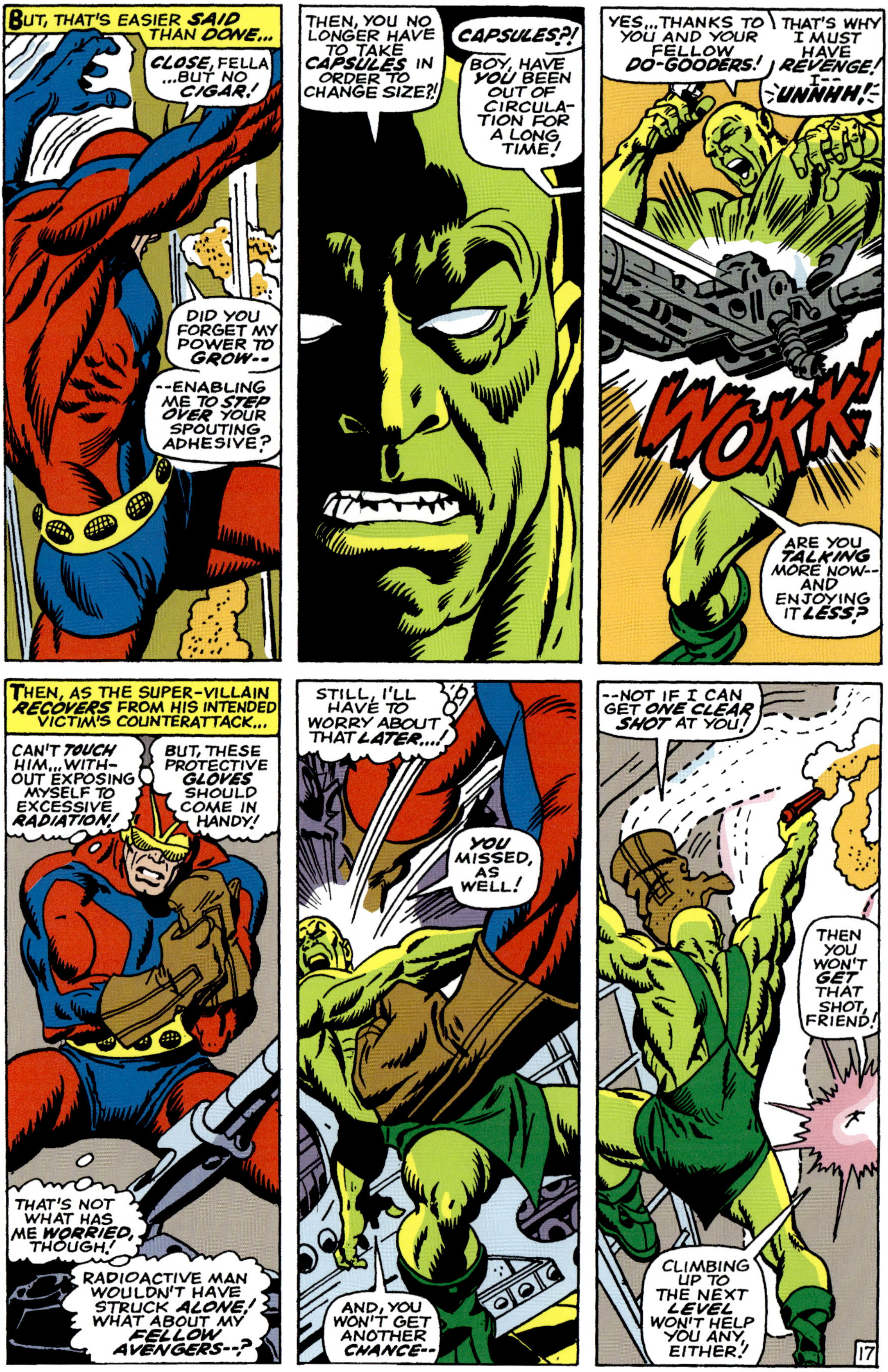
BUT, THAT'S EASIER SAID THAN DONE...
CLOSE, FELLA ...BUT NO CIGAR!
DID YOU FORGET MY POWER TO GROW--
--ENABLING ME TO STEP OVER YOUR SPOUTING ADHESIVE?
THEN, YOU NO LONGER HAVE TO TAKE CAPSULES IN ORDER TO CHANGE SIZE?!
CAPSULES?!
BOY, HAVE YOU BEEN OUT OF CIRCULATION FOR A LONG TIME!
YES... THANKS TO YOU AND YOUR FELLOW DO-GOODERS!
THAT'S WHY I MUST HAVE REVENGE! I--
UNNHH!
WOKK!
ARE YOU TALKING MORE NOW--AND ENJOYING IT LESS?
THEN, AS THE SUPER-VILLAIN RECOVERS FROM HIS INTENDED VICTIM'S COUNTERATTACK...
CAN'T TOUCH HIM... WITHOUT EXPOSING MYSELF TO EXCESSIVE RADIATION!
BUT, THESE PROTECTIVE GLOVES SHOULD COME IN HANDY!
THAT'S NOT WHAT HAS ME WORRIED, THOUGH!
RADIOACTIVE MAN WOULDN'T HAVE STRUCK ALONE! WHAT ABOUT MY FELLOW AVENGERS--?
STILL, I'LL HAVE TO WORRY ABOUT THAT LATER...!
YOU MISSED, AS WELL!
AND, YOU WON'T GET ANOTHER CHANCE--
--NOT IF I CAN GET ONE CLEAR SHOT AT YOU!
THEN YOU WON'T GET THAT SHOT, FRIEND!
CLIMBING UP TO THE NEXT LEVEL WON'T HELP YOU ANY, EITHER!
17

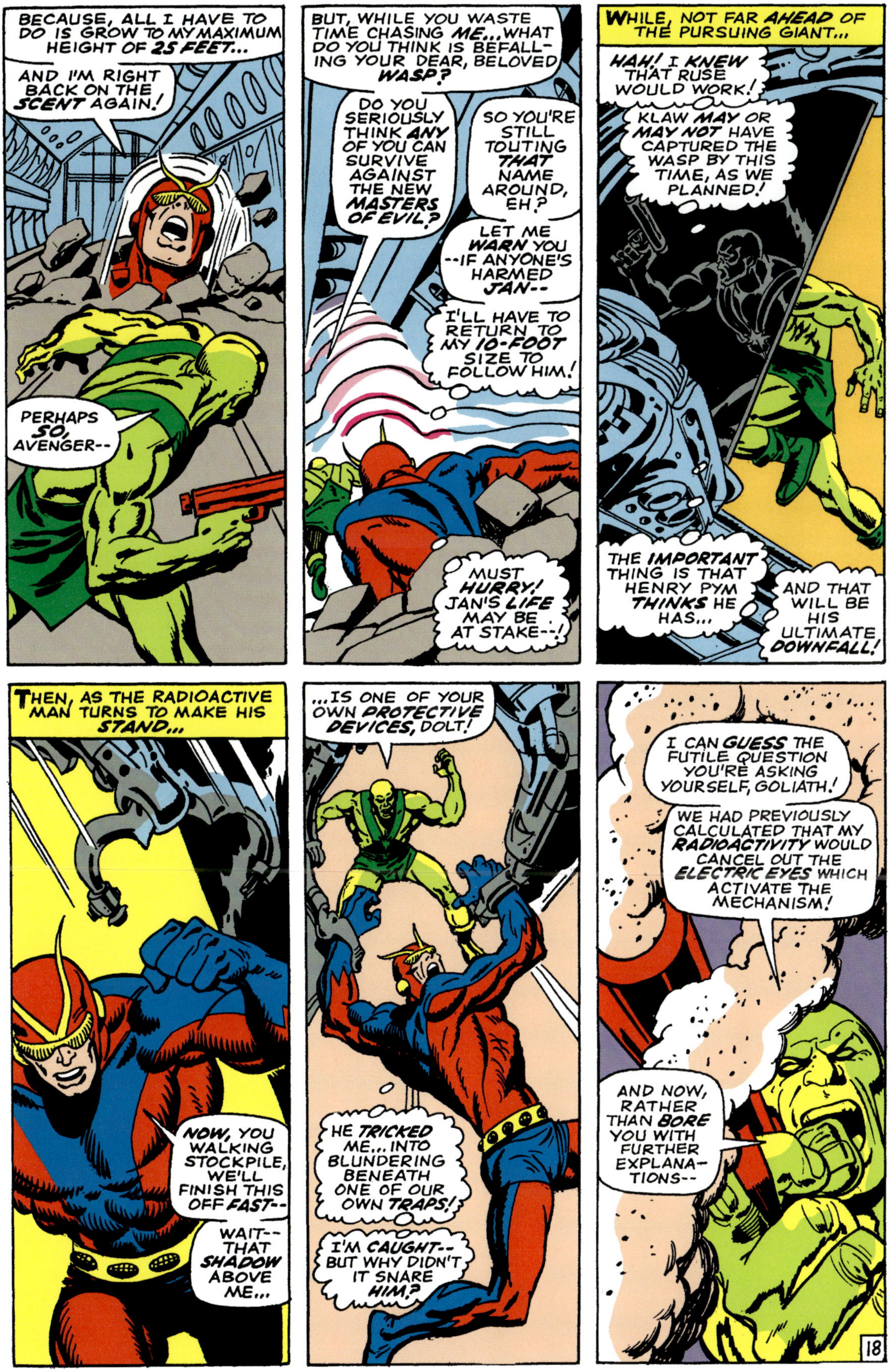

BECAUSE, ALL I HAVE TO DO IS GROW TO MY MAXIMUM HEIGHT OF 25 FEET...
AND I'M RIGHT BACK ON THE SCENT AGAIN!
PERHAPS SO, AVENGER--
BUT, WHILE YOU WASTE TIME CHASING ME... WHAT DO YOU THINK IS BEFALLING YOUR DEAR, BELOVED WASP?
DO YOU SERIOUSLY THINK ANY OF YOU CAN SURVIVE AGAINST THE NEW MASTERS OF EVIL?
SO YOU'RE STILL TOUTING THAT NAME AROUND, EH?
LET ME WARN YOU --IF ANYONE'S HARMED JAN--
I'LL HAVE TO RETURN TO MY 10-FOOT SIZE TO FOLLOW HIM!
MUST HURRY! JAN'S LIFE MAY BE AT STAKE--!
WHILE, NOT FAR AHEAD OF THE PURSUING GIANT...
HAH! I KNEW THAT RUSE WOULD WORK!
KLAW MAY OR MAY NOT HAVE CAPTURED THE WASP BY THIS TIME, AS WE PLANNED!
THE IMPORTANT THING IS THAT HENRY PYM THINKS HE HAS...
AND THAT WILL BE HIS ULTIMATE DOWNFALL!
THEN, AS THE RADIOACTIVE MAN TURNS TO MAKE HIS STAND...
NOW, YOU WALKING STOCKPILE, WE'LL FINISH THIS OFF FAST--
WAIT-- THAT SHADOW ABOVE ME...
...IS ONE OF YOUR OWN PROTECTIVE DEVICES, DOLT!
HE TRICKED ME... INTO BLUNDERING BENEATH ONE OF OUR OWN TRAPS!
I'M CAUGHT-- BUT WHY DIDN'T IT SNARE HIM?
I CAN GUESS THE FUTILE QUESTION YOU'RE ASKING YOURSELF, GOLIATH!
WE HAD PREVIOUSLY CALCULATED THAT MY RADIOACTIVITY WOULD CANCEL OUT THE ELECTRIC EYES WHICH ACTIVATE THE MECHANISM!
AND NOW, RATHER THAN BORE YOU WITH FURTHER EXPLANATIONS--
18

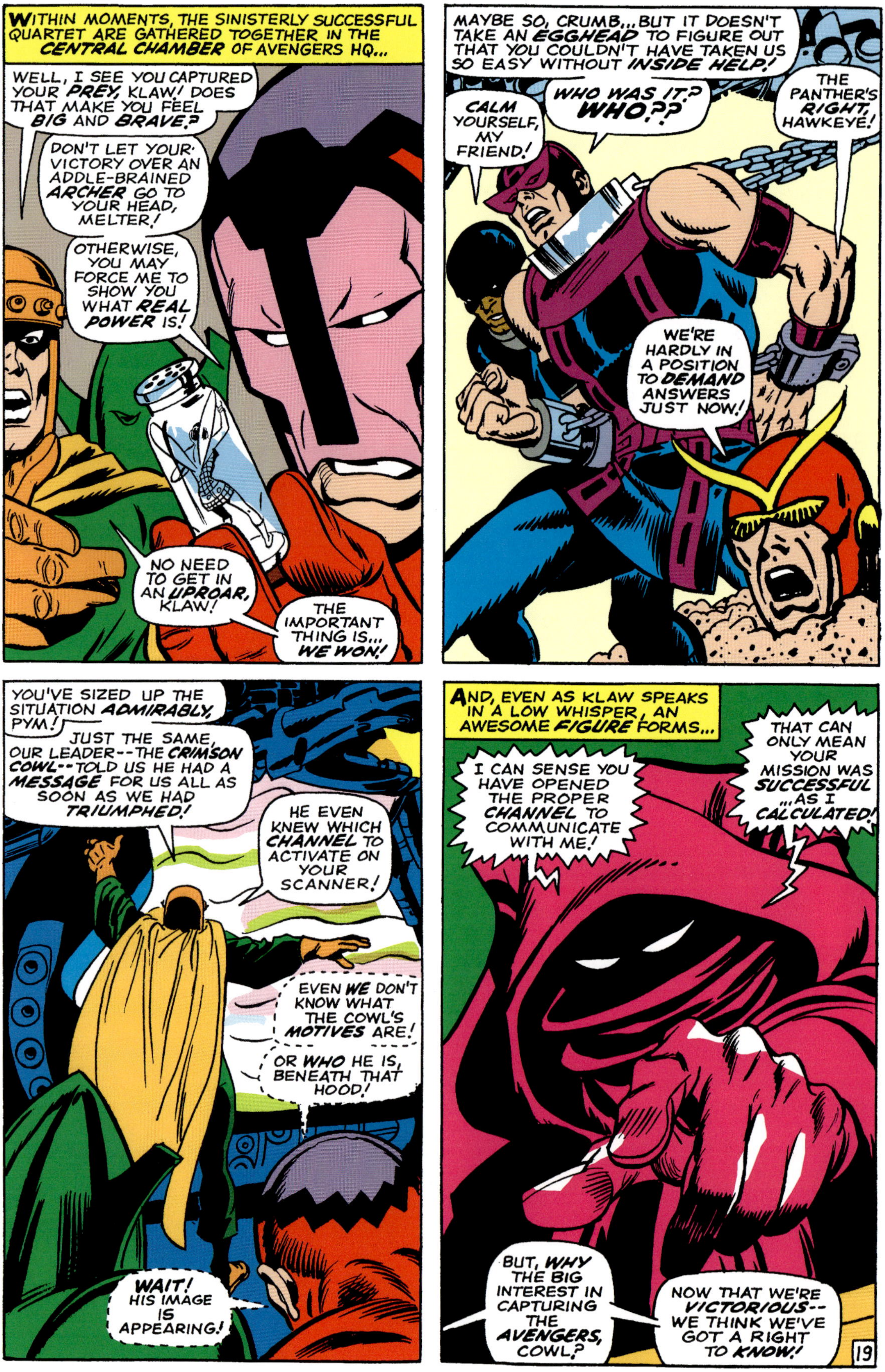

Panel 1 (caption): WITHIN MOMENTS, THE SINISTERLY SUCCESSFUL QUARTET ARE GATHERED TOGETHER IN THE *CENTRAL CHAMBER* OF AVENGERS HQ...

WELL, I SEE YOU CAPTURED YOUR *PREY*, KLAW! DOES THAT MAKE YOU FEEL *BIG* AND *BRAVE?*

DON'T LET YOUR VICTORY OVER AN *ADDLE-BRAINED ARCHER* GO TO YOUR HEAD, MELTER!

OTHERWISE, YOU MAY FORCE ME TO SHOW YOU WHAT *REAL POWER* IS!

NO NEED TO GET IN AN *UPROAR*, KLAW!

THE IMPORTANT THING IS... *WE WON!*

Panel 2: MAYBE SO, CRUMB,...BUT IT DOESN'T TAKE AN *EGGHEAD* TO FIGURE OUT THAT YOU COULDN'T HAVE TAKEN US SO EASY WITHOUT *INSIDE HELP!*

CALM YOURSELF, MY FRIEND!

WHO WAS IT? WHO??

THE PANTHER'S *RIGHT*, HAWKEYE!

WE'RE HARDLY IN A POSITION TO *DEMAND* ANSWERS JUST NOW!

Panel 3: YOU'VE SIZED UP THE SITUATION *ADMIRABLY*, PYM!

JUST THE SAME, OUR LEADER--THE *CRIMSON COWL*--TOLD US HE HAD A *MESSAGE* FOR US ALL AS SOON AS WE HAD *TRIUMPHED!*

HE EVEN KNEW WHICH *CHANNEL* TO ACTIVATE ON YOUR SCANNER!

EVEN *WE* DON'T KNOW WHAT THE COWL'S *MOTIVES* ARE!

OR *WHO* HE IS, BENEATH THAT HOOD!

WAIT! HIS IMAGE IS APPEARING!

Panel 4 (caption): AND, EVEN AS KLAW SPEAKS IN A LOW WHISPER, AN AWESOME *FIGURE* FORMS...

I CAN SENSE YOU HAVE OPENED THE PROPER *CHANNEL* TO COMMUNICATE WITH ME!

THAT CAN ONLY MEAN YOUR MISSION WAS *SUCCESSFUL* ...AS I *CALCULATED!*

BUT, *WHY* THE BIG INTEREST IN CAPTURING THE *AVENGERS*, COWL?

NOW THAT WE'RE *VICTORIOUS*-- WE THINK WE'VE GOT A RIGHT TO *KNOW!*

19

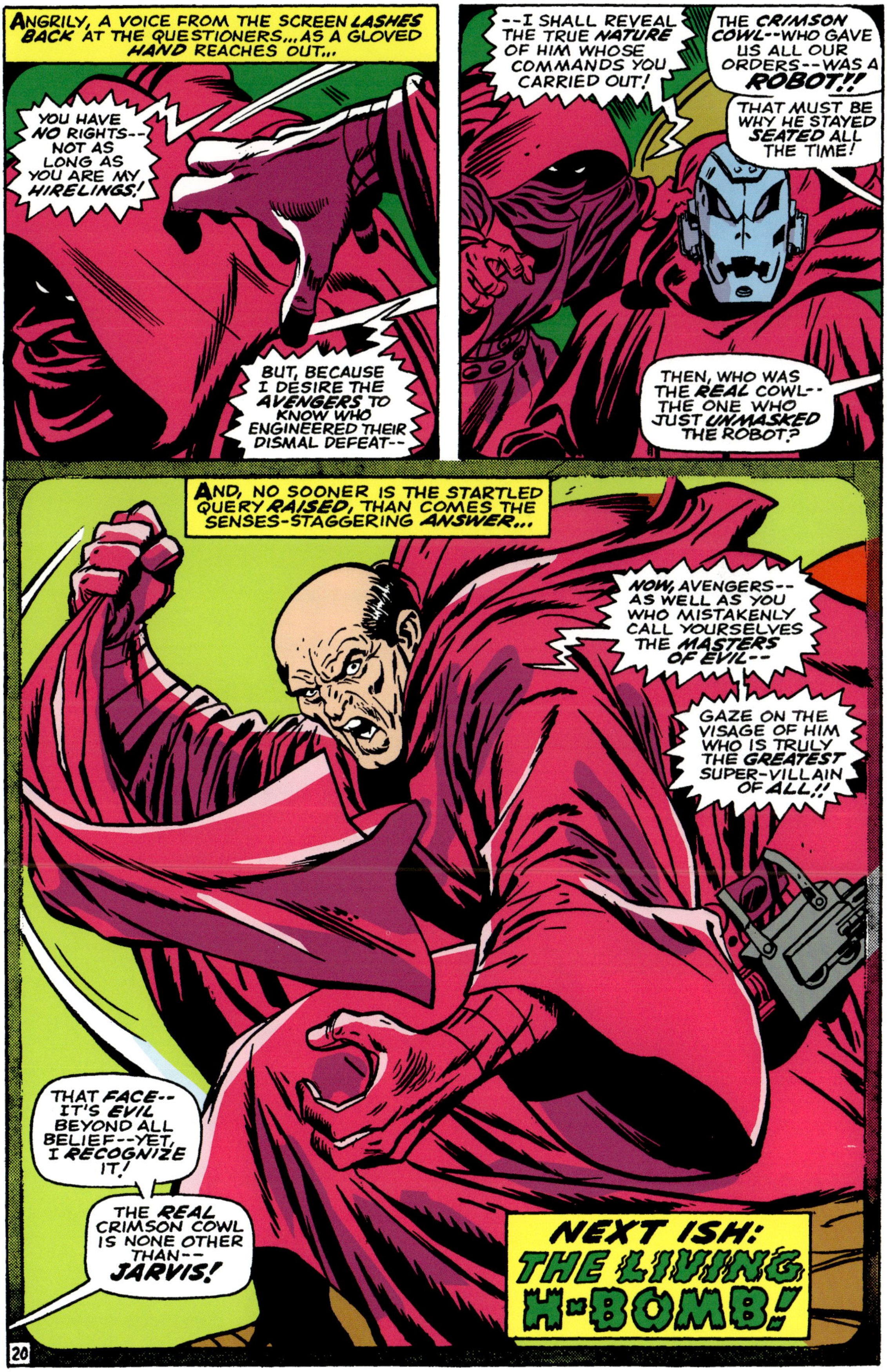
ANGRILY, A VOICE FROM THE SCREEN LASHES BACK AT THE QUESTIONERS...AS A GLOVED HAND REACHES OUT...
YOU HAVE NO RIGHTS--NOT AS LONG AS YOU ARE MY HIRELINGS!
BUT, BECAUSE I DESIRE THE AVENGERS TO KNOW WHO ENGINEERED THEIR DISMAL DEFEAT--
--I SHALL REVEAL THE TRUE NATURE OF HIM WHOSE COMMANDS YOU CARRIED OUT!
THE CRIMSON COWL--WHO GAVE US ALL OUR ORDERS--WAS A ROBOT!!
THAT MUST BE WHY HE STAYED SEATED ALL THE TIME!
THEN, WHO WAS THE REAL COWL--THE ONE WHO JUST UNMASKED THE ROBOT?
AND, NO SOONER IS THE STARTLED QUERY RAISED, THAN COMES THE SENSES-STAGGERING ANSWER...
NOW, AVENGERS--AS WELL AS YOU WHO MISTAKENLY CALL YOURSELVES THE MASTERS OF EVIL--
GAZE ON THE VISAGE OF HIM WHO IS TRULY THE GREATEST SUPER-VILLAIN OF ALL!!
THAT FACE--IT'S EVIL BEYOND ALL BELIEF--YET, I RECOGNIZE IT!
THE REAL CRIMSON COWL IS NONE OTHER THAN--JARVIS!
NEXT ISH: THE LIVING H-BOMB!
20

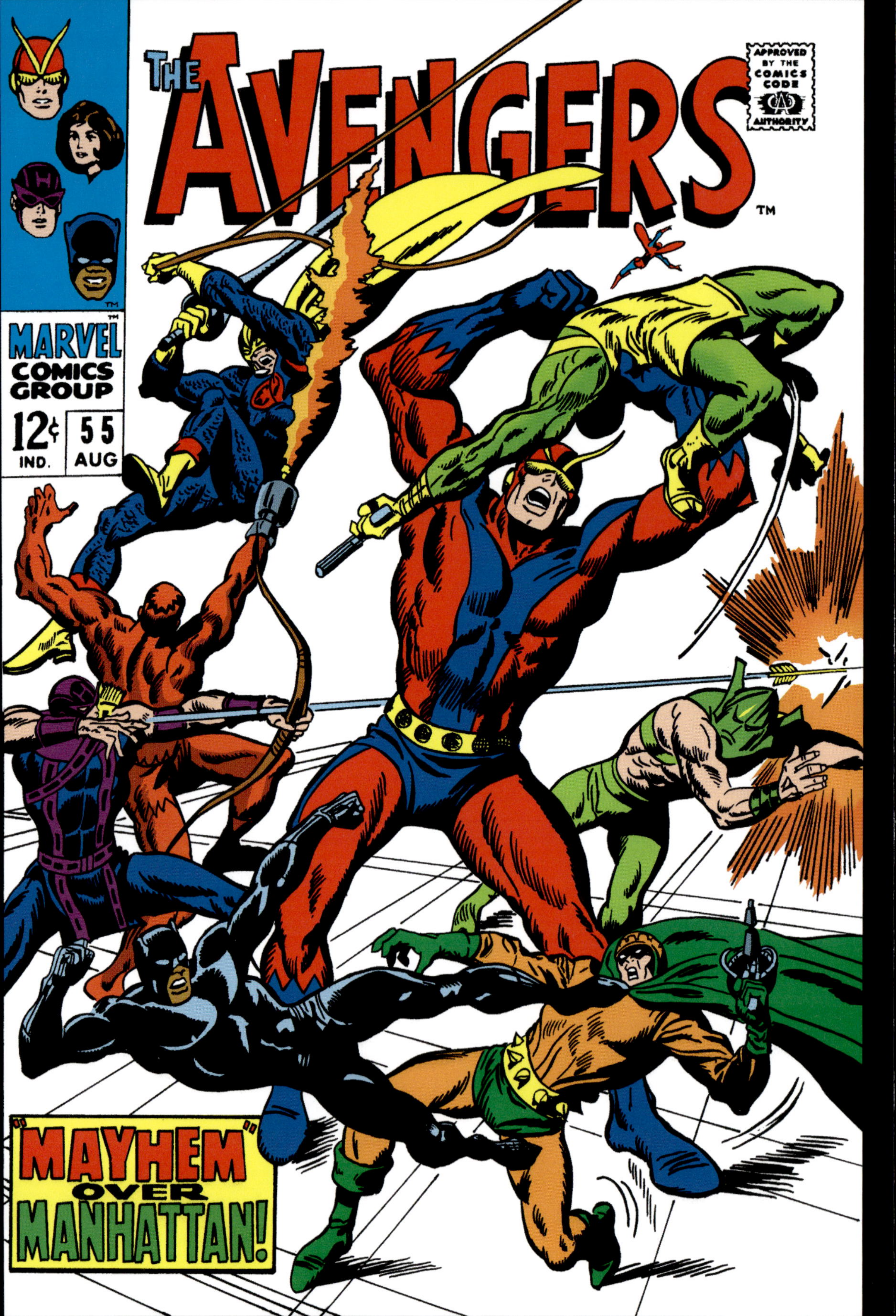

THE AVENGERS
APPROVED BY THE COMICS CODE AUTHORITY
MARVEL COMICS GROUP
12¢ IND.
55 AUG
"MAYHEM" OVER MANHATTAN!

THE MIGHTY AVENGERS!™
NEVER HAVE THE FORTUNES OF THE AVENGERS BEEN AT LOWER EBB! CAPTURED BY A QUARTET OF THEIR MOST DEADLY FOES, UNDER THE LEADERSHIP OF THE MYSTERIOUS CRIMSON COWL, OUR AWESOME ASSEMBLERS FACE A GRISLY FATE... A FATE THAT MAY ONLY BE PREVENTED BY...
"MAYHEM" OVER MANHATTAN!
SCOUT SHIP ONE TO CRIMSON COWL!
WE ARE NOW BLASTING OFF FROM TOP OF TONY STARK'S MANSION... WITH MISSION ACCOMPLISHED!
THE AVENGERS ARE OURS!!
VROOOOSH!
STAN LEE, EDITOR
ROY THOMAS, WRITER
JOHN BUSCEMA, ARTIST
INKED BY GEORGE KLEIN
LETTERED BY SAM ROSEN
WITH A LILTIN' LINEUP LIKE THAT, PILGRIM, YOU KNOW YOU'VE GOT ANOTHER MARVEL MASTERWORK ON YOUR HANDS!

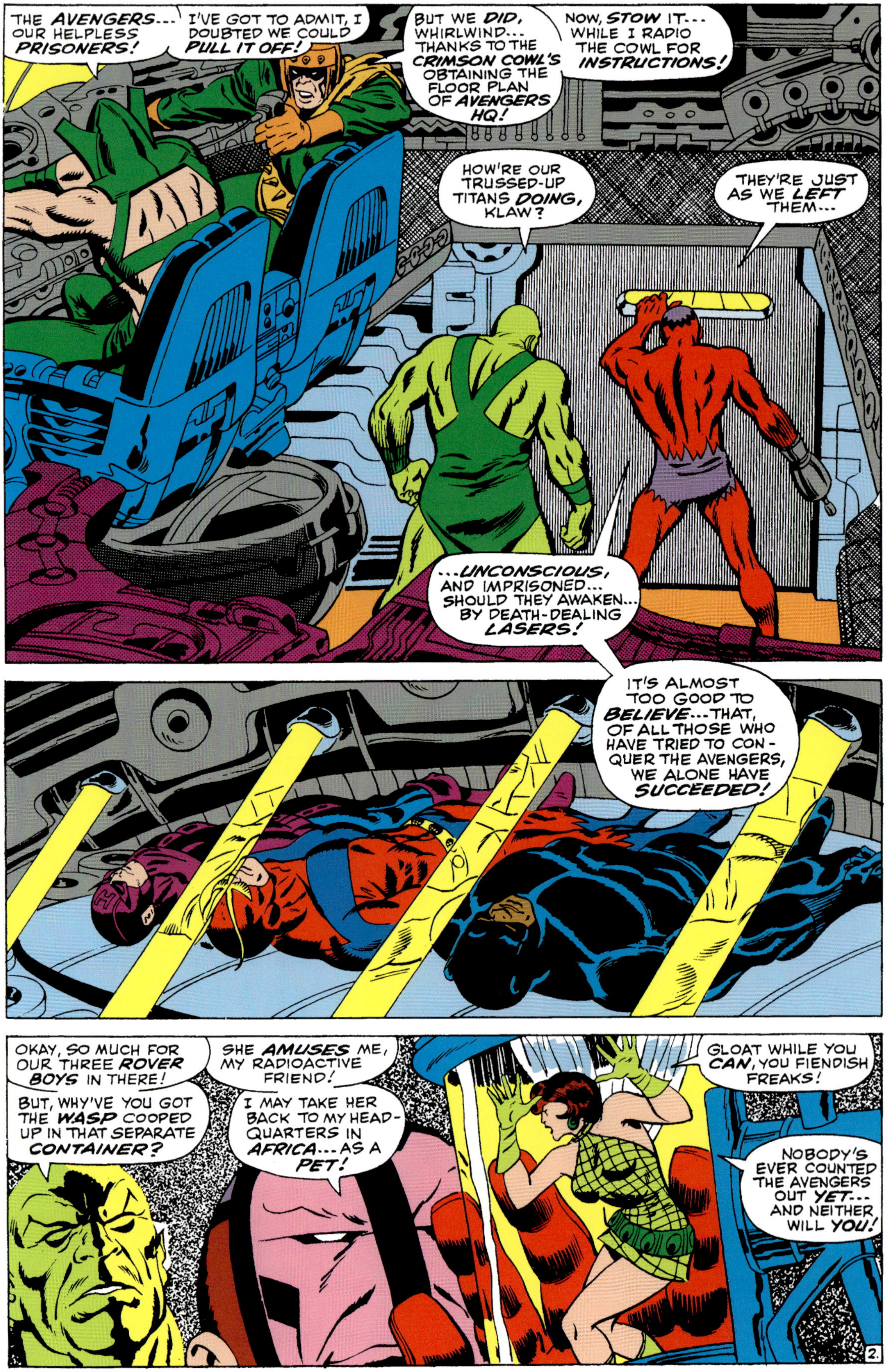
THE AVENGERS--- OUR HELPLESS PRISONERS!
I'VE GOT TO ADMIT, I DOUBTED WE COULD PULL IT OFF!
BUT WE DID, WHIRLWIND--- THANKS TO THE CRIMSON COWL'S OBTAINING THE FLOOR PLAN OF AVENGERS HQ!
NOW, STOW IT--- WHILE I RADIO THE COWL FOR INSTRUCTIONS!
HOW'RE OUR TRUSSED-UP TITANS DOING, KLAW?
THEY'RE JUST AS WE LEFT THEM---
...UNCONSCIOUS, AND IMPRISONED... SHOULD THEY AWAKEN... BY DEATH-DEALING LASERS!
IT'S ALMOST TOO GOOD TO BELIEVE---THAT, OF ALL THOSE WHO HAVE TRIED TO CONQUER THE AVENGERS, WE ALONE HAVE SUCCEEDED!
OKAY, SO MUCH FOR OUR THREE ROVER BOYS IN THERE!
BUT, WHY'VE YOU GOT THE WASP COOPED UP IN THAT SEPARATE CONTAINER?
SHE AMUSES ME, MY RADIOACTIVE FRIEND!
I MAY TAKE HER BACK TO MY HEADQUARTERS IN AFRICA--- AS A PET!
GLOAT WHILE YOU CAN, YOU FIENDISH FREAKS!
NOBODY'S EVER COUNTED THE AVENGERS OUT YET--- AND NEITHER WILL YOU!
2.

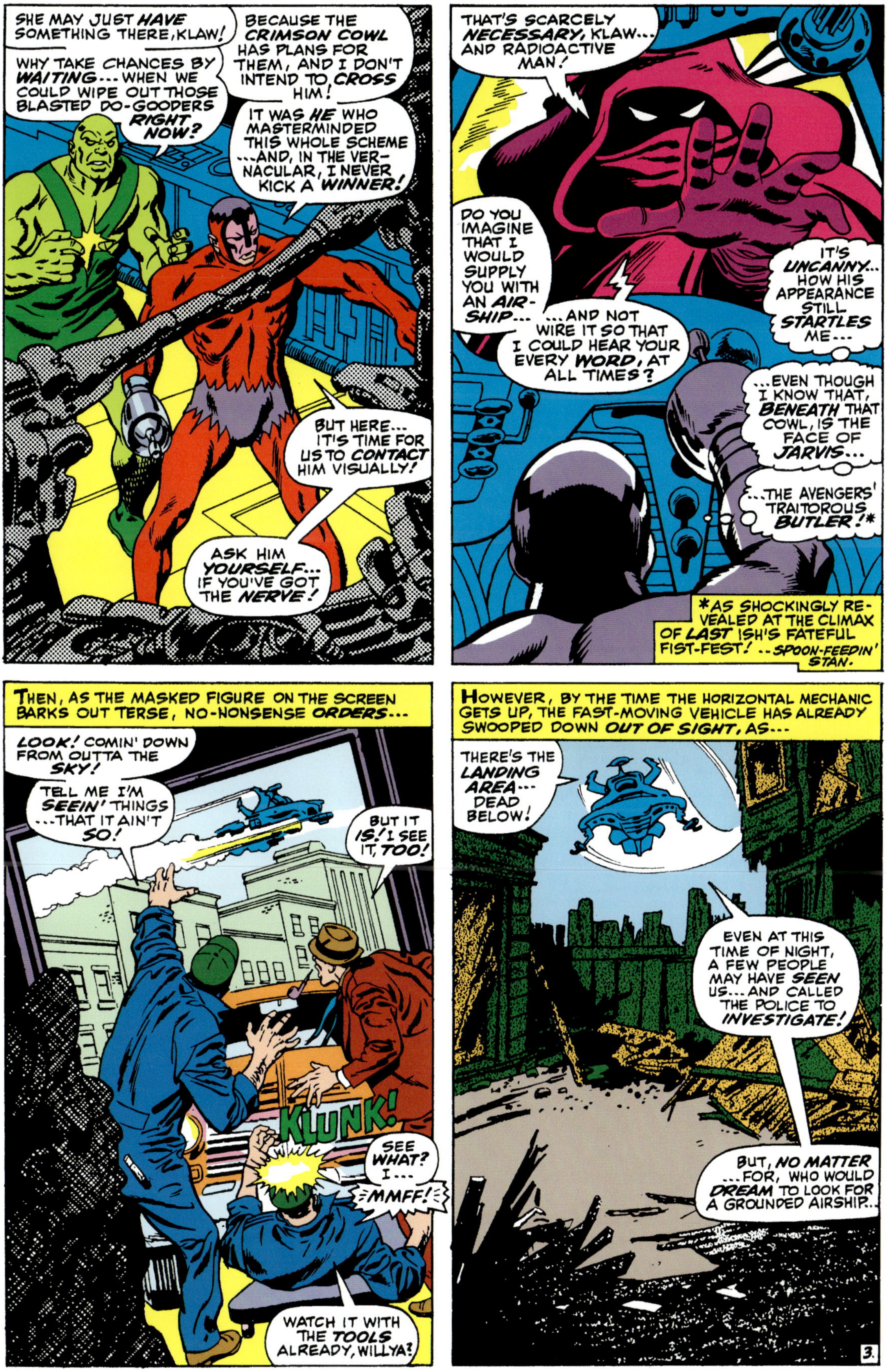
SHE MAY JUST HAVE SOMETHING THERE, KLAW!
WHY TAKE CHANCES BY WAITING... WHEN WE COULD WIPE OUT THOSE BLASTED DO-GOODERS RIGHT NOW?
BECAUSE THE CRIMSON COWL HAS PLANS FOR THEM, AND I DON'T INTEND TO CROSS HIM!
IT WAS HE WHO MASTERMINDED THIS WHOLE SCHEME ...AND, IN THE VERNACULAR, I NEVER KICK A WINNER!
BUT HERE... IT'S TIME FOR US TO CONTACT HIM VISUALLY!
ASK HIM YOURSELF... IF YOU'VE GOT THE NERVE!
THAT'S SCARCELY NECESSARY, KLAW... AND RADIOACTIVE MAN!
DO YOU IMAGINE THAT I WOULD SUPPLY YOU WITH AN AIR-SHIP...
...AND NOT WIRE IT SO THAT I COULD HEAR YOUR EVERY WORD, AT ALL TIMES?
IT'S UNCANNY... HOW HIS APPEARANCE STILL STARTLES ME...
...EVEN THOUGH I KNOW THAT, BENEATH THAT COWL, IS THE FACE OF JARVIS...
...THE AVENGERS' TRAITOROUS BUTLER!*
*AS SHOCKINGLY REVEALED AT THE CLIMAX OF LAST ISH'S FATEFUL FIST-FEST! --SPOON-FEEDIN' STAN.
THEN, AS THE MASKED FIGURE ON THE SCREEN BARKS OUT TERSE, NO-NONSENSE ORDERS...
LOOK! COMIN' DOWN FROM OUTTA THE SKY!
TELL ME I'M SEEIN' THINGS ...THAT IT AIN'T SO!
BUT IT IS! I SEE IT, TOO!
KLUNK!
SEE WHAT? I...
MMFF!
WATCH IT WITH THE TOOLS ALREADY, WILLYA?
HOWEVER, BY THE TIME THE HORIZONTAL MECHANIC GETS UP, THE FAST-MOVING VEHICLE HAS ALREADY SWOOPED DOWN OUT OF SIGHT, AS...
THERE'S THE LANDING AREA... DEAD BELOW!
EVEN AT THIS TIME OF NIGHT, A FEW PEOPLE MAY HAVE SEEN US... AND CALLED THE POLICE TO INVESTIGATE!
BUT, NO MATTER ...FOR, WHO WOULD DREAM TO LOOK FOR A GROUNDED AIRSHIP..
3.

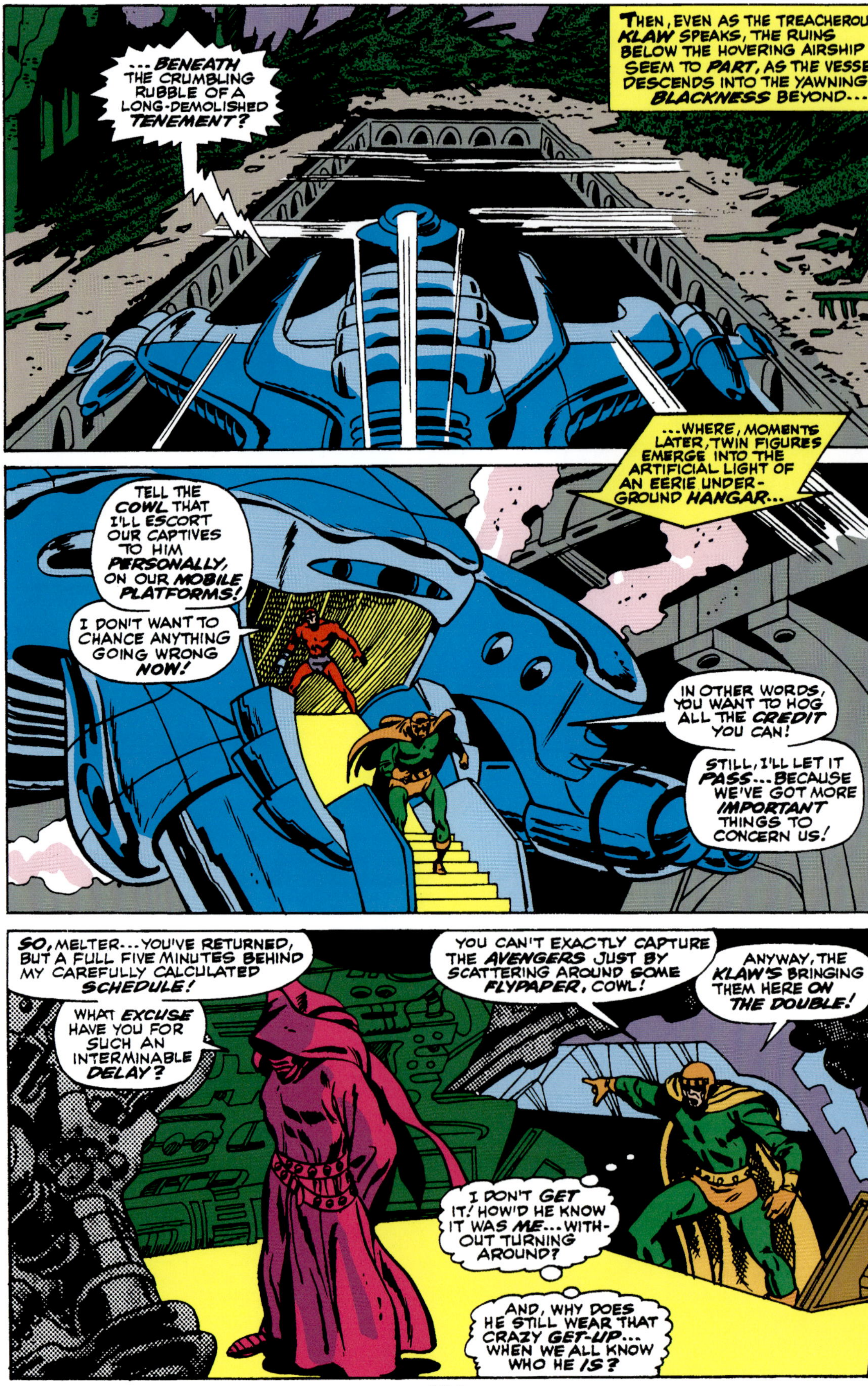
THEN, EVEN AS THE TREACHEROUS KLAW SPEAKS, THE RUINS BELOW THE HOVERING AIRSHIP SEEM TO PART, AS THE VESSEL DESCENDS INTO THE YAWNING BLACKNESS BEYOND...
...BENEATH THE CRUMBLING RUBBLE OF A LONG-DEMOLISHED TENEMENT?
...WHERE, MOMENTS LATER, TWIN FIGURES EMERGE INTO THE ARTIFICIAL LIGHT OF AN EERIE UNDER-GROUND HANGAR...
TELL THE COWL THAT I'LL ESCORT OUR CAPTIVES TO HIM PERSONALLY, ON OUR MOBILE PLATFORMS!
I DON'T WANT TO CHANCE ANYTHING GOING WRONG NOW!
IN OTHER WORDS, YOU WANT TO HOG ALL THE CREDIT YOU CAN!
STILL, I'LL LET IT PASS... BECAUSE WE'VE GOT MORE IMPORTANT THINGS TO CONCERN US!
SO, MELTER... YOU'VE RETURNED, BUT A FULL FIVE MINUTES BEHIND MY CAREFULLY CALCULATED SCHEDULE!
WHAT EXCUSE HAVE YOU FOR SUCH AN INTERMINABLE DELAY?
YOU CAN'T EXACTLY CAPTURE THE AVENGERS JUST BY SCATTERING AROUND SOME FLYPAPER, COWL!
ANYWAY, THE KLAW'S BRINGING THEM HERE ON THE DOUBLE!
I DON'T GET IT! HOW'D HE KNOW IT WAS ME... WITH-OUT TURNING AROUND?
AND, WHY DOES HE STILL WEAR THAT CRAZY GET-UP... WHEN WE ALL KNOW WHO HE IS?
4

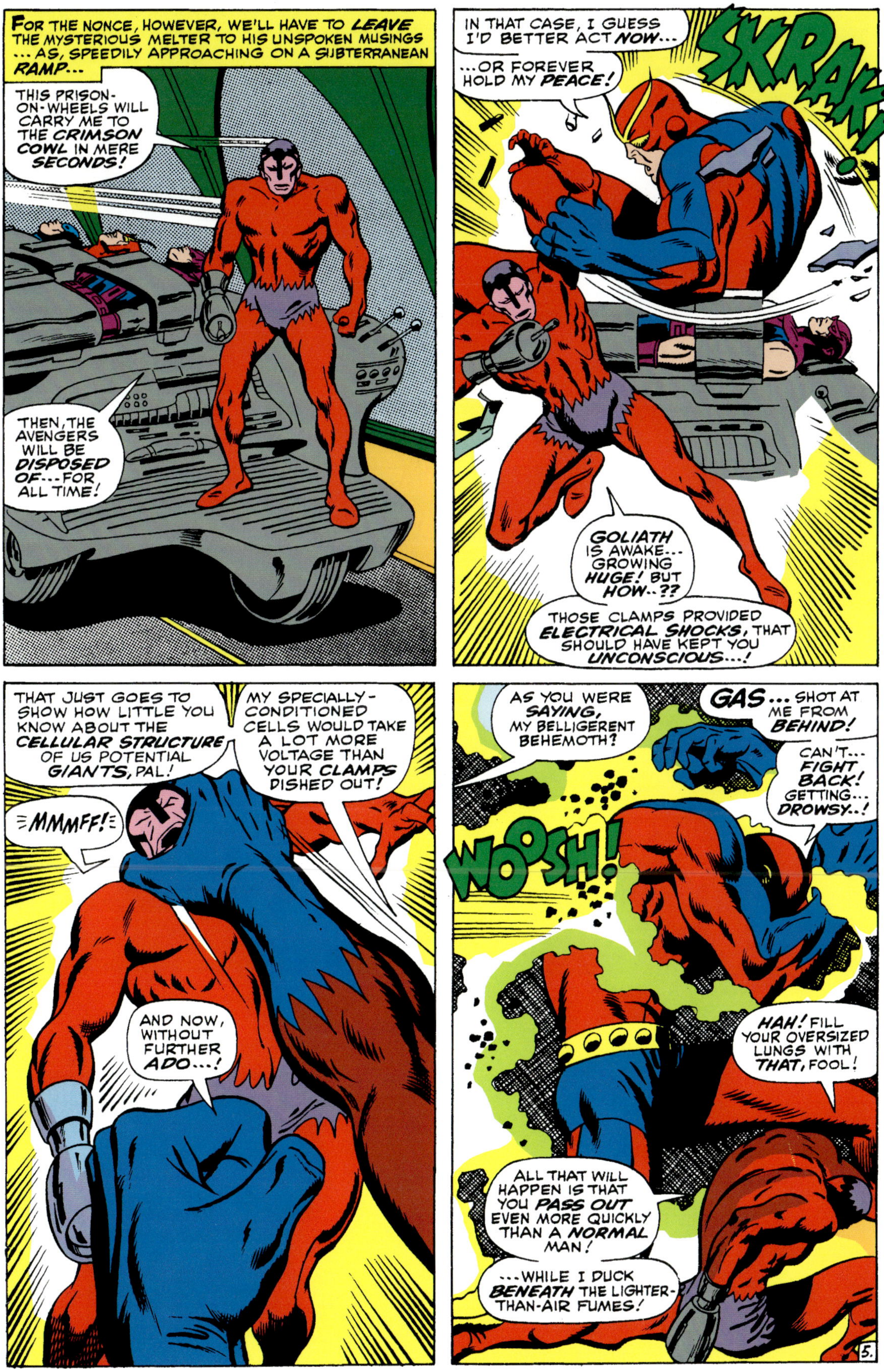
FOR THE NONCE, HOWEVER, WE'LL HAVE TO LEAVE THE MYSTERIOUS MELTER TO HIS UNSPOKEN MUSINGS ...AS, SPEEDILY APPROACHING ON A SUBTERRANEAN RAMP...
THIS PRISON-ON-WHEELS WILL CARRY ME TO THE CRIMSON COWL IN MERE SECONDS!
THEN, THE AVENGERS WILL BE DISPOSED OF---FOR ALL TIME!
IN THAT CASE, I GUESS I'D BETTER ACT NOW...
...OR FOREVER HOLD MY PEACE!
SKRAK!
GOLIATH IS AWAKE... GROWING HUGE! BUT HOW..??
THOSE CLAMPS PROVIDED ELECTRICAL SHOCKS, THAT SHOULD HAVE KEPT YOU UNCONSCIOUS...!
THAT JUST GOES TO SHOW HOW LITTLE YOU KNOW ABOUT THE CELLULAR STRUCTURE OF US POTENTIAL GIANTS, PAL!
MY SPECIALLY-CONDITIONED CELLS WOULD TAKE A LOT MORE VOLTAGE THAN YOUR CLAMPS DISHED OUT!
MMMFF!
AND NOW, WITHOUT FURTHER ADO...!
AS YOU WERE SAYING, MY BELLIGERENT BEHEMOTH?
GAS... SHOT AT ME FROM BEHIND!
CAN'T... FIGHT BACK! GETTING... DROWSY..!
WOOSH!
HAH! FILL YOUR OVERSIZED LUNGS WITH THAT, FOOL!
ALL THAT WILL HAPPEN IS THAT YOU PASS OUT EVEN MORE QUICKLY THAN A NORMAL MAN!
...WHILE I DUCK BENEATH THE LIGHTER-THAN-AIR FUMES!
5.

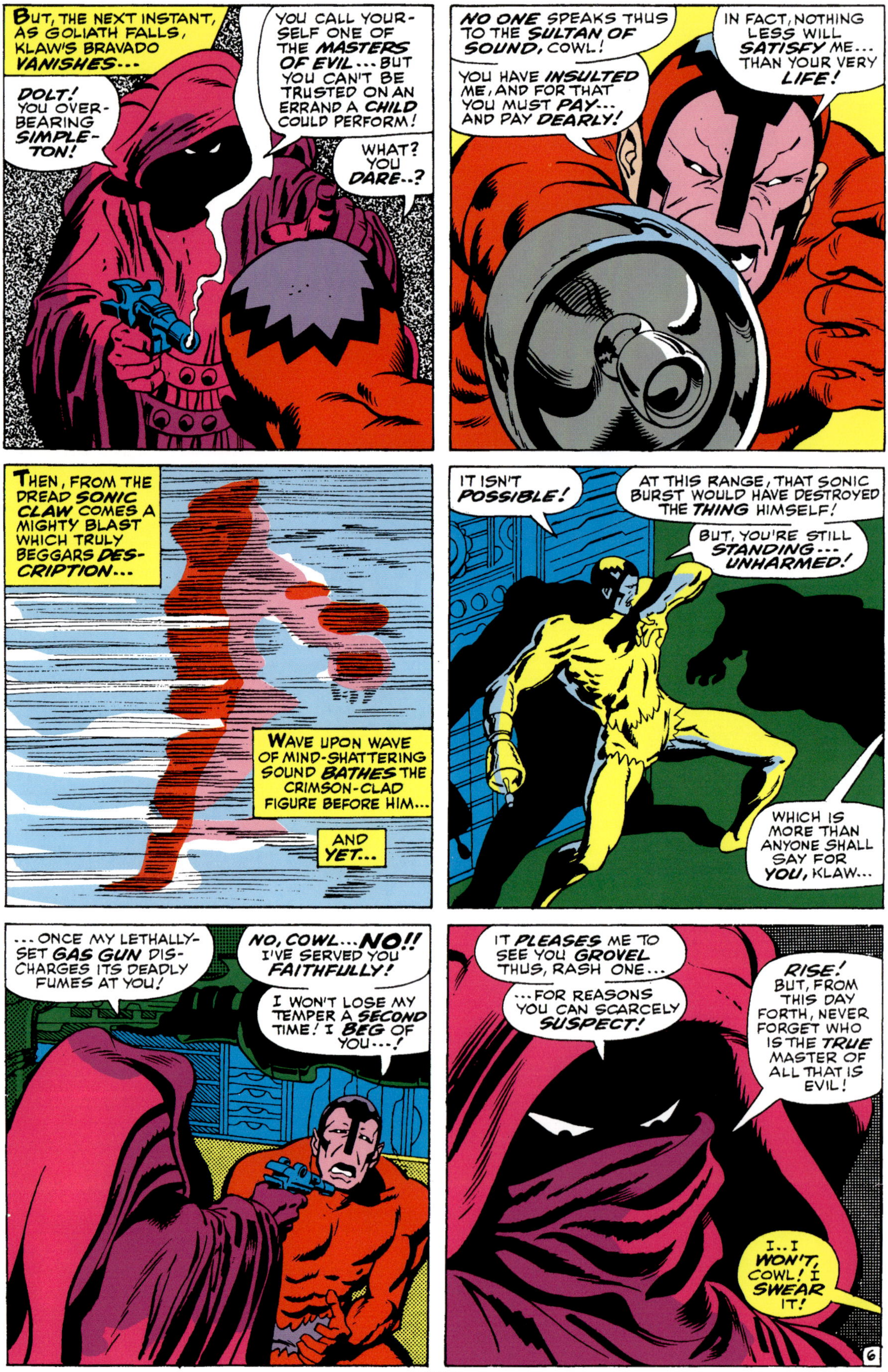

But, the next instant, as Goliath falls, Klaw's bravado vanishes...
Dolt! You overbearing simpleton!
You call yourself one of the Masters of Evil... but you can't be trusted on an errand a child could perform!
What? You dare..?
No one speaks thus to the Sultan of Sound, Cowl!
You have insulted me, and for that you must pay... and pay dearly!
In fact, nothing less will satisfy me... than your very life!
Then, from the dread sonic claw comes a mighty blast which truly beggars description...
Wave upon wave of mind-shattering sound bathes the crimson-clad figure before him...
And yet...
It isn't possible!
At this range, that sonic burst would have destroyed the Thing himself!
But, you're still standing... unharmed!
Which is more than anyone shall say for you, Klaw...
...once my lethally-set gas gun discharges its deadly fumes at you!
No, Cowl... no!! I've served you faithfully!
I won't lose my temper a second time! I beg of you...!
It pleases me to see you grovel thus, rash one...
...for reasons you can scarcely suspect!
Rise! But, from this day forth, never forget who is the true master of all that is evil!
I..I won't, Cowl! I swear it!
6

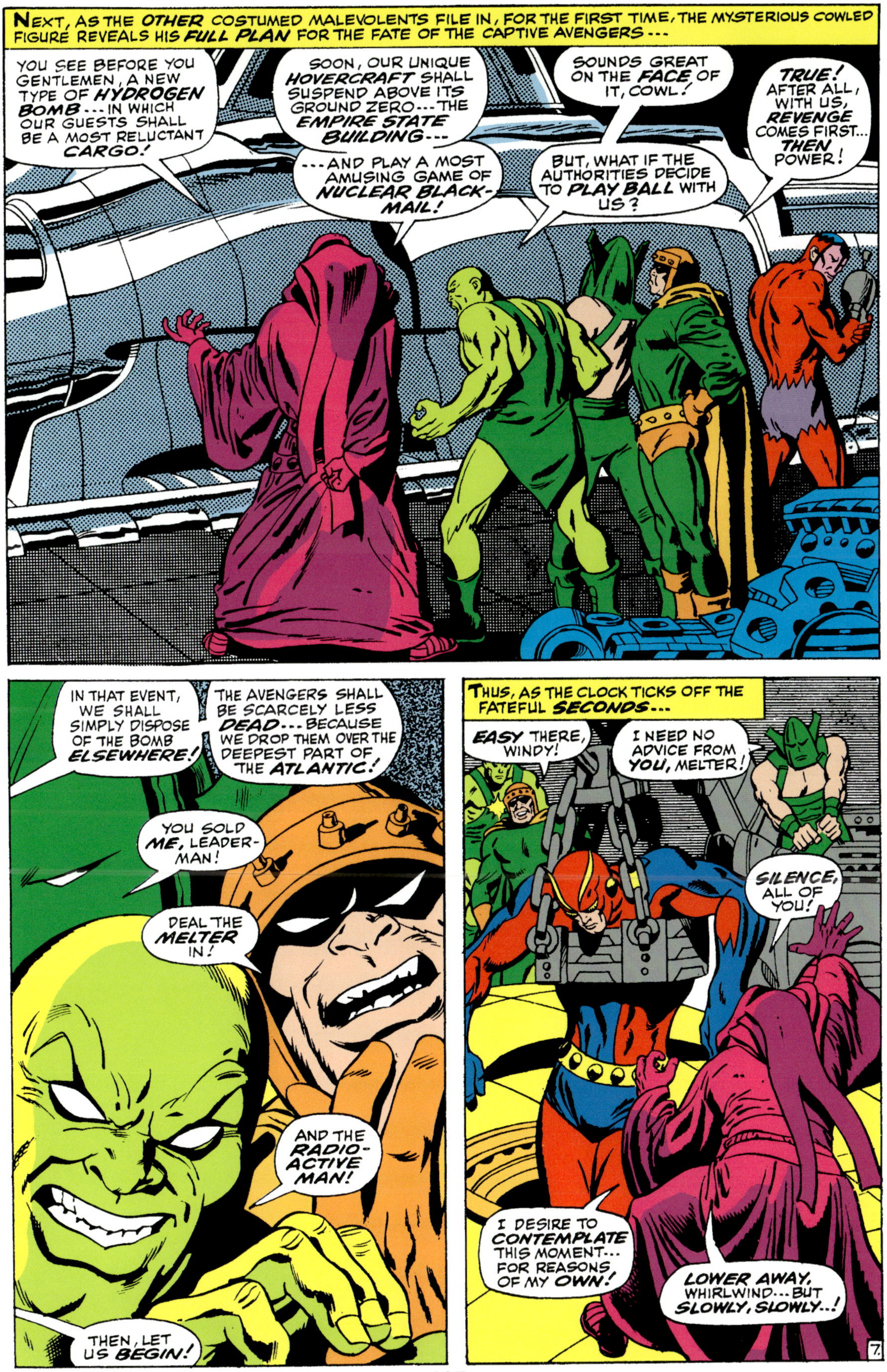
NEXT, AS THE OTHER COSTUMED MALEVOLENTS FILE IN, FOR THE FIRST TIME, THE MYSTERIOUS COWLED FIGURE REVEALS HIS FULL PLAN FOR THE FATE OF THE CAPTIVE AVENGERS---
YOU SEE BEFORE YOU GENTLEMEN, A NEW TYPE OF HYDROGEN BOMB--- IN WHICH OUR GUESTS SHALL BE A MOST RELUCTANT CARGO!
SOON, OUR UNIQUE HOVERCRAFT SHALL SUSPEND ABOVE ITS GROUND ZERO--- THE EMPIRE STATE BUILDING---
---AND PLAY A MOST AMUSING GAME OF NUCLEAR BLACK-MAIL!
SOUNDS GREAT ON THE FACE OF IT, COWL!
BUT, WHAT IF THE AUTHORITIES DECIDE TO PLAY BALL WITH US?
TRUE! AFTER ALL, WITH US, REVENGE COMES FIRST... THEN POWER!
IN THAT EVENT, WE SHALL SIMPLY DISPOSE OF THE BOMB ELSEWHERE!
THE AVENGERS SHALL BE SCARCELY LESS DEAD--- BECAUSE WE DROP THEM OVER THE DEEPEST PART OF THE ATLANTIC!
YOU SOLD ME, LEADER-MAN!
DEAL THE MELTER IN!
AND THE RADIO-ACTIVE MAN!
THEN, LET US BEGIN!
THUS, AS THE CLOCK TICKS OFF THE FATEFUL SECONDS---
EASY THERE, WINDY!
I NEED NO ADVICE FROM YOU, MELTER!
SILENCE, ALL OF YOU!
I DESIRE TO CONTEMPLATE THIS MOMENT--- FOR REASONS OF MY OWN!
LOWER AWAY, WHIRLWIND--- BUT SLOWLY, SLOWLY--!
7

Panel 1:
IT IS DONE!

THE TIMING WAS LETTER-PERFECT --- FOR THEY BEGIN TO REVIVE!

AND, IT IS MY WISH THAT THEY BE AWAKE WHEN THEY MEET THEIR DEATHS --- THAT THEY MAY KNOW STARK, UNREASONING FEAR!

≡UHHNNN!≡ THE LIGHTS ARE COMIN' ON AGAIN, ALL OVER THE WORLD!

Panel 2:
SLAM!

BUT, PERHAPS IT IS TOO LATE FOR US, HAWKEYE'!

SOMEONE JUST SLAMMED A THICK STEEL HATCH ABOVE US..!

HELP... HELP ME, PLEASE..!

THAT VOICE!

IT'S GOTTA BE...THE WASP!

Panel 3:
RETRIEVING A SMALL METAL CANNISTER IN THE FAR PART OF THE HOLD, THE REDOUBTABLE ARCHER OPENS IT, AND---

THANKS, TALL, DARK, AND HANDSOME!

THERE WASN'T ENOUGH AIR IN THERE FOR A GNAT TO BREATHE, LET ALONE A WASP!

ANYTIME, LADY...BUT, IF MY SIZIN' UP OF OUR FIX IS RIGHT---

HAVIN' ENOUGH OXYGEN IS SOON GONNA BE THE LEAST OF OUR WORRIES!

BUT...WHERE'S HANK? IS HE ALL RIGHT..?

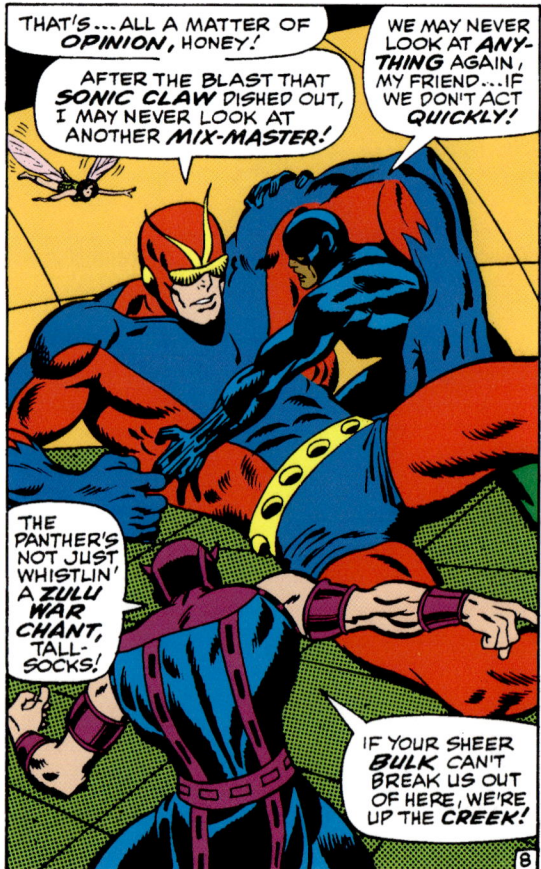

Panel 4:
THAT'S...ALL A MATTER OF OPINION, HONEY!

AFTER THE BLAST THAT SONIC CLAW DISHED OUT, I MAY NEVER LOOK AT ANOTHER MIX-MASTER!

WE MAY NEVER LOOK AT ANYTHING AGAIN, MY FRIEND...IF WE DON'T ACT QUICKLY!

THE PANTHER'S NOT JUST WHISTLIN' A ZULU WAR CHANT, TALL-SOCKS!

IF YOUR SHEER BULK CAN'T BREAK US OUT OF HERE, WE'RE UP THE CREEK!

8

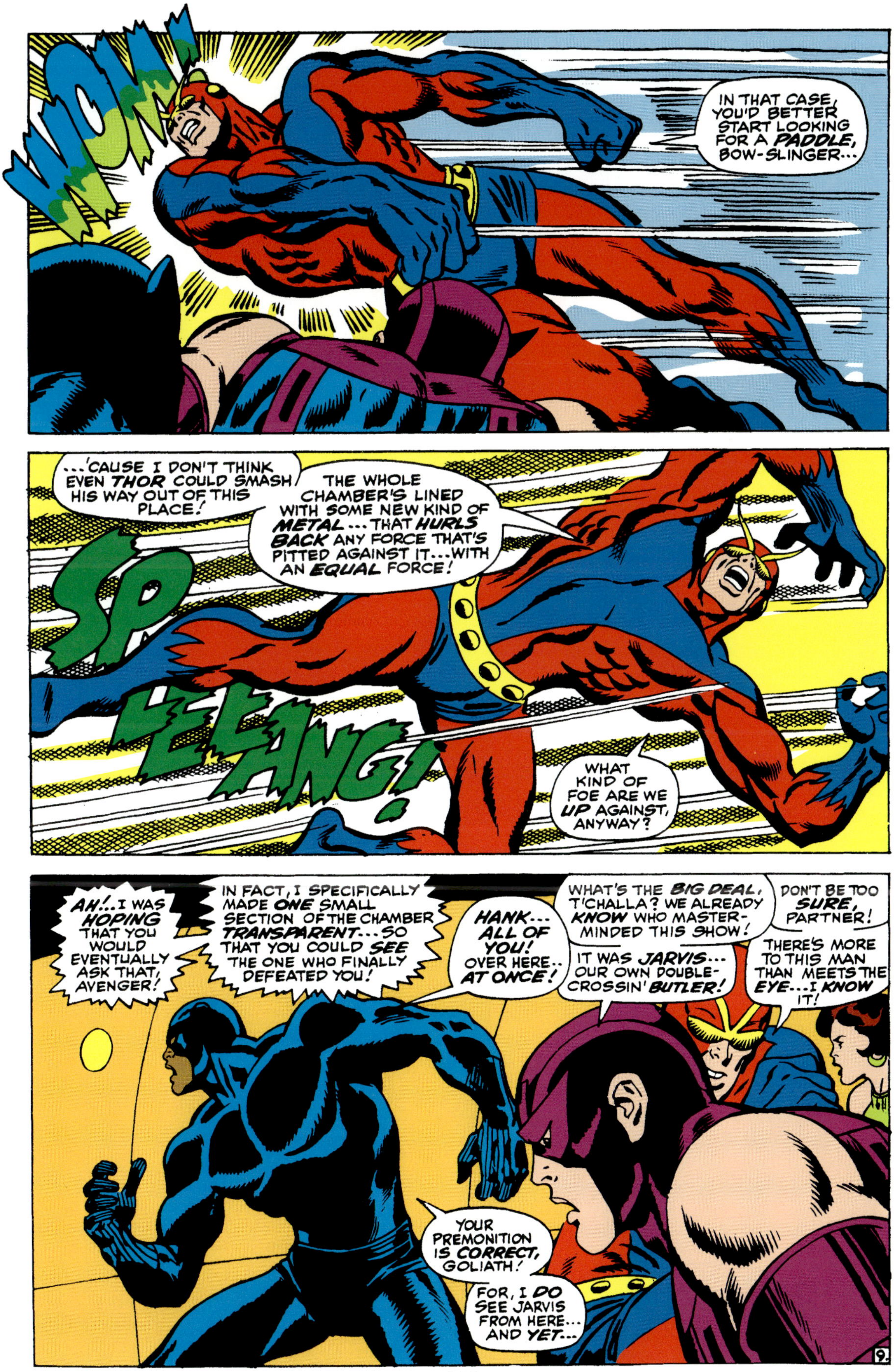
WOK!
IN THAT CASE, YOU'D BETTER START LOOKING FOR A PADDLE, BOW-SLINGER...
...'CAUSE I DON'T THINK EVEN THOR COULD SMASH HIS WAY OUT OF THIS PLACE!
THE WHOLE CHAMBER'S LINED WITH SOME NEW KIND OF METAL... THAT HURLS BACK ANY FORCE THAT'S PITTED AGAINST IT... WITH AN EQUAL FORCE!
SPLEEANG!
WHAT KIND OF FOE ARE WE UP AGAINST, ANYWAY?
AH!.. I WAS HOPING THAT YOU WOULD EVENTUALLY ASK THAT, AVENGER!
IN FACT, I SPECIFICALLY MADE ONE SMALL SECTION OF THE CHAMBER TRANSPARENT... SO THAT YOU COULD SEE THE ONE WHO FINALLY DEFEATED YOU!
HANK... ALL OF YOU! OVER HERE.. AT ONCE!
WHAT'S THE BIG DEAL, T'CHALLA? WE ALREADY KNOW WHO MASTER-MINDED THIS SHOW!
IT WAS JARVIS... OUR OWN DOUBLE-CROSSIN' BUTLER!
DON'T BE TOO SURE, PARTNER!
THERE'S MORE TO THIS MAN THAN MEETS THE EYE... I KNOW IT!
YOUR PREMONITION IS CORRECT, GOLIATH!
FOR, I DO SEE JARVIS FROM HERE... AND YET...
9.

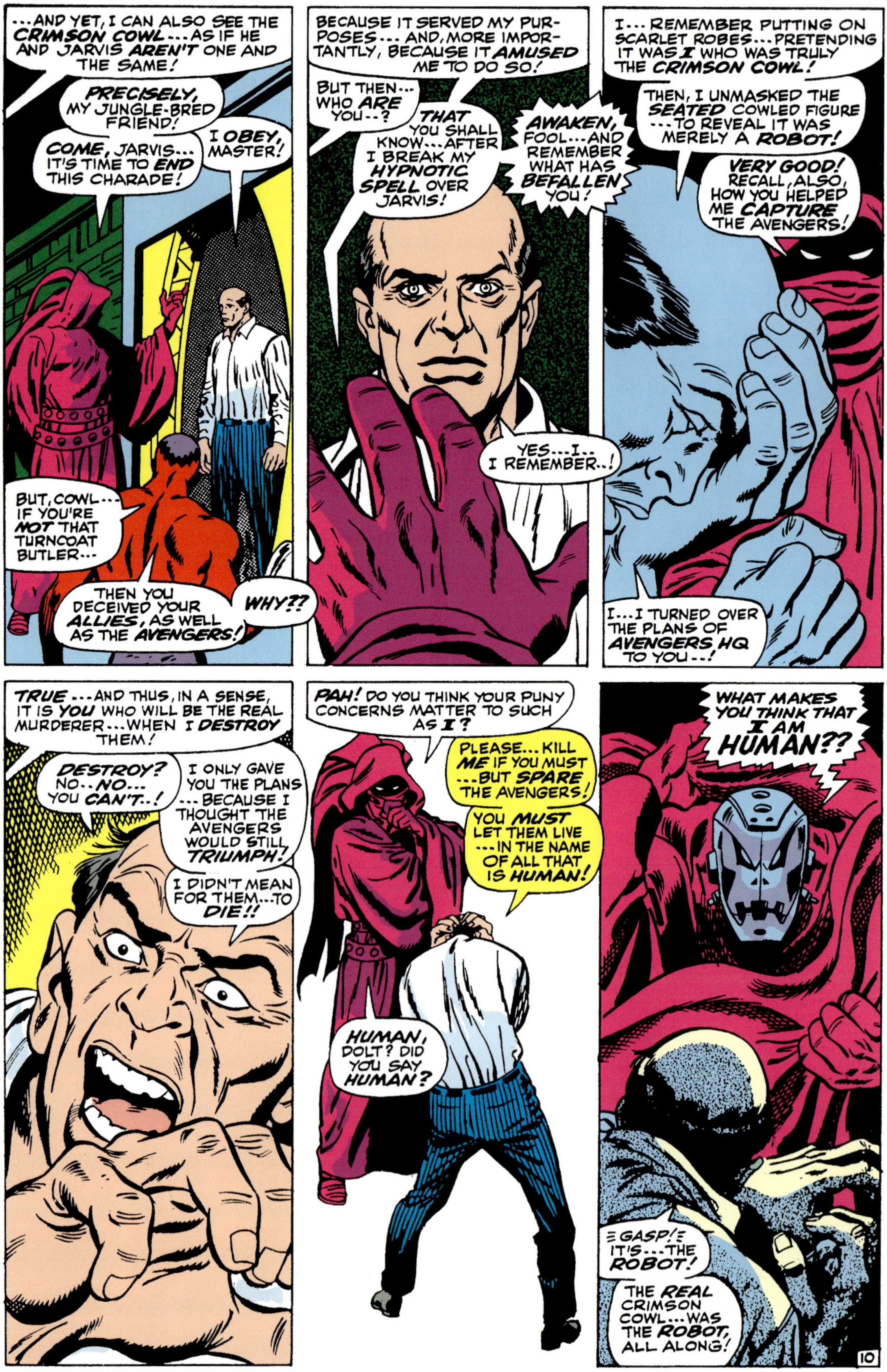

...AND YET, I CAN ALSO SEE THE CRIMSON COWL...AS IF HE AND JARVIS AREN'T ONE AND THE SAME!
PRECISELY, MY JUNGLE-BRED FRIEND!
COME, JARVIS... IT'S TIME TO END THIS CHARADE!
I OBEY, MASTER!
BUT, COWL... IF YOU'RE NOT THAT TURNCOAT BUTLER...
THEN YOU DECEIVED YOUR ALLIES, AS WELL AS THE AVENGERS!
WHY??
BECAUSE IT SERVED MY PURPOSES... AND, MORE IMPORTANTLY, BECAUSE IT AMUSED ME TO DO SO!
BUT THEN... WHO ARE YOU--?
THAT YOU SHALL KNOW...AFTER I BREAK MY HYPNOTIC SPELL OVER JARVIS!
AWAKEN, FOOL...AND REMEMBER WHAT HAS BEFALLEN YOU!
YES...I.. I REMEMBER..!
I... REMEMBER PUTTING ON SCARLET ROBES...PRETENDING IT WAS I WHO WAS TRULY THE CRIMSON COWL!
THEN, I UNMASKED THE SEATED COWLED FIGURE ...TO REVEAL IT WAS MERELY A ROBOT!
VERY GOOD! RECALL, ALSO, HOW YOU HELPED ME CAPTURE THE AVENGERS!
I...I TURNED OVER THE PLANS OF AVENGERS HQ TO YOU--!
TRUE...AND THUS, IN A SENSE, IT IS YOU WHO WILL BE THE REAL MURDERER...WHEN I DESTROY THEM!
DESTROY? NO..NO... YOU CAN'T..!
I ONLY GAVE YOU THE PLANS ...BECAUSE I THOUGHT THE AVENGERS WOULD STILL TRIUMPH!
I DIDN'T MEAN FOR THEM...TO DIE!!
PAH! DO YOU THINK YOUR PUNY CONCERNS MATTER TO SUCH AS I?
PLEASE... KILL ME IF YOU MUST ...BUT SPARE THE AVENGERS!
YOU MUST LET THEM LIVE ...IN THE NAME OF ALL THAT IS HUMAN!
HUMAN, DOLT? DID YOU SAY HUMAN?
WHAT MAKES YOU THINK THAT I AM HUMAN??
=GASP!= IT'S...THE ROBOT!
THE REAL CRIMSON COWL...WAS THE ROBOT, ALL ALONG!
10

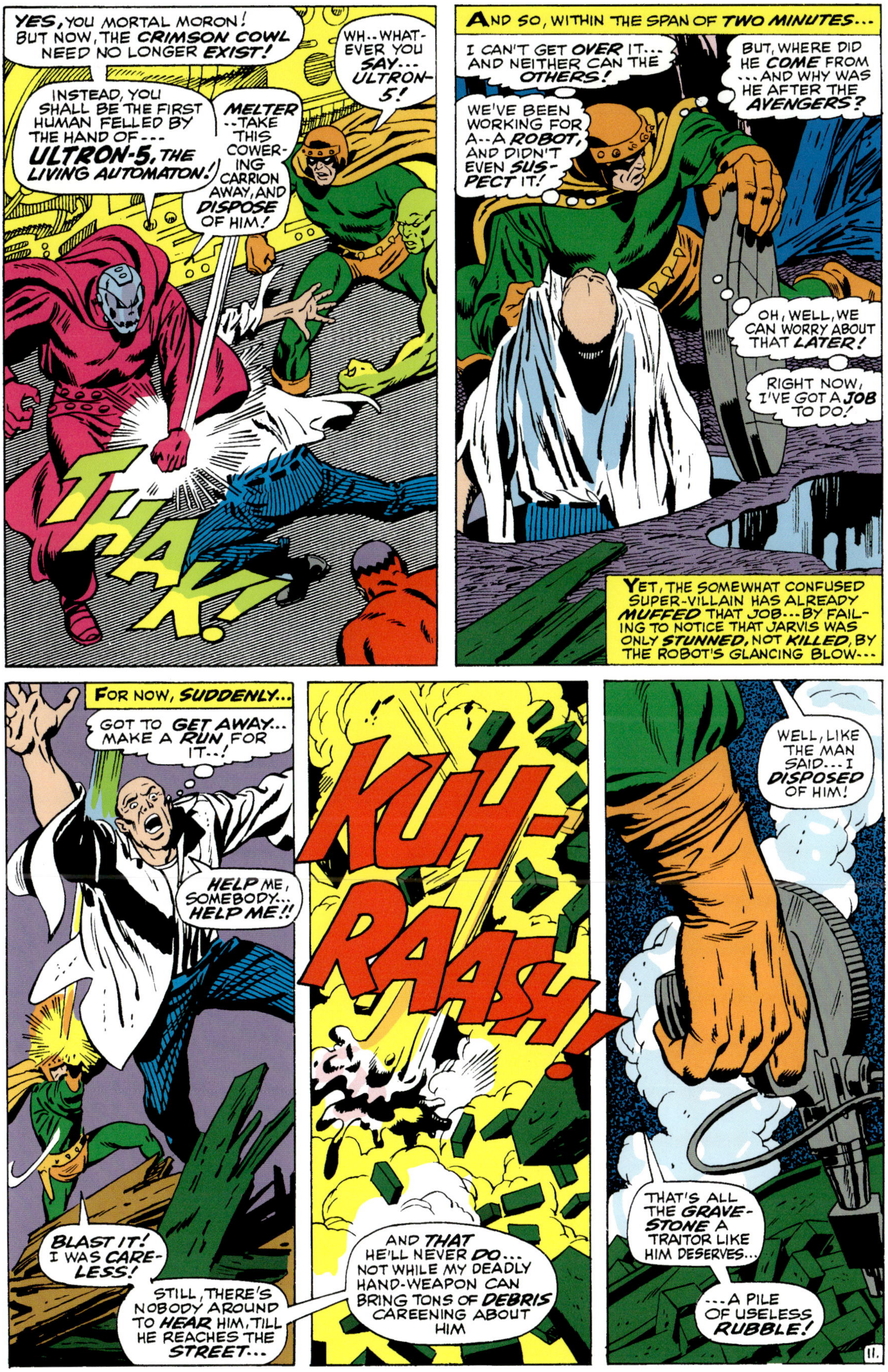
YES, YOU MORTAL MORON! BUT NOW, THE CRIMSON COWL NEED NO LONGER EXIST!
INSTEAD, YOU SHALL BE THE FIRST HUMAN FELLED BY THE HAND OF--- ULTRON-5, THE LIVING AUTOMATON!
WH..WHAT-EVER YOU SAY... ULTRON-5!
MELTER--TAKE THIS COWER-ING CARRION AWAY, AND DISPOSE OF HIM!
THAK!
AND SO, WITHIN THE SPAN OF TWO MINUTES...
I CAN'T GET OVER IT... AND NEITHER CAN THE OTHERS!
BUT, WHERE DID HE COME FROM ...AND WHY WAS HE AFTER THE AVENGERS?
WE'VE BEEN WORKING FOR A--A ROBOT, AND DIDN'T EVEN SUS-PECT IT!
OH, WELL, WE CAN WORRY ABOUT THAT LATER!
RIGHT NOW, I'VE GOT A JOB TO DO!
YET, THE SOMEWHAT CONFUSED SUPER-VILLAIN HAS ALREADY MUFFED THAT JOB---BY FAIL-ING TO NOTICE THAT JARVIS WAS ONLY STUNNED, NOT KILLED, BY THE ROBOT'S GLANCING BLOW---
FOR NOW, SUDDENLY...
GOT TO GET AWAY... MAKE A RUN FOR IT..!
HELP ME, SOMEBODY... HELP ME!!
BLAST IT! I WAS CARE-LESS!
STILL, THERE'S NOBODY AROUND TO HEAR HIM, TILL HE REACHES THE STREET...
KUH-RAASH!
AND THAT HE'LL NEVER DO... NOT WHILE MY DEADLY HAND-WEAPON CAN BRING TONS OF DEBRIS CAREENING ABOUT HIM
WELL, LIKE THE MAN SAID... I DISPOSED OF HIM!
THAT'S ALL THE GRAVE-STONE A TRAITOR LIKE HIM DESERVES...
...A PILE OF USELESS RUBBLE!
11.

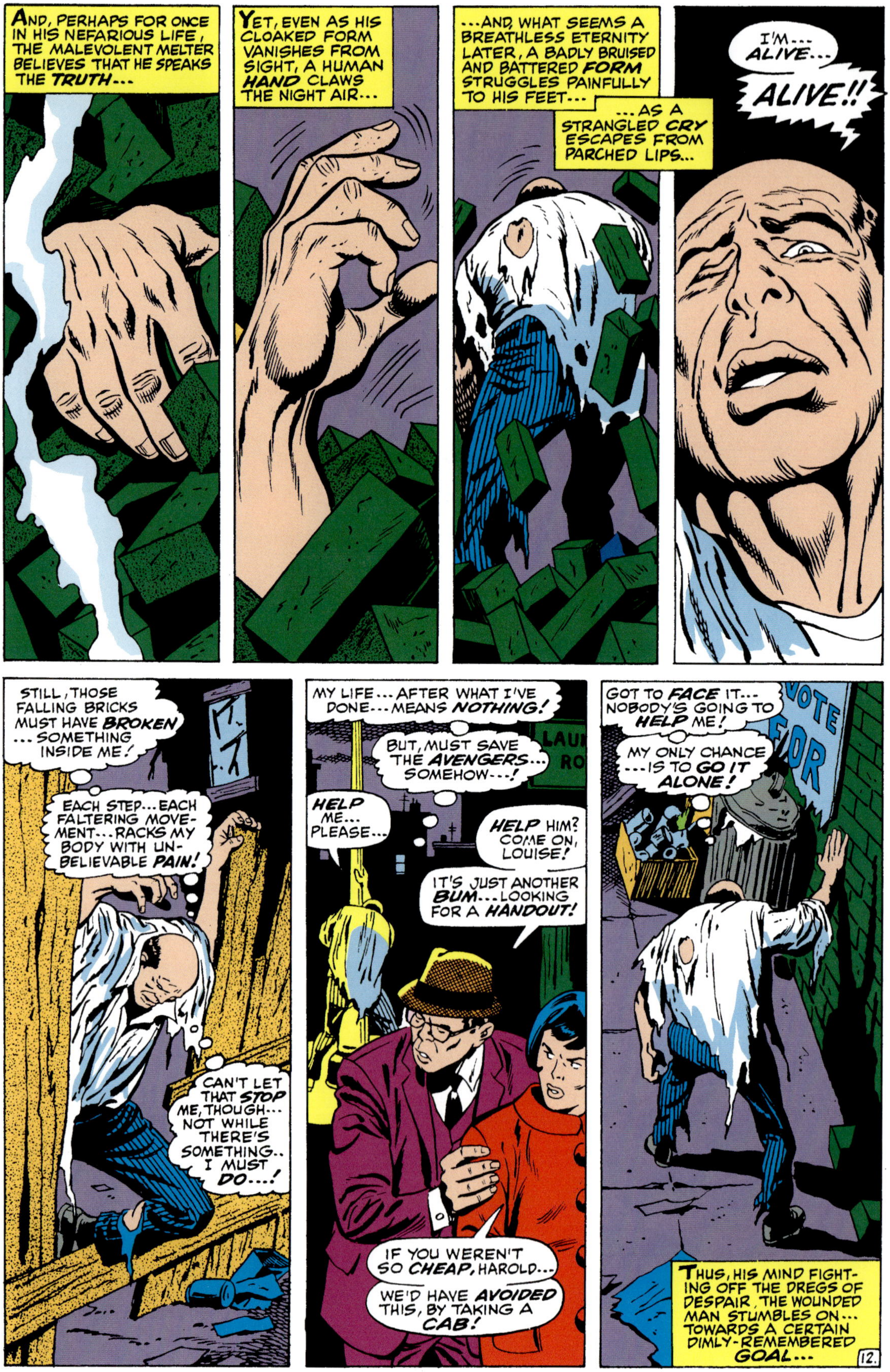
AND, PERHAPS FOR ONCE IN HIS NEFARIOUS LIFE, THE MALEVOLENT MELTER BELIEVES THAT HE SPEAKS THE TRUTH...
YET, EVEN AS HIS CLOAKED FORM VANISHES FROM SIGHT, A HUMAN HAND CLAWS THE NIGHT AIR...
...AND, WHAT SEEMS A BREATHLESS ETERNITY LATER, A BADLY BRUISED AND BATTERED FORM STRUGGLES PAINFULLY TO HIS FEET...
...AS A STRANGLED CRY ESCAPES FROM PARCHED LIPS...
I'M... ALIVE...
ALIVE!!
STILL, THOSE FALLING BRICKS MUST HAVE BROKEN ... SOMETHING INSIDE ME!
EACH STEP... EACH FALTERING MOVEMENT... RACKS MY BODY WITH UNBELIEVABLE PAIN!
CAN'T LET THAT STOP ME, THOUGH... NOT WHILE THERE'S SOMETHING.. I MUST DO...!
MY LIFE... AFTER WHAT I'VE DONE... MEANS NOTHING!
BUT, MUST SAVE THE AVENGERS... SOMEHOW...!
HELP ME... PLEASE...
HELP HIM? COME ON, LOUISE!
IT'S JUST ANOTHER BUM... LOOKING FOR A HANDOUT!
IF YOU WEREN'T SO CHEAP, HAROLD...
WE'D HAVE AVOIDED THIS, BY TAKING A CAB!
GOT TO FACE IT... NOBODY'S GOING TO HELP ME!
MY ONLY CHANCE ...IS TO GO IT ALONE!
VOTE FOR
THUS, HIS MIND FIGHTING OFF THE DREGS OF DESPAIR, THE WOUNDED MAN STUMBLES ON... TOWARDS A CERTAIN DIMLY-REMEMBERED GOAL...
12.

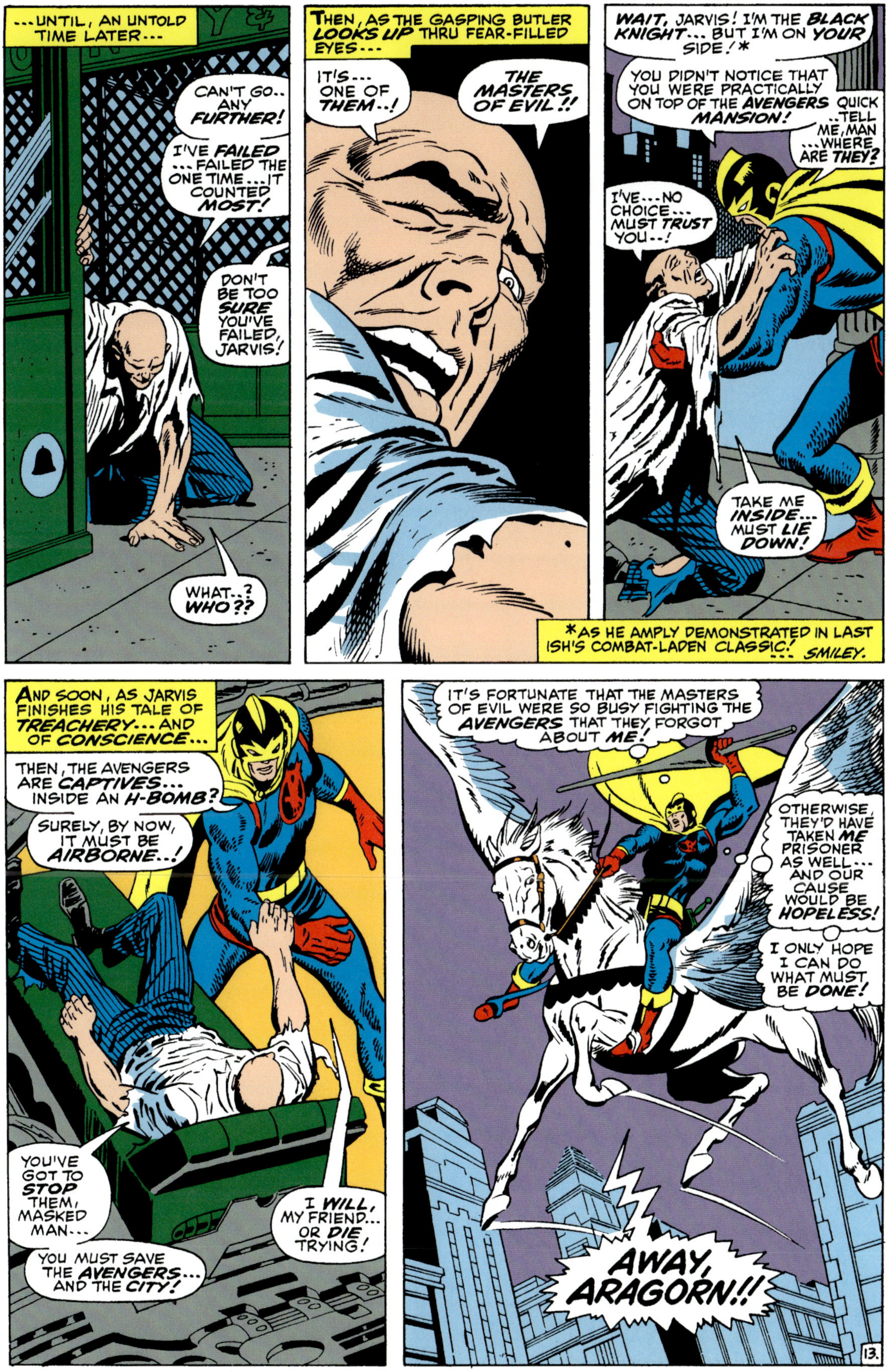

...UNTIL, AN UNTOLD TIME LATER---
CAN'T GO.. ANY FURTHER!
I'VE FAILED ...FAILED THE ONE TIME...IT COUNTED MOST!
DON'T BE TOO SURE YOU'VE FAILED, JARVIS!
WHAT..? WHO??
THEN, AS THE GASPING BUTLER LOOKS UP THRU FEAR-FILLED EYES---
IT'S--- ONE OF THEM..!
THE MASTERS OF EVIL!!
WAIT, JARVIS! I'M THE BLACK KNIGHT... BUT I'M ON YOUR SIDE!*
YOU DIDN'T NOTICE THAT YOU WERE PRACTICALLY ON TOP OF THE AVENGERS MANSION! QUICK ..TELL ME, MAN ...WHERE ARE THEY?
I'VE---NO CHOICE--- MUST TRUST YOU--!
TAKE ME INSIDE... MUST LIE DOWN!
*AS HE AMPLY DEMONSTRATED IN LAST ISH'S COMBAT-LADEN CLASSIC! ... SMILEY.
AND SOON, AS JARVIS FINISHES HIS TALE OF TREACHERY... AND OF CONSCIENCE...
THEN, THE AVENGERS ARE CAPTIVES... INSIDE AN H-BOMB?
SURELY, BY NOW, IT MUST BE AIRBORNE..!
YOU'VE GOT TO STOP THEM, MASKED MAN...
YOU MUST SAVE THE AVENGERS... AND THE CITY!
I WILL, MY FRIEND... OR DIE TRYING!
IT'S FORTUNATE THAT THE MASTERS OF EVIL WERE SO BUSY FIGHTING THE AVENGERS THAT THEY FORGOT ABOUT ME!
OTHERWISE, THEY'D HAVE TAKEN ME PRISONER AS WELL... AND OUR CAUSE WOULD BE HOPELESS!
I ONLY HOPE I CAN DO WHAT MUST BE DONE!
AWAY, ARAGORN!!
13.

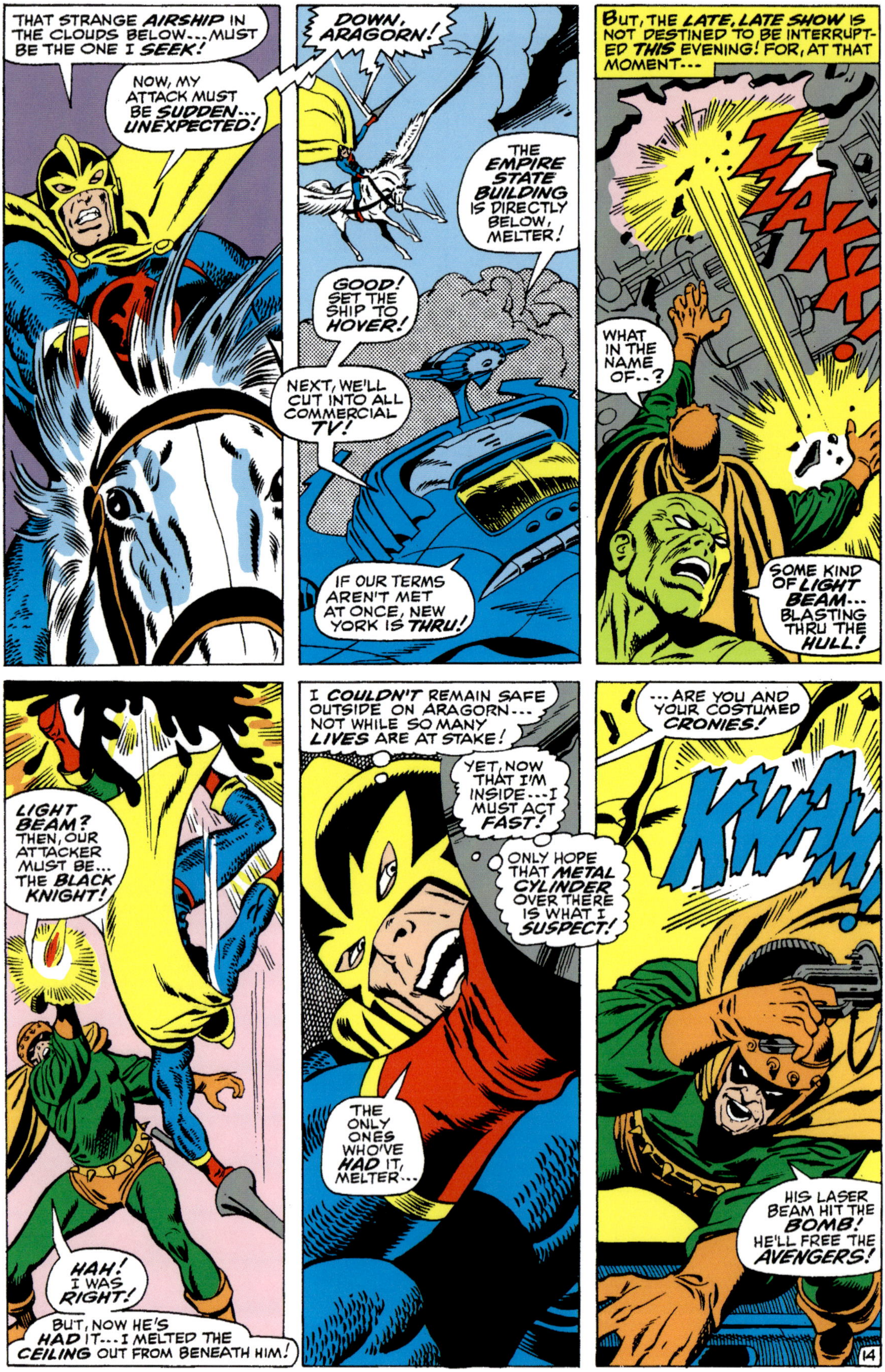
THAT STRANGE AIRSHIP IN THE CLOUDS BELOW... MUST BE THE ONE I SEEK!
NOW, MY ATTACK MUST BE SUDDEN... UNEXPECTED!
DOWN, ARAGORN!
THE EMPIRE STATE BUILDING IS DIRECTLY BELOW, MELTER!
GOOD! SET THE SHIP TO HOVER!
NEXT, WE'LL CUT INTO ALL COMMERCIAL TV!
IF OUR TERMS AREN'T MET AT ONCE, NEW YORK IS THRU!
BUT, THE LATE, LATE SHOW IS NOT DESTINED TO BE INTERRUPTED THIS EVENING! FOR, AT THAT MOMENT---
ZZAKK!
WHAT IN THE NAME OF--?
SOME KIND OF LIGHT BEAM... BLASTING THRU THE HULL!
LIGHT BEAM? THEN, OUR ATTACKER MUST BE... THE BLACK KNIGHT!
HAH! I WAS RIGHT!
BUT, NOW HE'S HAD IT... I MELTED THE CEILING OUT FROM BENEATH HIM!
I COULDN'T REMAIN SAFE OUTSIDE ON ARAGORN--- NOT WHILE SO MANY LIVES ARE AT STAKE!
YET, NOW THAT I'M INSIDE---I MUST ACT FAST!
ONLY HOPE THAT METAL CYLINDER OVER THERE IS WHAT I SUSPECT!
THE ONLY ONES WHO'VE HAD IT, MELTER...
...ARE YOU AND YOUR COSTUMED CRONIES!
KWAM!
HIS LASER BEAM HIT THE BOMB! HE'LL FREE THE AVENGERS!
14

Panel 1:
CORRECTION, OUR CHEERFUL LITTLE CHUM...

WE'RE FREE!

FROM THE EXPRESSION ON THEIR FACES, HANK...

I GATHER THEY'VE ALREADY NOTICED OUR PRESENCE!

Panel 2:
BUT, JUST IN CASE THEY DIDN'T---!

JUST LET ME LAY MY RADIO-ACTIVE HANDS ON YOU, PANTHER...

AND YOU'LL SOON WISH YOU WERE SAFE BACK IN THE JUNGLE!

≡ UNNHH! ≡

Panel 3:
I MUST ADMIT, MY GLOWING FRIEND, THAT I DO PREFER THE COMPANY OF LIONS AND LEOPARDS!

THEY'RE MUCH MORE TRUSTWORTHY THAN THE PREDATORS ONE FINDS IN SO-CALLED CIVILIZATION!

SMAK!

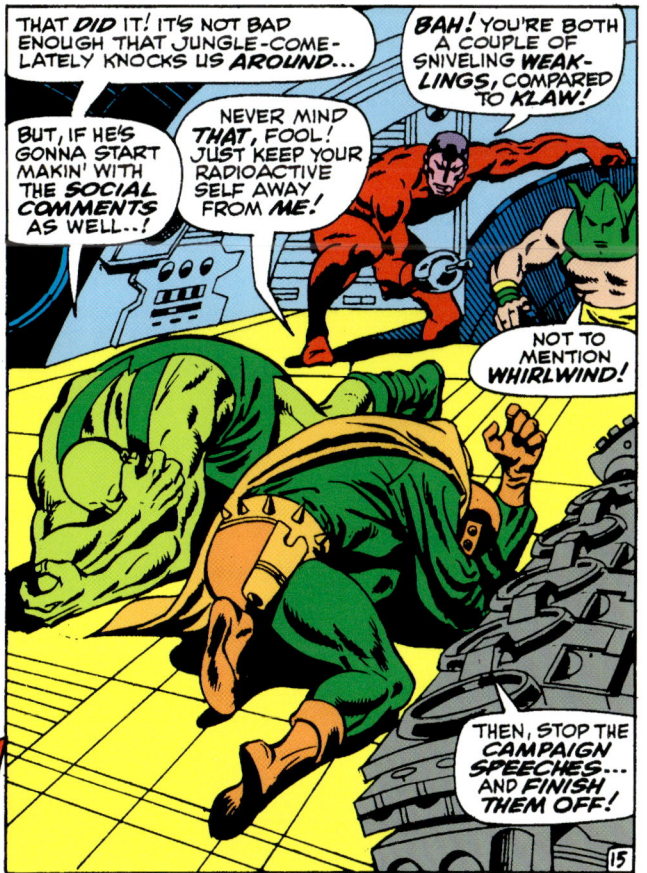

Panel 4:
THAT DID IT! IT'S NOT BAD ENOUGH THAT JUNGLE-COME-LATELY KNOCKS US AROUND...

BUT, IF HE'S GONNA START MAKIN' WITH THE SOCIAL COMMENTS AS WELL..!

NEVER MIND THAT, FOOL! JUST KEEP YOUR RADIOACTIVE SELF AWAY FROM ME!

BAH! YOU'RE BOTH A COUPLE OF SNIVELING WEAK-LINGS, COMPARED TO KLAW!

NOT TO MENTION WHIRLWIND!

THEN, STOP THE CAMPAIGN SPEECHES... AND FINISH THEM OFF!

15

115

Panel 1:
THE NEXT INSTANT, ALMOST AS THE MELTER *SPEAKS*...

LOOK OUT, AVENGERS! KLAW'S AIMING HIS *SONIC BLASTER* THIS W... ≈UNNHH!≈

≈OOOFF!≈ SORRY ABOUT THAT, MAN-MOUNTAIN!

LUCKILY, I MANAGED TO *EVADE* THE BURST!

BUT, WHERE IS THEIR LEADER...THE AUTOMATON CALLED *ULTRON-5?*

Panel 2:
AND, JUST IN CASE SOME-BODY OUT THERE IS *KEEPING SCORE*...

CAN'T THOSE BLUNDERING HIRELINGS OF MINE DO *ANY-THING* RIGHT?

I RETIRED TO A *SECOND* HIDEAWAY, FROM WHICH TO BROAD-CAST MY *ULTIMATUM* TO THE CITY!

NOW, THOSE BUMBLERS HAVE PLACED MY ENTIRE SCHEME IN *JEOPARDY!*

Panel 3:
TO TELL THE TRUTH, HOWEVER, WE'RE NOT QUITE CERTAIN THAT THE AVENGERS *SHARE* OUR METAL MASTERMIND'S ESTIMATES...

THE SINISTER *WHIRLWIND* IS FASTER THAN EVEN *I* HAD SUSPECTED!

ONLY MY PANTHER-LIKE *REFLEXES* ENABLED ME TO LEAP TO *SAFETY!*

DID YOU SAY TO *SAFETY*, YOU INFERNAL JUMPING-JACK?

NOT WHILE THE MELTER'S *GUN* IS SET TO DISSOLVE ---*HUMAN FLESH!*

Panel 4:
THOK!

LET'S NOT GET *GRUE-SOME* ABOUT IT, CHARLIE!

BY THE WAY, THIS BOW AND ARROW ARE WHAT THE WELL-BRED ARCHER IS *IMPROVISING* THIS YEAR!

A *PISTON*... A *CROWBAR*... A HUNK'A *WIRE*... AND IT'S *INSTANT ROBIN HOOD!*

NO, DON'T TRY TO *TALK*... I KNOW YOU'RE ALL *CHOKED UP!*

16

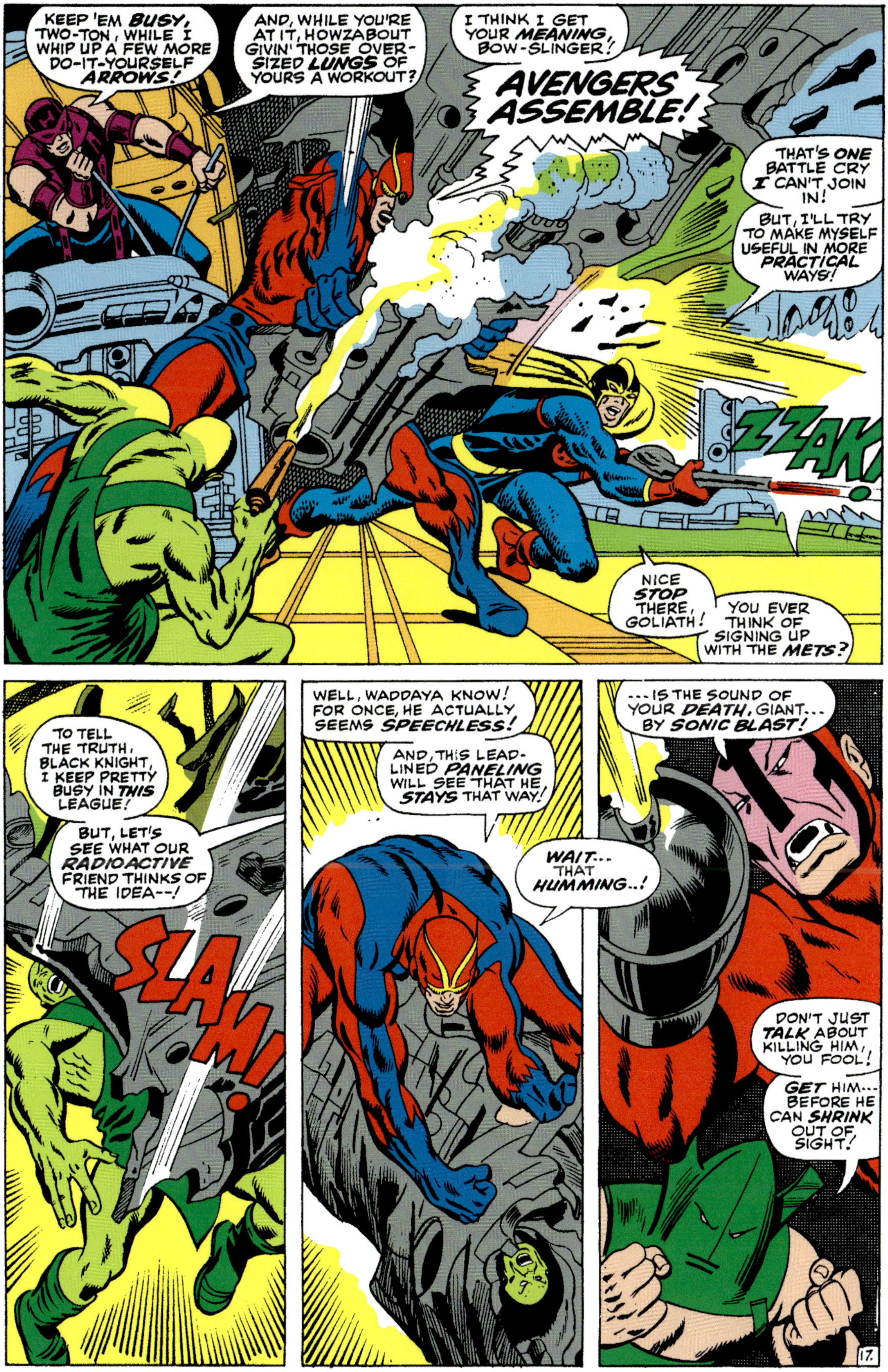
KEEP 'EM BUSY, TWO-TON, WHILE I WHIP UP A FEW MORE DO-IT-YOURSELF ARROWS!
AND, WHILE YOU'RE AT IT, HOWZABOUT GIVIN' THOSE OVER-SIZED LUNGS OF YOURS A WORKOUT?
I THINK I GET YOUR MEANING, BOW-SLINGER!
AVENGERS ASSEMBLE!
THAT'S ONE BATTLE CRY I CAN'T JOIN IN!
BUT, I'LL TRY TO MAKE MYSELF USEFUL IN MORE PRACTICAL WAYS!
ZZAK!
NICE STOP THERE, GOLIATH!
YOU EVER THINK OF SIGNING UP WITH THE METS?
TO TELL THE TRUTH, BLACK KNIGHT, I KEEP PRETTY BUSY IN THIS LEAGUE!
BUT, LET'S SEE WHAT OUR RADIOACTIVE FRIEND THINKS OF THE IDEA--!
SLAM!
WELL, WADDAYA KNOW! FOR ONCE, HE ACTUALLY SEEMS SPEECHLESS!
AND, THIS LEAD-LINED PANELING WILL SEE THAT HE STAYS THAT WAY!
WAIT... THAT HUMMING..!
...IS THE SOUND OF YOUR DEATH, GIANT... BY SONIC BLAST!
DON'T JUST TALK ABOUT KILLING HIM, YOU FOOL!
GET HIM... BEFORE HE CAN SHRINK OUT OF SIGHT!
17

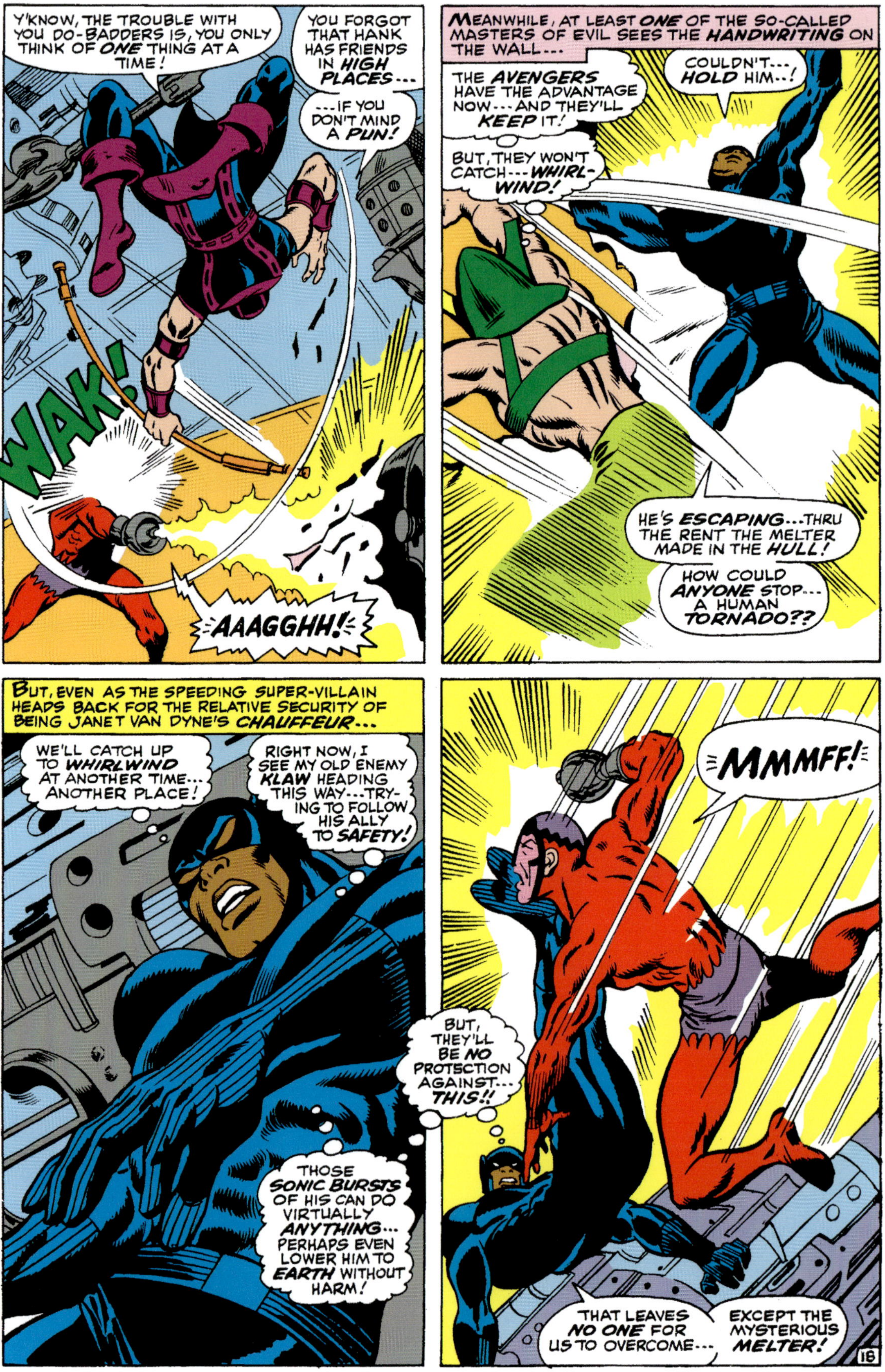

Y'KNOW, THE TROUBLE WITH YOU DO-BADDERS IS, YOU ONLY THINK OF ONE THING AT A TIME!
YOU FORGOT THAT HANK HAS FRIENDS IN HIGH PLACES...
...IF YOU DON'T MIND A PUN!
WAK!
AAAGGHH!
MEANWHILE, AT LEAST ONE OF THE SO-CALLED MASTERS OF EVIL SEES THE HANDWRITING ON THE WALL...
THE AVENGERS HAVE THE ADVANTAGE NOW... AND THEY'LL KEEP IT!
BUT, THEY WON'T CATCH... WHIRLWIND!
COULDN'T... HOLD HIM...!
HE'S ESCAPING...THRU THE RENT THE MELTER MADE IN THE HULL!
HOW COULD ANYONE STOP... A HUMAN TORNADO??
BUT, EVEN AS THE SPEEDING SUPER-VILLAIN HEADS BACK FOR THE RELATIVE SECURITY OF BEING JANET VAN DYNE'S CHAUFFEUR...
WE'LL CATCH UP TO WHIRLWIND AT ANOTHER TIME... ANOTHER PLACE!
RIGHT NOW, I SEE MY OLD ENEMY KLAW HEADING THIS WAY...TRY-ING TO FOLLOW HIS ALLY TO SAFETY!
THOSE SONIC BURSTS OF HIS CAN DO VIRTUALLY ANYTHING... PERHAPS EVEN LOWER HIM TO EARTH WITHOUT HARM!
MMMFF!
BUT, THEY'LL BE NO PROTECTION AGAINST... THIS!!
THAT LEAVES NO ONE FOR US TO OVERCOME...
EXCEPT THE MYSTERIOUS MELTER!
18

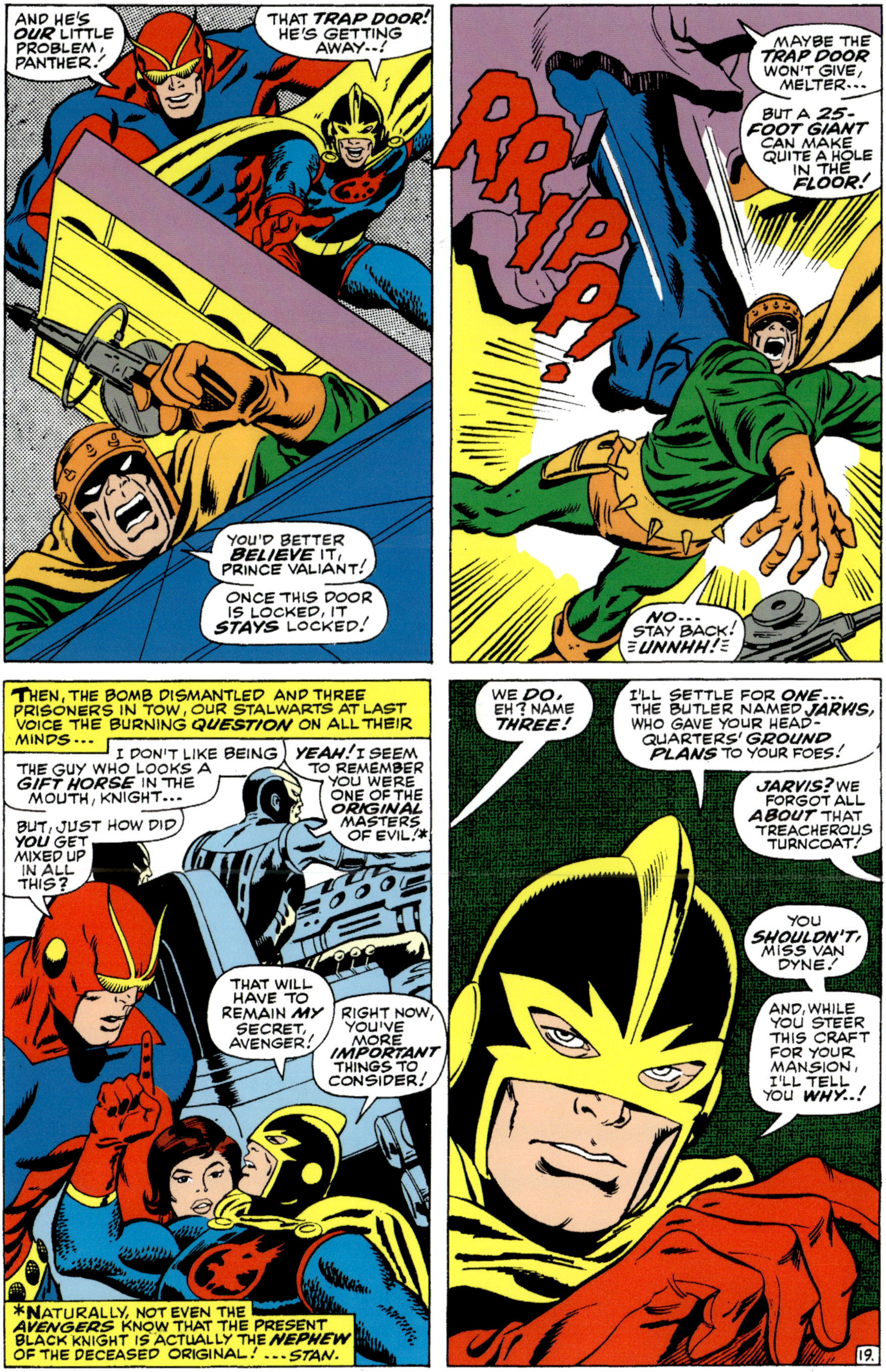
AND HE'S OUR LITTLE PROBLEM, PANTHER!
THAT TRAP DOOR! HE'S GETTING AWAY--!
YOU'D BETTER BELIEVE IT, PRINCE VALIANT!
ONCE THIS DOOR IS LOCKED, IT STAYS LOCKED!
MAYBE THE TRAP DOOR WON'T GIVE, MELTER...
BUT A 25-FOOT GIANT CAN MAKE QUITE A HOLE IN THE FLOOR!
RRIPP!
NO... STAY BACK! UNNHH!
THEN, THE BOMB DISMANTLED AND THREE PRISONERS IN TOW, OUR STALWARTS AT LAST VOICE THE BURNING QUESTION ON ALL THEIR MINDS...
I DON'T LIKE BEING THE GUY WHO LOOKS A GIFT HORSE IN THE MOUTH, KNIGHT...
BUT, JUST HOW DID YOU GET MIXED UP IN ALL THIS?
YEAH! I SEEM TO REMEMBER YOU WERE ONE OF THE ORIGINAL MASTERS OF EVIL!*
THAT WILL HAVE TO REMAIN MY SECRET, AVENGER!
RIGHT NOW, YOU'VE MORE IMPORTANT THINGS TO CONSIDER!
*NATURALLY, NOT EVEN THE AVENGERS KNOW THAT THE PRESENT BLACK KNIGHT IS ACTUALLY THE NEPHEW OF THE DECEASED ORIGINAL! ...STAN.
WE DO, EH? NAME THREE!
I'LL SETTLE FOR ONE... THE BUTLER NAMED JARVIS, WHO GAVE YOUR HEAD-QUARTERS' GROUND PLANS TO YOUR FOES!
JARVIS? WE FORGOT ALL ABOUT THAT TREACHEROUS TURNCOAT!
YOU SHOULDN'T, MISS VAN DYNE!
AND, WHILE YOU STEER THIS CRAFT FOR YOUR MANSION, I'LL TELL YOU WHY..!
19.

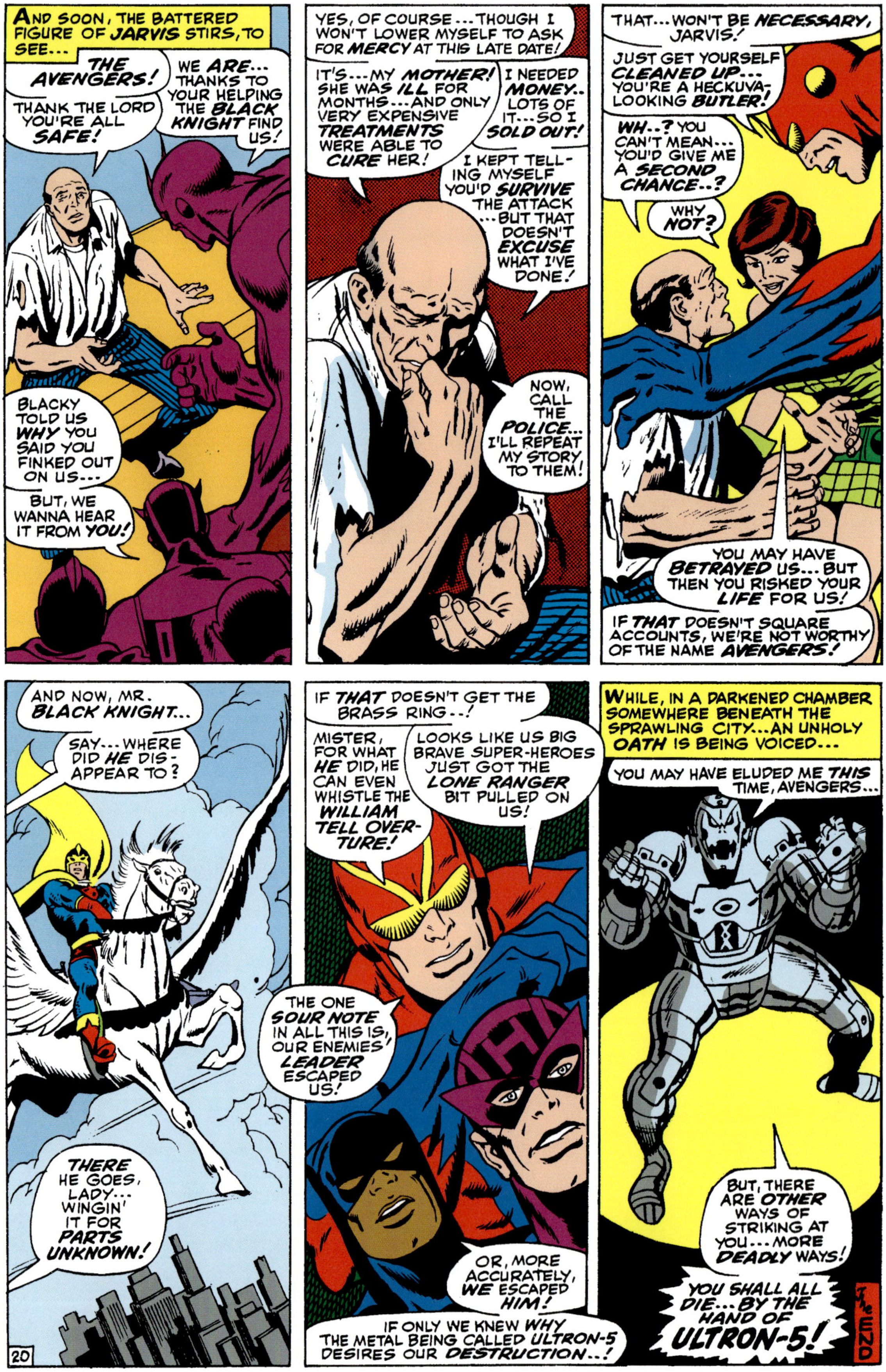
AND SOON, THE BATTERED FIGURE OF JARVIS STIRS, TO SEE...
THE AVENGERS!
THANK THE LORD YOU'RE ALL SAFE!
WE ARE... THANKS TO YOUR HELPING THE BLACK KNIGHT FIND US!
BLACKY TOLD US WHY YOU SAID YOU FINKED OUT ON US...
BUT, WE WANNA HEAR IT FROM YOU!
YES, OF COURSE... THOUGH I WON'T LOWER MYSELF TO ASK FOR MERCY AT THIS LATE DATE!
IT'S... MY MOTHER! SHE WAS ILL FOR MONTHS... AND ONLY VERY EXPENSIVE TREATMENTS WERE ABLE TO CURE HER!
I NEEDED MONEY.. LOTS OF IT... SO I SOLD OUT!
I KEPT TELLING MYSELF YOU'D SURVIVE THE ATTACK ... BUT THAT DOESN'T EXCUSE WHAT I'VE DONE!
NOW, CALL THE POLICE... I'LL REPEAT MY STORY TO THEM!
THAT... WON'T BE NECESSARY, JARVIS!
JUST GET YOURSELF CLEANED UP... YOU'RE A HECKUVA-LOOKING BUTLER!
WH..? YOU CAN'T MEAN... YOU'D GIVE ME A SECOND CHANCE..?
WHY NOT?
YOU MAY HAVE BETRAYED US... BUT THEN YOU RISKED YOUR LIFE FOR US!
IF THAT DOESN'T SQUARE ACCOUNTS, WE'RE NOT WORTHY OF THE NAME AVENGERS!
AND NOW, MR. BLACK KNIGHT...
SAY... WHERE DID HE DISAPPEAR TO?
THERE HE GOES, LADY... WINGIN' IT FOR PARTS UNKNOWN!
20
IF THAT DOESN'T GET THE BRASS RING--!
MISTER, FOR WHAT HE DID, HE CAN EVEN WHISTLE THE WILLIAM TELL OVERTURE!
LOOKS LIKE US BIG BRAVE SUPER-HEROES JUST GOT THE LONE RANGER BIT PULLED ON US!
THE ONE SOUR NOTE IN ALL THIS IS, OUR ENEMIES' LEADER ESCAPED US!
OR, MORE ACCURATELY, WE ESCAPED HIM!
IF ONLY WE KNEW WHY THE METAL BEING CALLED ULTRON-5 DESIRES OUR DESTRUCTION..!
WHILE, IN A DARKENED CHAMBER SOMEWHERE BENEATH THE SPRAWLING CITY... AN UNHOLY OATH IS BEING VOICED...
YOU MAY HAVE ELUDED ME THIS TIME, AVENGERS...
BUT, THERE ARE OTHER WAYS OF STRIKING AT YOU... MORE DEADLY WAYS!
YOU SHALL ALL DIE... BY THE HAND OF ULTRON-5!
THE END

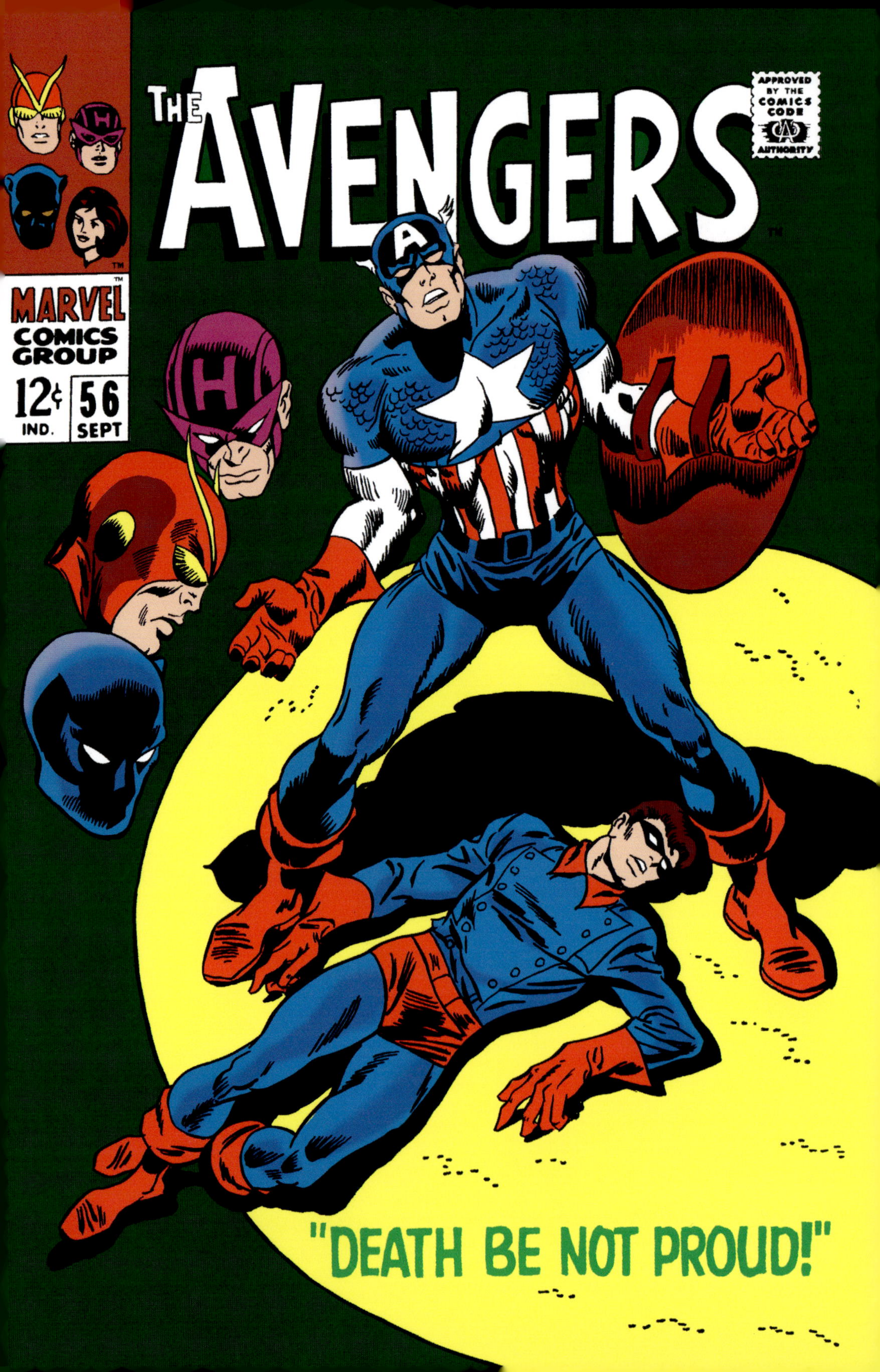
THE AVENGERS
MARVEL COMICS GROUP
12¢ IND.
56 SEPT
APPROVED BY THE COMICS CODE AUTHORITY
"DEATH BE NOT PROUD!"

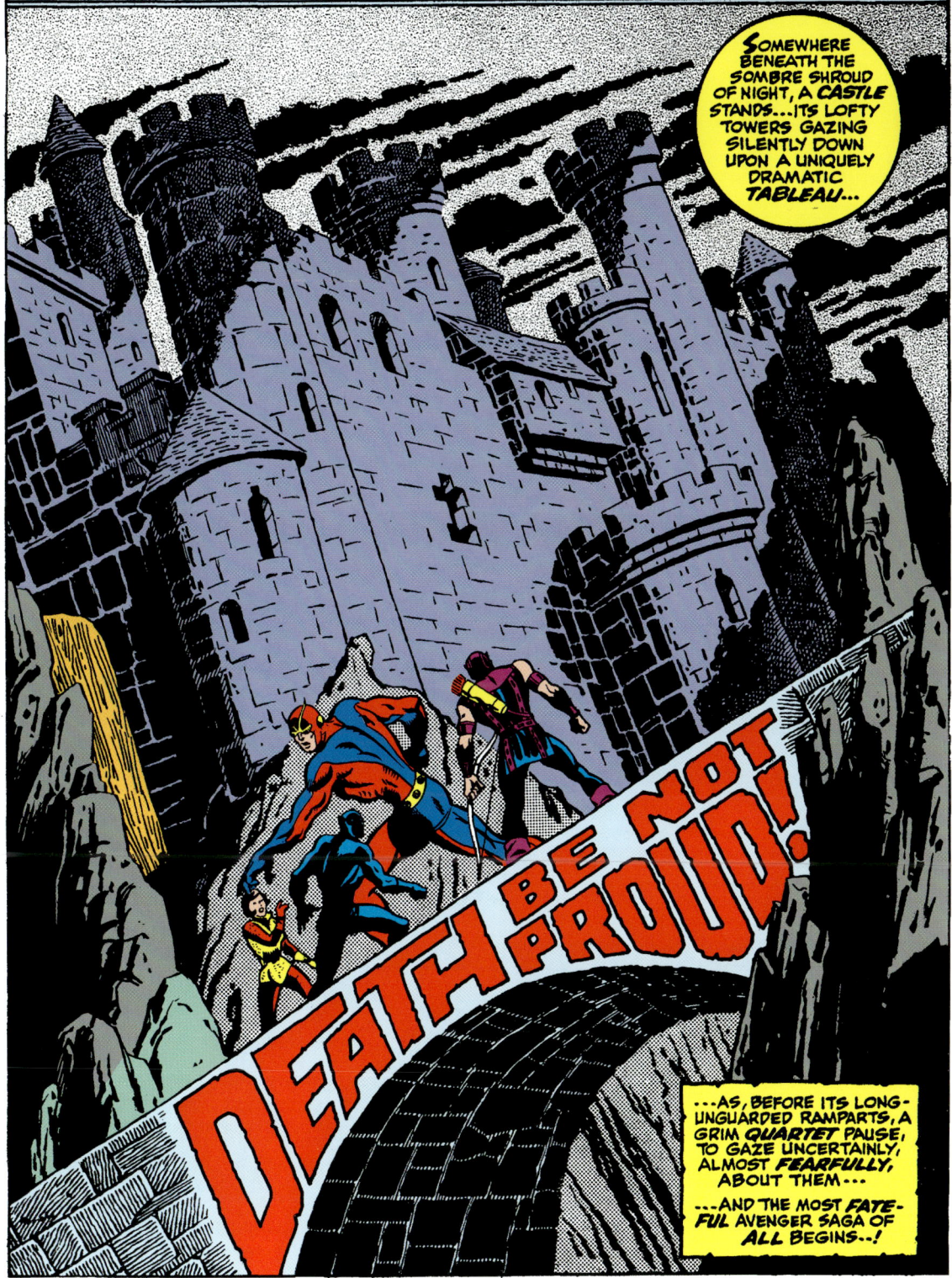

PRODUCED BY AS TALENTED A TEAM OF STRIVING STALWARTS AS EVER PUT PEN OR PENCIL TO PAPER!!
STAN LEE • ROY THOMAS • JOHN BUSCEMA • GEORGE KLEIN • SAM ROSEN
EDITOR!   WRITER!   ARTIST!   INKER!   LETTERER!

SOMEWHERE BENEATH THE SOMBRE SHROUD OF NIGHT, A *CASTLE* STANDS...ITS LOFTY TOWERS GAZING SILENTLY DOWN UPON A UNIQUELY DRAMATIC *TABLEAU*...

DEATH BE NOT PROUD!

---AS, BEFORE ITS LONG-UNGUARDED RAMPARTS, A GRIM *QUARTET* PAUSE, TO GAZE UNCERTAINLY, ALMOST *FEARFULLY*, ABOUT THEM---

---AND THE MOST *FATEFUL* AVENGER SAGA OF *ALL* BEGINS--!

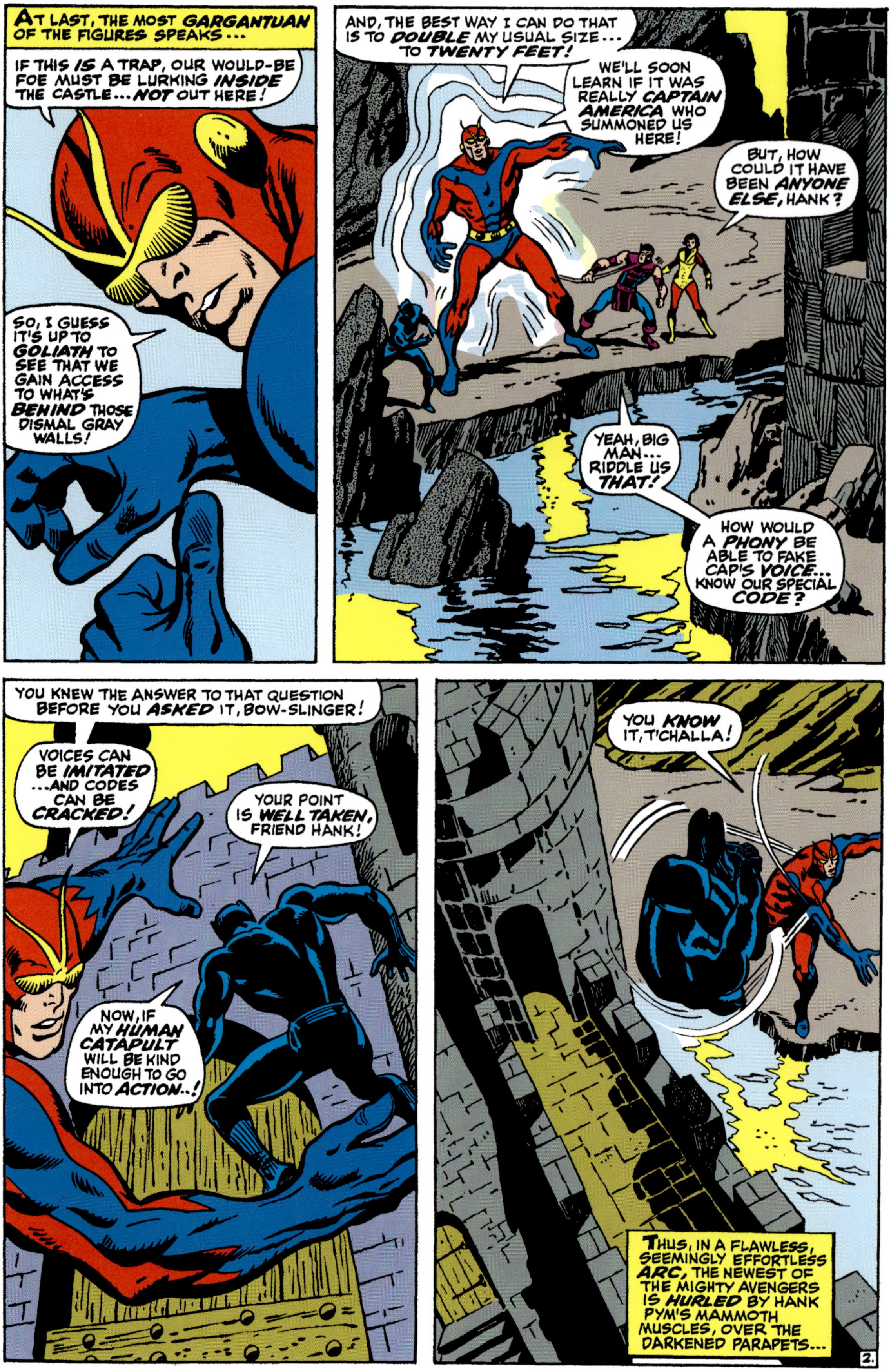
AT LAST, THE MOST GARGANTUAN OF THE FIGURES SPEAKS...
IF THIS IS A TRAP, OUR WOULD-BE FOE MUST BE LURKING INSIDE THE CASTLE... NOT OUT HERE!
SO, I GUESS IT'S UP TO GOLIATH TO SEE THAT WE GAIN ACCESS TO WHAT'S BEHIND THOSE DISMAL GRAY WALLS!
AND, THE BEST WAY I CAN DO THAT IS TO DOUBLE MY USUAL SIZE... TO TWENTY FEET!
WE'LL SOON LEARN IF IT WAS REALLY CAPTAIN AMERICA WHO SUMMONED US HERE!
BUT, HOW COULD IT HAVE BEEN ANYONE ELSE, HANK?
YEAH, BIG MAN... RIDDLE US THAT!
HOW WOULD A PHONY BE ABLE TO FAKE CAP'S VOICE... KNOW OUR SPECIAL CODE?
YOU KNEW THE ANSWER TO THAT QUESTION BEFORE YOU ASKED IT, BOW-SLINGER!
VOICES CAN BE IMITATED ...AND CODES CAN BE CRACKED!
YOUR POINT IS WELL TAKEN, FRIEND HANK!
NOW, IF MY HUMAN CATAPULT WILL BE KIND ENOUGH TO GO INTO ACTION..!
YOU KNOW IT, T'CHALLA!
THUS, IN A FLAWLESS, SEEMINGLY EFFORTLESS ARC, THE NEWEST OF THE MIGHTY AVENGERS IS HURLED BY HANK PYM'S MAMMOTH MUSCLES, OVER THE DARKENED PARAPETS...
2.

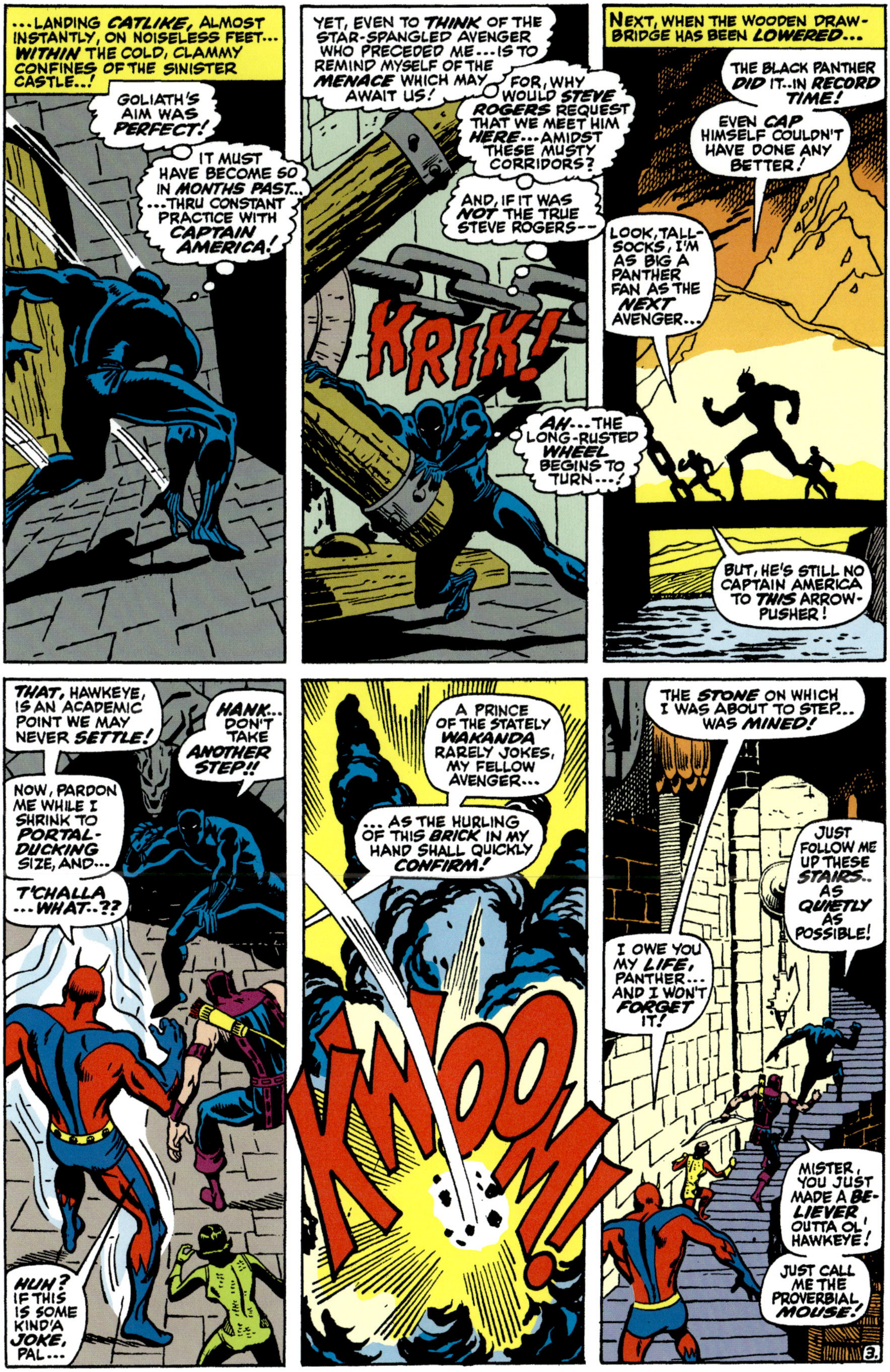
...LANDING CATLIKE, ALMOST INSTANTLY, ON NOISELESS FEET... WITHIN THE COLD, CLAMMY CONFINES OF THE SINISTER CASTLE..!
GOLIATH'S AIM WAS PERFECT!
IT MUST HAVE BECOME SO IN MONTHS PAST... ...THRU CONSTANT PRACTICE WITH CAPTAIN AMERICA!
YET, EVEN TO THINK OF THE STAR-SPANGLED AVENGER WHO PRECEDED ME... IS TO REMIND MYSELF OF THE MENACE WHICH MAY AWAIT US!
FOR, WHY WOULD STEVE ROGERS REQUEST THAT WE MEET HIM HERE... AMIDST THESE MUSTY CORRIDORS?
AND, IF IT WAS NOT THE TRUE STEVE ROGERS--
KRIK!
AH... THE LONG-RUSTED WHEEL BEGINS TO TURN...!
NEXT, WHEN THE WOODEN DRAW-BRIDGE HAS BEEN LOWERED...
THE BLACK PANTHER DID IT.. IN RECORD TIME!
EVEN CAP HIMSELF COULDN'T HAVE DONE ANY BETTER!
LOOK, TALL-SOCKS, I'M AS BIG A PANTHER FAN AS THE NEXT AVENGER...
BUT, HE'S STILL NO CAPTAIN AMERICA TO THIS ARROW-PUSHER!
THAT, HAWKEYE, IS AN ACADEMIC POINT WE MAY NEVER SETTLE!
HANK... DON'T TAKE ANOTHER STEP!!
NOW, PARDON ME WHILE I SHRINK TO PORTAL-DUCKING SIZE, AND...
T'CHALLA ...WHAT..??
HUH? IF THIS IS SOME KIND'A JOKE, PAL...
A PRINCE OF THE STATELY WAKANDA RARELY JOKES, MY FELLOW AVENGER...
... AS THE HURLING OF THIS BRICK IN MY HAND SHALL QUICKLY CONFIRM!
KNOOM!!
THE STONE ON WHICH I WAS ABOUT TO STEP... WAS MINED!
JUST FOLLOW ME UP THESE STAIRS.. AS QUIETLY AS POSSIBLE!
I OWE YOU MY LIFE, PANTHER... AND I WON'T FORGET IT!
MISTER, YOU JUST MADE A BE-LIEVER OUTTA OL' HAWKEYE!
JUST CALL ME THE PROVERBIAL MOUSE!
3.

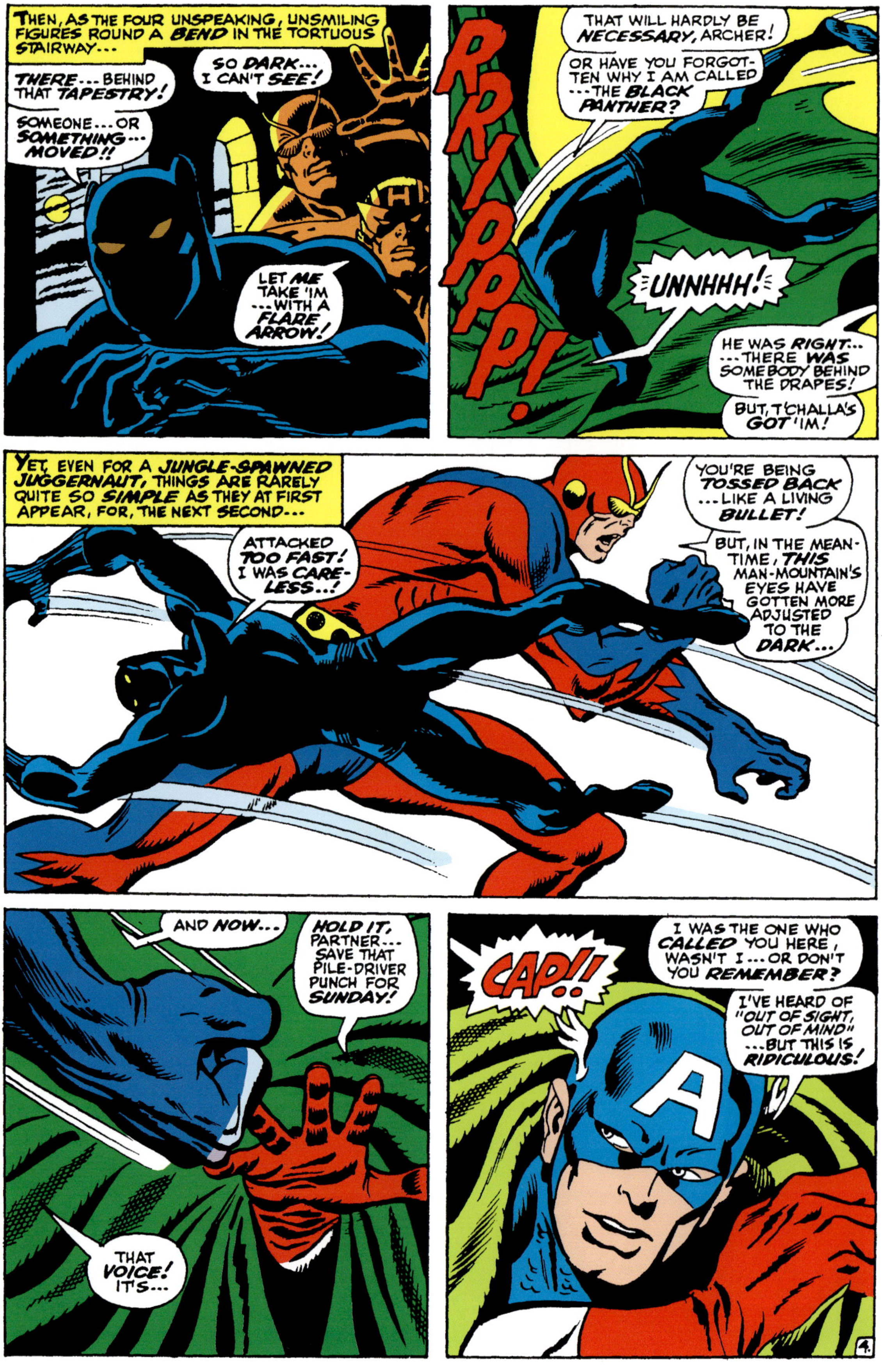

THEN, AS THE FOUR UNSPEAKING, UNSMILING FIGURES ROUND A BEND IN THE TORTUOUS STAIRWAY...
THERE... BEHIND THAT TAPESTRY!
SOMEONE... OR SOMETHING... MOVED!!
SO DARK... I CAN'T SEE!
LET ME TAKE 'IM ...WITH A FLARE ARROW!
THAT WILL HARDLY BE NECESSARY, ARCHER!
OR HAVE YOU FORGOTTEN WHY I AM CALLED ...THE BLACK PANTHER?
RRIPPP!
UNNHHH!
HE WAS RIGHT... ...THERE WAS SOMEBODY BEHIND THE DRAPES!
BUT, T'CHALLA'S GOT 'IM!
YET, EVEN FOR A JUNGLE-SPAWNED JUGGERNAUT, THINGS ARE RARELY QUITE SO SIMPLE AS THEY AT FIRST APPEAR, FOR, THE NEXT SECOND...
ATTACKED TOO FAST! I WAS CARELESS..!
YOU'RE BEING TOSSED BACK ...LIKE A LIVING BULLET!
BUT, IN THE MEANTIME, THIS MAN-MOUNTAIN'S EYES HAVE GOTTEN MORE ADJUSTED TO THE DARK...
AND NOW...
HOLD IT, PARTNER... SAVE THAT PILE-DRIVER PUNCH FOR SUNDAY!
THAT VOICE! IT'S...
CAP!!
I WAS THE ONE WHO CALLED YOU HERE, WASN'T I... OR DON'T YOU REMEMBER?
I'VE HEARD OF "OUT OF SIGHT, OUT OF MIND" ...BUT THIS IS RIDICULOUS!
4

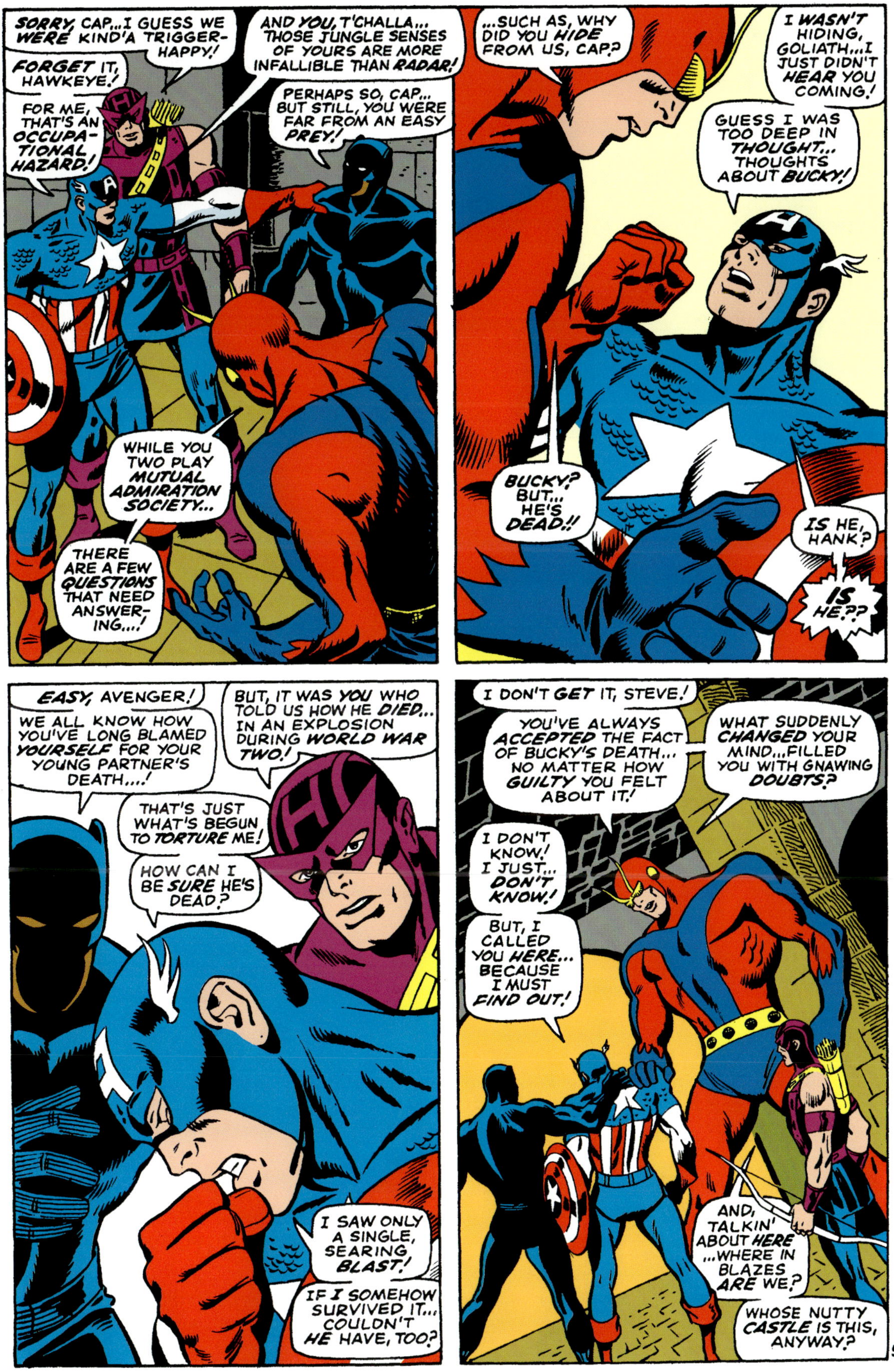

SORRY, CAP...I GUESS WE WERE KIND'A TRIGGER-HAPPY!
FORGET IT, HAWKEYE!
FOR ME, THAT'S AN OCCUPA-TIONAL HAZARD!
AND YOU, T'CHALLA... THOSE JUNGLE SENSES OF YOURS ARE MORE INFALLIBLE THAN RADAR!
PERHAPS SO, CAP... BUT STILL, YOU WERE FAR FROM AN EASY PREY!
WHILE YOU TWO PLAY MUTUAL ADMIRATION SOCIETY...
THERE ARE A FEW QUESTIONS THAT NEED ANSWER-ING...!
...SUCH AS, WHY DID YOU HIDE FROM US, CAP?
I WASN'T HIDING, GOLIATH...I JUST DIDN'T HEAR YOU COMING!
GUESS I WAS TOO DEEP IN THOUGHT... THOUGHTS ABOUT BUCKY!
BUCKY? BUT... HE'S DEAD!!
IS HE, HANK?
IS HE??
EASY, AVENGER!
WE ALL KNOW HOW YOU'VE LONG BLAMED YOURSELF FOR YOUR YOUNG PARTNER'S DEATH...!
BUT, IT WAS YOU WHO TOLD US HOW HE DIED... IN AN EXPLOSION DURING WORLD WAR TWO!
THAT'S JUST WHAT'S BEGUN TO TORTURE ME!
HOW CAN I BE SURE HE'S DEAD?
I SAW ONLY A SINGLE, SEARING BLAST!
IF I SOMEHOW SURVIVED IT... COULDN'T HE HAVE, TOO?
I DON'T GET IT, STEVE!
YOU'VE ALWAYS ACCEPTED THE FACT OF BUCKY'S DEATH... NO MATTER HOW GUILTY YOU FELT ABOUT IT!
WHAT SUDDENLY CHANGED YOUR MIND...FILLED YOU WITH GNAWING DOUBTS?
I DON'T KNOW! I JUST... DON'T KNOW!
BUT, I CALLED YOU HERE... BECAUSE I MUST FIND OUT!
AND, TALKIN' ABOUT HERE ...WHERE IN BLAZES ARE WE?
WHOSE NUTTY CASTLE IS THIS, ANYWAY?
5.

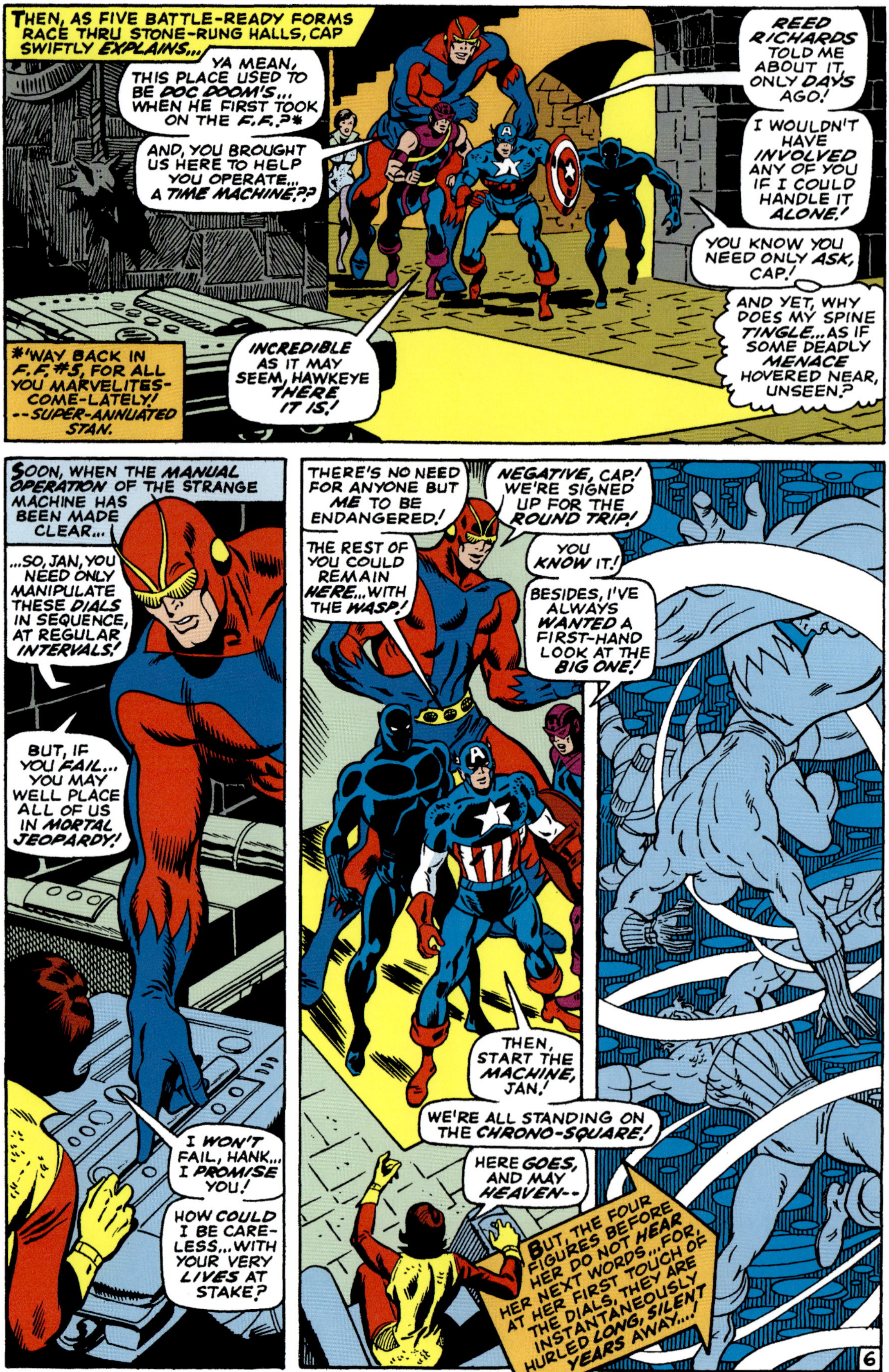
THEN, AS FIVE BATTLE-READY FORMS RACE THRU STONE-RUNG HALLS, CAP SWIFTLY EXPLAINS...
YA MEAN, THIS PLACE USED TO BE DOC DOOM'S... WHEN HE FIRST TOOK ON THE F.F.?*
AND, YOU BROUGHT US HERE TO HELP YOU OPERATE... A TIME MACHINE?
INCREDIBLE AS IT MAY SEEM, HAWKEYE THERE IT IS!
REED RICHARDS TOLD ME ABOUT IT, ONLY DAYS AGO!
I WOULDN'T HAVE INVOLVED ANY OF YOU IF I COULD HANDLE IT ALONE!
YOU KNOW YOU NEED ONLY ASK, CAP!
AND YET, WHY DOES MY SPINE TINGLE... AS IF SOME DEADLY MENACE HOVERED NEAR, UNSEEN?
*'WAY BACK IN F.F. #5, FOR ALL YOU MARVELITES-COME-LATELY! --SUPER-ANNUATED STAN.
SOON, WHEN THE MANUAL OPERATION OF THE STRANGE MACHINE HAS BEEN MADE CLEAR...
...SO, JAN, YOU NEED ONLY MANIPULATE THESE DIALS IN SEQUENCE, AT REGULAR INTERVALS!
BUT, IF YOU FAIL... YOU MAY WELL PLACE ALL OF US IN MORTAL JEOPARDY!
I WON'T FAIL, HANK... I PROMISE YOU!
HOW COULD I BE CARE-LESS... WITH YOUR VERY LIVES AT STAKE?
THERE'S NO NEED FOR ANYONE BUT ME TO BE ENDANGERED!
THE REST OF YOU COULD REMAIN HERE... WITH THE WASP!
NEGATIVE, CAP! WE'RE SIGNED UP FOR THE ROUND TRIP!
YOU KNOW IT!
BESIDES, I'VE ALWAYS WANTED A FIRST-HAND LOOK AT THE BIG ONE!
THEN, START THE MACHINE, JAN!
WE'RE ALL STANDING ON THE CHRONO-SQUARE!
HERE GOES, AND MAY HEAVEN--
BUT, THE FOUR FIGURES BEFORE HER DO NOT HEAR HER NEXT WORDS... FOR, AT HER FIRST TOUCH OF THE DIALS, THEY ARE INSTANTANEOUSLY HURLED LONG, SILENT YEARS AWAY...!
6

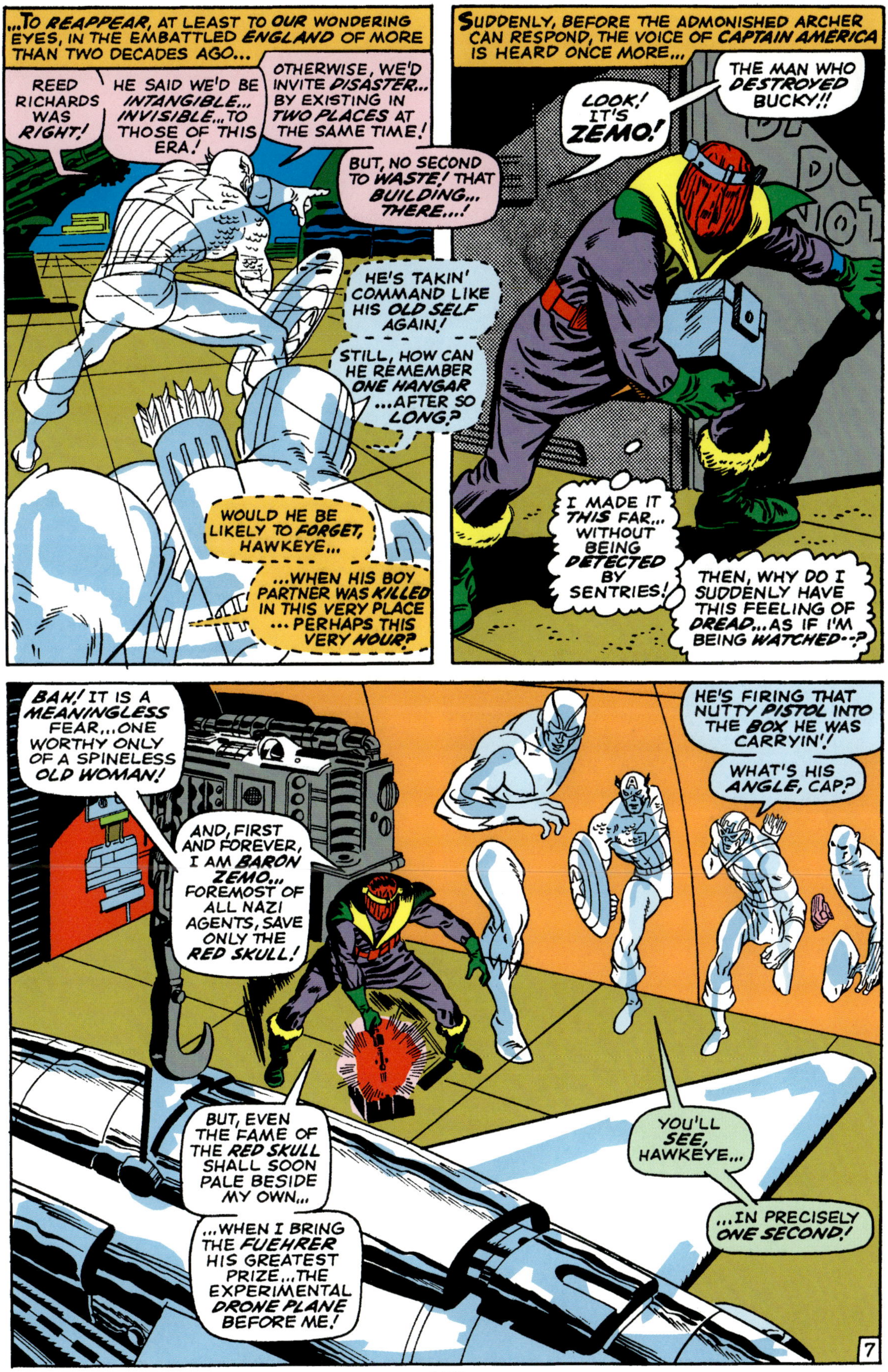
...TO REAPPEAR, AT LEAST TO OUR WONDERING EYES, IN THE EMBATTLED ENGLAND OF MORE THAN TWO DECADES AGO...
REED RICHARDS WAS RIGHT!
HE SAID WE'D BE INTANGIBLE... INVISIBLE... TO THOSE OF THIS ERA!
OTHERWISE, WE'D INVITE DISASTER... BY EXISTING IN TWO PLACES AT THE SAME TIME!
BUT, NO SECOND TO WASTE! THAT BUILDING... THERE...!
HE'S TAKIN' COMMAND LIKE HIS OLD SELF AGAIN!
STILL, HOW CAN HE REMEMBER ONE HANGAR ...AFTER SO LONG?
WOULD HE BE LIKELY TO FORGET, HAWKEYE...
...WHEN HIS BOY PARTNER WAS KILLED IN THIS VERY PLACE ... PERHAPS THIS VERY HOUR?
SUDDENLY, BEFORE THE ADMONISHED ARCHER CAN RESPOND, THE VOICE OF CAPTAIN AMERICA IS HEARD ONCE MORE...
LOOK! IT'S ZEMO!
THE MAN WHO DESTROYED BUCKY!!
I MADE IT THIS FAR... WITHOUT BEING DETECTED BY SENTRIES!
THEN, WHY DO I SUDDENLY HAVE THIS FEELING OF DREAD... AS IF I'M BEING WATCHED--?
BAH! IT IS A MEANINGLESS FEAR... ONE WORTHY ONLY OF A SPINELESS OLD WOMAN!
AND, FIRST AND FOREVER, I AM BARON ZEMO... FOREMOST OF ALL NAZI AGENTS, SAVE ONLY THE RED SKULL!
BUT, EVEN THE FAME OF THE RED SKULL SHALL SOON PALE BESIDE MY OWN...
...WHEN I BRING THE FUEHRER HIS GREATEST PRIZE... THE EXPERIMENTAL DRONE PLANE BEFORE ME!
HE'S FIRING THAT NUTTY PISTOL INTO THE BOX HE WAS CARRYIN'!
WHAT'S HIS ANGLE, CAP?
YOU'LL SEE, HAWKEYE...
...IN PRECISELY ONE SECOND!
7

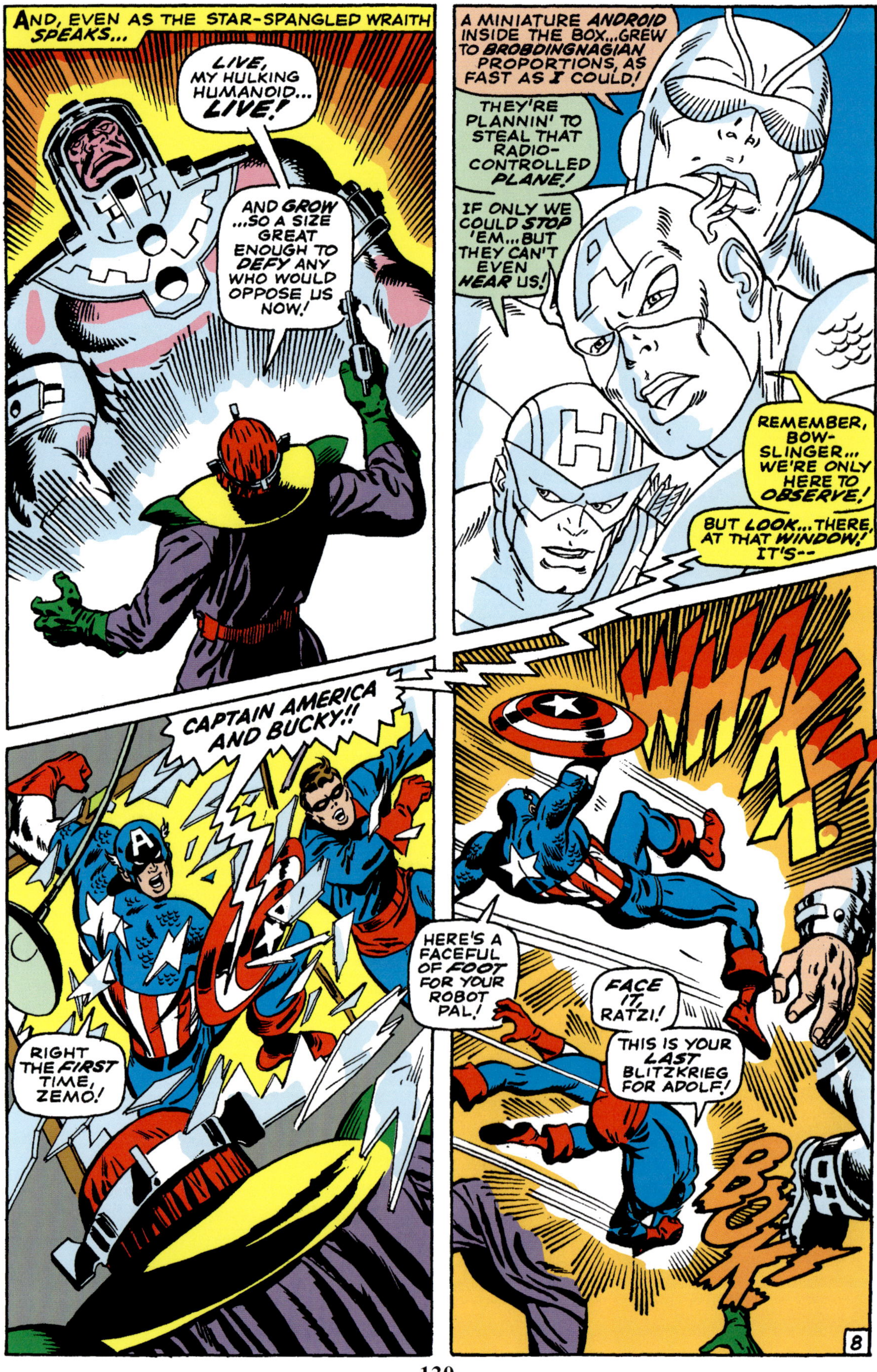
AND, EVEN AS THE STAR-SPANGLED WRAITH SPEAKS...
LIVE, MY HULKING HUMANOID... LIVE!
AND GROW ...SO A SIZE GREAT ENOUGH TO DEFY ANY WHO WOULD OPPOSE US NOW!
A MINIATURE ANDROID INSIDE THE BOX...GREW TO BROBDINGNAGIAN PROPORTIONS, AS FAST AS I COULD!
THEY'RE PLANNIN' TO STEAL THAT RADIO-CONTROLLED PLANE!
IF ONLY WE COULD STOP 'EM...BUT THEY CAN'T EVEN HEAR US!
REMEMBER, BOW-SLINGER... WE'RE ONLY HERE TO OBSERVE!
BUT LOOK...THERE, AT THAT WINDOW! IT'S--
CAPTAIN AMERICA AND BUCKY!!
RIGHT THE FIRST TIME, ZEMO!
WHAK!!
HERE'S A FACEFUL OF FOOT FOR YOUR ROBOT PAL!
FACE IT, RATZI!
THIS IS YOUR LAST BLITZKRIEG FOR ADOLF!
BOK!
8

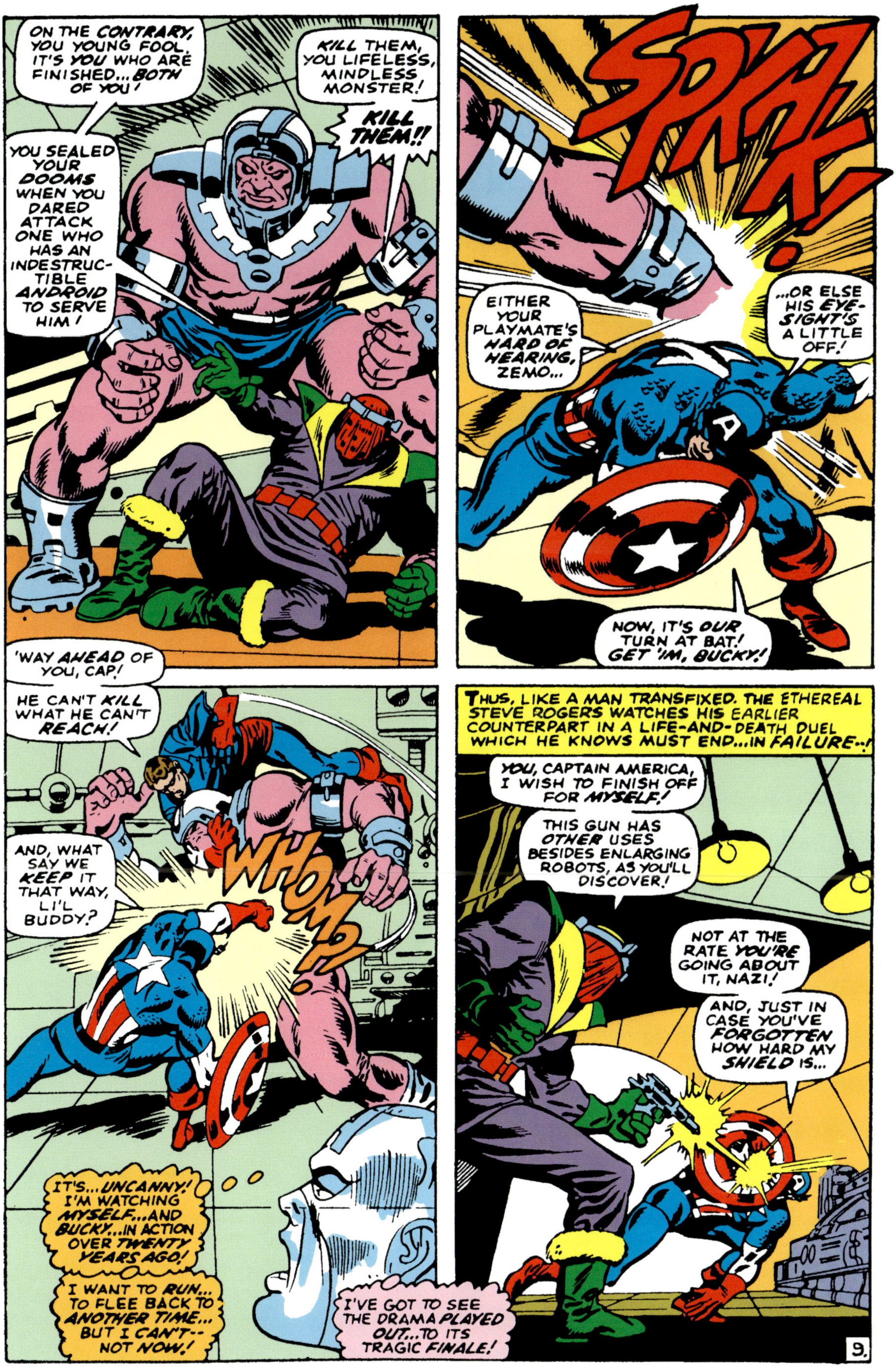

ON THE CONTRARY, YOU YOUNG FOOL, IT'S YOU WHO ARE FINISHED...BOTH OF YOU!
YOU SEALED YOUR DOOMS WHEN YOU DARED ATTACK ONE WHO HAS AN INDESTRUCTIBLE ANDROID TO SERVE HIM!
KILL THEM, YOU LIFELESS, MINDLESS MONSTER!
KILL THEM!!
SPAKK!
EITHER YOUR PLAYMATE'S HARD OF HEARING, ZEMO...
...OR ELSE HIS EYE-SIGHT'S A LITTLE OFF!
NOW, IT'S OUR TURN AT BAT! GET 'IM, BUCKY!
'WAY AHEAD OF YOU, CAP!
HE CAN'T KILL WHAT HE CAN'T REACH!
AND, WHAT SAY WE KEEP IT THAT WAY, LI'L BUDDY?
WHOMP!
IT'S...UNCANNY! I'M WATCHING MYSELF...AND BUCKY...IN ACTION OVER TWENTY YEARS AGO!
I WANT TO RUN... TO FLEE BACK TO ANOTHER TIME... BUT I CAN'T-- NOT NOW!
I'VE GOT TO SEE THE DRAMA PLAYED OUT...TO ITS TRAGIC FINALE!
THUS, LIKE A MAN TRANSFIXED, THE ETHEREAL STEVE ROGERS WATCHES HIS EARLIER COUNTERPART IN A LIFE-AND-DEATH DUEL WHICH HE KNOWS MUST END...IN FAILURE--!
YOU, CAPTAIN AMERICA, I WISH TO FINISH OFF FOR MYSELF!
THIS GUN HAS OTHER USES BESIDES ENLARGING ROBOTS, AS YOU'LL DISCOVER!
NOT AT THE RATE YOU'RE GOING ABOUT IT, NAZI!
AND, JUST IN CASE YOU'VE FORGOTTEN HOW HARD MY SHIELD IS...
9.

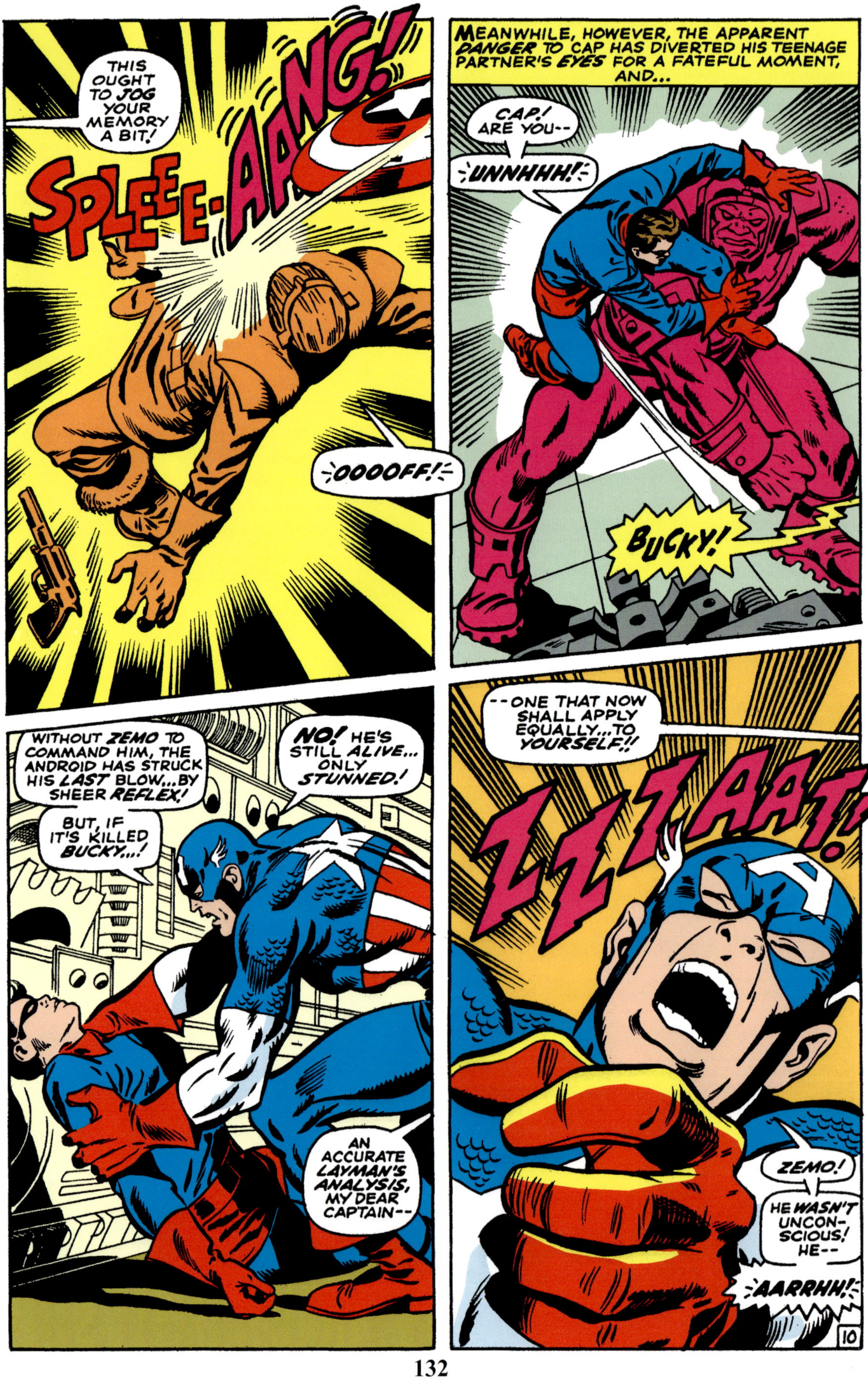
THIS OUGHT TO JOG YOUR MEMORY A BIT!
SPLEEE-AANG!
OOOOFF!
MEANWHILE, HOWEVER, THE APPARENT DANGER TO CAP HAS DIVERTED HIS TEENAGE PARTNER'S EYES FOR A FATEFUL MOMENT, AND...
CAP! ARE YOU--
UNNHHH!
BUCKY!
WITHOUT ZEMO TO COMMAND HIM, THE ANDROID HAS STRUCK HIS LAST BLOW...BY SHEER REFLEX!
BUT, IF IT'S KILLED BUCKY...!
NO! HE'S STILL ALIVE... ONLY STUNNED!
AN ACCURATE LAYMAN'S ANALYSIS, MY DEAR CAPTAIN--
--ONE THAT NOW SHALL APPLY EQUALLY...TO YOURSELF!!
ZZZTAAT!
ZEMO!
HE WASN'T UNCONSCIOUS! HE--
AARRHH!
10

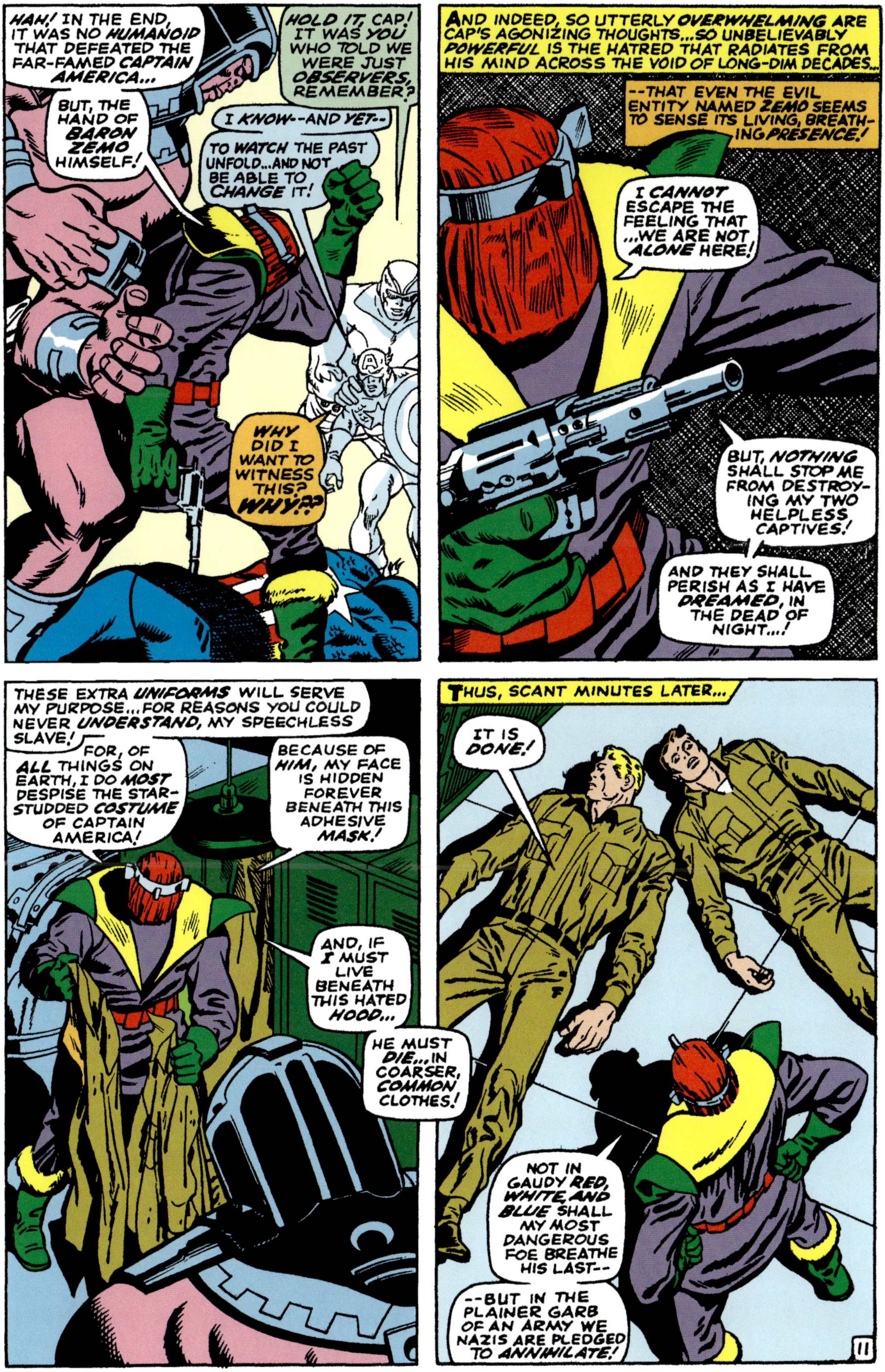
HAH! IN THE END, IT WAS NO HUMANOID THAT DEFEATED THE FAR-FAMED CAPTAIN AMERICA...
BUT, THE HAND OF BARON ZEMO HIMSELF!
HOLD IT, CAP! IT WAS YOU WHO TOLD WE WERE JUST OBSERVERS, REMEMBER?
I KNOW--AND YET--
TO WATCH THE PAST UNFOLD...AND NOT BE ABLE TO CHANGE IT!
WHY DID I WANT TO WITNESS THIS? WHY!??
AND INDEED, SO UTTERLY OVERWHELMING ARE CAP'S AGONIZING THOUGHTS...SO UNBELIEVABLY POWERFUL IS THE HATRED THAT RADIATES FROM HIS MIND ACROSS THE VOID OF LONG-DIM DECADES...
--THAT EVEN THE EVIL ENTITY NAMED ZEMO SEEMS TO SENSE ITS LIVING, BREATHING PRESENCE!
I CANNOT ESCAPE THE FEELING THAT ...WE ARE NOT ALONE HERE!
BUT, NOTHING SHALL STOP ME FROM DESTROYING MY TWO HELPLESS CAPTIVES!
AND THEY SHALL PERISH AS I HAVE DREAMED, IN THE DEAD OF NIGHT...!
THESE EXTRA UNIFORMS WILL SERVE MY PURPOSE...FOR REASONS YOU COULD NEVER UNDERSTAND, MY SPEECHLESS SLAVE!
FOR, OF ALL THINGS ON EARTH, I DO MOST DESPISE THE STAR-STUDDED COSTUME OF CAPTAIN AMERICA!
BECAUSE OF HIM, MY FACE IS HIDDEN FOREVER BENEATH THIS ADHESIVE MASK!
AND, IF I MUST LIVE BENEATH THIS HATED HOOD...
HE MUST DIE...IN COARSER, COMMON CLOTHES!
THUS, SCANT MINUTES LATER...
IT IS DONE!
NOT IN GAUDY RED, WHITE, AND BLUE SHALL MY MOST DANGEROUS FOE BREATHE HIS LAST--
--BUT IN THE PLAINER GARB OF AN ARMY WE NAZIS ARE PLEDGED TO ANNIHILATE!
11

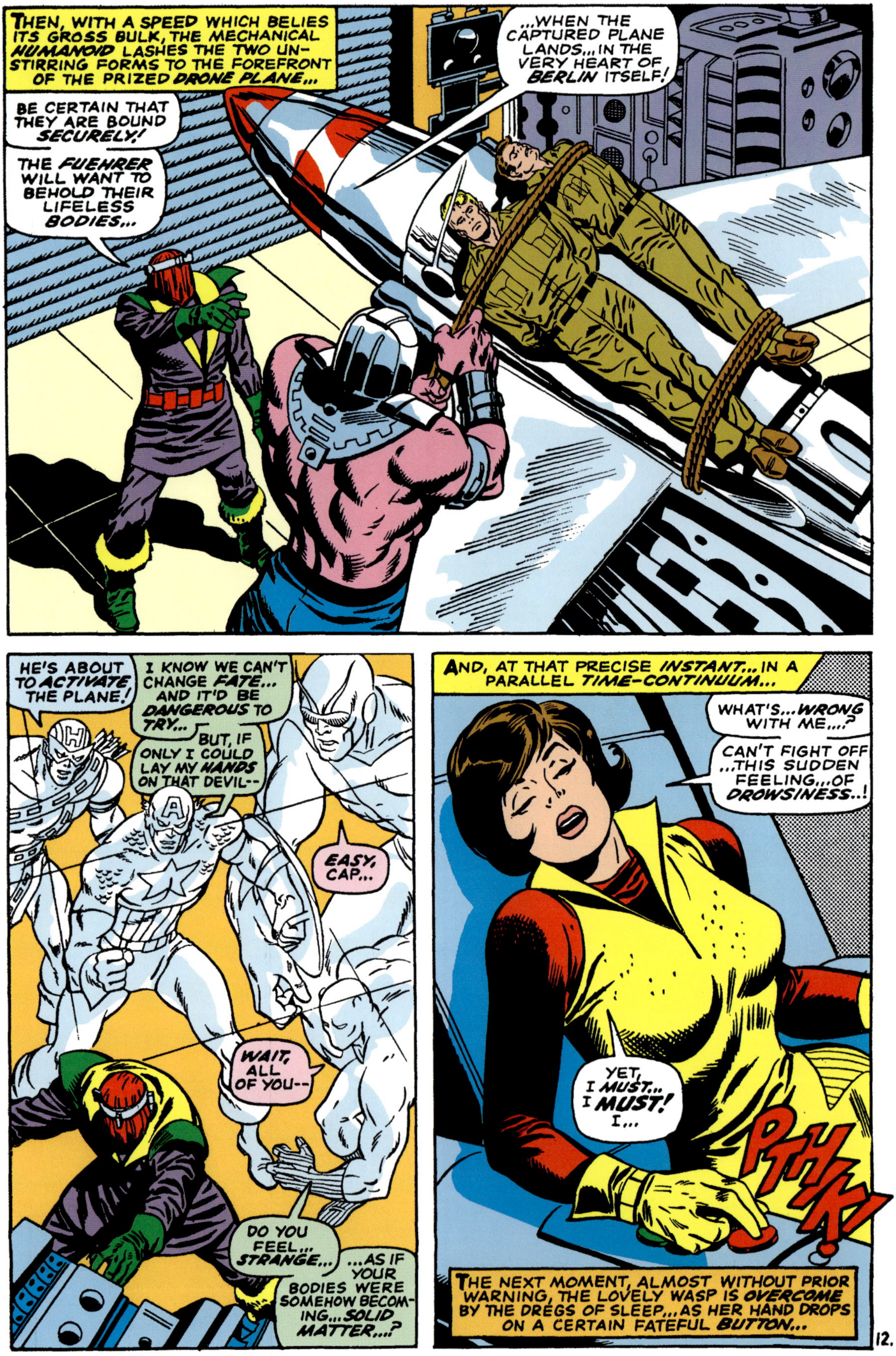

THEN, WITH A SPEED WHICH BELIES ITS GROSS BULK, THE MECHANICAL HUMANOID LASHES THE TWO UN-STIRRING FORMS TO THE FOREFRONT OF THE PRIZED DRONE PLANE...
BE CERTAIN THAT THEY ARE BOUND SECURELY!
THE FUEHRER WILL WANT TO BEHOLD THEIR LIFELESS BODIES...
...WHEN THE CAPTURED PLANE LANDS,...IN THE VERY HEART OF BERLIN ITSELF!
HE'S ABOUT TO ACTIVATE THE PLANE!
I KNOW WE CAN'T CHANGE FATE... AND IT'D BE DANGEROUS TO TRY... BUT, IF ONLY I COULD LAY MY HANDS ON THAT DEVIL--
EASY, CAP...
WAIT, ALL OF YOU--
DO YOU FEEL... STRANGE...
...AS IF YOUR BODIES WERE SOMEHOW BECOM-ING... SOLID MATTER...?
AND, AT THAT PRECISE INSTANT... IN A PARALLEL TIME-CONTINUUM...
WHAT'S... WRONG WITH ME...?
CAN'T FIGHT OFF ...THIS SUDDEN FEELING... OF DROWSINESS..!
YET, I MUST... I MUST! I...
PTHIK!
THE NEXT MOMENT, ALMOST WITHOUT PRIOR WARNING, THE LOVELY WASP IS OVERCOME BY THE DREGS OF SLEEP,.. AS HER HAND DROPS ON A CERTAIN FATEFUL BUTTON...
12.

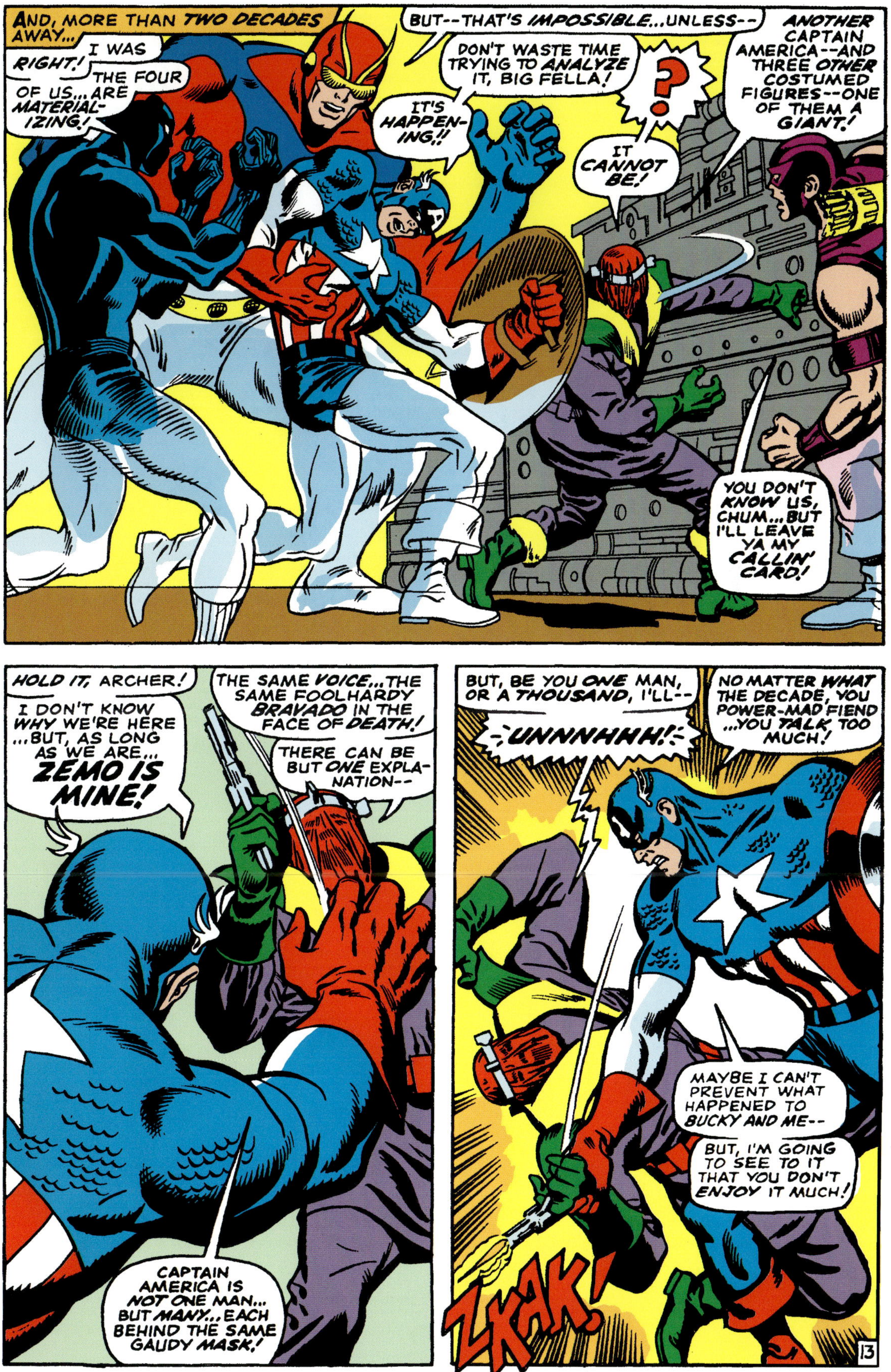
AND, MORE THAN TWO DECADES AWAY...
I WAS RIGHT! THE FOUR OF US... ARE MATERIALIZING!
BUT--THAT'S IMPOSSIBLE...UNLESS--
DON'T WASTE TIME TRYING TO ANALYZE IT, BIG FELLA!
IT'S HAPPENING!!
?
IT CANNOT BE!
ANOTHER CAPTAIN AMERICA--AND THREE OTHER COSTUMED FIGURES--ONE OF THEM A GIANT!
YOU DON'T KNOW US, CHUM...BUT I'LL LEAVE YA MY CALLIN' CARD!
HOLD IT, ARCHER!
I DON'T KNOW WHY WE'RE HERE ...BUT, AS LONG AS WE ARE... ZEMO IS MINE!
THE SAME VOICE...THE SAME FOOLHARDY BRAVADO IN THE FACE OF DEATH!
THERE CAN BE BUT ONE EXPLANATION--
CAPTAIN AMERICA IS NOT ONE MAN... BUT MANY... EACH BEHIND THE SAME GAUDY MASK!
BUT, BE YOU ONE MAN, OR A THOUSAND, I'LL--
UNNNHHH!
NO MATTER WHAT THE DECADE, YOU POWER-MAD FIEND ...YOU TALK TOO MUCH!
MAYBE I CAN'T PREVENT WHAT HAPPENED TO BUCKY AND ME--
BUT, I'M GOING TO SEE TO IT THAT YOU DON'T ENJOY IT MUCH!
ZKAK!
13

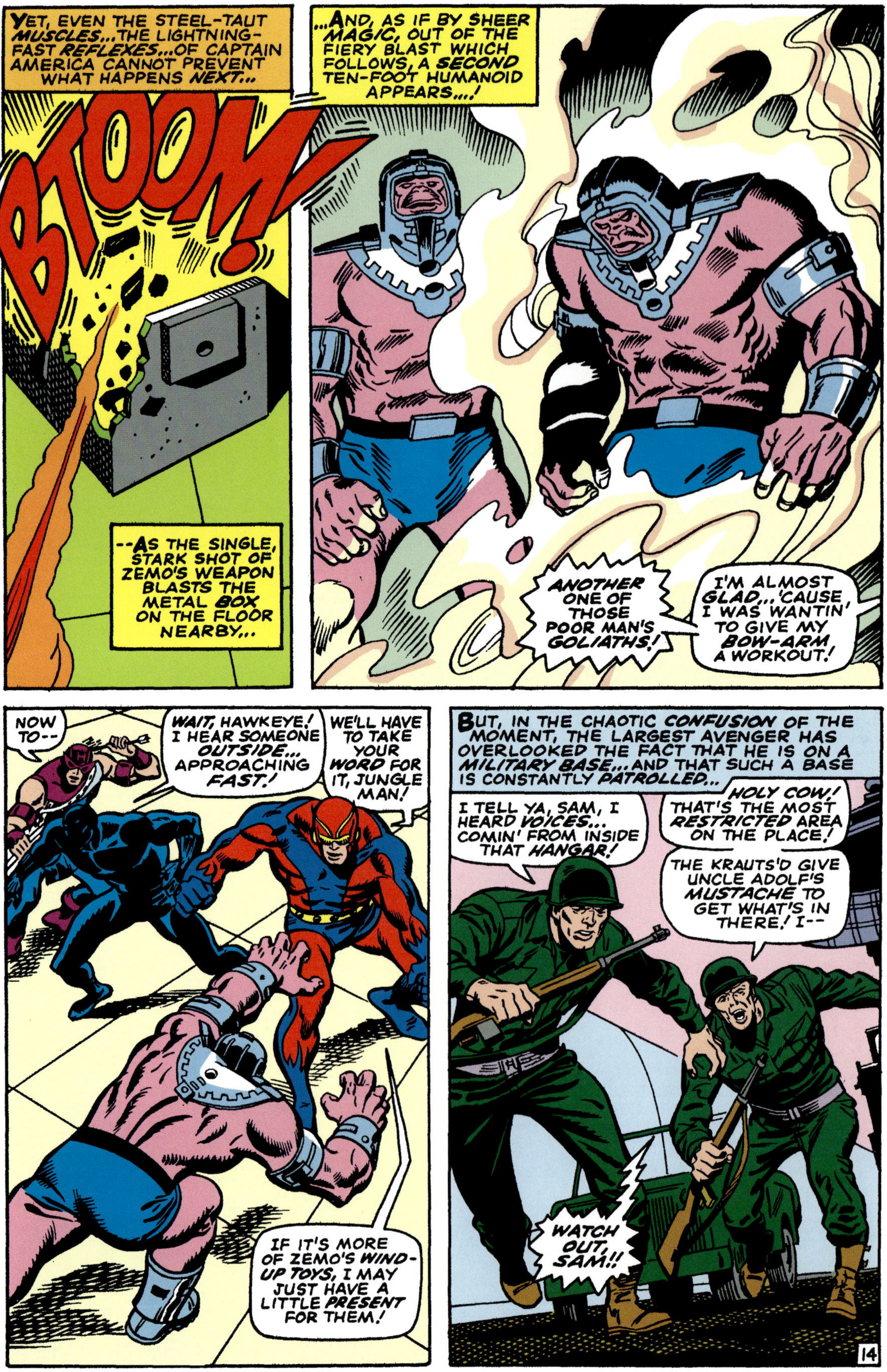
YET, EVEN THE STEEL-TAUT MUSCLES... THE LIGHTNING-FAST REFLEXES... OF CAPTAIN AMERICA CANNOT PREVENT WHAT HAPPENS NEXT...
BTOOM!
--AS THE SINGLE, STARK SHOT OF ZEMO'S WEAPON BLASTS THE METAL BOX ON THE FLOOR NEARBY...
...AND, AS IF BY SHEER MAGIC, OUT OF THE FIERY BLAST WHICH FOLLOWS, A SECOND TEN-FOOT HUMANOID APPEARS...!
ANOTHER ONE OF THOSE POOR MAN'S GOLIATHS!
I'M ALMOST GLAD... 'CAUSE I WAS WANTIN' TO GIVE MY BOW-ARM A WORKOUT!
NOW TO--
WAIT, HAWKEYE! I HEAR SOMEONE OUTSIDE... APPROACHING FAST!
WE'LL HAVE TO TAKE YOUR WORD FOR IT, JUNGLE MAN!
IF IT'S MORE OF ZEMO'S WIND-UP TOYS, I MAY JUST HAVE A LITTLE PRESENT FOR THEM!
BUT, IN THE CHAOTIC CONFUSION OF THE MOMENT, THE LARGEST AVENGER HAS OVERLOOKED THE FACT THAT HE IS ON A MILITARY BASE... AND THAT SUCH A BASE IS CONSTANTLY PATROLLED...
I TELL YA, SAM, I HEARD VOICES... COMIN' FROM INSIDE THAT HANGAR!
HOLY COW! THAT'S THE MOST RESTRICTED AREA ON THE PLACE!
THE KRAUTS'D GIVE UNCLE ADOLF'S MUSTACHE TO GET WHAT'S IN THERE! I--
WATCH OUT, SAM!!
14

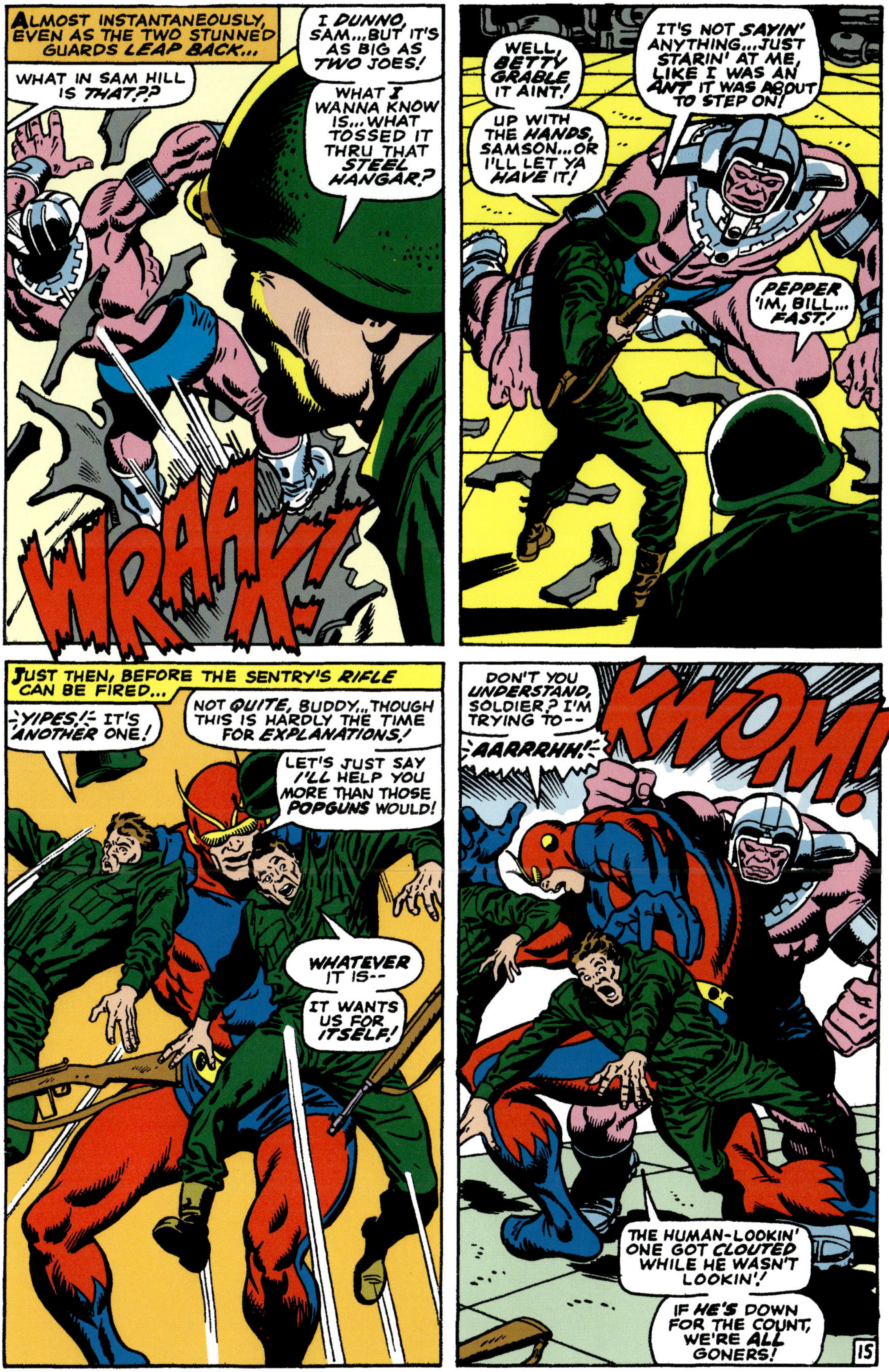
ALMOST INSTANTANEOUSLY, EVEN AS THE TWO STUNNED GUARDS LEAP BACK...
WHAT IN SAM HILL IS THAT??
I DUNNO, SAM...BUT IT'S AS BIG AS TWO JOES!
WHAT I WANNA KNOW IS...WHAT TOSSED IT THRU THAT STEEL HANGAR?
WRAAK!
WELL, BETTY GRABLE IT AINT!
IT'S NOT SAYIN' ANYTHING...JUST STARIN' AT ME, LIKE I WAS AN ANT IT WAS ABOUT TO STEP ON!
UP WITH THE HANDS, SAMSON...OR I'LL LET YA HAVE IT!
PEPPER 'IM, BILL... FAST!
JUST THEN, BEFORE THE SENTRY'S RIFLE CAN BE FIRED...
YIPES! IT'S ANOTHER ONE!
NOT QUITE, BUDDY...THOUGH THIS IS HARDLY THE TIME FOR EXPLANATIONS!
LET'S JUST SAY I'LL HELP YOU MORE THAN THOSE POPGUNS WOULD!
WHATEVER IT IS--
IT WANTS US FOR ITSELF!
DON'T YOU UNDERSTAND, SOLDIER? I'M TRYING TO--
AARRRHH!
KWOM!
THE HUMAN-LOOKIN' ONE GOT CLOUTED WHILE HE WASN'T LOOKIN'!
IF HE'S DOWN FOR THE COUNT, WE'RE ALL GONERS!
15

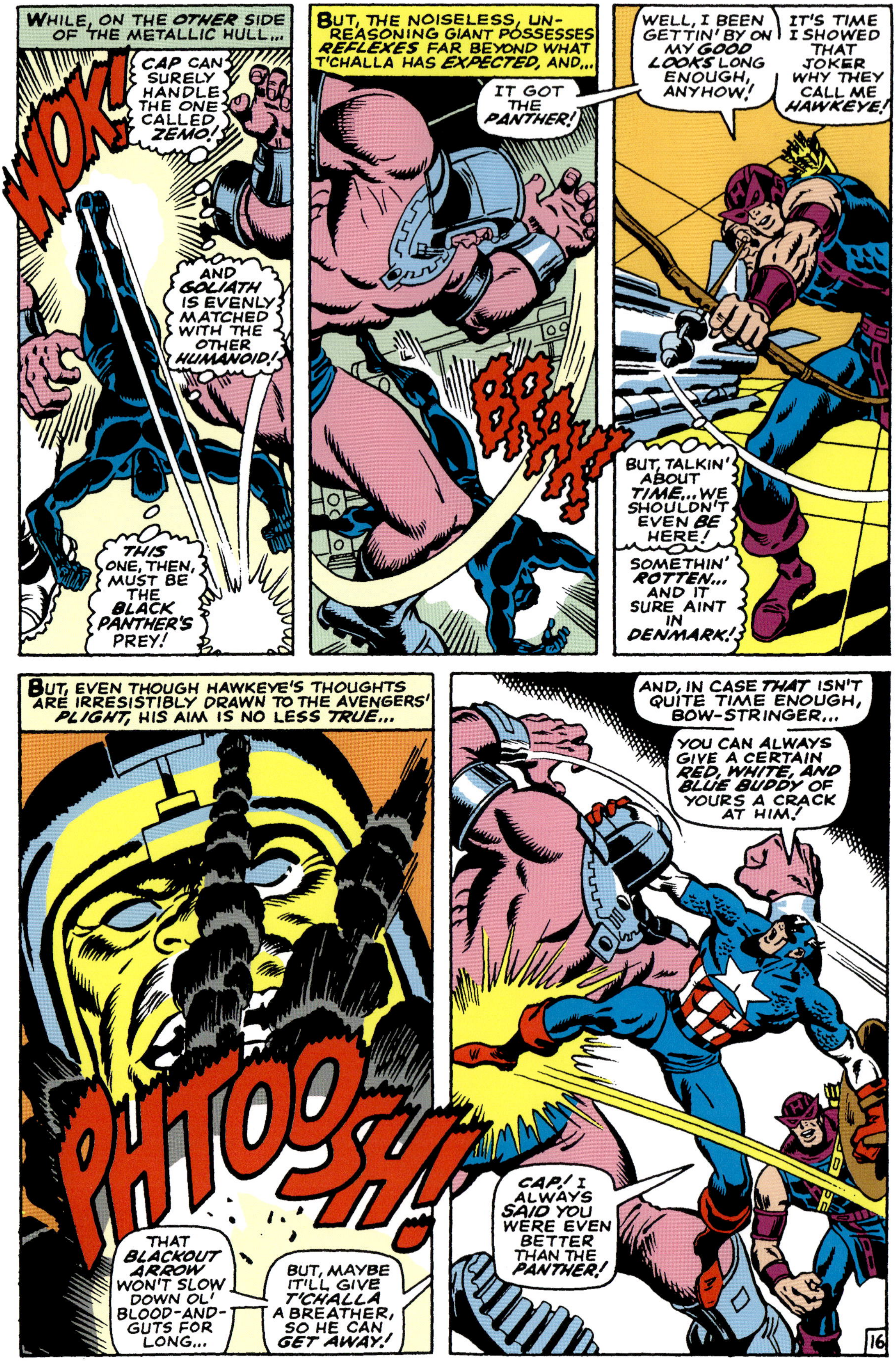
WHILE, ON THE OTHER SIDE OF THE METALLIC HULL...
WOK!
CAP CAN SURELY HANDLE THE ONE CALLED ZEMO!
AND GOLIATH IS EVENLY MATCHED WITH THE OTHER HUMANOID!
THIS ONE, THEN, MUST BE THE BLACK PANTHER'S PREY!
BUT, THE NOISELESS, UNREASONING GIANT POSSESSES REFLEXES FAR BEYOND WHAT T'CHALLA HAS EXPECTED, AND...
IT GOT THE PANTHER!
BRAK!
WELL, I BEEN GETTIN' BY ON MY GOOD LOOKS LONG ENOUGH, ANYHOW!
IT'S TIME I SHOWED THAT JOKER WHY THEY CALL ME HAWKEYE!
BUT, TALKIN' ABOUT TIME... WE SHOULDN'T EVEN BE HERE!
SOMETHIN' ROTTEN... AND IT SURE AINT IN DENMARK!
BUT, EVEN THOUGH HAWKEYE'S THOUGHTS ARE IRRESISTIBLY DRAWN TO THE AVENGERS' PLIGHT, HIS AIM IS NO LESS TRUE...
PHTOOSH!
THAT BLACKOUT ARROW WON'T SLOW DOWN OL' BLOOD-AND-GUTS FOR LONG...
BUT, MAYBE IT'LL GIVE T'CHALLA A BREATHER, SO HE CAN GET AWAY!
AND, IN CASE THAT ISN'T QUITE TIME ENOUGH, BOW-STRINGER...
YOU CAN ALWAYS GIVE A CERTAIN RED, WHITE, AND BLUE BUDDY OF YOURS A CRACK AT HIM!
CAP! I ALWAYS SAID YOU WERE EVEN BETTER THAN THE PANTHER!
16

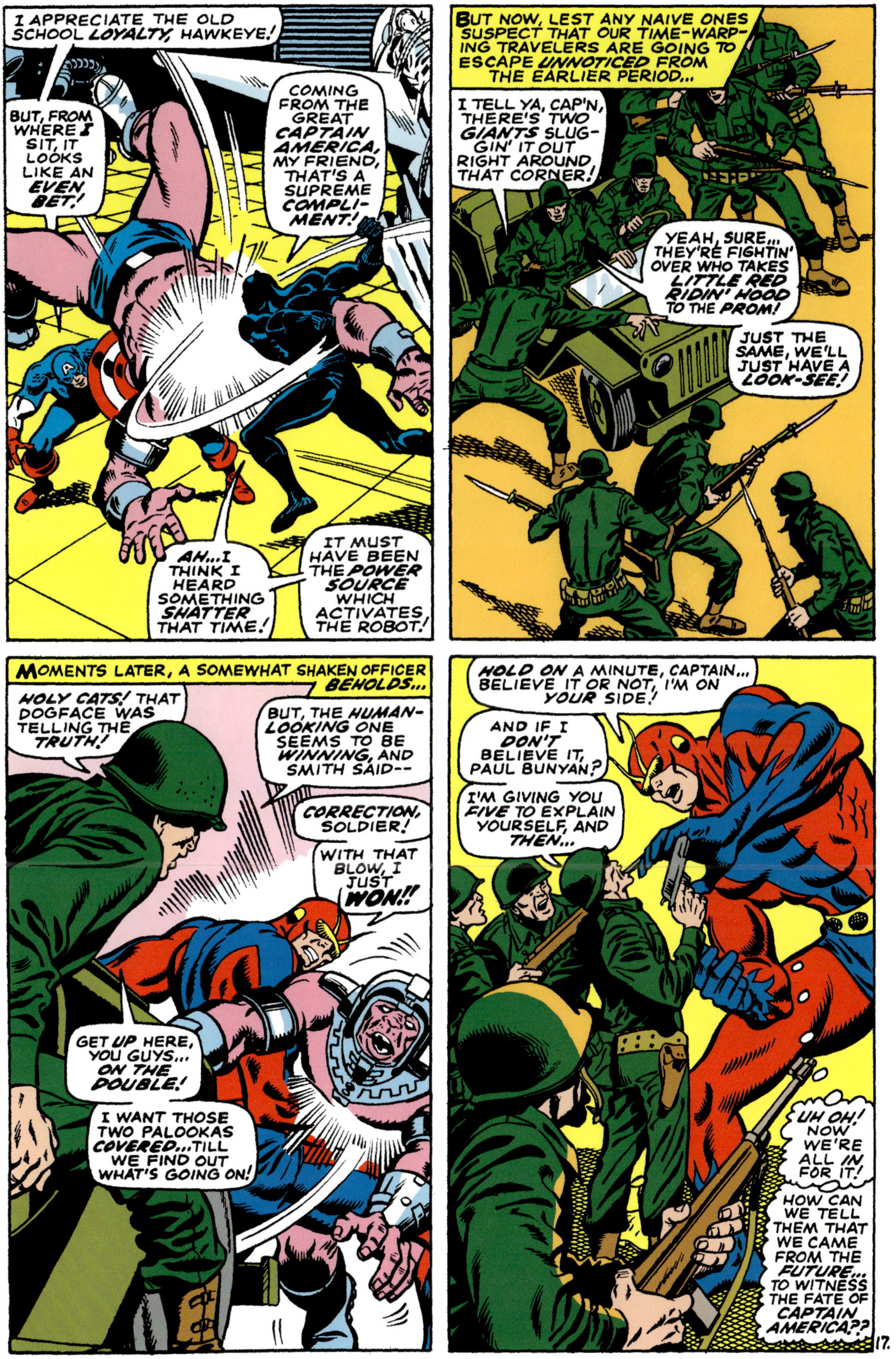
I APPRECIATE THE OLD SCHOOL LOYALTY, HAWKEYE!
BUT, FROM WHERE I SIT, IT LOOKS LIKE AN EVEN BET!
COMING FROM THE GREAT CAPTAIN AMERICA, MY FRIEND, THAT'S A SUPREME COMPLIMENT!
AH...I THINK I HEARD SOMETHING SHATTER THAT TIME!
IT MUST HAVE BEEN THE POWER SOURCE WHICH ACTIVATES THE ROBOT!
BUT NOW, LEST ANY NAIVE ONES SUSPECT THAT OUR TIME-WARPING TRAVELERS ARE GOING TO ESCAPE UNNOTICED FROM THE EARLIER PERIOD...
I TELL YA, CAP'N, THERE'S TWO GIANTS SLUGGIN' IT OUT RIGHT AROUND THAT CORNER!
YEAH, SURE... THEY'RE FIGHTIN' OVER WHO TAKES LITTLE RED RIDIN' HOOD TO THE PROM!
JUST THE SAME, WE'LL JUST HAVE A LOOK-SEE!
MOMENTS LATER, A SOMEWHAT SHAKEN OFFICER BEHOLDS...
HOLY CATS! THAT DOGFACE WAS TELLING THE TRUTH!
BUT, THE HUMAN-LOOKING ONE SEEMS TO BE WINNING, AND SMITH SAID--
CORRECTION, SOLDIER!
WITH THAT BLOW, I JUST WON!!
GET UP HERE, YOU GUYS... ON THE DOUBLE!
I WANT THOSE TWO PALOOKAS COVERED...TILL WE FIND OUT WHAT'S GOING ON!
HOLD ON A MINUTE, CAPTAIN... BELIEVE IT OR NOT, I'M ON YOUR SIDE!
AND IF I DON'T BELIEVE IT, PAUL BUNYAN?
I'M GIVING YOU FIVE TO EXPLAIN YOURSELF, AND THEN...
UH OH! NOW WE'RE ALL IN FOR IT!
HOW CAN WE TELL THEM THAT WE CAME FROM THE FUTURE... TO WITNESS THE FATE OF CAPTAIN AMERICA??
17.

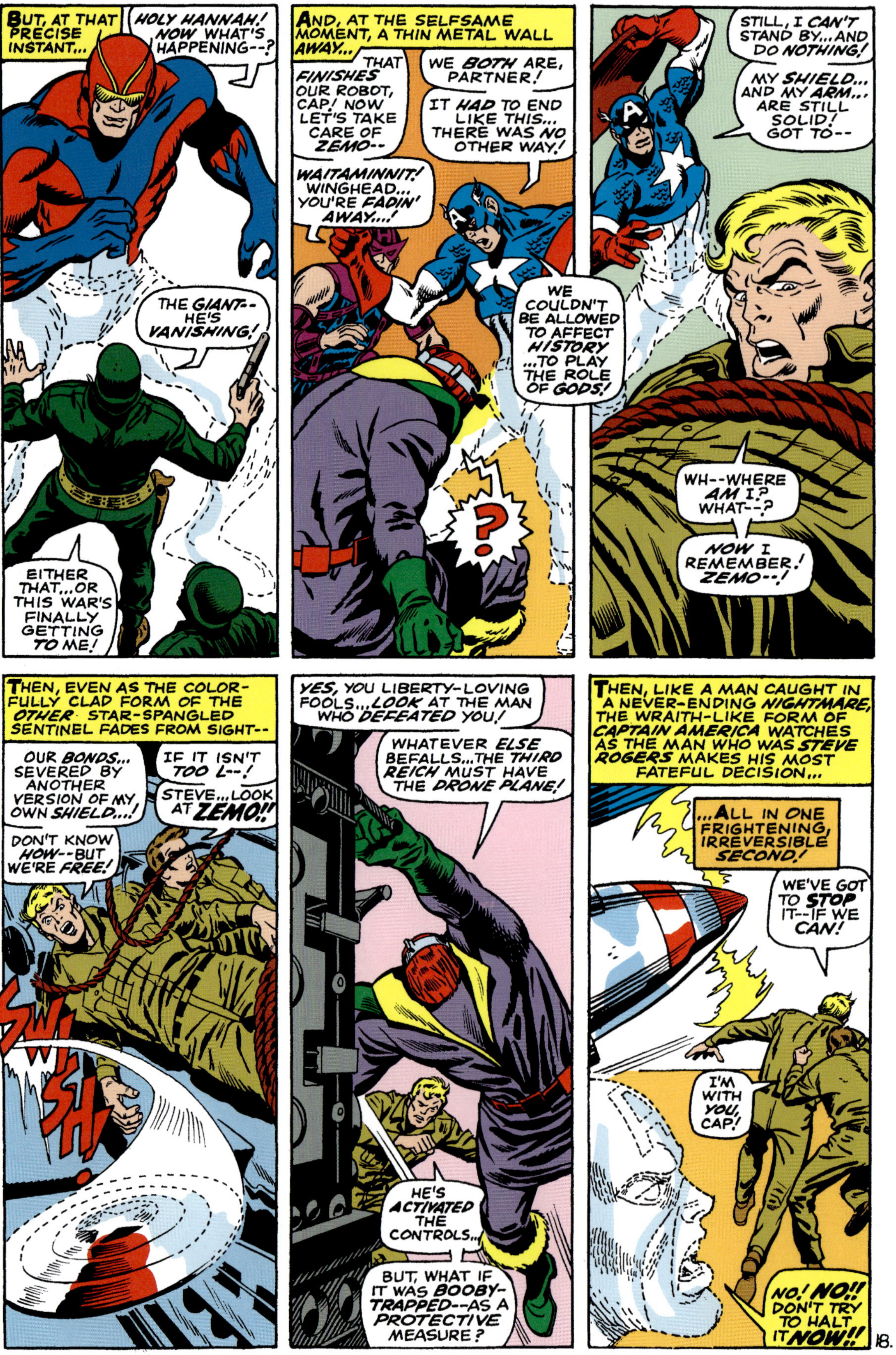

BUT, AT THAT PRECISE INSTANT...
HOLY HANNAH! NOW WHAT'S HAPPENING--?
THE GIANT--HE'S VANISHING!
EITHER THAT...OR THIS WAR'S FINALLY GETTING TO ME!
AND, AT THE SELFSAME MOMENT, A THIN METAL WALL AWAY...
THAT FINISHES OUR ROBOT, CAP! NOW LET'S TAKE CARE OF ZEMO--
WE BOTH ARE, PARTNER!
IT HAD TO END LIKE THIS... THERE WAS NO OTHER WAY!
WAITAMINNIT! WINGHEAD... YOU'RE FADIN' AWAY...!
WE COULDN'T BE ALLOWED TO AFFECT HISTORY ...TO PLAY THE ROLE OF GODS!
?
STILL, I CAN'T STAND BY...AND DO NOTHING!
MY SHIELD... AND MY ARM... ARE STILL SOLID! GOT TO--
WH--WHERE AM I? WHAT--?
NOW I REMEMBER! ZEMO--!
THEN, EVEN AS THE COLORFULLY CLAD FORM OF THE OTHER STAR-SPANGLED SENTINEL FADES FROM SIGHT--
OUR BONDS... SEVERED BY ANOTHER VERSION OF MY OWN SHIELD...!
IF IT ISN'T TOO L--!
STEVE...LOOK AT ZEMO!!
DON'T KNOW HOW--BUT WE'RE FREE!
SWISH!
YES, YOU LIBERTY-LOVING FOOLS...LOOK AT THE MAN WHO DEFEATED YOU!
WHATEVER ELSE BEFALLS...THE THIRD REICH MUST HAVE THE DRONE PLANE!
HE'S ACTIVATED THE CONTROLS...
BUT, WHAT IF IT WAS BOOBY-TRAPPED--AS A PROTECTIVE MEASURE?
THEN, LIKE A MAN CAUGHT IN A NEVER-ENDING NIGHTMARE, THE WRAITH-LIKE FORM OF CAPTAIN AMERICA WATCHES AS THE MAN WHO WAS STEVE ROGERS MAKES HIS MOST FATEFUL DECISION...
...ALL IN ONE FRIGHTENING, IRREVERSIBLE SECOND!
WE'VE GOT TO STOP IT--IF WE CAN!
I'M WITH YOU, CAP!
NO! NO!! DON'T TRY TO HALT IT NOW!!
18.

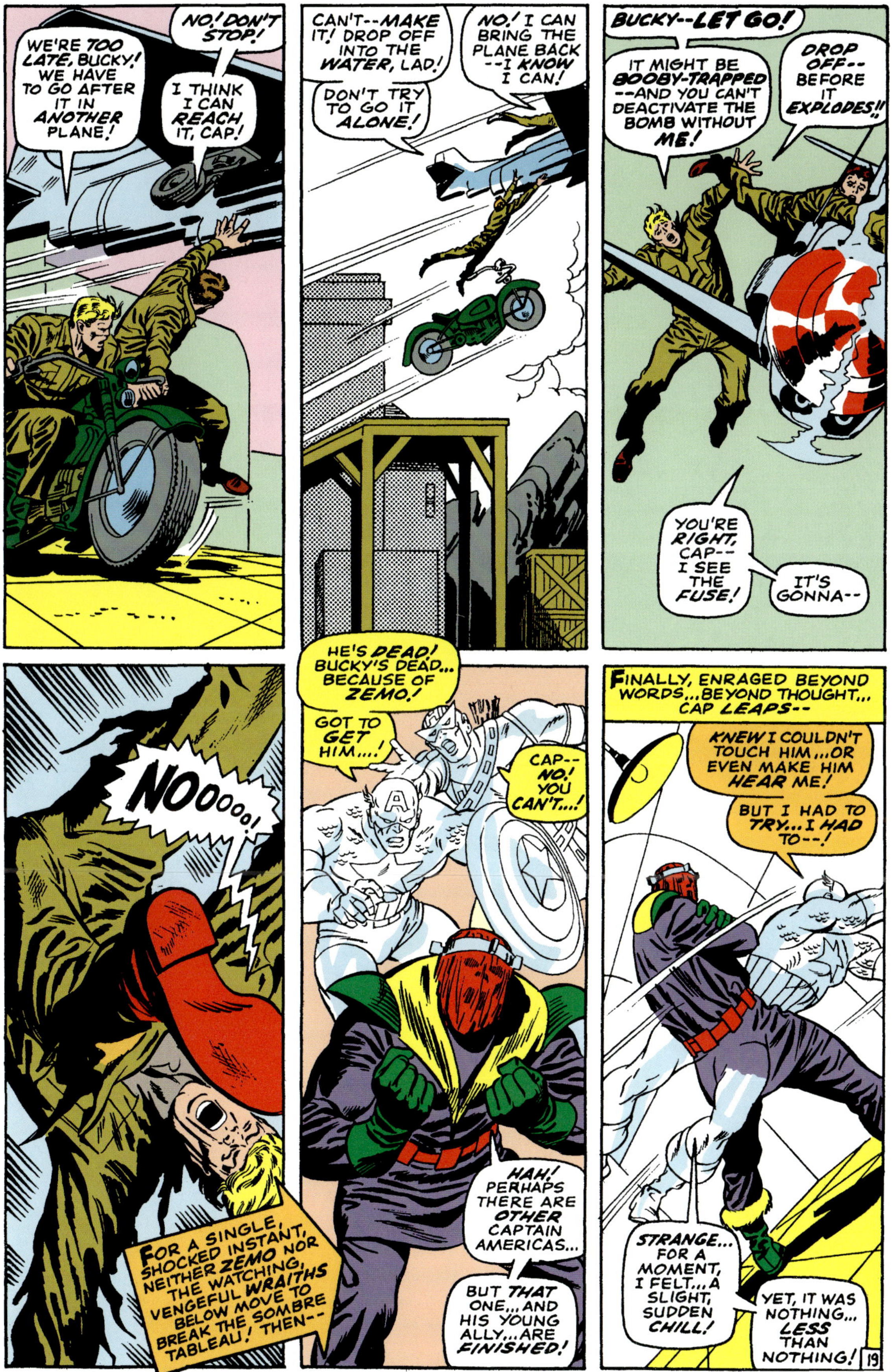
WE'RE TOO LATE, BUCKY! WE HAVE TO GO AFTER IT IN ANOTHER PLANE!
NO! DON'T STOP!
I THINK I CAN REACH IT, CAP!
CAN'T--MAKE IT! DROP OFF INTO THE WATER, LAD!
NO! I CAN BRING THE PLANE BACK --I KNOW I CAN!
DON'T TRY TO GO IT ALONE!
BUCKY--LET GO!
IT MIGHT BE BOOBY-TRAPPED --AND YOU CAN'T DEACTIVATE THE BOMB WITHOUT ME!
DROP OFF-- BEFORE IT EXPLODES!!
YOU'RE RIGHT, CAP-- I SEE THE FUSE!
IT'S GONNA--
NOOooo!
FOR A SINGLE, SHOCKED INSTANT, NEITHER ZEMO NOR THE WATCHING, VENGEFUL WRAITHS BELOW MOVE TO BREAK THE SOMBRE TABLEAU! THEN--
HE'S DEAD! BUCKY'S DEAD... BECAUSE OF ZEMO!
GOT TO GET HIM....!
CAP-- NO! YOU CAN'T...!
HAH! PERHAPS THERE ARE OTHER CAPTAIN AMERICAS...
BUT THAT ONE... AND HIS YOUNG ALLY... ARE FINISHED!
FINALLY, ENRAGED BEYOND WORDS... BEYOND THOUGHT... CAP LEAPS--
KNEW I COULDN'T TOUCH HIM... OR EVEN MAKE HIM HEAR ME!
BUT I HAD TO TRY... I HAD TO--!
STRANGE... FOR A MOMENT, I FELT... A SLIGHT, SUDDEN CHILL!
YET, IT WAS NOTHING... LESS THAN NOTHING!
19

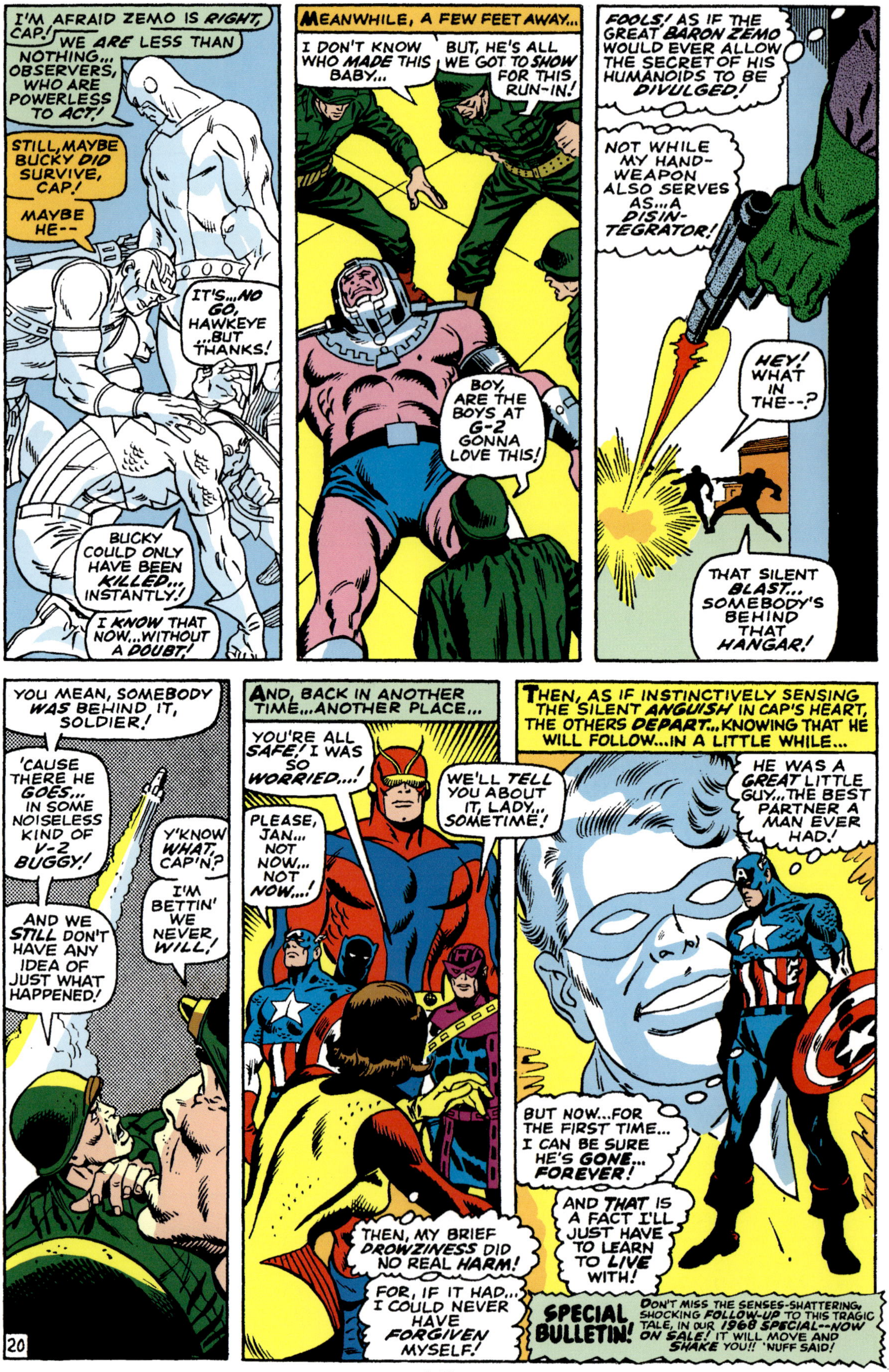

I'M AFRAID ZEMO IS RIGHT, CAP! WE ARE LESS THAN NOTHING... OBSERVERS, WHO ARE POWERLESS TO ACT!
STILL, MAYBE BUCKY DID SURVIVE, CAP!
MAYBE HE--
IT'S... NO GO, HAWKEYE ...BUT THANKS!
BUCKY COULD ONLY HAVE BEEN KILLED..., INSTANTLY!
I KNOW THAT NOW... WITHOUT A DOUBT!
MEANWHILE, A FEW FEET AWAY...
I DON'T KNOW WHO MADE THIS BABY...
BUT, HE'S ALL WE GOT TO SHOW FOR THIS RUN-IN!
BOY, ARE THE BOYS AT G-2 GONNA LOVE THIS!
FOOLS! AS IF THE GREAT BARON ZEMO WOULD EVER ALLOW THE SECRET OF HIS HUMANOIDS TO BE DIVULGED!
NOT WHILE MY HAND-WEAPON ALSO SERVES AS... A DISIN-TEGRATOR!
HEY! WHAT IN THE--?
THAT SILENT BLAST... SOMEBODY'S BEHIND THAT HANGAR!
YOU MEAN, SOMEBODY WAS BEHIND IT, SOLDIER!
'CAUSE THERE HE GOES... IN SOME NOISELESS KIND OF V-2 BUGGY!
Y'KNOW WHAT, CAP'N?
I'M BETTIN' WE NEVER WILL!
AND WE STILL DON'T HAVE ANY IDEA OF JUST WHAT HAPPENED!
20
AND, BACK IN ANOTHER TIME... ANOTHER PLACE...
YOU'RE ALL SAFE! I WAS SO WORRIED...!
WE'LL TELL YOU ABOUT IT, LADY... SOMETIME!
PLEASE, JAN... NOT NOW... NOT NOW...!
THEN, MY BRIEF DROWZINESS DID NO REAL HARM!
FOR, IF IT HAD... I COULD NEVER HAVE FORGIVEN MYSELF!
THEN, AS IF INSTINCTIVELY SENSING THE SILENT ANGUISH IN CAP'S HEART, THE OTHERS DEPART... KNOWING THAT HE WILL FOLLOW... IN A LITTLE WHILE...
HE WAS A GREAT LITTLE GUY... THE BEST PARTNER A MAN EVER HAD!
BUT NOW... FOR THE FIRST TIME... I CAN BE SURE HE'S GONE... FOREVER!
AND THAT IS A FACT I'LL JUST HAVE TO LEARN TO LIVE WITH!
SPECIAL BULLETIN! DON'T MISS THE SENSES-SHATTERING, SHOCKING FOLLOW-UP TO THIS TRAGIC TALE, IN OUR 1968 SPECIAL--NOW ON SALE! IT WILL MOVE AND SHAKE YOU!! 'NUFF SAID!

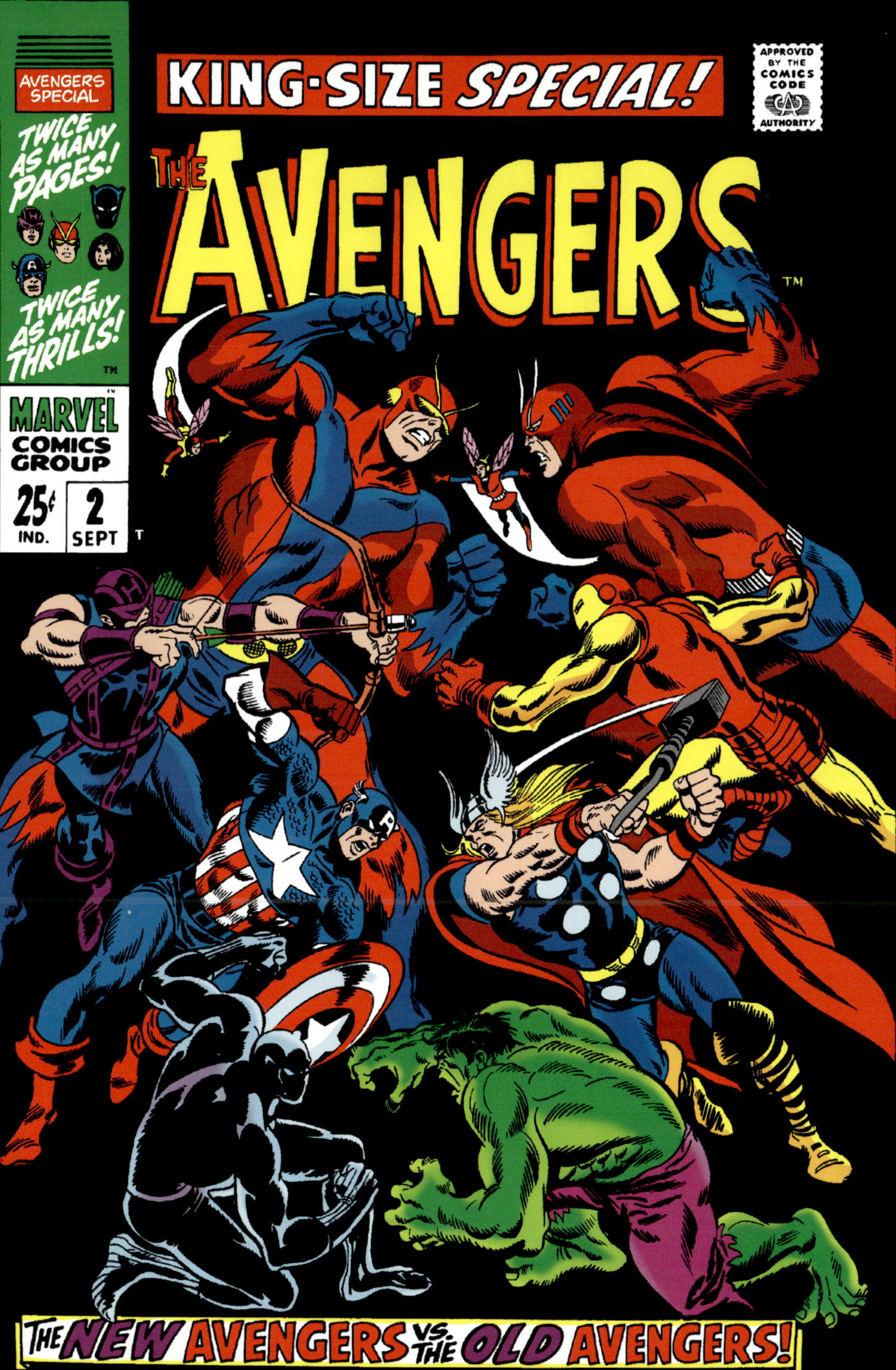
AVENGERS SPECIAL
TWICE AS MANY PAGES!
TWICE AS MANY THRILLS!
MARVEL COMICS GROUP
25¢ IND.
2 SEPT
KING-SIZE SPECIAL!
APPROVED BY THE COMICS CODE AUTHORITY
THE AVENGERS
THE NEW AVENGERS VS. THE OLD AVENGERS!

THE MIGHTY AVENGERS!™
"...AND TIME, THE RUSHING RIVER..."
THE AVENGERS... SPEARHEADED BY THE FAMILIAR FORM OF CAPTAIN AMERICA ...HAVE RETURNED FROM THEIR MISSION INTO THE PAST, NOT REALIZING THAT A FANTASTIC, EVEN MORE FOREBODING PRESENT AWAITS THEM--!
I TELL YOU, CAP, I DON'T LIKE IT!
THERE'S SOMETHING ABOUT THE WAY EVERYONE'S STARING AT US..!
JUST THE HIGH PRICE OF BEIN' PUBLIC IDOLS, MAN-MOUNTAIN!
NO, HAWKEYE... IT'S SOMETHING MORE! I SENSE IT, TOO!
IT'S ALMOST AS IF... NONE OF THEM EVER SAW OR HEARD OF US BEFORE..!
PERHAPS THE MOST INCREDIBLE AVENGERS THRILLER YET, PRESENTED WITH PRIDE BY: STAN LEE·EDITOR ROY THOMAS·WRITER DON HECK WERNER ROTH ARTISTS VINCE COLLETTA·INKER JOE ROSEN·LETTERER
HONORARY AVENGERS ALL!!
AND WITH THAT STRANGELY PROPHETIC PRONOUNCEMENT, THE MIGHTY AVENGERS STEP FROM THE PAGES OF ISSUE #56--AND INTO AN AWESOME ADVENTURE YOU WILL NEVER FORGET--!

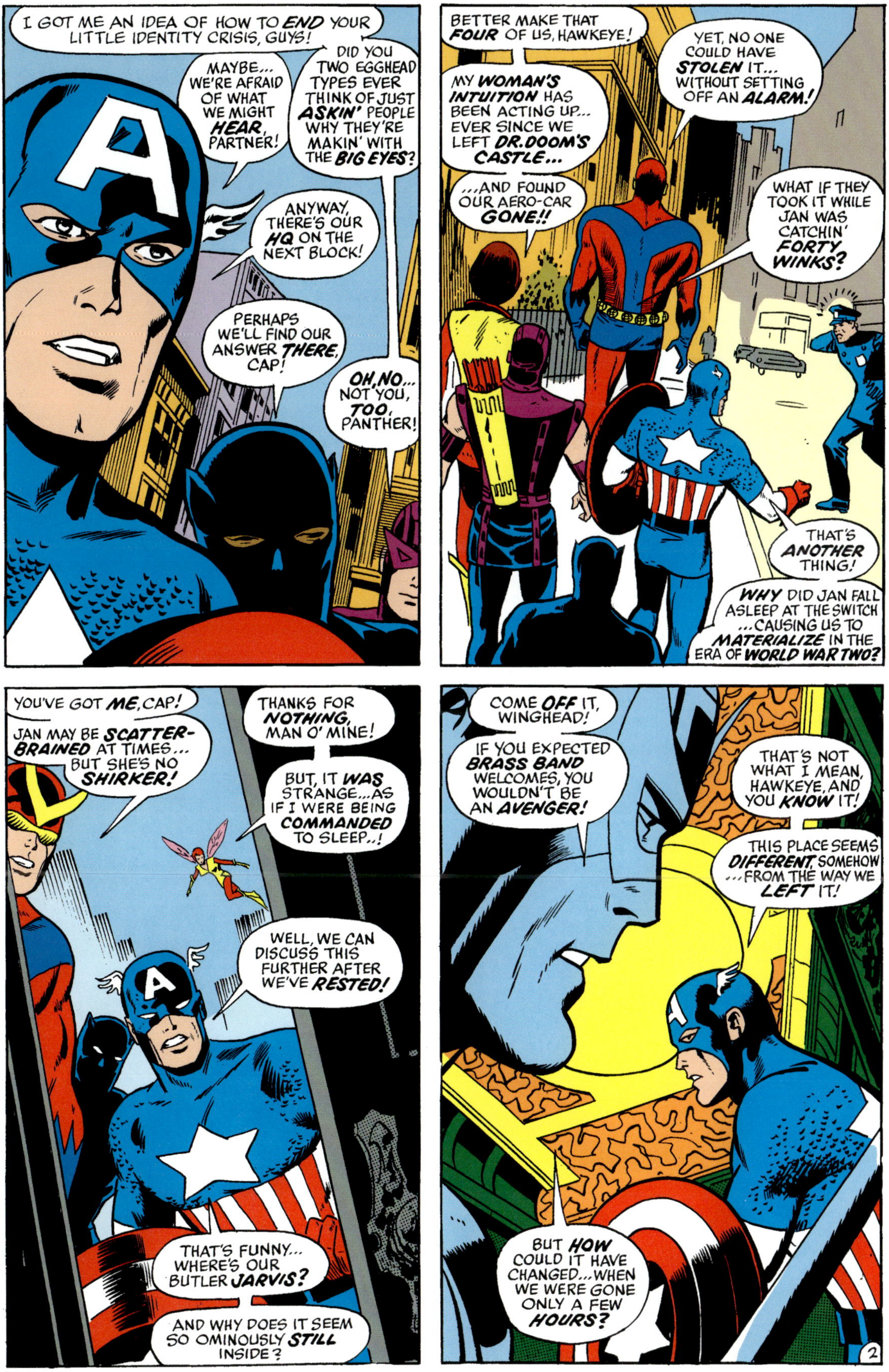
I GOT ME AN IDEA OF HOW TO END YOUR LITTLE IDENTITY CRISIS, GUYS!
MAYBE... WE'RE AFRAID OF WHAT WE MIGHT HEAR, PARTNER!
DID YOU TWO EGGHEAD TYPES EVER THINK OF JUST ASKIN' PEOPLE WHY THEY'RE MAKIN' WITH THE BIG EYES?
ANYWAY, THERE'S OUR HQ ON THE NEXT BLOCK!
PERHAPS WE'LL FIND OUR ANSWER THERE, CAP!
OH, NO... NOT YOU, TOO, PANTHER!
BETTER MAKE THAT FOUR OF US, HAWKEYE!
MY WOMAN'S INTUITION HAS BEEN ACTING UP... EVER SINCE WE LEFT DR. DOOM'S CASTLE...
...AND FOUND OUR AERO-CAR GONE!!
YET, NO ONE COULD HAVE STOLEN IT... WITHOUT SETTING OFF AN ALARM!
WHAT IF THEY TOOK IT WHILE JAN WAS CATCHIN' FORTY WINKS?
THAT'S ANOTHER THING!
WHY DID JAN FALL ASLEEP AT THE SWITCH ...CAUSING US TO MATERIALIZE IN THE ERA OF WORLD WAR TWO?
YOU'VE GOT ME, CAP!
JAN MAY BE SCATTER-BRAINED AT TIMES... BUT SHE'S NO SHIRKER!
THANKS FOR NOTHING, MAN O' MINE!
BUT, IT WAS STRANGE... AS IF I WERE BEING COMMANDED TO SLEEP..!
WELL, WE CAN DISCUSS THIS FURTHER AFTER WE'VE RESTED!
THAT'S FUNNY... WHERE'S OUR BUTLER JARVIS?
AND WHY DOES IT SEEM SO OMINOUSLY STILL INSIDE?
COME OFF IT, WINGHEAD!
IF YOU EXPECTED BRASS BAND WELCOMES, YOU WOULDN'T BE AN AVENGER!
THAT'S NOT WHAT I MEAN, HAWKEYE, AND YOU KNOW IT!
THIS PLACE SEEMS DIFFERENT, SOMEHOW ...FROM THE WAY WE LEFT IT!
BUT HOW COULD IT HAVE CHANGED... WHEN WE WERE GONE ONLY A FEW HOURS?
2

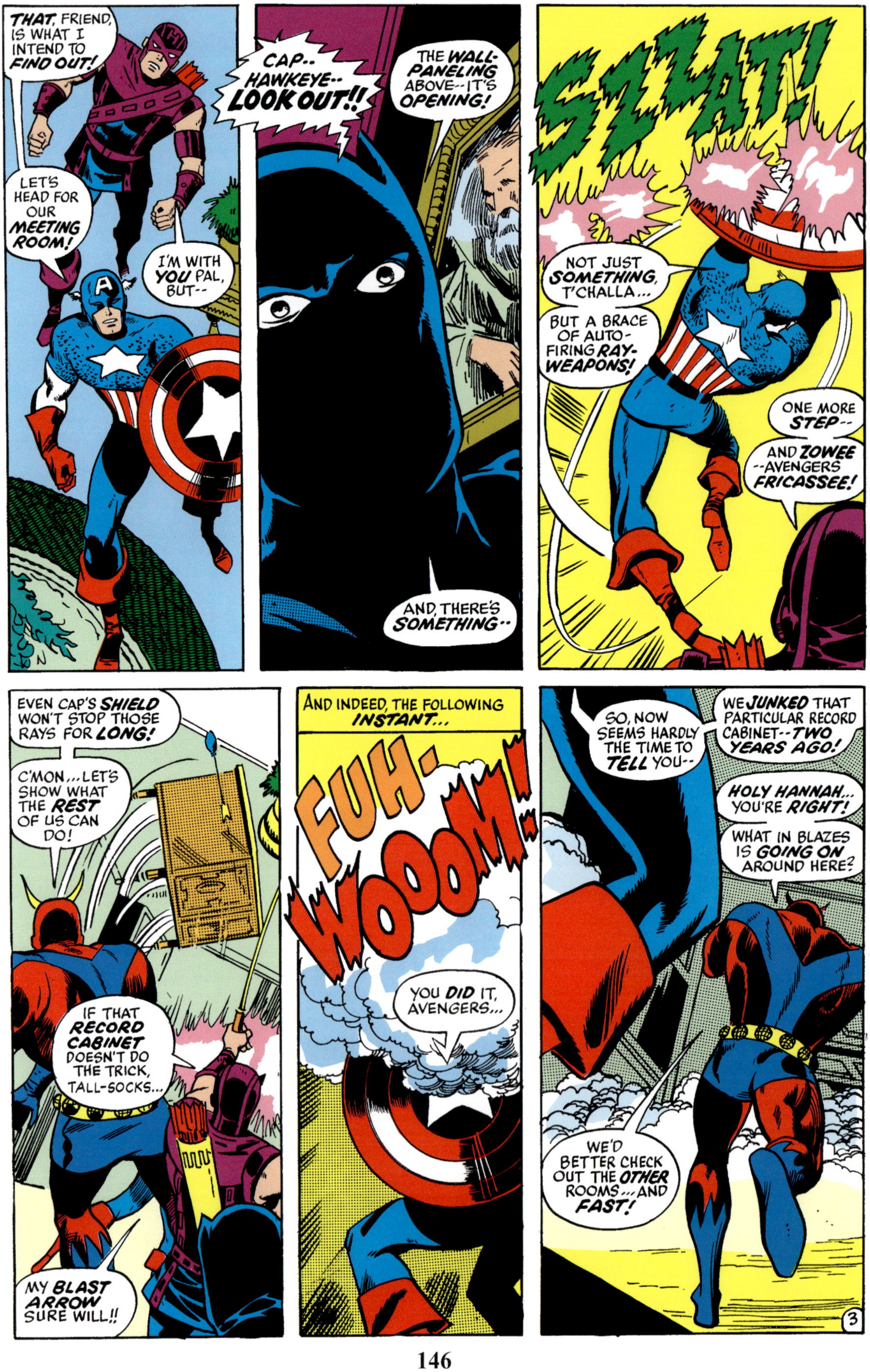
THAT, FRIEND, IS WHAT I INTEND TO FIND OUT!
LET'S HEAD FOR OUR MEETING ROOM!
I'M WITH YOU PAL, BUT--
CAP-- HAWKEYE-- LOOK OUT!!
THE WALL-PANELING ABOVE--IT'S OPENING!
AND, THERE'S SOMETHING--
SZZAT!
NOT JUST SOMETHING, T'CHALLA...
BUT A BRACE OF AUTO-FIRING RAY-WEAPONS!
ONE MORE STEP--
AND ZOWEE --AVENGERS FRICASSEE!
EVEN CAP'S SHIELD WON'T STOP THOSE RAYS FOR LONG!
C'MON...LET'S SHOW WHAT THE REST OF US CAN DO!
IF THAT RECORD CABINET DOESN'T DO THE TRICK, TALL-SOCKS...
MY BLAST ARROW SURE WILL!!
AND INDEED, THE FOLLOWING INSTANT...
FUH-WOOOM!
YOU DID IT, AVENGERS...
SO, NOW SEEMS HARDLY THE TIME TO TELL YOU--
WE JUNKED THAT PARTICULAR RECORD CABINET--TWO YEARS AGO!
HOLY HANNAH... YOU'RE RIGHT!
WHAT IN BLAZES IS GOING ON AROUND HERE?
WE'D BETTER CHECK OUT THE OTHER ROOMS...AND FAST!
3

THEN, INSTINCTIVELY... AS IF DRAWN BY SOME IRRESISTIBLE INNER COMPULSION... THE FIVE FRENZIED FIGURES HURTLE DOWN A SPIRALING STAIRWAY-- SUDDENLY ROUNDING A CORNER TO CONFRONT A ONCE-FAMED TABLEAU--!
IT CAN'T BE! IT ISN'T POSSIBLE--!
THERE--AROUND OUR MEETING-TABLE--THE FIVE ORIGINAL AVENGERS!
AND, TWO OF THEM, JAN --ARE YOU AND I!!
BY THE BRISTLING BEARD OF ODIN!
WHAT INSOLENT INTRUDERS ARE THESE... WHO DARE BROOK THE MIGHTY AVENGERS IN THEIR VERY LAIR?
WHOEVER IT IS... THEY'LL BE SORRY THEY TANGLED WITH THE HULK!
EASY, MY GREEN-SKINNED FRIEND!
MAYBE THOSE COSTUMED CLOWNS HAVE AN EXPLANATION..
BUT, IT SURE BETTER BE A GOOD ONE!
CAP, WHAT IS THIS? WHY WOULD THOR AND THE OTHERS BE HERE?
I--THINK I MAY BEGIN TO SUSPECT THE ANSWER, BOW-SLINGER...
AND, I DON'T LIKE IT... NOT ONE BIT!
4

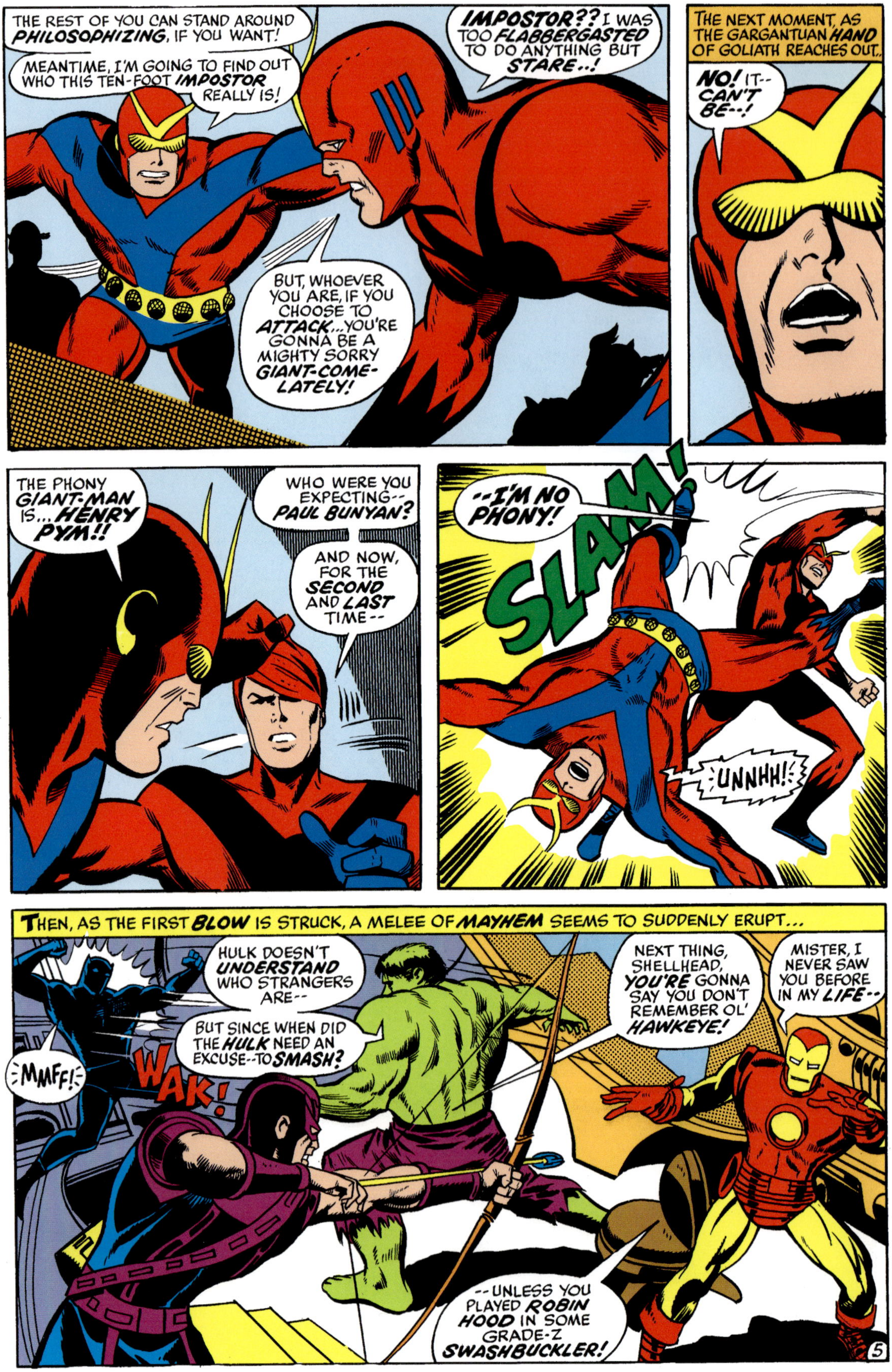
THE REST OF YOU CAN STAND AROUND PHILOSOPHIZING, IF YOU WANT!
MEANTIME, I'M GOING TO FIND OUT WHO THIS TEN-FOOT IMPOSTOR REALLY IS!
IMPOSTOR?? I WAS TOO FLABBERGASTED TO DO ANYTHING BUT STARE..!
BUT, WHOEVER YOU ARE, IF YOU CHOOSE TO ATTACK... YOU'RE GONNA BE A MIGHTY SORRY GIANT-COME-LATELY!
THE NEXT MOMENT, AS THE GARGANTUAN HAND OF GOLIATH REACHES OUT...
NO! IT-- CAN'T BE--!
THE PHONY GIANT-MAN IS... HENRY PYM!!
WHO WERE YOU EXPECTING-- PAUL BUNYAN?
AND NOW, FOR THE SECOND AND LAST TIME--
--I'M NO PHONY!
SLAM!
UNNHH!
THEN, AS THE FIRST BLOW IS STRUCK, A MELEE OF MAYHEM SEEMS TO SUDDENLY ERUPT...
HULK DOESN'T UNDERSTAND WHO STRANGERS ARE--
BUT SINCE WHEN DID THE HULK NEED AN EXCUSE--TO SMASH?
MMFF!
WAK!
NEXT THING, SHELLHEAD, YOU'RE GONNA SAY YOU DON'T REMEMBER OL' HAWKEYE!
MISTER, I NEVER SAW YOU BEFORE IN MY LIFE--
--UNLESS YOU PLAYED ROBIN HOOD IN SOME GRADE-Z SWASHBUCKLER!
5

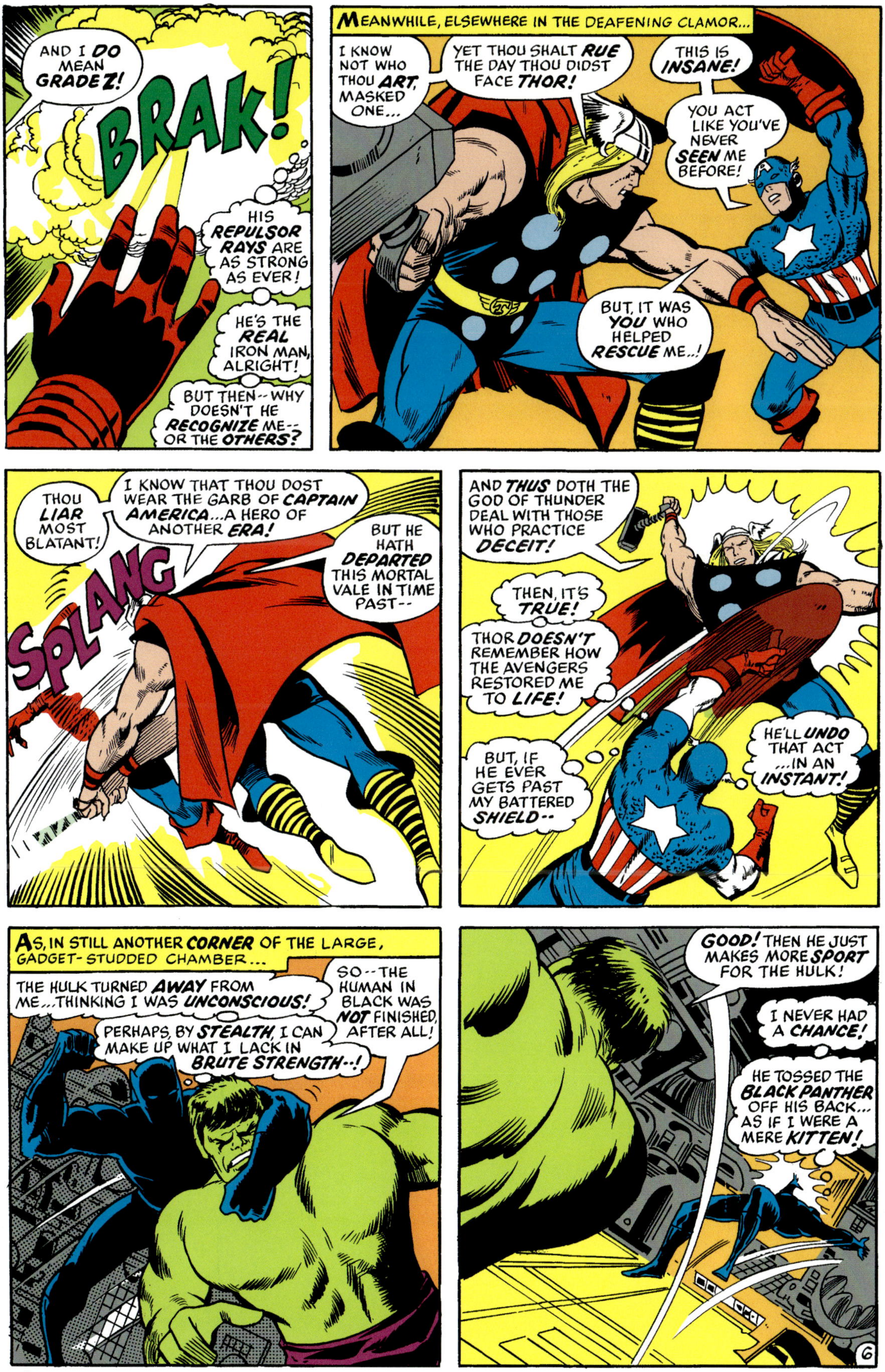
AND I DO MEAN GRADE Z!
BRAK!
HIS REPULSOR RAYS ARE AS STRONG AS EVER!
HE'S THE REAL IRON MAN, ALRIGHT!
BUT THEN--WHY DOESN'T HE RECOGNIZE ME--OR THE OTHERS?
MEANWHILE, ELSEWHERE IN THE DEAFENING CLAMOR...
I KNOW NOT WHO THOU ART, MASKED ONE...
YET THOU SHALT RUE THE DAY THOU DIDST FACE THOR!
THIS IS INSANE!
YOU ACT LIKE YOU'VE NEVER SEEN ME BEFORE!
BUT, IT WAS YOU WHO HELPED RESCUE ME...!
THOU LIAR MOST BLATANT!
I KNOW THAT THOU DOST WEAR THE GARB OF CAPTAIN AMERICA...A HERO OF ANOTHER ERA!
BUT HE HATH DEPARTED THIS MORTAL VALE IN TIME PAST--
SPLANG
AND THUS DOTH THE GOD OF THUNDER DEAL WITH THOSE WHO PRACTICE DECEIT!
THEN, IT'S TRUE!
THOR DOESN'T REMEMBER HOW THE AVENGERS RESTORED ME TO LIFE!
BUT, IF HE EVER GETS PAST MY BATTERED SHIELD--
HE'LL UNDO THAT ACT ...IN AN INSTANT!
AS, IN STILL ANOTHER CORNER OF THE LARGE, GADGET-STUDDED CHAMBER...
THE HULK TURNED AWAY FROM ME...THINKING I WAS UNCONSCIOUS!
PERHAPS, BY STEALTH, I CAN MAKE UP WHAT I LACK IN BRUTE STRENGTH--!
SO--THE HUMAN IN BLACK WAS NOT FINISHED, AFTER ALL!
GOOD! THEN HE JUST MAKES MORE SPORT FOR THE HULK!
I NEVER HAD A CHANCE!
HE TOSSED THE BLACK PANTHER OFF HIS BACK... AS IF I WERE A MERE KITTEN!
6

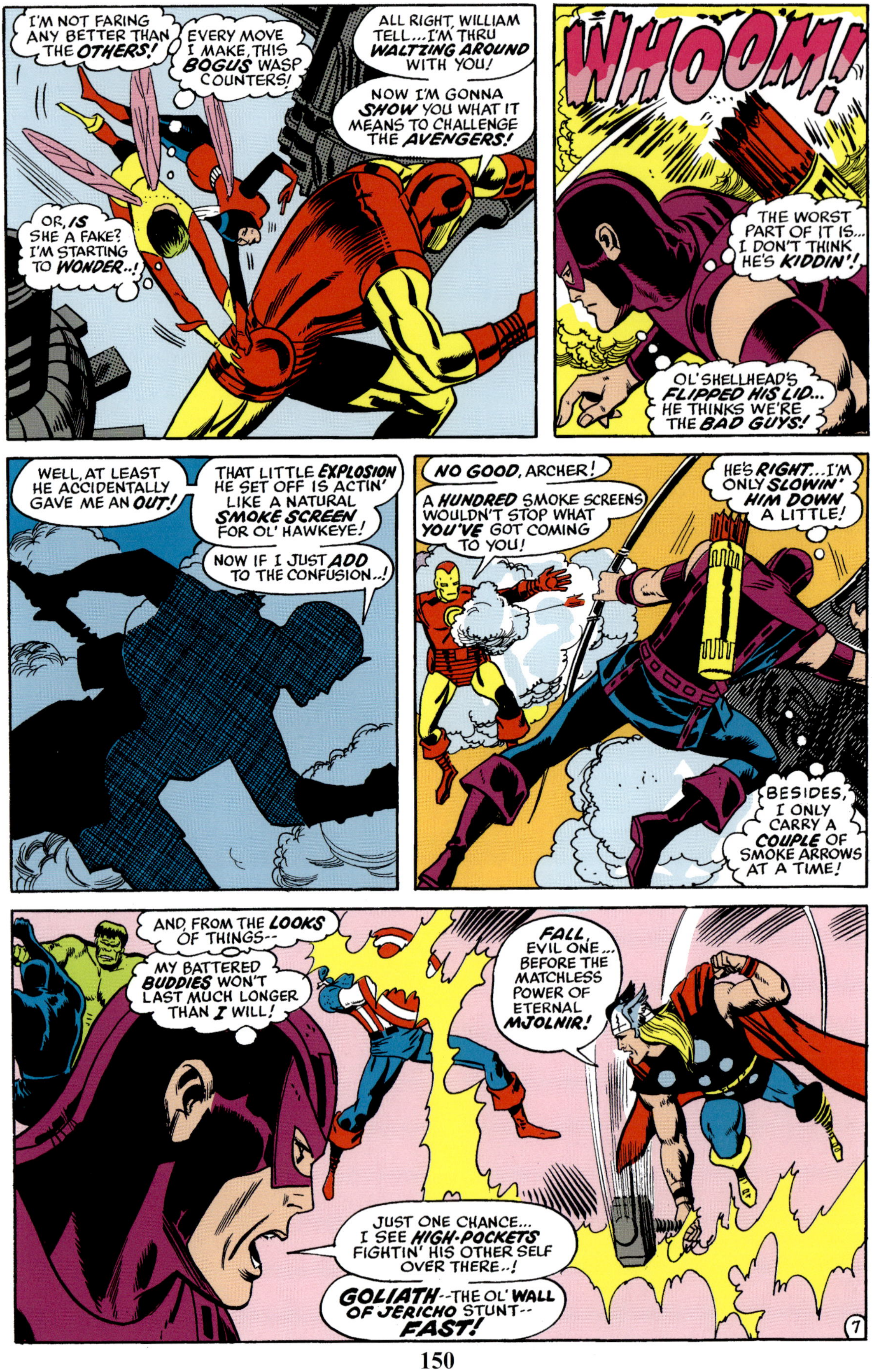

I'M NOT FARING ANY BETTER THAN THE OTHERS!
EVERY MOVE I MAKE, THIS BOGUS WASP COUNTERS!
OR, IS SHE A FAKE? I'M STARTING TO WONDER..!
ALL RIGHT, WILLIAM TELL... I'M THRU WALTZING AROUND WITH YOU!
NOW I'M GONNA SHOW YOU WHAT IT MEANS TO CHALLENGE THE AVENGERS!
WHOOM!
THE WORST PART OF IT IS... I DON'T THINK HE'S KIDDIN'!
OL' SHELLHEAD'S FLIPPED HIS LID... HE THINKS WE'RE THE BAD GUYS!
WELL, AT LEAST HE ACCIDENTALLY GAVE ME AN OUT!
THAT LITTLE EXPLOSION HE SET OFF IS ACTIN' LIKE A NATURAL SMOKE SCREEN FOR OL' HAWKEYE!
NOW IF I JUST ADD TO THE CONFUSION..!
NO GOOD, ARCHER!
A HUNDRED SMOKE SCREENS WOULDN'T STOP WHAT YOU'VE GOT COMING TO YOU!
HE'S RIGHT... I'M ONLY SLOWIN' HIM DOWN A LITTLE!
BESIDES, I ONLY CARRY A COUPLE OF SMOKE ARROWS AT A TIME!
AND, FROM THE LOOKS OF THINGS--
MY BATTERED BUDDIES WON'T LAST MUCH LONGER THAN I WILL!
FALL, EVIL ONE... BEFORE THE MATCHLESS POWER OF ETERNAL MJOLNIR!
JUST ONE CHANCE... I SEE HIGH-POCKETS FIGHTIN' HIS OTHER SELF OVER THERE..!
GOLIATH--THE OL' WALL OF JERICHO STUNT--FAST!
7

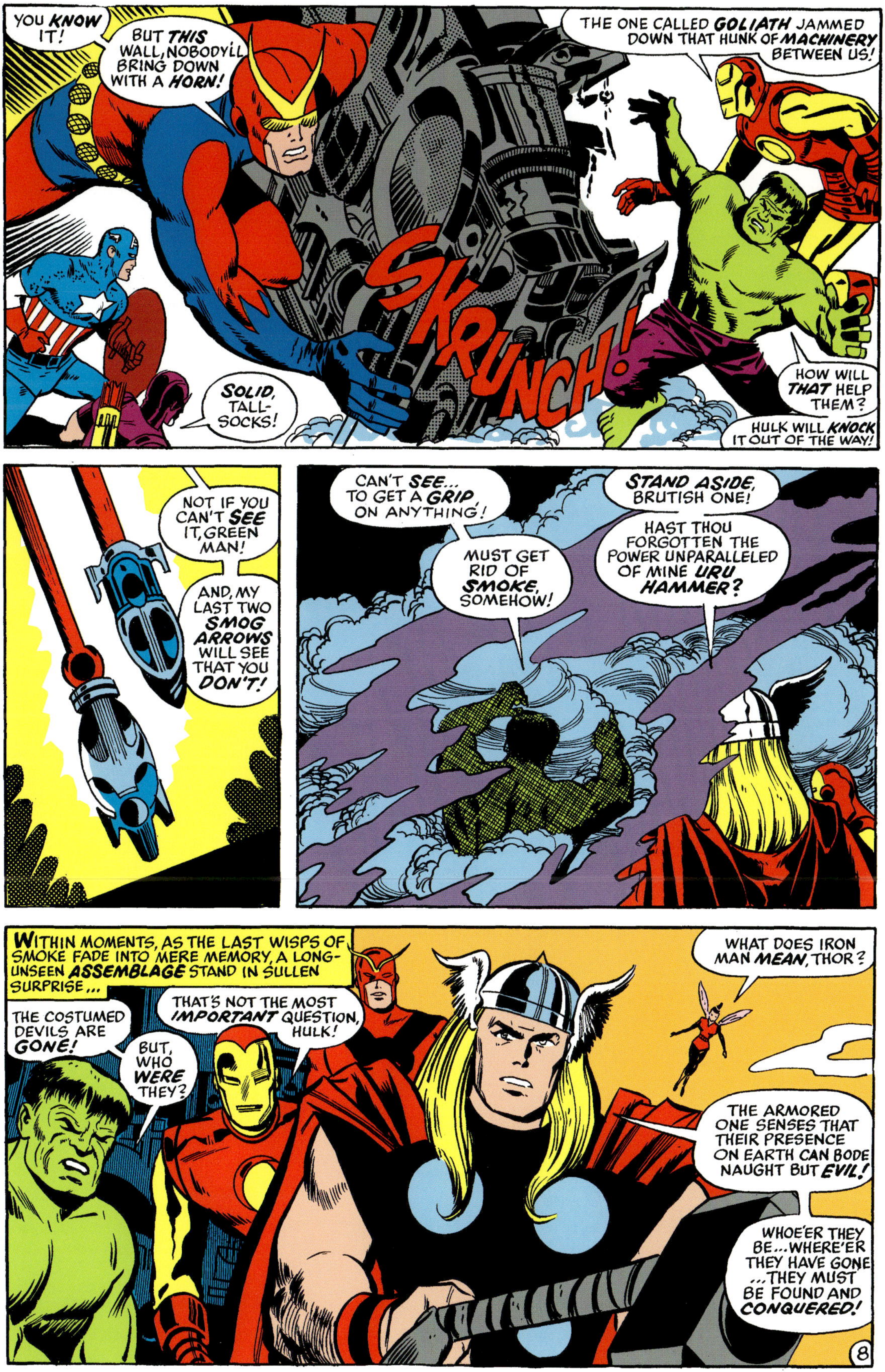
YOU KNOW IT!
BUT THIS WALL, NOBODY'LL BRING DOWN WITH A HORN!
THE ONE CALLED GOLIATH JAMMED DOWN THAT HUNK OF MACHINERY BETWEEN US!
SKRUNCH!
SOLID, TALL-SOCKS!
HOW WILL THAT HELP THEM?
HULK WILL KNOCK IT OUT OF THE WAY!
NOT IF YOU CAN'T SEE IT, GREEN MAN!
AND, MY LAST TWO SMOG ARROWS WILL SEE THAT YOU DON'T!
CAN'T SEE... TO GET A GRIP ON ANYTHING!
MUST GET RID OF SMOKE, SOMEHOW!
STAND ASIDE, BRUTISH ONE!
HAST THOU FORGOTTEN THE POWER UNPARALLELED OF MINE URU HAMMER?
WITHIN MOMENTS, AS THE LAST WISPS OF SMOKE FADE INTO MERE MEMORY, A LONG-UNSEEN ASSEMBLAGE STAND IN SULLEN SURPRISE...
THE COSTUMED DEVILS ARE GONE!
BUT, WHO WERE THEY?
THAT'S NOT THE MOST IMPORTANT QUESTION, HULK!
WHAT DOES IRON MAN MEAN, THOR?
THE ARMORED ONE SENSES THAT THEIR PRESENCE ON EARTH CAN BODE NAUGHT BUT EVIL!
WHOE'ER THEY BE...WHERE'ER THEY HAVE GONE ...THEY MUST BE FOUND AND CONQUERED!
8

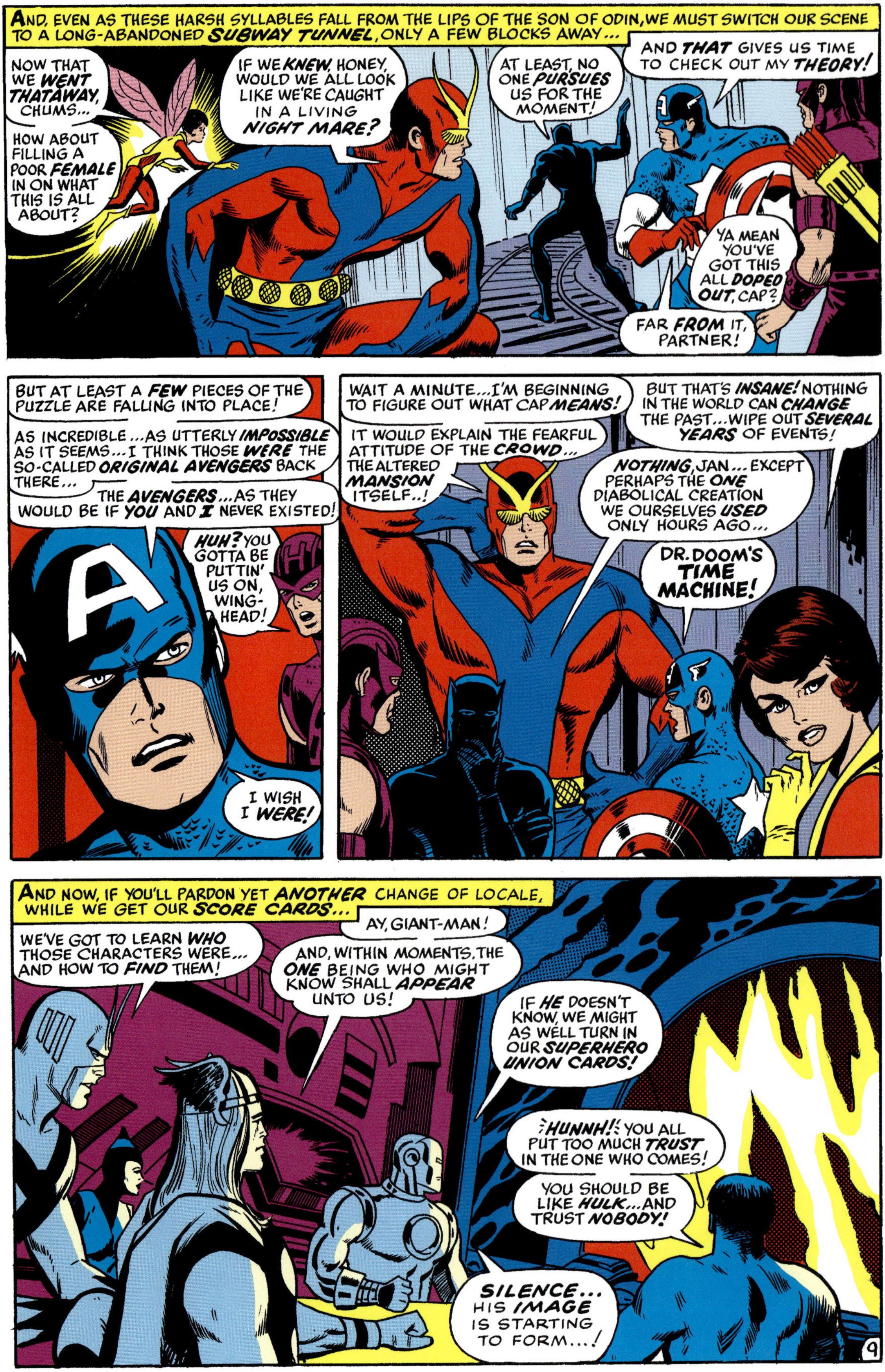
AND, EVEN AS THESE HARSH SYLLABLES FALL FROM THE LIPS OF THE SON OF ODIN, WE MUST SWITCH OUR SCENE TO A LONG-ABANDONED SUBWAY TUNNEL, ONLY A FEW BLOCKS AWAY...
NOW THAT WE WENT THATAWAY, CHUMS...
HOW ABOUT FILLING A POOR FEMALE IN ON WHAT THIS IS ALL ABOUT?
IF WE KNEW, HONEY, WOULD WE ALL LOOK LIKE WE'RE CAUGHT IN A LIVING NIGHT MARE?
AT LEAST, NO ONE PURSUES US FOR THE MOMENT!
AND THAT GIVES US TIME TO CHECK OUT MY THEORY!
YA MEAN YOU'VE GOT THIS ALL DOPED OUT, CAP?
FAR FROM IT, PARTNER!
BUT AT LEAST A FEW PIECES OF THE PUZZLE ARE FALLING INTO PLACE!
AS INCREDIBLE... AS UTTERLY IMPOSSIBLE AS IT SEEMS... I THINK THOSE WERE THE SO-CALLED ORIGINAL AVENGERS BACK THERE...
THE AVENGERS... AS THEY WOULD BE IF YOU AND I NEVER EXISTED!
HUH? YOU GOTTA BE PUTTIN' US ON, WING-HEAD!
I WISH I WERE!
WAIT A MINUTE... I'M BEGINNING TO FIGURE OUT WHAT CAP MEANS!
IT WOULD EXPLAIN THE FEARFUL ATTITUDE OF THE CROWD... THE ALTERED MANSION ITSELF..!
BUT THAT'S INSANE! NOTHING IN THE WORLD CAN CHANGE THE PAST... WIPE OUT SEVERAL YEARS OF EVENTS!
NOTHING, JAN... EXCEPT PERHAPS THE ONE DIABOLICAL CREATION WE OURSELVES USED ONLY HOURS AGO...
DR. DOOM'S TIME MACHINE!
AND NOW, IF YOU'LL PARDON YET ANOTHER CHANGE OF LOCALE, WHILE WE GET OUR SCORE CARDS...
WE'VE GOT TO LEARN WHO THOSE CHARACTERS WERE... AND HOW TO FIND THEM!
AY, GIANT-MAN!
AND, WITHIN MOMENTS, THE ONE BEING WHO MIGHT KNOW SHALL APPEAR UNTO US!
IF HE DOESN'T KNOW, WE MIGHT AS WELL TURN IN OUR SUPERHERO UNION CARDS!
HUNNH!! YOU ALL PUT TOO MUCH TRUST IN THE ONE WHO COMES!
YOU SHOULD BE LIKE HULK... AND TRUST NOBODY!
SILENCE... HIS IMAGE IS STARTING TO FORM...!
9

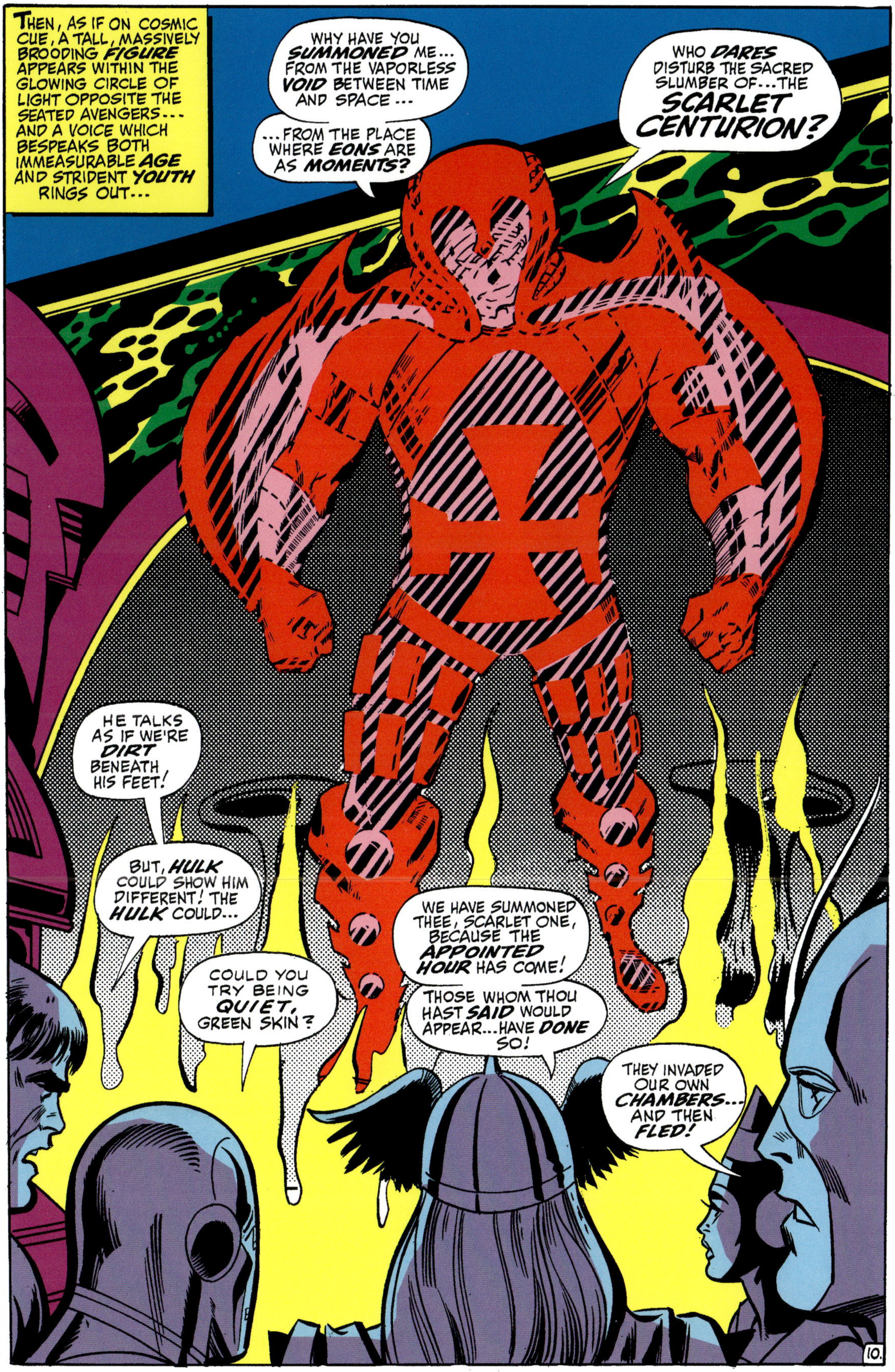
THEN, AS IF ON COSMIC CUE, A TALL, MASSIVELY BROODING FIGURE APPEARS WITHIN THE GLOWING CIRCLE OF LIGHT OPPOSITE THE SEATED AVENGERS... AND A VOICE WHICH BESPEAKS BOTH IMMEASURABLE AGE AND STRIDENT YOUTH RINGS OUT...
WHY HAVE YOU SUMMONED ME... FROM THE VAPORLESS VOID BETWEEN TIME AND SPACE...
...FROM THE PLACE WHERE EONS ARE AS MOMENTS?
WHO DARES DISTURB THE SACRED SLUMBER OF...THE SCARLET CENTURION?
HE TALKS AS IF WE'RE DIRT BENEATH HIS FEET!
BUT, HULK COULD SHOW HIM DIFFERENT! THE HULK COULD...
COULD YOU TRY BEING QUIET, GREEN SKIN?
WE HAVE SUMMONED THEE, SCARLET ONE, BECAUSE THE APPOINTED HOUR HAS COME!
THOSE WHOM THOU HAST SAID WOULD APPEAR...HAVE DONE SO!
THEY INVADED OUR OWN CHAMBERS... AND THEN FLED!
10.

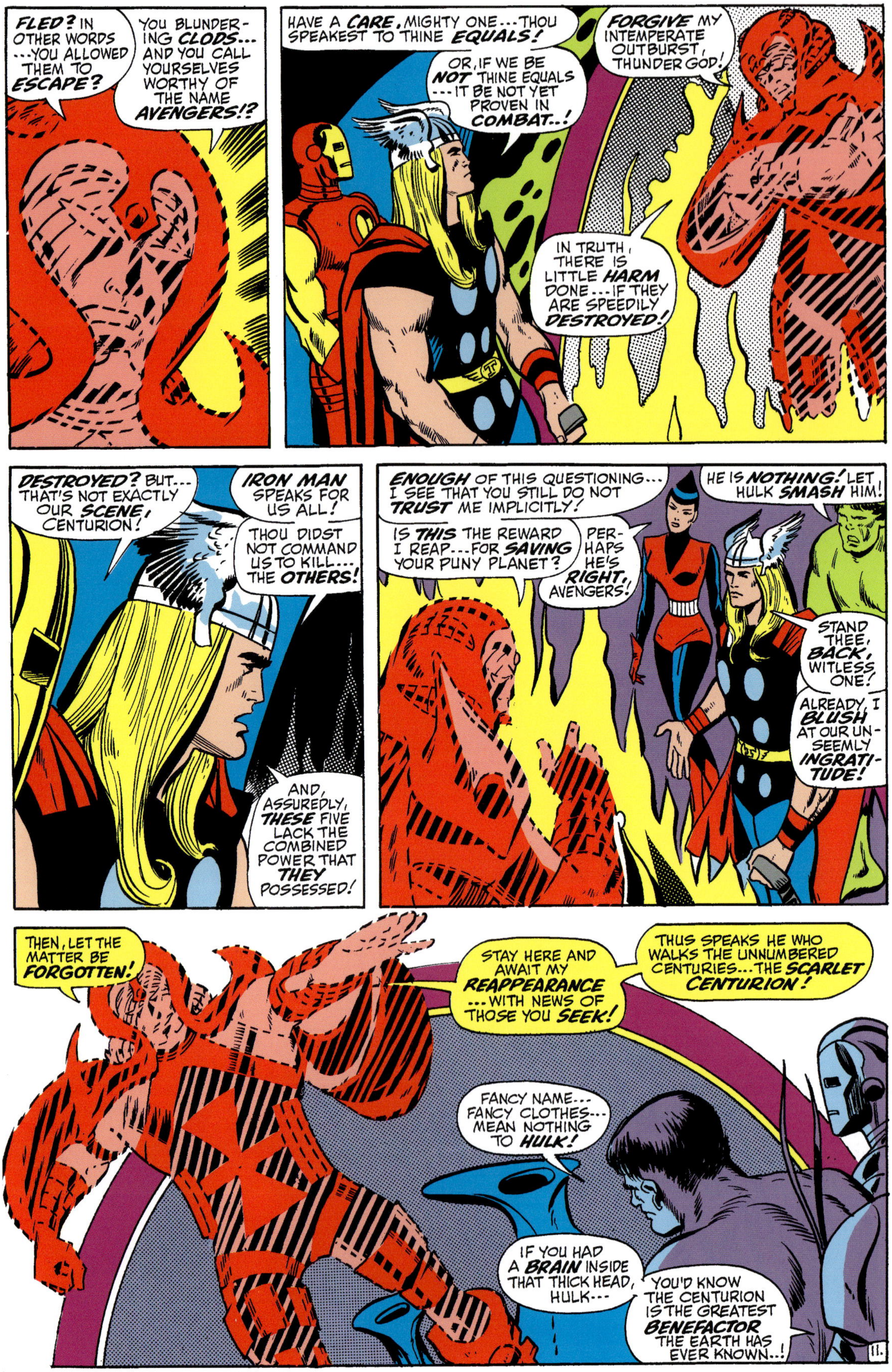
FLED? IN OTHER WORDS ...YOU ALLOWED THEM TO ESCAPE?
YOU BLUNDERING CLODS... AND YOU CALL YOURSELVES WORTHY OF THE NAME AVENGERS!?
HAVE A CARE, MIGHTY ONE... THOU SPEAKEST TO THINE EQUALS!
OR, IF WE BE NOT THINE EQUALS ... IT BE NOT YET PROVEN IN COMBAT..!
FORGIVE MY INTEMPERATE OUTBURST, THUNDER GOD!
IN TRUTH, THERE IS LITTLE HARM DONE... IF THEY ARE SPEEDILY DESTROYED!
DESTROYED? BUT... THAT'S NOT EXACTLY OUR SCENE, CENTURION!
IRON MAN SPEAKS FOR US ALL!
THOU DIDST NOT COMMAND US TO KILL... THE OTHERS!
AND, ASSUREDLY, THESE FIVE LACK THE COMBINED POWER THAT THEY POSSESSED!
ENOUGH OF THIS QUESTIONING... I SEE THAT YOU STILL DO NOT TRUST ME IMPLICITLY!
IS THIS THE REWARD I REAP... FOR SAVING YOUR PUNY PLANET?
PERHAPS HE'S RIGHT, AVENGERS!
HE IS NOTHING! LET HULK SMASH HIM!
STAND THEE BACK, WITLESS ONE!
ALREADY, I BLUSH AT OUR UNSEEMLY INGRATITUDE!
THEN, LET THE MATTER BE FORGOTTEN!
STAY HERE AND AWAIT MY REAPPEARANCE ... WITH NEWS OF THOSE YOU SEEK!
THUS SPEAKS HE WHO WALKS THE UNNUMBERED CENTURIES... THE SCARLET CENTURION!
FANCY NAME... FANCY CLOTHES... MEAN NOTHING TO HULK!
IF YOU HAD A BRAIN INSIDE THAT THICK HEAD, HULK...
YOU'D KNOW THE CENTURION IS THE GREATEST BENEFACTOR THE EARTH HAS EVER KNOWN..!
11.

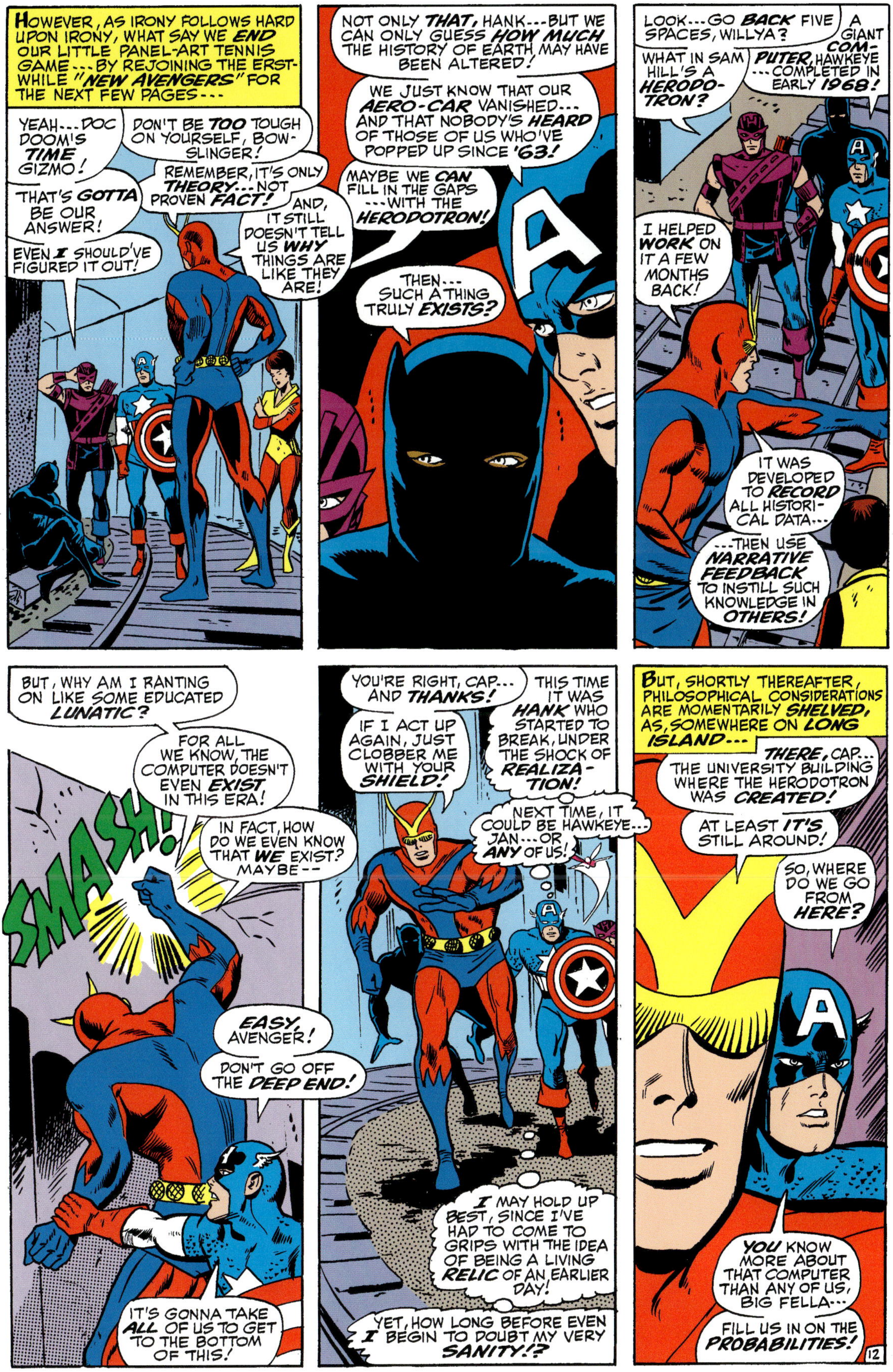
HOWEVER, AS IRONY FOLLOWS HARD UPON IRONY, WHAT SAY WE END OUR LITTLE PANEL-ART TENNIS GAME--- BY REJOINING THE ERSTWHILE "NEW AVENGERS" FOR THE NEXT FEW PAGES---
YEAH--- DOC DOOM'S TIME GIZMO!
THAT'S GOTTA BE OUR ANSWER!
EVEN I SHOULD'VE FIGURED IT OUT!
DON'T BE TOO TOUGH ON YOURSELF, BOW-SLINGER!
REMEMBER, IT'S ONLY THEORY--- NOT PROVEN FACT!
AND, IT STILL DOESN'T TELL US WHY THINGS ARE LIKE THEY ARE!
NOT ONLY THAT, HANK---BUT WE CAN ONLY GUESS HOW MUCH THE HISTORY OF EARTH MAY HAVE BEEN ALTERED!
WE JUST KNOW THAT OUR AERO-CAR VANISHED--- AND THAT NOBODY'S HEARD OF THOSE OF US WHO'VE POPPED UP SINCE '63!
MAYBE WE CAN FILL IN THE GAPS ---WITH THE HERODOTRON!
THEN--- SUCH A THING TRULY EXISTS?
LOOK---GO BACK FIVE SPACES, WILLYA?
WHAT IN SAM HILL'S A HERODOTRON?
A GIANT COMPUTER, HAWKEYE ---COMPLETED IN EARLY 1968!
I HELPED WORK ON IT A FEW MONTHS BACK!
IT WAS DEVELOPED TO RECORD ALL HISTORICAL DATA---
---THEN USE NARRATIVE FEEDBACK TO INSTILL SUCH KNOWLEDGE IN OTHERS!
BUT, WHY AM I RANTING ON LIKE SOME EDUCATED LUNATIC?
FOR ALL WE KNOW, THE COMPUTER DOESN'T EVEN EXIST IN THIS ERA!
IN FACT, HOW DO WE EVEN KNOW THAT WE EXIST? MAYBE--
SMASH!
EASY, AVENGER!
DON'T GO OFF THE DEEP END!
IT'S GONNA TAKE ALL OF US TO GET TO THE BOTTOM OF THIS!
YOU'RE RIGHT, CAP--- AND THANKS!
IF I ACT UP AGAIN, JUST CLOBBER ME WITH YOUR SHIELD!
THIS TIME IT WAS HANK WHO STARTED TO BREAK, UNDER THE SHOCK OF REALIZATION!
NEXT TIME, IT COULD BE HAWKEYE--- JAN---OR ANY OF US!
I MAY HOLD UP BEST, SINCE I'VE HAD TO COME TO GRIPS WITH THE IDEA OF BEING A LIVING RELIC OF AN EARLIER DAY!
YET, HOW LONG BEFORE EVEN I BEGIN TO DOUBT MY VERY SANITY!?
BUT, SHORTLY THEREAFTER, PHILOSOPHICAL CONSIDERATIONS ARE MOMENTARILY SHELVED, AS, SOMEWHERE ON LONG ISLAND---
THERE, CAP--- THE UNIVERSITY BUILDING WHERE THE HERODOTRON WAS CREATED!
AT LEAST IT'S STILL AROUND!
SO, WHERE DO WE GO FROM HERE?
YOU KNOW MORE ABOUT THAT COMPUTER THAN ANY OF US, BIG FELLA---
FILL US IN ON THE PROBABILITIES!
12

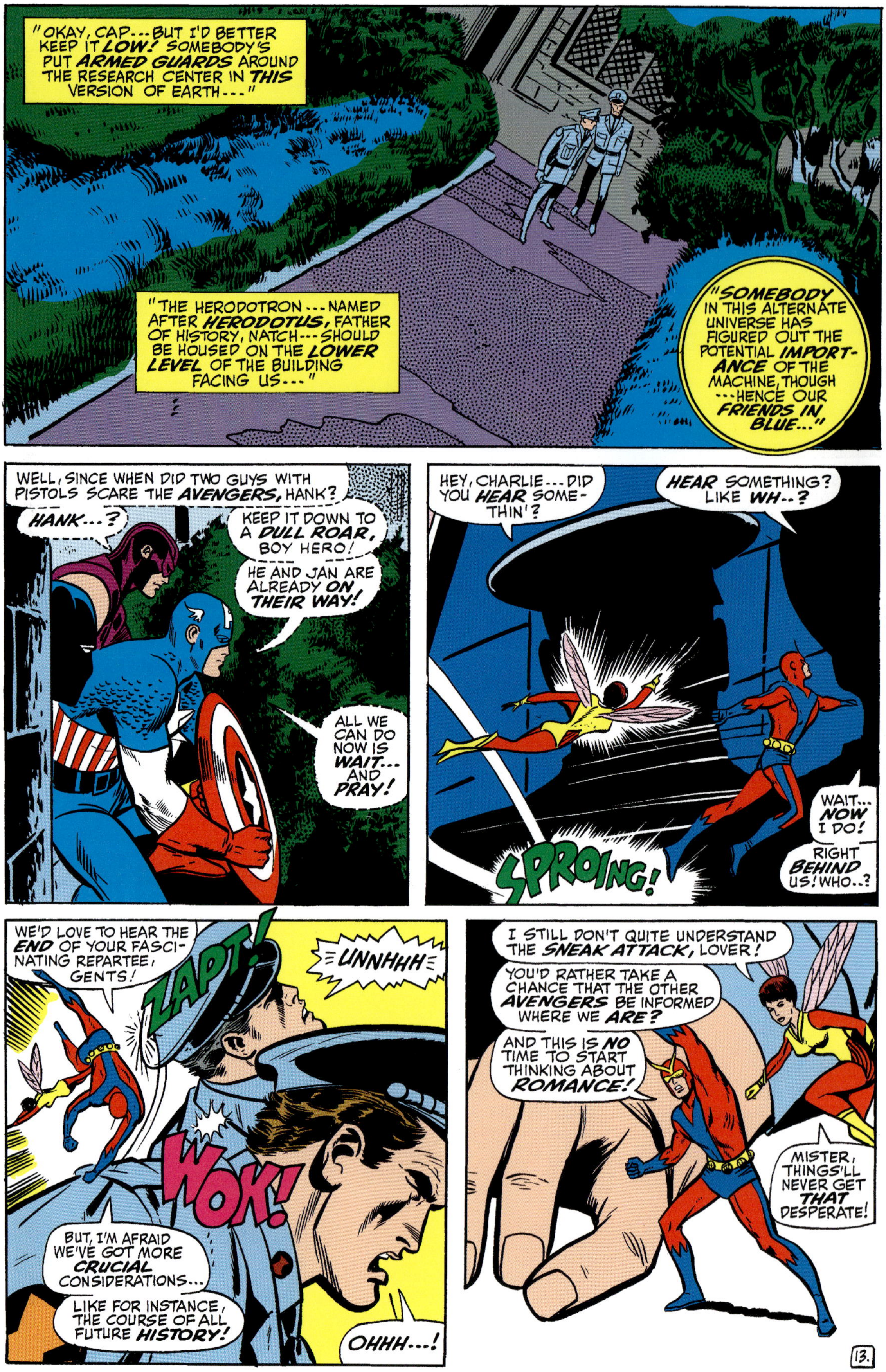

"OKAY, CAP--- BUT I'D BETTER KEEP IT LOW! SOMEBODY'S PUT ARMED GUARDS AROUND THE RESEARCH CENTER IN THIS VERSION OF EARTH---"
"THE HERODOTRON --- NAMED AFTER HERODOTUS, FATHER OF HISTORY, NATCH--- SHOULD BE HOUSED ON THE LOWER LEVEL OF THE BUILDING FACING US---"
"SOMEBODY IN THIS ALTERNATE UNIVERSE HAS FIGURED OUT THE POTENTIAL IMPORTANCE OF THE MACHINE, THOUGH --- HENCE OUR FRIENDS IN BLUE..."
WELL, SINCE WHEN DID TWO GUYS WITH PISTOLS SCARE THE AVENGERS, HANK?
HANK...?
KEEP IT DOWN TO A DULL ROAR, BOY HERO!
HE AND JAN ARE ALREADY ON THEIR WAY!
ALL WE CAN DO NOW IS WAIT... AND PRAY!
HEY, CHARLIE--- DID YOU HEAR SOMETHIN'?
HEAR SOMETHING? LIKE WH--?
SPROING!
WAIT... NOW I DO!
RIGHT BEHIND US! WHO--?
WE'D LOVE TO HEAR THE END OF YOUR FASCINATING REPARTEE, GENTS!
ZAPT!
UNNHHH
WOK!
BUT, I'M AFRAID WE'VE GOT MORE CRUCIAL CONSIDERATIONS...
LIKE FOR INSTANCE, THE COURSE OF ALL FUTURE HISTORY!
OHHH---!
I STILL DON'T QUITE UNDERSTAND THE SNEAK ATTACK, LOVER!
YOU'D RATHER TAKE A CHANCE THAT THE OTHER AVENGERS BE INFORMED WHERE WE ARE?
AND THIS IS NO TIME TO START THINKING ABOUT ROMANCE!
MISTER, THINGS'LL NEVER GET THAT DESPERATE!
13.

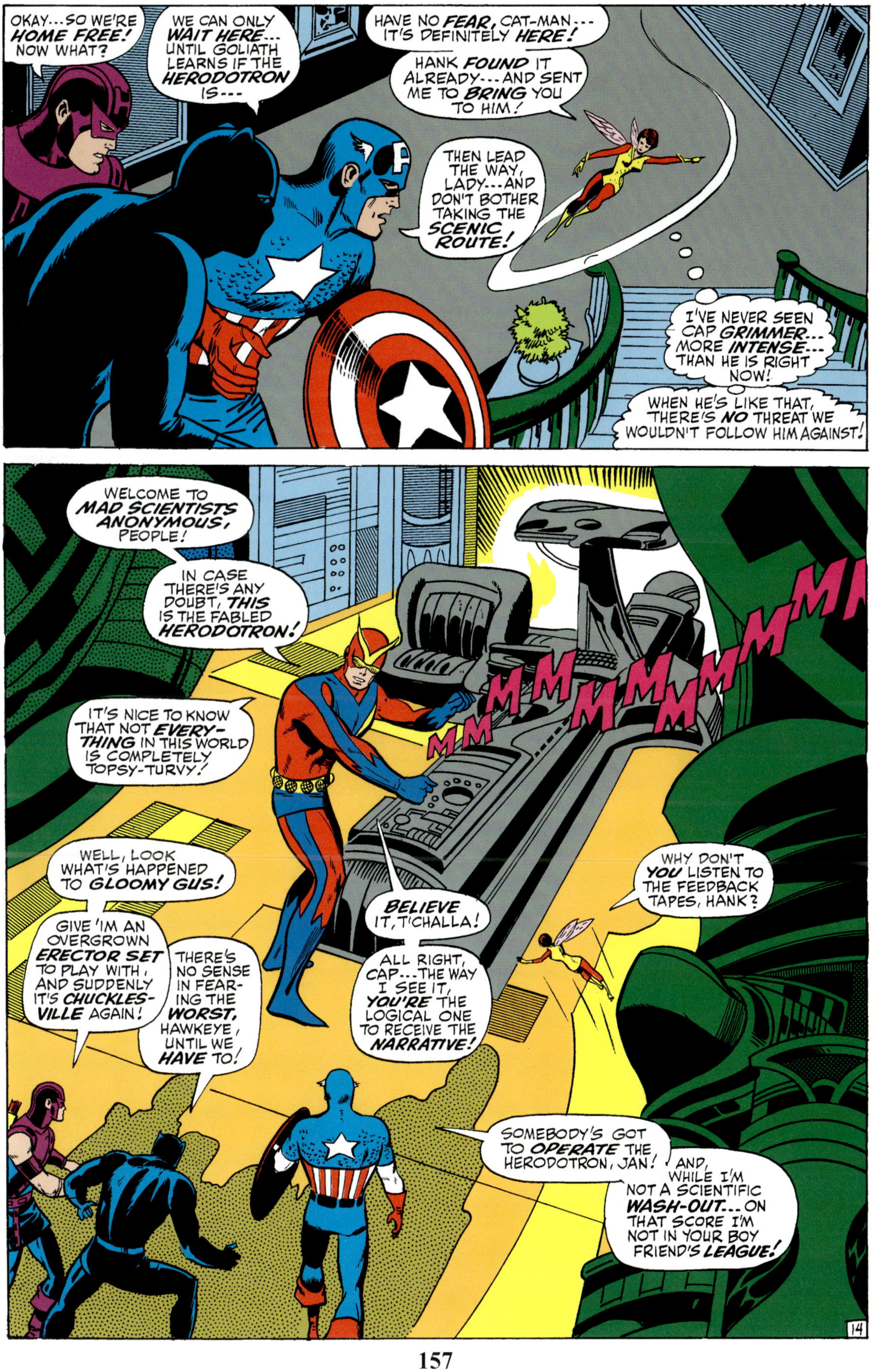
OKAY... SO WE'RE HOME FREE! NOW WHAT?
WE CAN ONLY WAIT HERE... UNTIL GOLIATH LEARNS IF THE HERODOTRON IS---
HAVE NO FEAR, CAT-MAN--- IT'S DEFINITELY HERE!
HANK FOUND IT ALREADY--- AND SENT ME TO BRING YOU TO HIM!
THEN LEAD THE WAY, LADY--- AND DON'T BOTHER TAKING THE SCENIC ROUTE!
I'VE NEVER SEEN CAP GRIMMER... MORE INTENSE--- THAN HE IS RIGHT NOW!
WHEN HE'S LIKE THAT, THERE'S NO THREAT WE WOULDN'T FOLLOW HIM AGAINST!
WELCOME TO MAD SCIENTISTS ANONYMOUS, PEOPLE!
IN CASE THERE'S ANY DOUBT, THIS IS THE FABLED HERODOTRON!
IT'S NICE TO KNOW THAT NOT EVERY-THING IN THIS WORLD IS COMPLETELY TOPSY-TURVY!
MMMMMMMMMMMMMMMMM
WELL, LOOK WHAT'S HAPPENED TO GLOOMY GUS!
GIVE 'IM AN OVERGROWN ERECTOR SET TO PLAY WITH, AND SUDDENLY IT'S CHUCKLES-VILLE AGAIN!
THERE'S NO SENSE IN FEAR-ING THE WORST, HAWKEYE, UNTIL WE HAVE TO!
BELIEVE IT, T'CHALLA!
ALL RIGHT, CAP--- THE WAY I SEE IT, YOU'RE THE LOGICAL ONE TO RECEIVE THE NARRATIVE!
WHY DON'T YOU LISTEN TO THE FEEDBACK TAPES, HANK?
SOMEBODY'S GOT TO OPERATE THE HERODOTRON, JAN!
AND, WHILE I'M NOT A SCIENTIFIC WASH-OUT... ON THAT SCORE I'M NOT IN YOUR BOY FRIEND'S LEAGUE!
14

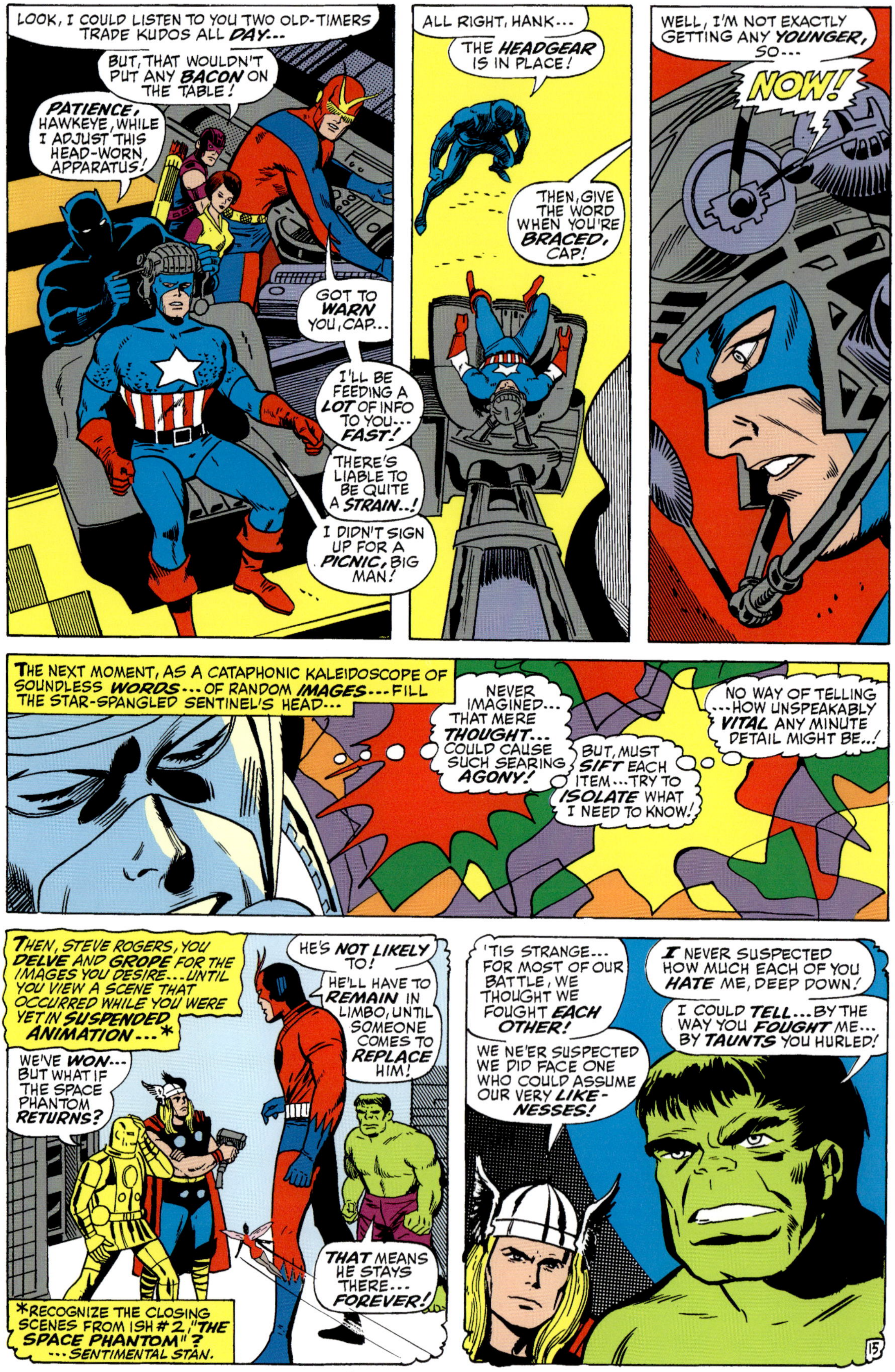

LOOK, I COULD LISTEN TO YOU TWO OLD-TIMERS TRADE KUDOS ALL DAY...
BUT, THAT WOULDN'T PUT ANY BACON ON THE TABLE!
PATIENCE, HAWKEYE, WHILE I ADJUST THIS HEAD-WORN APPARATUS!
GOT TO WARN YOU, CAP...
I'LL BE FEEDING A LOT OF INFO TO YOU... FAST!
THERE'S LIABLE TO BE QUITE A STRAIN..!
I DIDN'T SIGN UP FOR A PICNIC, BIG MAN!
ALL RIGHT, HANK...
THE HEADGEAR IS IN PLACE!
THEN, GIVE THE WORD WHEN YOU'RE BRACED, CAP!
WELL, I'M NOT EXACTLY GETTING ANY YOUNGER, SO---
NOW!
THE NEXT MOMENT, AS A CATAPHONIC KALEIDOSCOPE OF SOUNDLESS WORDS... OF RANDOM IMAGES--- FILL THE STAR-SPANGLED SENTINEL'S HEAD...
NEVER IMAGINED... THAT MERE THOUGHT... COULD CAUSE SUCH SEARING AGONY!
BUT, MUST SIFT EACH ITEM... TRY TO ISOLATE WHAT I NEED TO KNOW!
NO WAY OF TELLING ...HOW UNSPEAKABLY VITAL ANY MINUTE DETAIL MIGHT BE..!
THEN, STEVE ROGERS, YOU DELVE AND GROPE FOR THE IMAGES YOU DESIRE... UNTIL YOU VIEW A SCENE THAT OCCURRED WHILE YOU WERE YET IN SUSPENDED ANIMATION...*
WE'VE WON... BUT WHAT IF THE SPACE PHANTOM RETURNS?
HE'S NOT LIKELY TO!
HE'LL HAVE TO REMAIN IN LIMBO, UNTIL SOMEONE COMES TO REPLACE HIM!
THAT MEANS HE STAYS THERE... FOREVER!
*RECOGNIZE THE CLOSING SCENES FROM ISH #2, "THE SPACE PHANTOM"? ---SENTIMENTAL STAN.
'TIS STRANGE... FOR MOST OF OUR BATTLE, WE THOUGHT WE FOUGHT EACH OTHER!
WE NE'ER SUSPECTED WE DID FACE ONE WHO COULD ASSUME OUR VERY LIKE-NESSES!
I NEVER SUSPECTED HOW MUCH EACH OF YOU HATE ME, DEEP DOWN!
I COULD TELL... BY THE WAY YOU FOUGHT ME... BY TAUNTS YOU HURLED!
15

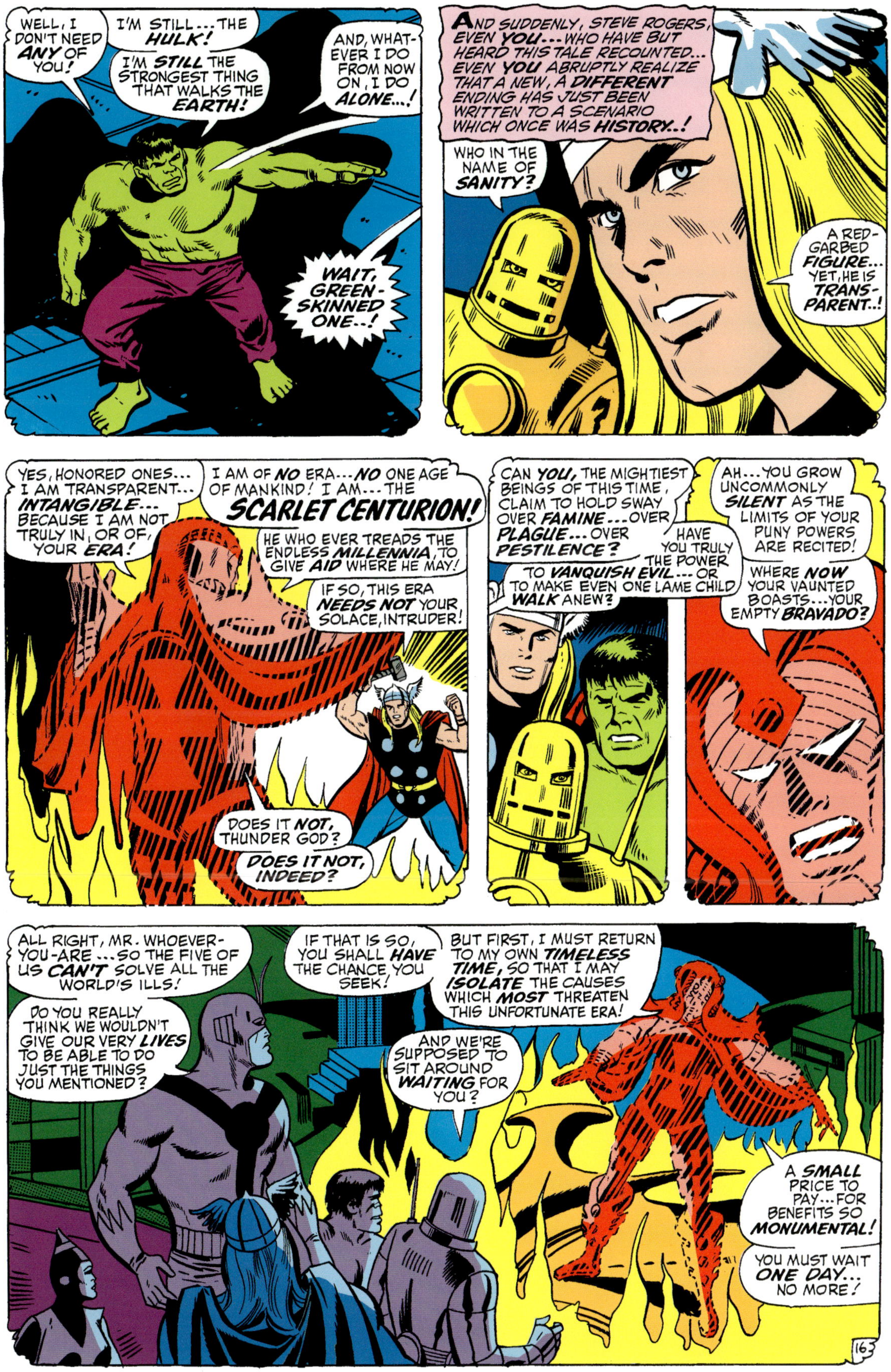
WELL, I DON'T NEED ANY OF YOU!
I'M STILL... THE HULK!
I'M STILL THE STRONGEST THING THAT WALKS THE EARTH!
AND, WHATEVER I DO FROM NOW ON, I DO ALONE...!
WAIT, GREEN-SKINNED ONE..!
AND SUDDENLY, STEVE ROGERS, EVEN YOU... WHO HAVE BUT HEARD THIS TALE RECOUNTED... EVEN YOU ABRUPTLY REALIZE THAT A NEW, A DIFFERENT ENDING HAS JUST BEEN WRITTEN TO A SCENARIO WHICH ONCE WAS HISTORY..!
WHO IN THE NAME OF SANITY?
A RED-GARBED FIGURE... YET, HE IS TRANSPARENT..!
YES, HONORED ONES... I AM TRANSPARENT... INTANGIBLE... BECAUSE I AM NOT TRULY IN, OR OF, YOUR ERA!
I AM OF NO ERA... NO ONE AGE OF MANKIND! I AM... THE SCARLET CENTURION!
HE WHO EVER TREADS THE ENDLESS MILLENNIA, TO GIVE AID WHERE HE MAY!
IF SO, THIS ERA NEEDS NOT YOUR SOLACE, INTRUDER!
DOES IT NOT, THUNDER GOD?
DOES IT NOT, INDEED?
CAN YOU, THE MIGHTIEST BEINGS OF THIS TIME, CLAIM TO HOLD SWAY OVER FAMINE... OVER PLAGUE... OVER PESTILENCE?
HAVE YOU TRULY THE POWER TO VANQUISH EVIL... OR TO MAKE EVEN ONE LAME CHILD WALK ANEW?
AH... YOU GROW UNCOMMONLY SILENT AS THE LIMITS OF YOUR PUNY POWERS ARE RECITED!
WHERE NOW YOUR VAUNTED BOASTS... YOUR EMPTY BRAVADO?
ALL RIGHT, MR. WHOEVER-YOU-ARE... SO THE FIVE OF US CAN'T SOLVE ALL THE WORLD'S ILLS!
DO YOU REALLY THINK WE WOULDN'T GIVE OUR VERY LIVES TO BE ABLE TO DO JUST THE THINGS YOU MENTIONED?
IF THAT IS SO, YOU SHALL HAVE THE CHANCE YOU SEEK!
BUT FIRST, I MUST RETURN TO MY OWN TIMELESS TIME, SO THAT I MAY ISOLATE THE CAUSES WHICH MOST THREATEN THIS UNFORTUNATE ERA!
AND WE'RE SUPPOSED TO SIT AROUND WAITING FOR YOU?
A SMALL PRICE TO PAY... FOR BENEFITS SO MONUMENTAL!
YOU MUST WAIT ONE DAY... NO MORE!
16

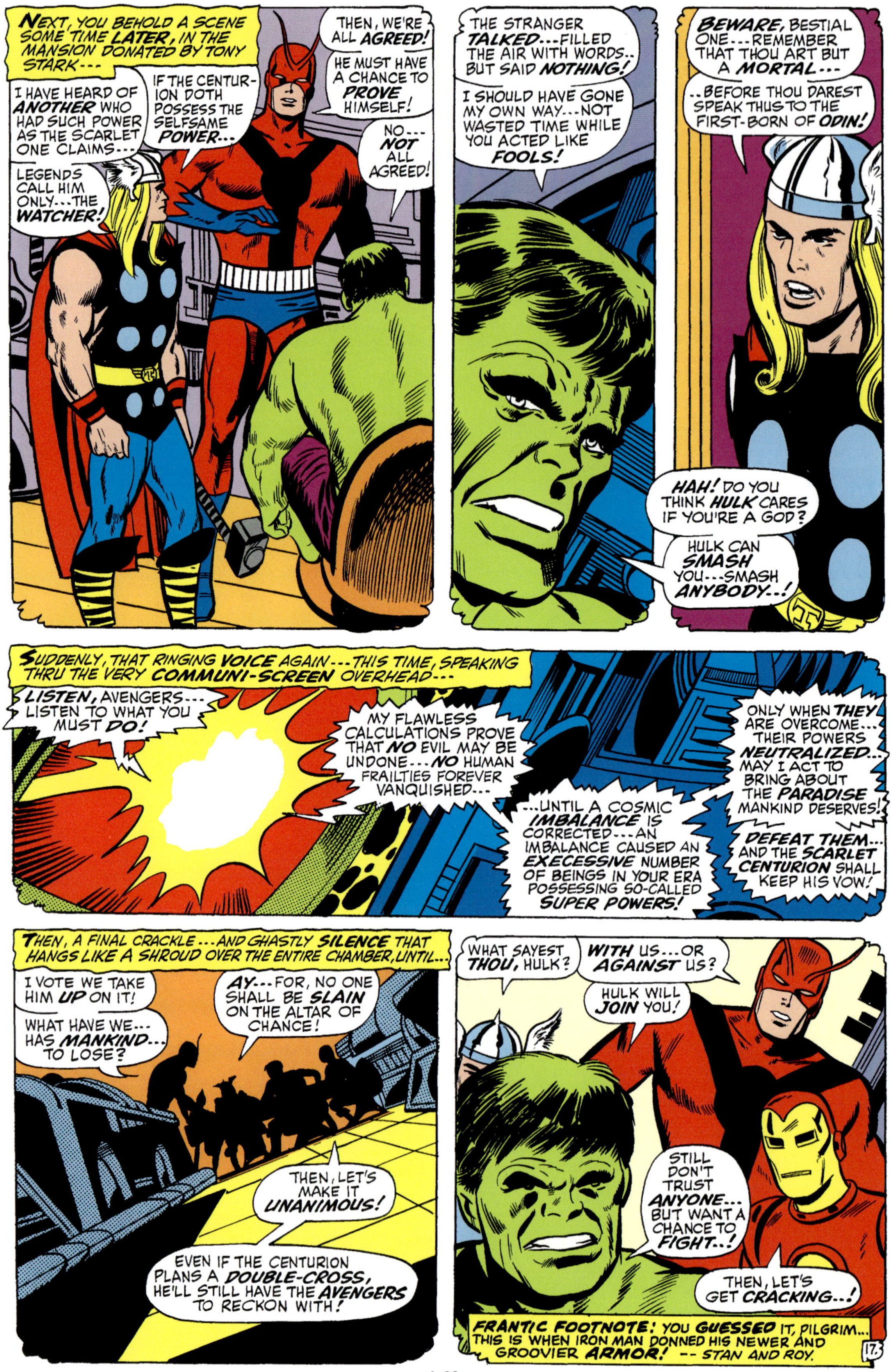
NEXT, YOU BEHOLD A SCENE SOME TIME LATER, IN THE MANSION DONATED BY TONY STARK---
I HAVE HEARD OF ANOTHER WHO HAD SUCH POWER AS THE SCARLET ONE CLAIMS---
LEGENDS CALL HIM ONLY---THE WATCHER!
IF THE CENTURION DOTH POSSESS THE SELFSAME POWER--
THEN, WE'RE ALL AGREED!
HE MUST HAVE A CHANCE TO PROVE HIMSELF!
NO--- NOT ALL AGREED!
THE STRANGER TALKED---FILLED THE AIR WITH WORDS.. BUT SAID NOTHING!
I SHOULD HAVE GONE MY OWN WAY---NOT WASTED TIME WHILE YOU ACTED LIKE FOOLS!
BEWARE, BESTIAL ONE---REMEMBER THAT THOU ART BUT A MORTAL---
..BEFORE THOU DAREST SPEAK THUS TO THE FIRST-BORN OF ODIN!
HAH! DO YOU THINK HULK CARES IF YOU'RE A GOD?
HULK CAN SMASH YOU---SMASH ANYBODY..!
SUDDENLY, THAT RINGING VOICE AGAIN---THIS TIME, SPEAKING THRU THE VERY COMMUNI-SCREEN OVERHEAD---
LISTEN, AVENGERS--- LISTEN TO WHAT YOU MUST DO!
MY FLAWLESS CALCULATIONS PROVE THAT NO EVIL MAY BE UNDONE---NO HUMAN FRAILTIES FOREVER VANQUISHED---
--UNTIL A COSMIC IMBALANCE IS CORRECTED---AN IMBALANCE CAUSED AN EXECESSIVE NUMBER OF BEINGS IN YOUR ERA POSSESSING SO-CALLED SUPER POWERS!
ONLY WHEN THEY ARE OVERCOME--- THEIR POWERS NEUTRALIZED.. MAY I ACT TO BRING ABOUT THE PARADISE MANKIND DESERVES!
DEFEAT THEM... AND THE SCARLET CENTURION SHALL KEEP HIS VOW!
THEN, A FINAL CRACKLE---AND GHASTLY SILENCE THAT HANGS LIKE A SHROUD OVER THE ENTIRE CHAMBER, UNTIL..
I VOTE WE TAKE HIM UP ON IT!
WHAT HAVE WE--- HAS MANKIND-- TO LOSE?
AY---FOR, NO ONE SHALL BE SLAIN ON THE ALTAR OF CHANCE!
THEN, LET'S MAKE IT UNANIMOUS!
EVEN IF THE CENTURION PLANS A DOUBLE-CROSS, HE'LL STILL HAVE THE AVENGERS TO RECKON WITH!
WHAT SAYEST THOU, HULK?
WITH US---OR AGAINST US?
HULK WILL JOIN YOU!
STILL DON'T TRUST ANYONE--- BUT WANT A CHANCE TO FIGHT..!
THEN, LET'S GET CRACKING..!
FRANTIC FOOTNOTE: YOU GUESSED IT, PILGRIM... THIS IS WHEN IRON MAN DONNED HIS NEWER AND GROOVIER ARMOR! -- STAN AND ROY.
17

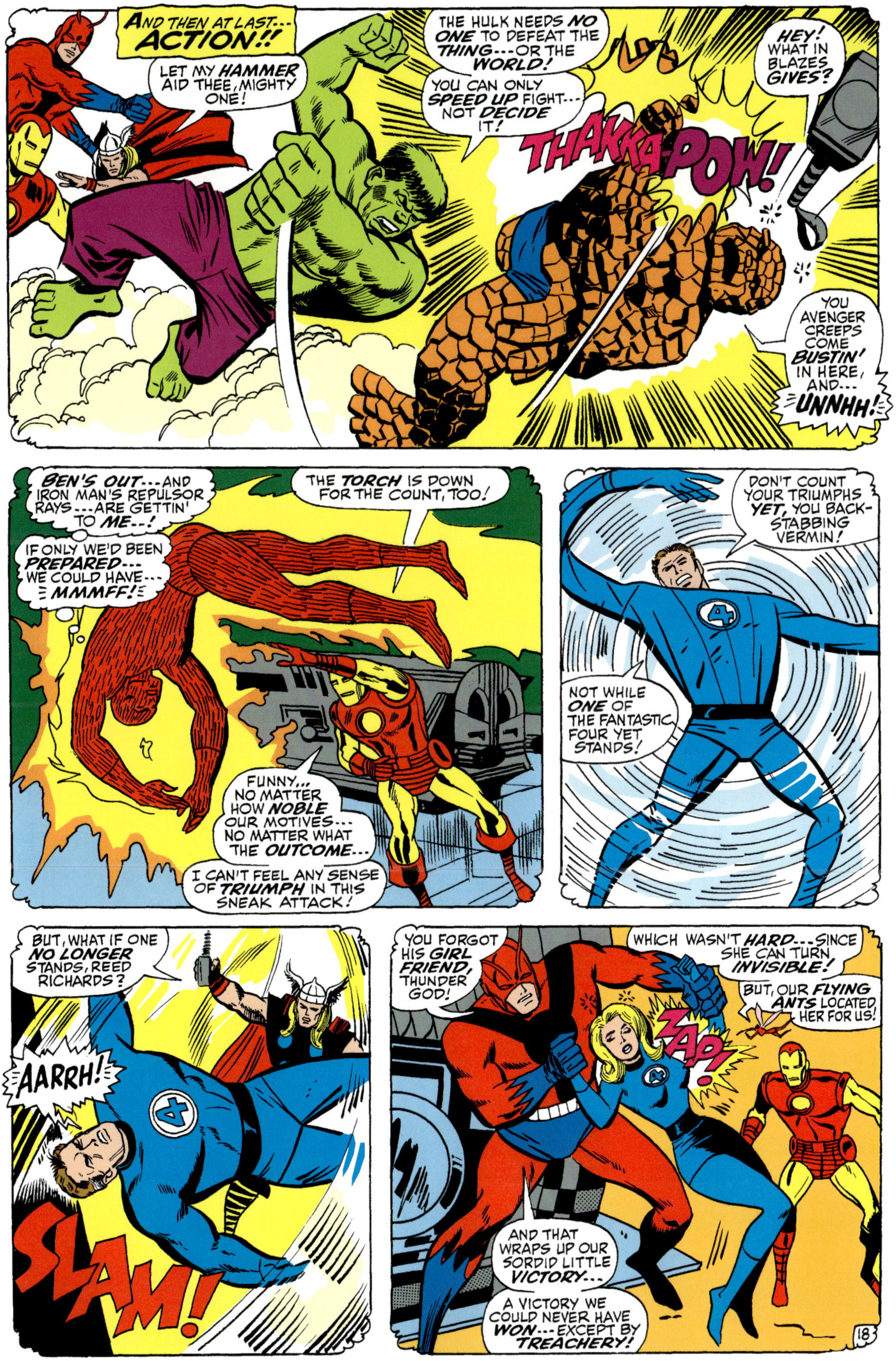
AND THEN AT LAST... ACTION!!
LET MY HAMMER AID THEE, MIGHTY ONE!
THE HULK NEEDS NO ONE TO DEFEAT THE THING---OR THE WORLD!
YOU CAN ONLY SPEED UP FIGHT--- NOT DECIDE IT!
THAKKA-POW!
HEY! WHAT IN BLAZES GIVES?
YOU AVENGER CREEPS COME BUSTIN' IN HERE, AND--- UNNHH!
BEN'S OUT---AND IRON MAN'S REPULSOR RAYS---ARE GETTIN' TO ME--!
IF ONLY WE'D BEEN PREPARED--- WE COULD HAVE--- MMMFF!
THE TORCH IS DOWN FOR THE COUNT, TOO!
FUNNY... NO MATTER HOW NOBLE OUR MOTIVES--- NO MATTER WHAT THE OUTCOME...
I CAN'T FEEL ANY SENSE OF TRIUMPH IN THIS SNEAK ATTACK!
DON'T COUNT YOUR TRIUMPHS YET, YOU BACK-STABBING VERMIN!
NOT WHILE ONE OF THE FANTASTIC FOUR YET STANDS!
BUT, WHAT IF ONE NO LONGER STANDS, REED RICHARDS?
AARRH!
SLAM!
YOU FORGOT HIS GIRL FRIEND, THUNDER GOD!
WHICH WASN'T HARD---SINCE SHE CAN TURN INVISIBLE!
BUT, OUR FLYING ANTS LOCATED HER FOR US!
ZAP!
AND THAT WRAPS UP OUR SORDID LITTLE VICTORY...
A VICTORY WE COULD NEVER HAVE WON---EXCEPT BY TREACHERY!
18

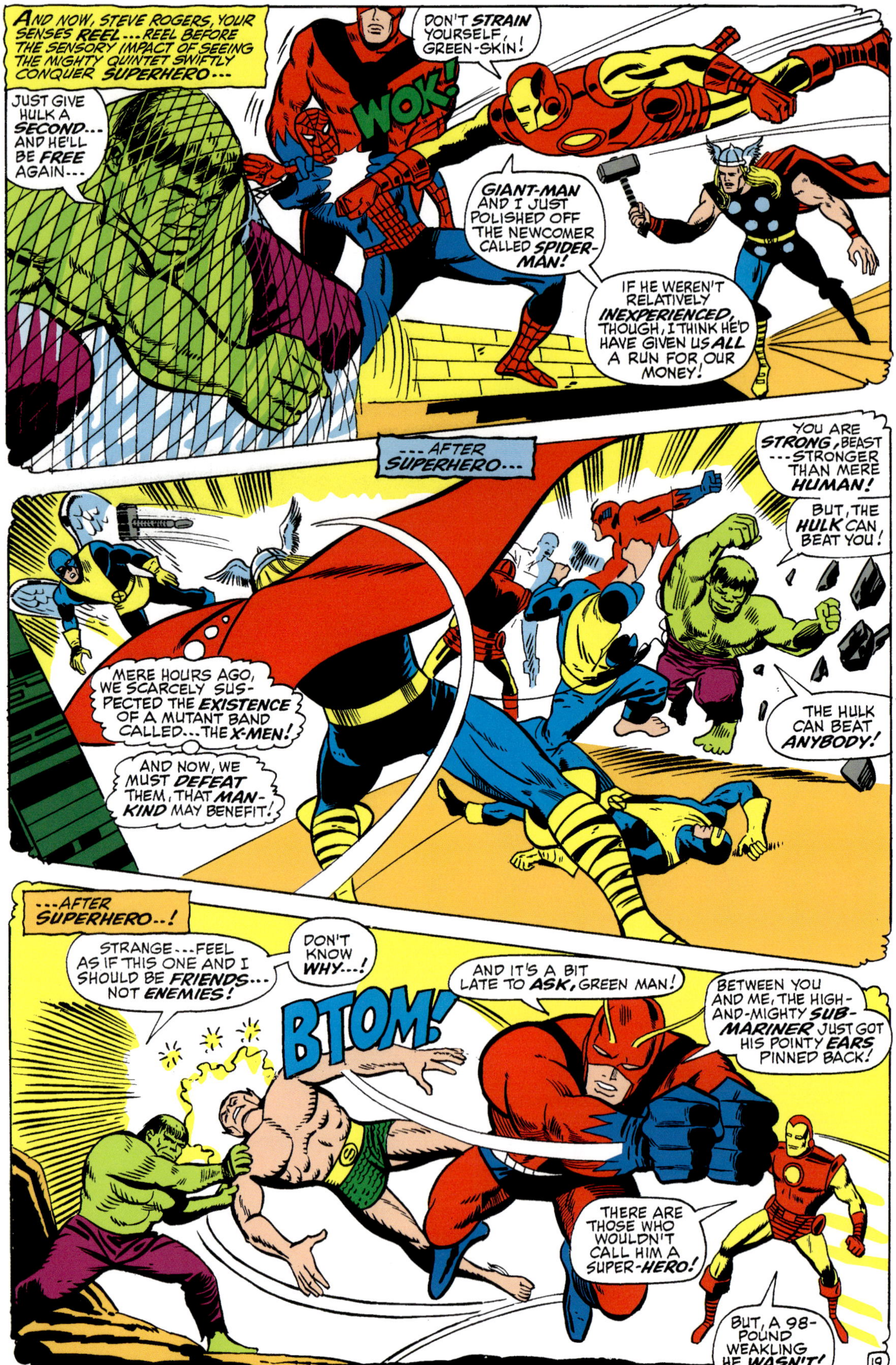
AND NOW, STEVE ROGERS, YOUR SENSES REEL... REEL BEFORE THE SENSORY IMPACT OF SEEING THE MIGHTY QUINTET SWIFTLY CONQUER SUPERHERO...
DON'T STRAIN YOURSELF, GREEN-SKIN!
WOK!
JUST GIVE HULK A SECOND... AND HE'LL BE FREE AGAIN...
GIANT-MAN AND I JUST POLISHED OFF THE NEWCOMER CALLED SPIDER-MAN!
IF HE WEREN'T RELATIVELY INEXPERIENCED, THOUGH, I THINK HE'D HAVE GIVEN US ALL A RUN FOR OUR MONEY!
...AFTER SUPERHERO...
YOU ARE STRONG, BEAST ---STRONGER THAN MERE HUMAN!
BUT, THE HULK CAN BEAT YOU!
MERE HOURS AGO, WE SCARCELY SUSPECTED THE EXISTENCE OF A MUTANT BAND CALLED... THE X-MEN!
AND NOW, WE MUST DEFEAT THEM, THAT MAN-KIND MAY BENEFIT!
THE HULK CAN BEAT ANYBODY!
...AFTER SUPERHERO..!
STRANGE...FEEL AS IF THIS ONE AND I SHOULD BE FRIENDS... NOT ENEMIES!
DON'T KNOW WHY...!
AND IT'S A BIT LATE TO ASK, GREEN MAN!
BTOM!
BETWEEN YOU AND ME, THE HIGH-AND-MIGHTY SUB-MARINER JUST GOT HIS POINTY EARS PINNED BACK!
THERE ARE THOSE WHO WOULDN'T CALL HIM A SUPER-HERO!
BUT, A 98-POUND WEAKLING HE WASN'T!
19

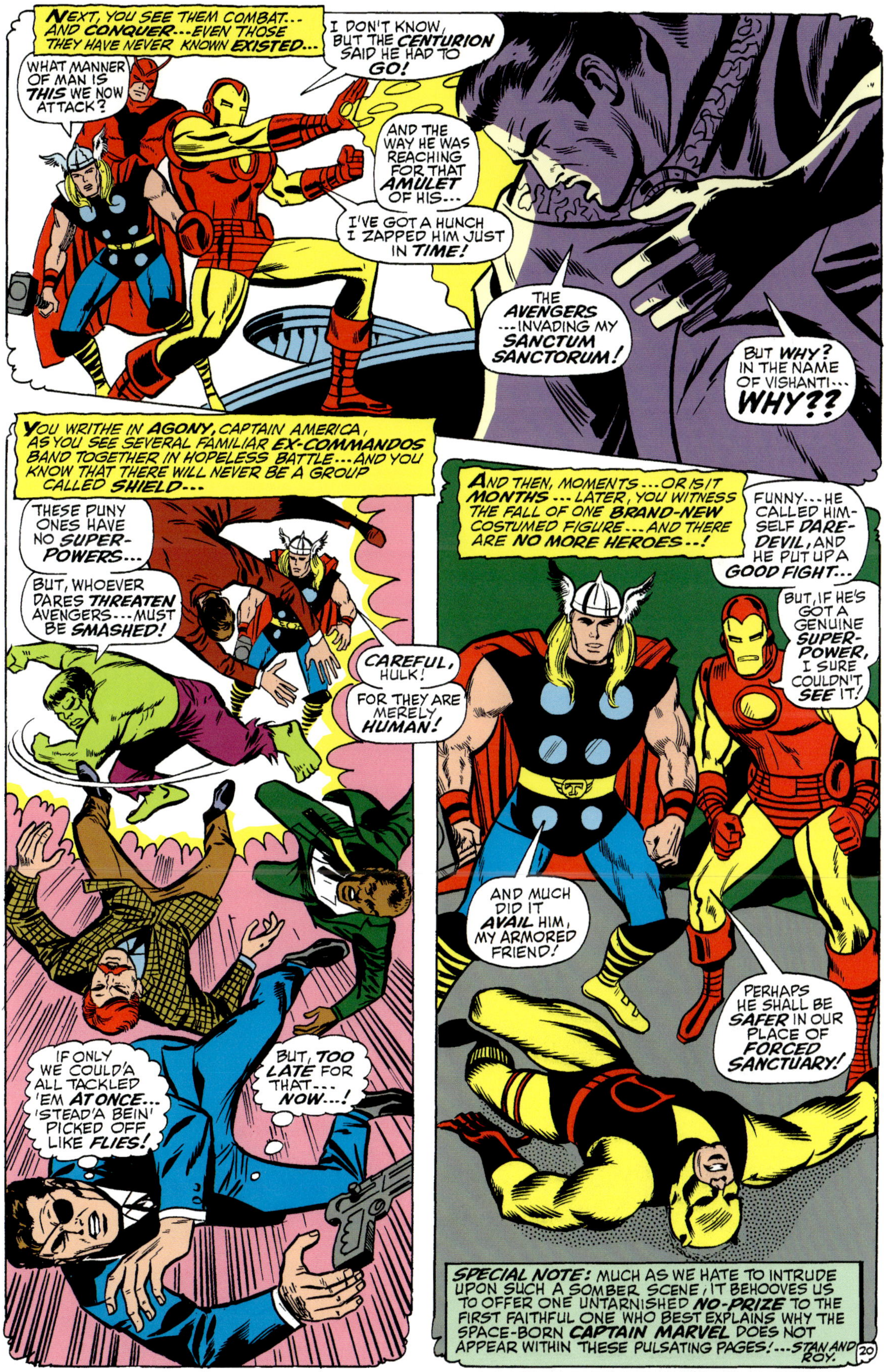
NEXT, YOU SEE THEM COMBAT... AND CONQUER... EVEN THOSE THEY HAVE NEVER KNOWN EXISTED...
WHAT MANNER OF MAN IS THIS WE NOW ATTACK?
I DON'T KNOW, BUT THE CENTURION SAID HE HAD TO GO!
AND THE WAY HE WAS REACHING FOR THAT AMULET OF HIS...
I'VE GOT A HUNCH I ZAPPED HIM JUST IN TIME!
THE AVENGERS ...INVADING MY SANCTUM SANCTORUM!
BUT WHY? IN THE NAME OF VISHANTI... WHY??
YOU WRITHE IN AGONY, CAPTAIN AMERICA, AS YOU SEE SEVERAL FAMILIAR EX-COMMANDOS BAND TOGETHER IN HOPELESS BATTLE... AND YOU KNOW THAT THERE WILL NEVER BE A GROUP CALLED SHIELD...
THESE PUNY ONES HAVE NO SUPER-POWERS...
BUT, WHOEVER DARES THREATEN AVENGERS... MUST BE SMASHED!
CAREFUL, HULK!
FOR THEY ARE MERELY HUMAN!
IF ONLY WE COULD'A ALL TACKLED 'EM AT ONCE... 'STEAD'A BEIN' PICKED OFF LIKE FLIES!
BUT, TOO LATE FOR THAT... NOW...!
AND THEN, MOMENTS... OR IS IT MONTHS... LATER, YOU WITNESS THE FALL OF ONE BRAND-NEW COSTUMED FIGURE... AND THERE ARE NO MORE HEROES...!
FUNNY... HE CALLED HIMSELF DAREDEVIL, AND HE PUT UP A GOOD FIGHT...
BUT, IF HE'S GOT A GENUINE SUPER-POWER, I SURE COULDN'T SEE IT!
AND MUCH DID IT AVAIL HIM, MY ARMORED FRIEND!
PERHAPS HE SHALL BE SAFER IN OUR PLACE OF FORCED SANCTUARY!
SPECIAL NOTE: MUCH AS WE HATE TO INTRUDE UPON SUCH A SOMBER SCENE, IT BEHOOVES US TO OFFER ONE UNTARNISHED NO-PRIZE TO THE FIRST FAITHFUL ONE WHO BEST EXPLAINS WHY THE SPACE-BORN CAPTAIN MARVEL DOES NOT APPEAR WITHIN THESE PULSATING PAGES! ...STAN AND ROY.
20

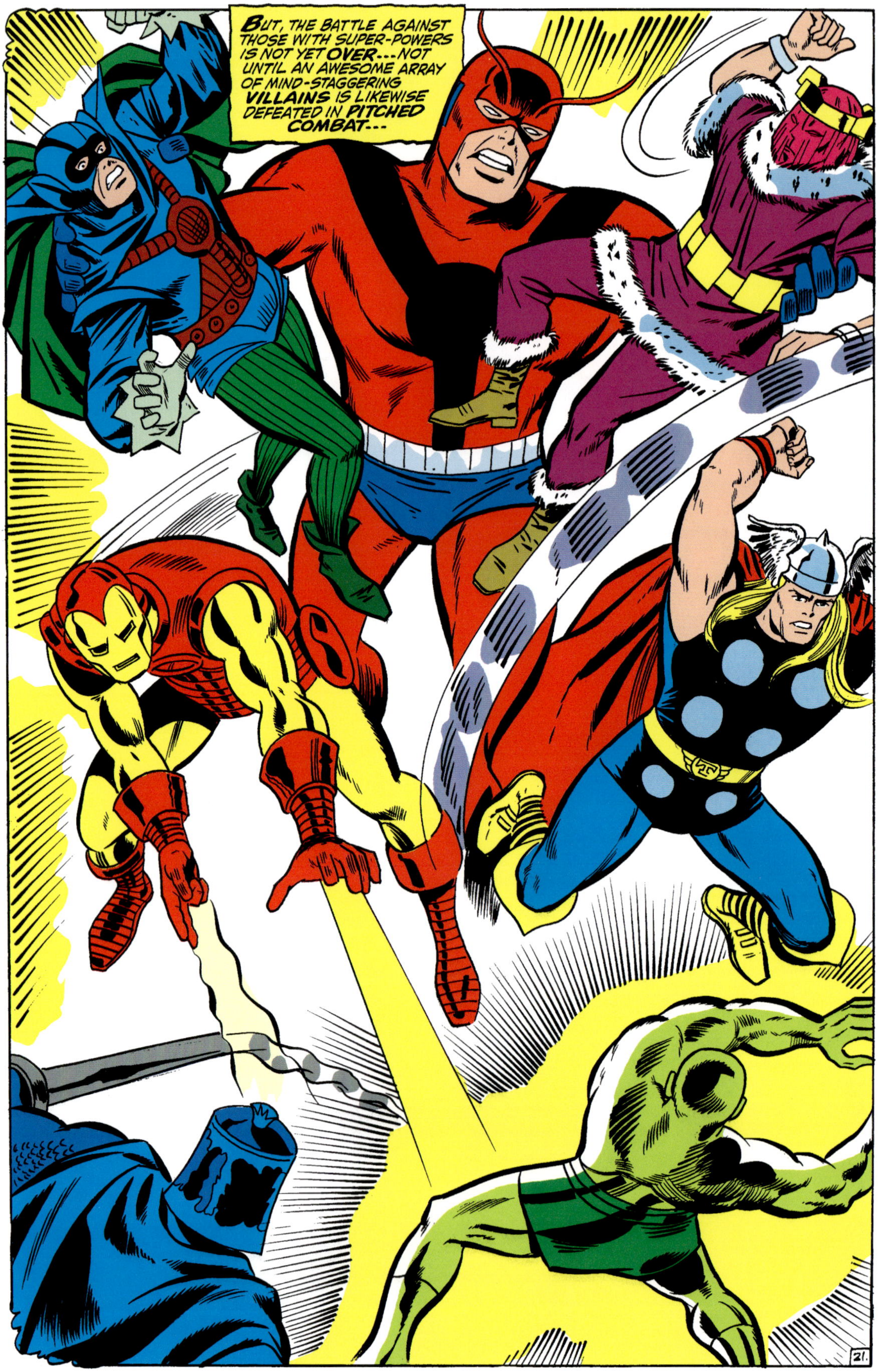
BUT, THE BATTLE AGAINST THOSE WITH SUPER-POWERS IS NOT YET OVER--- NOT UNTIL AN AWESOME ARRAY OF MIND-STAGGERING VILLAINS IS LIKEWISE DEFEATED IN PITCHED COMBAT---
21.

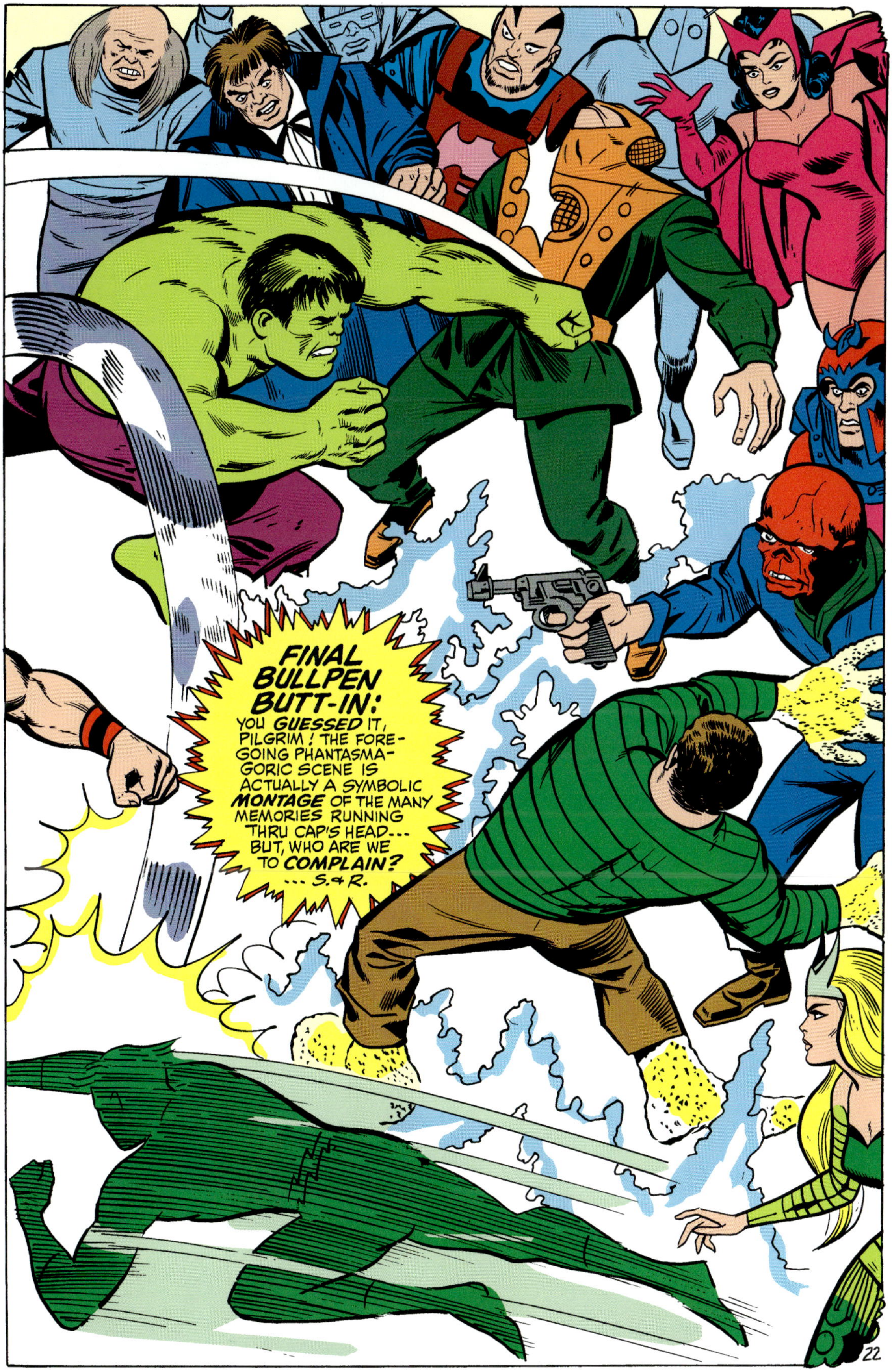
FINAL BULLPEN BUTT-IN:
YOU GUESSED IT, PILGRIM! THE FORE-GOING PHANTASMA-GORIC SCENE IS ACTUALLY A SYMBOLIC MONTAGE OF THE MANY MEMORIES RUNNING THRU CAP'S HEAD... BUT, WHO ARE WE TO COMPLAIN? ... S. & R.
22

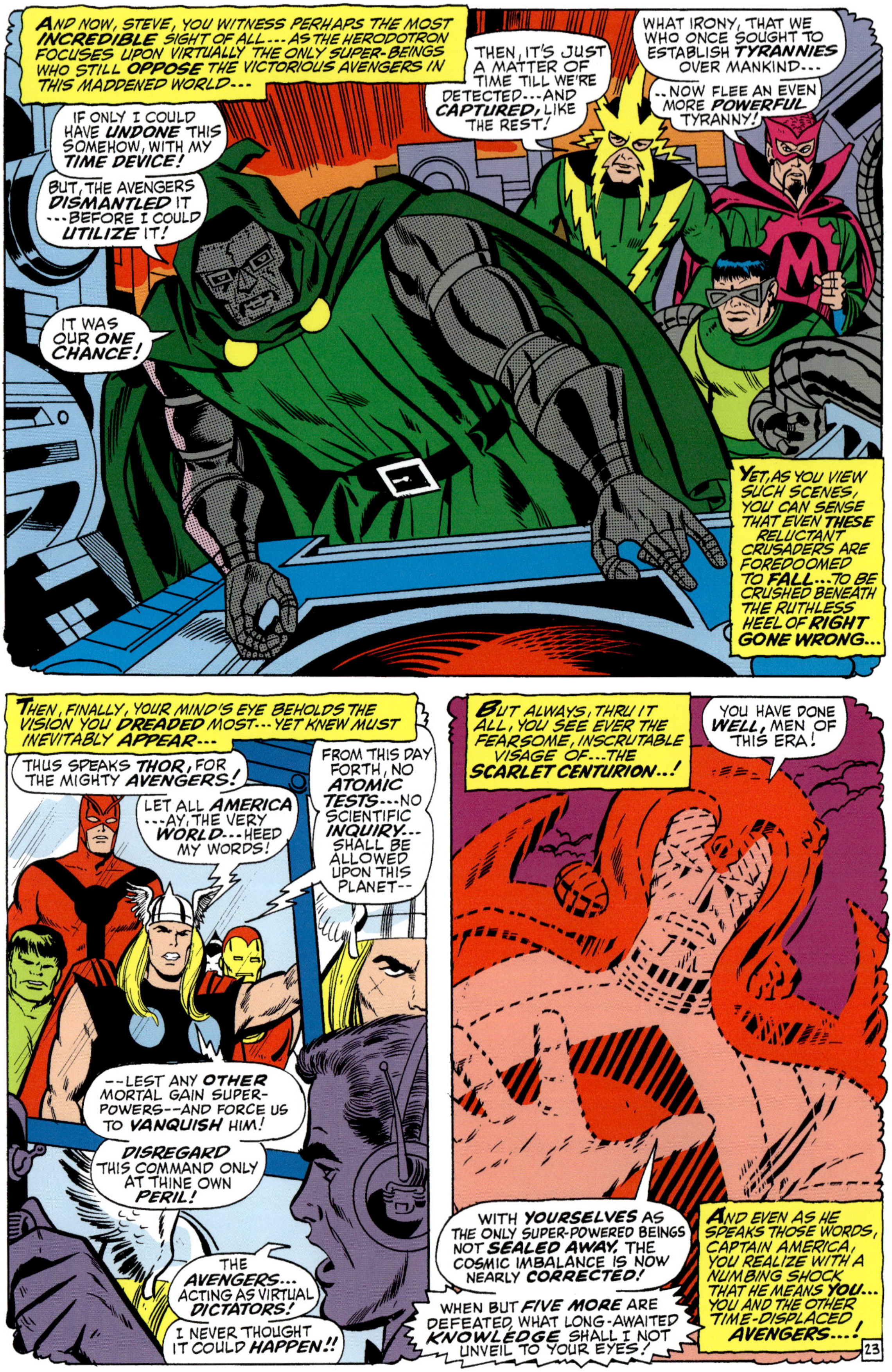
AND NOW, STEVE, YOU WITNESS PERHAPS THE MOST INCREDIBLE SIGHT OF ALL--- AS THE HERODOTRON FOCUSES UPON VIRTUALLY THE ONLY SUPER-BEINGS WHO STILL OPPOSE THE VICTORIOUS AVENGERS IN THIS MADDENED WORLD---
IF ONLY I COULD HAVE UNDONE THIS SOMEHOW, WITH MY TIME DEVICE!
BUT, THE AVENGERS DISMANTLED IT ---BEFORE I COULD UTILIZE IT!
IT WAS OUR ONE CHANCE!
THEN, IT'S JUST A MATTER OF TIME TILL WE'RE DETECTED---AND CAPTURED, LIKE THE REST!
WHAT IRONY, THAT WE WHO ONCE SOUGHT TO ESTABLISH TYRANNIES OVER MANKIND---
..NOW FLEE AN EVEN MORE POWERFUL TYRANNY!
YET, AS YOU VIEW SUCH SCENES, YOU CAN SENSE THAT EVEN THESE RELUCTANT CRUSADERS ARE FOREDOOMED TO FALL...TO BE CRUSHED BENEATH THE RUTHLESS HEEL OF RIGHT GONE WRONG...
THEN, FINALLY, YOUR MIND'S EYE BEHOLDS THE VISION YOU DREADED MOST--- YET KNEW MUST INEVITABLY APPEAR---
THUS SPEAKS THOR, FOR THE MIGHTY AVENGERS!
LET ALL AMERICA ---AY, THE VERY WORLD---HEED MY WORDS!
FROM THIS DAY FORTH, NO ATOMIC TESTS---NO SCIENTIFIC INQUIRY--- SHALL BE ALLOWED UPON THIS PLANET--
--LEST ANY OTHER MORTAL GAIN SUPER-POWERS--AND FORCE US TO VANQUISH HIM!
DISREGARD THIS COMMAND ONLY AT THINE OWN PERIL!
THE AVENGERS... ACTING AS VIRTUAL DICTATORS!
I NEVER THOUGHT IT COULD HAPPEN!!
BUT ALWAYS, THRU IT ALL, YOU SEE EVER THE FEARSOME, INSCRUTABLE VISAGE OF...THE SCARLET CENTURION..!
YOU HAVE DONE WELL, MEN OF THIS ERA!
WITH YOURSELVES AS THE ONLY SUPER-POWERED BEINGS NOT SEALED AWAY, THE COSMIC IMBALANCE IS NOW NEARLY CORRECTED!
WHEN BUT FIVE MORE ARE DEFEATED, WHAT LONG-AWAITED KNOWLEDGE SHALL I NOT UNVEIL TO YOUR EYES!
AND EVEN AS HE SPEAKS THOSE WORDS, CAPTAIN AMERICA, YOU REALIZE WITH A NUMBING SHOCK THAT HE MEANS YOU... YOU AND THE OTHER TIME-DISPLACED AVENGERS...!
23

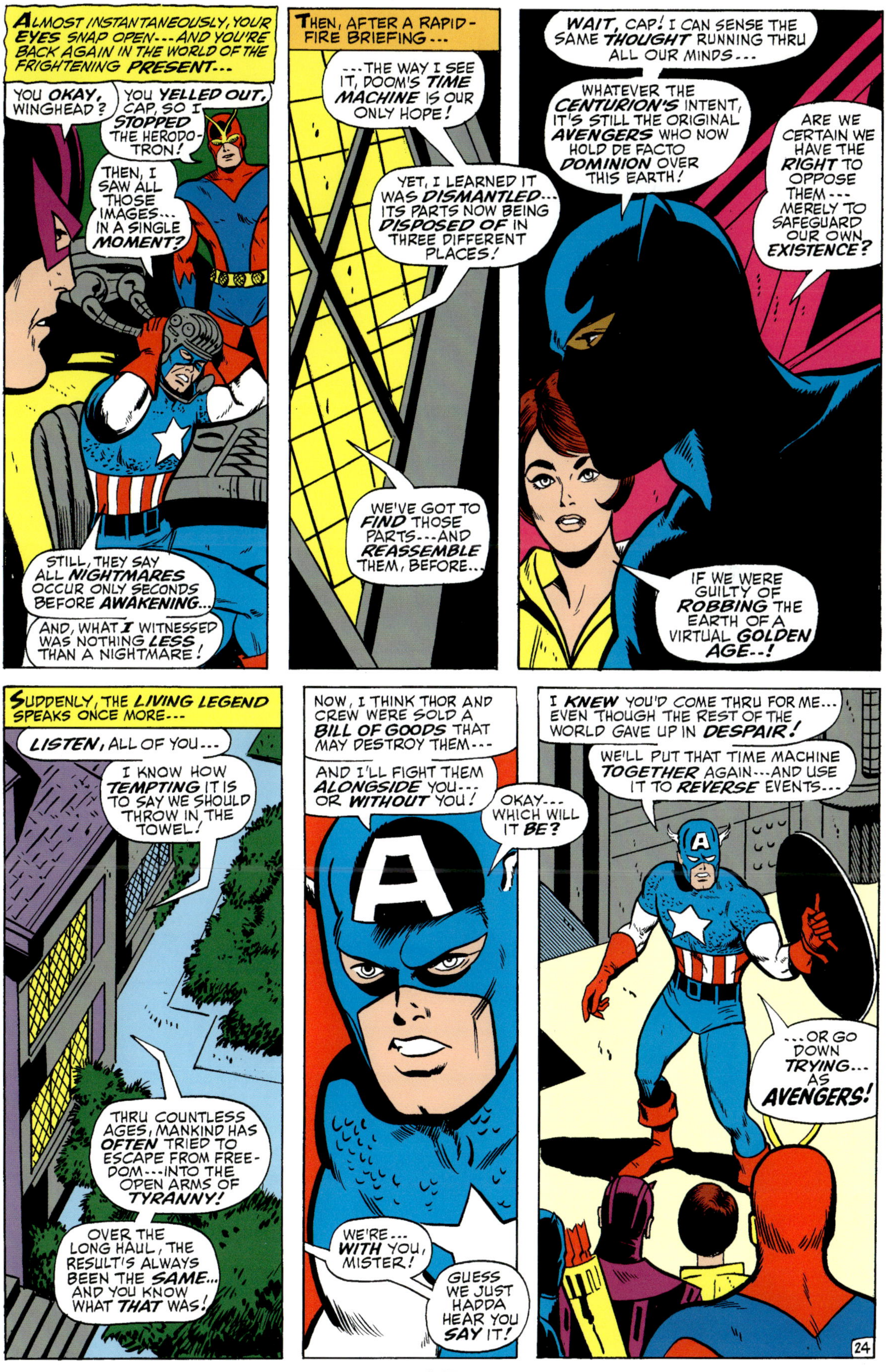
ALMOST INSTANTANEOUSLY, YOUR EYES SNAP OPEN---AND YOU'RE BACK AGAIN IN THE WORLD OF THE FRIGHTENING PRESENT---
YOU OKAY, WINGHEAD?
YOU YELLED OUT, CAP, SO I STOPPED THE HERODOTRON!
THEN, I SAW ALL THOSE IMAGES... IN A SINGLE MOMENT?
STILL, THEY SAY ALL NIGHTMARES OCCUR ONLY SECONDS BEFORE AWAKENING...
AND, WHAT I WITNESSED WAS NOTHING LESS THAN A NIGHTMARE!
THEN, AFTER A RAPID-FIRE BRIEFING---
---THE WAY I SEE IT, DOOM'S TIME MACHINE IS OUR ONLY HOPE!
YET, I LEARNED IT WAS DISMANTLED... ITS PARTS NOW BEING DISPOSED OF IN THREE DIFFERENT PLACES!
WE'VE GOT TO FIND THOSE PARTS---AND REASSEMBLE THEM, BEFORE...
WAIT, CAP! I CAN SENSE THE SAME THOUGHT RUNNING THRU ALL OUR MINDS---
WHATEVER THE CENTURION'S INTENT, IT'S STILL THE ORIGINAL AVENGERS WHO NOW HOLD DE FACTO DOMINION OVER THIS EARTH!
ARE WE CERTAIN WE HAVE THE RIGHT TO OPPOSE THEM--- MERELY TO SAFEGUARD OUR OWN EXISTENCE?
IF WE WERE GUILTY OF ROBBING THE EARTH OF A VIRTUAL GOLDEN AGE--!
SUDDENLY, THE LIVING LEGEND SPEAKS ONCE MORE---
LISTEN, ALL OF YOU---
I KNOW HOW TEMPTING IT IS TO SAY WE SHOULD THROW IN THE TOWEL!
THRU COUNTLESS AGES, MANKIND HAS OFTEN TRIED TO ESCAPE FROM FREEDOM---INTO THE OPEN ARMS OF TYRANNY!
OVER THE LONG HAUL, THE RESULT'S ALWAYS BEEN THE SAME... AND YOU KNOW WHAT THAT WAS!
NOW, I THINK THOR AND CREW WERE SOLD A BILL OF GOODS THAT MAY DESTROY THEM---
AND I'LL FIGHT THEM ALONGSIDE YOU--- OR WITHOUT YOU!
OKAY--- WHICH WILL IT BE?
WE'RE--- WITH YOU, MISTER!
GUESS WE JUST HADDA HEAR YOU SAY IT!
I KNEW YOU'D COME THRU FOR ME... EVEN THOUGH THE REST OF THE WORLD GAVE UP IN DESPAIR!
WE'LL PUT THAT TIME MACHINE TOGETHER AGAIN---AND USE IT TO REVERSE EVENTS---
...OR GO DOWN TRYING... AS AVENGERS!
24

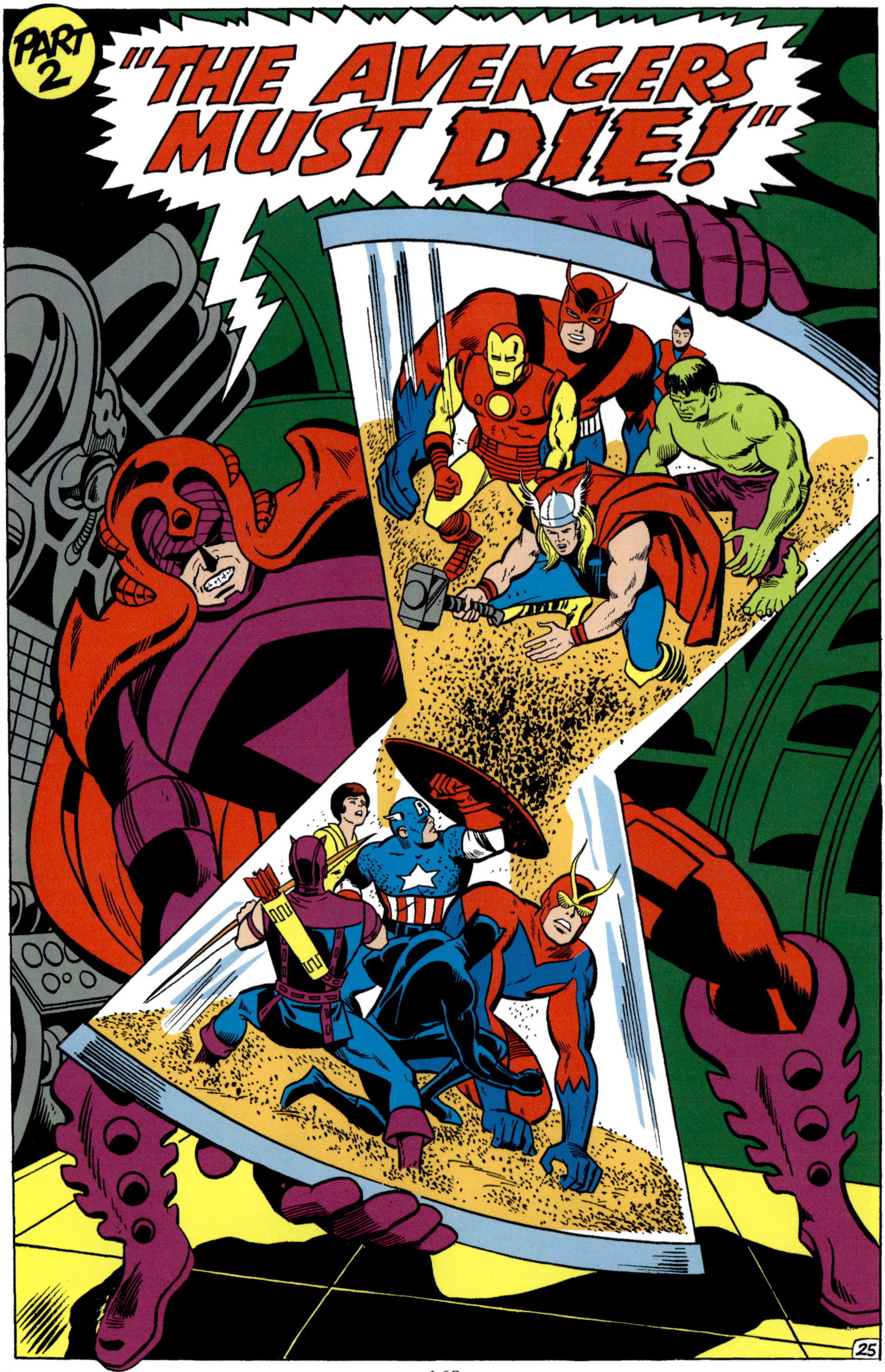
PART 2
"THE AVENGERS MUST DIE!"
25

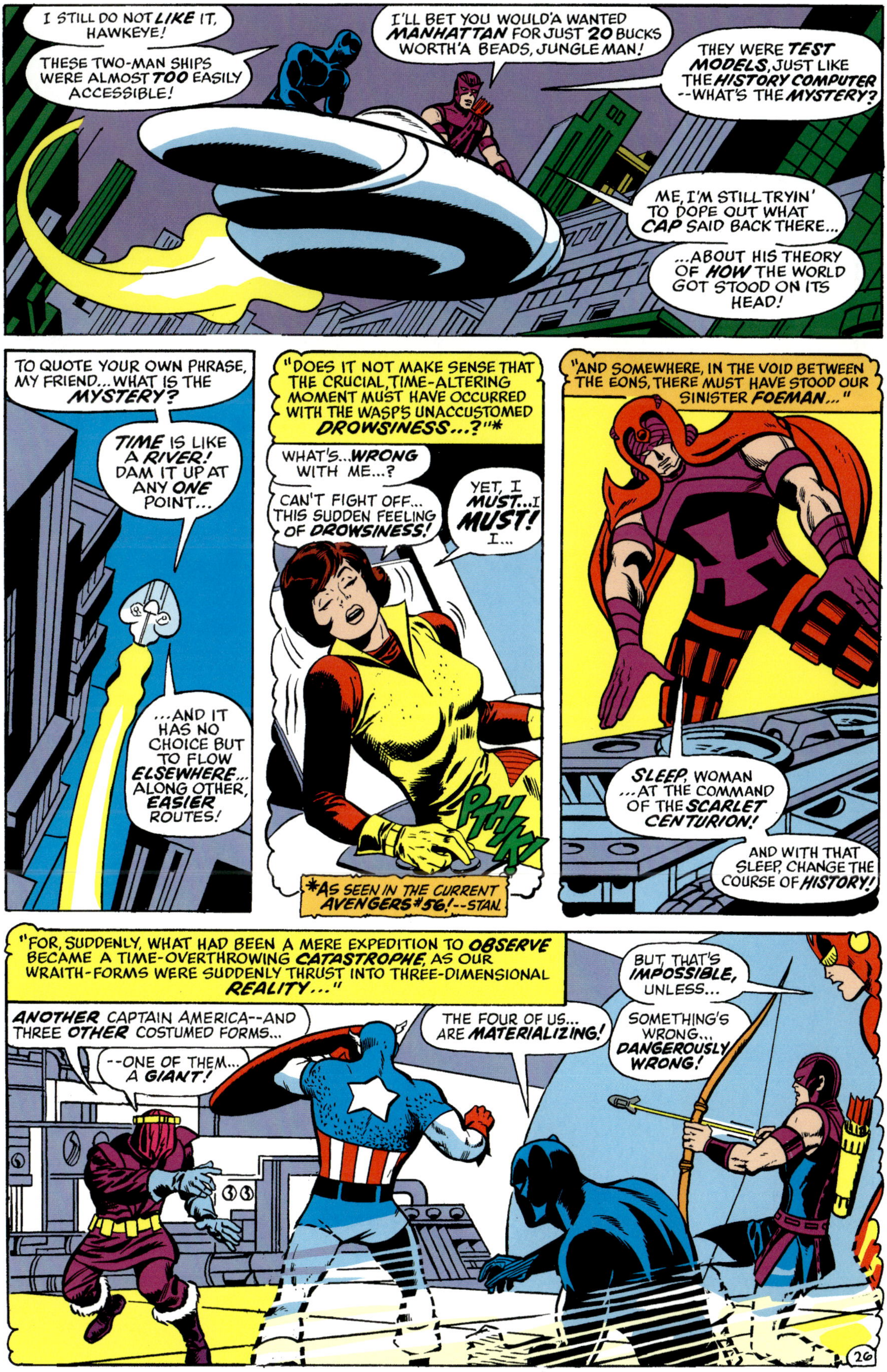
I STILL DO NOT LIKE IT, HAWKEYE!
THESE TWO-MAN SHIPS WERE ALMOST TOO EASILY ACCESSIBLE!
I'LL BET YOU WOULD'A WANTED MANHATTAN FOR JUST 20 BUCKS WORTH'A BEADS, JUNGLE MAN!
THEY WERE TEST MODELS, JUST LIKE THE HISTORY COMPUTER --WHAT'S THE MYSTERY?
ME, I'M STILL TRYIN' TO DOPE OUT WHAT CAP SAID BACK THERE...
...ABOUT HIS THEORY OF HOW THE WORLD GOT STOOD ON ITS HEAD!
TO QUOTE YOUR OWN PHRASE, MY FRIEND... WHAT IS THE MYSTERY?
TIME IS LIKE A RIVER! DAM IT UP AT ANY ONE POINT...
...AND IT HAS NO CHOICE BUT TO FLOW ELSEWHERE... ALONG OTHER, EASIER ROUTES!
"DOES IT NOT MAKE SENSE THAT THE CRUCIAL, TIME-ALTERING MOMENT MUST HAVE OCCURRED WITH THE WASP'S UNACCUSTOMED DROWSINESS...?"*
WHAT'S... WRONG WITH ME...?
CAN'T FIGHT OFF... THIS SUDDEN FEELING OF DROWSINESS!
YET, I MUST... I MUST! I...
PTHK!
*AS SEEN IN THE CURRENT AVENGERS #56! --STAN.
"AND SOMEWHERE, IN THE VOID BETWEEN THE EONS, THERE MUST HAVE STOOD OUR SINISTER FOEMAN..."
SLEEP, WOMAN ...AT THE COMMAND OF THE SCARLET CENTURION!
AND WITH THAT SLEEP, CHANGE THE COURSE OF HISTORY!
"FOR, SUDDENLY, WHAT HAD BEEN A MERE EXPEDITION TO OBSERVE BECAME A TIME-OVERTHROWING CATASTROPHE, AS OUR WRAITH-FORMS WERE SUDDENLY THRUST INTO THREE-DIMENSIONAL REALITY..."
ANOTHER CAPTAIN AMERICA--AND THREE OTHER COSTUMED FORMS...
--ONE OF THEM... A GIANT!
THE FOUR OF US... ARE MATERIALIZING!
BUT, THAT'S IMPOSSIBLE, UNLESS...
SOMETHING'S WRONG... DANGEROUSLY WRONG!
26

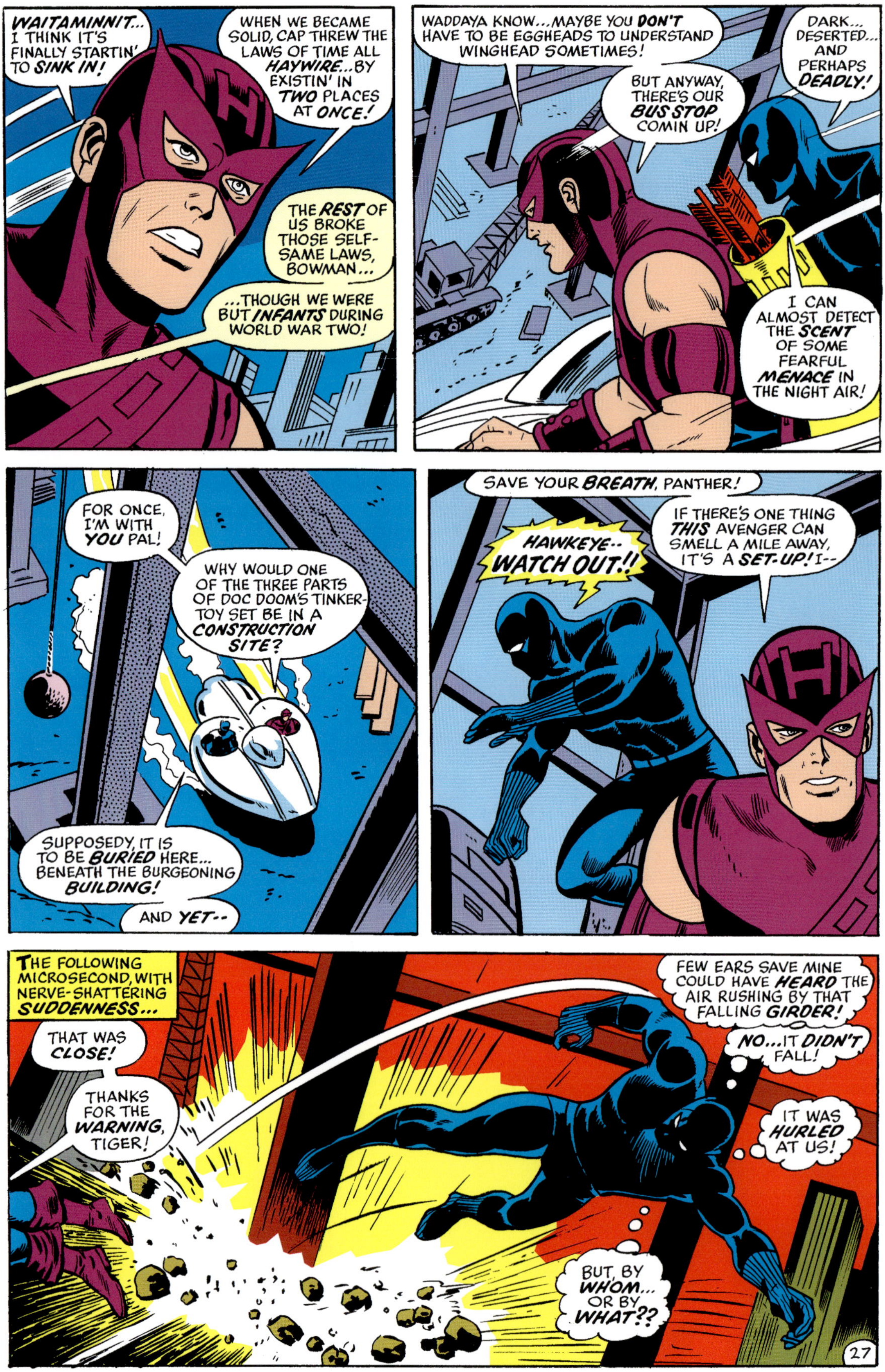
WAITAMINNIT... I THINK IT'S FINALLY STARTIN' TO SINK IN!
WHEN WE BECAME SOLID, CAP THREW THE LAWS OF TIME ALL HAYWIRE... BY EXISTIN' IN TWO PLACES AT ONCE!
THE REST OF US BROKE THOSE SELF-SAME LAWS, BOWMAN...
...THOUGH WE WERE BUT INFANTS DURING WORLD WAR TWO!
WADDAYA KNOW... MAYBE YOU DON'T HAVE TO BE EGGHEADS TO UNDERSTAND WINGHEAD SOMETIMES!
BUT ANYWAY, THERE'S OUR BUS STOP COMIN UP!
DARK... DESERTED... AND PERHAPS DEADLY!
I CAN ALMOST DETECT THE SCENT OF SOME FEARFUL MENACE IN THE NIGHT AIR!
FOR ONCE, I'M WITH YOU PAL!
WHY WOULD ONE OF THE THREE PARTS OF DOC DOOM'S TINKER-TOY SET BE IN A CONSTRUCTION SITE?
SUPPOSEDY, IT IS TO BE BURIED HERE... BENEATH THE BURGEONING BUILDING!
AND YET--
SAVE YOUR BREATH, PANTHER!
IF THERE'S ONE THING THIS AVENGER CAN SMELL A MILE AWAY, IT'S A SET-UP! I--
HAWKEYE-- WATCH OUT!!
THE FOLLOWING MICROSECOND, WITH NERVE-SHATTERING SUDDENNESS...
THAT WAS CLOSE!
THANKS FOR THE WARNING, TIGER!
FEW EARS SAVE MINE COULD HAVE HEARD THE AIR RUSHING BY THAT FALLING GIRDER!
NO... IT DIDN'T FALL!
IT WAS HURLED AT US!
BUT, BY WHOM... OR BY WHAT??
27

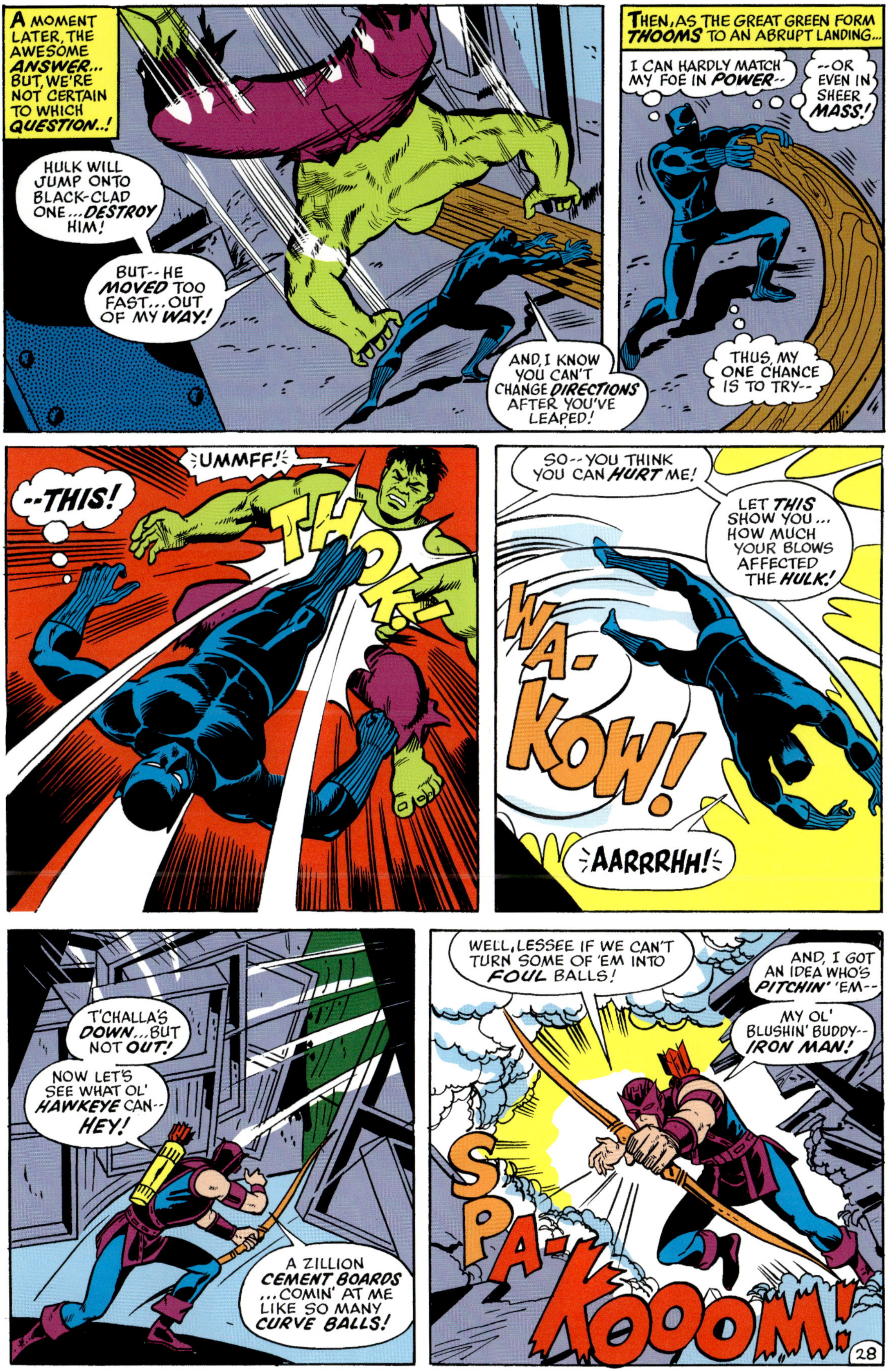
A MOMENT LATER, THE AWESOME ANSWER... BUT, WE'RE NOT CERTAIN TO WHICH QUESTION..!
HULK WILL JUMP ONTO BLACK-CLAD ONE...DESTROY HIM!
BUT--HE MOVED TOO FAST...OUT OF MY WAY!
AND, I KNOW YOU CAN'T CHANGE DIRECTIONS AFTER YOU'VE LEAPED!
THEN, AS THE GREAT GREEN FORM THOOMS TO AN ABRUPT LANDING...
I CAN HARDLY MATCH MY FOE IN POWER--
--OR EVEN IN SHEER MASS!
THUS, MY ONE CHANCE IS TO TRY--
--THIS!
UMMFF!
THOK!
SO--YOU THINK YOU CAN HURT ME!
LET THIS SHOW YOU... HOW MUCH YOUR BLOWS AFFECTED THE HULK!
WA-KOW!
AARRRHH!
T'CHALLA'S DOWN...BUT NOT OUT!
NOW LET'S SEE WHAT OL' HAWKEYE CAN--HEY!
A ZILLION CEMENT BOARDS ...COMIN' AT ME LIKE SO MANY CURVE BALLS!
WELL, LESSEE IF WE CAN'T TURN SOME OF 'EM INTO FOUL BALLS!
AND, I GOT AN IDEA WHO'S PITCHIN' 'EM--
MY OL' BLUSHIN' BUDDY--IRON MAN!
SPA-KOOOOM!
28

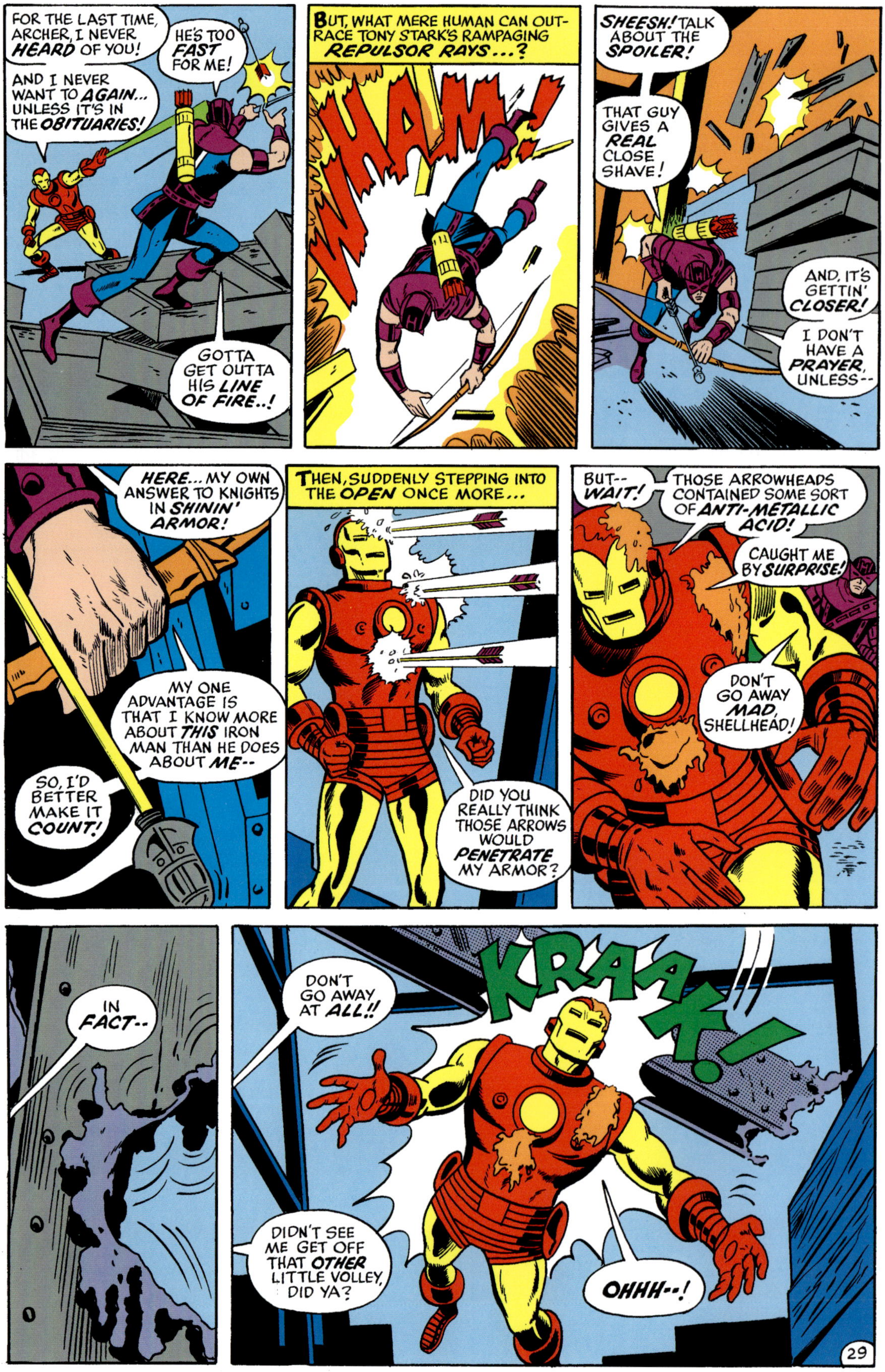

FOR THE LAST TIME, ARCHER, I NEVER HEARD OF YOU!
HE'S TOO FAST FOR ME!
AND I NEVER WANT TO AGAIN... UNLESS IT'S IN THE OBITUARIES!
GOTTA GET OUTTA HIS LINE OF FIRE..!
BUT, WHAT MERE HUMAN CAN OUT-RACE TONY STARK'S RAMPAGING REPULSOR RAYS...?
WHAM!
SHEESH! TALK ABOUT THE SPOILER!
THAT GUY GIVES A REAL CLOSE SHAVE!
AND, IT'S GETTIN' CLOSER!
I DON'T HAVE A PRAYER, UNLESS--
HERE... MY OWN ANSWER TO KNIGHTS IN SHININ' ARMOR!
MY ONE ADVANTAGE IS THAT I KNOW MORE ABOUT THIS IRON MAN THAN HE DOES ABOUT ME--
SO, I'D BETTER MAKE IT COUNT!
THEN, SUDDENLY STEPPING INTO THE OPEN ONCE MORE...
DID YOU REALLY THINK THOSE ARROWS WOULD PENETRATE MY ARMOR?
BUT-- WAIT!
THOSE ARROWHEADS CONTAINED SOME SORT OF ANTI-METALLIC ACID!
CAUGHT ME BY SURPRISE!
DON'T GO AWAY MAD, SHELLHEAD!
IN FACT--
DON'T GO AWAY AT ALL!!
KRAAK!
DIDN'T SEE ME GET OFF THAT OTHER LITTLE VOLLEY, DID YA?
OHHH--!
29

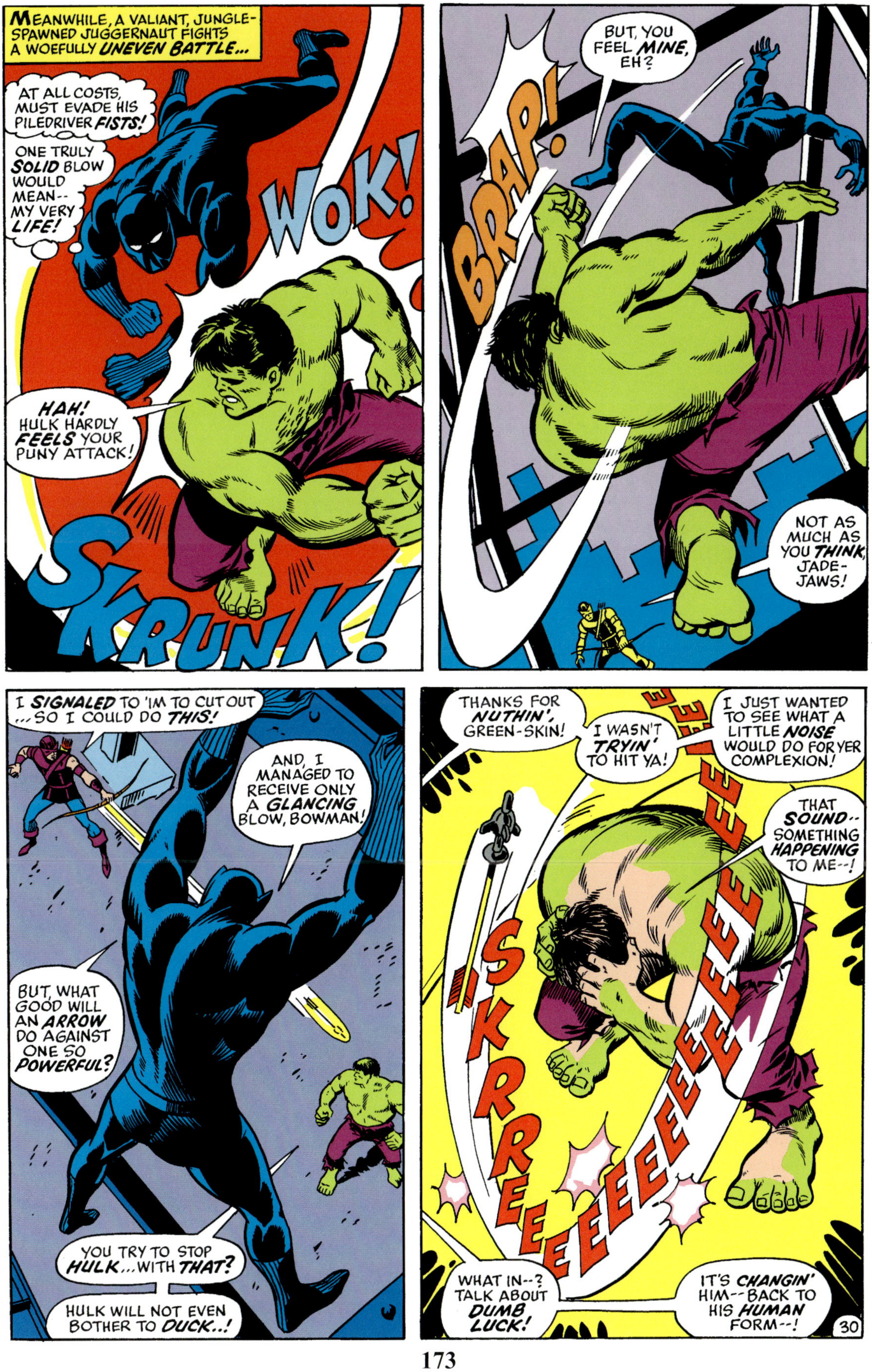
MEANWHILE, A VALIANT, JUNGLE-SPAWNED JUGGERNAUT FIGHTS A WOEFULLY UNEVEN BATTLE...
AT ALL COSTS, MUST EVADE HIS PILEDRIVER FISTS!
ONE TRULY SOLID BLOW WOULD MEAN-- MY VERY LIFE!
WOK!
HAH! HULK HARDLY FEELS YOUR PUNY ATTACK!
SKRUNK!
BUT, YOU FEEL MINE, EH?
BRAP!
NOT AS MUCH AS YOU THINK, JADE-JAWS!
I SIGNALED TO 'IM TO CUT OUT ...SO I COULD DO THIS!
AND, I MANAGED TO RECEIVE ONLY A GLANCING BLOW, BOWMAN!
BUT, WHAT GOOD WILL AN ARROW DO AGAINST ONE SO POWERFUL?
YOU TRY TO STOP HULK... WITH THAT?
HULK WILL NOT EVEN BOTHER TO DUCK..!
THANKS FOR NUTHIN', GREEN-SKIN!
I WASN'T TRYIN' TO HIT YA!
I JUST WANTED TO SEE WHAT A LITTLE NOISE WOULD DO FOR YER COMPLEXION!
THAT SOUND-- SOMETHING HAPPENING TO ME--!
SKREEEEEEEEEEEEEE
WHAT IN--? TALK ABOUT DUMB LUCK!
IT'S CHANGIN' HIM--BACK TO HIS HUMAN FORM--!
30

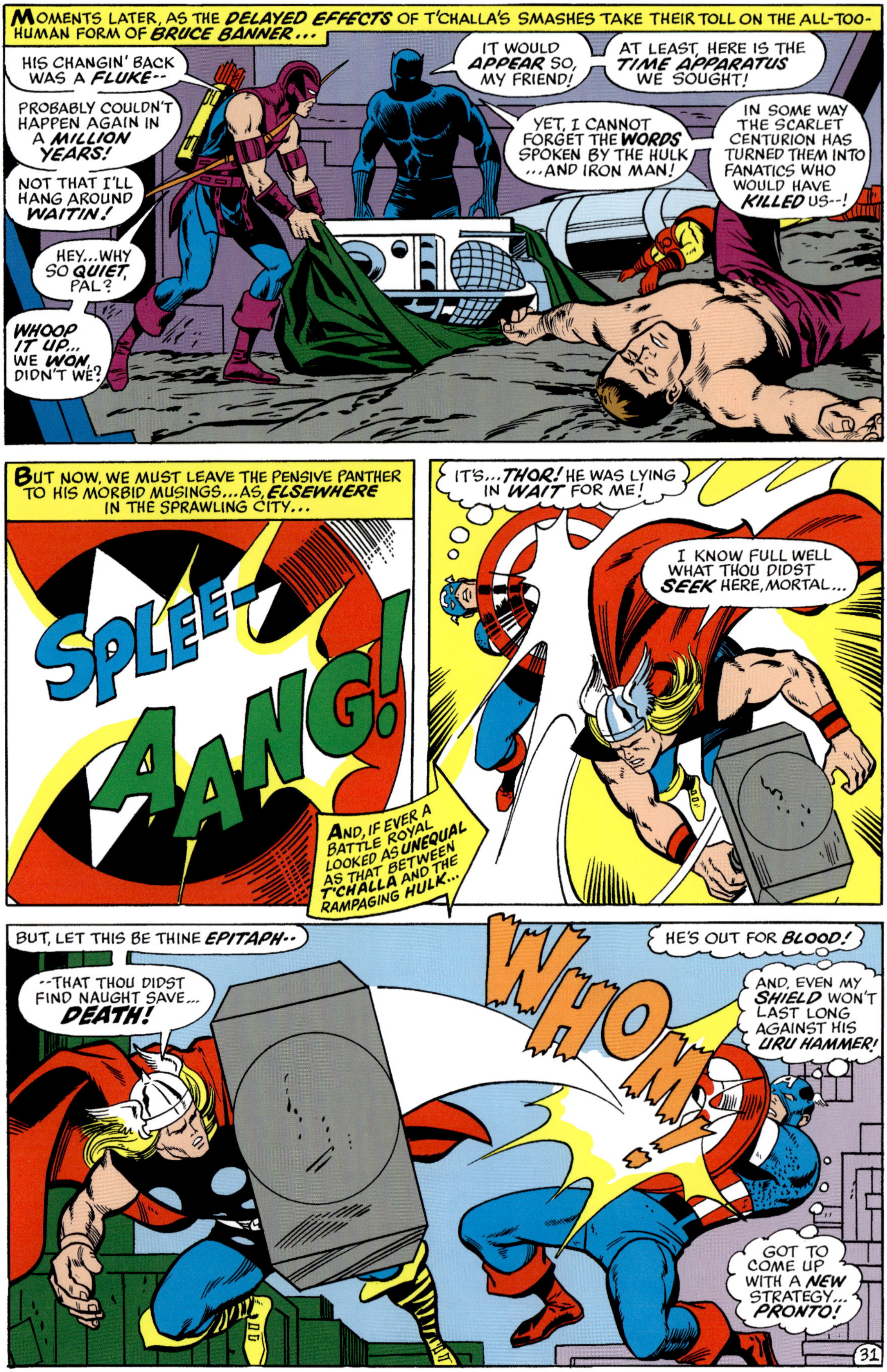
MOMENTS LATER, AS THE DELAYED EFFECTS OF T'CHALLA'S SMASHES TAKE THEIR TOLL ON THE ALL-TOO-HUMAN FORM OF BRUCE BANNER...
HIS CHANGIN' BACK WAS A FLUKE--
PROBABLY COULDN'T HAPPEN AGAIN IN A MILLION YEARS!
NOT THAT I'LL HANG AROUND WAITIN!
HEY...WHY SO QUIET, PAL?
WHOOP IT UP... WE WON, DIDN'T WE?
IT WOULD APPEAR SO, MY FRIEND!
AT LEAST, HERE IS THE TIME APPARATUS WE SOUGHT!
YET, I CANNOT FORGET THE WORDS SPOKEN BY THE HULK ...AND IRON MAN!
IN SOME WAY THE SCARLET CENTURION HAS TURNED THEM INTO FANATICS WHO WOULD HAVE KILLED US--!
BUT NOW, WE MUST LEAVE THE PENSIVE PANTHER TO HIS MORBID MUSINGS...AS, ELSEWHERE IN THE SPRAWLING CITY...
SPLEE-AANG!
AND, IF EVER A BATTLE ROYAL LOOKED AS UNEQUAL AS THAT BETWEEN T'CHALLA AND THE RAMPAGING HULK...
IT'S...THOR! HE WAS LYING IN WAIT FOR ME!
I KNOW FULL WELL WHAT THOU DIDST SEEK HERE, MORTAL...
BUT, LET THIS BE THINE EPITAPH--
--THAT THOU DIDST FIND NAUGHT SAVE... DEATH!
WHOOM!
HE'S OUT FOR BLOOD!
AND, EVEN MY SHIELD WON'T LAST LONG AGAINST HIS URU HAMMER!
GOT TO COME UP WITH A NEW STRATEGY... PRONTO!
31

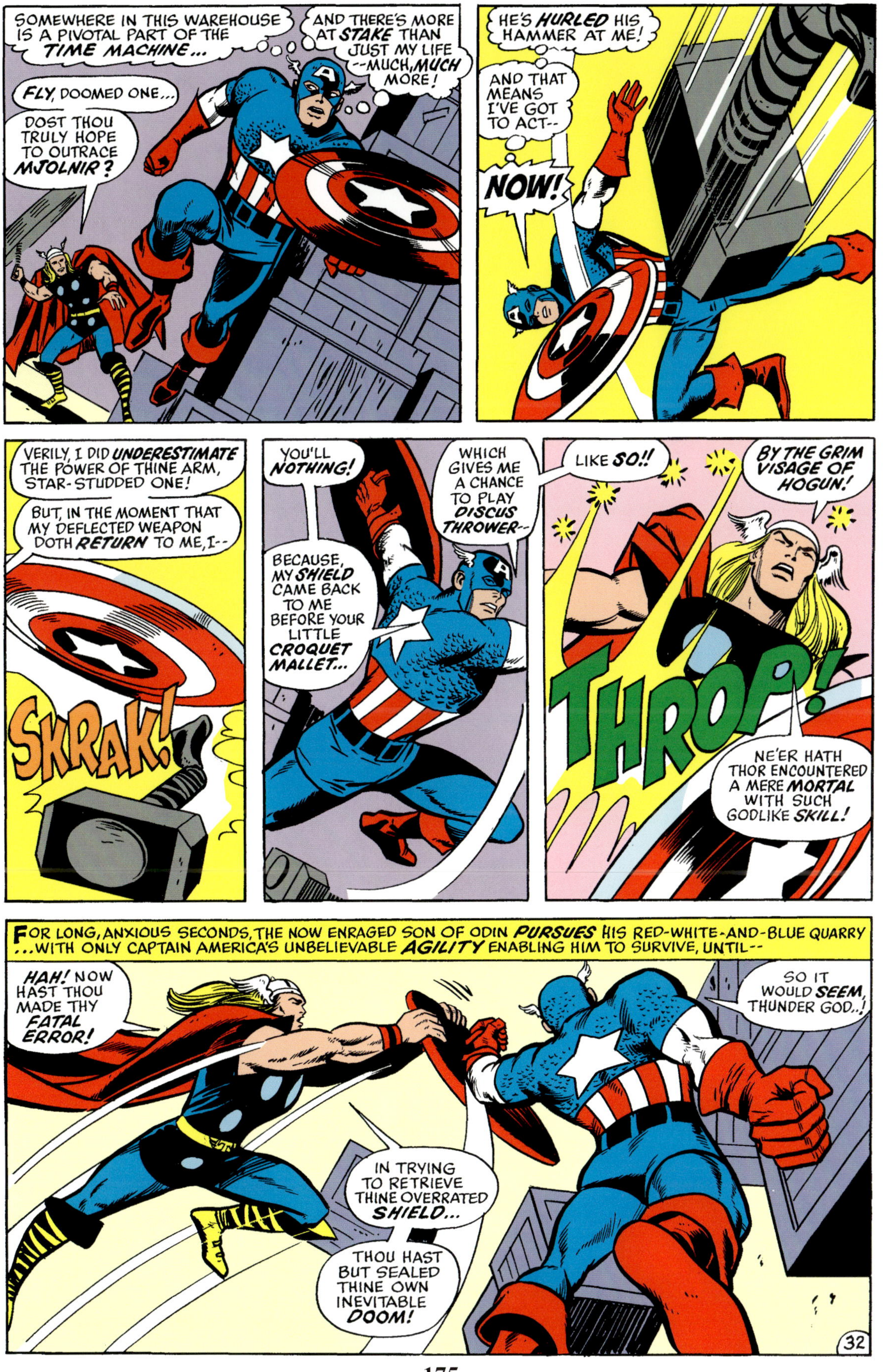

SOMEWHERE IN THIS WAREHOUSE IS A PIVOTAL PART OF THE TIME MACHINE...
AND THERE'S MORE AT STAKE THAN JUST MY LIFE --MUCH, MUCH MORE!
FLY, DOOMED ONE...
DOST THOU TRULY HOPE TO OUTRACE MJOLNIR?
HE'S HURLED HIS HAMMER AT ME!
AND THAT MEANS I'VE GOT TO ACT--
NOW!
VERILY, I DID UNDERESTIMATE THE POWER OF THINE ARM, STAR-STUDDED ONE!
BUT, IN THE MOMENT THAT MY DEFLECTED WEAPON DOTH RETURN TO ME, I--
SKRAK!
YOU'LL NOTHING!
BECAUSE, MY SHIELD CAME BACK TO ME BEFORE YOUR LITTLE CROQUET MALLET...
WHICH GIVES ME A CHANCE TO PLAY DISCUS THROWER--
LIKE SO!!
BY THE GRIM VISAGE OF HOGUN!
THROP!
NE'ER HATH THOR ENCOUNTERED A MERE MORTAL WITH SUCH GODLIKE SKILL!
FOR LONG, ANXIOUS SECONDS, THE NOW ENRAGED SON OF ODIN PURSUES HIS RED-WHITE-AND-BLUE QUARRY ...WITH ONLY CAPTAIN AMERICA'S UNBELIEVABLE AGILITY ENABLING HIM TO SURVIVE, UNTIL--
HAH! NOW HAST THOU MADE THY FATAL ERROR!
SO IT WOULD SEEM, THUNDER GOD..!
IN TRYING TO RETRIEVE THINE OVERRATED SHIELD...
THOU HAST BUT SEALED THINE OWN INEVITABLE DOOM!
32

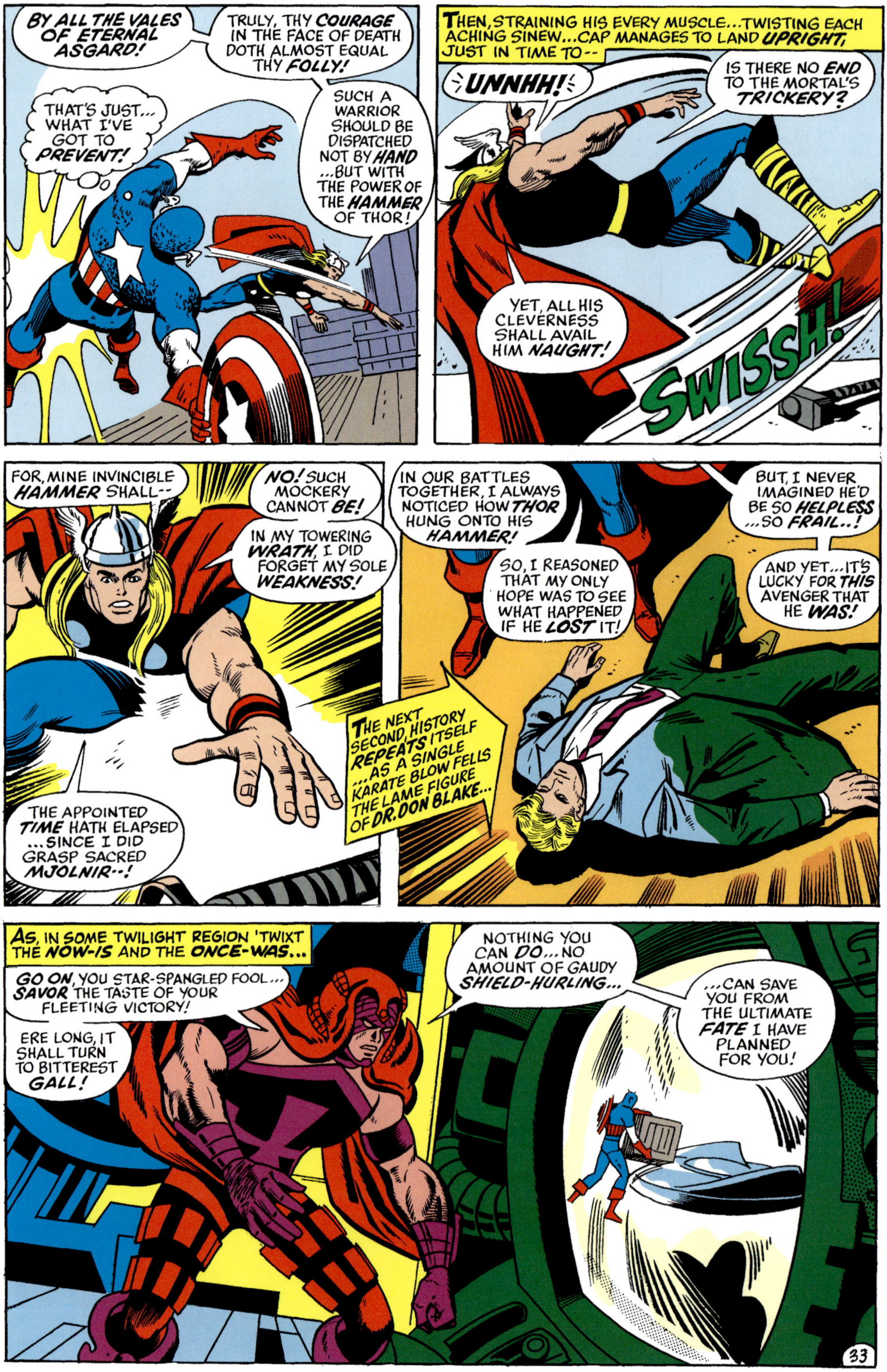

BY ALL THE VALES OF ETERNAL ASGARD!
TRULY, THY COURAGE IN THE FACE OF DEATH DOTH ALMOST EQUAL THY FOLLY!
THAT'S JUST... WHAT I'VE GOT TO PREVENT!
SUCH A WARRIOR SHOULD BE DISPATCHED NOT BY HAND ...BUT WITH THE POWER OF THE HAMMER OF THOR!
THEN, STRAINING HIS EVERY MUSCLE...TWISTING EACH ACHING SINEW...CAP MANAGES TO LAND UPRIGHT, JUST IN TIME TO--
UNNHH!
IS THERE NO END TO THE MORTAL'S TRICKERY?
YET, ALL HIS CLEVERNESS SHALL AVAIL HIM NAUGHT!
SWISSH!
FOR, MINE INVINCIBLE HAMMER SHALL--
NO! SUCH MOCKERY CANNOT BE!
IN MY TOWERING WRATH, I DID FORGET MY SOLE WEAKNESS!
THE APPOINTED TIME HATH ELAPSED ...SINCE I DID GRASP SACRED MJOLNIR--!
THE NEXT SECOND, HISTORY REPEATS ITSELF ...AS A SINGLE KARATE BLOW FELLS THE LAME FIGURE OF DR. DON BLAKE...
IN OUR BATTLES TOGETHER, I ALWAYS NOTICED HOW THOR HUNG ONTO HIS HAMMER!
SO, I REASONED THAT MY ONLY HOPE WAS TO SEE WHAT HAPPENED IF HE LOST IT!
BUT, I NEVER IMAGINED HE'D BE SO HELPLESS ...SO FRAIL..!
AND YET...IT'S LUCKY FOR THIS AVENGER THAT HE WAS!
AS, IN SOME TWILIGHT REGION 'TWIXT THE NOW-IS AND THE ONCE-WAS...
GO ON, YOU STAR-SPANGLED FOOL... SAVOR THE TASTE OF YOUR FLEETING VICTORY!
ERE LONG, IT SHALL TURN TO BITTEREST GALL!
NOTHING YOU CAN DO...NO AMOUNT OF GAUDY SHIELD-HURLING...
...CAN SAVE YOU FROM THE ULTIMATE FATE I HAVE PLANNED FOR YOU!
33

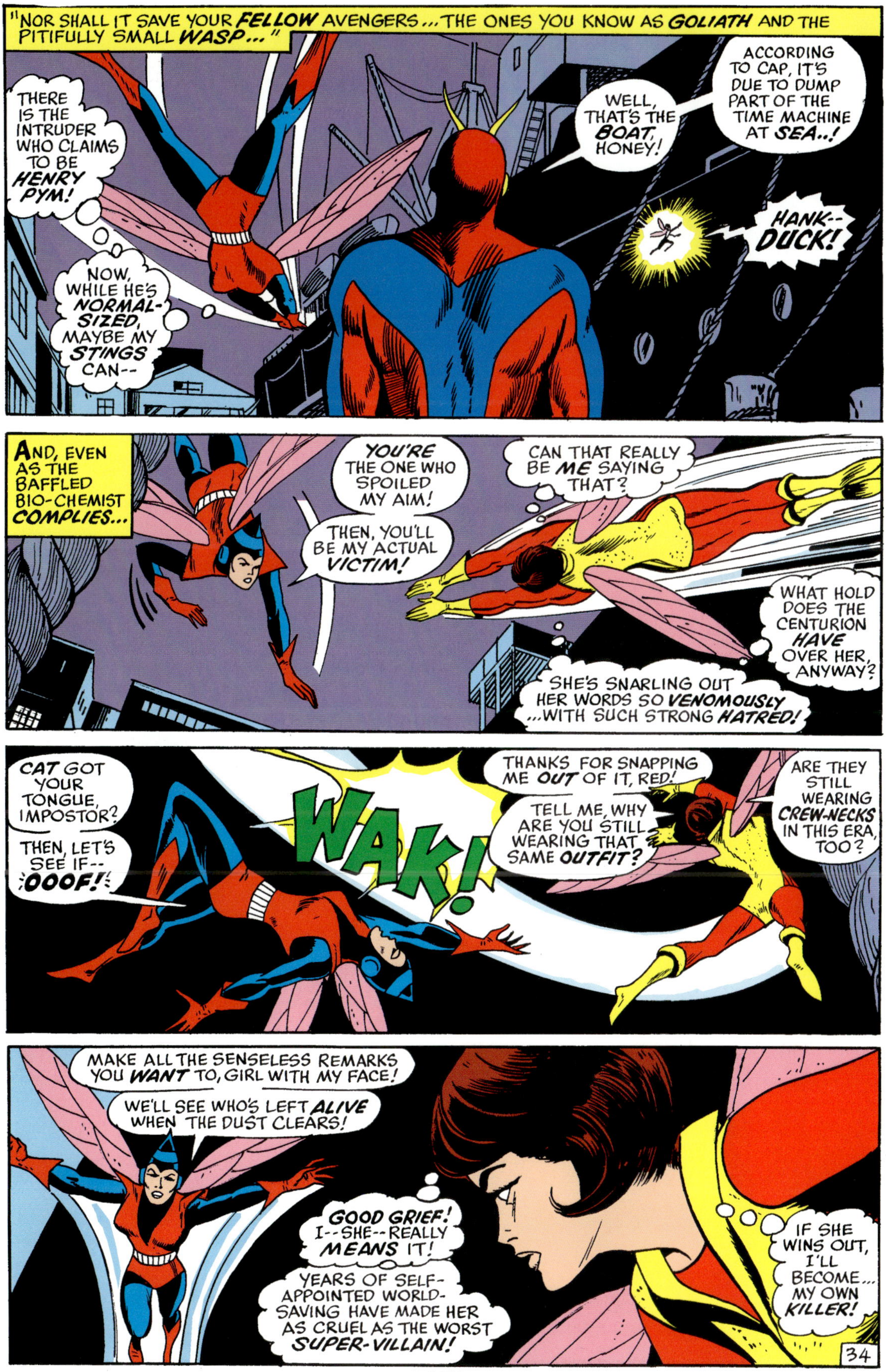
"NOR SHALL IT SAVE YOUR FELLOW AVENGERS ... THE ONES YOU KNOW AS GOLIATH AND THE PITIFULLY SMALL WASP..."
THERE IS THE INTRUDER WHO CLAIMS TO BE HENRY PYM!
NOW, WHILE HE'S NORMAL-SIZED, MAYBE MY STINGS CAN--
WELL, THAT'S THE BOAT, HONEY!
ACCORDING TO CAP, IT'S DUE TO DUMP PART OF THE TIME MACHINE AT SEA..!
HANK--DUCK!
AND, EVEN AS THE BAFFLED BIO-CHEMIST COMPLIES...
YOU'RE THE ONE WHO SPOILED MY AIM!
THEN, YOU'LL BE MY ACTUAL VICTIM!
CAN THAT REALLY BE ME SAYING THAT?
WHAT HOLD DOES THE CENTURION HAVE OVER HER, ANYWAY?
SHE'S SNARLING OUT HER WORDS SO VENOMOUSLY ...WITH SUCH STRONG HATRED!
CAT GOT YOUR TONGUE, IMPOSTOR?
THEN, LET'S SEE IF--
OOOF!
WAK!
THANKS FOR SNAPPING ME OUT OF IT, RED!
TELL ME, WHY ARE YOU STILL WEARING THAT SAME OUTFIT?
ARE THEY STILL WEARING CREW-NECKS IN THIS ERA, TOO?
MAKE ALL THE SENSELESS REMARKS YOU WANT TO, GIRL WITH MY FACE!
WE'LL SEE WHO'S LEFT ALIVE WHEN THE DUST CLEARS!
GOOD GRIEF! I--SHE--REALLY MEANS IT!
YEARS OF SELF-APPOINTED WORLD-SAVING HAVE MADE HER AS CRUEL AS THE WORST SUPER-VILLAIN!
IF SHE WINS OUT, I'LL BECOME... MY OWN KILLER!
34

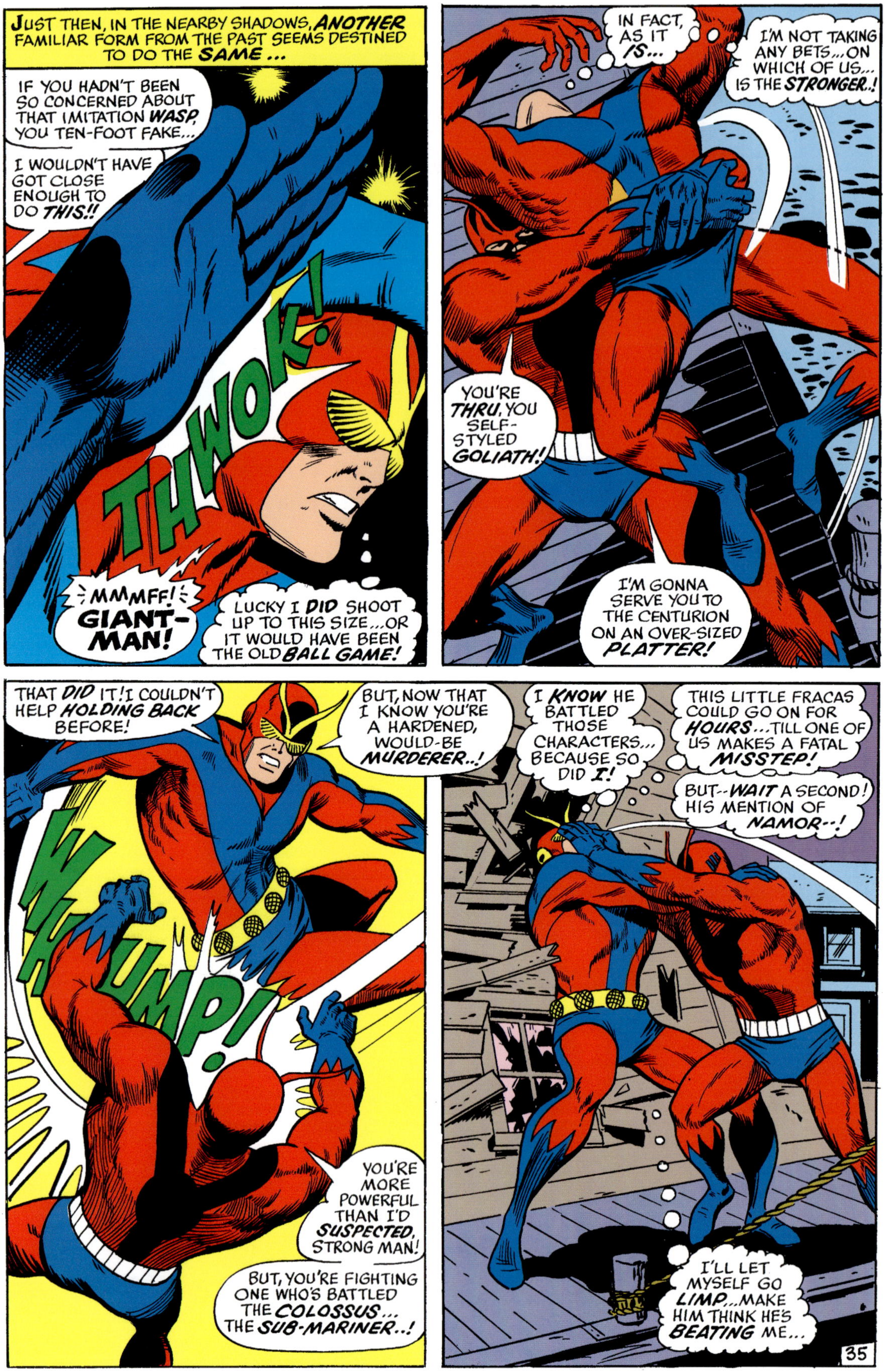
JUST THEN, IN THE NEARBY SHADOWS, ANOTHER FAMILIAR FORM FROM THE PAST SEEMS DESTINED TO DO THE SAME...
IF YOU HADN'T BEEN SO CONCERNED ABOUT THAT IMITATION WASP, YOU TEN-FOOT FAKE...
I WOULDN'T HAVE GOT CLOSE ENOUGH TO DO THIS!!
THWOK!
MMMFF! GIANT-MAN!
LUCKY I DID SHOOT UP TO THIS SIZE...OR IT WOULD HAVE BEEN THE OLD BALL GAME!
IN FACT, AS IT IS...
I'M NOT TAKING ANY BETS...ON WHICH OF US... IS THE STRONGER..!
YOU'RE THRU, YOU SELF-STYLED GOLIATH!
I'M GONNA SERVE YOU TO THE CENTURION ON AN OVER-SIZED PLATTER!
THAT DID IT! I COULDN'T HELP HOLDING BACK BEFORE!
BUT, NOW THAT I KNOW YOU'RE A HARDENED, WOULD-BE MURDERER..!
WHUMP!
YOU'RE MORE POWERFUL THAN I'D SUSPECTED, STRONG MAN!
BUT, YOU'RE FIGHTING ONE WHO'S BATTLED THE COLOSSUS... THE SUB-MARINER..!
I KNOW HE BATTLED THOSE CHARACTERS... BECAUSE SO DID I!
THIS LITTLE FRACAS COULD GO ON FOR HOURS... TILL ONE OF US MAKES A FATAL MISSTEP!
BUT--WAIT A SECOND! HIS MENTION OF NAMOR--!
I'LL LET MYSELF GO LIMP... MAKE HIM THINK HE'S BEATING ME...
35

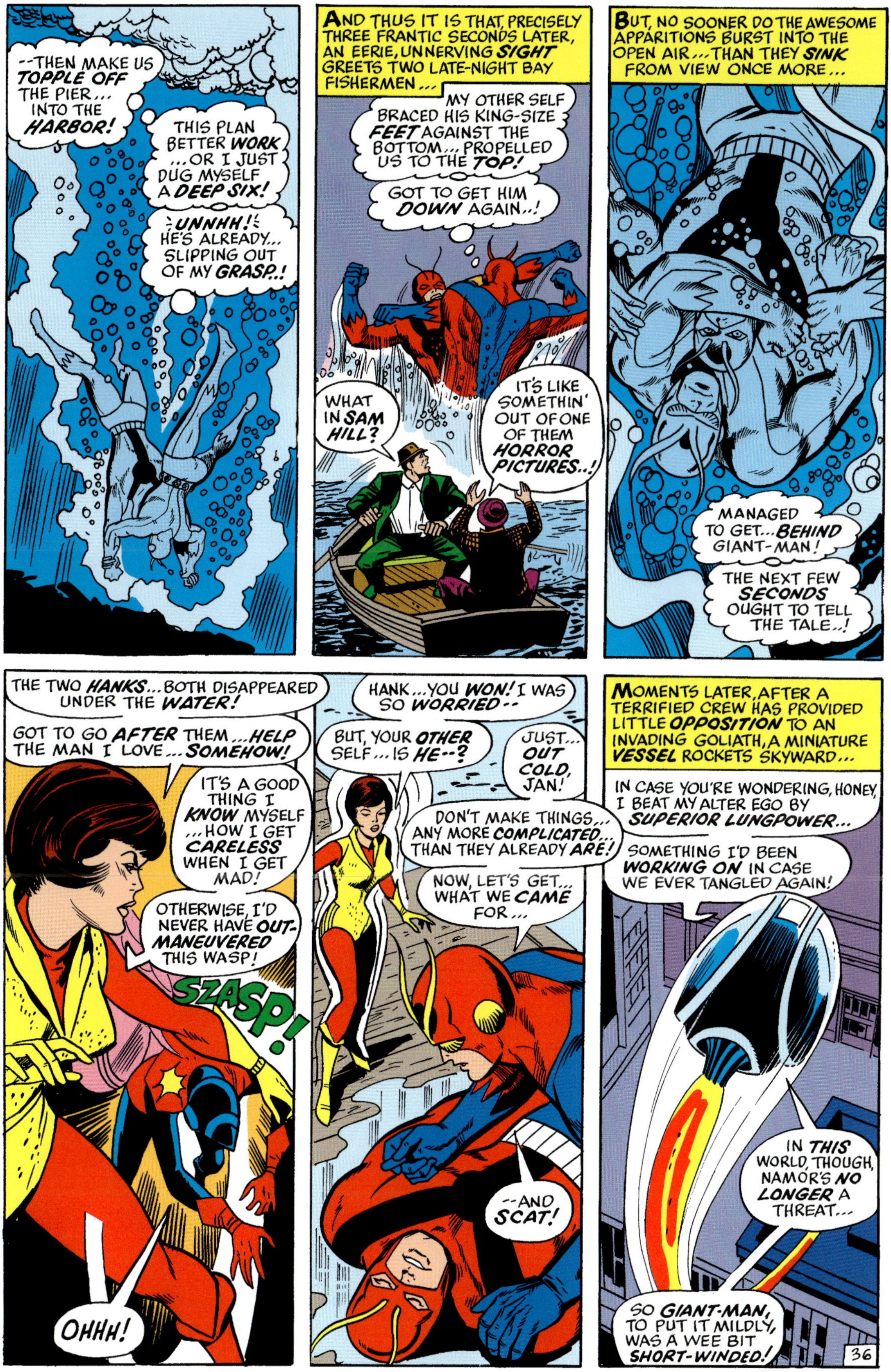
--THEN MAKE US TOPPLE OFF THE PIER... INTO THE HARBOR!
THIS PLAN BETTER WORK ...OR I JUST DUG MYSELF A DEEP SIX!
UNNHH! HE'S ALREADY... SLIPPING OUT OF MY GRASP..!
AND THUS IT IS THAT, PRECISELY THREE FRANTIC SECONDS LATER, AN EERIE, UNNERVING SIGHT GREETS TWO LATE-NIGHT BAY FISHERMEN...
MY OTHER SELF BRACED HIS KING-SIZE FEET AGAINST THE BOTTOM... PROPELLED US TO THE TOP!
GOT TO GET HIM DOWN AGAIN..!
WHAT IN SAM HILL?
IT'S LIKE SOMETHIN' OUT OF ONE OF THEM HORROR PICTURES..!
BUT, NO SOONER DO THE AWESOME APPARITIONS BURST INTO THE OPEN AIR... THAN THEY SINK FROM VIEW ONCE MORE...
MANAGED TO GET... BEHIND GIANT-MAN!
THE NEXT FEW SECONDS OUGHT TO TELL THE TALE..!
THE TWO HANKS... BOTH DISAPPEARED UNDER THE WATER!
GOT TO GO AFTER THEM... HELP THE MAN I LOVE... SOMEHOW!
IT'S A GOOD THING I KNOW MYSELF ...HOW I GET CARELESS WHEN I GET MAD!
OTHERWISE, I'D NEVER HAVE OUT-MANEUVERED THIS WASP!
SZASP!
OHHH!
HANK... YOU WON! I WAS SO WORRIED--
BUT, YOUR OTHER SELF... IS HE--?
JUST... OUT COLD, JAN!
DON'T MAKE THINGS... ANY MORE COMPLICATED... THAN THEY ALREADY ARE!
NOW, LET'S GET... WHAT WE CAME FOR...
--AND SCAT!
MOMENTS LATER, AFTER A TERRIFIED CREW HAS PROVIDED LITTLE OPPOSITION TO AN INVADING GOLIATH, A MINIATURE VESSEL ROCKETS SKYWARD...
IN CASE YOU'RE WONDERING, HONEY, I BEAT MY ALTER EGO BY SUPERIOR LUNGPOWER...
SOMETHING I'D BEEN WORKING ON IN CASE WE EVER TANGLED AGAIN!
IN THIS WORLD, THOUGH, NAMOR'S NO LONGER A THREAT...
SO GIANT-MAN, TO PUT IT MILDLY, WAS A WEE BIT SHORT-WINDED!
36

A SHORT TIME LATER, IN A FORSAKEN SPOT SOMEWHERE IN THE HINTERLANDS...
PERSONALLY, JAN, I'M SURPRISED THAT THE CENTURION...OR THE AVENGERS...DIDN'T HAVE DOOM'S CASTLE DEMOLISHED!
I STILL CAN'T ESCAPE THE FEELING THAT ONE PIECE OF OUR LITTLE PUZZLE IS STILL MISSING...
AND THAT'S ASSUMING THAT CAP AND THE REST GOT WHAT THEY WENT AFTER!

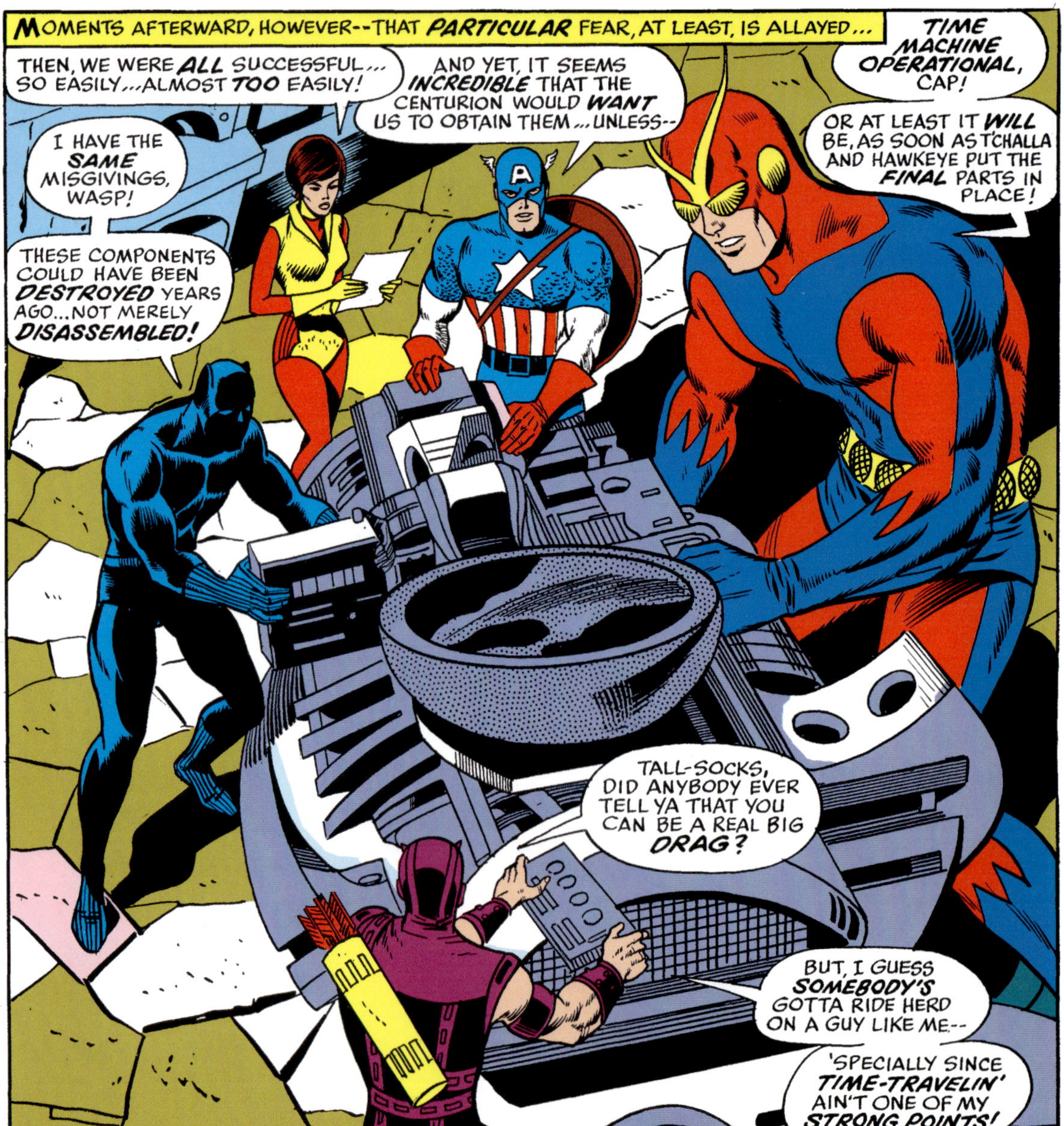
MOMENTS AFTERWARD, HOWEVER--THAT PARTICULAR FEAR, AT LEAST, IS ALLAYED...
THEN, WE WERE ALL SUCCESSFUL... SO EASILY...ALMOST TOO EASILY!
AND YET, IT SEEMS INCREDIBLE THAT THE CENTURION WOULD WANT US TO OBTAIN THEM...UNLESS--
TIME MACHINE OPERATIONAL, CAP!
OR AT LEAST IT WILL BE, AS SOON AS T'CHALLA AND HAWKEYE PUT THE FINAL PARTS IN PLACE!
I HAVE THE SAME MISGIVINGS, WASP!
THESE COMPONENTS COULD HAVE BEEN DESTROYED YEARS AGO...NOT MERELY DISASSEMBLED!
TALL-SOCKS, DID ANYBODY EVER TELL YA THAT YOU CAN BE A REAL BIG DRAG?
BUT, I GUESS SOMEBODY'S GOTTA RIDE HERD ON A GUY LIKE ME--
'SPECIALLY SINCE TIME-TRAVELIN' AIN'T ONE OF MY STRONG POINTS!
37

NOW WE'RE SET!
GREAT! ARE OUR CONFUSED COUNTERPARTS STILL COMFY, JAN?
YOU KNOW IT, LEADER-MAN!
ALTHOUGH I STILL DON'T SEE WHY YOU WANTED ANY CAPTURED AVENGERS BROUGHT BACK HERE!
LOOK AT IT THIS WAY, JAN... AT LEAST WE CAN KEEP AN EYE ON THEM!
ALL RIGHT, HANK... LET 'ER RIP!
THEN, AS THE LONG-UNUSED DEVICE BEGINS TO HUM WITH PULSATING RHYTHM...
WAIT! WE'RE NOT ALONE HERE... I CAN SENSE IT!
HE'S RIGHT! I CAN ALMOST FEEL OTHER EYES ON US!
BUT, WHO--?
MMMMMMMMMMMMMMMMMN
WHO ELSE, MY DEAR WASP, BUT I--YOUR FRIEND AND FORMER BENEFACTOR--THE SCARLET CENTURION!?
THAT VOICE... SO MERCILESS... SO UNSPEAKABLY EVIL..!
BY YOUR ARCHAIC STANDARDS, I SUPPOSE THAT MERCILESSNESS WOULD BE EQUATED WITH EVIL!
BUT, AS YOU KNOW, MY TIME IS NOT YOUR TIME...
AND YOUR STANDARDS HOLD NO MEANING FOR ONE SUCH AS I!
OHHH--!
THOSE LIGHTS--HIS VOICE--
SOMETHIN' ABOUT 'EM--GETTIN' TO ME--!
38

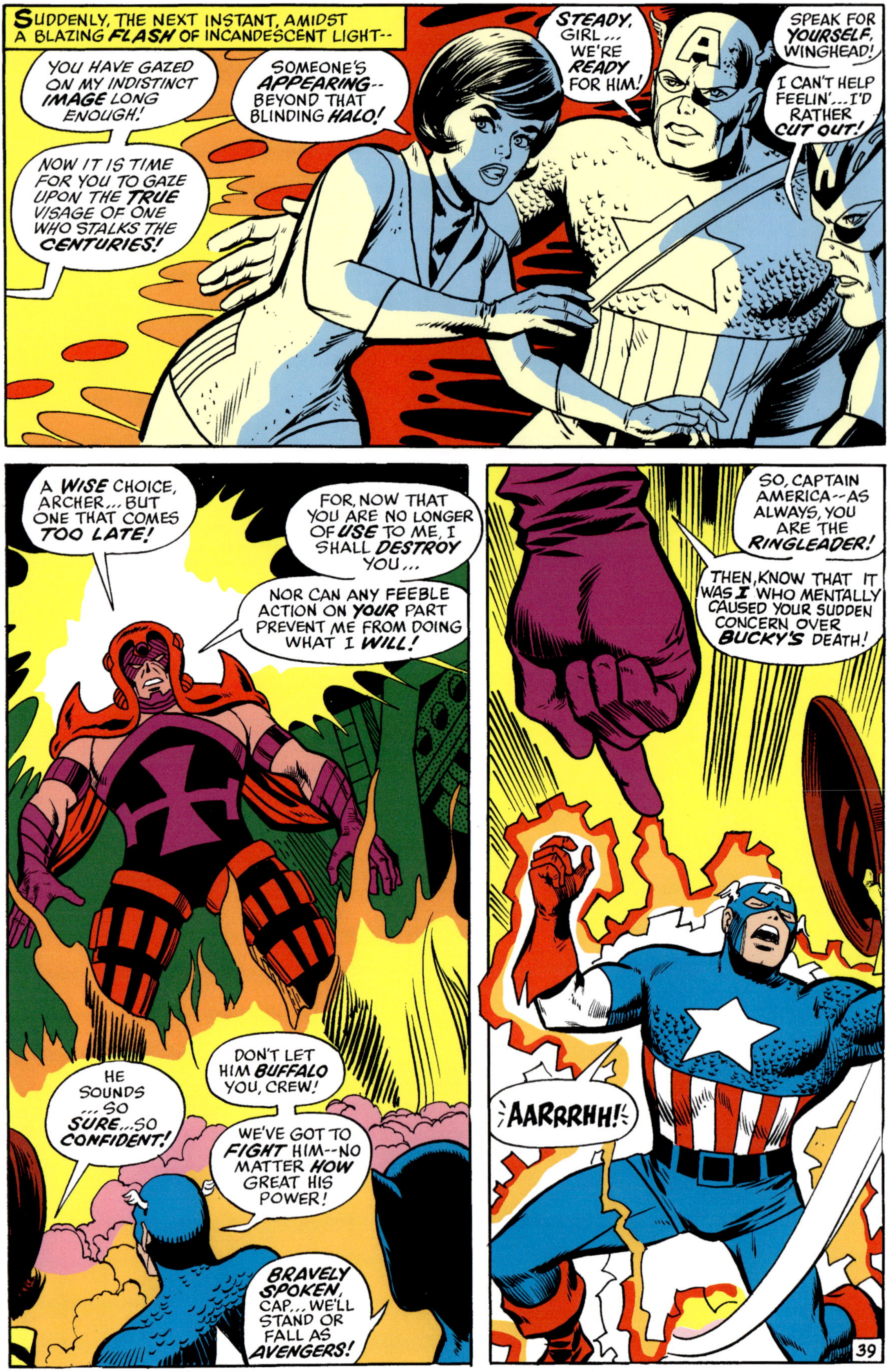
SUDDENLY, THE NEXT INSTANT, AMIDST A BLAZING FLASH OF INCANDESCENT LIGHT--
YOU HAVE GAZED ON MY INDISTINCT IMAGE LONG ENOUGH!
NOW IT IS TIME FOR YOU TO GAZE UPON THE TRUE VISAGE OF ONE WHO STALKS THE CENTURIES!
SOMEONE'S APPEARING-- BEYOND THAT BLINDING HALO!
STEADY, GIRL... WE'RE READY FOR HIM!
SPEAK FOR YOURSELF, WINGHEAD!
I CAN'T HELP FEELIN'...I'D RATHER CUT OUT!
A WISE CHOICE, ARCHER... BUT ONE THAT COMES TOO LATE!
FOR, NOW THAT YOU ARE NO LONGER OF USE TO ME, I SHALL DESTROY YOU...
NOR CAN ANY FEEBLE ACTION ON YOUR PART PREVENT ME FROM DOING WHAT I WILL!
HE SOUNDS ...SO SURE...SO CONFIDENT!
DON'T LET HIM BUFFALO YOU, CREW!
WE'VE GOT TO FIGHT HIM--NO MATTER HOW GREAT HIS POWER!
BRAVELY SPOKEN, CAP... WE'LL STAND OR FALL AS AVENGERS!
SO, CAPTAIN AMERICA--AS ALWAYS, YOU ARE THE RINGLEADER!
THEN, KNOW THAT IT WAS I WHO MENTALLY CAUSED YOUR SUDDEN CONCERN OVER BUCKY'S DEATH!
AARRRHH!
39

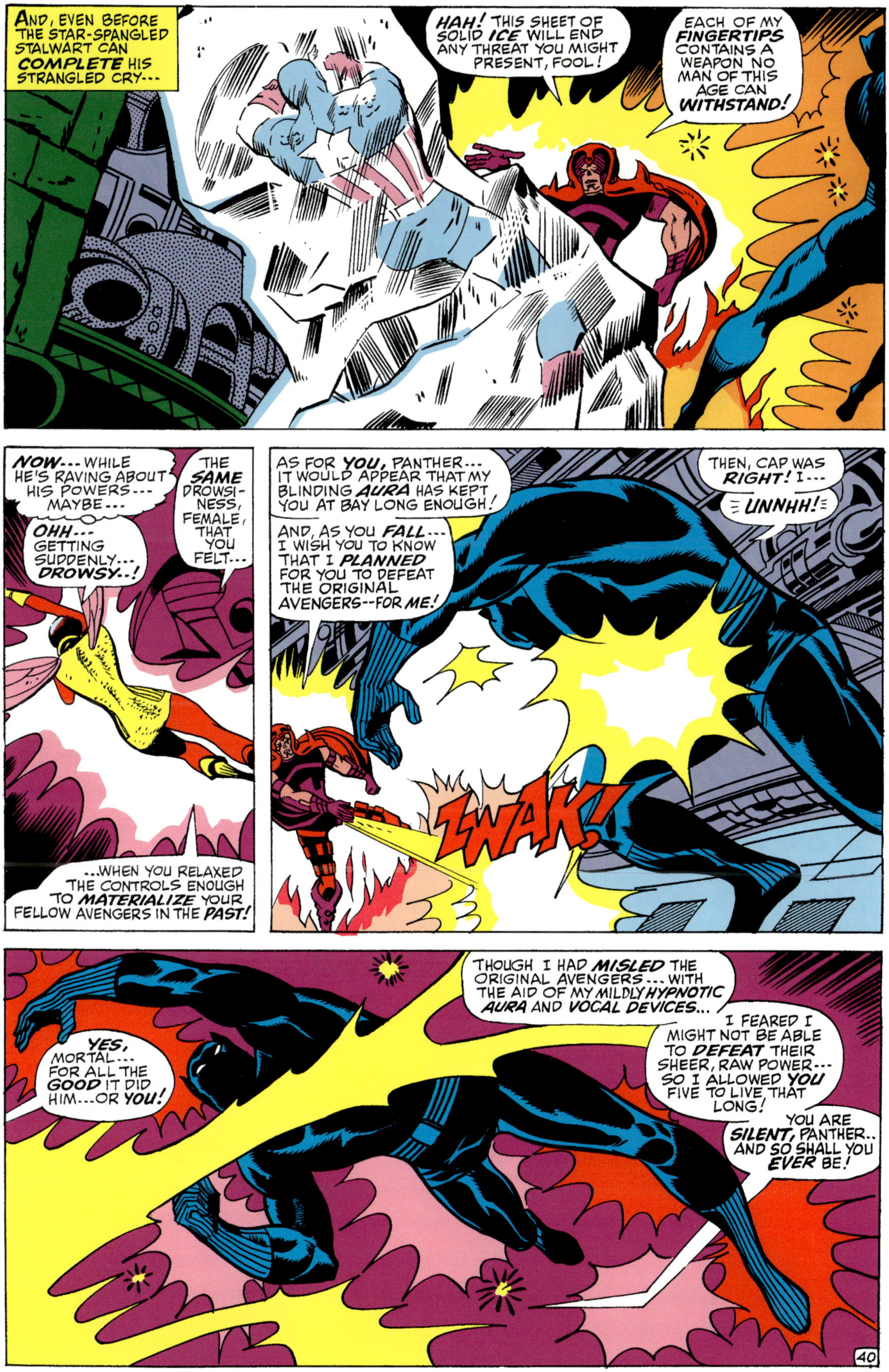

AND, EVEN BEFORE THE STAR-SPANGLED STALWART CAN COMPLETE HIS STRANGLED CRY---
HAH! THIS SHEET OF SOLID ICE WILL END ANY THREAT YOU MIGHT PRESENT, FOOL!
EACH OF MY FINGERTIPS CONTAINS A WEAPON NO MAN OF THIS AGE CAN WITHSTAND!
NOW--- WHILE HE'S RAVING ABOUT HIS POWERS--- MAYBE---
OHH--- GETTING SUDDENLY--- DROWSY--!
THE SAME DROWSINESS, FEMALE, THAT YOU FELT---
--WHEN YOU RELAXED THE CONTROLS ENOUGH TO MATERIALIZE YOUR FELLOW AVENGERS IN THE PAST!
AS FOR YOU, PANTHER--- IT WOULD APPEAR THAT MY BLINDING AURA HAS KEPT YOU AT BAY LONG ENOUGH!
AND, AS YOU FALL--- I WISH YOU TO KNOW THAT I PLANNED FOR YOU TO DEFEAT THE ORIGINAL AVENGERS--FOR ME!
THEN, CAP WAS RIGHT! I---
UNNHH!
ZWAK!
YES, MORTAL--- FOR ALL THE GOOD IT DID HIM---OR YOU!
THOUGH I HAD MISLED THE ORIGINAL AVENGERS--- WITH THE AID OF MY MILDLY HYPNOTIC AURA AND VOCAL DEVICES...
I FEARED I MIGHT NOT BE ABLE TO DEFEAT THEIR SHEER, RAW POWER--- SO I ALLOWED YOU FIVE TO LIVE THAT LONG!
YOU ARE SILENT, PANTHER.. AND SO SHALL YOU EVER BE!
40

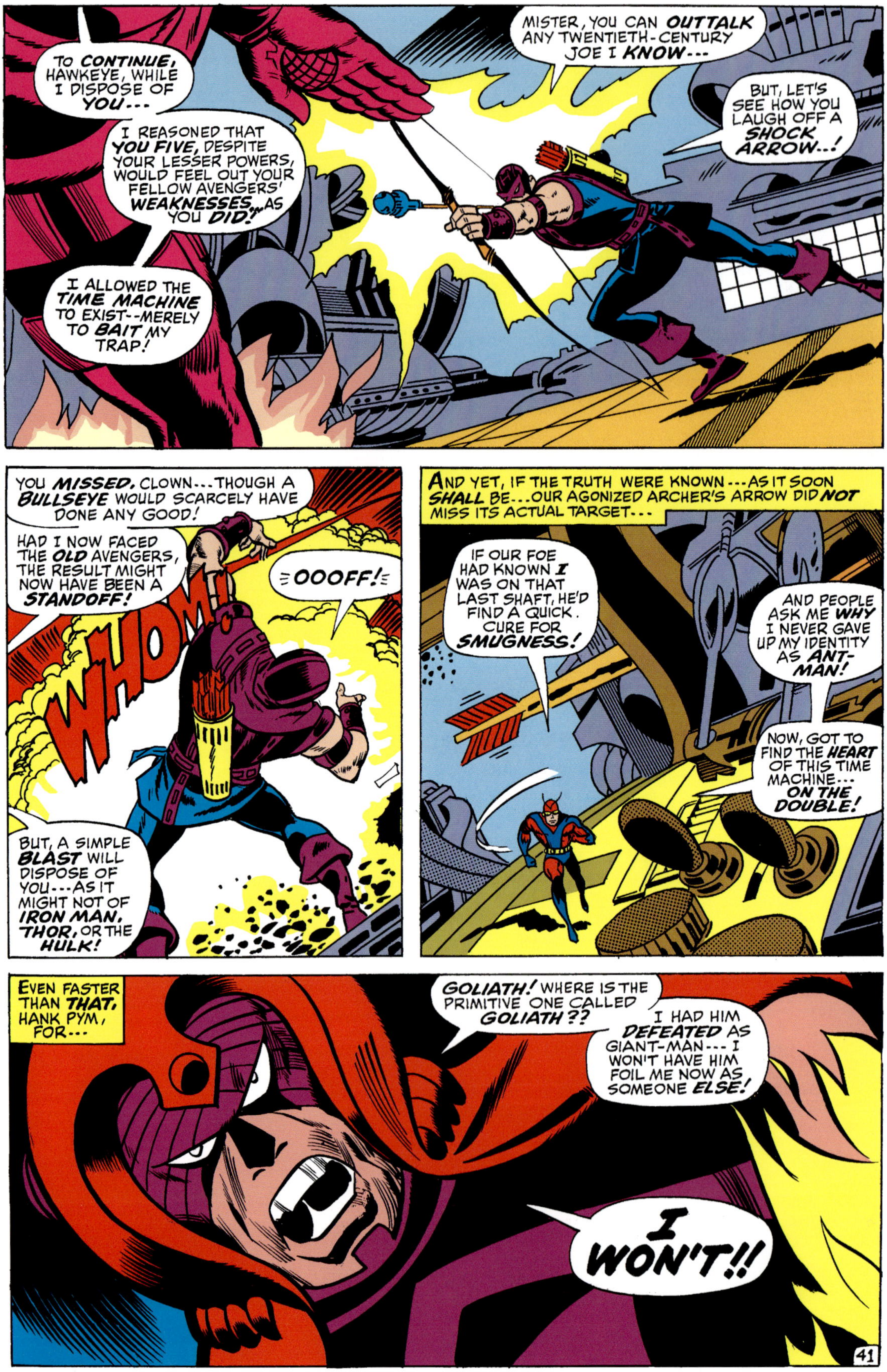
TO CONTINUE, HAWKEYE, WHILE I DISPOSE OF YOU...
I REASONED THAT YOU FIVE, DESPITE YOUR LESSER POWERS, WOULD FEEL OUT YOUR FELLOW AVENGERS' WEAKNESSES,,,AS YOU DID!
I ALLOWED THE TIME MACHINE TO EXIST--MERELY TO BAIT MY TRAP!
MISTER, YOU CAN OUTTALK ANY TWENTIETH-CENTURY JOE I KNOW...
BUT, LET'S SEE HOW YOU LAUGH OFF A SHOCK ARROW..!
YOU MISSED, CLOWN...THOUGH A BULLSEYE WOULD SCARCELY HAVE DONE ANY GOOD!
HAD I NOW FACED THE OLD AVENGERS, THE RESULT MIGHT NOW HAVE BEEN A STANDOFF!
OOOFF!
WHOM!
BUT, A SIMPLE BLAST WILL DISPOSE OF YOU...AS IT MIGHT NOT OF IRON MAN, THOR, OR THE HULK!
AND YET, IF THE TRUTH WERE KNOWN...AS IT SOON SHALL BE...OUR AGONIZED ARCHER'S ARROW DID NOT MISS ITS ACTUAL TARGET...
IF OUR FOE HAD KNOWN I WAS ON THAT LAST SHAFT, HE'D FIND A QUICK CURE FOR SMUGNESS!
AND PEOPLE ASK ME WHY I NEVER GAVE UP MY IDENTITY AS ANT-MAN!
NOW, GOT TO FIND THE HEART OF THIS TIME MACHINE... ON THE DOUBLE!
EVEN FASTER THAN THAT, HANK PYM, FOR...
GOLIATH! WHERE IS THE PRIMITIVE ONE CALLED GOLIATH??
I HAD HIM DEFEATED AS GIANT-MAN... I WON'T HAVE HIM FOIL ME NOW AS SOMEONE ELSE!
I WON'T!!
41

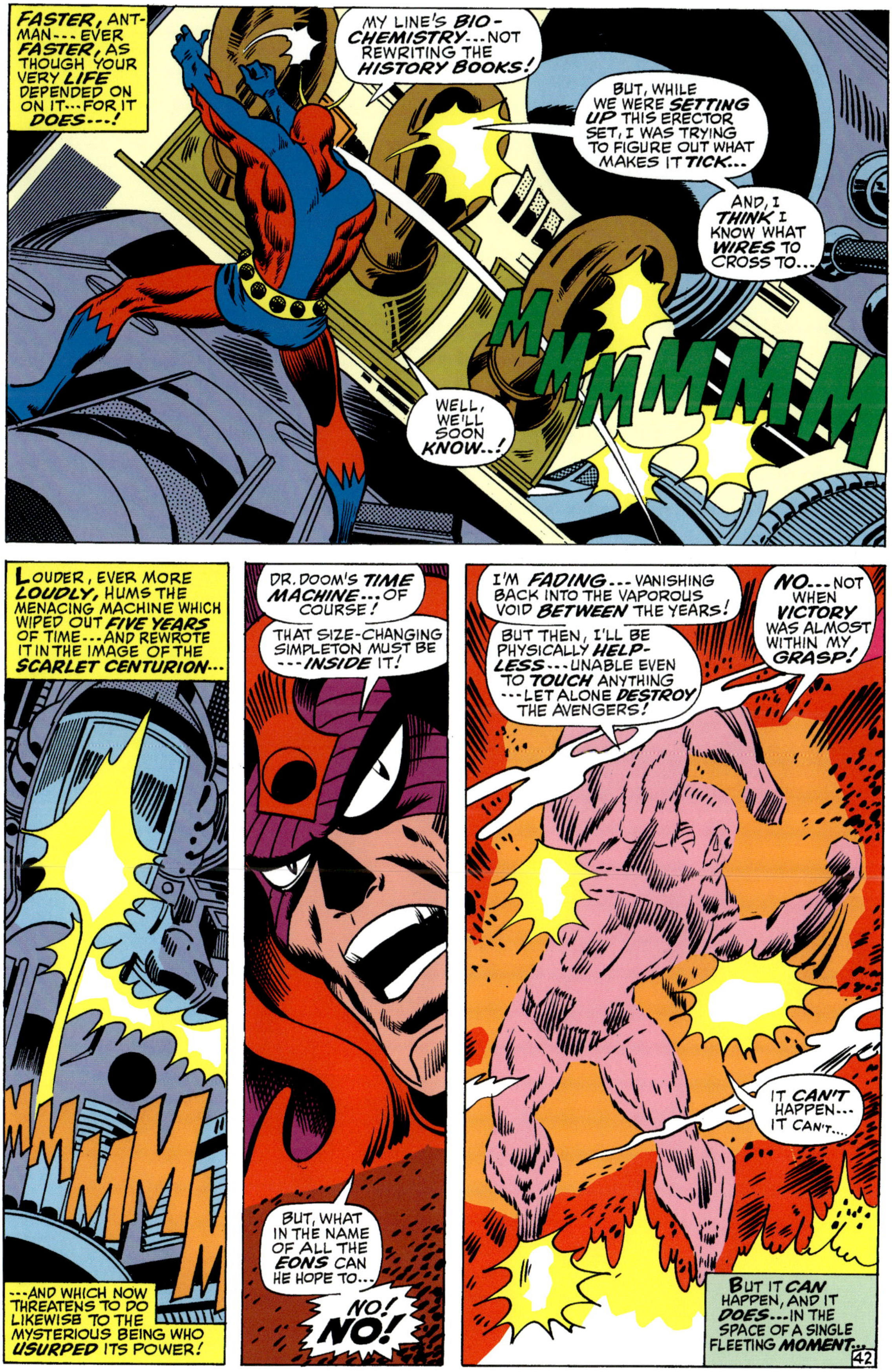

FASTER, ANT-MAN--- EVER FASTER, AS THOUGH YOUR VERY LIFE DEPENDED ON ON IT---FOR IT DOES---!
MY LINE'S BIO-CHEMISTRY---NOT REWRITING THE HISTORY BOOKS!
BUT, WHILE WE WERE SETTING UP THIS ERECTOR SET, I WAS TRYING TO FIGURE OUT WHAT MAKES IT TICK...
AND, I THINK I KNOW WHAT WIRES TO CROSS TO...
WELL, WE'LL SOON KNOW..!
MMMMMMM
LOUDER, EVER MORE LOUDLY, HUMS THE MENACING MACHINE WHICH WIPED OUT FIVE YEARS OF TIME---AND REWROTE IT IN THE IMAGE OF THE SCARLET CENTURION---
MMMMM
---AND WHICH NOW THREATENS TO DO LIKEWISE TO THE MYSTERIOUS BEING WHO USURPED ITS POWER!
DR. DOOM'S TIME MACHINE---OF COURSE!
THAT SIZE-CHANGING SIMPLETON MUST BE ---INSIDE IT!
BUT, WHAT IN THE NAME OF ALL THE EONS CAN HE HOPE TO...
NO! NO!
I'M FADING--- VANISHING BACK INTO THE VAPOROUS VOID BETWEEN THE YEARS!
BUT THEN, I'LL BE PHYSICALLY HELP-LESS---UNABLE EVEN TO TOUCH ANYTHING ---LET ALONE DESTROY THE AVENGERS!
NO---NOT WHEN VICTORY WAS ALMOST WITHIN MY GRASP!
IT CAN'T HAPPEN--- IT CAN'T...
BUT IT CAN HAPPEN, AND IT DOES---IN THE SPACE OF A SINGLE FLEETING MOMENT...
42

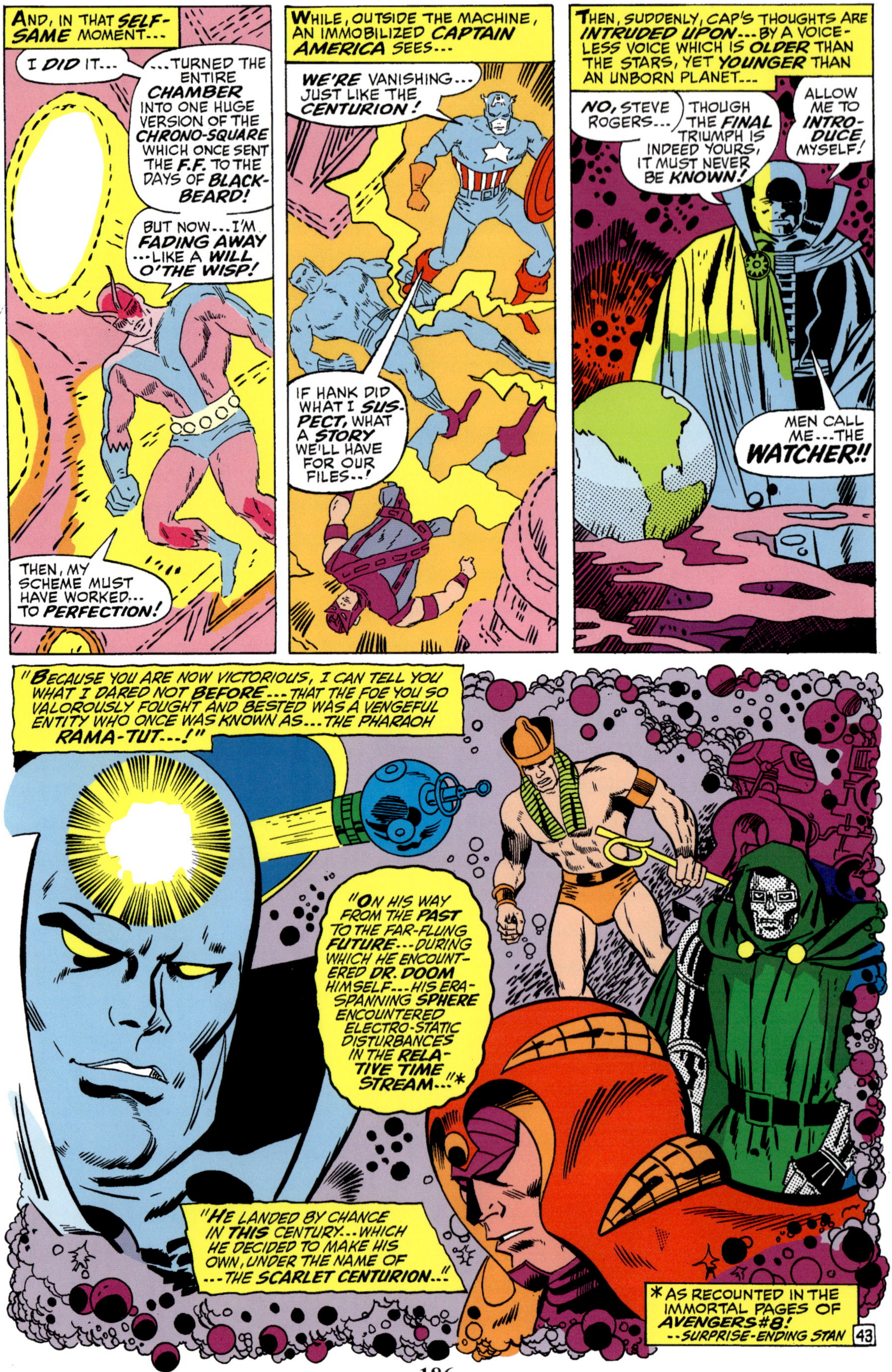

Panel 1: AND, IN THAT *SELF-SAME* MOMENT...

I *DID* IT... ...TURNED THE ENTIRE *CHAMBER* INTO ONE HUGE VERSION OF THE *CHRONO-SQUARE* WHICH ONCE SENT THE *F.F.* TO THE DAYS OF *BLACK-BEARD!*

BUT NOW...I'M *FADING AWAY* ...LIKE A *WILL O' THE WISP!*

THEN, MY *SCHEME* MUST HAVE WORKED... TO *PERFECTION!*

Panel 2: WHILE, OUTSIDE THE MACHINE, AN IMMOBILIZED *CAPTAIN AMERICA* SEES...

WE'RE *VANISHING*... JUST LIKE THE *CENTURION!*

IF HANK DID WHAT I *SUS-PECT*, WHAT A *STORY* WE'LL HAVE FOR OUR FILES--!

Panel 3: THEN, SUDDENLY, CAP'S THOUGHTS ARE *INTRUDED UPON*---BY A VOICE-LESS VOICE WHICH IS *OLDER* THAN THE STARS, YET *YOUNGER* THAN AN UNBORN PLANET...

NO, STEVE ROGERS... THOUGH THE *FINAL* TRIUMPH IS INDEED YOURS, IT MUST NEVER BE *KNOWN!*

ALLOW ME TO *INTRO-DUCE* MYSELF!

MEN CALL ME---THE *WATCHER!!*

Panel 4: "BECAUSE YOU ARE NOW *VICTORIOUS*, I CAN TELL YOU WHAT I DARED NOT *BEFORE*---THAT THE FOE YOU SO VALOROUSLY FOUGHT AND BESTED WAS A VENGEFUL ENTITY WHO ONCE WAS KNOWN AS....THE PHARAOH *RAMA-TUT*---!"

"ON HIS WAY FROM THE *PAST* TO THE FAR-FLUNG *FUTURE*---DURING WHICH HE ENCOUNT-ERED *DR. DOOM* HIMSELF---HIS ERA-SPANNING *SPHERE* ENCOUNTERED ELECTRO-STATIC DISTURBANCES IN THE *RELA-TIVE TIME STREAM*...!*"

"HE LANDED BY CHANCE IN *THIS* CENTURY---WHICH HE DECIDED TO MAKE HIS OWN, UNDER THE NAME OF ---*THE SCARLET CENTURION*..."

*AS RECOUNTED IN THE *IMMORTAL* PAGES OF *AVENGERS #8!* --SURPRISE-ENDING STAN

43

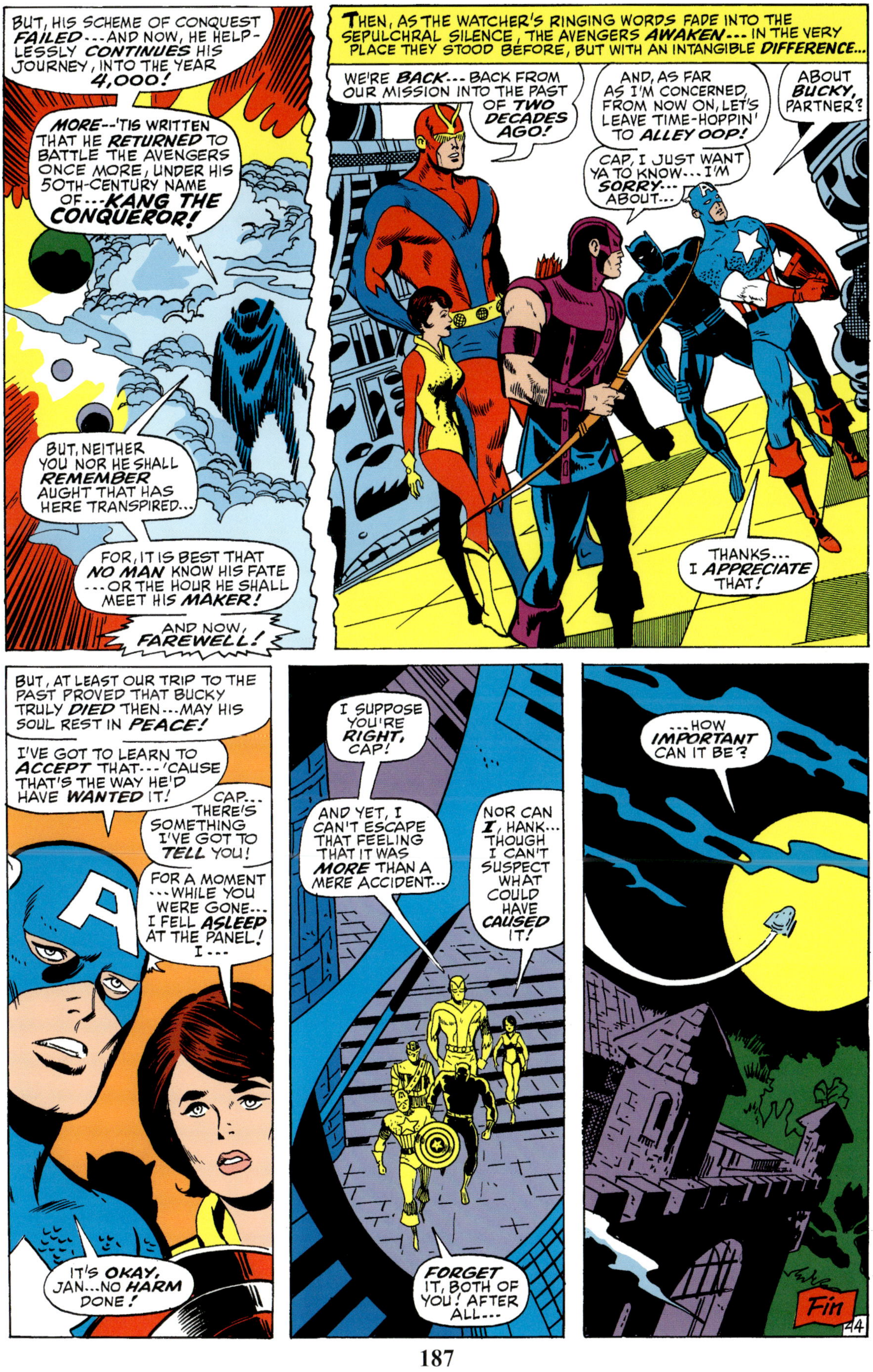

BUT, HIS SCHEME OF CONQUEST FAILED---AND NOW, HE HELPLESSLY CONTINUES HIS JOURNEY, INTO THE YEAR 4,000!
MORE--'TIS WRITTEN THAT HE RETURNED TO BATTLE THE AVENGERS ONCE MORE, UNDER HIS 50TH-CENTURY NAME OF---KANG THE CONQUEROR!
BUT, NEITHER YOU NOR HE SHALL REMEMBER AUGHT THAT HAS HERE TRANSPIRED...
FOR, IT IS BEST THAT NO MAN KNOW HIS FATE ---OR THE HOUR HE SHALL MEET HIS MAKER!
AND NOW, FAREWELL!
THEN, AS THE WATCHER'S RINGING WORDS FADE INTO THE SEPULCHRAL SILENCE, THE AVENGERS AWAKEN--- IN THE VERY PLACE THEY STOOD BEFORE, BUT WITH AN INTANGIBLE DIFFERENCE...
WE'RE BACK--- BACK FROM OUR MISSION INTO THE PAST OF TWO DECADES AGO!
AND, AS FAR AS I'M CONCERNED, FROM NOW ON, LET'S LEAVE TIME-HOPPIN' TO ALLEY OOP!
CAP, I JUST WANT YA TO KNOW--- I'M SORRY--- ABOUT---
ABOUT BUCKY, PARTNER?
THANKS... I APPRECIATE THAT!
BUT, AT LEAST OUR TRIP TO THE PAST PROVED THAT BUCKY TRULY DIED THEN---MAY HIS SOUL REST IN PEACE!
I'VE GOT TO LEARN TO ACCEPT THAT---'CAUSE THAT'S THE WAY HE'D HAVE WANTED IT!
CAP... THERE'S SOMETHING I'VE GOT TO TELL YOU!
FOR A MOMENT ---WHILE YOU WERE GONE... I FELL ASLEEP AT THE PANEL! I---
IT'S OKAY, JAN...NO HARM DONE!
I SUPPOSE YOU'RE RIGHT, CAP!
AND YET, I CAN'T ESCAPE THAT FEELING THAT IT WAS MORE THAN A MERE ACCIDENT...
NOR CAN I, HANK... THOUGH I CAN'T SUSPECT WHAT COULD HAVE CAUSED IT!
FORGET IT, BOTH OF YOU! AFTER ALL---
...HOW IMPORTANT CAN IT BE?
Fin
44

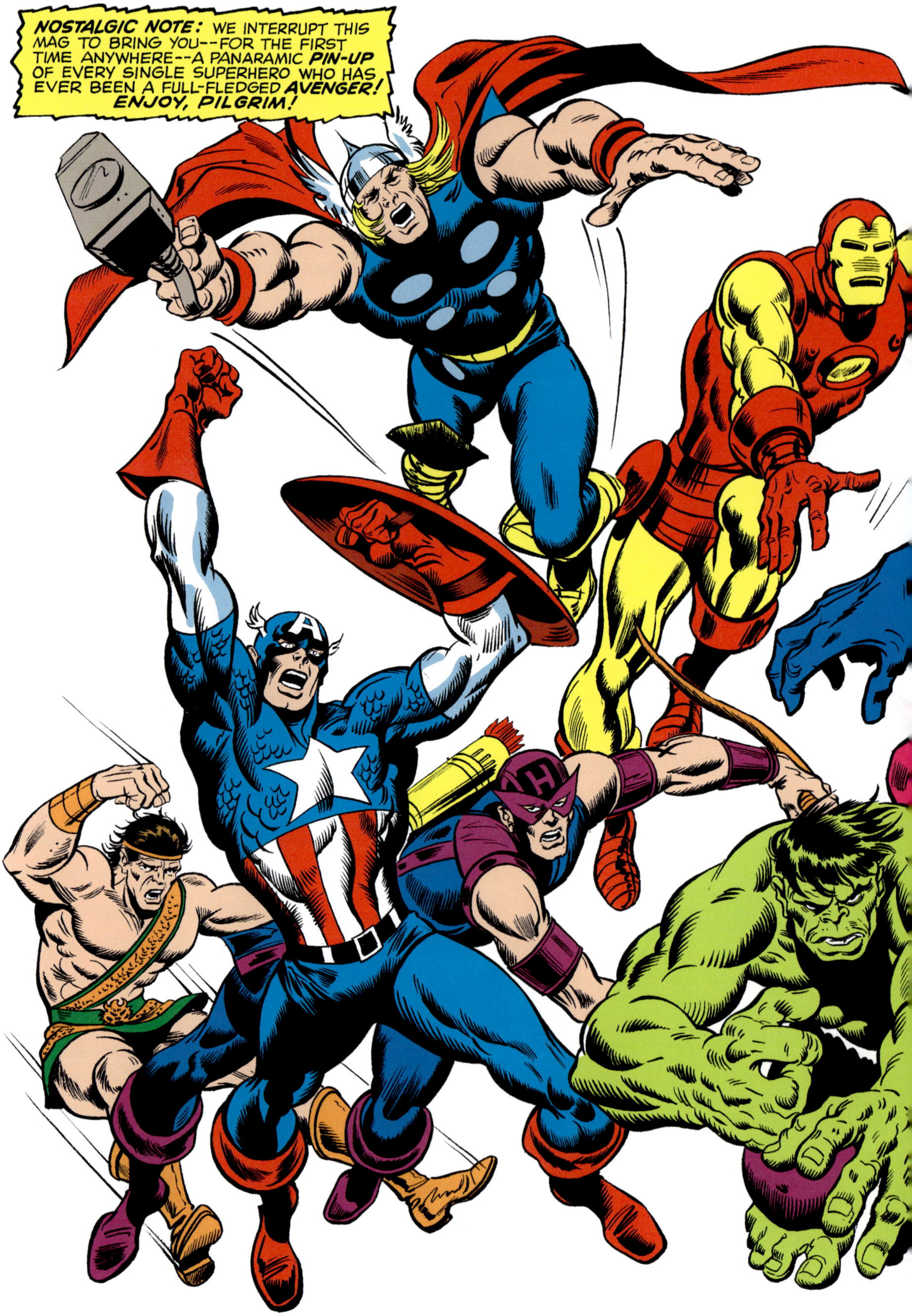
NOSTALGIC NOTE: WE INTERRUPT THIS MAG TO BRING YOU--FOR THE FIRST TIME ANYWHERE--A PANARAMIC PIN-UP OF EVERY SINGLE SUPERHERO WHO HAS EVER BEEN A FULL-FLEDGED AVENGER! ENJOY, PILGRIM!

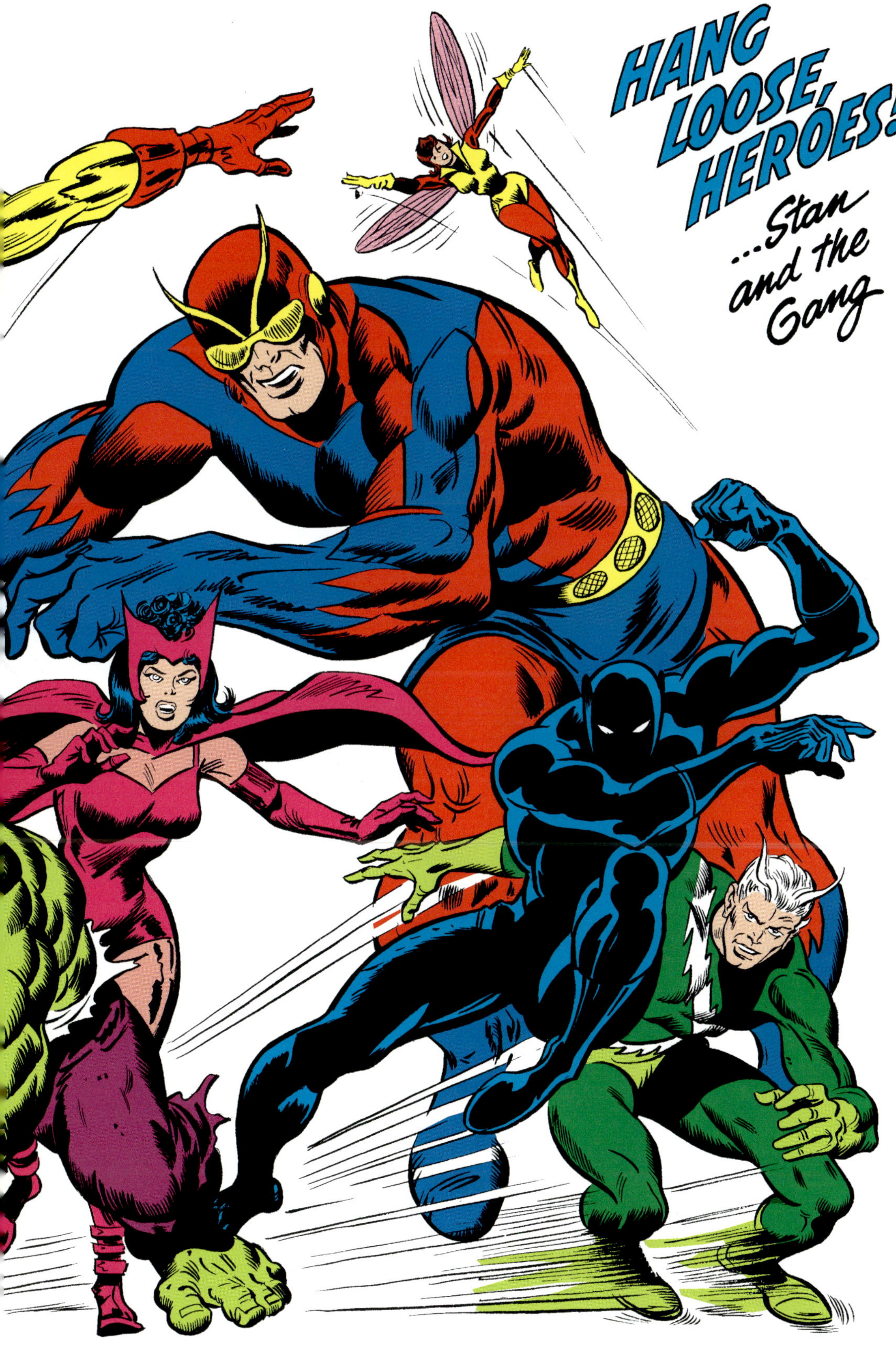
HANG LOOSE, HEROES!
...Stan and the Gang

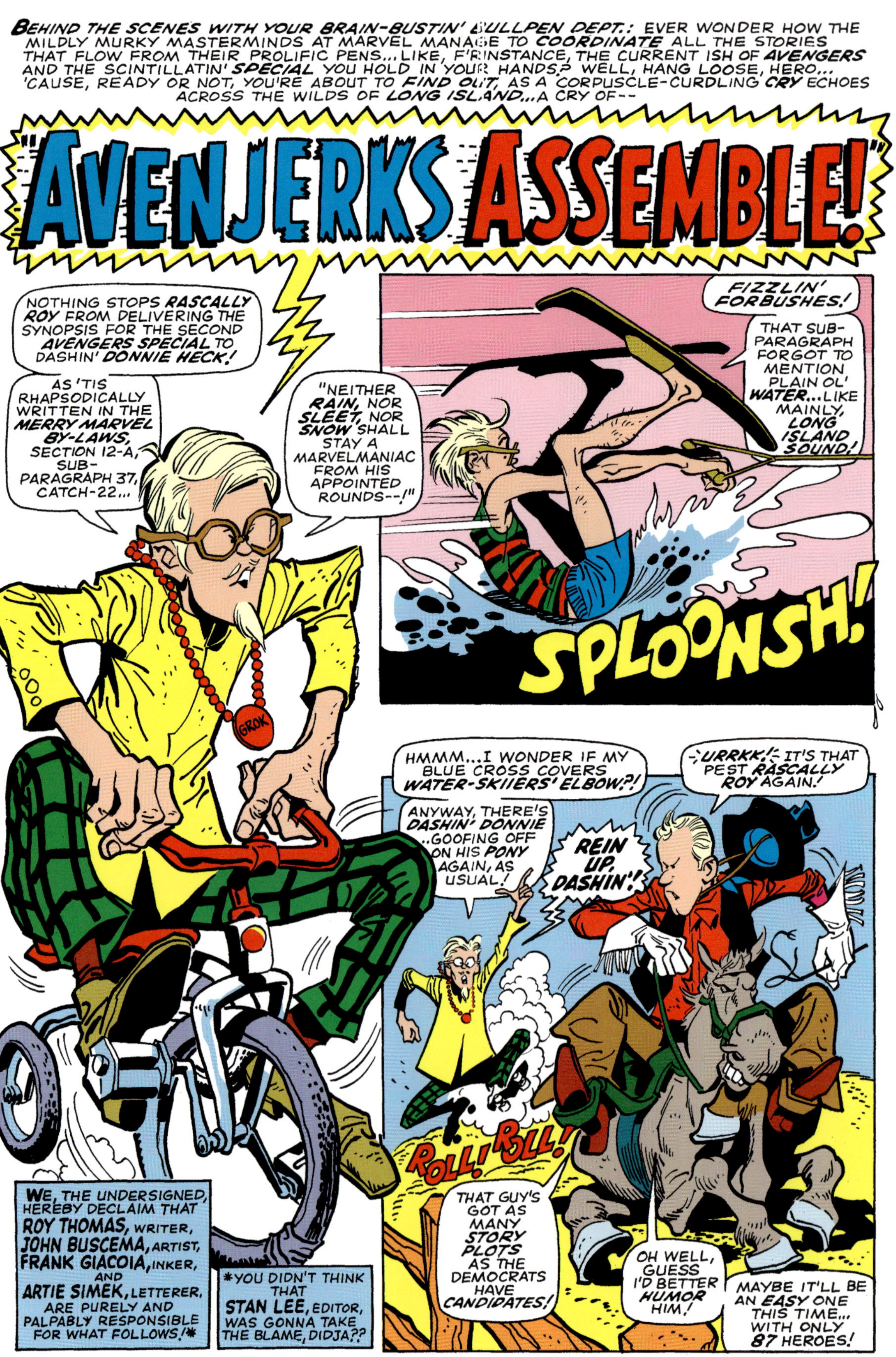
BEHIND THE SCENES WITH YOUR BRAIN-BUSTIN' BULLPEN DEPT.: EVER WONDER HOW THE MILDLY MURKY MASTERMINDS AT MARVEL MANAGE TO COORDINATE ALL THE STORIES THAT FLOW FROM THEIR PROLIFIC PENS... LIKE, F'RINSTANCE, THE CURRENT ISH OF AVENGERS AND THE SCINTILLATIN' SPECIAL YOU HOLD IN YOUR HANDS?? WELL, HANG LOOSE, HERO... 'CAUSE, READY OR NOT, YOU'RE ABOUT TO FIND OUT, AS A CORPUSCLE-CURDLING CRY ECHOES ACROSS THE WILDS OF LONG ISLAND... A CRY OF--
"AVENJERKS ASSEMBLE!"
NOTHING STOPS RASCALLY ROY FROM DELIVERING THE SYNOPSIS FOR THE SECOND AVENGERS SPECIAL TO DASHIN' DONNIE HECK!
AS 'TIS RHAPSODICALLY WRITTEN IN THE MERRY MARVEL BY-LAWS, SECTION 12-A, SUB-PARAGRAPH 37, CATCH-22...
"NEITHER RAIN, NOR SLEET, NOR SNOW SHALL STAY A MARVELMANIAC FROM HIS APPOINTED ROUNDS--!"
GROK
FIZZLIN' FORBUSHES!
THAT SUB-PARAGRAPH FORGOT TO MENTION PLAIN OL' WATER... LIKE MAINLY, LONG ISLAND SOUND!
SPLOONSH!
HMMM... I WONDER IF MY BLUE CROSS COVERS WATER-SKIIERS' ELBOW?!
ANYWAY, THERE'S DASHIN' DONNIE ..GOOFING OFF ON HIS PONY AGAIN, AS USUAL!
REIN UP, DASHIN'!
-URRKK!- IT'S THAT PEST RASCALLY ROY AGAIN!
ROLL! ROLL!
THAT GUY'S GOT AS MANY STORY PLOTS AS THE DEMOCRATS HAVE CANDIDATES!
OH WELL, GUESS I'D BETTER HUMOR HIM!
MAYBE IT'LL BE AN EASY ONE THIS TIME... WITH ONLY 87 HEROES!
WE, THE UNDERSIGNED, HEREBY DECLAIM THAT ROY THOMAS, WRITER, JOHN BUSCEMA, ARTIST, FRANK GIACOIA, INKER, AND ARTIE SIMEK, LETTERER, ARE PURELY AND PALPABLY RESPONSIBLE FOR WHAT FOLLOWS!*
*YOU DIDN'T THINK THAT STAN LEE, EDITOR, WAS GONNA TAKE THE BLAME, DIDJA??

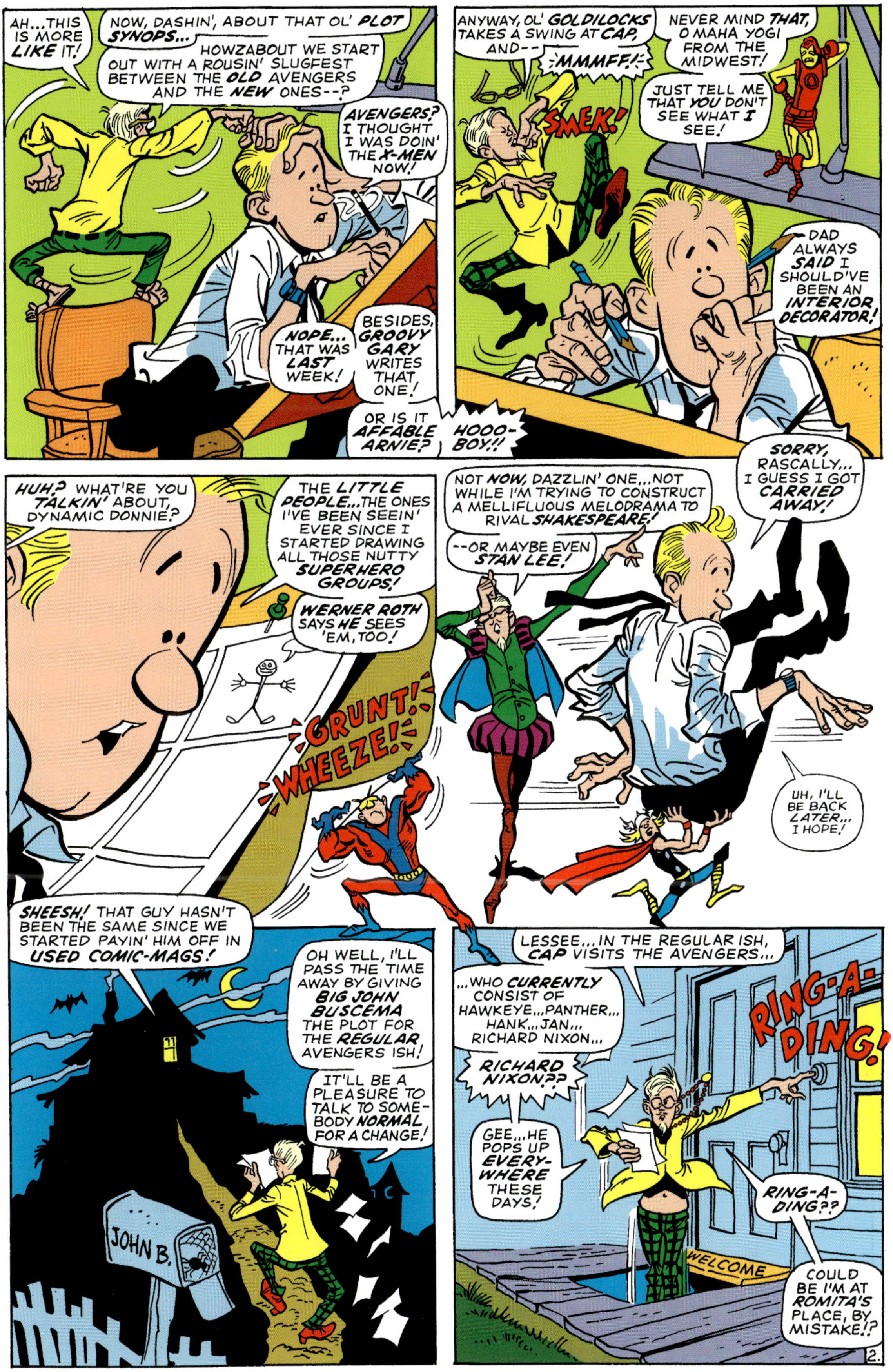

AH...THIS IS MORE LIKE IT!
NOW, DASHIN', ABOUT THAT OL' PLOT SYNOPS...
HOWZABOUT WE START OUT WITH A ROUSIN' SLUGFEST BETWEEN THE OLD AVENGERS AND THE NEW ONES--?
AVENGERS? I THOUGHT I WAS DOIN' THE X-MEN NOW.!
NOPE... THAT WAS LAST WEEK!
BESIDES, GROOVY GARY WRITES THAT ONE!
OR IS IT AFFABLE ARNIE?
HOOO-BOY!!
ANYWAY, OL' GOLDILOCKS TAKES A SWING AT CAP, AND--
MMMFF!
SMEK!
NEVER MIND THAT, O MAHA YOGI FROM THE MIDWEST!
JUST TELL ME THAT YOU DON'T SEE WHAT I SEE!
DAD ALWAYS SAID I SHOULD'VE BEEN AN INTERIOR DECORATOR!
HUH? WHAT'RE YOU TALKIN' ABOUT, DYNAMIC DONNIE?
THE LITTLE PEOPLE...THE ONES I'VE BEEN SEEIN' EVER SINCE I STARTED DRAWING ALL THOSE NUTTY SUPERHERO GROUPS!
WERNER ROTH SAYS HE SEES 'EM, TOO!
GRUNT!
WHEEZE!
NOT NOW, DAZZLIN' ONE,...NOT WHILE I'M TRYING TO CONSTRUCT A MELLIFLUOUS MELODRAMA TO RIVAL SHAKESPEARE!
--OR MAYBE EVEN STAN LEE!
SORRY, RASCALLY... I GUESS I GOT CARRIED AWAY!
UH, I'LL BE BACK LATER... I HOPE!
SHEESH! THAT GUY HASN'T BEEN THE SAME SINCE WE STARTED PAYIN' HIM OFF IN USED COMIC-MAGS!
OH WELL, I'LL PASS THE TIME AWAY BY GIVING BIG JOHN BUSCEMA THE PLOT FOR THE REGULAR AVENGERS ISH!
IT'LL BE A PLEASURE TO TALK TO SOME-BODY NORMAL FOR A CHANGE!
JOHN B.
LESSEE... IN THE REGULAR ISH, CAP VISITS THE AVENGERS...
...WHO CURRENTLY CONSIST OF HAWKEYE... PANTHER... HANK... JAN... RICHARD NIXON...
RICHARD NIXON??
GEE... HE POPS UP EVERY-WHERE THESE DAYS!
RING-A-DING!
RING-A-DING??
WELCOME
COULD BE I'M AT ROMITA'S PLACE, BY MISTAKE!?
2.

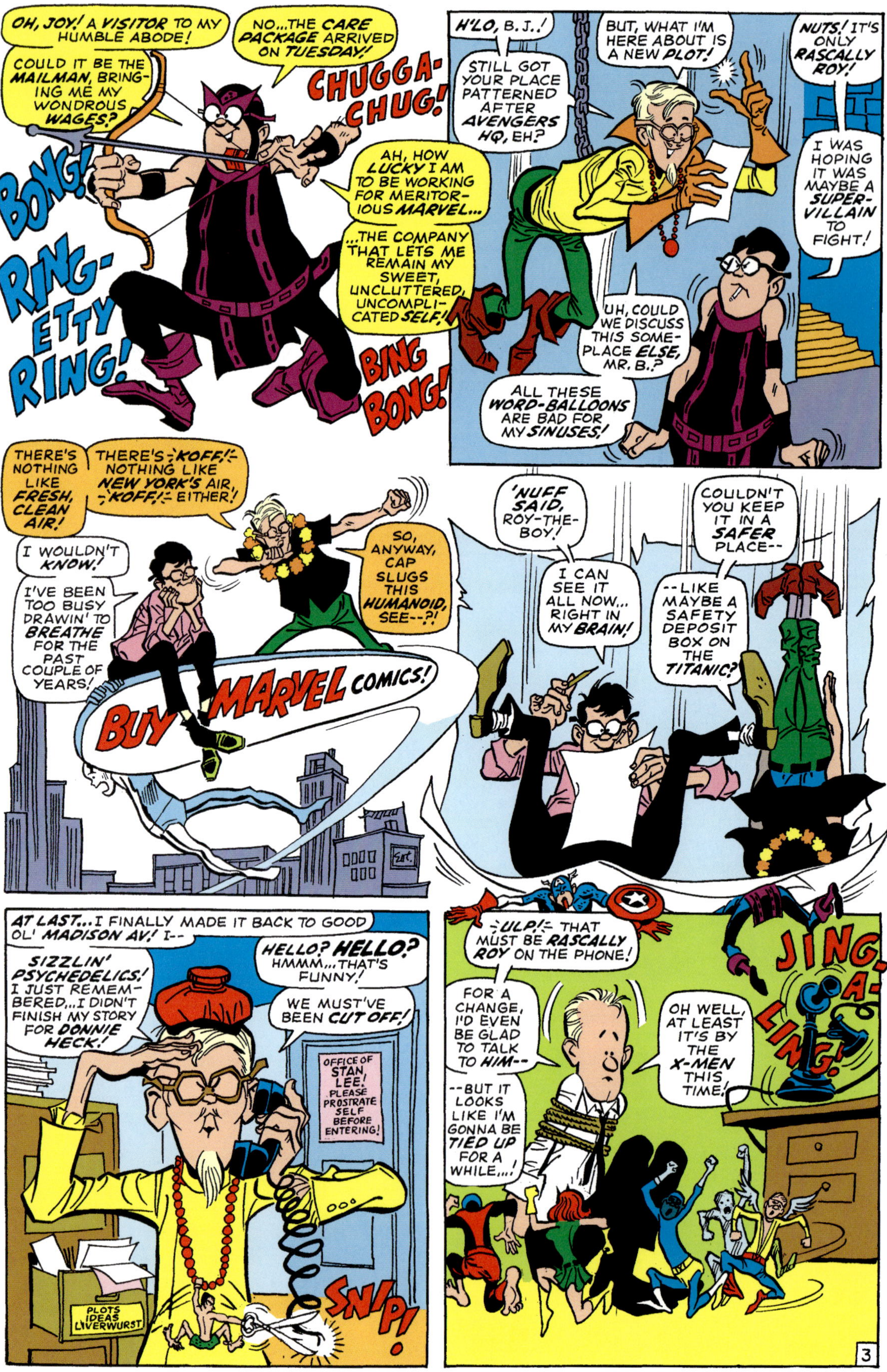

OH, JOY! A VISITOR TO MY HUMBLE ABODE!
COULD IT BE THE MAILMAN, BRINGING ME MY WONDROUS WAGES?
NO...THE CARE PACKAGE ARRIVED ON TUESDAY!
CHUGGA-CHUG!
BONG!
RING-ETTY RING!
AH, HOW LUCKY I AM TO BE WORKING FOR MERITORIOUS MARVEL...
...THE COMPANY THAT LETS ME REMAIN MY SWEET, UNCLUTTERED, UNCOMPLICATED SELF!
BING BONG!
H'LO, B.J.!
STILL GOT YOUR PLACE PATTERNED AFTER AVENGERS HQ, EH?
BUT, WHAT I'M HERE ABOUT IS A NEW PLOT!
NUTS! IT'S ONLY RASCALLY ROY!
I WAS HOPING IT WAS MAYBE A SUPER-VILLAIN TO FIGHT!
UH, COULD WE DISCUSS THIS SOMEPLACE ELSE, MR. B.?
ALL THESE WORD-BALLOONS ARE BAD FOR MY SINUSES!
THERE'S NOTHING LIKE FRESH, CLEAN AIR!
THERE'S -KOFF!- NOTHING LIKE NEW YORK'S AIR, -KOFF!- EITHER!
I WOULDN'T KNOW!
I'VE BEEN TOO BUSY DRAWIN' TO BREATHE FOR THE PAST COUPLE OF YEARS!
SO, ANYWAY, CAP SLUGS THIS HUMANOID, SEE--?!
BUY MARVEL COMICS!
'NUFF SAID, ROY-THE-BOY!
I CAN SEE IT ALL NOW... RIGHT IN MY BRAIN!
COULDN'T YOU KEEP IT IN A SAFER PLACE--
--LIKE MAYBE A SAFETY DEPOSIT BOX ON THE TITANIC?
AT LAST...I FINALLY MADE IT BACK TO GOOD OL' MADISON AV! I--
SIZZLIN' PSYCHEDELICS! I JUST REMEMBERED... I DIDN'T FINISH MY STORY FOR DONNIE HECK!
HELLO? HELLO? HMMM... THAT'S FUNNY!
WE MUST'VE BEEN CUT OFF!
OFFICE OF STAN LEE! PLEASE PROSTRATE SELF BEFORE ENTERING!
PLOTS IDEAS LIVERWURST
SNIP!
-ULP!- THAT MUST BE RASCALLY ROY ON THE PHONE!
FOR A CHANGE, I'D EVEN BE GLAD TO TALK TO HIM--
--BUT IT LOOKS LIKE I'M GONNA BE TIED UP FOR A WHILE...!
OH WELL, AT LEAST IT'S BY THE X-MEN THIS TIME!
JING-A-LING!
3

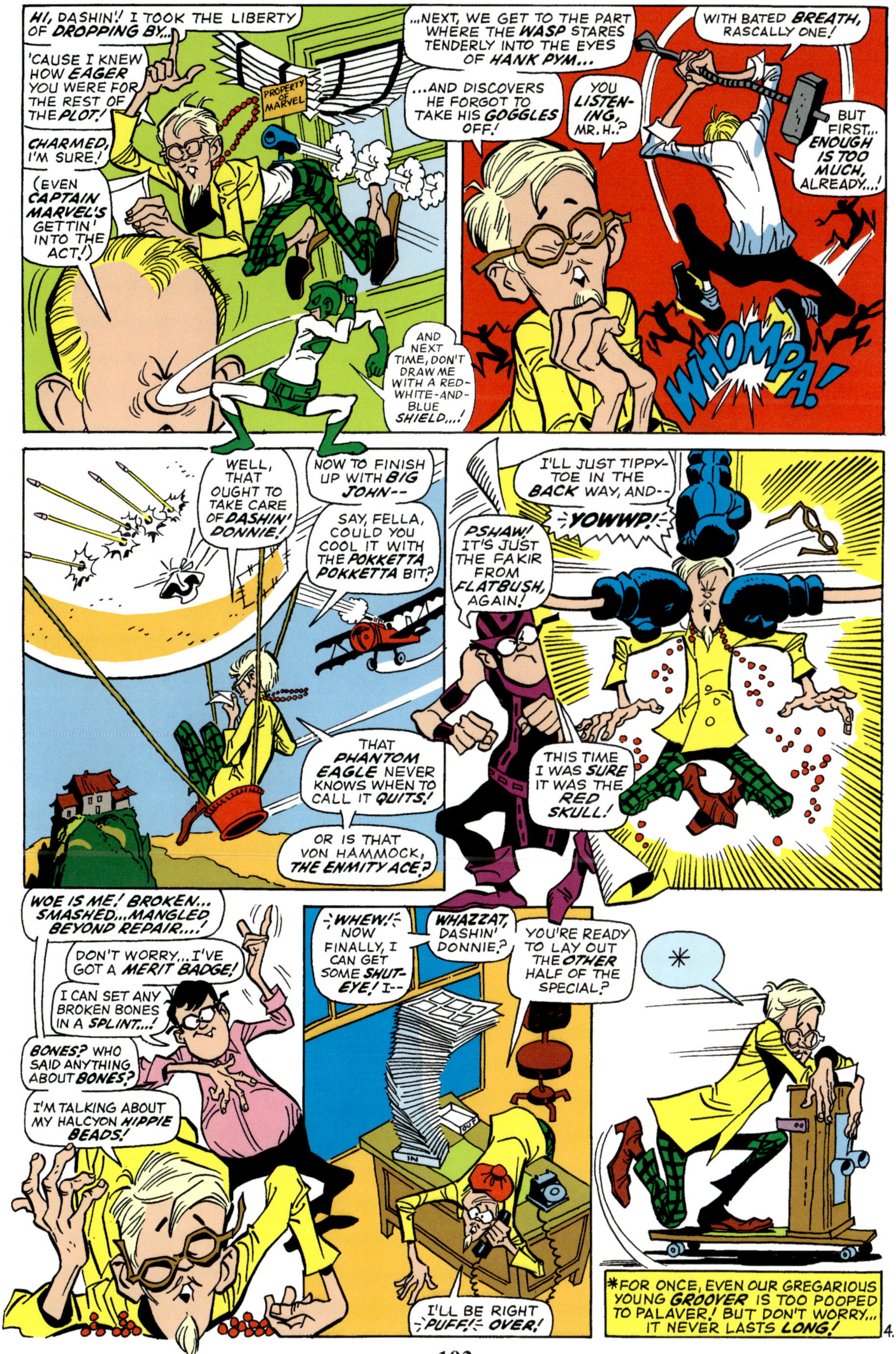
HI, DASHIN'! I TOOK THE LIBERTY OF DROPPING BY...
'CAUSE I KNEW HOW EAGER YOU WERE FOR THE REST OF THE PLOT!
PROPERTY OF MARVEL
CHARMED, I'M SURE!
(EVEN CAPTAIN MARVEL'S GETTIN' INTO THE ACT!)
AND NEXT TIME, DON'T DRAW ME WITH A RED-WHITE-AND-BLUE SHIELD...!
...NEXT, WE GET TO THE PART WHERE THE WASP STARES TENDERLY INTO THE EYES OF HANK PYM...
...AND DISCOVERS HE FORGOT TO TAKE HIS GOGGLES OFF!
YOU LISTEN-ING, MR. H..?
WITH BATED BREATH, RASCALLY ONE!
BUT FIRST... ENOUGH IS TOO MUCH, ALREADY...!
WHOMPA!
WELL, THAT OUGHT TO TAKE CARE OF DASHIN' DONNIE!
NOW TO FINISH UP WITH BIG JOHN--
SAY, FELLA, COULD YOU COOL IT WITH THE POKKETTA POKKETTA BIT?
THAT PHANTOM EAGLE NEVER KNOWS WHEN TO CALL IT QUITS!
OR IS THAT VON HAMMOCK, THE ENMITY ACE?
I'LL JUST TIPPY-TOE IN THE BACK WAY, AND--
YOWWP!
PSHAW! IT'S JUST THE FAKIR FROM FLATBUSH, AGAIN!
THIS TIME I WAS SURE IT WAS THE RED SKULL!
WOE IS ME! BROKEN... SMASHED...MANGLED BEYOND REPAIR...!
DON'T WORRY...I'VE GOT A MERIT BADGE!
I CAN SET ANY BROKEN BONES IN A SPLINT...!
BONES? WHO SAID ANYTHING ABOUT BONES?
I'M TALKING ABOUT MY HALCYON HIPPIE BEADS!
WHEW! NOW FINALLY, I CAN GET SOME SHUT-EYE! I--
WHAZZAT, DASHIN' DONNIE?
YOU'RE READY TO LAY OUT THE OTHER HALF OF THE SPECIAL?
I'LL BE RIGHT PUFF! OVER!
*
*FOR ONCE, EVEN OUR GREGARIOUS YOUNG GROOVER IS TOO POOPED TO PALAVER! BUT DON'T WORRY... IT NEVER LASTS LONG!
4.

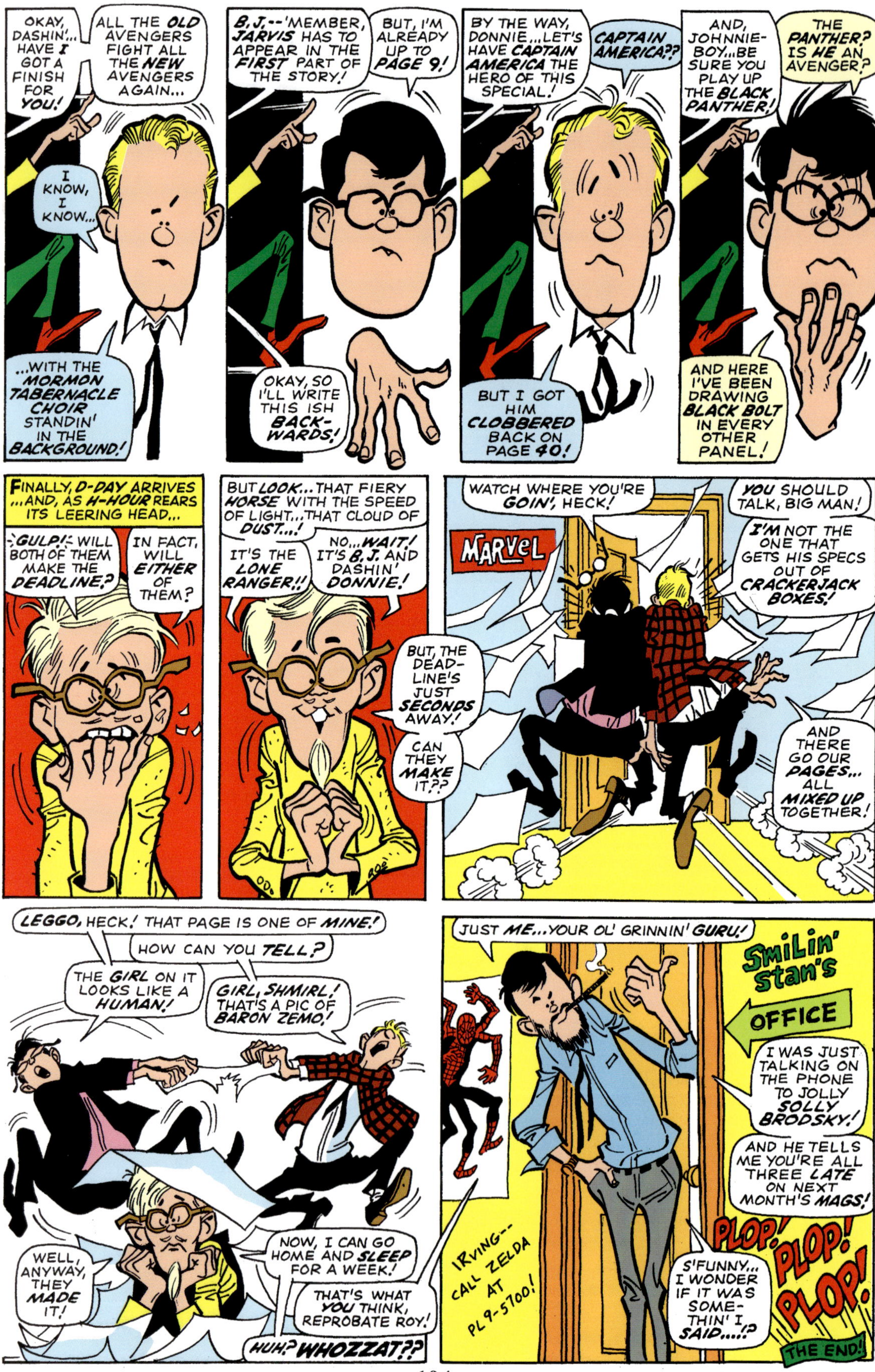
OKAY, DASHIN'... HAVE I GOT A FINISH FOR YOU!
ALL THE OLD AVENGERS FIGHT ALL THE NEW AVENGERS AGAIN...
I KNOW, I KNOW...
...WITH THE MORMON TABERNACLE CHOIR STANDIN' IN THE BACKGROUND!
B.J.--'MEMBER, JARVIS HAS TO APPEAR IN THE FIRST PART OF THE STORY!
BUT, I'M ALREADY UP TO PAGE 9!
OKAY, SO I'LL WRITE THIS ISH BACK-WARDS!
BY THE WAY, DONNIE...LET'S HAVE CAPTAIN AMERICA THE HERO OF THIS SPECIAL!
CAPTAIN AMERICA??
BUT I GOT HIM CLOBBERED BACK ON PAGE 40!
AND, JOHNNIE-BOY...BE SURE YOU PLAY UP THE BLACK PANTHER!
THE PANTHER? IS HE AN AVENGER?
AND HERE I'VE BEEN DRAWING BLACK BOLT IN EVERY OTHER PANEL!
FINALLY, D-DAY ARRIVES ...AND, AS H-HOUR REARS ITS LEERING HEAD...
GULP! WILL BOTH OF THEM MAKE THE DEADLINE?
IN FACT, WILL EITHER OF THEM?
BUT LOOK...THAT FIERY HORSE WITH THE SPEED OF LIGHT...THAT CLOUD OF DUST...!
IT'S THE LONE RANGER!!
NO...WAIT! IT'S B.J. AND DASHIN' DONNIE!
BUT, THE DEAD-LINE'S JUST SECONDS AWAY!
CAN THEY MAKE IT??
WATCH WHERE YOU'RE GOIN', HECK!
YOU SHOULD TALK, BIG MAN!
I'M NOT THE ONE THAT GETS HIS SPECS OUT OF CRACKERJACK BOXES!
MARVEL
AND THERE GO OUR PAGES... ALL MIXED UP TOGETHER!
LEGGO, HECK! THAT PAGE IS ONE OF MINE!
HOW CAN YOU TELL?
THE GIRL ON IT LOOKS LIKE A HUMAN!
GIRL, SHMIRL! THAT'S A PIC OF BARON ZEMO!
WELL, ANYWAY, THEY MADE IT!
NOW, I CAN GO HOME AND SLEEP FOR A WEEK!
THAT'S WHAT YOU THINK, REPROBATE ROY!
HUH? WHOZZAT??
JUST ME...YOUR OL' GRINNIN' GURU!
SMILIN' STAN'S
OFFICE
I WAS JUST TALKING ON THE PHONE TO JOLLY SOLLY BRODSKY!
AND HE TELLS ME YOU'RE ALL THREE LATE ON NEXT MONTH'S MAGS!
IRVING-- CALL ZELDA AT PL 9-5700!
PLOP! PLOP! PLOP!
S'FUNNY... I WONDER IF IT WAS SOME-THIN' I SAID...!?
THE END!

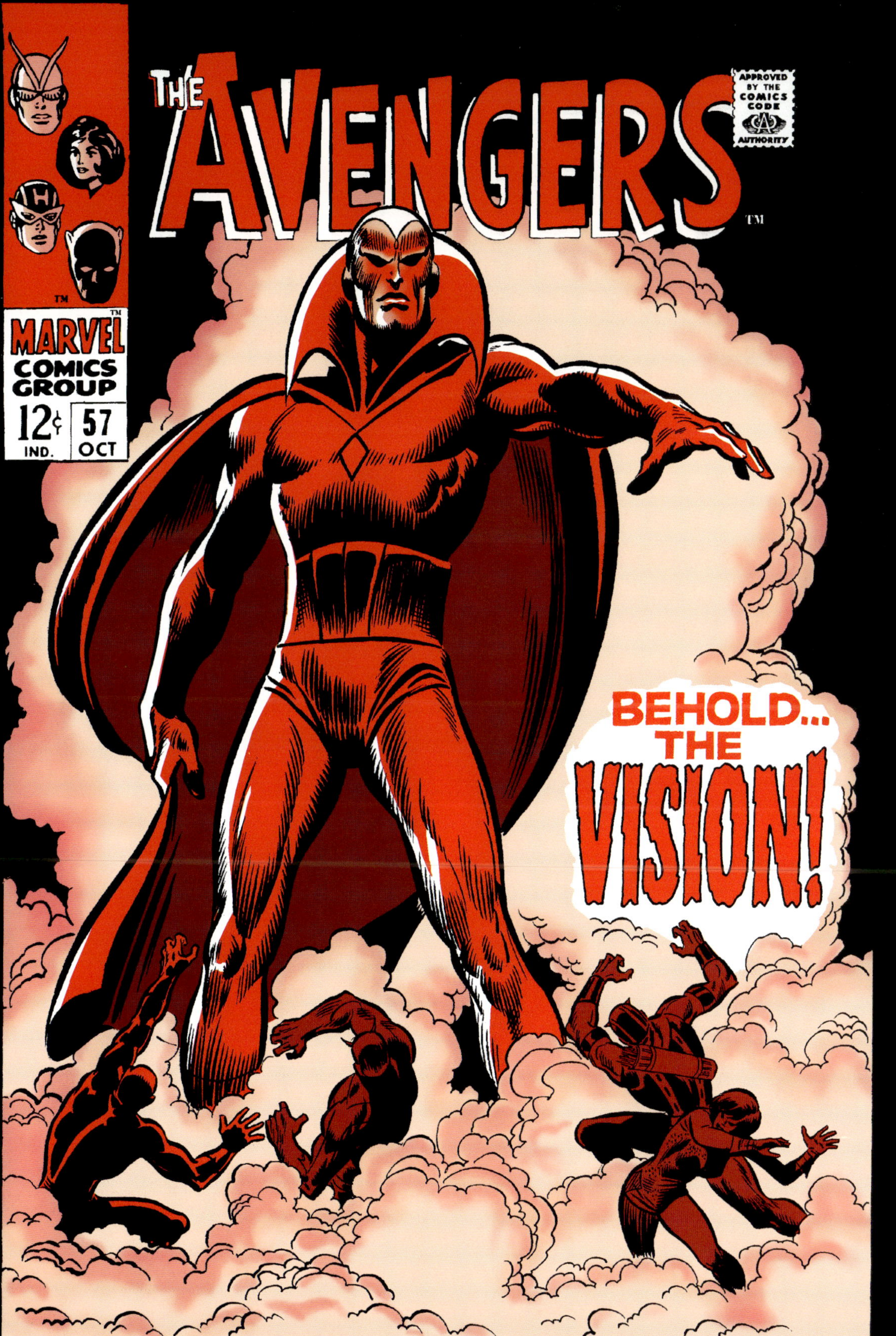
THE AVENGERS
TM
APPROVED BY THE COMICS CODE AUTHORITY
MARVEL COMICS GROUP
12¢ IND.
57 OCT
BEHOLD... THE VISION!

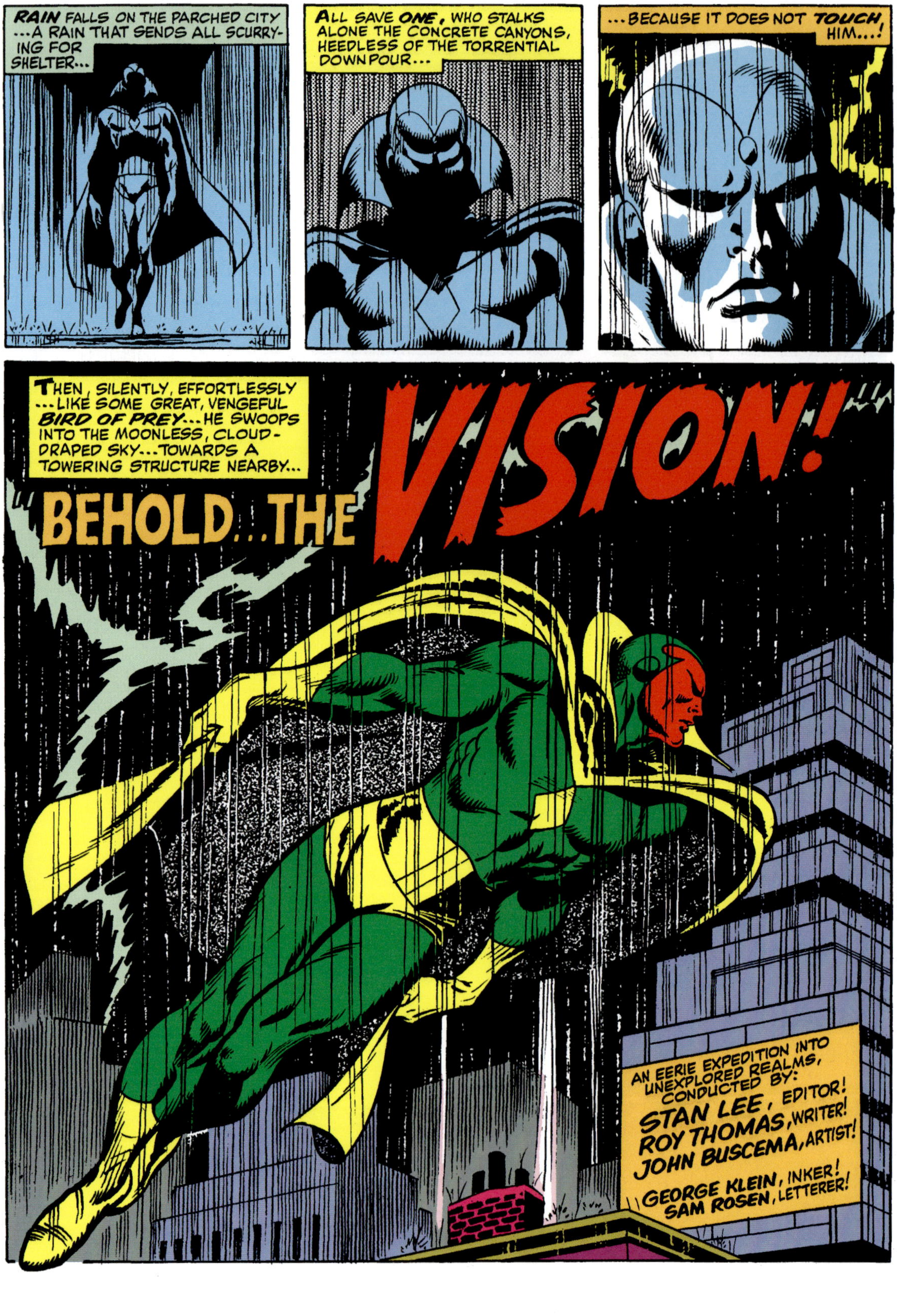
RAIN FALLS ON THE PARCHED CITY ...A RAIN THAT SENDS ALL SCURRYING FOR SHELTER...
ALL SAVE ONE, WHO STALKS ALONE THE CONCRETE CANYONS, HEEDLESS OF THE TORRENTIAL DOWNPOUR...
...BECAUSE IT DOES NOT TOUCH HIM...!
THEN, SILENTLY, EFFORTLESSLY ...LIKE SOME GREAT, VENGEFUL BIRD OF PREY...HE SWOOPS INTO THE MOONLESS, CLOUD-DRAPED SKY...TOWARDS A TOWERING STRUCTURE NEARBY...
"BEHOLD...THE VISION!"
AN EERIE EXPEDITION INTO UNEXPLORED REALMS, CONDUCTED BY:
STAN LEE, EDITOR!
ROY THOMAS, WRITER!
JOHN BUSCEMA, ARTIST!
GEORGE KLEIN, INKER!
SAM ROSEN, LETTERER!

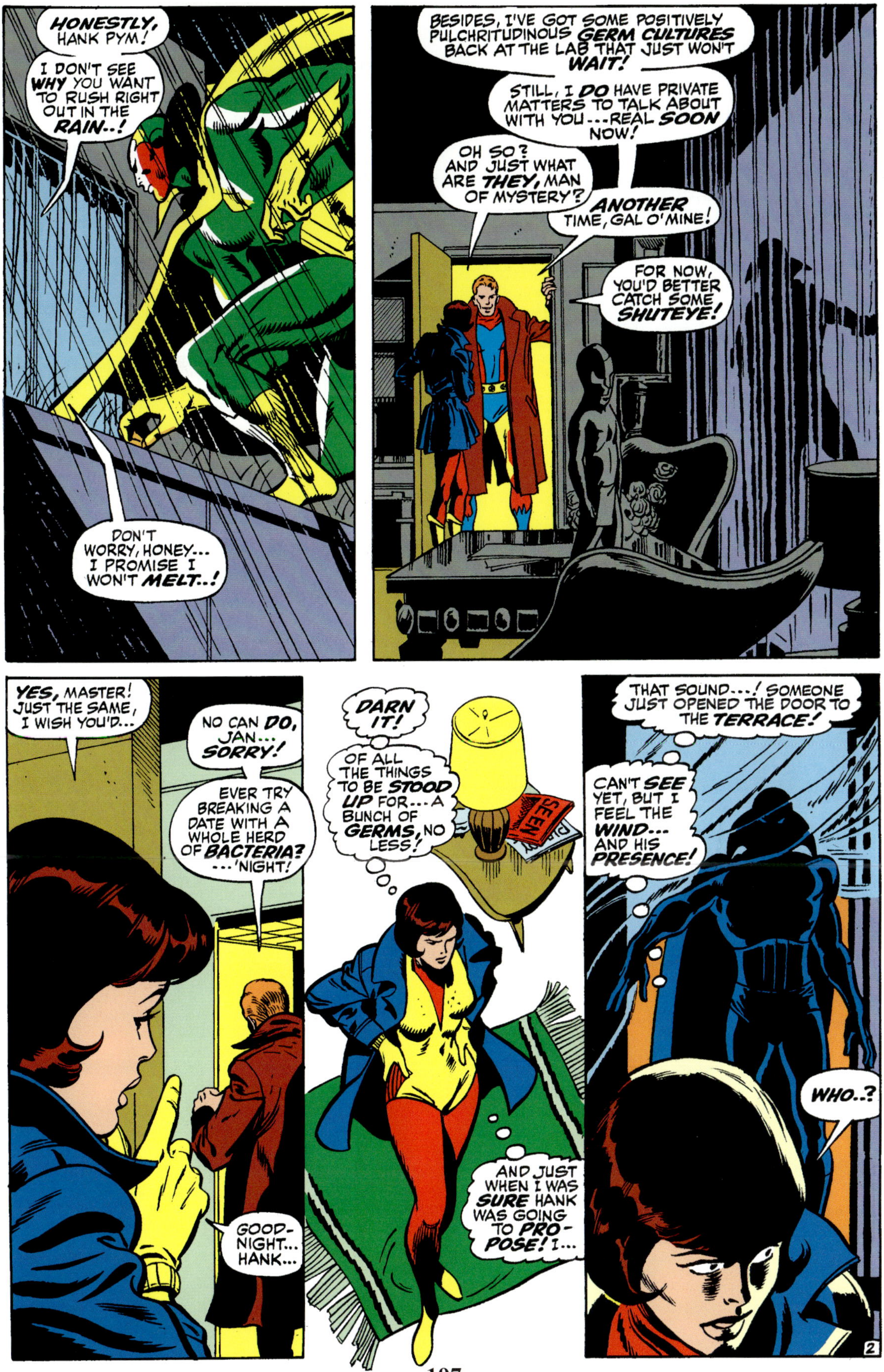
HONESTLY, HANK PYM!
I DON'T SEE WHY YOU WANT TO RUSH RIGHT OUT IN THE RAIN..!
DON'T WORRY, HONEY... I PROMISE I WON'T MELT..!
BESIDES, I'VE GOT SOME POSITIVELY PULCHRITUDINOUS GERM CULTURES BACK AT THE LAB THAT JUST WON'T WAIT!
STILL, I DO HAVE PRIVATE MATTERS TO TALK ABOUT WITH YOU---REAL SOON NOW!
OH SO? AND JUST WHAT ARE THEY, MAN OF MYSTERY?
ANOTHER TIME, GAL O'MINE!
FOR NOW, YOU'D BETTER CATCH SOME SHUTEYE!
YES, MASTER! JUST THE SAME, I WISH YOU'D...
NO CAN DO, JAN... SORRY!
EVER TRY BREAKING A DATE WITH A WHOLE HERD OF BACTERIA? ---'NIGHT!
GOOD-NIGHT... HANK...
DARN IT!
OF ALL THE THINGS TO BE STOOD UP FOR---A BUNCH OF GERMS, NO LESS!
SEEN
AND JUST WHEN I WAS SURE HANK WAS GOING TO PRO-POSE! I...
THAT SOUND---! SOMEONE JUST OPENED THE DOOR TO THE TERRACE!
CAN'T SEE YET, BUT I FEEL THE WIND... AND HIS PRESENCE!
WHO..?
2

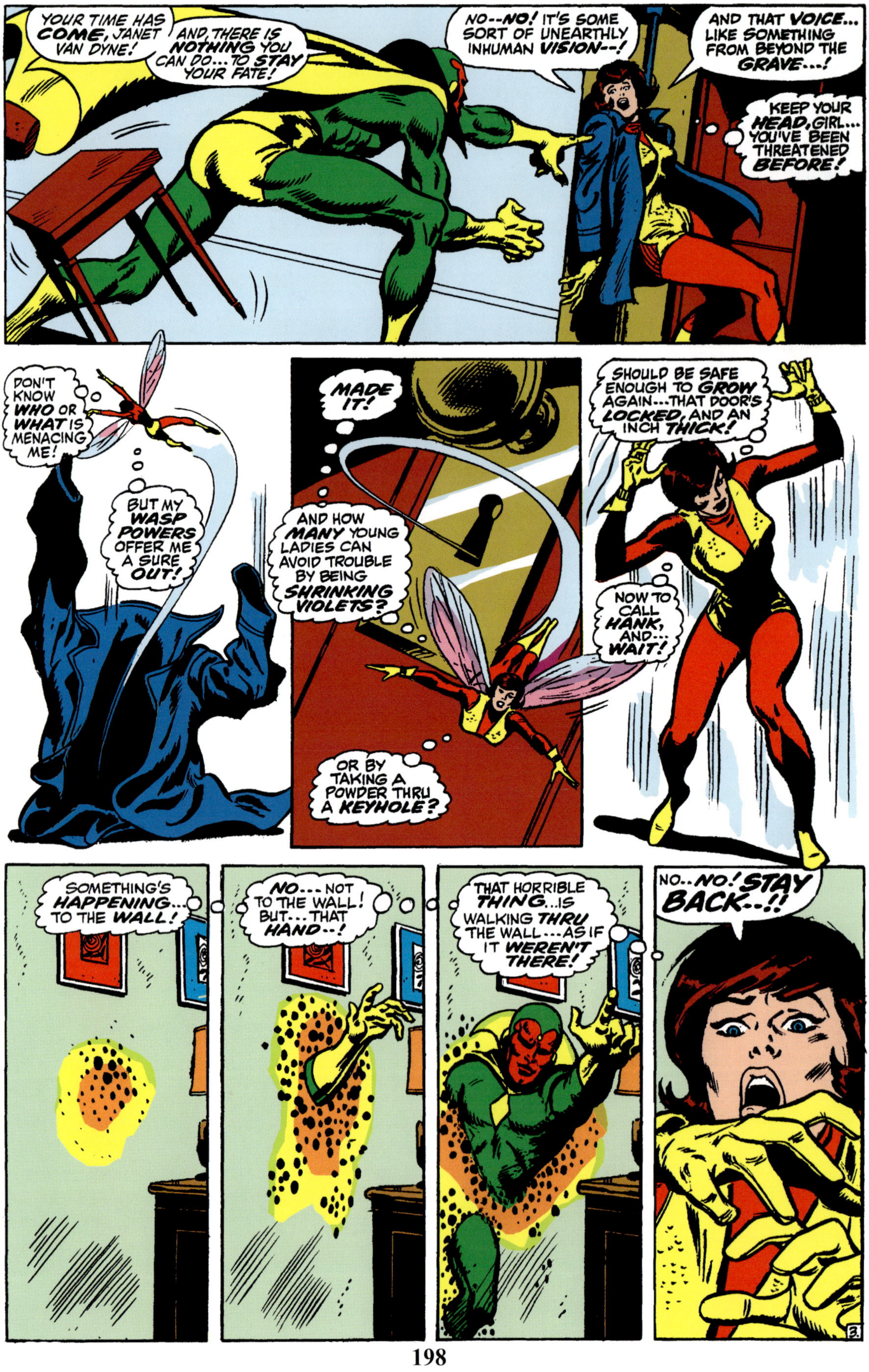
YOUR TIME HAS COME, JANET VAN DYNE!
AND THERE IS NOTHING YOU CAN DO... TO STAY YOUR FATE!
NO--NO! IT'S SOME SORT OF UNEARTHLY INHUMAN VISION--!
AND THAT VOICE... LIKE SOMETHING FROM BEYOND THE GRAVE...!
KEEP YOUR HEAD, GIRL... YOU'VE BEEN THREATENED BEFORE!
DON'T KNOW WHO OR WHAT IS MENACING ME!
BUT MY WASP POWERS OFFER ME A SURE OUT!
MADE IT!
AND HOW MANY YOUNG LADIES CAN AVOID TROUBLE BY BEING SHRINKING VIOLETS?
OR BY TAKING A POWDER THRU A KEYHOLE?
SHOULD BE SAFE ENOUGH TO GROW AGAIN...THAT DOOR'S LOCKED, AND AN INCH THICK!
NOW TO CALL HANK, AND... WAIT!
SOMETHING'S HAPPENING... TO THE WALL!
NO... NOT TO THE WALL! BUT... THAT HAND--!
THAT HORRIBLE THING...IS WALKING THRU THE WALL...AS IF IT WEREN'T THERE!
NO..NO! STAY BACK..!!
3.

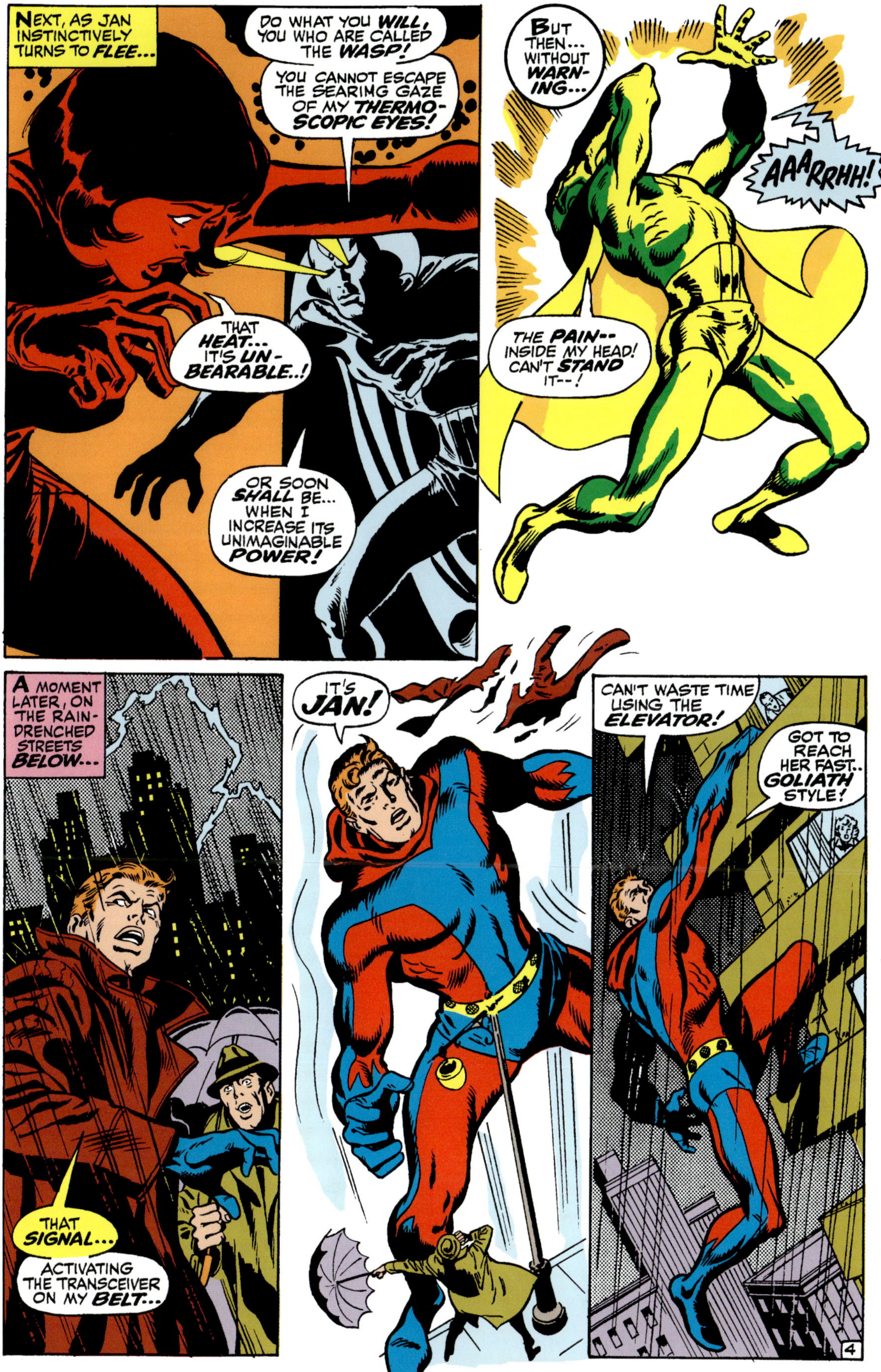
NEXT, AS JAN INSTINCTIVELY TURNS TO FLEE...
DO WHAT YOU WILL, YOU WHO ARE CALLED THE WASP!
YOU CANNOT ESCAPE THE SEARING GAZE OF MY THERMO-SCOPIC EYES!
THAT HEAT... IT'S UN-BEARABLE..!
OR SOON SHALL BE... WHEN I INCREASE ITS UNIMAGINABLE POWER!
BUT THEN... WITHOUT WARN-ING...
AAARRHH!
THE PAIN-- INSIDE MY HEAD! CAN'T STAND IT--!
A MOMENT LATER, ON THE RAIN-DRENCHED STREETS BELOW...
THAT SIGNAL...
ACTIVATING THE TRANSCEIVER ON MY BELT...
IT'S JAN!
CAN'T WASTE TIME USING THE ELEVATOR!
GOT TO REACH HER FAST.. GOLIATH STYLE!
4

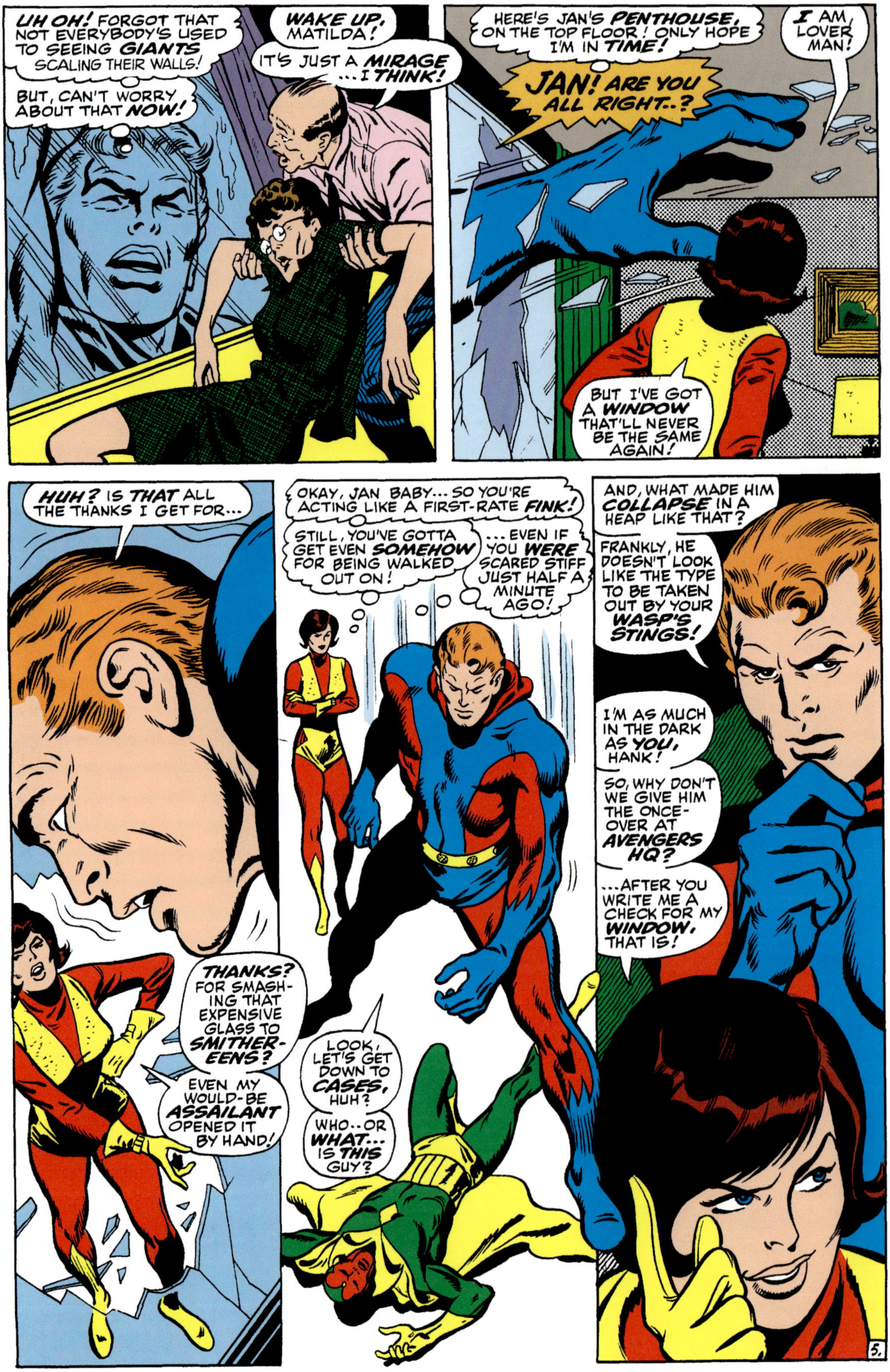

UH OH! FORGOT THAT NOT EVERYBODY'S USED TO SEEING GIANTS SCALING THEIR WALLS!
BUT, CAN'T WORRY ABOUT THAT NOW!
WAKE UP, MATILDA!
IT'S JUST A MIRAGE ...I THINK!
HERE'S JAN'S PENTHOUSE, ON THE TOP FLOOR! ONLY HOPE I'M IN TIME!
JAN! ARE YOU ALL RIGHT..?
I AM, LOVER MAN!
BUT I'VE GOT A WINDOW THAT'LL NEVER BE THE SAME AGAIN!
HUH? IS THAT ALL THE THANKS I GET FOR...
THANKS? FOR SMASHING THAT EXPENSIVE GLASS TO SMITHEREENS?
EVEN MY WOULD-BE ASSAILANT OPENED IT BY HAND!
OKAY, JAN BABY... SO YOU'RE ACTING LIKE A FIRST-RATE FINK!
STILL, YOU'VE GOTTA GET EVEN SOMEHOW FOR BEING WALKED OUT ON!
...EVEN IF YOU WERE SCARED STIFF JUST HALF A MINUTE AGO!
LOOK, LET'S GET DOWN TO CASES, HUH?
WHO..OR WHAT... IS THIS GUY?
AND, WHAT MADE HIM COLLAPSE IN A HEAP LIKE THAT?
FRANKLY, HE DOESN'T LOOK LIKE THE TYPE TO BE TAKEN OUT BY YOUR WASP'S STINGS!
I'M AS MUCH IN THE DARK AS YOU, HANK!
SO, WHY DON'T WE GIVE HIM THE ONCE-OVER AT AVENGERS HQ?
...AFTER YOU WRITE ME A CHECK FOR MY WINDOW, THAT IS!
5.

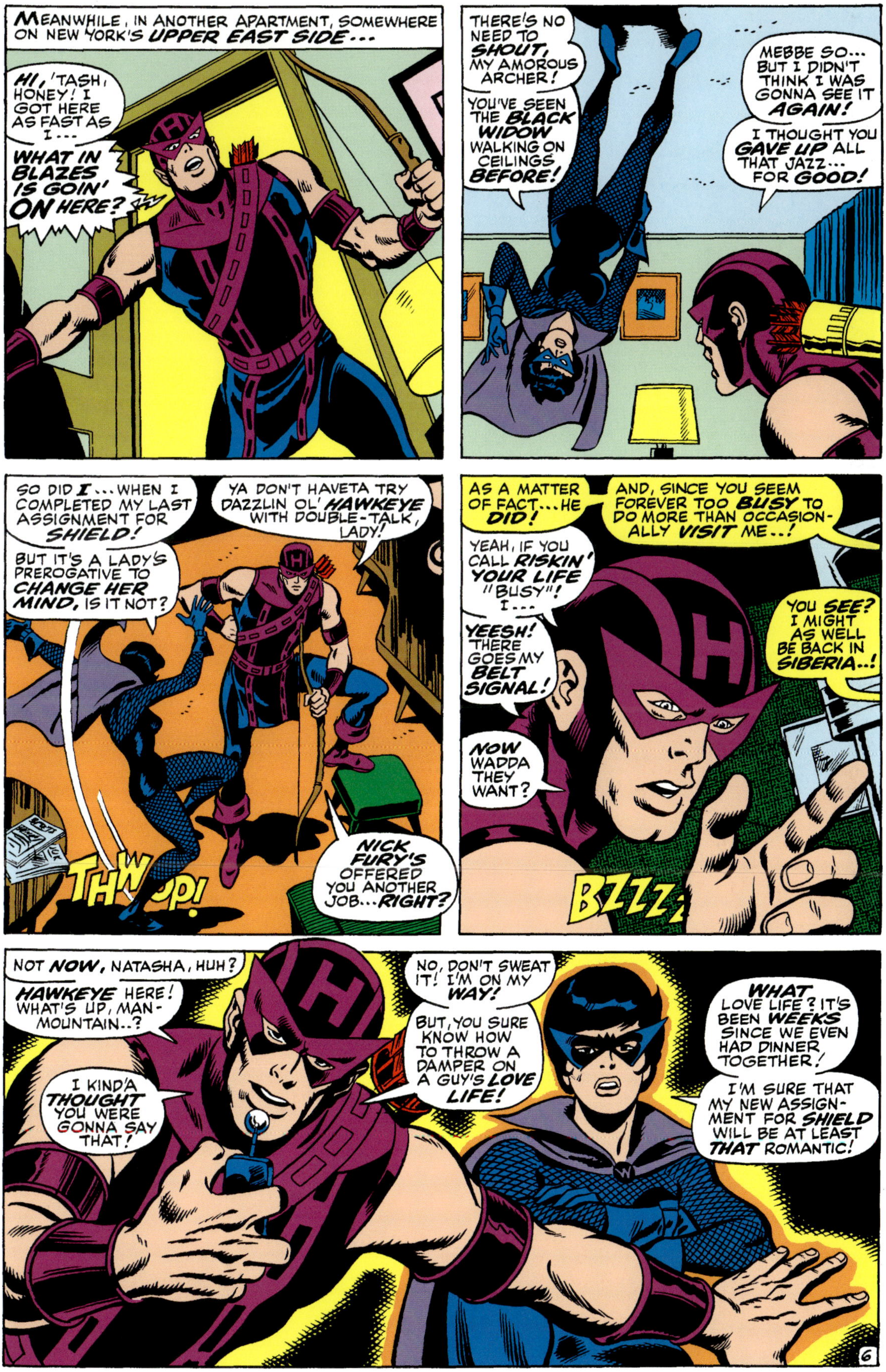
MEANWHILE, IN ANOTHER APARTMENT, SOMEWHERE ON NEW YORK'S UPPER EAST SIDE...
HI, 'TASH, HONEY! I GOT HERE AS FAST AS I...
WHAT IN BLAZES IS GOIN' ON HERE?
THERE'S NO NEED TO SHOUT, MY AMOROUS ARCHER!
YOU'VE SEEN THE BLACK WIDOW WALKING ON CEILINGS BEFORE!
MEBBE SO... BUT I DIDN'T THINK I WAS GONNA SEE IT AGAIN!
I THOUGHT YOU GAVE UP ALL THAT JAZZ... FOR GOOD!
SO DID I... WHEN I COMPLETED MY LAST ASSIGNMENT FOR SHIELD!
BUT IT'S A LADY'S PREROGATIVE TO CHANGE HER MIND, IS IT NOT?
YA DON'T HAVETA TRY DAZZLIN OL' HAWKEYE WITH DOUBLE-TALK, LADY!
NICK FURY'S OFFERED YOU ANOTHER JOB...RIGHT?
THWOP!
AS A MATTER OF FACT...HE DID!
AND, SINCE YOU SEEM FOREVER TOO BUSY TO DO MORE THAN OCCASION-ALLY VISIT ME..!
YEAH, IF YOU CALL RISKIN' YOUR LIFE "BUSY"! I...
YOU SEE? I MIGHT AS WELL BE BACK IN SIBERIA..!
YEESH! THERE GOES MY BELT SIGNAL!
NOW WADDA THEY WANT?
BZZZ
NOT NOW, NATASHA, HUH?
HAWKEYE HERE! WHAT'S UP, MAN-MOUNTAIN..?
I KIND'A THOUGHT YOU WERE GONNA SAY THAT!
NO, DON'T SWEAT IT! I'M ON MY WAY!
BUT, YOU SURE KNOW HOW TO THROW A DAMPER ON A GUY'S LOVE LIFE!
WHAT LOVE LIFE? IT'S BEEN WEEKS SINCE WE EVEN HAD DINNER TOGETHER!
I'M SURE THAT MY NEW ASSIGN-MENT FOR SHIELD WILL BE AT LEAST THAT ROMANTIC!
6

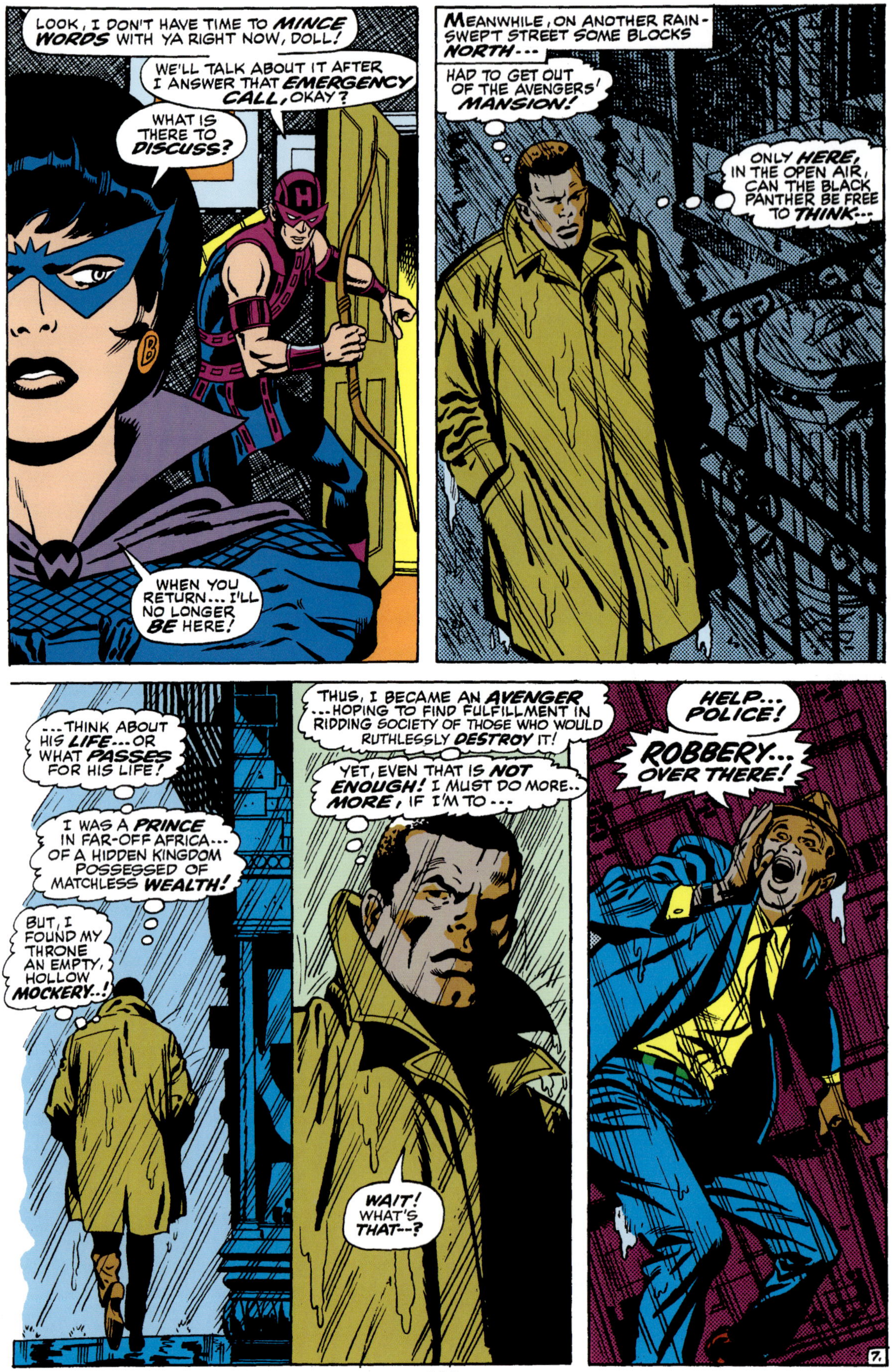
LOOK, I DON'T HAVE TIME TO MINCE WORDS WITH YA RIGHT NOW, DOLL!
WE'LL TALK ABOUT IT AFTER I ANSWER THAT EMERGENCY CALL, OKAY?
WHAT IS THERE TO DISCUSS?
WHEN YOU RETURN... I'LL NO LONGER BE HERE!
MEANWHILE, ON ANOTHER RAIN-SWEPT STREET SOME BLOCKS NORTH---
HAD TO GET OUT OF THE AVENGERS' MANSION!
ONLY HERE, IN THE OPEN AIR, CAN THE BLACK PANTHER BE FREE TO THINK...
...THINK ABOUT HIS LIFE...OR WHAT PASSES FOR HIS LIFE?
I WAS A PRINCE IN FAR-OFF AFRICA... OF A HIDDEN KINGDOM POSSESSED OF MATCHLESS WEALTH!
BUT, I FOUND MY THRONE AN EMPTY, HOLLOW MOCKERY..!
THUS, I BECAME AN AVENGER ...HOPING TO FIND FULFILLMENT IN RIDDING SOCIETY OF THOSE WHO WOULD RUTHLESSLY DESTROY IT!
YET, EVEN THAT IS NOT ENOUGH! I MUST DO MORE.. MORE, IF I'M TO ...
WAIT! WHAT'S THAT--?
HELP... POLICE!
ROBBERY... OVER THERE!
7.

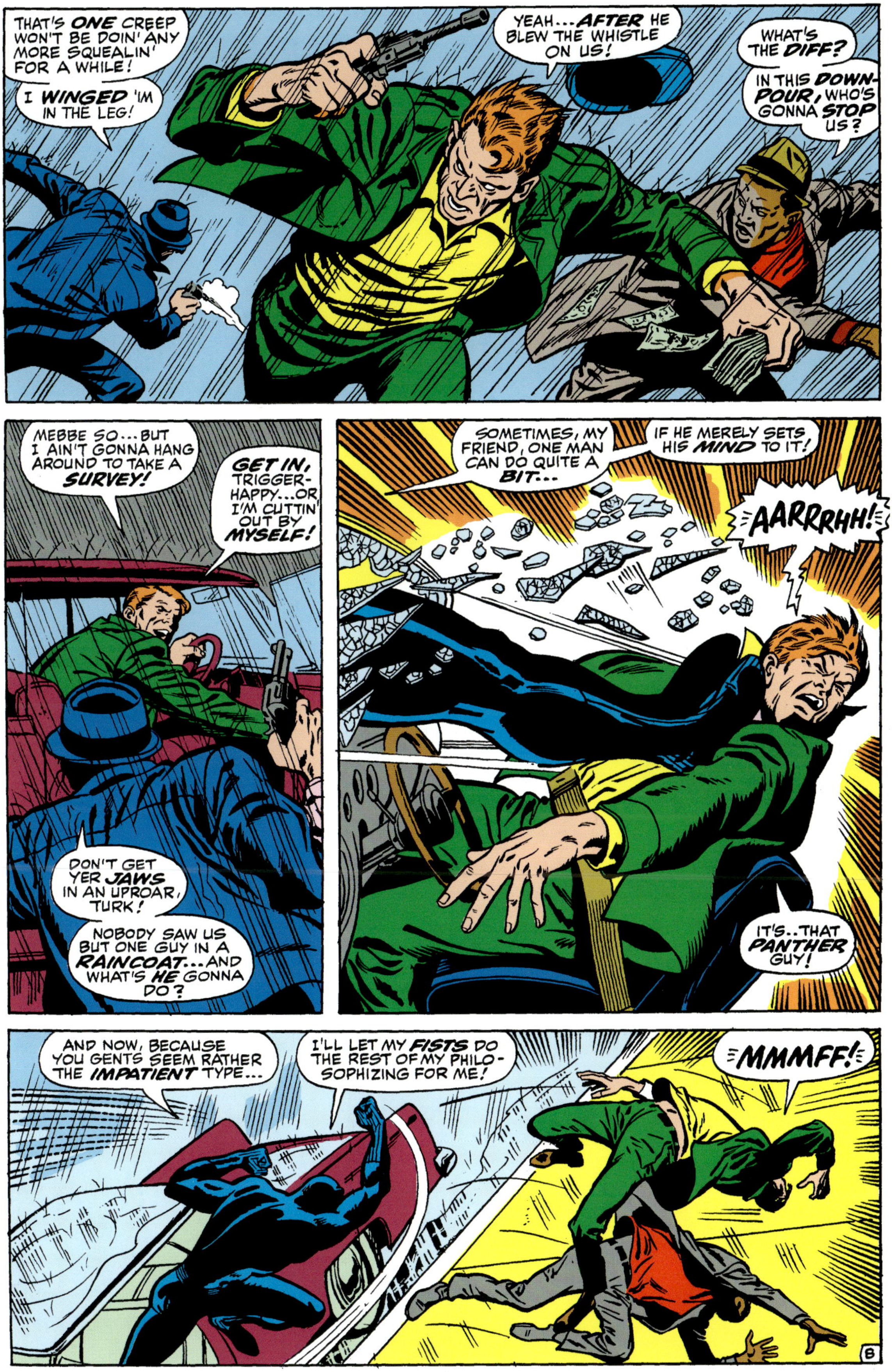
THAT'S ONE CREEP WON'T BE DOIN' ANY MORE SQUEALIN' FOR A WHILE!
I WINGED 'IM IN THE LEG!
YEAH... AFTER HE BLEW THE WHISTLE ON US!
WHAT'S THE DIFF?
IN THIS DOWNPOUR, WHO'S GONNA STOP US?
MEBBE SO... BUT I AIN'T GONNA HANG AROUND TO TAKE A SURVEY!
GET IN, TRIGGER-HAPPY... OR I'M CUTTIN' OUT BY MYSELF!
DON'T GET YER JAWS IN AN UPROAR, TURK!
NOBODY SAW US BUT ONE GUY IN A RAINCOAT... AND WHAT'S HE GONNA DO?
SOMETIMES, MY FRIEND, ONE MAN CAN DO QUITE A BIT...
IF HE MERELY SETS HIS MIND TO IT!
AARRRHH!
IT'S.. THAT PANTHER GUY!
AND NOW, BECAUSE YOU GENTS SEEM RATHER THE IMPATIENT TYPE...
I'LL LET MY FISTS DO THE REST OF MY PHILOSOPHIZING FOR ME!
MMMFF!
8

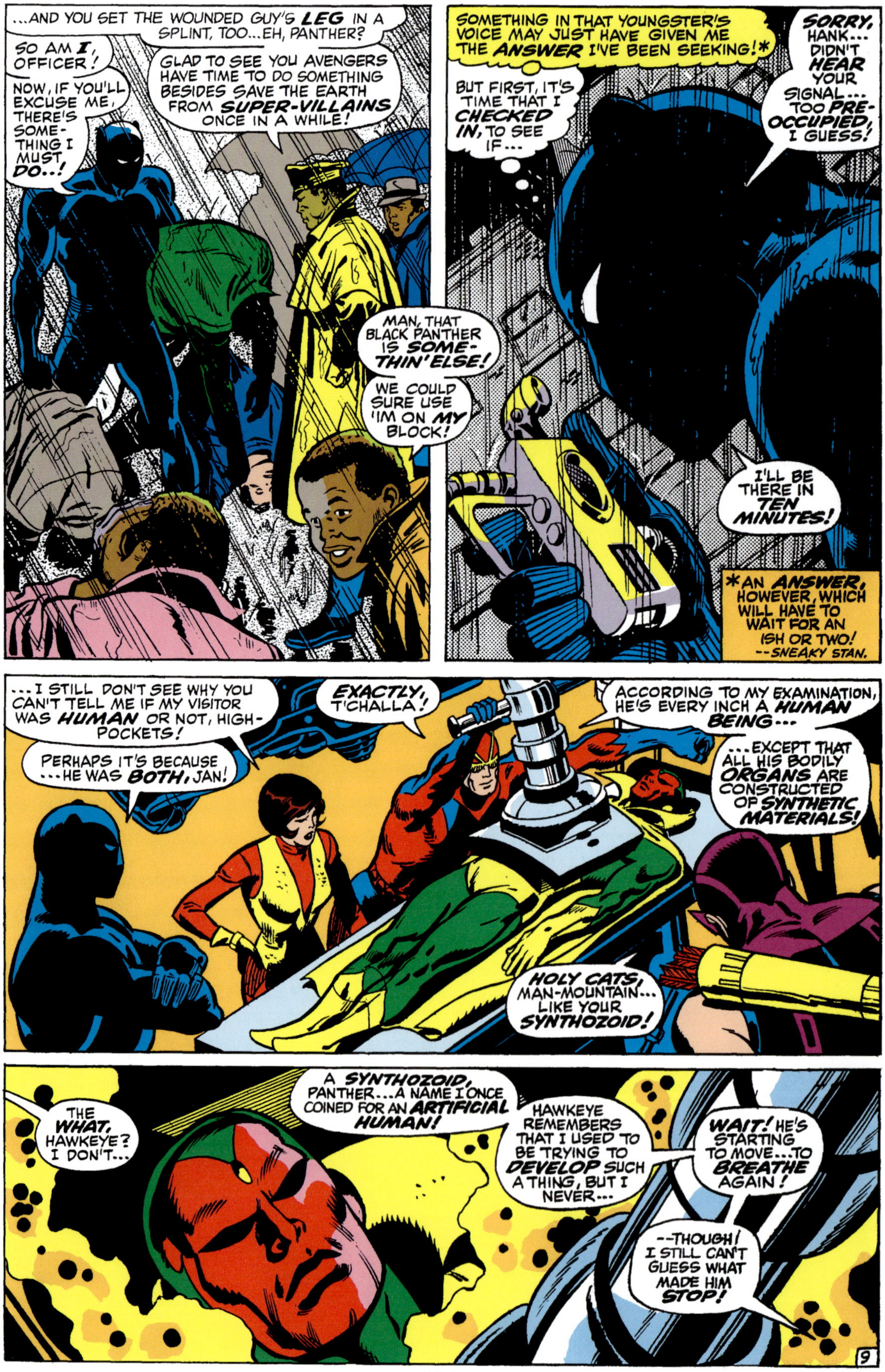
...AND YOU SET THE WOUNDED GUY'S LEG IN A SPLINT, TOO...EH, PANTHER?
SO AM I, OFFICER!
NOW, IF YOU'LL EXCUSE ME, THERE'S SOMETHING I MUST DO..!
GLAD TO SEE YOU AVENGERS HAVE TIME TO DO SOMETHING BESIDES SAVE THE EARTH FROM SUPER-VILLAINS ONCE IN A WHILE!
MAN, THAT BLACK PANTHER IS SOMETHIN' ELSE!
WE COULD SURE USE 'IM ON MY BLOCK!
SOMETHING IN THAT YOUNGSTER'S VOICE MAY JUST HAVE GIVEN ME THE ANSWER I'VE BEEN SEEKING!*
BUT FIRST, IT'S TIME THAT I CHECKED IN, TO SEE IF...
SORRY, HANK... DIDN'T HEAR YOUR SIGNAL... TOO PREOCCUPIED, I GUESS!
I'LL BE THERE IN TEN MINUTES!
*AN ANSWER, HOWEVER, WHICH WILL HAVE TO WAIT FOR AN ISH OR TWO! --SNEAKY STAN.
...I STILL DON'T SEE WHY YOU CAN'T TELL ME IF MY VISITOR WAS HUMAN OR NOT, HIGH-POCKETS!
PERHAPS IT'S BECAUSE ...HE WAS BOTH, JAN!
EXACTLY, T'CHALLA!
ACCORDING TO MY EXAMINATION, HE'S EVERY INCH A HUMAN BEING...
...EXCEPT THAT ALL HIS BODILY ORGANS ARE CONSTRUCTED OF SYNTHETIC MATERIALS!
HOLY CATS, MAN-MOUNTAIN... LIKE YOUR SYNTHOZOID!
THE WHAT, HAWKEYE? I DON'T...
A SYNTHOZOID, PANTHER...A NAME I ONCE COINED FOR AN ARTIFICIAL HUMAN!
HAWKEYE REMEMBERS THAT I USED TO BE TRYING TO DEVELOP SUCH A THING, BUT I NEVER...
WAIT! HE'S STARTING TO MOVE...TO BREATHE AGAIN!
--THOUGH! I STILL CAN'T GUESS WHAT MADE HIM STOP!
9

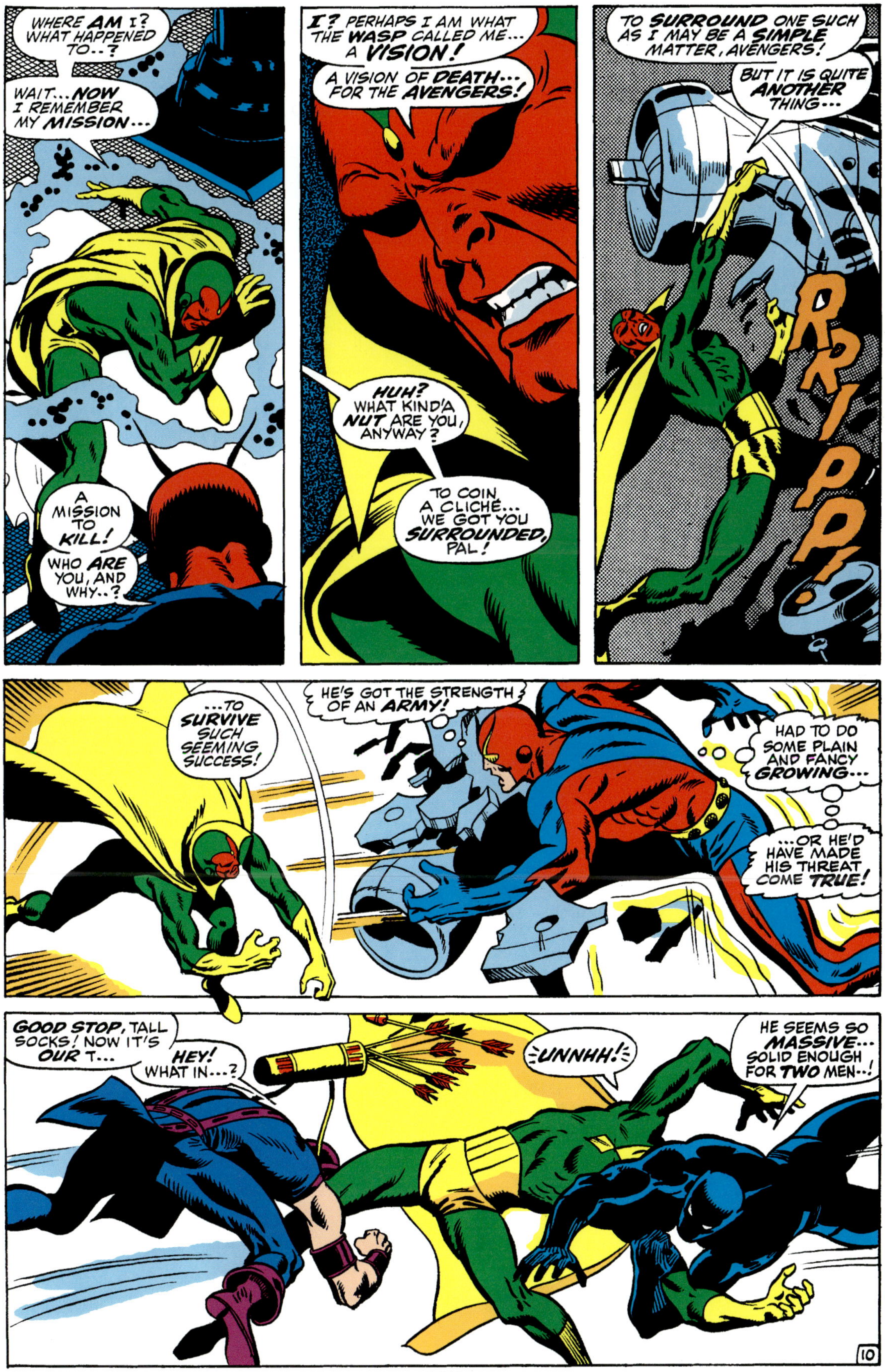
WHERE AM I? WHAT HAPPENED TO..?
WAIT...NOW I REMEMBER MY MISSION...
A MISSION TO KILL!
WHO ARE YOU, AND WHY..?
I? PERHAPS I AM WHAT THE WASP CALLED ME... A VISION!
A VISION OF DEATH... FOR THE AVENGERS!
HUH? WHAT KIND'A NUT ARE YOU, ANYWAY?
TO COIN A CLICHÉ... WE GOT YOU SURROUNDED, PAL!
TO SURROUND ONE SUCH AS I MAY BE A SIMPLE MATTER, AVENGERS!
BUT IT IS QUITE ANOTHER THING...
RRIPP!
...TO SURVIVE SUCH SEEMING SUCCESS!
HE'S GOT THE STRENGTH OF AN ARMY!
HAD TO DO SOME PLAIN AND FANCY GROWING...
...OR HE'D HAVE MADE HIS THREAT COME TRUE!
GOOD STOP, TALL SOCKS! NOW IT'S OUR T...
HEY! WHAT IN...?
UNNHH!
HE SEEMS SO MASSIVE... SOLID ENOUGH FOR TWO MEN..!
10

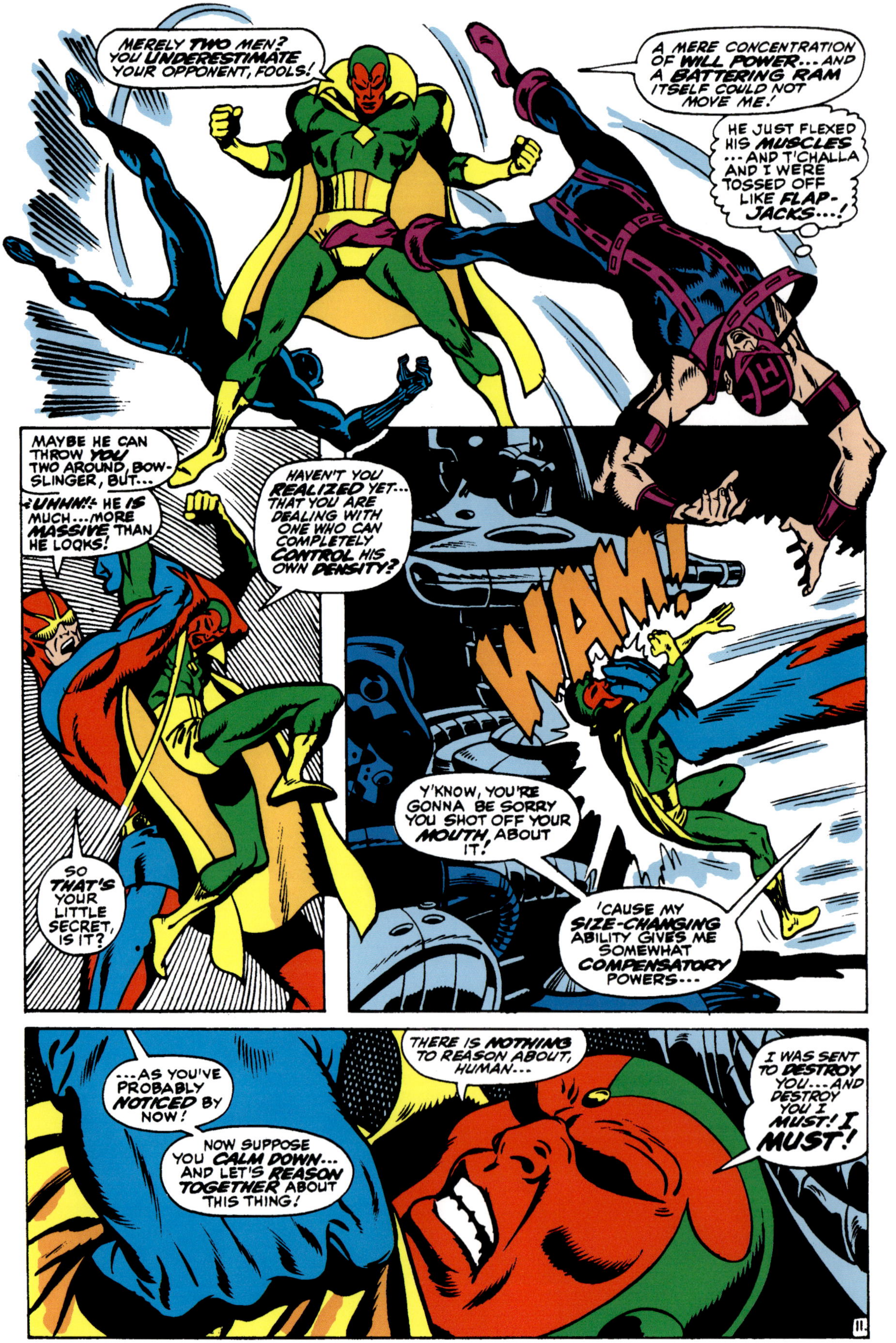
MERELY TWO MEN? YOU UNDERESTIMATE YOUR OPPONENT, FOOLS!
A MERE CONCENTRATION OF WILL POWER... AND A BATTERING RAM ITSELF COULD NOT MOVE ME!
HE JUST FLEXED HIS MUSCLES... AND T'CHALLA AND I WERE TOSSED OFF LIKE FLAP-JACKS...!
MAYBE HE CAN THROW YOU TWO AROUND, BOW-SLINGER, BUT...
UNHH! HE IS MUCH... MORE MASSIVE THAN HE LOOKS!
HAVEN'T YOU REALIZED YET... THAT YOU ARE DEALING WITH ONE WHO CAN COMPLETELY CONTROL HIS OWN DENSITY?
SO THAT'S YOUR LITTLE SECRET, IS IT?
WAM!
Y'KNOW, YOU'RE GONNA BE SORRY YOU SHOT OFF YOUR MOUTH, ABOUT IT!
'CAUSE MY SIZE-CHANGING ABILITY GIVES ME SOMEWHAT COMPENSATORY POWERS...
...AS YOU'VE PROBABLY NOTICED BY NOW!
NOW SUPPOSE YOU CALM DOWN... AND LET'S REASON TOGETHER ABOUT THIS THING!
THERE IS NOTHING TO REASON ABOUT, HUMAN...
I WAS SENT TO DESTROY YOU... AND DESTROY YOU I MUST! I MUST!
11.

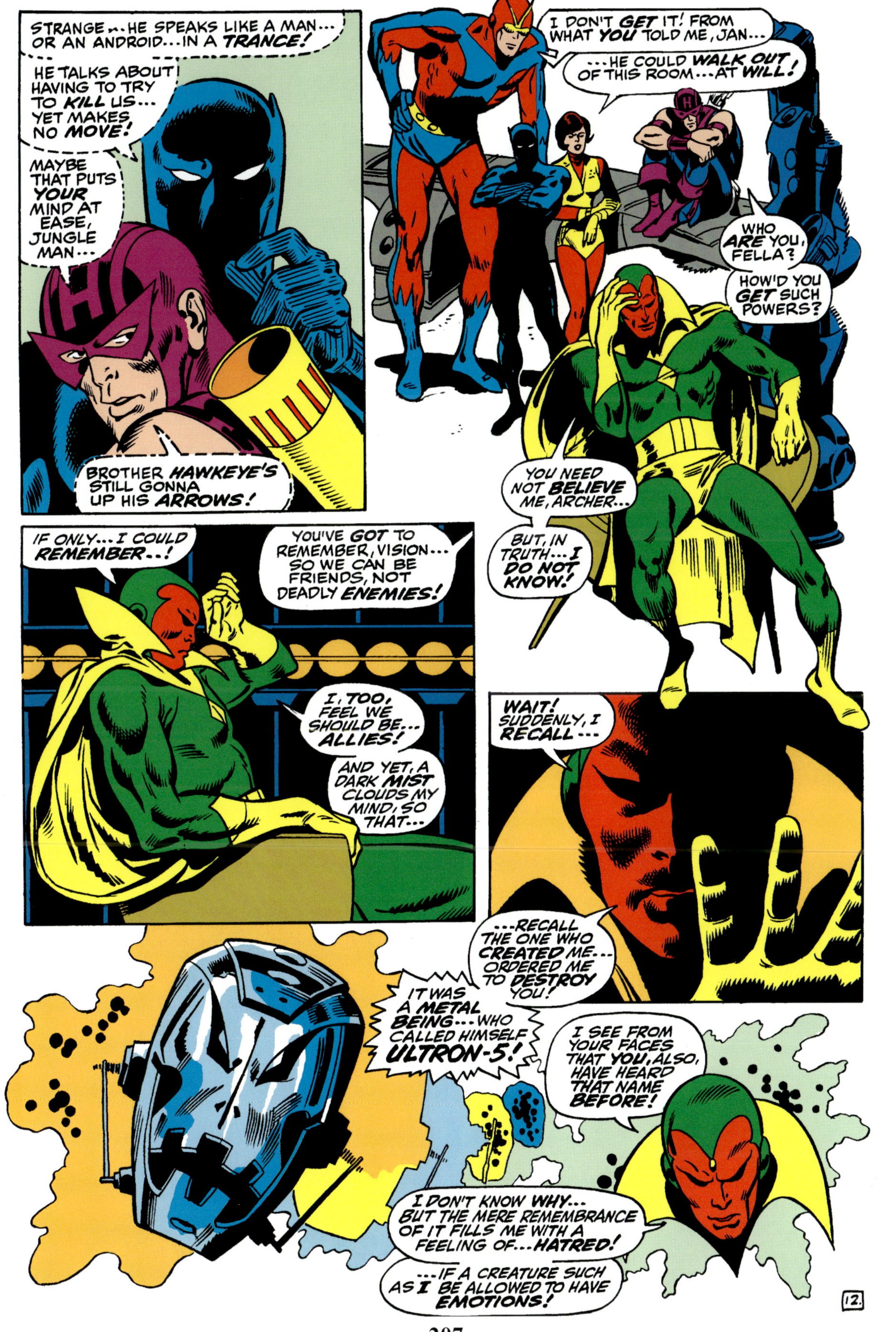
STRANGE...HE SPEAKS LIKE A MAN... OR AN ANDROID...IN A TRANCE!
HE TALKS ABOUT HAVING TO TRY TO KILL US... YET MAKES NO MOVE!
MAYBE THAT PUTS YOUR MIND AT EASE, JUNGLE MAN...
BROTHER HAWKEYE'S STILL GONNA UP HIS ARROWS!
I DON'T GET IT! FROM WHAT YOU TOLD ME, JAN...
...HE COULD WALK OUT OF THIS ROOM...AT WILL!
WHO ARE YOU, FELLA?
HOW'D YOU GET SUCH POWERS?
YOU NEED NOT BELIEVE ME, ARCHER...
BUT, IN TRUTH...I DO NOT KNOW!
IF ONLY...I COULD REMEMBER...!
YOU'VE GOT TO REMEMBER, VISION... SO WE CAN BE FRIENDS, NOT DEADLY ENEMIES!
I, TOO, FEEL WE SHOULD BE... ALLIES!
AND YET, A DARK MIST CLOUDS MY MIND, SO THAT...
WAIT! SUDDENLY, I RECALL...
...RECALL THE ONE WHO CREATED ME... ORDERED ME TO DESTROY YOU!
IT WAS A METAL BEING...WHO CALLED HIMSELF ULTRON-5!
I SEE FROM YOUR FACES THAT YOU, ALSO, HAVE HEARD THAT NAME BEFORE!
I DON'T KNOW WHY... BUT THE MERE REMEMBRANCE OF IT FILLS ME WITH A FEELING OF...HATRED!
...IF A CREATURE SUCH AS I BE ALLOWED TO HAVE EMOTIONS!
12

Panel 1:

VISION: IT IS UNCANNY... BUT, NOW THAT I HAVE PLUMBED MY DIM MEMORIES BACK AS FAR AS THEY WILL GO...

VISION: I NO LONGER FEEL ANY DESIRE TO ATTACK YOU!

VISION: IN FACT, IF YOU WISH... I'LL LEAD YOU TO HIM WHO... CREATED ME!

BLACK PANTHER: WE'VE BEEN HUNTING THAT METAL MANIAC FOR WEEKS!

BLACK PANTHER: SO, WE'VE GOT TO TAKE A CHANCE ON YOU!

HAWKEYE: STILL, JUST IN CASE THERE'S SOME TRICK UP YOUR SLEEVE...

HAWKEYE: I'M KEEPIN' A SHOCK ARROW TRAINED RIGHT ON YOUR SYNTHETIC KISSER!

Panel 2:

CAPTION: MOMENTS LATER, A SLEEK AIR-CRUISER SOARS INTO THE SKY... ITS OCCUPANTS CLOAKED IN SOMBRE SILENCE...

CAPTION: --- EXCEPT FOR THE STRANGELY UNNATURAL VOICE WHICH ISSUES DIRECTIONS --- DIRECTIONS WHICH SOON LEAD TO ...

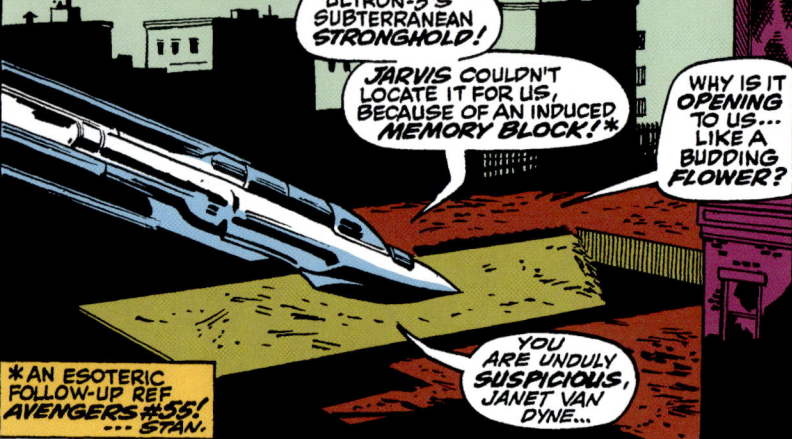

VISION: ULTRON-5'S SUBTERRANEAN STRONGHOLD!

VISION: JARVIS COULDN'T LOCATE IT FOR US, BECAUSE OF AN INDUCED MEMORY BLOCK!*

WASP: WHY IS IT OPENING TO US... LIKE A BUDDING FLOWER?

VISION: YOU ARE UNDULY SUSPICIOUS, JANET VAN DYNE...

CAPTION: *AN ESOTERIC FOLLOW-UP REF AVENGERS #55! --- STAN.

Panel 3:

VISION: ---REMEMBER, MY CREATOR'S PROTECTIVE DEVICES WERE SET TO RE-ADMIT ME!

GOLIATH: SPEAKING OF YOUR SUPPOSED CREATOR... JUST WHO IS HE... AND WHY IS HE SO FANATICAL ABOUT DESTROYING THE AVENGERS?

VISION: THAT, GOLIATH, EVEN I DO NOT KNOW...

13

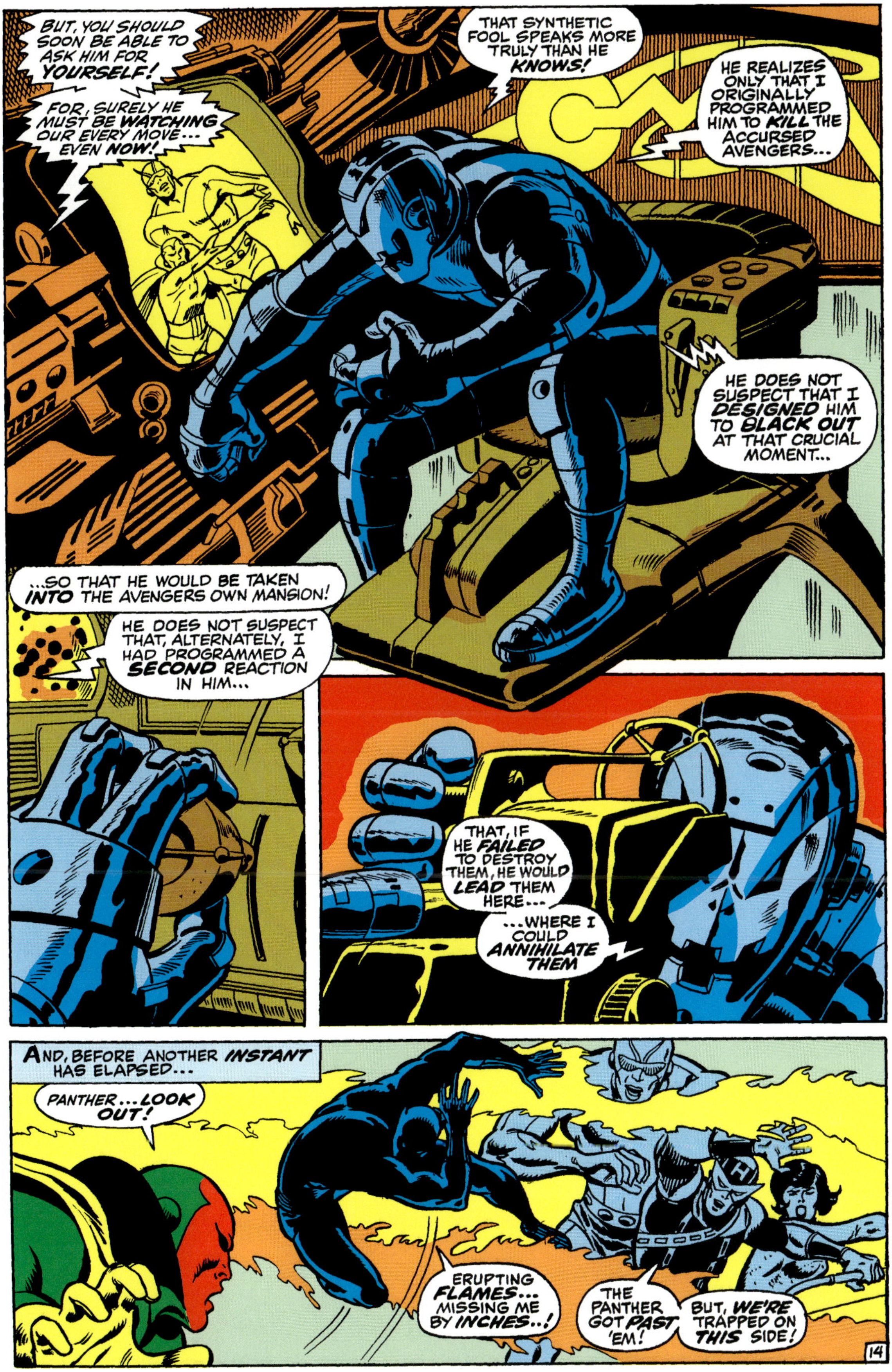
BUT, YOU SHOULD SOON BE ABLE TO ASK HIM FOR YOURSELF!
FOR, SURELY HE MUST BE WATCHING OUR EVERY MOVE... EVEN NOW!
THAT SYNTHETIC FOOL SPEAKS MORE TRULY THAN HE KNOWS!
HE REALIZES ONLY THAT I ORIGINALLY PROGRAMMED HIM TO KILL THE ACCURSED AVENGERS...
HE DOES NOT SUSPECT THAT I DESIGNED HIM TO BLACK OUT AT THAT CRUCIAL MOMENT...
...SO THAT HE WOULD BE TAKEN INTO THE AVENGERS OWN MANSION!
HE DOES NOT SUSPECT THAT, ALTERNATELY, I HAD PROGRAMMED A SECOND REACTION IN HIM...
THAT, IF HE FAILED TO DESTROY THEM, HE WOULD LEAD THEM HERE...
...WHERE I COULD ANNIHILATE THEM
AND, BEFORE ANOTHER INSTANT HAS ELAPSED...
PANTHER... LOOK OUT!
ERUPTING FLAMES... MISSING ME BY INCHES..!
THE PANTHER GOT PAST 'EM!
BUT, WE'RE TRAPPED ON THIS SIDE!
14

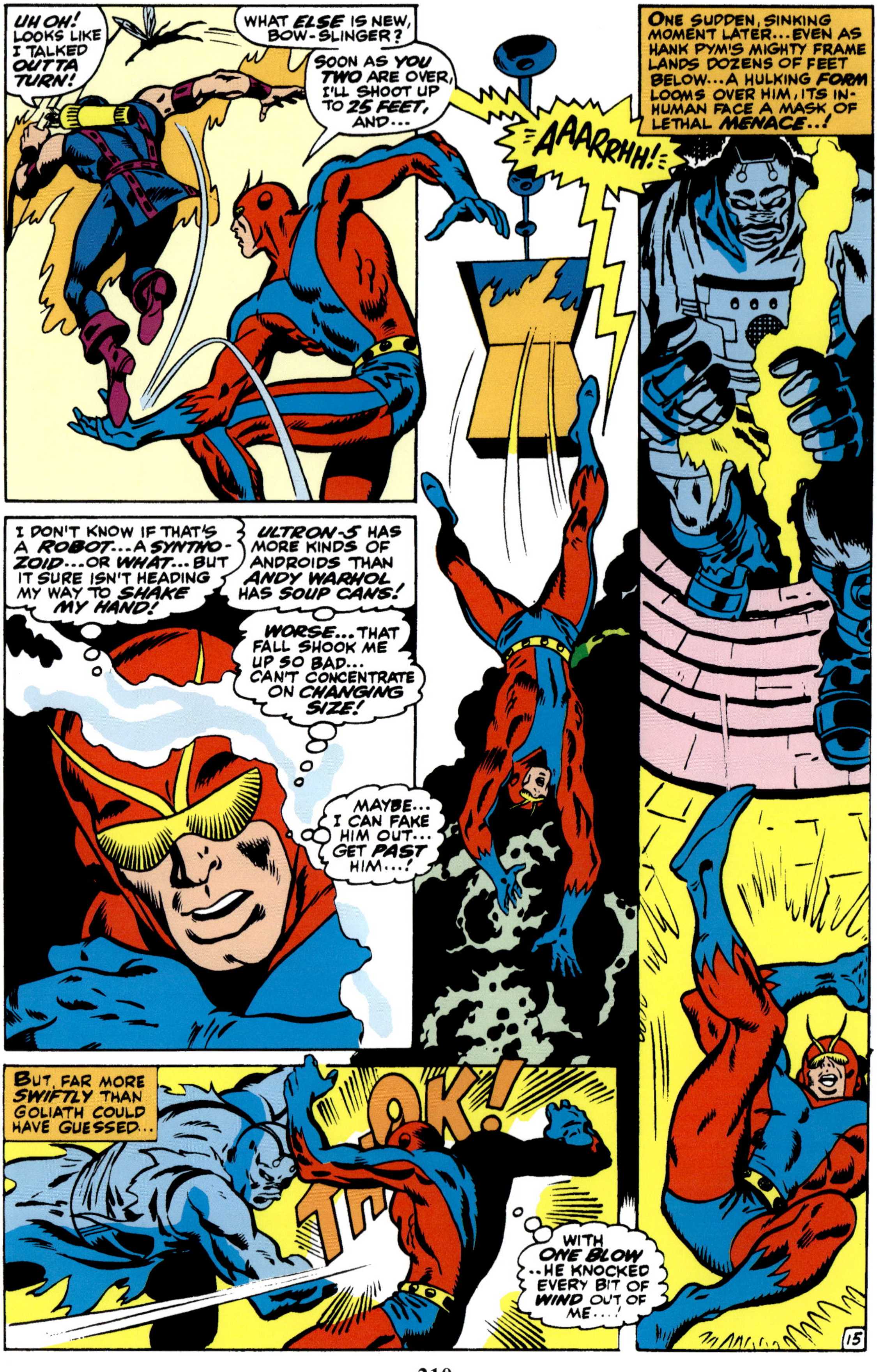

UH OH! LOOKS LIKE I TALKED OUTTA TURN!
WHAT ELSE IS NEW, BOW-SLINGER?
SOON AS YOU TWO ARE OVER, I'LL SHOOT UP TO 25 FEET, AND...
ONE SUDDEN, SINKING MOMENT LATER... EVEN AS HANK PYM'S MIGHTY FRAME LANDS DOZENS OF FEET BELOW... A HULKING FORM LOOMS OVER HIM, ITS IN-HUMAN FACE A MASK OF LETHAL MENACE..!
AAARRHH!
I DON'T KNOW IF THAT'S A ROBOT... A SYNTHO-ZOID... OR WHAT... BUT IT SURE ISN'T HEADING MY WAY TO SHAKE MY HAND!
ULTRON-5 HAS MORE KINDS OF ANDROIDS THAN ANDY WARHOL HAS SOUP CANS!
WORSE... THAT FALL SHOOK ME UP SO BAD... CAN'T CONCENTRATE ON CHANGING SIZE!
MAYBE... I CAN FAKE HIM OUT... GET PAST HIM...!
BUT, FAR MORE SWIFTLY THAN GOLIATH COULD HAVE GUESSED...
THOK!
WITH ONE BLOW ..HE KNOCKED EVERY BIT OF WIND OUT OF ME...!
15

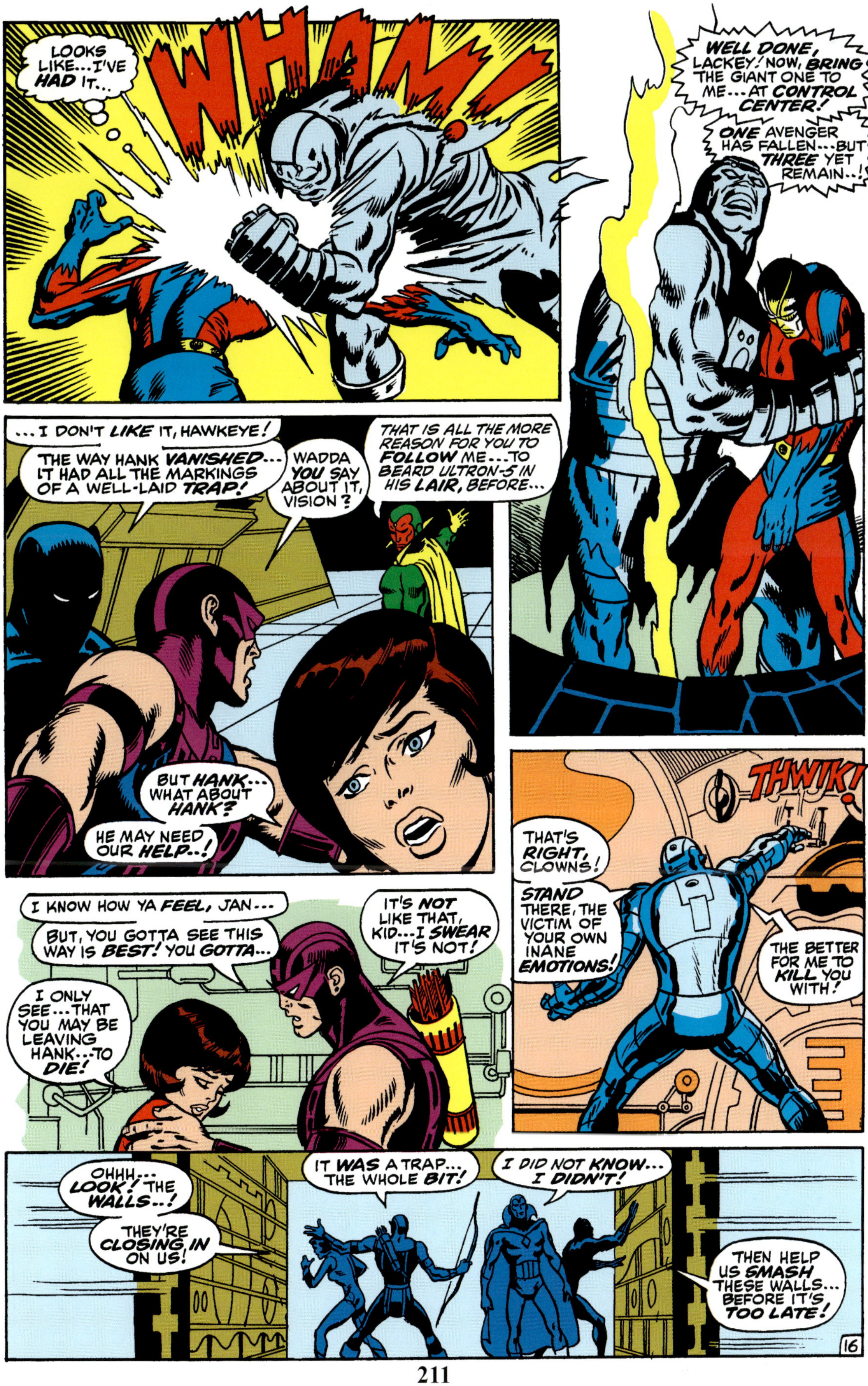
LOOKS LIKE...I'VE HAD IT...
WHAM!
WELL DONE, LACKEY! NOW, BRING THE GIANT ONE TO ME...AT CONTROL CENTER!
ONE AVENGER HAS FALLEN...BUT THREE YET REMAIN..!
...I DON'T LIKE IT, HAWKEYE!
THE WAY HANK VANISHED... IT HAD ALL THE MARKINGS OF A WELL-LAID TRAP!
WADDA YOU SAY ABOUT IT, VISION?
THAT IS ALL THE MORE REASON FOR YOU TO FOLLOW ME...TO BEARD ULTRON-5 IN HIS LAIR, BEFORE...
BUT HANK... WHAT ABOUT HANK?
HE MAY NEED OUR HELP..!
THWIK!
THAT'S RIGHT, CLOWNS!
STAND THERE, THE VICTIM OF YOUR OWN INANE EMOTIONS!
THE BETTER FOR ME TO KILL YOU WITH!
I KNOW HOW YA FEEL, JAN...
BUT, YOU GOTTA SEE THIS WAY IS BEST! YOU GOTTA...
IT'S NOT LIKE THAT, KID...I SWEAR IT'S NOT!
I ONLY SEE...THAT YOU MAY BE LEAVING HANK...TO DIE!
OHHH... LOOK! THE WALLS..!
THEY'RE CLOSING IN ON US!
IT WAS A TRAP... THE WHOLE BIT!
I DID NOT KNOW... I DIDN'T!
THEN HELP US SMASH THESE WALLS... BEFORE IT'S TOO LATE!
16

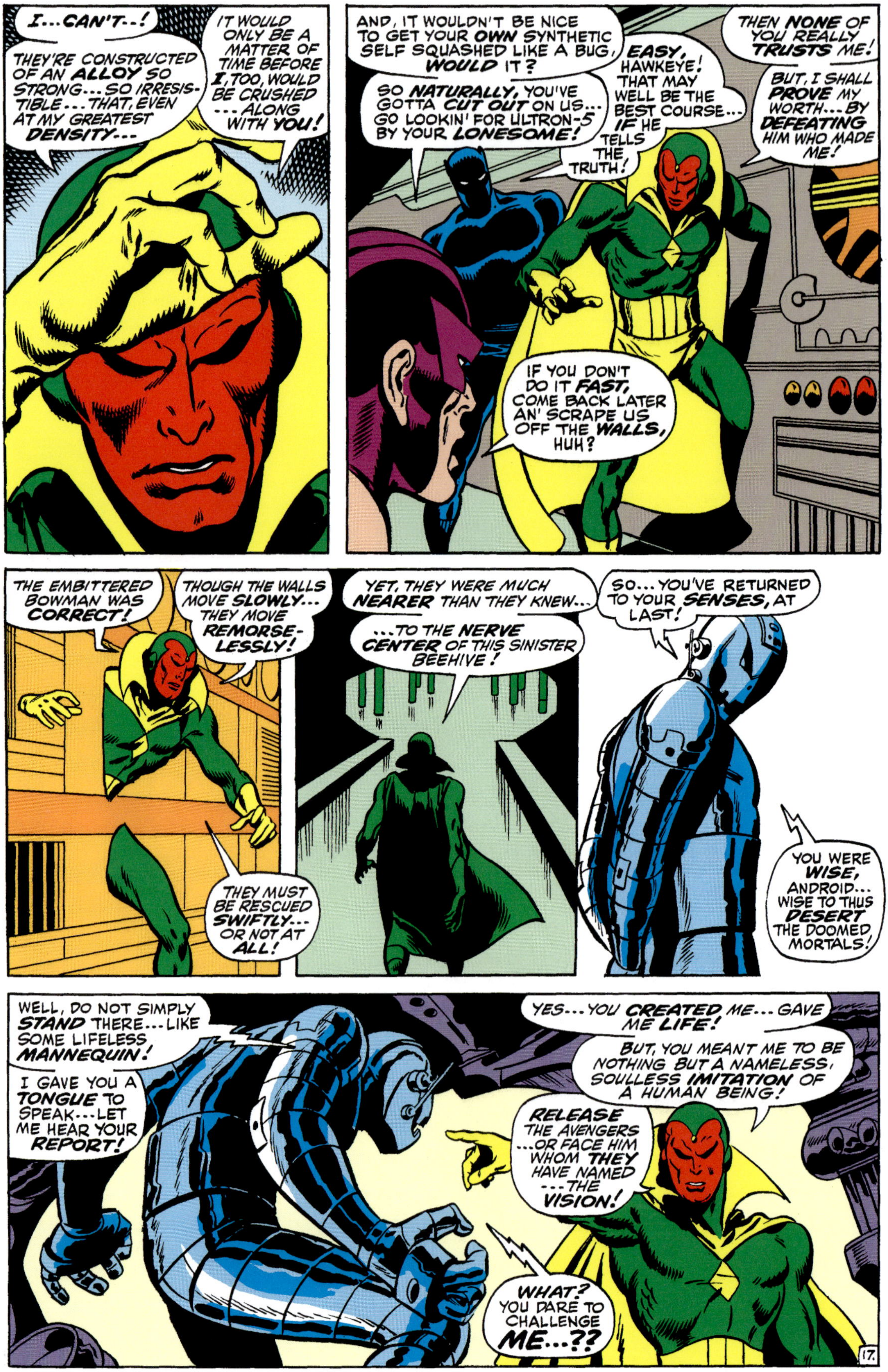

I...CAN'T..!
THEY'RE CONSTRUCTED OF AN ALLOY SO STRONG...SO IRRESISTIBLE...THAT, EVEN AT MY GREATEST DENSITY...
IT WOULD ONLY BE A MATTER OF TIME BEFORE I, TOO, WOULD BE CRUSHED ...ALONG WITH YOU!
AND, IT WOULDN'T BE NICE TO GET YOUR OWN SYNTHETIC SELF SQUASHED LIKE A BUG, WOULD IT?
SO NATURALLY, YOU'VE GOTTA CUT OUT ON US... GO LOOKIN' FOR ULTRON-5 BY YOUR LONESOME!
EASY, HAWKEYE! THAT MAY WELL BE THE BEST COURSE... IF HE TELLS THE TRUTH!
THEN NONE OF YOU REALLY TRUSTS ME!
BUT, I SHALL PROVE MY WORTH... BY DEFEATING HIM WHO MADE ME!
IF YOU DON'T DO IT FAST, COME BACK LATER AN' SCRAPE US OFF THE WALLS, HUH?
THE EMBITTERED BOWMAN WAS CORRECT!
THOUGH THE WALLS MOVE SLOWLY... THEY MOVE REMORSELESSLY!
THEY MUST BE RESCUED SWIFTLY... OR NOT AT ALL!
YET, THEY WERE MUCH NEARER THAN THEY KNEW...
...TO THE NERVE CENTER OF THIS SINISTER BEEHIVE!
SO... YOU'VE RETURNED TO YOUR SENSES, AT LAST!
YOU WERE WISE, ANDROID... WISE TO THUS DESERT THE DOOMED MORTALS!
WELL, DO NOT SIMPLY STAND THERE... LIKE SOME LIFELESS MANNEQUIN!
I GAVE YOU A TONGUE TO SPEAK... LET ME HEAR YOUR REPORT!
YES... YOU CREATED ME... GAVE ME LIFE!
BUT, YOU MEANT ME TO BE NOTHING BUT A NAMELESS, SOULLESS IMITATION OF A HUMAN BEING!
RELEASE THE AVENGERS ...OR FACE HIM WHOM THEY HAVE NAMED ...THE VISION!
WHAT? YOU DARE TO CHALLENGE ME...??
17

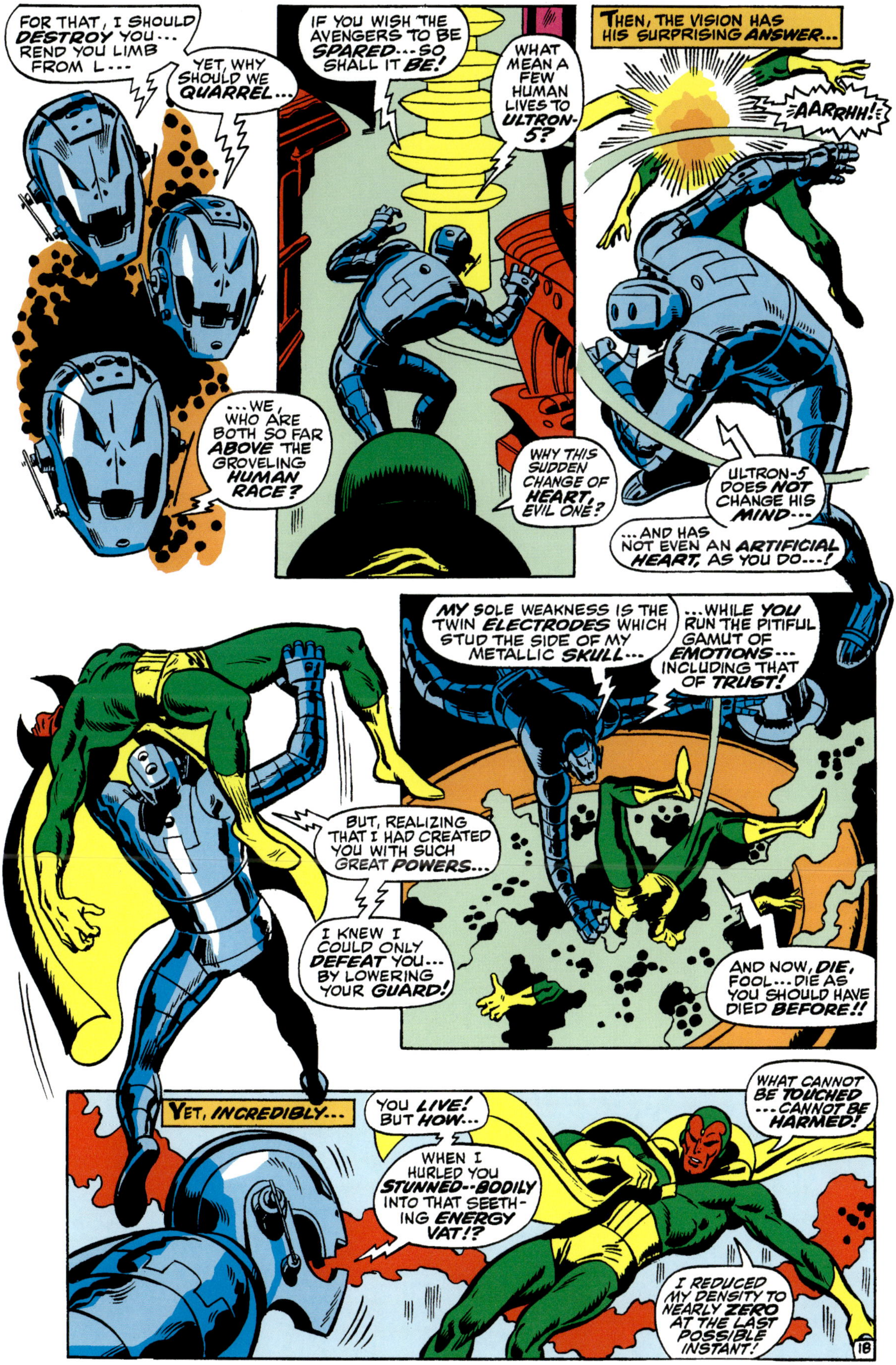
FOR THAT, I SHOULD DESTROY YOU... REND YOU LIMB FROM L---
YET, WHY SHOULD WE QUARREL...
...WE, WHO ARE BOTH SO FAR ABOVE THE GROVELING HUMAN RACE?
IF YOU WISH THE AVENGERS TO BE SPARED...SO SHALL IT BE!
WHAT MEAN A FEW HUMAN LIVES TO ULTRON-5?
WHY THIS SUDDEN CHANGE OF HEART, EVIL ONE?
THEN, THE VISION HAS HIS SURPRISING ANSWER...
AARRHH!
ULTRON-5 DOES NOT CHANGE HIS MIND...
...AND HAS NOT EVEN AN ARTIFICIAL HEART, AS YOU DO...!
MY SOLE WEAKNESS IS THE TWIN ELECTRODES WHICH STUD THE SIDE OF MY METALLIC SKULL...
...WHILE YOU RUN THE PITIFUL GAMUT OF EMOTIONS...INCLUDING THAT OF TRUST!
BUT, REALIZING THAT I HAD CREATED YOU WITH SUCH GREAT POWERS...
I KNEW I COULD ONLY DEFEAT YOU... BY LOWERING YOUR GUARD!
AND NOW, DIE, FOOL...DIE AS YOU SHOULD HAVE DIED BEFORE!!
YET, INCREDIBLY...
YOU LIVE! BUT HOW...
WHEN I HURLED YOU STUNNED--BODILY INTO THAT SEETHING ENERGY VAT!?
WHAT CANNOT BE TOUCHED ...CANNOT BE HARMED!
I REDUCED MY DENSITY TO NEARLY ZERO AT THE LAST POSSIBLE INSTANT!
18

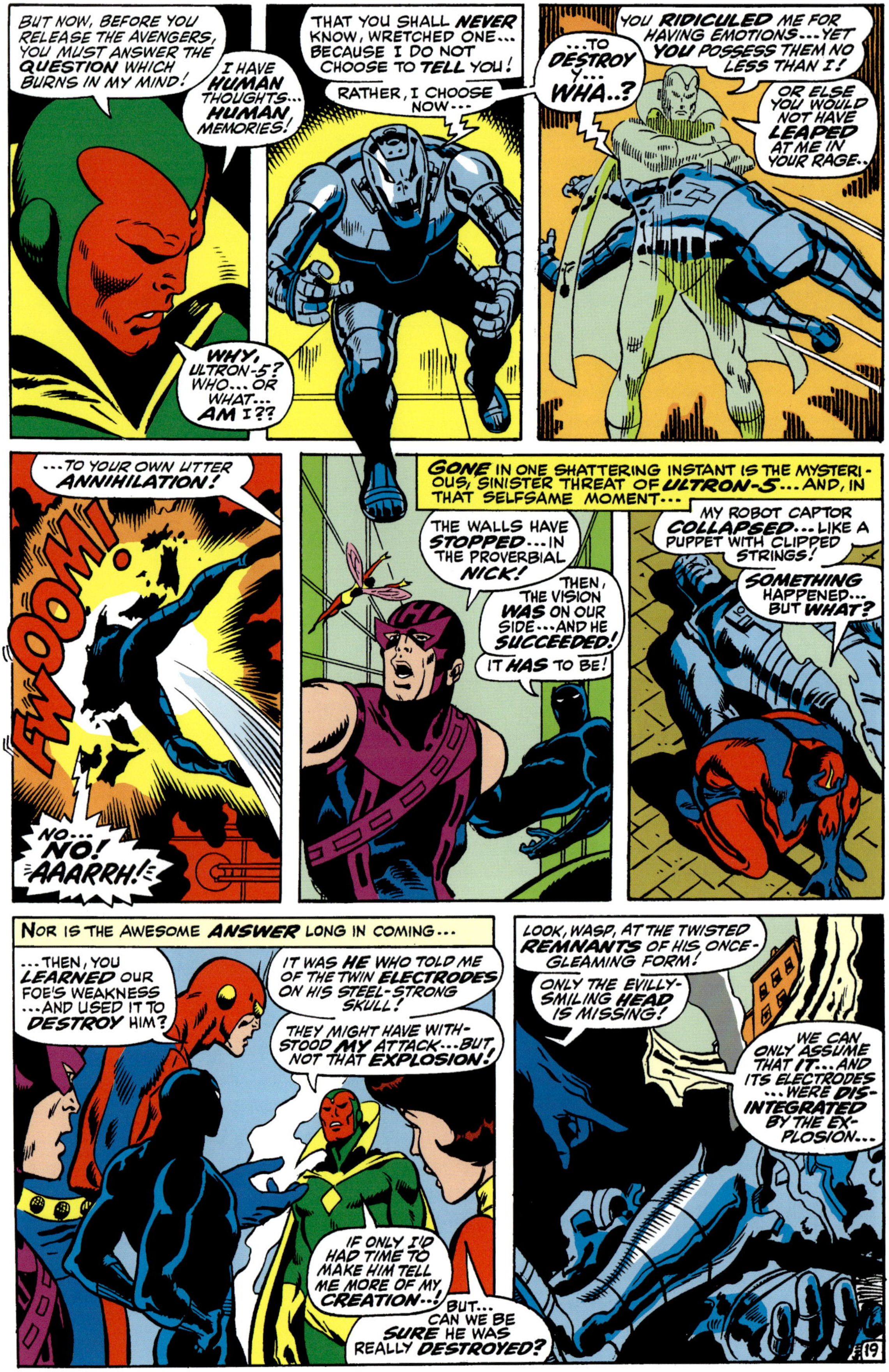
BUT NOW, BEFORE YOU RELEASE THE AVENGERS, YOU MUST ANSWER THE QUESTION WHICH BURNS IN MY MIND!
I HAVE HUMAN THOUGHTS... HUMAN MEMORIES!
WHY, ULTRON-5? WHO... OR WHAT... AM I??
THAT YOU SHALL NEVER KNOW, WRETCHED ONE... BECAUSE I DO NOT CHOOSE TO TELL YOU!
RATHER, I CHOOSE NOW...
...TO DESTROY Y... WHA..?
YOU RIDICULED ME FOR HAVING EMOTIONS... YET YOU POSSESS THEM NO LESS THAN I!
OR ELSE YOU WOULD NOT HAVE LEAPED AT ME IN YOUR RAGE..
...TO YOUR OWN UTTER ANNIHILATION!
FWOOM!
NO... NO! AAARRH!
GONE IN ONE SHATTERING INSTANT IS THE MYSTERIOUS, SINISTER THREAT OF ULTRON-5... AND, IN THAT SELFSAME MOMENT...
THE WALLS HAVE STOPPED... IN THE PROVERBIAL NICK!
THEN, THE VISION WAS ON OUR SIDE... AND HE SUCCEEDED!
IT HAS TO BE!
MY ROBOT CAPTOR COLLAPSED... LIKE A PUPPET WITH CLIPPED STRINGS!
SOMETHING HAPPENED... BUT WHAT?
NOR IS THE AWESOME ANSWER LONG IN COMING...
...THEN, YOU LEARNED OUR FOE'S WEAKNESS ...AND USED IT TO DESTROY HIM?
IT WAS HE WHO TOLD ME OF THE TWIN ELECTRODES ON HIS STEEL-STRONG SKULL!
THEY MIGHT HAVE WITHSTOOD MY ATTACK... BUT NOT THAT EXPLOSION!
IF ONLY I'D HAD TIME TO MAKE HIM TELL ME MORE OF MY CREATION..!
BUT... CAN WE BE SURE HE WAS REALLY DESTROYED?
LOOK, WASP, AT THE TWISTED REMNANTS OF HIS ONCE-GLEAMING FORM!
ONLY THE EVILLY-SMILING HEAD IS MISSING!
WE CAN ONLY ASSUME THAT IT... AND ITS ELECTRODES ...WERE DISINTEGRATED BY THE EXPLOSION...
19

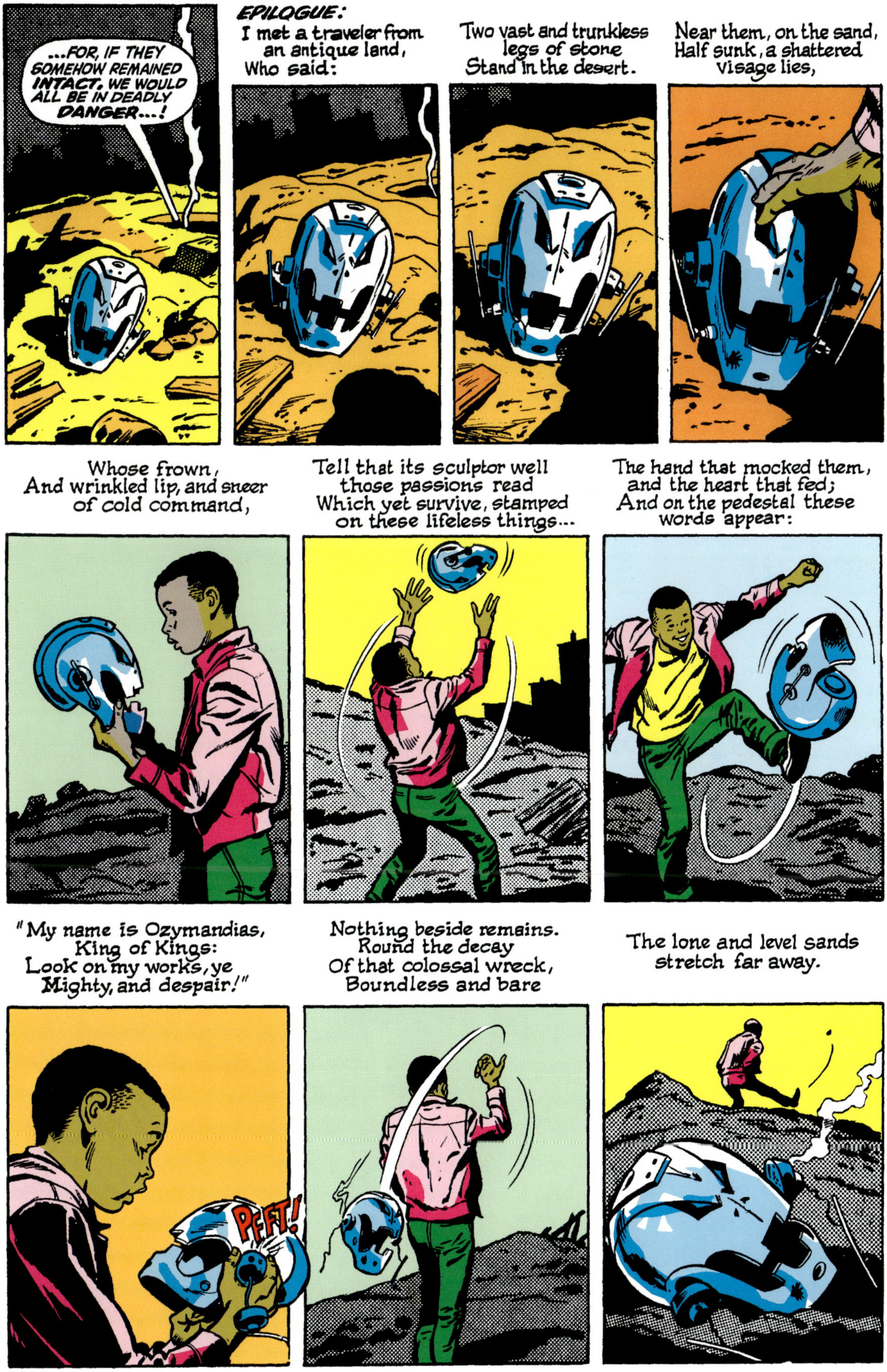
...FOR, IF THEY SOMEHOW REMAINED INTACT, WE WOULD ALL BE IN DEADLY DANGER...!
EPILOGUE:
I met a traveler from an antique land, Who said:
Two vast and trunkless legs of stone Stand in the desert.
Near them, on the sand, Half sunk, a shattered visage lies,
Whose frown, And wrinkled lip, and sneer of cold command,
Tell that its sculptor well those passions read Which yet survive, stamped on these lifeless things...
The hand that mocked them, and the heart that fed; And on the pedestal these words appear:
"My name is Ozymandias, King of Kings: Look on my works, ye Mighty, and despair!"
PFFT!
Nothing beside remains. Round the decay Of that colossal wreck, Boundless and bare
The lone and level sands stretch far away.

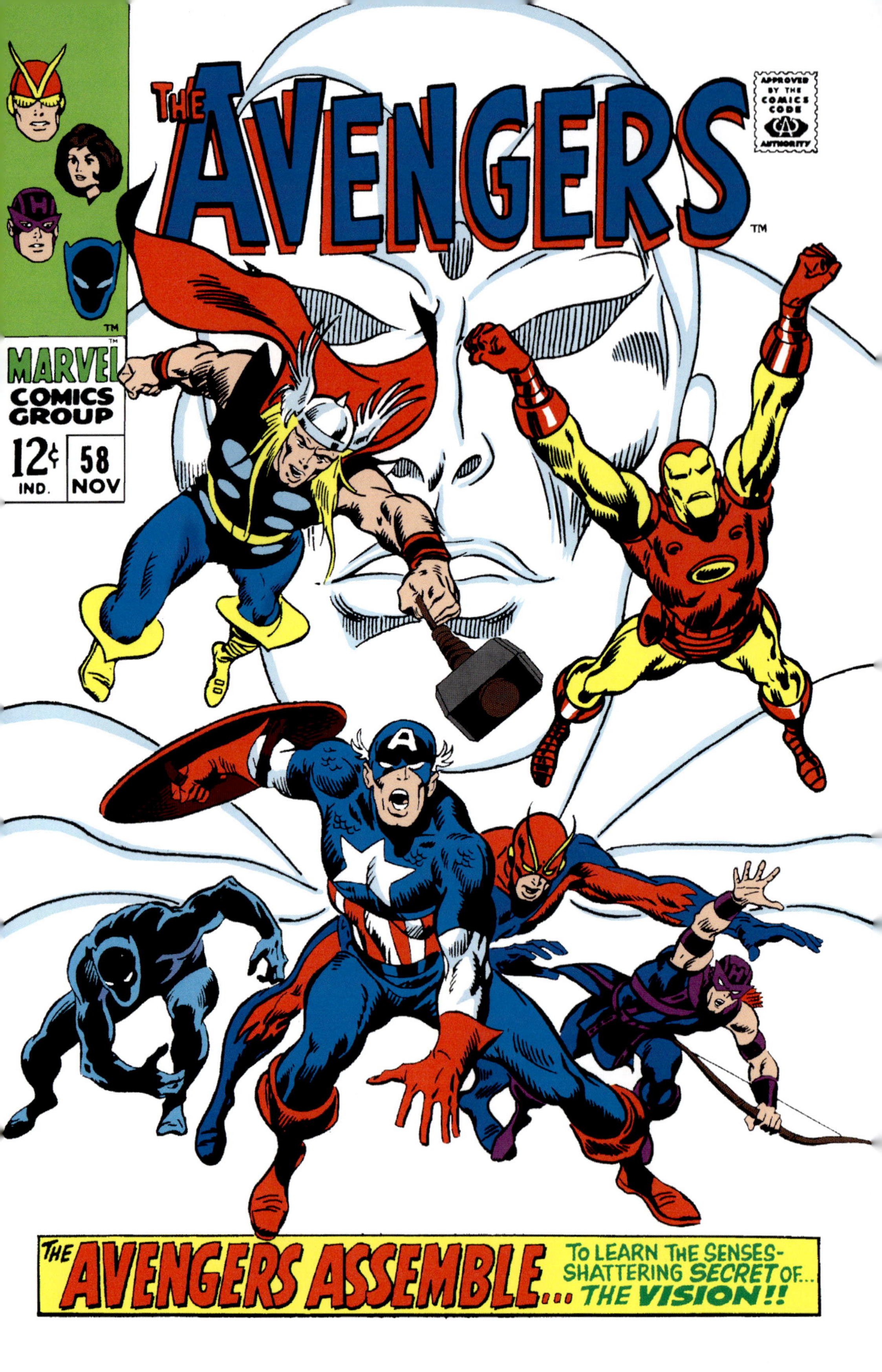

THE AVENGERS
APPROVED BY THE COMICS CODE AUTHORITY
MARVEL COMICS GROUP
12¢ IND.
58 NOV
THE AVENGERS ASSEMBLE... TO LEARN THE SENSES-SHATTERING SECRET OF... THE VISION!!

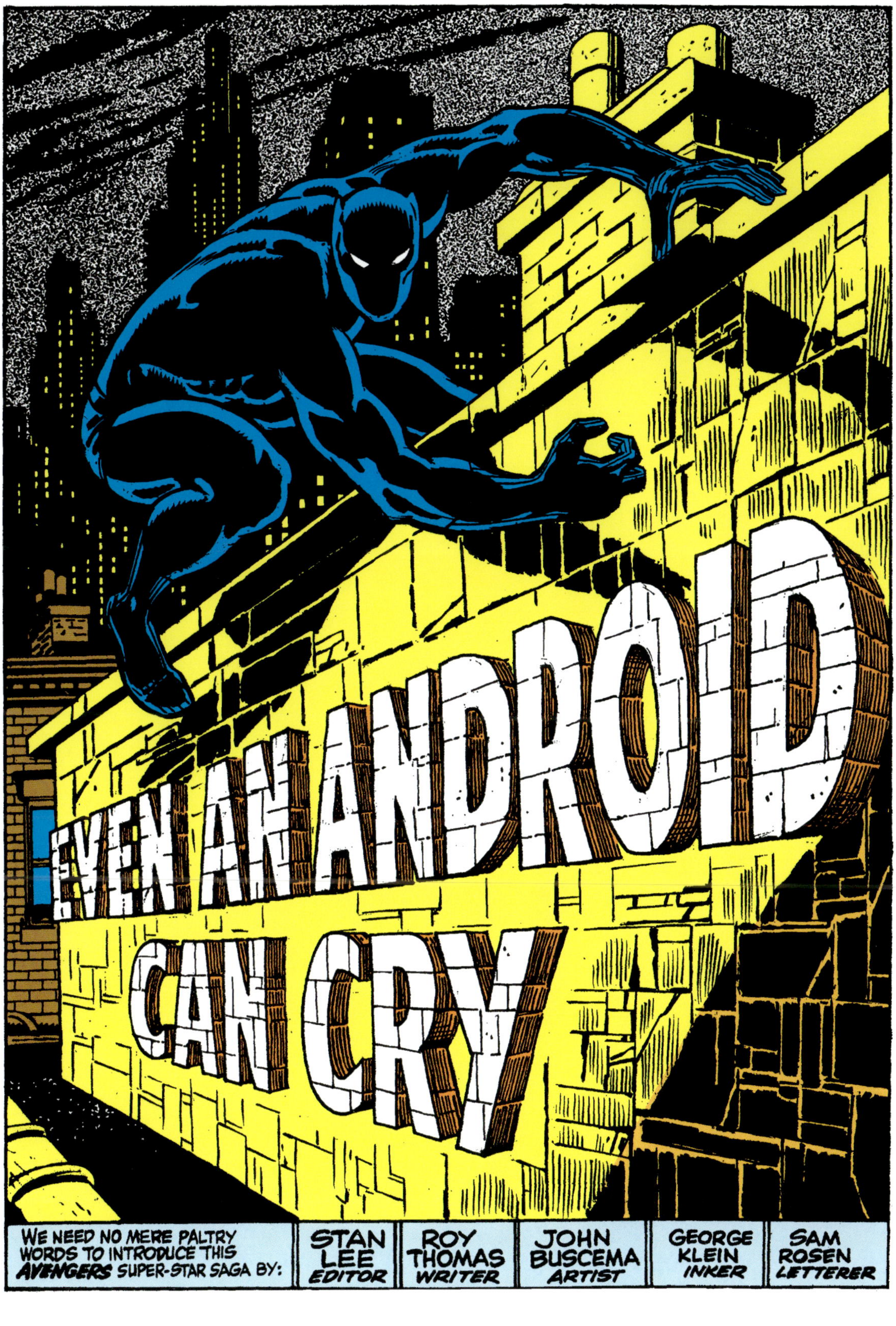
EVEN AN ANDROID CAN CRY
WE NEED NO MERE PALTRY WORDS TO INTRODUCE THIS AVENGERS SUPER-STAR SAGA BY:
STAN LEE EDITOR
ROY THOMAS WRITER
JOHN BUSCEMA ARTIST
GEORGE KLEIN INKER
SAM ROSEN LETTERER

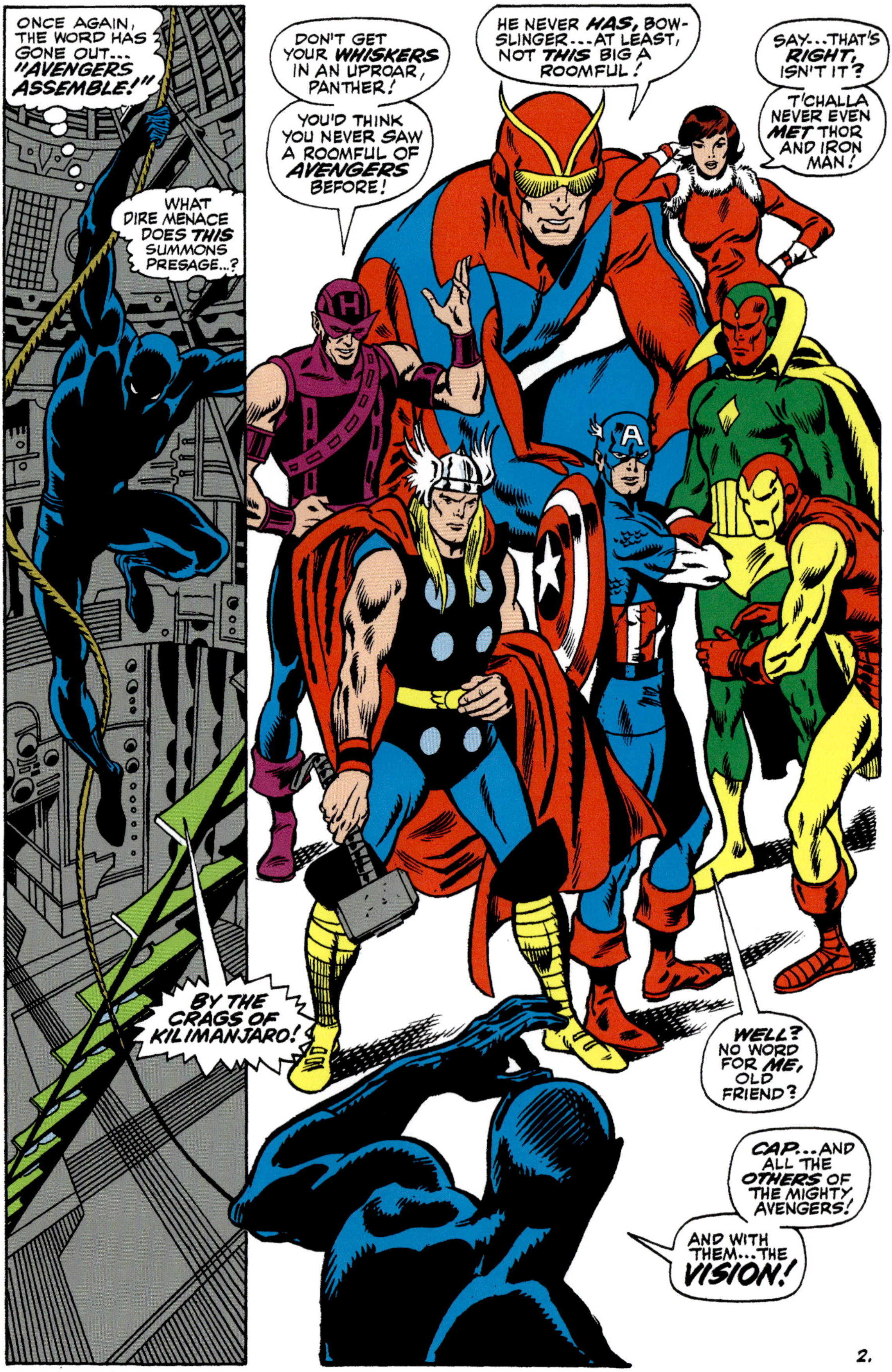
ONCE AGAIN, THE WORD HAS GONE OUT... "AVENGERS ASSEMBLE!"
WHAT DIRE MENACE DOES THIS SUMMONS PRESAGE...?
BY THE CRAGS OF KILIMANJARO!
DON'T GET YOUR WHISKERS IN AN UPROAR, PANTHER!
YOU'D THINK YOU NEVER SAW A ROOMFUL OF AVENGERS BEFORE!
HE NEVER HAS, BOW-SLINGER...AT LEAST, NOT THIS BIG A ROOMFUL!
SAY...THAT'S RIGHT, ISN'T IT?
T'CHALLA NEVER EVEN MET THOR AND IRON MAN!
WELL? NO WORD FOR ME, OLD FRIEND?
CAP...AND ALL THE OTHERS OF THE MIGHTY AVENGERS!
AND WITH THEM...THE VISION!
2.

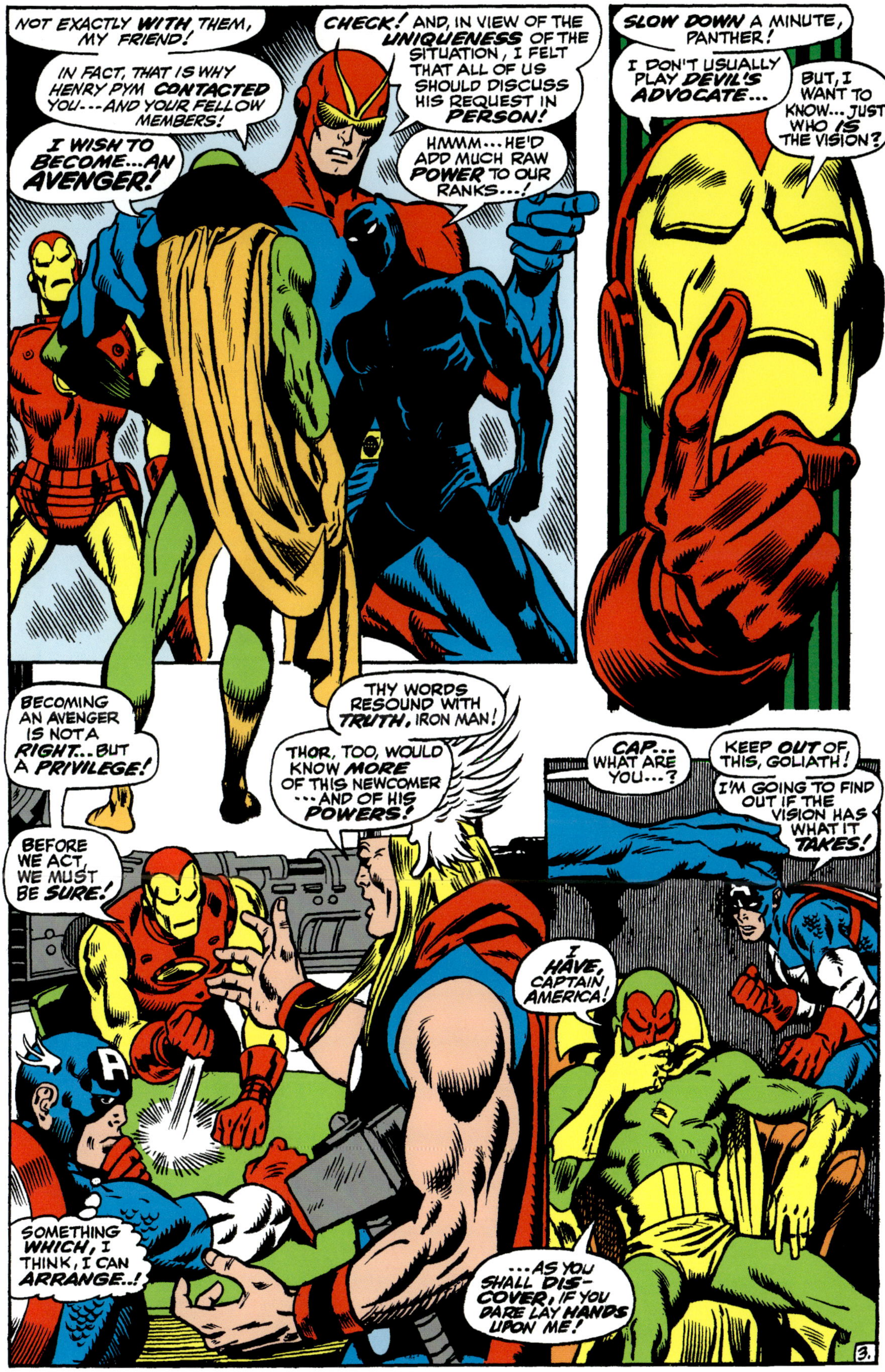
NOT EXACTLY WITH THEM, MY FRIEND!
IN FACT, THAT IS WHY HENRY PYM CONTACTED YOU---AND YOUR FELLOW MEMBERS!
CHECK! AND, IN VIEW OF THE UNIQUENESS OF THE SITUATION, I FELT THAT ALL OF US SHOULD DISCUSS HIS REQUEST IN PERSON!
I WISH TO BECOME...AN AVENGER!
HMMM...HE'D ADD MUCH RAW POWER TO OUR RANKS...!
SLOW DOWN A MINUTE, PANTHER!
I DON'T USUALLY PLAY DEVIL'S ADVOCATE...
BUT, I WANT TO KNOW...JUST WHO IS THE VISION?
BECOMING AN AVENGER IS NOT A RIGHT...BUT A PRIVILEGE!
BEFORE WE ACT, WE MUST BE SURE!
THY WORDS RESOUND WITH TRUTH, IRON MAN!
THOR, TOO, WOULD KNOW MORE OF THIS NEWCOMER ---AND OF HIS POWERS!
SOMETHING WHICH, I THINK, I CAN ARRANGE..!
CAP... WHAT ARE YOU...?
KEEP OUT OF THIS, GOLIATH!
I'M GOING TO FIND OUT IF THE VISION HAS WHAT IT TAKES!
I HAVE, CAPTAIN AMERICA!
...AS YOU SHALL DISCOVER, IF YOU DARE LAY HANDS UPON ME!
3.

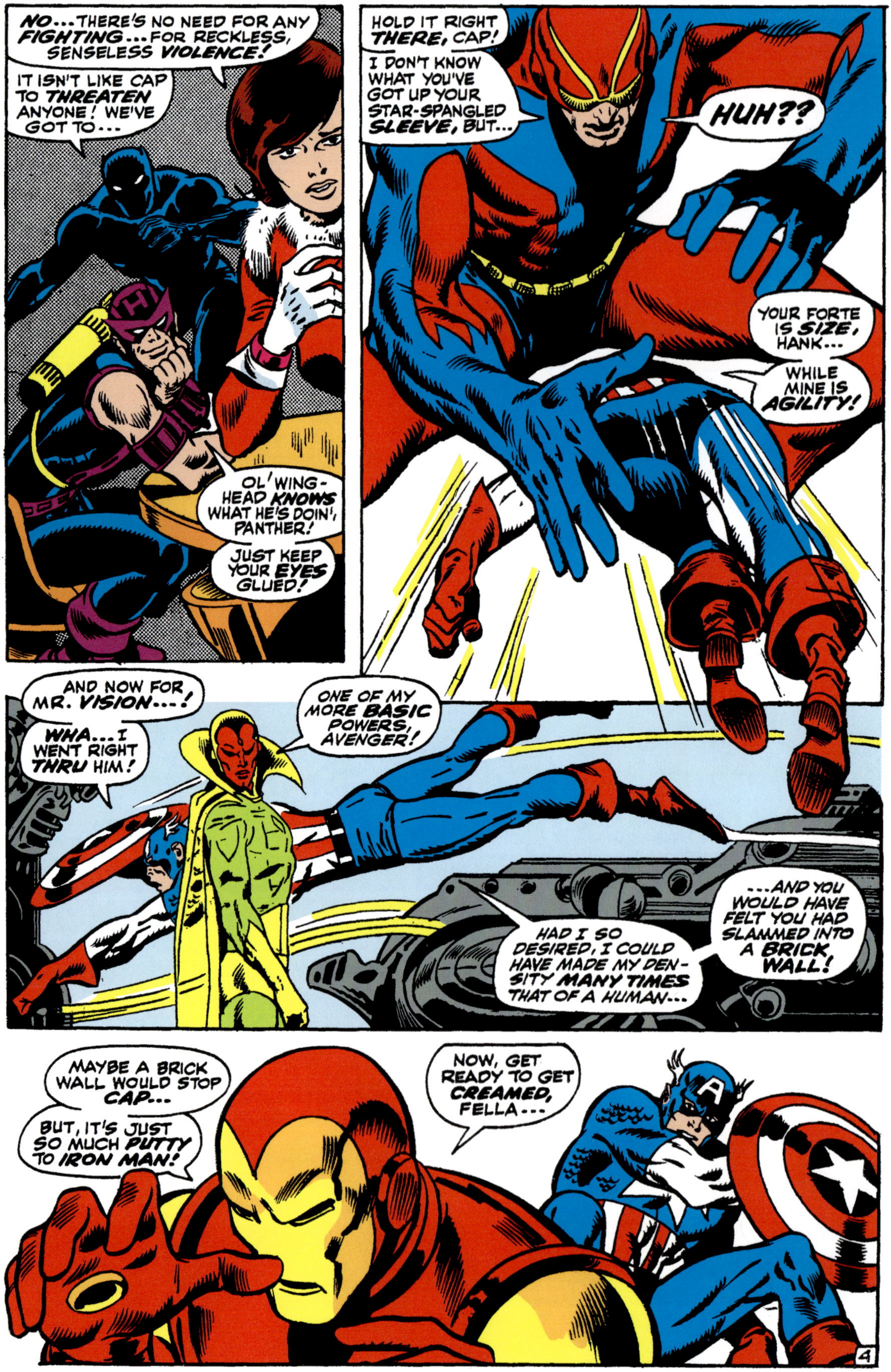
NO... THERE'S NO NEED FOR ANY FIGHTING... FOR RECKLESS, SENSELESS VIOLENCE!
IT ISN'T LIKE CAP TO THREATEN ANYONE! WE'VE GOT TO...
OL' WING-HEAD KNOWS WHAT HE'S DOIN', PANTHER!
JUST KEEP YOUR EYES GLUED!
HOLD IT RIGHT THERE, CAP!
I DON'T KNOW WHAT YOU'VE GOT UP YOUR STAR-SPANGLED SLEEVE, BUT...
HUH??
YOUR FORTE IS SIZE, HANK...
WHILE MINE IS AGILITY!
AND NOW FOR MR. VISION...!
WHA... I WENT RIGHT THRU HIM!
ONE OF MY MORE BASIC POWERS, AVENGER!
HAD I SO DESIRED, I COULD HAVE MADE MY DENSITY MANY TIMES THAT OF A HUMAN...
...AND YOU WOULD HAVE FELT YOU HAD SLAMMED INTO A BRICK WALL!
MAYBE A BRICK WALL WOULD STOP CAP...
BUT, IT'S JUST SO MUCH PUTTY TO IRON MAN!
NOW, GET READY TO GET CREAMED, FELLA...
4

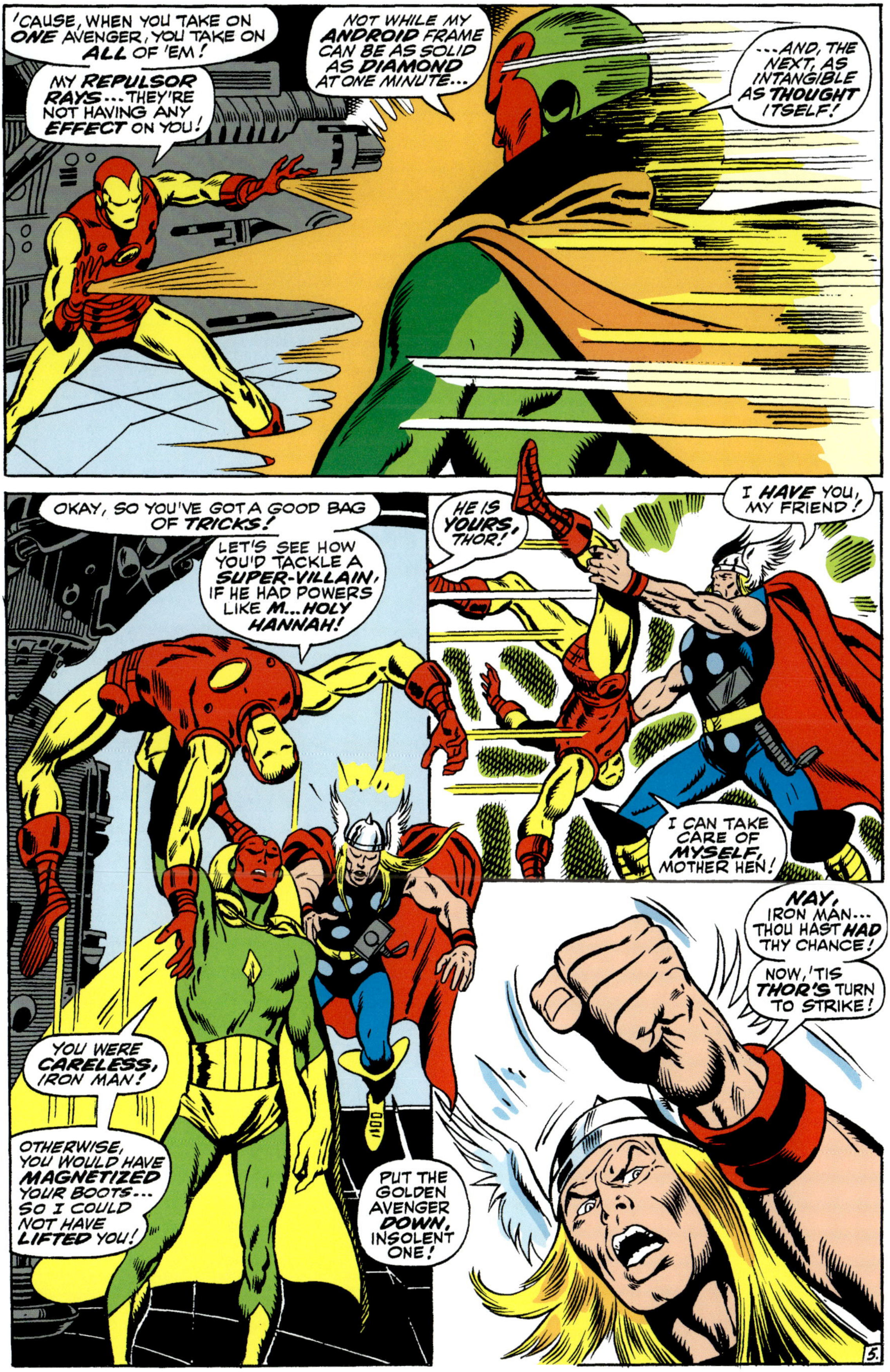
'CAUSE, WHEN YOU TAKE ON ONE AVENGER, YOU TAKE ON ALL OF 'EM!
MY REPULSOR RAYS... THEY'RE NOT HAVING ANY EFFECT ON YOU!
NOT WHILE MY ANDROID FRAME CAN BE AS SOLID AS DIAMOND AT ONE MINUTE...
...AND, THE NEXT, AS INTANGIBLE AS THOUGHT ITSELF!
OKAY, SO YOU'VE GOT A GOOD BAG OF TRICKS!
LET'S SEE HOW YOU'D TACKLE A SUPER-VILLAIN, IF HE HAD POWERS LIKE M...HOLY HANNAH!
YOU WERE CARELESS, IRON MAN!
OTHERWISE, YOU WOULD HAVE MAGNETIZED YOUR BOOTS... SO I COULD NOT HAVE LIFTED YOU!
PUT THE GOLDEN AVENGER DOWN, INSOLENT ONE!
HE IS YOURS, THOR!
I HAVE YOU, MY FRIEND!
I CAN TAKE CARE OF MYSELF, MOTHER HEN!
NAY, IRON MAN... THOU HAST HAD THY CHANCE!
NOW, 'TIS THOR'S TURN TO STRIKE!
5.

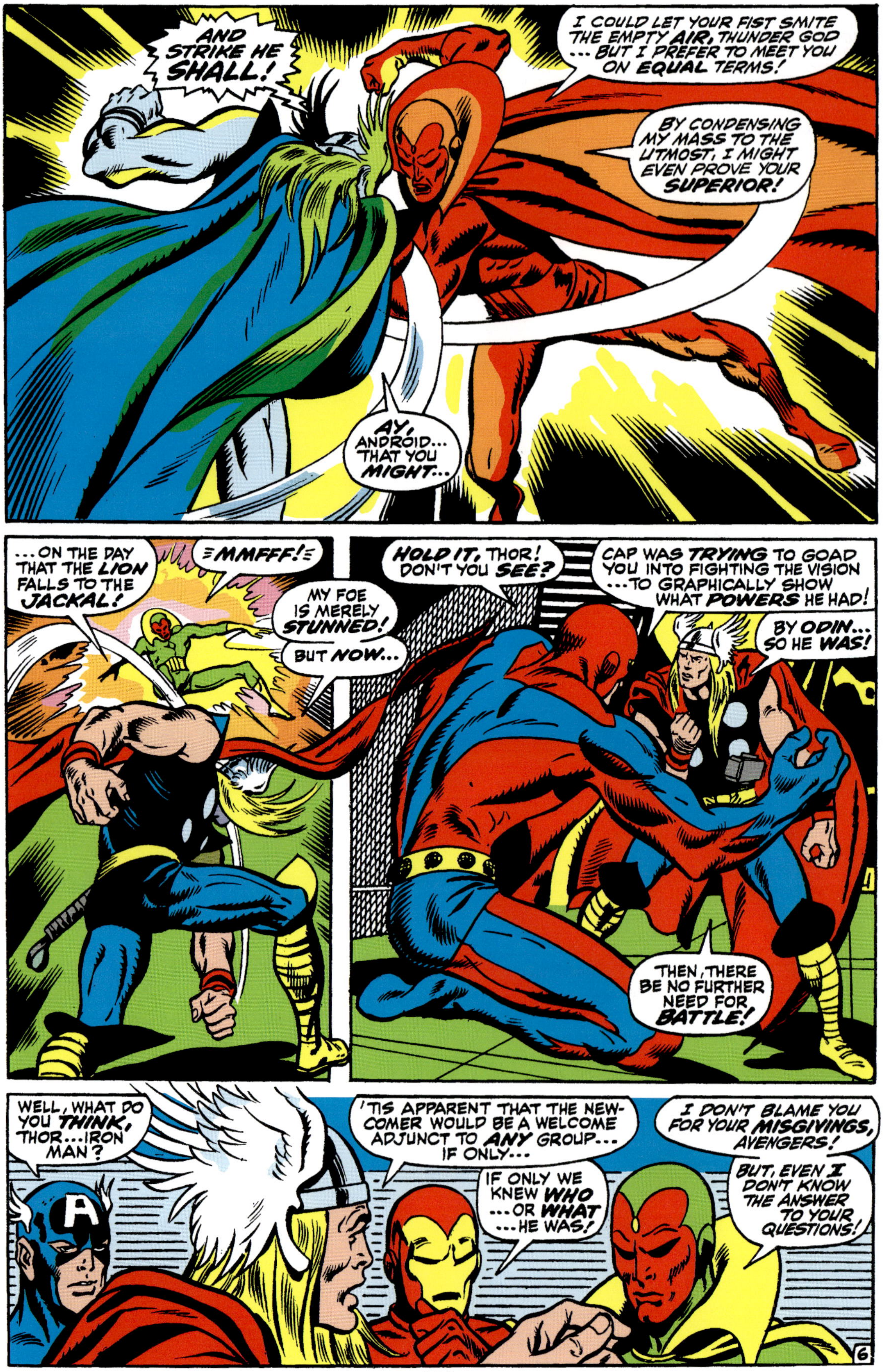
AND STRIKE HE SHALL!
I COULD LET YOUR FIST SMITE THE EMPTY AIR, THUNDER GOD ... BUT I PREFER TO MEET YOU ON EQUAL TERMS!
BY CONDENSING MY MASS TO THE UTMOST, I MIGHT EVEN PROVE YOUR SUPERIOR!
AY, ANDROID... THAT YOU MIGHT...
...ON THE DAY THAT THE LION FALLS TO THE JACKAL!
MMFFF!
MY FOE IS MERELY STUNNED!
BUT NOW...
HOLD IT, THOR! DON'T YOU SEE?
CAP WAS TRYING TO GOAD YOU INTO FIGHTING THE VISION ...TO GRAPHICALLY SHOW WHAT POWERS HE HAD!
BY ODIN... SO HE WAS!
THEN, THERE BE NO FURTHER NEED FOR BATTLE!
WELL, WHAT DO YOU THINK, THOR...IRON MAN?
'TIS APPARENT THAT THE NEW-COMER WOULD BE A WELCOME ADJUNCT TO ANY GROUP... IF ONLY...
IF ONLY WE KNEW WHO ...OR WHAT ...HE WAS!
I DON'T BLAME YOU FOR YOUR MISGIVINGS, AVENGERS!
BUT, EVEN I DON'T KNOW THE ANSWER TO YOUR QUESTIONS!
6

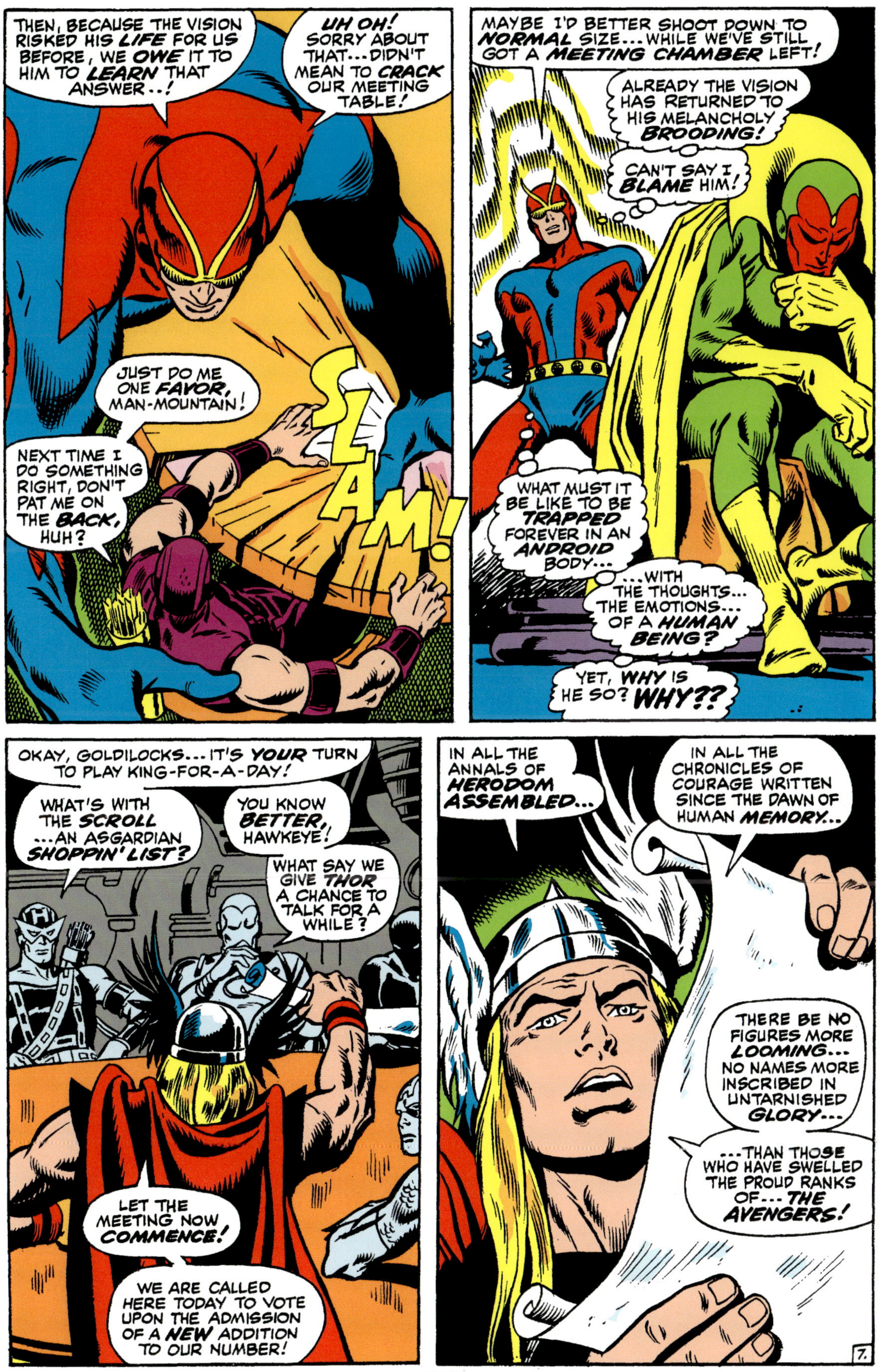
THEN, BECAUSE THE VISION RISKED HIS LIFE FOR US BEFORE, WE OWE IT TO HIM TO LEARN THAT ANSWER..!
UH OH! SORRY ABOUT THAT... DIDN'T MEAN TO CRACK OUR MEETING TABLE!
SLAM!
JUST DO ME ONE FAVOR, MAN-MOUNTAIN!
NEXT TIME I DO SOMETHING RIGHT, DON'T PAT ME ON THE BACK, HUH?
MAYBE I'D BETTER SHOOT DOWN TO NORMAL SIZE... WHILE WE'VE STILL GOT A MEETING CHAMBER LEFT!
ALREADY THE VISION HAS RETURNED TO HIS MELANCHOLY BROODING!
CAN'T SAY I BLAME HIM!
WHAT MUST IT BE LIKE TO BE TRAPPED FOREVER IN AN ANDROID BODY...
...WITH THE THOUGHTS... THE EMOTIONS... OF A HUMAN BEING?
YET, WHY IS HE SO? WHY??
OKAY, GOLDILOCKS... IT'S YOUR TURN TO PLAY KING-FOR-A-DAY!
WHAT'S WITH THE SCROLL ...AN ASGARDIAN SHOPPIN' LIST?
YOU KNOW BETTER, HAWKEYE!
WHAT SAY WE GIVE THOR A CHANCE TO TALK FOR A WHILE?
LET THE MEETING NOW COMMENCE!
WE ARE CALLED HERE TODAY TO VOTE UPON THE ADMISSION OF A NEW ADDITION TO OUR NUMBER!
IN ALL THE ANNALS OF HERODOM ASSEMBLED...
IN ALL THE CHRONICLES OF COURAGE WRITTEN SINCE THE DAWN OF HUMAN MEMORY...
THERE BE NO FIGURES MORE LOOMING... NO NAMES MORE INSCRIBED IN UNTARNISHED GLORY...
...THAN THOSE WHO HAVE SWELLED THE PROUD RANKS OF... THE AVENGERS!
7.

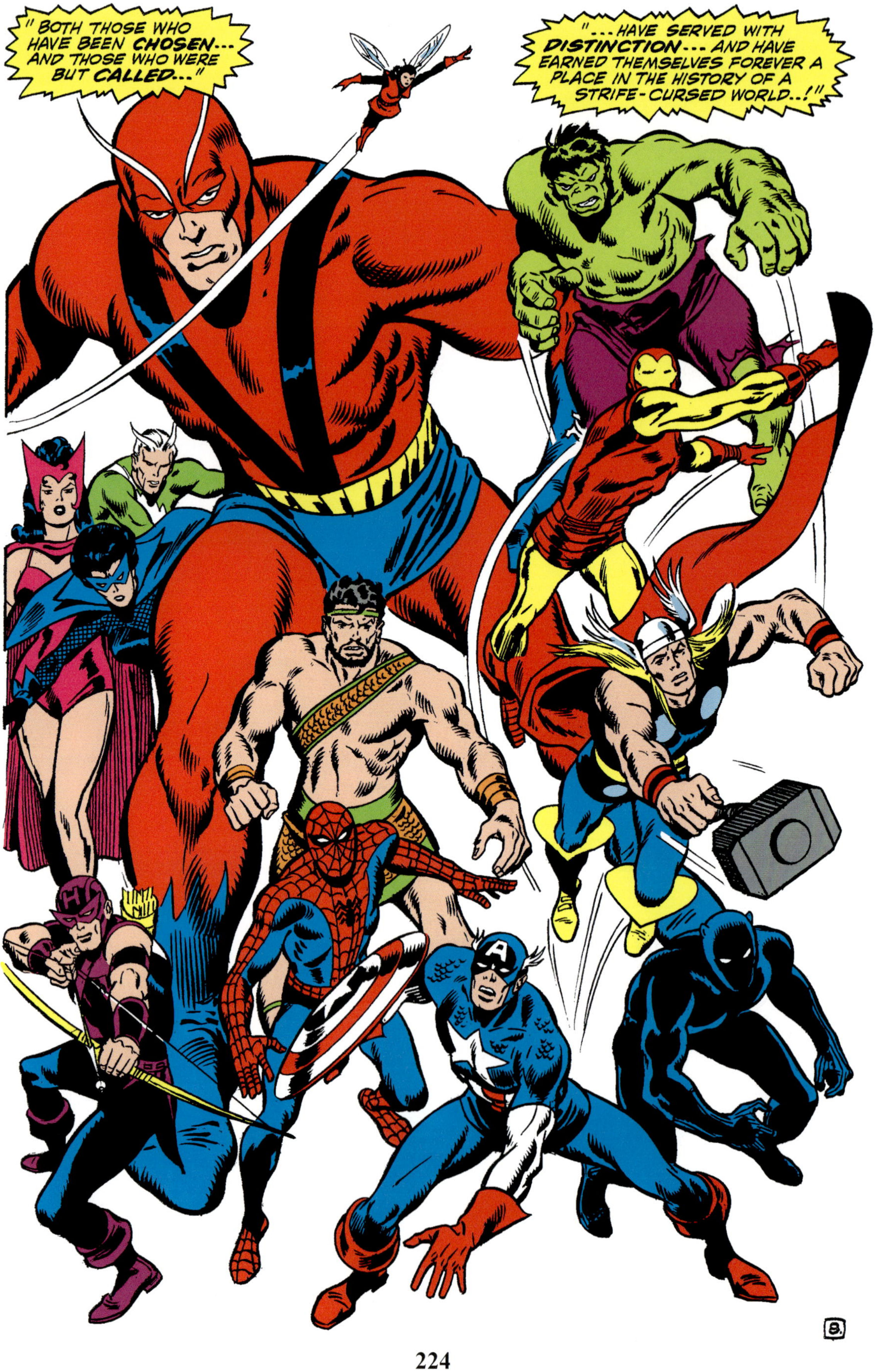
" BOTH THOSE WHO HAVE BEEN CHOSEN... AND THOSE WHO WERE BUT CALLED..."
"...HAVE SERVED WITH DISTINCTION... AND HAVE EARNED THEMSELVES FOREVER A PLACE IN THE HISTORY OF A STRIFE-CURSED WORLD..!"
8.

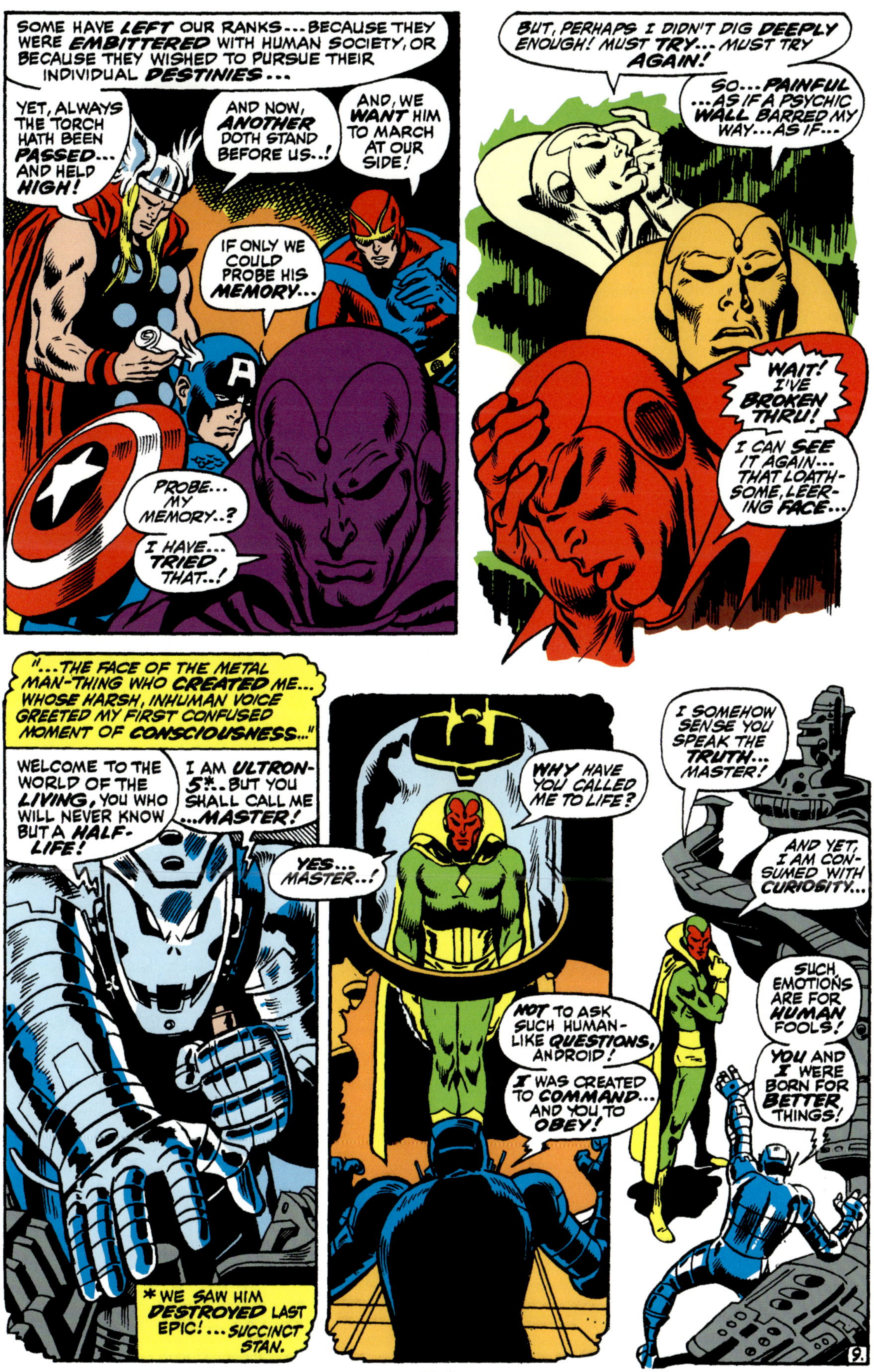
SOME HAVE LEFT OUR RANKS... BECAUSE THEY WERE EMBITTERED WITH HUMAN SOCIETY, OR BECAUSE THEY WISHED TO PURSUE THEIR INDIVIDUAL DESTINIES...
YET, ALWAYS THE TORCH HATH BEEN PASSED... AND HELD HIGH!
AND NOW, ANOTHER DOTH STAND BEFORE US..!
AND, WE WANT HIM TO MARCH AT OUR SIDE!
IF ONLY WE COULD PROBE HIS MEMORY...
PROBE... MY MEMORY..?
I HAVE... TRIED THAT..!
BUT, PERHAPS I DIDN'T DIG DEEPLY ENOUGH! MUST TRY... MUST TRY AGAIN!
SO... PAINFUL ...AS IF A PSYCHIC WALL BARRED MY WAY... AS IF...
WAIT! I'VE BROKEN THRU!
I CAN SEE IT AGAIN... THAT LOATH-SOME, LEER-ING FACE...
"...THE FACE OF THE METAL MAN-THING WHO CREATED ME... WHOSE HARSH, INHUMAN VOICE GREETED MY FIRST CONFUSED MOMENT OF CONSCIOUSNESS..."
WELCOME TO THE WORLD OF THE LIVING, YOU WHO WILL NEVER KNOW BUT A HALF-LIFE!
I AM ULTRON-5*.. BUT YOU SHALL CALL ME ...MASTER!
YES... MASTER..!
*WE SAW HIM DESTROYED LAST EPIC! ...SUCCINCT STAN.
WHY HAVE YOU CALLED ME TO LIFE?
NOT TO ASK SUCH HUMAN-LIKE QUESTIONS, ANDROID!
I WAS CREATED TO COMMAND... AND YOU TO OBEY!
I SOMEHOW SENSE YOU SPEAK THE TRUTH... MASTER!
AND YET, I AM CON-SUMED WITH CURIOSITY...
SUCH EMOTIONS ARE FOR HUMAN FOOLS!
YOU AND I WERE BORN FOR BETTER THINGS!
9.

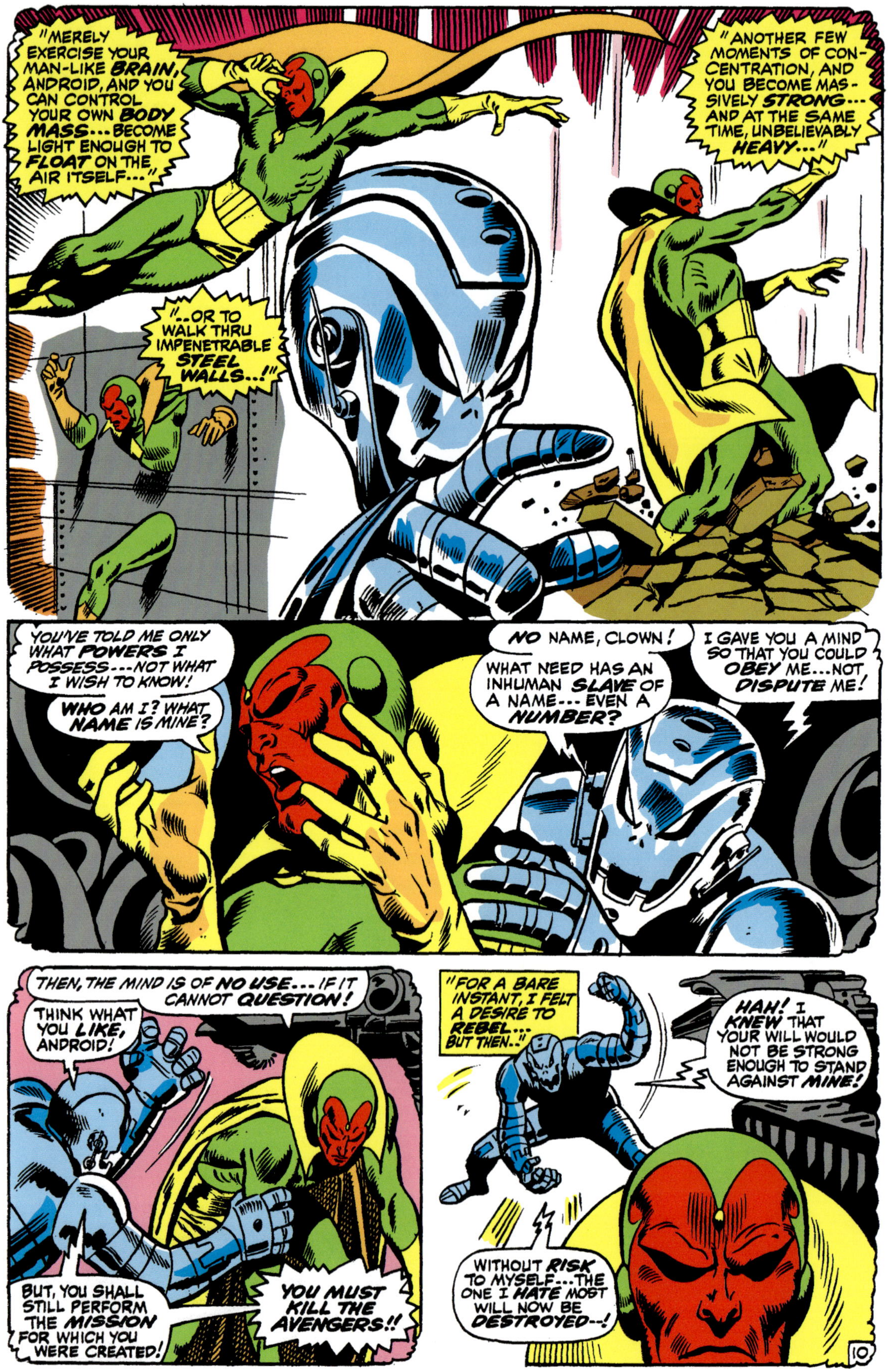

"MERELY EXERCISE YOUR MAN-LIKE BRAIN, ANDROID, AND YOU CAN CONTROL YOUR OWN BODY MASS... BECOME LIGHT ENOUGH TO FLOAT ON THE AIR ITSELF..."
"..OR TO WALK THRU IMPENETRABLE STEEL WALLS..!"
"ANOTHER FEW MOMENTS OF CON-CENTRATION, AND YOU BECOME MAS-SIVELY STRONG... AND AT THE SAME TIME, UNBELIEVABLY HEAVY..."
YOU'VE TOLD ME ONLY WHAT POWERS I POSSESS--- NOT WHAT I WISH TO KNOW!
WHO AM I? WHAT NAME IS MINE?
NO NAME, CLOWN!
WHAT NEED HAS AN INHUMAN SLAVE OF A NAME--- EVEN A NUMBER?
I GAVE YOU A MIND SO THAT YOU COULD OBEY ME... NOT DISPUTE ME!
THEN, THE MIND IS OF NO USE... IF IT CANNOT QUESTION!
THINK WHAT YOU LIKE, ANDROID!
BUT, YOU SHALL STILL PERFORM THE MISSION FOR WHICH YOU WERE CREATED!
YOU MUST KILL THE AVENGERS!!
"FOR A BARE INSTANT, I FELT A DESIRE TO REBEL... BUT THEN.."
HAH! I KNEW THAT YOUR WILL WOULD NOT BE STRONG ENOUGH TO STAND AGAINST MINE!
WITHOUT RISK TO MYSELF... THE ONE I HATE MOST WILL NOW BE DESTROYED--!
10

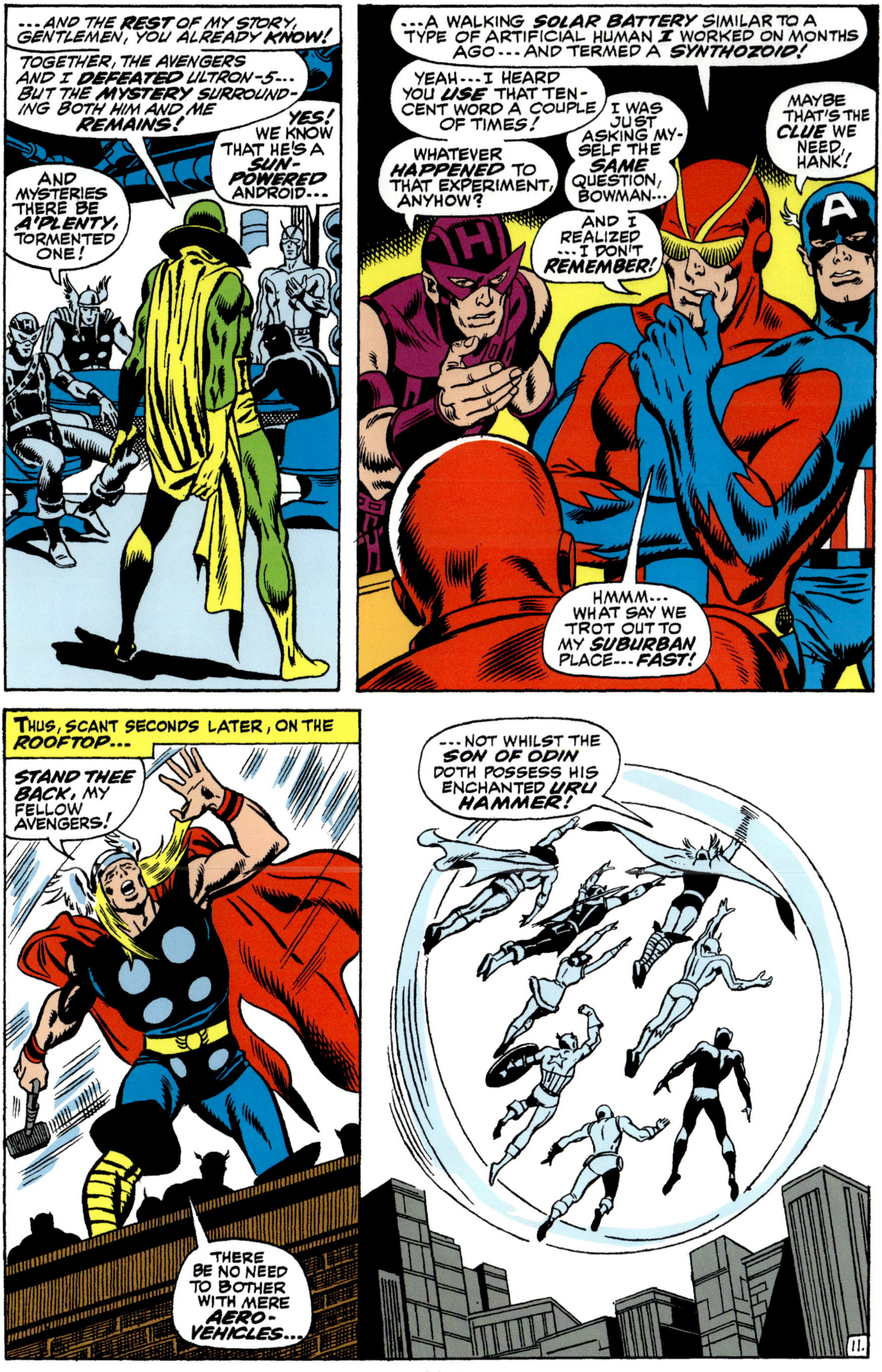
...AND THE REST OF MY STORY, GENTLEMEN, YOU ALREADY KNOW!
TOGETHER, THE AVENGERS AND I DEFEATED ULTRON-5... BUT THE MYSTERY SURROUNDING BOTH HIM AND ME REMAINS!
YES! WE KNOW THAT HE'S A SUN-POWERED ANDROID...
AND MYSTERIES THERE BE A'PLENTY, TORMENTED ONE!
...A WALKING SOLAR BATTERY SIMILAR TO A TYPE OF ARTIFICIAL HUMAN I WORKED ON MONTHS AGO... AND TERMED A SYNTHOZOID!
YEAH... I HEARD YOU USE THAT TEN-CENT WORD A COUPLE OF TIMES!
WHATEVER HAPPENED TO THAT EXPERIMENT, ANYHOW?
I WAS JUST ASKING MYSELF THE SAME QUESTION, BOWMAN...
AND I REALIZED ...I DON'T REMEMBER!
MAYBE THAT'S THE CLUE WE NEED, HANK!
HMMM... WHAT SAY WE TROT OUT TO MY SUBURBAN PLACE... FAST!
THUS, SCANT SECONDS LATER, ON THE ROOFTOP...
STAND THEE BACK, MY FELLOW AVENGERS!
THERE BE NO NEED TO BOTHER WITH MERE AERO-VEHICLES...
...NOT WHILST THE SON OF ODIN DOTH POSSESS HIS ENCHANTED URU HAMMER!
11.

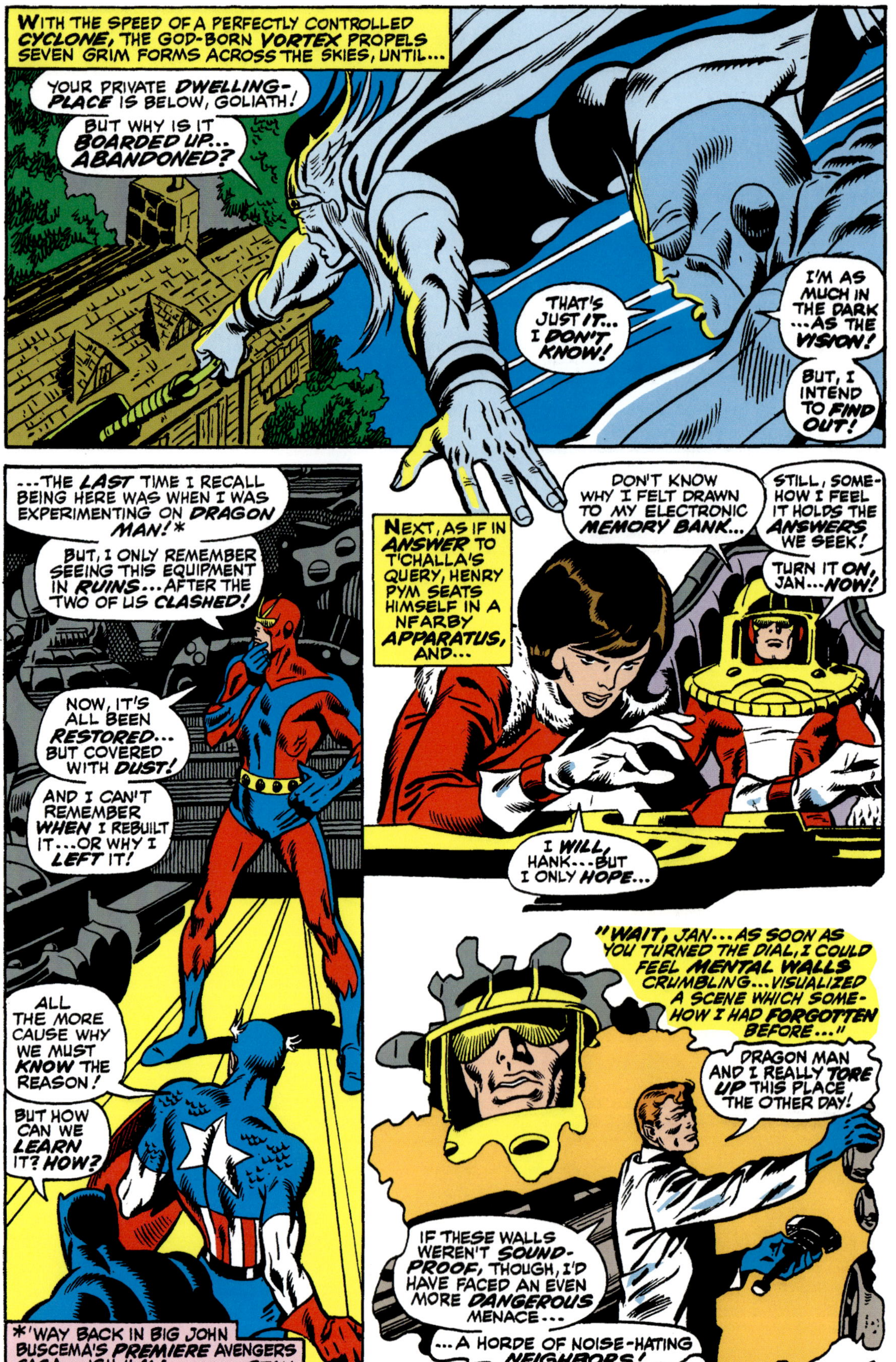

WITH THE SPEED OF A PERFECTLY CONTROLLED CYCLONE, THE GOD-BORN VORTEX PROPELS SEVEN GRIM FORMS ACROSS THE SKIES, UNTIL...
YOUR PRIVATE DWELLING-PLACE IS BELOW, GOLIATH!
BUT WHY IS IT BOARDED UP... ABANDONED?
THAT'S JUST IT... I DON'T KNOW!
I'M AS MUCH IN THE DARK ...AS THE VISION!
BUT, I INTEND TO FIND OUT!
...THE LAST TIME I RECALL BEING HERE WAS WHEN I WAS EXPERIMENTING ON DRAGON MAN!*
BUT, I ONLY REMEMBER SEEING THIS EQUIPMENT IN RUINS... AFTER THE TWO OF US CLASHED!
NOW, IT'S ALL BEEN RESTORED... BUT COVERED WITH DUST!
AND I CAN'T REMEMBER WHEN I REBUILT IT... OR WHY I LEFT IT!
ALL THE MORE CAUSE WHY WE MUST KNOW THE REASON!
BUT HOW CAN WE LEARN IT? HOW?
*'WAY BACK IN BIG JOHN BUSCEMA'S PREMIERE AVENGERS SAGA... ISH #41! ...STAN.
NEXT, AS IF IN ANSWER TO T'CHALLA'S QUERY, HENRY PYM SEATS HIMSELF IN A NFARBY APPARATUS, AND...
DON'T KNOW WHY I FELT DRAWN TO MY ELECTRONIC MEMORY BANK...
STILL, SOMEHOW I FEEL IT HOLDS THE ANSWERS WE SEEK!
TURN IT ON, JAN... NOW!
I WILL, HANK... BUT I ONLY HOPE...
"WAIT, JAN... AS SOON AS YOU TURNED THE DIAL, I COULD FEEL MENTAL WALLS CRUMBLING... VISUALIZED A SCENE WHICH SOMEHOW I HAD FORGOTTEN BEFORE..."
DRAGON MAN AND I REALLY TORE UP THIS PLACE THE OTHER DAY!
IF THESE WALLS WEREN'T SOUND-PROOF, THOUGH, I'D HAVE FACED AN EVEN MORE DANGEROUS MENACE...
...A HORDE OF NOISE-HATING NEIGHBORS!
12.

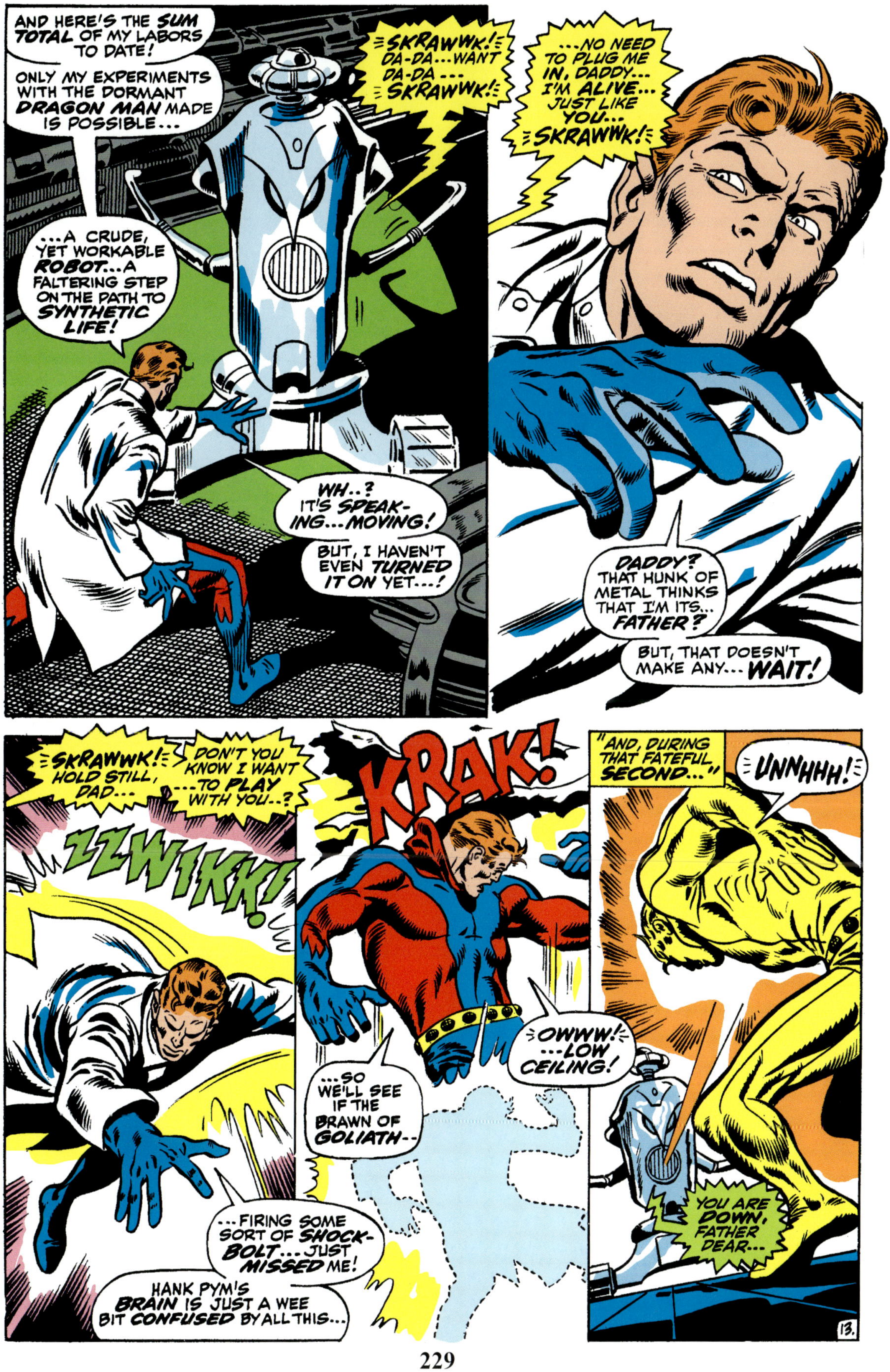
AND HERE'S THE SUM TOTAL OF MY LABORS TO DATE!
ONLY MY EXPERIMENTS WITH THE DORMANT DRAGON MAN MADE IS POSSIBLE...
...A CRUDE, YET WORKABLE ROBOT...A FALTERING STEP ON THE PATH TO SYNTHETIC LIFE!
SKRAWWK! DA-DA...WANT DA-DA... SKRAWWK!
WH..? IT'S SPEAKING...MOVING!
BUT, I HAVEN'T EVEN TURNED IT ON YET...!
...NO NEED TO PLUG ME IN, DADDY... I'M ALIVE... JUST LIKE YOU... SKRAWWK!
DADDY? THAT HUNK OF METAL THINKS THAT I'M ITS... FATHER?
BUT, THAT DOESN'T MAKE ANY... WAIT!
SKRAWWK! HOLD STILL, DAD...
DON'T YOU KNOW I WANT ...TO PLAY WITH YOU..?
ZZWIKK!
...FIRING SOME SORT OF SHOCK-BOLT... JUST MISSED ME!
HANK PYM'S BRAIN IS JUST A WEE BIT CONFUSED BY ALL THIS...
KRAK!
OWWW! ...LOW CEILING!
...SO WE'LL SEE IF THE BRAWN OF GOLIATH--
"AND, DURING THAT FATEFUL SECOND..."
UNNHHH!
YOU ARE DOWN, FATHER DEAR...
13.

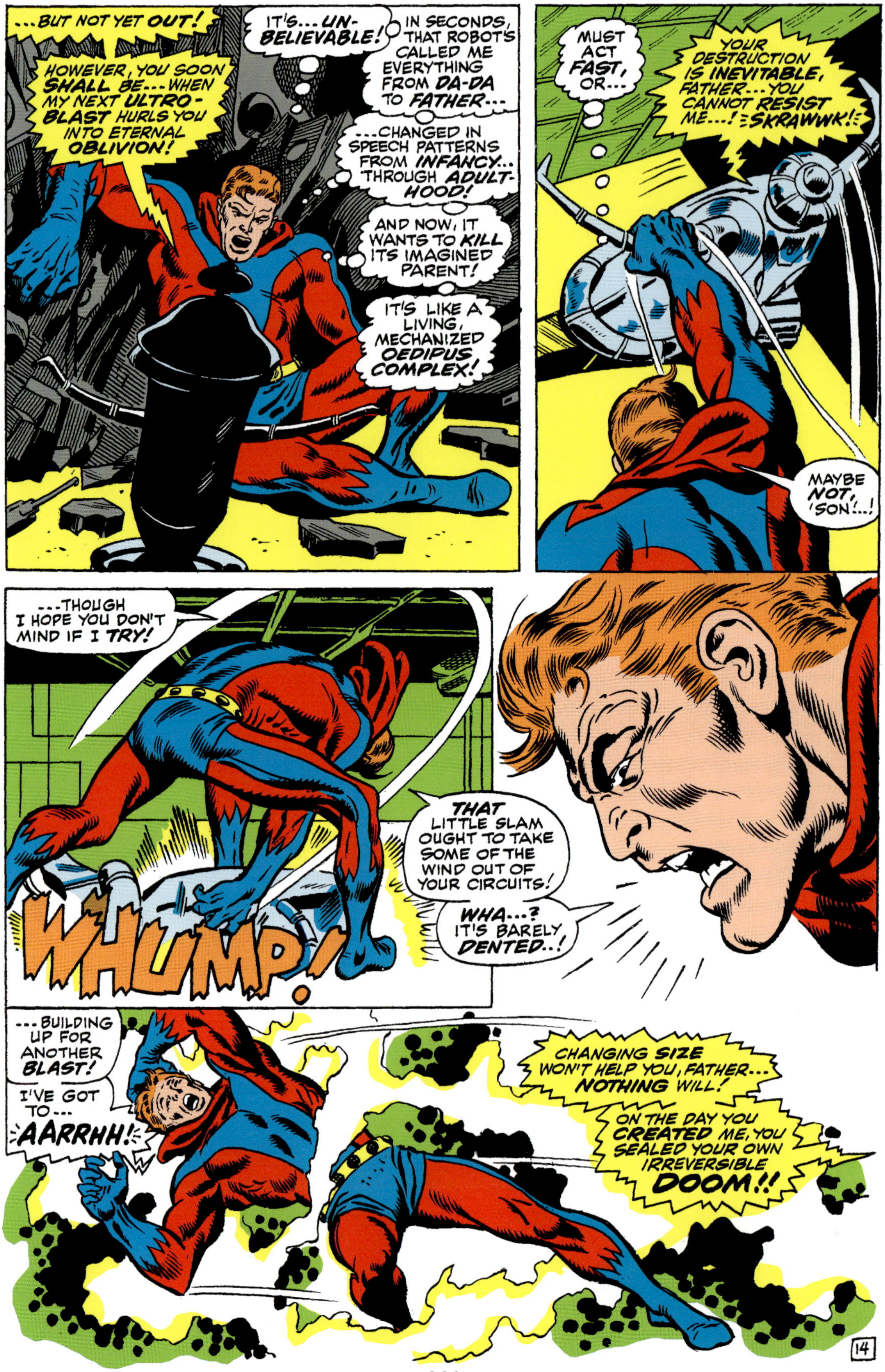
...BUT NOT YET OUT!
HOWEVER, YOU SOON SHALL BE... WHEN MY NEXT ULTRO-BLAST HURLS YOU INTO ETERNAL OBLIVION!
IT'S... UN-BELIEVABLE!
IN SECONDS, THAT ROBOT'S CALLED ME EVERYTHING FROM DA-DA TO FATHER...
...CHANGED IN SPEECH PATTERNS FROM INFANCY... THROUGH ADULT-HOOD!
AND NOW, IT WANTS TO KILL ITS IMAGINED PARENT!
IT'S LIKE A LIVING, MECHANIZED OEDIPUS COMPLEX!
MUST ACT FAST, OR...
YOUR DESTRUCTION IS INEVITABLE, FATHER... YOU CANNOT RESIST ME...! SKRAWWK!
MAYBE NOT, 'SON'...!
...THOUGH I HOPE YOU DON'T MIND IF I TRY!
THAT LITTLE SLAM OUGHT TO TAKE SOME OF THE WIND OUT OF YOUR CIRCUITS!
WHUMP!
WHA...? IT'S BARELY DENTED..!
...BUILDING UP FOR ANOTHER BLAST!
I'VE GOT TO... AARRHH!
CHANGING SIZE WON'T HELP YOU, FATHER... NOTHING WILL!
ON THE DAY YOU CREATED ME, YOU SEALED YOUR OWN IRREVERSIBLE DOOM!!
14

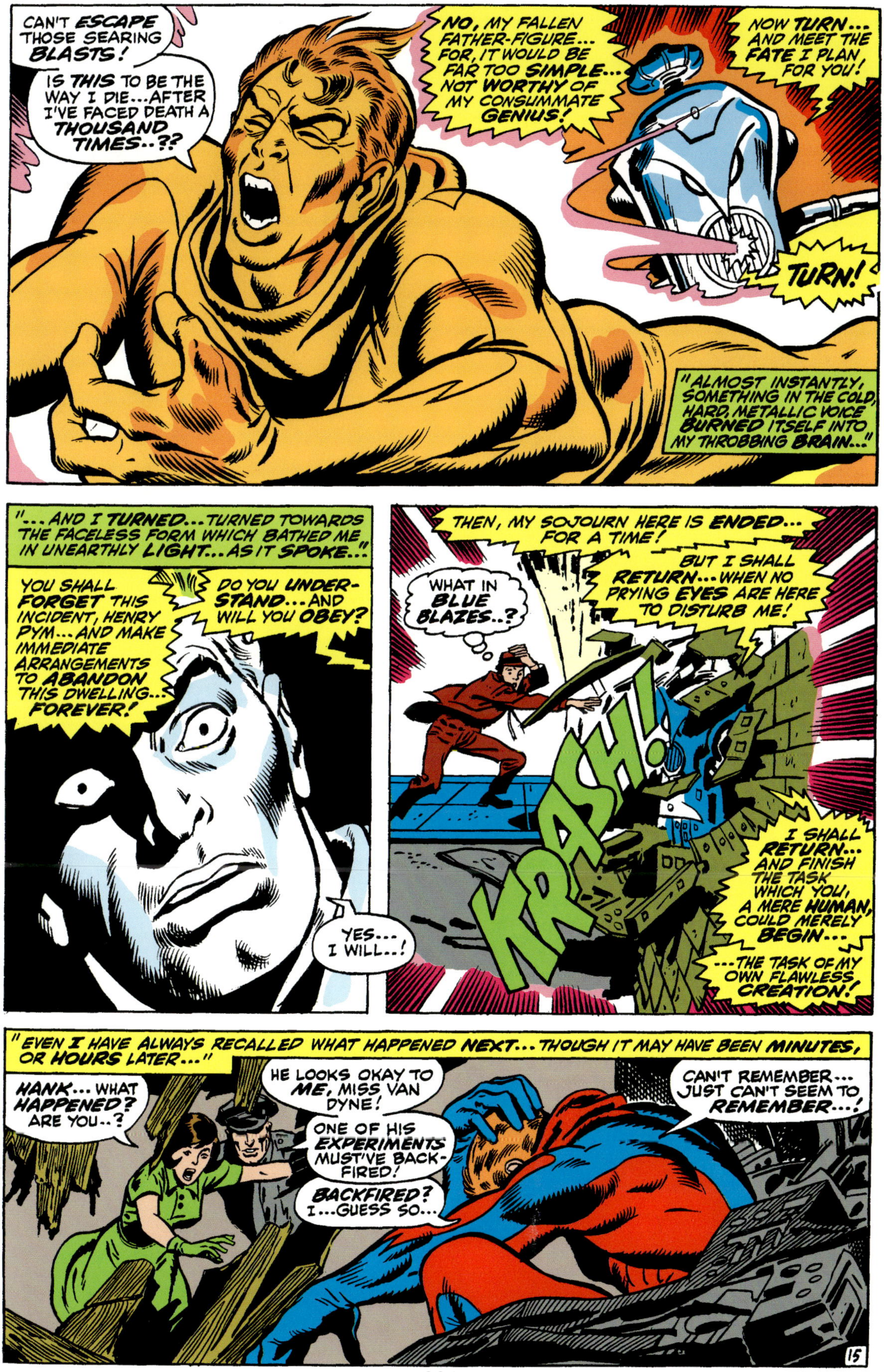
CAN'T ESCAPE THOSE SEARING BLASTS!
IS THIS TO BE THE WAY I DIE...AFTER I'VE FACED DEATH A THOUSAND TIMES..??
NO, MY FALLEN FATHER-FIGURE... FOR, IT WOULD BE FAR TOO SIMPLE... NOT WORTHY OF MY CONSUMMATE GENIUS!
NOW TURN... AND MEET THE FATE I PLAN FOR YOU!
TURN!
"ALMOST INSTANTLY, SOMETHING IN THE COLD, HARD, METALLIC VOICE BURNED ITSELF INTO MY THROBBING BRAIN..."
"...AND I TURNED...TURNED TOWARDS THE FACELESS FORM WHICH BATHED ME IN UNEARTHLY LIGHT...AS IT SPOKE..."
YOU SHALL FORGET THIS INCIDENT, HENRY PYM...AND MAKE IMMEDIATE ARRANGEMENTS TO ABANDON THIS DWELLING... FOREVER!
DO YOU UNDERSTAND...AND WILL YOU OBEY?
YES... I WILL..!
THEN, MY SOJOURN HERE IS ENDED... FOR A TIME!
WHAT IN BLUE BLAZES..?
BUT I SHALL RETURN...WHEN NO PRYING EYES ARE HERE TO DISTURB ME!
KRASH!
I SHALL RETURN... AND FINISH THE TASK WHICH YOU, A MERE HUMAN, COULD MERELY BEGIN...
...THE TASK OF MY OWN FLAWLESS CREATION!
"EVEN I HAVE ALWAYS RECALLED WHAT HAPPENED NEXT... THOUGH IT MAY HAVE BEEN MINUTES, OR HOURS LATER..."
HANK... WHAT HAPPENED? ARE YOU..?
HE LOOKS OKAY TO ME, MISS VAN DYNE!
ONE OF HIS EXPERIMENTS MUST'VE BACK-FIRED!
BACKFIRED? I...GUESS SO...
CAN'T REMEMBER... JUST CAN'T SEEM TO REMEMBER...!
15

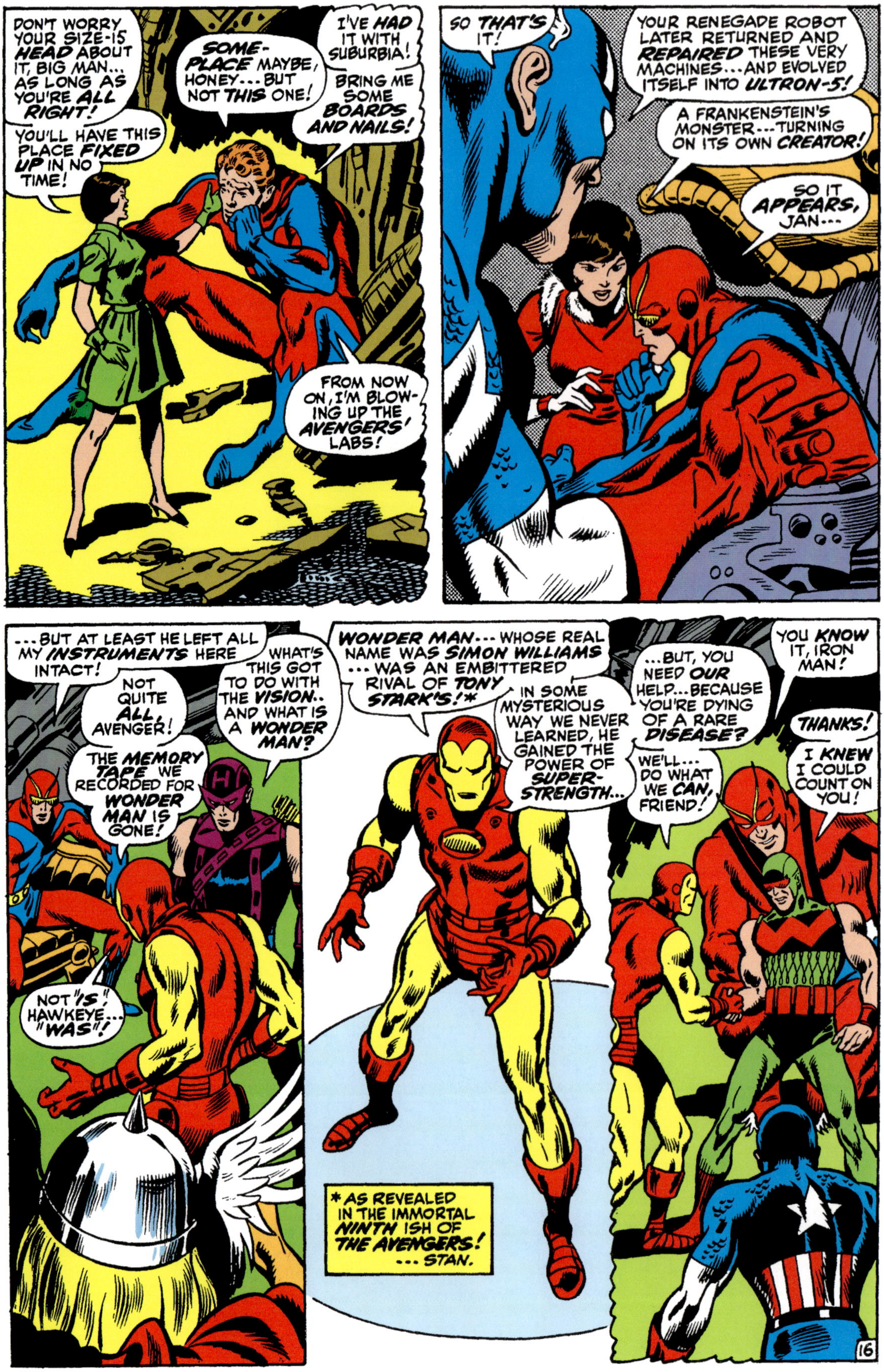
DON'T WORRY YOUR SIZE-IS HEAD ABOUT IT, BIG MAN... AS LONG AS YOU'RE ALL RIGHT!
YOU'LL HAVE THIS PLACE FIXED UP IN NO TIME!
SOME-PLACE MAYBE, HONEY... BUT NOT THIS ONE!
I'VE HAD IT WITH SUBURBIA!
BRING ME SOME BOARDS AND NAILS!
FROM NOW ON, I'M BLOW-ING UP THE AVENGERS' LABS!
SO THAT'S IT!
YOUR RENEGADE ROBOT LATER RETURNED AND REPAIRED THESE VERY MACHINES... AND EVOLVED ITSELF INTO ULTRON-5!
A FRANKENSTEIN'S MONSTER---TURNING ON ITS OWN CREATOR!
SO IT APPEARS, JAN...
...BUT AT LEAST HE LEFT ALL MY INSTRUMENTS HERE INTACT!
NOT QUITE ALL, AVENGER!
WHAT'S THIS GOT TO DO WITH THE VISION.. AND WHAT IS A WONDER MAN?
THE MEMORY TAPE WE RECORDED FOR WONDER MAN IS GONE!
NOT "IS"! HAWKEYE... "WAS"!
WONDER MAN... WHOSE REAL NAME WAS SIMON WILLIAMS ... WAS AN EMBITTERED RIVAL OF TONY STARK'S!*
IN SOME MYSTERIOUS WAY WE NEVER LEARNED, HE GAINED THE POWER OF SUPER-STRENGTH...
* AS REVEALED IN THE IMMORTAL NINTH ISH OF THE AVENGERS! ... STAN.
...BUT, YOU NEED OUR HELP... BECAUSE YOU'RE DYING OF A RARE DISEASE?
WE'LL... DO WHAT WE CAN, FRIEND!
YOU KNOW IT, IRON MAN!
THANKS!
I KNEW I COULD COUNT ON YOU!
16

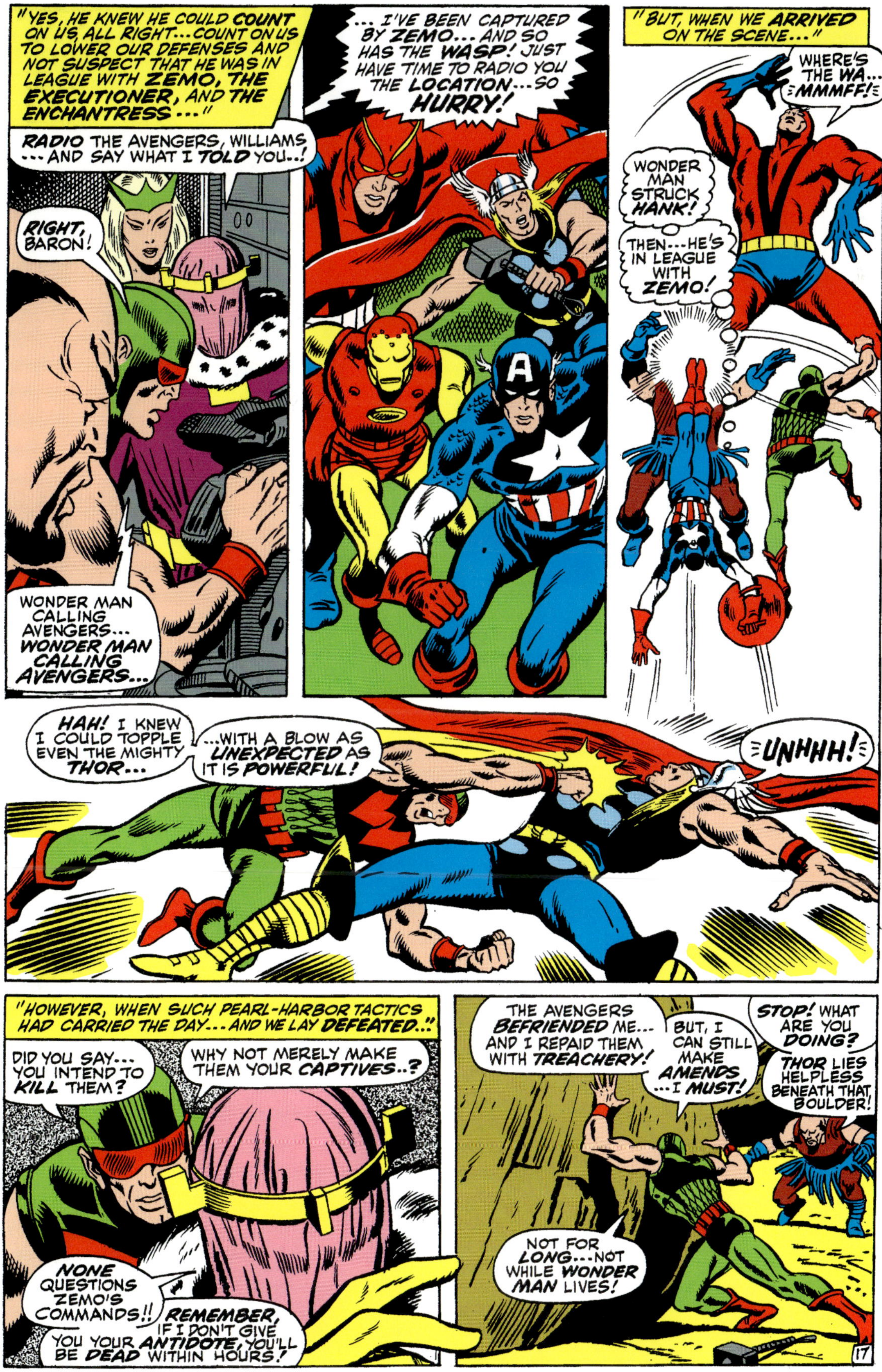
"YES, HE KNEW HE COULD COUNT ON US, ALL RIGHT... COUNT ON US TO LOWER OUR DEFENSES AND NOT SUSPECT THAT HE WAS IN LEAGUE WITH ZEMO, THE EXECUTIONER, AND THE ENCHANTRESS..."
RADIO THE AVENGERS, WILLIAMS ... AND SAY WHAT I TOLD YOU..!
RIGHT, BARON!
WONDER MAN CALLING AVENGERS... WONDER MAN CALLING AVENGERS...
... I'VE BEEN CAPTURED BY ZEMO... AND SO HAS THE WASP! JUST HAVE TIME TO RADIO YOU THE LOCATION... SO HURRY!
"BUT, WHEN WE ARRIVED ON THE SCENE..."
WHERE'S THE WA... MMMFF!
WONDER MAN STRUCK HANK!
THEN... HE'S IN LEAGUE WITH ZEMO!
HAH! I KNEW I COULD TOPPLE EVEN THE MIGHTY THOR...
...WITH A BLOW AS UNEXPECTED AS IT IS POWERFUL!
UNHHH!
"HOWEVER, WHEN SUCH PEARL-HARBOR TACTICS HAD CARRIED THE DAY... AND WE LAY DEFEATED..!"
DID YOU SAY... YOU INTEND TO KILL THEM?
WHY NOT MERELY MAKE THEM YOUR CAPTIVES..?
NONE QUESTIONS ZEMO'S COMMANDS!!
REMEMBER, IF I DON'T GIVE YOU YOUR ANTIDOTE, YOU'LL BE DEAD WITHIN HOURS!
THE AVENGERS BEFRIENDED ME... AND I REPAID THEM WITH TREACHERY!
BUT, I CAN STILL MAKE AMENDS ...I MUST!
STOP! WHAT ARE YOU DOING?
THOR LIES HELPLESS BENEATH THAT BOULDER!
NOT FOR LONG... NOT WHILE WONDER MAN LIVES!
17

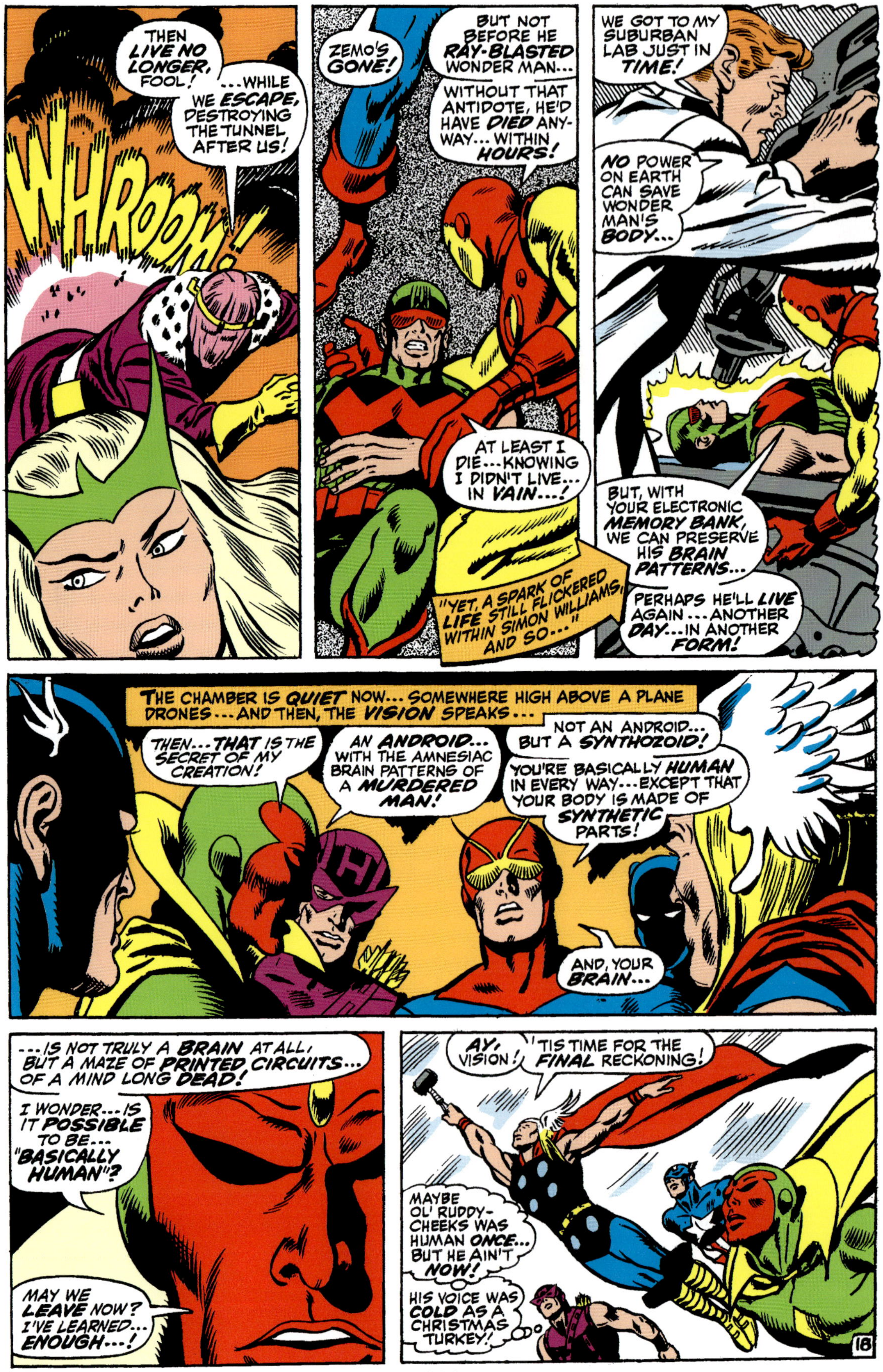
THEN LIVE NO LONGER, FOOL!
...WHILE WE ESCAPE, DESTROYING THE TUNNEL AFTER US!
WHROOM!
ZEMO'S GONE!
BUT NOT BEFORE HE RAY-BLASTED WONDER MAN...
WITHOUT THAT ANTIDOTE, HE'D HAVE DIED ANY-WAY... WITHIN HOURS!
AT LEAST I DIE...KNOWING I DIDN'T LIVE... IN VAIN...!
"YET, A SPARK OF LIFE STILL FLICKERED WITHIN SIMON WILLIAMS, AND SO..."
WE GOT TO MY SUBURBAN LAB JUST IN TIME!
NO POWER ON EARTH CAN SAVE WONDER MAN'S BODY...
BUT, WITH YOUR ELECTRONIC MEMORY BANK, WE CAN PRESERVE HIS BRAIN PATTERNS...
PERHAPS HE'LL LIVE AGAIN ... ANOTHER DAY...IN ANOTHER FORM!
THE CHAMBER IS QUIET NOW... SOMEWHERE HIGH ABOVE A PLANE DRONES ... AND THEN, THE VISION SPEAKS ...
THEN... THAT IS THE SECRET OF MY CREATION!
AN ANDROID... WITH THE AMNESIAC BRAIN PATTERNS OF A MURDERED MAN!
NOT AN ANDROID... BUT A SYNTHOZOID!
YOU'RE BASICALLY HUMAN IN EVERY WAY... EXCEPT THAT YOUR BODY IS MADE OF SYNTHETIC PARTS!
AND, YOUR BRAIN...
...IS NOT TRULY A BRAIN AT ALL, BUT A MAZE OF PRINTED CIRCUITS... OF A MIND LONG DEAD!
I WONDER... IS IT POSSIBLE TO BE... "BASICALLY HUMAN"?
MAY WE LEAVE NOW? I'VE LEARNED... ENOUGH...!
AY, VISION!
'TIS TIME FOR THE FINAL RECKONING!
MAYBE OL' RUDDY-CHEEKS WAS HUMAN ONCE... BUT HE AIN'T NOW!
HIS VOICE WAS COLD AS A CHRISTMAS TURKEY!
18

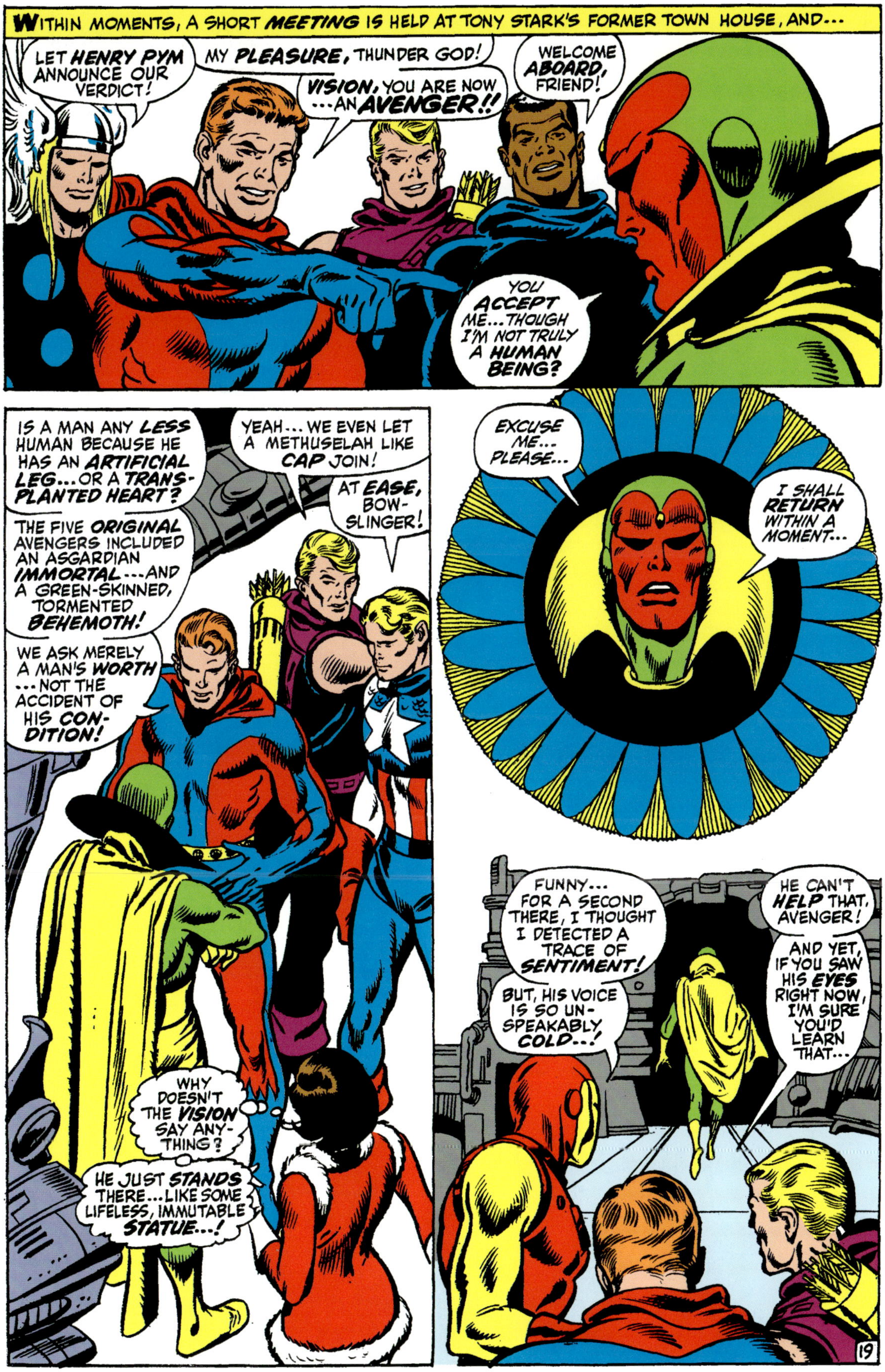
WITHIN MOMENTS, A SHORT MEETING IS HELD AT TONY STARK'S FORMER TOWN HOUSE, AND...
LET HENRY PYM ANNOUNCE OUR VERDICT!
MY PLEASURE, THUNDER GOD!
VISION, YOU ARE NOW ...AN AVENGER!!
WELCOME ABOARD, FRIEND!
YOU ACCEPT ME...THOUGH I'M NOT TRULY A HUMAN BEING?
IS A MAN ANY LESS HUMAN BECAUSE HE HAS AN ARTIFICIAL LEG...OR A TRANS-PLANTED HEART?
THE FIVE ORIGINAL AVENGERS INCLUDED AN ASGARDIAN IMMORTAL...AND A GREEN-SKINNED, TORMENTED BEHEMOTH!
WE ASK MERELY A MAN'S WORTH ...NOT THE ACCIDENT OF HIS CON-DITION!
YEAH... WE EVEN LET A METHUSELAH LIKE CAP JOIN!
AT EASE, BOW-SLINGER!
WHY DOESN'T THE VISION SAY ANY-THING?
HE JUST STANDS THERE...LIKE SOME LIFELESS, IMMUTABLE STATUE...!
EXCUSE ME... PLEASE...
I SHALL RETURN WITHIN A MOMENT...
FUNNY... FOR A SECOND THERE, I THOUGHT I DETECTED A TRACE OF SENTIMENT!
BUT, HIS VOICE IS SO UN-SPEAKABLY COLD...!
HE CAN'T HELP THAT, AVENGER!
AND YET, IF YOU SAW HIS EYES RIGHT NOW, I'M SURE YOU'D LEARN THAT...
19

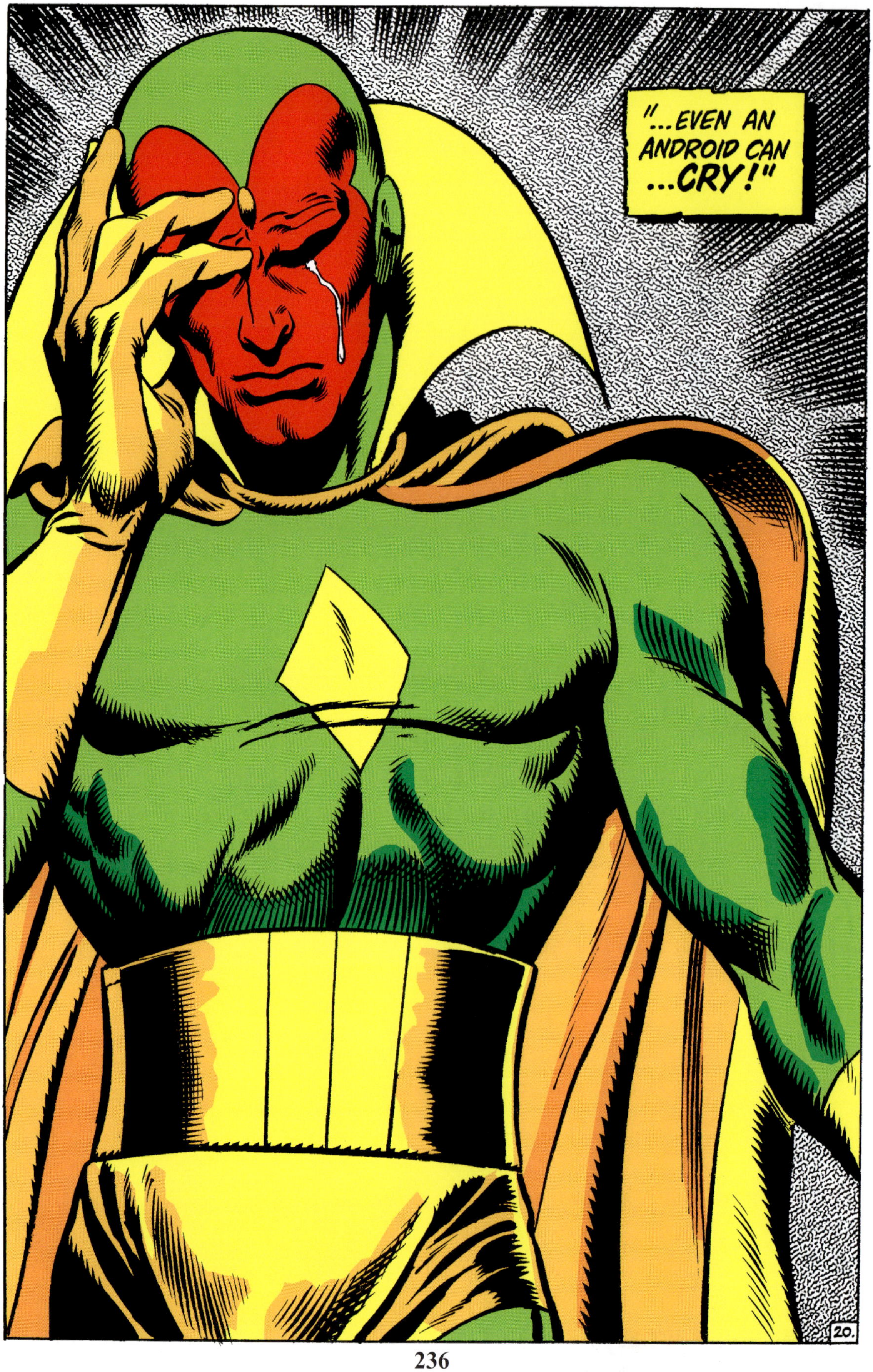
"...EVEN AN ANDROID CAN ...CRY!"
20.

SPECIAL BONUS:

Steve Ditko's reinterpretation of *The Avengers* #54 cover from the 1979 reprin

Marvel Triple Action #47

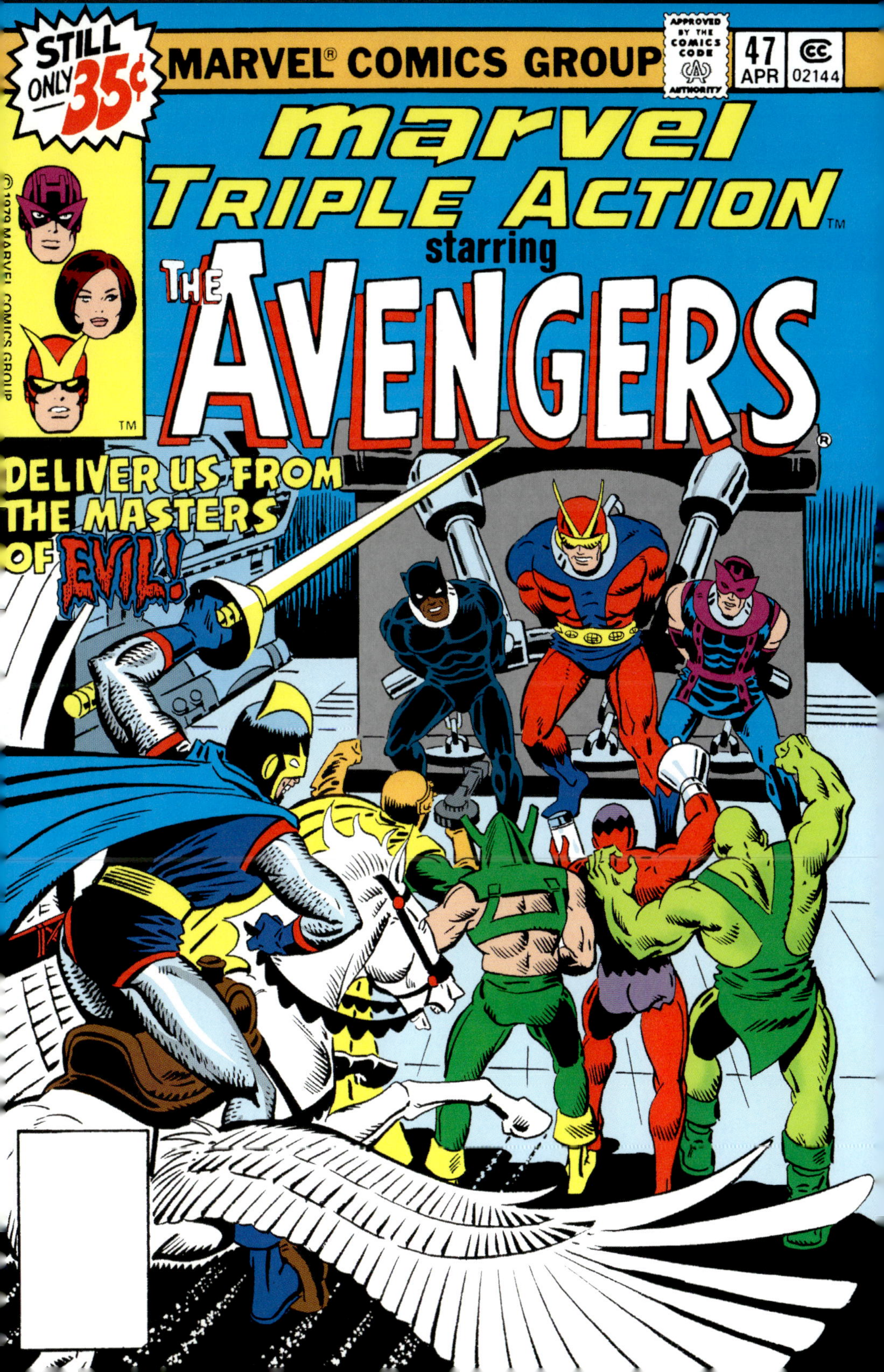

STILL ONLY 35¢
MARVEL® COMICS GROUP
APPROVED BY THE COMICS CODE AUTHORITY
47 APR
CC 02144
marvel TRIPLE ACTION™
starring
THE AVENGERS®
© 1979 MARVEL COMICS GROUP
DELIVER US FROM THE MASTERS OF EVIL!

John Buscema's unedited cover art for *The Avengers #51*.

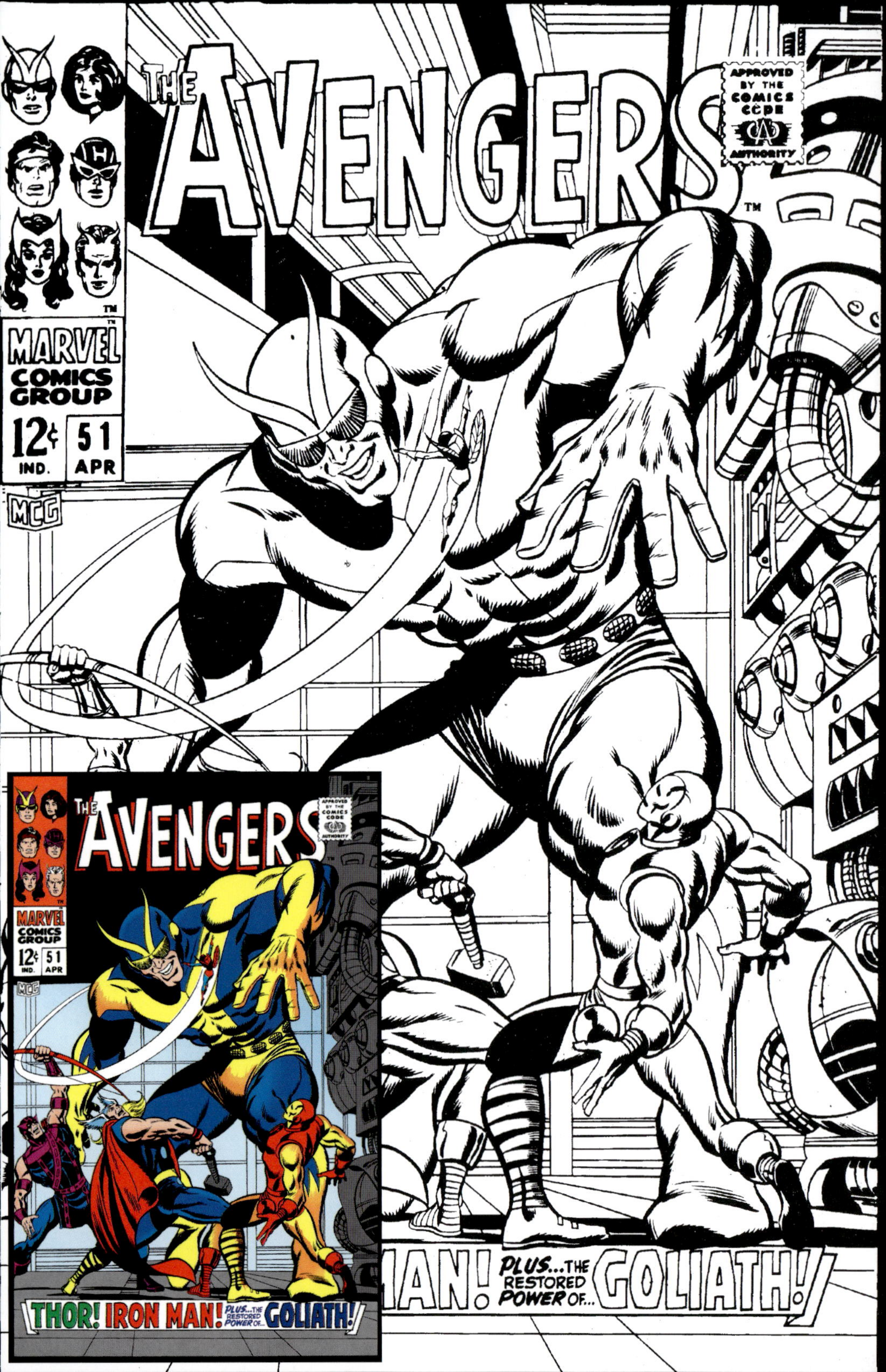
THE AVENGERS
APPROVED BY THE COMICS CODE AUTHORITY
MARVEL COMICS GROUP
12¢ IND.
51 APR
MCG
AN! PLUS...THE RESTORED POWER OF... GOLIATH!
THE AVENGERS
APPROVED BY THE COMICS CODE AUTHORITY
MARVEL COMICS GROUP
12¢ IND.
51 APR
MCG
THOR! IRON MAN! PLUS...THE RESTORED POWER OF... GOLIATH!

rare glimpse at John Buscema's pencils from this period. Photo taken the
St. Louis Gateway Con. Inks by George Klein are presented below.

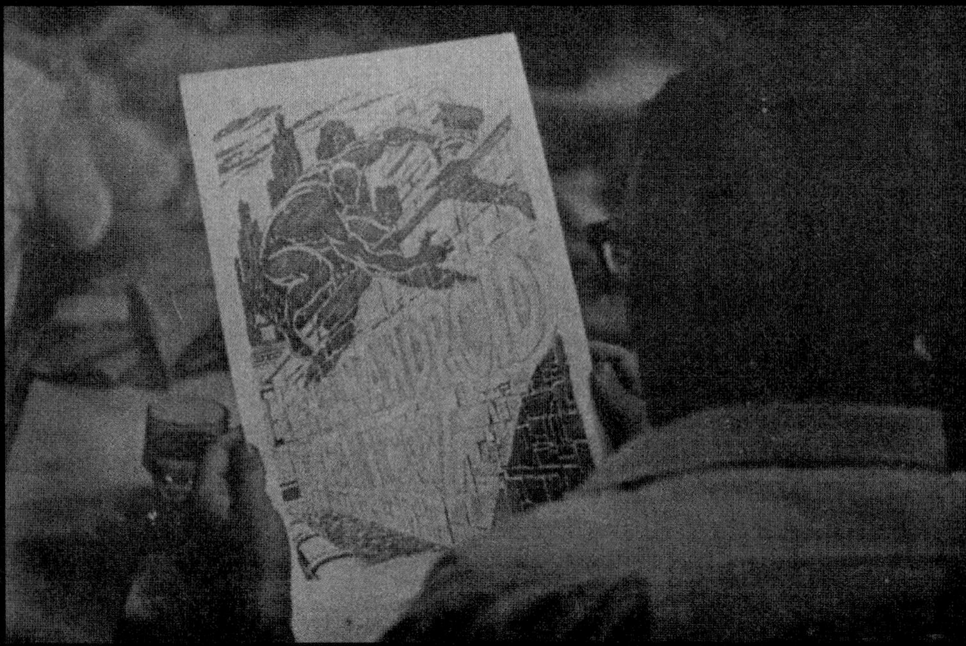

Photo courtesy Michel Maillot & Roy Thomas

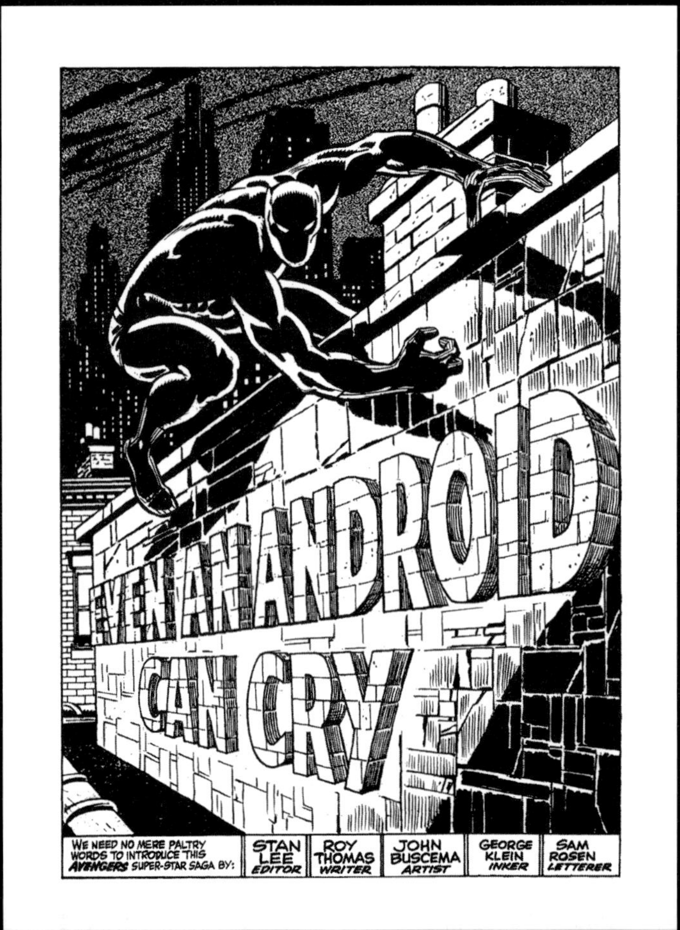
EVEN AN ANDROID CAN CRY
WE NEED NO MERE PALTRY WORDS TO INTRODUCE THIS AVENGERS SUPER-STAR SAGA BY:
STAN LEE EDITOR
ROY THOMAS WRITER
JOHN BUSCEMA ARTIST
GEORGE KLEIN INKER
SAM ROSEN LETTERER

Always best to learn from a master: *The Avengers #51*, page 8 layout possibly by John Buscema with pencils by an undetermined bullpen member.

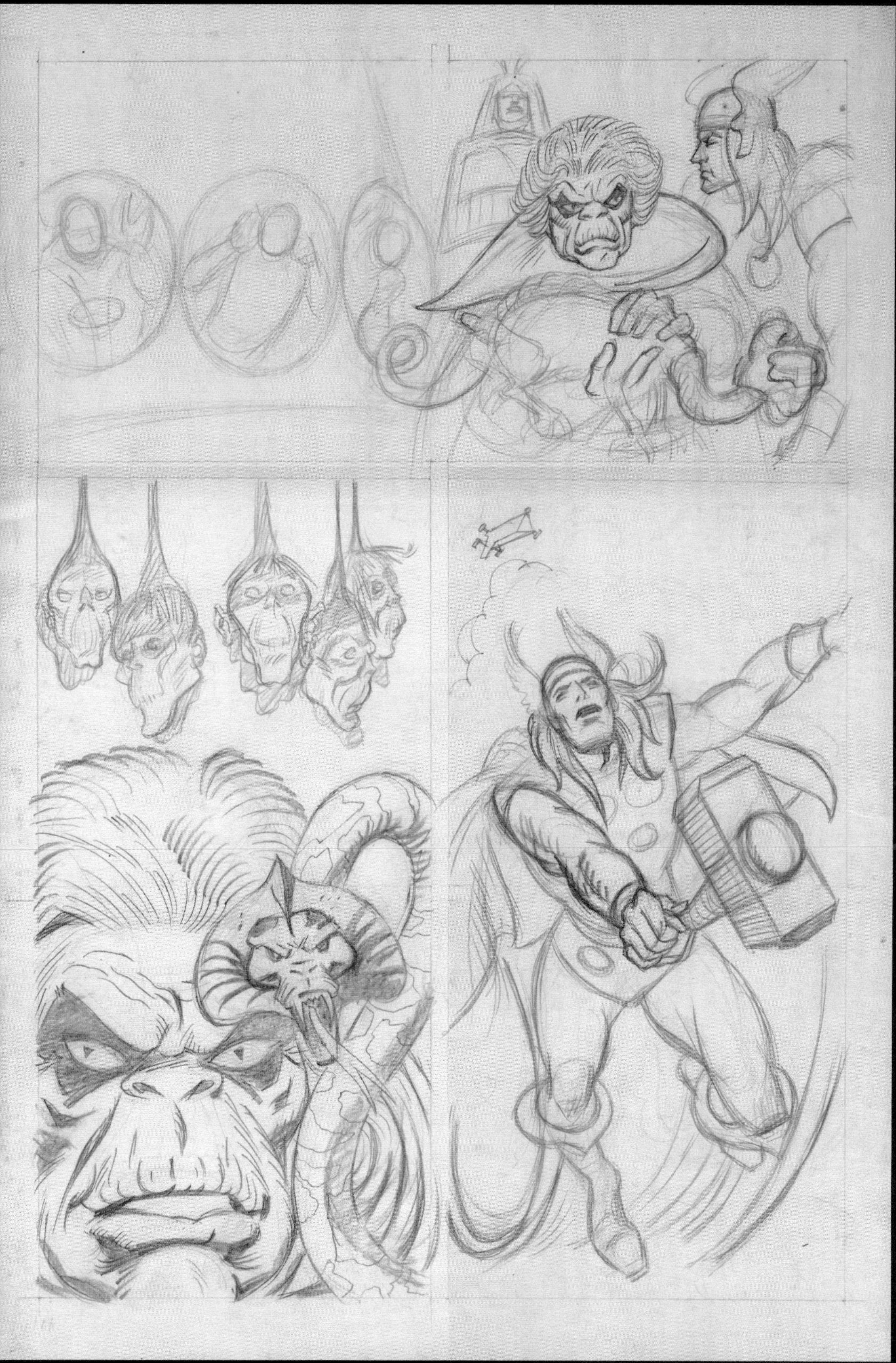

Courtesy Kelly Borkert

Original art for *The Avengers #58*, page 19 by John Buscema & George Klein

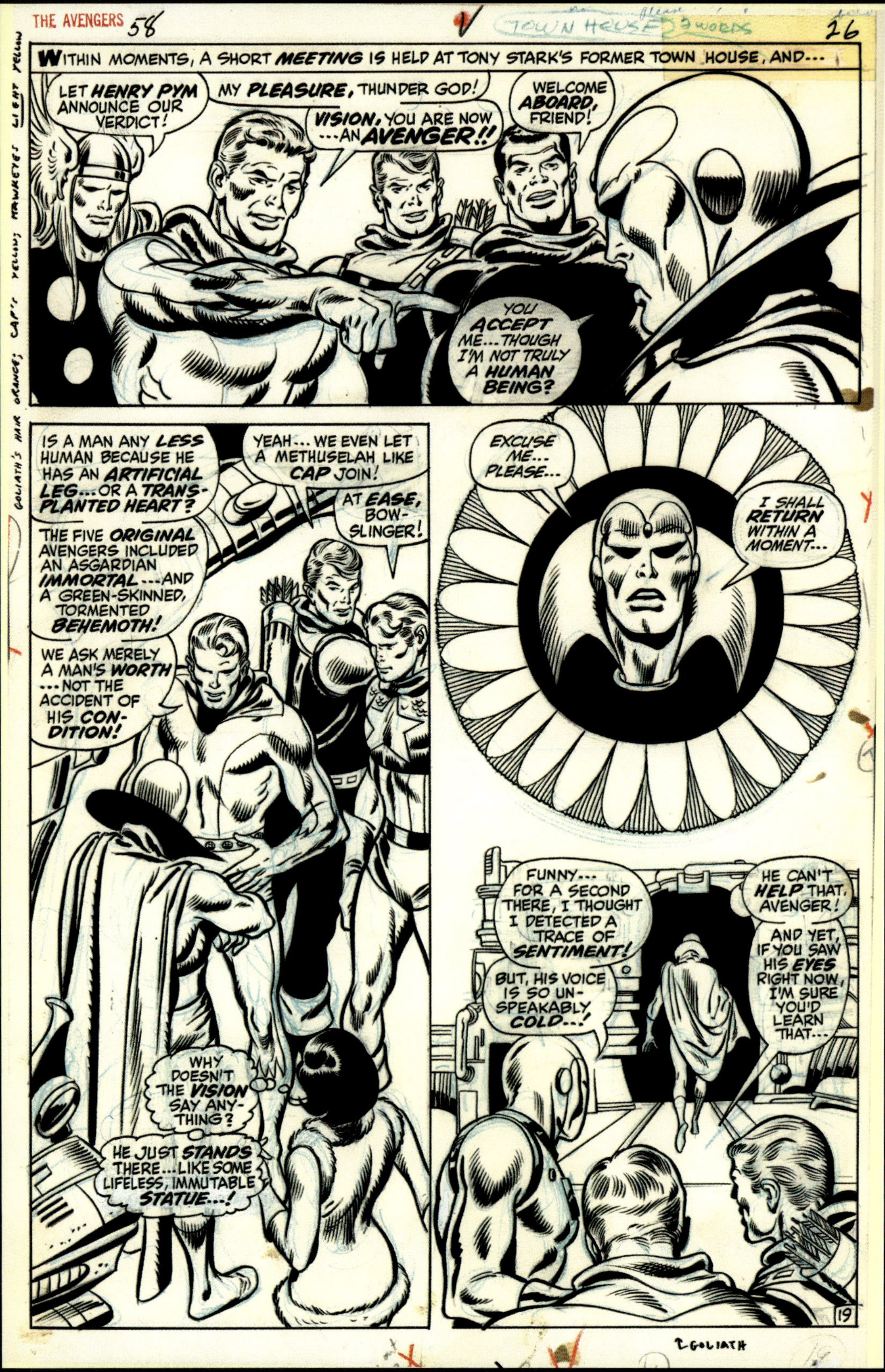

THE AVENGERS 58
26
WITHIN MOMENTS, A SHORT MEETING IS HELD AT TONY STARK'S FORMER TOWN HOUSE, AND...
LET HENRY PYM ANNOUNCE OUR VERDICT!
MY PLEASURE, THUNDER GOD!
VISION, YOU ARE NOW ...AN AVENGER!!
WELCOME ABOARD, FRIEND!
YOU ACCEPT ME... THOUGH I'M NOT TRULY A HUMAN BEING?
IS A MAN ANY LESS HUMAN BECAUSE HE HAS AN ARTIFICIAL LEG... OR A TRANS-PLANTED HEART?
YEAH... WE EVEN LET A METHUSELAH LIKE CAP JOIN!
AT EASE, BOW-SLINGER!
THE FIVE ORIGINAL AVENGERS INCLUDED AN ASGARDIAN IMMORTAL ...AND A GREEN-SKINNED, TORMENTED BEHEMOTH!
WE ASK MERELY A MAN'S WORTH ...NOT THE ACCIDENT OF HIS CON-DITION!
WHY DOESN'T THE VISION SAY ANY-THING?
HE JUST STANDS THERE... LIKE SOME LIFELESS, IMMUTABLE STATUE...!
EXCUSE ME... PLEASE...
I SHALL RETURN WITHIN A MOMENT...
FUNNY... FOR A SECOND THERE, I THOUGHT I DETECTED A TRACE OF SENTIMENT!
BUT, HIS VOICE IS SO UN-SPEAKABLY COLD...!
HE CAN'T HELP THAT, AVENGER!
AND YET, IF YOU SAW HIS EYES RIGHT NOW, I'M SURE YOU'D LEARN THAT...
19

Courtesy Scott Williams

Original art for *The Avengers #58*, page 20 by John Buscema & George Klein

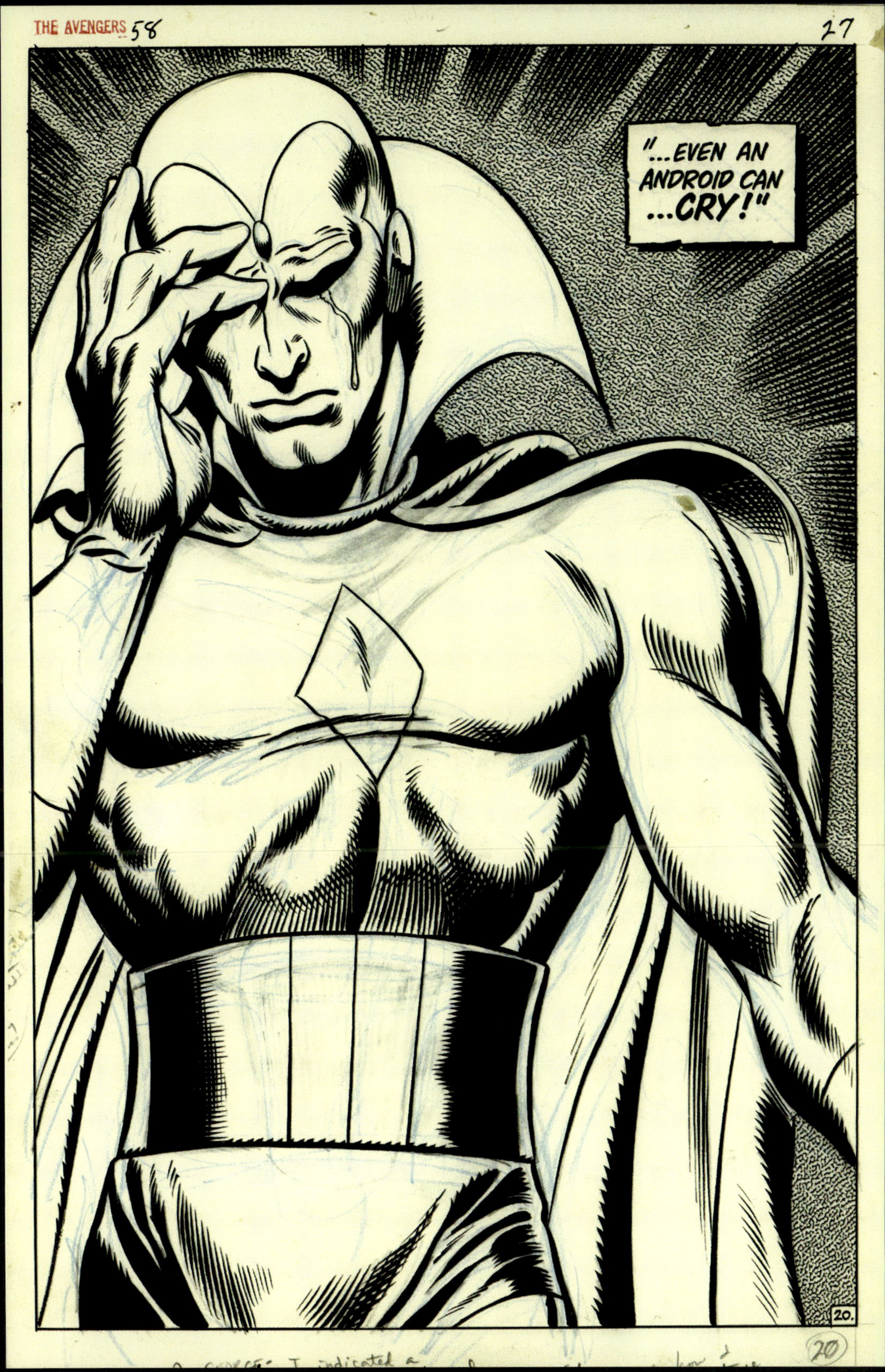
THE AVENGERS 58
27
"...EVEN AN ANDROID CAN ...CRY!"
20.

Courtesy Scott Williams

BIOGRAPHIES

ROY THOMAS

Roy Thomas broke into the comics business in 1965, a bright-eyed young man from Missouri, who would come to personally represent the inevitable promise of the medium finally made manifest: the fan that was raised on the stories was now creating them. Along with fellow fan and teenager Jerry Bails, Roy developed the first known organized comic fandom in the pages of *Alter Ego*, their self-published fanzine that connected together longtime and avid readers of comic books.

Leaving a teaching job, Roy took his deep knowledge of comics characters and their history and moved to New York City, taking a position at DC Comics. His job at DC lasted little over a week before he moved across town to Marvel Comics, starting his career earnest. As staff writer under Stan Lee, his duties quickly matured from proofreading and spot writing to more serious work as an assistant editor, where his acumen at remembering the minutiae of Marvel history came in handy for his forgetful boss.

Titles as disparate as *Modeling With Millie, Kid Colt*, and *Sgt. Fury* were written under his auspices, but his burning desire to write his own super-hero comics was finally sated with the Iron Man story in *Tales of Suspense #73* and quickly followed by a number of Dr. Strange scripts.

Stan must have liked what he was reading because Roy "The Boy" (as he was called around the Bullpen) was given his own books for keeps. Roy closed out the year 1966 holding the reins to both *Sgt. Fury* and *The X-Men*. The latter book was a big deal for him personally, as his true love in writing was not *just* super-hero books, but super-hero *team* books! Along with artist Werner Roth, Roy carried *X-Men* through its '60s-era tenure, creating characters like Banshee, Sunfire, and Havok along the way. His seminal run with Neal Adams on the series is to this day regarded as a watershed moment within comics' most-popular franchise.

Proving his mettle on *X-Men* led him to *The Avengers*, and it was with this team that Roy really started crafting his legacy. In the adventures of the Earth's Mightiest Heroes, Roy introduced the Vision, drafted the Black Panther into membership, and brought a touch of the cosmic to the Marvel U. with the "Kree/Skrull War." All in all, Roy logged serious time as the writer of *Daredevil, Sub-Mariner* and *The Incredible Hulk*.

The 1970s brought Roy's adaptation of Robert E. Howard's *Conan the Barbarian* to Marvel Comics, a character that remains one of the industry's most popular to this day. He also developed new super-team books around the Defenders and the WWII-era Invaders.

By 1972, Roy's esteem at Marvel was so great that he was selected to succeed Stan Lee as Editor-In-Chief after the maestro of Marvel moved on to duties as Publisher. His tenure as EIC lasted for over two years before he moved on to DC Comics, where he was able to live a lifelong dream by reviving the Justice Society of America in the pages of *All-Star Squadron*.

His enviable credits at DC and Marvel continued to add up over the ensuing years, and Thomas is still active today with *Stoker's Dracula* at Marvel and publishing the latest volume of *Alter Ego*. He lives in South Carolina with his wife Dann, and an amazing menagerie of animals that must make the neighbors nervous.

JOHN BUSCEMA

Though known primarily for his long tenure as one of Marvel Comics' most prolific pencilers, John Buscema began his celebrated career at the age of twenty-one with Timely Comics. After Timely closed up its in-house bullpen and sent most freelancers chasing down new art assignments, John pursued comics work for a time before he bagged the comics scene altogether and went to work in advertising in 1958.

When he finally returned to comics, however, he did so with a vengeance. Stan Lee recruited him away from the field of advertising and quickly ensconced him into the upper ranks of Marvel artists. Picking up where *Avengers* mainstay Don Heck left off, "Big John" settled into a long run of his own showcasing the exploits of Earth's Mightiest Heroes. The much-anticipated *Silver Surfer* series was launched with John at the helm, and top-shelf books like *Fantastic Four* and *Thor* were entrusted to his care after Jack Kirby left Marvel for DC Comics.

John's bold, muscular artwork commanded the comic book page with realistic figurework that represented the next evolutionary step in post-Kirby Marvel Comics style. His respect within Marvel as an artist's artist was of such renown that he literally wrote the book on it, composing *How To Draw the Marvel Way*, the classic "how to" book in comic-book illustration.

He worked from the '70s through the '90s on nearly every title in the Marvel stable, including his personal favorite title *Conan the Barbarian* with Roy Thomas, providing steady work throughout his career. He retired from regular work in 1996, but returned every now and then to the comics scene until he passed away after a battle with cancer in 2002.

GARY FRIEDRICH

The early days of Gary Friedrich's life as a comics writer has a similar arc to that of teenage pal Roy Thomas, and while he may not have had as long a career that his friend and fellow fan developed, he was still able make a significant contribution to Marvel, especially in the period during Stan Lee's transition from writer to Publisher. Hailing from the same Missouri environs as Roy Thomas, the pair befriended each other in their high school days and established a bond through their love of comics; for Gary, it was the super-hero revival taking place in late-50s DC Comics that first peaked his interest, but it was Stan Lee's Marvel Age of Comics that really inspired him. After Roy made the trip to New York City and got his own career started in earnest, he made it clear to his pal back in Missouri that there might be a job in comics waiting for him if he made the attempt. Shortly after getting off the bus from the Show Me State, Gary got his first work from Dick Giordano to write various Charlton comics, including *Blue Beetle* backup stories penciled by none other than Steve Ditko!

At the same time, he was able to pick up some work at Marvel, his first effort being the western *Ghost Rider*, a new series created in tandem with Dick Ayers and his pal, Roy Thomas. Other contributions during this time included other westerns like *Rawhide Kid* and *Two-Gun Kid*, as well as other non-superhero titles like *Captain Savage*—for which Gary wrote virtually the entire nineteen issue run—and *Sgt. Fury*, wherein he started a four-year run that saw him cautiously but profoundly merge a sense of social commentary and allegory into the long-running war title. Beyond his regular work on these titles, Gary was able to do spot writing on titles that were in transition between regular writers, including *X-Men*, *Incredible Hulk* and *Captain Marvel*.

The early '70s saw Gary behind the helm of Marvel's last new war title, *Combat Kelly*, but his most significant contribution of the era was taking place in the pages of the showcase title *Marvel Spotlight*. Not wanting a high-concept character name like Ghost Rider to languish after the western iteration had left newsstands, Gary took the name and, along with Roy Thomas and artist Mike Ploog, created the flaming skulled, chopper-riding Johnny Blaze, a tormented soul on the run from Satan himself! He wrote the first dozen stories featuring the iconic character, and in the meantime wrote a faithful adaptation of Mary Shelley's classic novel in the pages of *Monster of Frankenstein*. These were to be his last major contributions to Marvel.

After a stint with the short-lived Atlas/Seaboard company in the mid-'70s, and then a brief run writing *Captain Britain* stories for Marvel UK, Gary left the comics scene, though he is still a featured guest at various comics conventions.

DON HECK

A native New Yorker, and artist's artist, Don Heck began his comics career working for Harvey Comics in 1949, but it was his dramatic covers for the Comic Media genre titles of the early '50s that got the attention of one Stan Lee. Don's future employer at Atlas/Marvel was engrossed by his stark images of battle-worn war heroes, creepy shrunken heads, gunshot victims, vampires, and bristling cowboy action. When Stan was searching through the list of free agent artists to hire for Atlas, Don was extended an immediate offer.

Don attacked his Atlas Comics assignments with aplomb,

turning in page after page of work across all genres, including science fiction, jungle, military and romance. In fact, it was while toiling as a romance artist that Don Heck's reputation for stunning renderings of female beauty took hold.

Perhaps Don Heck's most lasting contributions to the world of comic books came after the Atlas Era imploded and the Marvel Age of Comics rose up from its ashes. He is perhaps best remembered for the adventures of Iron Man, the character which he first defined with Stan Lee in the pages of *Tales of Suspense* #39. He also earned renown during his long tenure as artist on *Avengers* with writers Stan Lee and Roy Thomas, introducing the fan-favorite archer, Hawkeye to the ranks of Earth's Mightiest Heroes.

Don worked throughout the 1970s on titles including *The Flash*, *Justice League of America* and *Dial H for Hero*, and then intermittently through the early 1990s for both Marvel and DC Comics. He passed away from lung cancer in 1995.

WERNER ROTH

Werner Roth may not be remembered as widely as Marvel Age giants like Kirby, Ditko or Buscema, but that cannot change the fact that he was a key contributor during the early years when Marvel's Silver Age legacy was still an unknown quantity. In fact, unlike those other artists, Werner Roth was an active participant in the earliest years of Marvel's Atlas Era: the beyond-beautiful heroine, *Venus*; *Matt Slade*, Western gunfighter; the horror/suspense stories of *Strange Tales, Menace* and *World of Fantasy*…Werner did it all! His two titles of longest creative standing were the Native American Western title *Apache Kid* and *Lorna, the Jungle Queen*, for which he turned in consistently lovely artwork.

After several years away from comics, he reemerged at Marvel drawing *X-Men*, the first permanent artist installed to fill the big shoes of Jack Kirby. Werner's *X-Men* work nonetheless has charm to burn, with freewheeling renderings of such frozen-in-time characters like The Locust, Kukulcan/El Tigre, and Factor Three. He also created the visual look of The Banshee, certainly one of his most memorable contributions to the *X-Men* legacy. After his run on the *X-Men* ended, Werner dabbled in comics for a bit in the '70s before retiring.

Biographical material researched and written by John Rhett Thomas.

THE
MARVEL MASTERWORKS
LIBRARY

The Amazing Spider-Man Vols. 1-8 By Stan Lee, Steve Ditko & John Romita
Sensational stories of everybody's favorite wall-crawler—your friendly neighborhood Spider-Man.

Ant-Man/Giant-Man Vol. 1 By Stan Lee, Jack Kirby, Don Heck & Larry Lieber
Thrilling science and microscopic adventures abound in the action-packed world of Hank Pym, Ant-Man and Janet Van Dyne, the Wasp!

Atlas Era Tales to Astonish Vol. 1 By Jack Kirby, Steve Ditko, Don Heck, Joe Sinnott & Stan Lee
Amazing tales of monsters and the farthest reaches of the imagination by comics' greatest talents.

Atlas Era Tales of Suspense Vol. 1 By Jack Kirby, Steve Ditko, Don Heck, Joe Sinnott & Stan Lee
Sci-fi fantasy wonders of other worldly aliens and incomprehensible monsters as crafted by the greatest talents of the Atlas Era!

The Avengers Vols. 1-6 By Stan Lee, Roy Thomas, Jack Kirby, Don Heck & John Buscema
Marvel's greatest stars assemble to form Earth's Mightiest Heroes.

Captain America Vols. 1-3 By Stan Lee, Jack Kirby, Gil Kane & Jim Steranko
America's Sentinel of Liberty in action-packed stories of amazing adventure and suspense.

Captain Marvel Vol. 1 By Stan Lee, Roy Thomas, Arnold Drake, Gene Colan & Don Heck
Born of the Kree, Marvel's Space-Born Super-Hero, Captain Mar-Vell protects planet Earth!

Doctor Strange Vols. 1-2 By Stan Lee, Steve Ditko, Bill Everett, Marie Severin & Dan Adkins
The original otherworldly tales of Dr. Stephen Strange, Master of the Mystic Arts!

Daredevil Vols. 1-3 By Stan Lee, Wallace Wood, John Romita & Gene Colan
Blind lawyer Matt Murdock is Daredevil, the Man Without Fear.

The Fantastic Four Vols. 1-10 By Stan Lee & Jack Kirby
Presenting the First Family of Super Heroes' unparalleled adventures beyond your wildest imagination.

Golden Age All-Winners Vol. 1 By Joe Simon, Jack Kirby, Carl Burgos, Bill Everett & Stan Lee
The greatest heroes of the Golden Age band together to fight the Nazi hordes and the forces of evil!

Golden Age Captain America Vol. 1 By Joe Simon & Jack Kirby
A top-secret serum turns Steve Rogers, 98-pound weakling, into America's greatest wartime weapon in battles with his kid sidekick, Bucky.

Golden Age Marvel Comics Vols. 1-2 By Carl Burgos & Bill Everett
Experience the birth of Marvel Comics from the very beginning! Featuring the Sub-Mariner, Ka-Zar, the Human Torch and more!

Golden Age Human Torch Vol. 1 By Carl Burgos & Bill Everett
Fiery adventures of the amazing creation, the Human Torch and Toro, the Flaming Kid.

Golden Age Sub-Mariner Vol. 1 By Bill Everett & Paul Gustavson
From his undersea kingdom of Atlantis, the mighty Sub-Mariner protects the Seven Seas from tyranny.

The Incredible Hulk Vols. 1-3 By Stan Lee, Jack Kirby, Steve Ditko, Bill Everett, John Buscema, Gil Kane & Marie Severin
When Dr. Robert Bruce Banner loses control, he becomes the unstoppable Hulk!

The Human Torch Vol. 1 By Stan Lee, Jack Kirby, Larry Lieber & Dick Ayers
Johnny Storm, the high-flying teen Human Torch, in solo adventures from the early days of the Fantastic Four!

The Invincible Iron Man Vols. 1-3 By Stan Lee, Don Heck & Gene Colan
Gravely injured, Tony Stark built a suit of amazing armor to become the Invincible Iron Man!

Rawhide Kid Vol. 1 By Stan Lee & Jack Kirby
Johnny Bart brings justice to the American frontier with the fastest six-shooters this side of the Mississippi. He is the Rawhide Kid!

Sgt. Fury Vol. 1 By Stan Lee, Jack Kirby & Dick Ayers
WWII tales of America's toughest army team, the Howling Commandos!

The Silver Surfer Vols. 1-2 By Stan Lee & John Buscema
The Sentinel of the Spaceways in his galaxy-spanning saga throughout the stars.

The Sub-Mariner Vol. 1 By Stan Lee, Gene Colan & Bill Everett
Namor, Prince of Atlantis, in his original adventures under the Seven Seas.

The Mighty Thor Vols. 1-5 By Stan Lee & Jack Kirby
The Asgardian Thunder God in mythic tales of epic battle and mystical adventure.

The X-Men Vols. 1-6 By Stan Lee, Roy Thomas, Arnold Drake, Jack Kirby, Werner Roth & Neal Adams
Gifted with strange and amazing powers, Professor Charles Xavier's teen team, the X-Men, leads the way in the quest to bring together man and mutant.

The Uncanny X-Men Vols. 1-5 By Chris Claremont, Dave Cockrum & John Byrne
Children of the Atom, they fight to defend a world that fears and hates them. They are the All-New, All-Different X-Men.